NEW ENGLAND
HOME COOKING

NEW ENGLAND HOME COOKING

350 Recipes from Town and Country, Land and Sea, Hearth and Home

BROOKE DOJNY

ILLUSTRATIONS BY JOHN MACDONALD

The Harvard Common Press
Boston, Massachusetts

The Harvard Common Press
535 Albany Street
Boston, Massachusetts 02118
www.harvardcommonpress.com

Printed in the United States of America
Printed on acid-free paper

Previously published as *The New England Cookbook,* ISBN 978-1-55832-139-7

Library of Congress Cataloging-in-Publication Data
Dojny, Brooke.
  [New England cookbook]
  New England home cooking : 350 recipes from town and country, land and sea, hearth, and home / Brooke Dojny.
      p. cm. — (America cooks)
  Originally published: New England cookbook. Boston, Mass. : Harvard Common Press, c1999.
  Includes index.
    Summary: "A witty, authoritative, and comprehensive celebration of cooking in the New England style with over 350 recipes for soups, salads, appetizers, breads, main courses, vegetables, jams and preserves, and desserts. Brooke Dojny, a native New Englander, has adapted traditional recipes to modern tastes by streamlining cooking methods and adding contemporary ingredients. She has also included such Yankee classics as North End Clams Casino, Wellfleet Oysters on the Half Shell with Mango Mignonette, Hashed Chicken with Dried Cranberries, Maine-Style Molasses Baked Yellow-Eyes, New England Cobb Salad, Shaker Whipped Winter Squash with Cape Cod Cranberries, Wood-Grilled Steak au Poivre with a Vegetable Bouquet, Pan-Seared Venison Steaks with Peppery Beach Plum Sauce, Succulent Braised Chicken Portuguese Style, Little Italy Calamari in Spicy Red Sauce, Grilled Chive-Tarragon Lobster, Reach House Blueberry Cobbler, and Chocolate Bread and Butter Pudding"— Provided by publisher.
  ISBN 978-1-55832-757-3 (pbk.)
  1. Cooking, American—New England style. I. Title.
TX715.2.N48D65 2011
641.5974—dc23
                                                                                          2011023317

Special bulk-order discounts are available on this and other Harvard Common Press books. Companies and organizations may purchase books for premiums or for resale, or may arrange a custom edition, by contacting the Marketing Director at the address above.

Cover design by Night & Day Design
Cover photography by Joyce Oudkerk Pool, assisted by
Morgan Bellinger; food styling by Jason Wheeler
Text design by Joyce C. Weston
Text illustrations by John MacDonald

10 9 8 7 6 5 4 3 2 1

For my father, Henry Brooke Maury, who took me clamming and let me help him clean fish, and who taught me to care about all the details

CONTENTS

ACKNOWLEDGMENTS

A book of this scope doesn't get written without generous contributions from many, many other people.

The seed for *New England Home Cooking* was planted by editor Dan Rosenberg, who then nurtured it, brilliantly, to fruition.

When I was forced by time and deadline constraints to stop traveling and researching and to start cooking and writing, Susan Capone Maloney filled in gaps and kept feeding me material. She willingly and unstintingly shared her memories and her knowledge, particularly of the coastal areas of Massachusetts and Rhode Island around Narragansett Bay. And her large collection of community cookbooks provided additional valuable source material.

Others gave similar help in the form of stories, memories, information, professional expertise, and ideas for recipes. These include Karyl Bannister, Nancy Barr, Paul Brayton, Hilliard Bloom, Barbara Carlson, Gus Charos, Eliot Coleman, Marylu Cordisco, Beverly Cox, Peter Cucciara, Barbara Damrosch, Phyllis Diiorio, The Durgin Park Management, Ann Marie Dustin, Sandy Eaton, Mike Elia, Jon Ellsworth, Sarah Everdell, Des FitzGerald, Dorothy Fox, Henry Gonsalves, Mary Goodbody, Bill Grant, Lyndon Grant, Patrick Grant, Rhoda Grant, Rich Hanson, Tom Harty, John Henderson, Corin Hewitt, Janie Hibler, Jennifer Huntley-Corbin, Ann E. Kerrigan, Barbara Kuck, Calvin Kurimai, Leslie Land, Barbara Lauterbach, Helen Limberis, Nunzio LoRusso, Paula Marcoux, Jack Maury, Mary Maynard, Libby Dietz Minsky, John Moulton, Mara Nascimento, Gretchen O'Grady, Freddy Pagliuca, Jeff Paige, Peter Perez, Betsy Perry, Roseanne Person, Bill Petitte, Marilyn A. Poulos, Jim Reilly, Roger Rist, Cathy Romano, Sandra Roxo, Carol Rusnak, Elizabeth Russell, Jackie Salvo, Brinna Sands, Jennifer Schroth, Cynthia Sewell, Gregory

Sharrow, Chris Singer, Suzanne Slater, Arnold and Luella Smith, Maddie Sobel, Avery Stephenson, Catherine Van Orman, Ann Walsh-Sullivan, Martha Welty, Allene White, Jasper White, Stephanie Whitney, Julia Wright, and Susan Young.

Deborah Callan brought professional expertise, a discerning palate, and her calm reassurance to the job of recipe testing.

I am grateful as always to friend and food-writing partner Melanie Barnard for her generosity and support.

The late food writer Richard Sax spoke to me throughout this project. He spoke from the pages of his superb book *Classic Home Desserts*, which I used as both a reference and a model, and I heard his voice in my ear, reminding me to strive for the highest standards of professional ethics.

I am indebted to my wonderful agent, Judith Weber, first for her patience and then for her remarkable professional skills.

And finally, my love and gratitude to my family—my mother, Hester Maury, my father, to whom this book is dedicated, my children, Matt and Maury Dojny, and especially to my forbearing (though seldom hungry) husband, Richard, whose steadfast support anchors our ship.

A VERY LUCKY GIRL

I had no idea what a lucky child I was. I thought every little girl in America woke up on Saturday morning, as I did in my house in Norwalk, in southern Connecticut, to the unmistakable perfume and sizzle of bacon cooking, and then ate the thick-cut, crisp-edged strips for breakfast with fluffy, eggy pancakes cascading with real maple syrup poured from a little glass jug. I thought every little girl's father caught flatfish and let her watch him clean them and then fried them and their popping orange roe in bacon fat in a cast-iron skillet for lunch. And that every mother made golden cornbread from scratch and served it on Saturday night to sop up the sauce from the sweet, molassesy baked beans—sometimes homemade, sometimes B&M from a can doctored up with onion and mustard. I thought a home-cooked dessert every night was every child's birthright—whether it be homely junket pudding or nutmeg-dusted baked custard or darkly mysterious Indian pudding or warm gingerbread with foamy sauce. And I thought every cookie jar was filled with spiced hermit cookies or Grandmother's brown-edged wafer cookies or snickerdoodles.

In the summer I thought everybody got to spend entire days at the beach digging in the mud for clams. And that on Cape Cod vacations everybody gathered buckets of beach plums for jelly and took a trip to Provincetown to see the Portuguese fishing boats and taste little slices of peppery linguiça offered from the end of a fish-scaling knife. Or that everyone got to make a daily stop at a white "clam shack" for a fried scallop or clam or lobster salad roll.

When I got a little older and began venturing further afield in Norwalk, which happened to be, unbeknownst to me at the time, an almost perfect microcosm of the New England ethnic melting pot, I still didn't know how lucky I was to get taken to shop for "foreign" groceries in Little Italy—for pungent provolone cheese, garlicky salamis, bread with a hard crust, avocados! And I didn't know how lucky I was that, on my circuitous walking route home from school, I could first duck into the Greek grocery store for a buttery, sugar-dusted cookie, then stop at Lynn Yobaggy's cellar to fish a few homemade Hungarian pickles out of the barrels, and end up at Libby Dietz's, where we could hope her mother had just baked a batch of an exotic (to me) Jewish fruit-and-nut-filled spiral pastry. Sometimes I would go to Lucille Gagne's house, where always, on the back of the stove, simmered a pot of yellow split pea soup with big chunks of streaky salt pork. And once or twice I sat in the corner of Diane Gaeta's kitchen watching her grandmother preside over the making of her tomato "gravy."

I didn't know how lucky I was—until I moved away from Norwalk and out of New England. Over the course of the next many years, living in New York and California, I learned to cook, delving into countless cuisines, taking detours through French, "gourmet," authentic ethnic everything, "New American," New Orleansean, high-fat, low-fat, no-fat, recipes that take five days to make, recipes that take five minutes to make, you name it, I studied it, cooked it, and then wrote about it. Until finally, after moving back to Connecticut and then to a summer house in Maine, I began to see that the circle was complete and that I had come home for good, both personally and professionally. It seems that I've spent my whole life preparing to write this book. Not only was I unconsciously "researching" New England foodways during my childhood, but all that experimenting ultimately led me back to the recognition and conviction that the kind of simple, honest cooking that is the hallmark of New England is the very best cooking in all the world.

HOME COOKING IN NEW ENGLAND

The Past Is a Present

Our American culinary identity is irrevocably intertwined with the cooking of early New England. The early colonials quickly embraced some of the best of Native American foodways, merging New World ingredients with their own English country cooking to create a cuisine that has formed the basis of the food traditions not only of a region but of an entire continent.

During that first bitter winter of 1620 at Plymouth, it was a cache of corn discovered by Miles Standish that saved many of the Pilgrims from starvation. Had it not been for the remarkably friendly local Indians, who taught them how to cook the corn into mush and primitive cakes, even more Pilgrims would have perished.

Soon thereafter, though, the colonists introduced basic English farming techniques to this "new" England. They imported cattle to help plow the fields and to provide meat and milk and butter and cheese, brought over sheep, chickens, and pigs, and imported seeds from England to plant grains, basic vegetable crops, and apple and other fruit orchards.

And then these colonists, who over the next decades were joined by hundreds and then thousands of other new arrivals, began to cook in earnest. By the mid- to late-1600s, the basic elements of an emerging regional cuisine were in place.

More than the imported foodstuffs, it was the ingredients indigenous to the New World that defined the character of this cuisine. In addition to the all-important corn, a colonial larder might include beans, cranberries, blueberries, wild plums, pumpkins and other squash, maple syrup and sugar, wild mushrooms, wild turkeys and other game birds, venison, oysters, hard- and soft-shell clams, eels, cod and other finfish, and (eventually) lobsters.

Cooking in big cast-iron cooking pots slung over the hearth, colonial housewives borrowed directly from Native Americans such dishes as corn and bean succotash, cornmeal cakes, and stewed cranberries, reinterpreted English boiled beef dinners and stews and stirred custard puddings, created new versions of seafood chowders, and invented dishes such as New World beans, slow-baked with maple over damped-down coals. They roasted wild turkeys and other game birds, and they baked their beloved English pies—filling them with maple-sweetened pumpkin and stewed native blueberries. As fishing grew more vital to the economy, fish became central to the table, and they learned new ways of cooking the plentiful cod (both fresh and dried), haddock, mackerel, smelt, bluefish, and shad.

By the dawn of the eighteenth century, a new and distinct regional cuisine had taken root, with dishes that we continue to cook today. Chowders, fish cakes, baked beans, succotash, cornbread, boiled dinner, roast turkey and cranberry sauce, pumpkin and berry pies—these traditional dishes form the central core of New England home cooking, linking past with present in an unbroken chain.

The Ethnic Infusion

The first English settlers did not come from a fishing culture. In fact, the Mayflower colonists had not even thought to bring fish hooks with them. But the Portuguese—especially men from the Azores—had a centuries-old fishing tradition, and they, along with Italian fishermen, soon migrated (or were recruited as crew by New England whalers) to the New World, settling in towns along the coast from Gloucester to New Bedford to Providence.

At first in a trickle and then in a flood, wave upon wave of immigrants rolled onto New England shores. In the nineteenth century, first the Irish came and then Germans and Jews and Italians. In the early twentieth century, Greeks, Poles, Scandinavians and Finns, and Hungarians arrived. French filtered south from Canada. Later people from Asia, the Middle East, the Caribbean, and South America arrived. All of these peoples, naturally, brought their food traditions with them. Some ethnic cooking in New England survives intact—particularly dishes deeply ingrained in holiday tradition, such as Polish pierogi or the Greek Easter bread. More commonly there has been an incredibly fertile food cross-pollination, a continuing dialectic, with each ethnic group in its turn coming to grips with the New England landscape, with the ocean, and with the radically changing seasons. Portuguese linguiça appeared at clambakes along the Massachusetts shore and in pizzerias in tiny towns in northern New Hampshire. Stuffed grape leaves were listed next to corned beef hash on menus at Greek-run diners in Rhode Island. Adobo seasoning sat beside the cranberry sauce in a Spanish grocery store in Connecticut. Turkey and lasagne appeared together on the Thanksgiving menu of Italian Yankees. Asian food stalls set up shop at a flea market in southern Vermont, and a French-Canadian tourtière concession stood next to a fried clam shack at a Maine street fair. And as other immigrants arrive this dynamic interchange continues.

The Current Scene

Through the centuries New England cooking has remained essentially home cooking. Unlike other regions of the United States—California, Florida, New York City—where the emerging regional cuisines are largely chef- and restaurant-driven, New England has never had an haute cuisine. People do "eat out"—at clam shacks and pizzerias, at restaurants and inns—but more New Englanders still "eat in" than in other areas of the country. Perhaps it is another function of the weather—especially in winter we come in out of the cold, staying indoors and cooking or baking for our families and friends.

Like every cuisine in every part of the world, what we cook and bake is continuously evolving, responding to ongoing changes in the ethnic make-up of our population and to changes in the American lifestyle in general and to the New England lifestyle in particular. But at our core, our New England food traditions still sustain us, connecting us in a very vital, tangible way (and also in a subtle, subconscious way) with our own rich history and past.

The best of contemporary New England home cooking is inspired by our enduring wealth of superb raw ingredients. In recent years, Yankee cooks are increasingly engaged in a rediscovery of locally grown and harvested provender, whether from ocean, farm, forest, or woodland. Using our inherited impulse toward simplicity, we cook with these ingredients with a renewed appreciation of their essential goodness, adapting older recipes to modern tastes by streamlining cooking methods (substituting olive oil for butter, for example) and adding infusions of flavor with contemporary ingredients such as fresh herbs and condiments. In an ever more homogenized world, New England continues to celebrate the common by carrying on our home cooking tradition, asserting both our Yankee individualism and an understanding of our collective past.

NEW ENGLAND
HOME COOKING

STARTERS, CLASSIC AND CONTEMPORARY

Sublime Smoked Salmon Pâté   31

Broiled Westport Wings with Blue Cheese Dressing   32

Grilled Cumberland Quail with Rosemary   33

Historically speaking, an appetizer course that preceded the main entree was not a fixture of the New England culinary tradition. Formal dining was the exception, snacking was frowned upon, and the cocktail party was a twentieth-century concept. Rather, the focus was on getting a warming, fueling meal on the table, inviting the family to pull up a chair, and then getting right to the serious business of eating it.

Although some of that staunch no-nonsense attitude lingers, we present-day Yankees love to entertain guests with hors d'oeuvres and snacks or put on a sit-down dinner with a formal first course as much as anybody else around the country. A host of imaginative ethnic cooks have contributed their more relaxed "grazing" customs to the New England snack scene. Such delectable appetizers as spicy Bicoastal Middle Eastern Eggplant (page 8), savory Baked Stuffed Mushrooms Siciliana (page 5), and creamy Turkey Hill Taramasalata (page 27) enhance our repertoire considerably.

Some of our glorious native seafood dishes, such as Citrus-Glazed Steamed Mussels (page 20), Connecticut Coast Steamers (page 12), or Wellfleet Oysters on the Half Shell (page 22), make perfect light first courses. And we happily turn to such "newer" New England specialties as Sublime Smoked Salmon Pâté (page 31) or Grilled Cumberland Quail with Rosemary (page 33) to complete this appetizing picture.

Yankee Summer Salsa

MAKES 2 GENEROUS CUPS; 4 TO 6 SERVINGS

Of all the New England states, Vermont has the highest concentration of start-up artisan food producers, making not only traditional products like maple syrup and farmstead cheeses but also foods with roots in other regions, such as salsas. I try to have a bottle of one of the better-quality New England–made salsas in my refrigerator at all times, but in summer, when Yankee garden or farm stand tomatoes are dead ripe and abounding, I make this fresh version almost daily. Here's a nifty tip: if your bowl of fresh salsa starts to get a little too depleted, stir some of the bottled stuff into the fresh to stretch it.

2 cups chopped seeded ripe tomatoes (from 1½ pounds)
1 cup chopped green or yellow bell pepper
1 cup chopped red or white onion
1 tablespoon fresh lime juice
1 fresh or pickled jalapeño pepper, minced (see Note)
1 teaspoon salt
½ teaspoon sugar
¼ cup chopped fresh cilantro

1. Combine all of the ingredients except the cilantro in a medium-sized bowl. Cover and refrigerate for at least 1 hour to blend the flavors or for up to 4 hours.
2. Spoon off and discard (or drink or add to a soup or stew) any excess liquid released by the salsa. Stir in the cilantro. Taste, and correct the seasoning if necessary.
3. Serve in a bowl surrounded by tortilla chips.

Note: For less heat, scrape out the ribs and seeds before chopping the jalapeño; for more fire, leave them in.

Tavern Fare

"The tavern's fare was simple, centering around a 'joint' of meat or stews with boiled vegetables and pastry of corn meal. Yankees did not favor water as a drink. Cider was a staple of the tavern bar, but even more so was rum—or, as it was more generally called, 'kill-devil.' Yankees, from yeomen to statesmen, had a special passion for this powerful liquor."

—Earle W. Newton, Foreword to *New England Cookbook*, by Eleanor Early (Random House 1954)

Baked Stuffed Mushrooms Siciliana

MAKES 24 SMALL MUSHROOMS; 4 TO 6 SERVINGS

Cathy Romano, who gave me my precious copy of Saugatuck, Connecticut's *Festival Italiano Cookbook*, says that stuffed mushrooms—one cook's version or another's—were always served at festive gatherings when she was growing up, and continue to be an extremely popular and much-requested recipe in most Italian-American cooks' repertoires. Sometimes sweet Italian sausage is used as a stuffing, but a good many fillings, such as this sweet-tart herbed breadcrumb mixture, are meatless. (Hint: If you don't mention the anchovies, suspicious people will just wonder why these are extra delicious!)

> 24 mushrooms, about 1 inch in diameter
> 2 tablespoons raisins or currants
> ½ cup dry white wine
> 3 tablespoons olive oil
> ¼ cup chopped onion
> 1 garlic clove, minced
> 1 tablespoon chopped anchovy fillets
> ½ cup fresh breadcrumbs
> 1 tablespoon chopped fresh flat-leaf parsley, plus sprigs for the platter
> 1 teaspoon chopped fresh rosemary or ¾ teaspoon dried
> ½ teaspoon fresh-ground black pepper
> Salt
> 3 tablespoons grated Parmesan cheese

1. Remove the stems from the mushrooms, chop the stems finely, and set aside. Soak the raisins in the wine in a small bowl until softened, about 15 minutes.
2. Meanwhile, heat 2 tablespoons of the oil in a large skillet. Add the onion, garlic, and chopped mushroom stems and cook over medium-high heat, stirring frequently, until softened, about 5 minutes. Add the anchovies and cook, stirring, until they dissolve, about 2 minutes. Add the soaked raisins and wine and boil, scraping up any browned bits from the bottom of the pan, until reduced by about half, 2 to 3 minutes. Add the breadcrumbs, parsley, rosemary, and pepper and cook, stirring, until heated through.

3. Preheat the oven to 400 degrees. Lightly grease or coat with cooking spray a rimmed baking sheet.

4. Sprinkle the cavities of the mushroom caps with salt and fill generously with the breadcrumb mixture. Arrange in the prepared pan. Sprinkle with the cheese and drizzle or brush with the remaining tablespoon of oil. (The mushrooms can be made ahead to this point. Hold at cool room temperature for a couple of hours or refrigerate for up to 6 hours. Return to room temperature before baking.)

5. Bake the mushrooms, uncovered, for about 20 minutes, until the filling begins to turn crisp and brown. To give a darker, richer look to the mushrooms, run under the broiler to finish cooking.

6. Serve on a parsley-lined platter.

Zucchini Pie Oreganata

MAKES ABOUT 36 SMALL SQUARES OR 10 WEDGES; 4 TO 6 SERVINGS

My father, an adventurous spirit, enjoyed visiting the Italian neighborhoods in Norwalk, Connecticut, during the 1950s, bringing home to our WASP table such delightful exotica as garlicky salami, chunks of potent provolone or nutty Parmesan, and, once, a wedge of freshly baked zucchini pie, wrapped in oil-soaked butcher paper. This recipe, based on one in an Italian community cookbook, is a re-creation of that indelible, oregano-scented taste memory. Use a fresh jar of good-quality imported oregano for the right result. (P.S. This recipe also would serve two or three people as a lovely lunch or light supper.)

2½ cups very thinly sliced zucchini
About 1 teaspoon coarse salt
2 tablespoons olive oil
¾ cup chopped onion
2 eggs
⅓ cup whole, lowfat, or skim milk
¾ cup Bisquick or similar baking mix
½ cup shredded mozzarella cheese
3 tablespoons grated Parmesan cheese
1 tablespoon minced fresh flat-leaf parsley

2 teaspoons dried oregano
½ teaspoon salt
¼ teaspoon black pepper
½ cup chopped seeded plum tomatoes, optional

1. Preheat the oven to 375 degrees. Spray a 9-inch-square baking dish or 9-inch pie plate with cooking spray or lightly coat with oil.
2. Place the sliced zucchini in a colander and sprinkle with the coarse salt. Let stand for 15 minutes while preparing the other ingredients.
3. Heat the oil in a skillet. Add the onion and cook for about 8 minutes over medium heat, stirring frequently, until softened.
4. In a large mixing bowl, lightly beat the eggs with the milk. Add the baking mix and whisk just until smooth. Stir in the sautéed onions along with the cheeses, parsley, oregano, salt, and pepper.
5. Rinse the zucchini, spread out on a double thickness of paper towels, and pat dry. Stir the zucchini into the batter and transfer the batter to the prepared pan. Bake for 25 minutes, until the top is flecked with brown and the pie tests done near the center. (If you are using the tomatoes, scatter them over the top after the first 15 minutes of baking.)
6. Cut into about 36 squares and serve as a finger-food hors d'oeuvre or, if made in a pie pan, cut into wedges and serve as a first course or snack. Serve warm or at room temperature.

Lunchtime in Portuguese America

The Henry Gonsalves Company in Smithfield, Rhode Island, sells Portuguese food products to "Portuguese America," as Henry E. Gonsalves, the firm's president, calls it. Every now and then, Mr. Gonsalves cooks lunch for his approximately twenty employees. "It's always grilled out back, because that's the only stove we've got here." One day it's fresh sardines brushed with lemon, oil, and garlic. Another time it's red snapper and prawns grilled with a similar basting sauce. "We have Portuguese rolls with the seafood, and get in a pan of potatoes (or 'Portuguese pasta,' as potatoes are sometimes known)—small white ones, halved and fried. It makes a nice treat once in a while."

Bicoastal Middle Eastern Eggplant

MAKES ABOUT 6 GENEROUS SERVINGS

I acquired this delectable eggplant recipe in Mill Valley, California, by way of Alice Sturgis Steinman, who grew up outside of Boston and frequented Eastern Lamejun, a large Middle Eastern food emporium in Belmont, Massachusetts, and begged from them a vague version of this recipe for their fabulous spiced eggplant. The secret ingredient is the orange-flower water, which can be acquired in a liquor store if you can't find it elsewhere.

> 1 medium eggplant, unpeeled, cut in ¾-inch cubes
> About 2 teaspoons coarse salt
> 3 tablespoons extra-virgin olive oil
> 1 yellow or green bell pepper, chopped
> 1 medium zucchini, cut in ½-inch cubes
> 1 medium tomato, seeded and cut in chunks
> 2 garlic cloves, minced
> 1 teaspoon ground cumin
> ½ teaspoon cayenne pepper
> Salt and fresh-ground black pepper
> ½ teaspoon orange-flower water
> Small crackers or quartered small pita breads
> About ½ cup plain yogurt
> Alfalfa sprouts

1. Toss the eggplant with the coarse salt in a colander, and set aside to drain for 30 minutes. Rinse, drain, and pat dry on paper towels.

2. Heat the oil in a large skillet. Add the eggplant and cook over medium heat, stirring occasionally, until soft, 10 to 15 minutes. Raise the heat to medium-high, add the bell pepper, zucchini, tomato, and garlic and cook, stirring, until all the vegetables begin to give off their juices, about 5 minutes. Simmer, uncovered, over medium heat until all the vegetables are very soft and most of the liquid is evaporated, about 15 minutes. Stir in the cumin and cayenne and season to taste with salt and pepper. When almost cool, stir in the orange-flower water. Cover and refrigerate for at least 2 hours or up to 3 days. Return to cool room temperature before serving.

3. Serve in a bowl surrounded by crackers or pitas, a small bowl of plain yogurt, and sprouts. Scoop up a small spoonful of eggplant with the cracker or bread, spoon a little yogurt over, and top with a few sprouts.

Crispy Raw-Vegetable Summer Rolls

MAKES 6 TO 10 SPRING ROLLS (18 TO 30 CUT-UP PIECES)

The Asian ingredients required to make this recipe are becoming more readily available in regular supermarkets or in the Asian markets that continue to crop up all around New England, as well as the rest of the country. This light, delicate summer roll makes a delectable hors d'oeuvre when sliced on a sharp diagonal into finger-food-sized pieces and served with a small bowl of the dipping sauce.

For the dipping sauce:

½ cup apricot preserves
3 tablespoons rice vinegar
2 tablespoons Thai or Vietnamese fish sauce (*nam pla*)
½ teaspoon Asian hot chili oil, or more to taste

For the summer rolls:

4 ounces dried rice stick noodles, broken into 2-inch lengths and
    softened (see Note), about 2 cups softened noodles
1½ cups shredded or grated carrots
1½ cups shredded or grated seeded European cucumber
2 tablespoons chopped fresh mint
3 tablespoons chunky peanut butter
1 tablespoon rice vinegar
1 tablespoon Thai or Vietnamese fish sauce (*nam pla*)
1 teaspoon grated fresh ginger
1 teaspoon minced garlic
6 to 10 rice pancake wrappers (7- to 8-inch)

1. To make the dipping sauce, whisk together all the ingredients for the sauce in a small bowl, adjusting the amount of chili oil to your taste. Set aside at room temperature.

2. In a large bowl, toss together the noodles, carrots, cucumber, and mint. Stir together the peanut butter, vinegar, fish sauce, ginger, and garlic in a small bowl until smooth. Add the peanut mixture to the vegetable mixture and toss gently with your hands until thoroughly combined.

3. To soften the rice pancakes, fill a glass pie plate with lukewarm water, dip each wrapper in the water for about 15 seconds, and pat dry on a clean dish towel. (The pancakes will turn almost translucent and are quite fragile, but any tears can be remedied by rolling the pancakes tightly around the filling.) Place a pancake on a work surface and arrange some of the vegetable filling down the center. Roll up tightly, tucking in the ends as you go. Repeat with the remaining filling and pancakes. (These can be made a couple of hours ahead. Cover and refrigerate.)

4. To serve, cut each roll on a sharp diagonal into 3 pieces and arrange on a platter. Pass with a bowl of the dipping sauce.

Note: To soften the rice stick noodles, soak them in cold water to cover for 20 minutes, or follow the directions on the package. Drain well before using.

Asia in Vermont

Are we dreaming? It's one of those only-in-America sights for sure. Here in Newfane, in southern Vermont, in the midst of a huge assemblage of New England dealers in antiques, collectibles, and, well, junk, stands a modest food stall wafting out such intoxicating aromas that crowds line up well before it officially opens. Run by one of the many families of Cambodian and Laotian refugees that have found their way to this state, this multigenerational operation (one of many such enterprises) not only boasts the active participation of grandma and grandchildren but comes complete with an adorable miniature pet pig tethered out back. Grilled skewered chicken and fish, big puffy-battered deep-fried shrimp, fried sweet potatoes, and fried bananas get the salivary glands working. But more often than not, we opt for one of their crispy raw vegetable spring rolls—crunchy fresh vegetables enclosed in a soft rice paper package and served on a paper plate with a sweet-hot dipping sauce. All thoughts of bargain hunting grind to an abrupt halt while we stand still to savor one of the best snacks this side of an alley in Phnom Penh or Vientiane.

Peabody Cheddar Wafers

MAKES 6 TO 8 DOZEN WAFERS; 8 TO 10 SERVINGS

In the 1940s, Lucetta Upham Peabody lived a proper Bostonian life in the winter and spent summers on Eggemoggin Reach in midcoast Maine. In both places she was an ardent, dedicated cook, skilled at acquiring and documenting the very best recipes of the day. Lucetta's personal handwritten recipe collection yields up this wonderfully cheese-rich, slightly peppery wafer—still, these many years later, the ideal (and very addictive) nibble with drinks. Keep a "log" of the dough in the freezer so that you can slice off and bake a fresh batch of these anytime!

> ¼ cup sesame seeds
> 1 cup all-purpose flour
> ¾ teaspoon baking powder
> ¾ teaspoon salt
> ¼ teaspoon cayenne pepper
> ¼ teaspoon black pepper
> 6 tablespoons chilled unsalted butter, cut into 12 pieces
> 2 cups (½ pound) grated sharp cheddar cheese

1. Toast the sesame seeds in a small skillet over medium heat, stirring almost constantly, until they are fragrant and one shade darker in color, 3 to 4 minutes. Transfer to waxed paper to cool.

2. Combine the flour, baking powder, salt, cayenne, and black pepper in a food processor. Pulse a few times to blend.

3. Add the butter and cheese and process until the mixture resembles coarse crumbs, about 15 seconds. Add 2 tablespoons cold water and process until the mixture clumps together and begins to form a ball on top of the blades, 15 to 30 seconds. Add up to 1 tablespoon more water if the dough is too dry.

4. Turn the dough out onto a sheet of plastic wrap and shape into 2 logs about 10 inches long and 1 inch in diameter. Roll the logs in the sesame seeds, pressing the seeds firmly into the dough so they adhere. Chill the dough in the freezer for 30 minutes or in the refrigerator for at least 2 hours. (The dough can be made 2 days ahead and refrigerated, or it may be frozen. Thaw slightly before slicing.)

5. Preheat the oven to 425 degrees.

6. With a sharp knife, cut the dough log into ⅛- to ¼-inch slices and arrange 1 inch apart on ungreased or parchment-lined baking sheets. Bake for 7 to 12 minutes, depending on thickness, until the wafers are golden and tinged with brown around the edges. Cool on wire racks. The wafers are best on the same day they are baked, but leftovers will keep fresh for a couple of days in a tightly sealed container.

Connecticut Coast Steamers with Drawn Butter

MAKES 6 SERVINGS

There are some heretical recipes these days that call for cooking steamer clams in wine or beer, with herbs and whole spices or other flavorings added. I say, no thanks, just give me the pure, salty-sweet, earthy taste of the clams themselves, with a mere quick swish through plain melted butter for enhancement. This is the way we ate them when we dug a "mess" from Long Island Sound's magnificent mudflats when I was growing up, and it's how I cook them still. Spread newspapers or a plastic cloth on a picnic table, provide plenty of napkins and beer, and dig right in!

> 3 quarts steamer clams
> ¼ pound (1 stick) unsalted butter
> 1 tablespoon fresh lemon juice

1. Soak the clams in cold water to cover in a large bowl or pot for a couple of hours, rinsing the clams and changing the water several times. If the clams are very muddy, scrub them with a brush. Drain well.

2. Combine the clams and ½ cup water in a large cooking pot and place over high heat. Cover and bring to a rolling boil. Reduce the heat to medium-low and cook for 5 minutes. Check the clams; if they are all open, remove from the heat. If some are still closed, continue to cook for a few more minutes.

3. Meanwhile, melt the butter in a small saucepan over low heat. Stir in the lemon juice and pour the butter into 2 small bowls.

4. Use a slotted spoon to transfer the clams to 1 or 2 serving bowls. Pour the cooking broth into a couple of small bowls, leaving behind any grit or sand in the bottom of the pot.

5. To eat the steamers, most people first pull the black skin off the edge and neck of the clam. Next, holding it by the neck, dip the clam in broth to rinse and reheat, then dunk in the butter, and, finally, pop into your mouth. For a taste of the essence of sea, sip some of the remaining broth, leaving any grit behind.

Fried Clams

Conventional wisdom has it that fried clams were invented in 1916 at Woodman's, in Essex on the North Shore of Massachusetts. The story goes that Lawrence Dexter "Chubby" Woodman was frying potato chips for a Fourth of July celebration when he serendipitously dropped some bivalves into the hot fat, and the rest is clam shack history. Woodman's is still run by seven members of the founding clan today. Most fried clam aficionados will tell you that true fried clams (unlike the ghastly fried clam strips perpetrated on an unsuspecting public and franchised by Howard Johnson's—an otherwise blameless food operation with great ice cream) are made with whole-belly soft-shell clams, dipped in a light batter or rolled in egg and crumbs, and deep-fried in hot fat to a crisp finish. Heaven in a cardboard carton.

Crispy Ipswich Fried Clams with Classic Tartar Sauce

MAKES 4 SERVINGS

Great debate rages about what constitutes the TRUE fried clam. Soft or hard shell? Batter or crumbs? Naturally, it all depends on who's dishing out the expert advice and from which geographical locale. I strongly favor soft-shell clams such as the delicate variety dug in the mudflats off Ipswich, Massachusetts, and for home frying I recommend this coating of crumbs that in the end is nearly a batter. The traditionalist, by the way, would skip the optional herbs in the tartar sauce, but you go right ahead and do what you want. To turn these into a traditional New England clam roll, simply stuff the fried clams into a grilled hot dog roll.

For Classic Tartar Sauce:

⅔ cup regular or lowfat mayonnaise

3 tablespoons drained sweet pickle relish

1 tablespoon finely minced or grated
    onion

2 to 3 teaspoons chopped fresh herbs,
    such as parsley, dill, tarragon, or basil,
    optional

For the clams:

1½ pounds (24 to 30) soft-shell clams,
    shucked (see Note)

⅔ cup all-purpose flour

¼ cup yellow or white cornmeal

2 eggs

½ cup whole, lowfat, or skim milk

½ teaspoon salt, plus more to taste

¼ teaspoon black pepper

Vegetable oil for frying

Lemon wedges

> ### Fannie Daddies
>
> Nobody seems to know
> where the name comes from,
> but according to Eleanor Early,
> noted expert on New England
> cookery, fried clams used to be
> known as "fannie daddies"
> on Cape Cod.

1. To make the tartar sauce, combine the mayonnaise, relish, onion, and herbs, if using, in a small bowl. Stir well to combine. Refrigerate until ready to use or for up to 1 week.

2. To prepare the clams, rinse them thoroughly (see page 64) and drain them on paper towels. They will not stay intact—you'll have some strips, some bellies, and some other pieces, which is fine.

3. Stir together the flour and cornmeal in a shallow dish. In another dish, lightly beat the eggs with the milk, ½ teaspoon salt, and the pepper. Heat about 2 inches of oil in a large, heavy, deep skillet or heat oil in a deep fryer to about 370 degrees, or until a drop of water sizzles on the surface.

4. Roll the clams lightly in the flour mixture, then dip in the egg mixture and again in the flour mixture, shaking off any excess. Place the clams on a rack until all are

coated. Fry the clams, about 8 at a time so as not to crowd the pan, turning once with tongs if you are using a skillet, until golden brown on both sides, 2 to 3 minutes total. Drain on paper towels. Sprinkle with salt to taste.

5. Serve with the tartar sauce and lemon wedges.

Note: Unlike hard-shells, soft-shell clams are not difficult to shuck if you use a good sharp, short, sturdy knife. The clams are also easier to shuck if you blanch them in boiling water for 8 seconds.

North End Clams Casino

MAKES 24 CLAMS; 4 TO 6 SERVINGS

This tasty appetizer appears on Italian restaurant menus all over Boston's North End and indeed throughout New England—the invention, it seems, of a creative restaurant chef a good many years ago. This is a study in delicious contrast. The raw clams, sprinkled with crunchy minced vegetables, then topped with bacon, are finished under the broiler so that the bacon crisps and the clams are just barely cooked.

24 cherrystone clams
4 slices bacon
3 tablespoons olive oil
3 tablespoons minced onion
3 tablespoons minced green bell pepper
2 tablespoons minced celery
1 small garlic clove, minced
1 teaspoon dried oregano
¼ teaspoon salt
¼ teaspoon black pepper
3 tablespoons chopped fresh flat-leaf parsley
Lemon wedges

1. Open the clams, removing and discarding the top half of each shell, and cut around each clam to release the body from the shell. Arrange on a baking sheet, propping up the shells if necessary with crumpled aluminum foil so they don't tip over.

2. Cut each bacon slice into 6 equal pieces. Stir-fry the bacon in a large skillet over medium-high heat until limp and a bit more than half cooked, about 6 minutes. Drain on paper towels.

3. Preheat the broiler.

4. Stir together the oil, onion, green pepper, celery, garlic, oregano, salt, and pepper in a small bowl. Spoon some of the chopped vegetable mixture over each clam and top with a bacon square.

5. Broil, about 6 inches from the heat, until the bacon is crisp and brown, watching carefully to prevent burning, 3 to 5 minutes. Sprinkle with parsley before serving and pass lemon wedges at the table.

Tonics

The generic term is soft drink, usually known west of the Hudson as *soda pop* or *pop*. But in New England, sweet carbonated beverages are called sodas, except around Boston and Cape Cod, where they're still sometimes referred to by that quaint old-fashioned term *tonic*. And in Lisbon Falls, Maine, there is a festival every summer to honor Moxie, a dark brown, bittersweet carbonated drink first bottled nearby, now almost extinct except in New England but forever famous for lending its name to a slang word meaning vigor, pep, or verve.

Rhode Island "Stuffies"

MAKES 4 TO 6 SERVINGS

Baked stuffed clams, affectionately known as "stuffies" around Narragansett Bay, are probably most often eaten as street food at fairs and festivals. When making them at home, though, you can up the percentage of chopped clams in the filling, thus ensuring that the vigorous, briny flavor of real clams (as opposed to a preponderance of bread-crumbs) dominates. Take these babies to a potluck cookout and just stand back and receive the accolades—guaranteed!

2½ cups (about 24) shucked hard-shell clams, plus ¼ to ½ cup of
their liquor (see Note)
3 tablespoons olive oil

1 cup chopped onion
½ cup minced green bell pepper
1 large garlic clove, minced
2 cups fresh breadcrumbs, or more if necessary
¼ cup chopped fresh parsley
2 tablespoons chopped fresh sage or 2 teaspoons crumbled dried
½ teaspoon salt
½ teaspoon fresh-ground black pepper
¼ teaspoon red pepper flakes
1 egg
24 clean hard-shell cherrystone or quahog clam shells (see Note)
2 to 3 tablespoons cold butter
Lemon wedges

1. Chop the clams medium fine in a food processor or by hand. Reserve the liquor.
2. Heat the oil in a large skillet. Add the onion, green pepper, and garlic and cook over medium heat, stirring occasionally, until the onion is softened, about 8 minutes. Remove from the heat and stir in the breadcrumbs, parsley, sage, salt, pepper, and red pepper flakes; add the chopped clams and toss to combine. Whisk the egg with the ¼ cup clam liquor (or broth; see Note), add to the stuffing mixture, and toss gently but thoroughly to combine. Add up to ¼ cup more liquor or broth if the mixture is dry or crumbly.
3. Fill the clam shells with stuffing, place a thin slice of butter on top of each one, and arrange on a rimmed baking sheet or pan. (The clams can be prepared ahead to this point. Cover and refrigerate for up to 1 day.)
4. Preheat the oven to 400 degrees.
5. Bake the clams, uncovered, until the stuffing is golden brown and heated through, 20 to 30 minutes. Serve with lemon wedges.

Note: The recipe assumes you will buy clam meats and shells separately from your fish-monger. If you wish instead to start with clams in the shell, open them with a knife if you have the skill, or scrub the shells and steam the clams in 1 cup of water in a tightly covered large pot until they open, 6 to 10 minutes. Strain the broth and use it instead of the reserved liquor in the stuffing. When you acquire some good-sized clam shells, save them to use again.

Clam Cakes

If you order clam cakes in Rhode Island, don't expect a delicate, lightly bound crab cake. *Clam cakes* is actually another name for clam fritters—hefty deep-fried dollops of baking powder batter embedded with chopped clams. In a stellar example of culinary lily-gilding, clam cakes or fritters are often served as a side dish to clam chowder around Narragansett Bay.

Narragansett Clam Fritters

MAKES ABOUT 3 DOZEN FRITTERS; 4 TO 6 SERVINGS

My friend Susan Maloney grew up in Fall River, Massachusetts, near Narragansett Bay, a seafood-rich body of water that cuts deep into the coastline of Rhode Island and southern Massachusetts. Susan extolled her Aunt Phyllis Corcoran's clam fritters for years, and when I finally got around to trying them, I had to agree that this is the very best clam fritter recipe I've ever tried. The mixture is proportioned exactly right—a high concentration of chopped clams suspended in a batter that fries up light and crispy every time. Be sure to follow the instruction to cook one test fritter first and taste it for seasoning.

1 egg
3 tablespoons vegetable oil
¾ cup clam juice (liquor drained from clams or bottled or a combination)
¼ cup whole, lowfat, or skim milk
1½ cups all-purpose flour
2 teaspoons baking powder
½ teaspoon salt, plus more if necessary
¼ teaspoon black pepper
1 cup finely chopped drained hard-shell clams
Vegetable oil for frying
Cider vinegar or lemon wedges
Bottled hot pepper sauce

1. Whisk together the egg and oil in a small bowl until blended. Whisk in the clam juice and milk.

2. Combine the flour, baking powder, salt, and pepper in a large bowl. Whisk in the liquid mixture just until blended and stir in the clams. The batter should be the consistency of thick cake batter. Adjust by adding a little more flour or liquid as necessary.

3. In a large, deep frying pan or Dutch oven, heat a couple of inches of oil to 370 degrees, or until a drop of water sizzles when it hits the surface. Dip a teaspoon (see Note) in the oil to coat it, then spoon out one rounded spoonful of batter, drop it into the hot oil, and cook for 2 to 3 minutes, turning once with tongs, until puffed and golden. Taste this first fritter for seasoning, adding more salt and pepper to the batter if necessary. Continue to fry the fritters, a few at a time so as not to crowd the pan, until all the batter is used. Drain them on paper towels.

4. Pass vinegar or lemon wedges and the bottle of hot sauce to season the fritters when serving.

Note: I like to use a long-handled iced tea spoon to portion out the batter. It keeps your hands from getting too close to the hot oil, and it also creates a nicely shaped and sized fritter.

Clams

There are two basic families of East Coast clams—hard-shell and soft-shell:

Hard-shell clams have a hard, rocklike, tightly closed shell that takes skill to open by hand, and is easier to lightly steam open for cooking. The shells should be tightly closed before cooking. Hard shells include:

• Quahogs (pronounced "co'hog"), usually about 3 inches or more across; good for chowders or stuffing

• Cherrystones, about 2½ inches across; can be eaten raw on the half-shell

• Littlenecks, youngest and smallest, less than 2 inches across; best for eating raw on the half-shell

Soft-shell clams, also known as steamer clams, have a soft, eggshell-like, textured shell and long black neck (siphon); they are easy to open by hand or by steaming. They come in a variety of sizes, from about 1½ to 3 inches across. The smaller size is preferable for most cooking uses, including steaming and deep-frying.

Citrus-Glazed Steamed Mussels

MAKES 4 SERVINGS

Now that most mussels are farm raised, they are relatively uniform in size, have little or no grit, and arrive at the market sans that pesky little black beard to yank off. Some people say that wild mussels have a more assertive flavor, but my palate does not detect the difference, so the cultivated ones seem like an excellent trade-off to me. You'll want to pass a basket of crusty peasant bread for mopping up every last drop of this scrumptious citrusy sauce.

> 3 tablespoons extra-virgin olive oil
> 1 cup finely chopped onion
> 3 garlic cloves, minced
> 3 anchovy fillets, chopped
> 1 teaspoon grated lemon zest
> ½ teaspoon grated lime zest
> ¼ teaspoon red pepper flakes
> 2 pounds farm-raised mussels, rinsed
> 1 cup dry white wine
> 1 tablespoon chopped fresh marjoram or 1 teaspoon dried
> 2 tablespoons chopped fresh flat-leaf parsley
> 1 tablespoon fresh lemon juice
> 2 teaspoons fresh lime juice
> Thin slices of lemon and lime for garnish

1. Heat the oil in a medium skillet over medium heat, and cook the onion, stirring occasionally, until softened, about 5 minutes. Add the garlic and anchovies and cook, mashing the anchovies until they dissolve, for 2 minutes. Stir in the lemon and lime zest and the red pepper flakes and remove from the heat. (This base can be made up to 3 hours ahead. Reserve at room temperature.)

2. Place the mussels, wine, and marjoram in a large saucepan or soup pot. Cover the pan and bring to a boil. Reduce the heat to medium and cook until the mussels open and the meat is just firm to the touch, 4 to 10 minutes, depending on size.

3. Use a slotted spoon to transfer the mussels to a shallow serving bowl or individual dishes. Slowly pour the mussel broth into the skillet containing the sauce base, leaving behind any grit or mud in the bottom of the cooking pot (see Note). Bring the liquid in the skillet to a boil over high heat and cook briskly until the sauce is slightly reduced, 2 to 4 minutes. Stir in the parsley and citrus juices.

4. Spoon the hot sauce over the mussels, garnish with lemon and lime slices, and serve.

Note: If mussels are farm-raised—clean and grit-free—you can simply add the onion mixture to the mussel broth, and reduce.

Half Shell Sauces

Raw clams and oysters on the half shell seem to beg for a simple sauce treatment, even if only to scantily cloak their nakedness as they lie resplendent on a chilly bed of crushed ice. A squeeze of fresh lemon juice is the minimal embellishment; a more elaborate adornment such as Mango Mignonette sauce (page 22) is gilding the lily (or bivalve). Here are four more topping possibilities, all well suited to either clams or oysters:

• Classic cocktail sauce made with equal parts of ketchup or chili sauce and horseradish (freshly grated or from a fresh new jar of prepared horseradish), sparked by a squeeze of lemon and several shakes of hot pepper sauce.

• Pickled Japanese ginger, cut in shreds, finished with a sprinkle of chopped fresh parsley.

• Wasabi (green Japanese horseradish) mixed to a paste with rice vinegar.

• Homemade red or green tomato salsa, chopped extra fine, with extra cilantro added.

Wellfleet Oysters on the Half Shell with Mango Mignonette

MAKES 3 DOZEN DRESSED OYSTERS

This concept of adding fruit to a classic mignonette sauce is adapted from Chris Schlesinger, an authoritative Boston chef and cookbook author. In my version of the recipe, finely diced mango lends its sweetness to the vinegar-based sauce, balancing the sharper flavors and enhancing the clean, flinty taste of ice-cold oysters. Wellfleets, from a shallow, nutrient-rich bay off Cape Cod, are considered one of New England's most prized oysters, but many other varieties, including Cotuits, Pemaquids, and Cedar Points (named for the closest-by bay or town), are also delicious.

For the sauce:

2 tablespoons minced shallots
2 tablespoons minced mango, preferably, or papaya or cantaloupe
2 tablespoons minced fresh parsley
1 tablespoon cracked black peppercorns
¾ cup white wine vinegar

3 dozen scrubbed oysters, opened
Crushed ice
Parsley sprigs for garnish

1. To make the sauce, combine the shallots, mango or other fruit, parsley, pepper, and vinegar in a small bowl. Refrigerate for at least 30 minutes to allow flavors to blend, or up to 6 hours.
2. Arrange the opened oysters on a bed of crushed ice on a large tray or individual plates. Garnish with parsley, spoon a little sauce onto each oyster, and serve.

Jazzed-Up Maine Shrimp Boil

MAKES 4 TO 6 SERVINGS

Tiny, tender, fresh Maine shrimp are a seasonal treat that we commemorate every midwinter with an indoor picnic-style feast. Sometimes I simply steam the shrimp briefly in water and then serve them with melted butter or cocktail sauce, but I recently experimented with this spicy boil using ingredients similar to those in a New Orleans recipe from my book *The Best of New Orleans*, and I thought the results were fantastic. Just be careful not to overcook the shrimp, or they will get crumbly and lose their flavor.

> 4 pounds fresh Maine or other small or medium shrimp in their shells
> 2 tablespoons olive oil
> 3 tablespoons butter
> 2 garlic cloves, minced
> 1 teaspoon salt
> 1 teaspoon cracked black peppercorns
> 2 teaspoons crumbled dried rosemary
> ½ teaspoon cayenne pepper
> 2 bay leaves, broken in half
> 2 12-ounce bottles ale or beer
> 1½ lemons

1. Break the heads off the shrimp and rinse the shrimp under cool water.
2. Heat the oil and 1 tablespoon of the butter in a large saucepan or soup pot. Add the garlic, salt, black pepper, rosemary, cayenne, and bay leaves and cook over medium heat, stirring frequently, for 2 minutes. Add the ale or beer, bring to a boil, and simmer over low heat, uncovered, for about 10 minutes, until the liquid is reduced by about half. Cut the whole lemon in quarters, squeeze the juice into the sauce, and add the rinds to the pot. (This base can be made several hours ahead and held at cool room temperature or refrigerated.)
3. Return the ale mixture to a simmer. Add the shrimp, stir well, and simmer for 1 to 2 minutes, or just until they turn bright pink.
4. Using a slotted spoon, spoon the shrimp out onto 1 or 2 serving platters. Add the remaining 2 tablespoons of butter to the pot, swirl until it melts, and pour the sauce into 2 or 3 bowls.

5. To eat, everyone uses their fingers to peel their own shrimp and dunk it into the sauce. Slice the half lemon and float it in 2 bowls of water on the table so that guests can periodically dip their fingers in for a refreshing rinse.

Sandy Eaton on Crab Picking

Together, Randy and Sandy Eaton of Brooklin, Maine, make a perfectly matched shellfish duo. Many lobstermen still toss away the pesky rock and sand crabs that crawl into their traps and do damage to the prized lobster catch. Not Randy. Instead, he brings them home to Sandy, who steams them outside her back door in a state-inspected large stainless-steel pot, ices them down, and picks out the sweet, snowy-white-with-pink-edges meat to sell fresh every day from her licensed kitchen. Because the product does not get processed or shipped out of state, this Maine delicacy is something of a secret except to residents, who wait eagerly every summer for "Fresh Crabmeat" signs to sprout along the coastal roadways.

When I called on her one summer morning at eight, Sandy had been up working for three hours, boiling, chilling, cracking bodies and claws with the handle of her small paring knife, and picking out the fresh meat with the pointed blade of the same knife. "Lots of women like doing this," she says as her deft fingers never stop cracking and picking. "We can do it from home, care for our children as we work, be our own boss." I follow her and daughter Lacey over a rock ledge to the shore, where Sandy pulls a heavy trap from the water to retrieve more crabs to begin the process all over again. In this part of the world, where lobster has always reigned supreme, crabs have been something of an afterthought. Nor has an appreciation for shedders, or soft-shell crabs, ever been much cultivated in New England. "I know a woman," relates Sandy, "who went for a visit down to Maryland. When she was served a fried soft-shell crab for dinner, she insisted on 'picking' it first because she couldn't believe that people really expected her to eat all those claws and shell!"

Sweet Summer Crab on Cucumber Rounds

MAKES 4 TO 6 SERVINGS

In coastal Maine, freshly picked sweet, snowy white rock or sand crabmeat is available almost all summer long. This simple crab salad mixture, sparked by just a couple of propitious seasonings, gets heaped onto crisp cucumber rounds. I make this very often every summer because, to my mind, it is everything an hors d'oeuvre should be—full of rich flavor yet not so heavy as to spoil the courses to come. Any excellent quality crab-meat—Maryland lump crab or pasteurized or canned crab—can be used.

½ pound fresh snowy white lump-style crabmeat, picked over
¼ cup regular or lowfat mayonnaise, plus more to taste
3 tablespoons minced scallions, including green tops
2 teaspoons chopped fresh tarragon or ¾ teaspoon dried, plus sprigs
   for garnish
1 tablespoon fresh lemon juice
¾ teaspoon grated lemon zest
⅛ teaspoon cayenne pepper
Salt
1 long European cucumber

1. Combine the crabmeat, mayonnaise, scallions, tarragon, lemon juice and zest, and cayenne in a mixing bowl. Mix well to combine, breaking up any larger lumps of crabmeat so that the seasonings are well distributed. Add a spoonful or so more mayonnaise if necessary to bind the mixture, then season with salt to taste. (Can be made up to 1 day ahead and refrigerated.)
2. Rinse off the cucumber and score it decoratively by drawing the tines of a fork all the way down its length on all sides. Cut into slices between ⅛ and ¼ inch thick. Sprinkle the slices with salt.
3. Heap the crab mixture onto the cucumber rounds and arrange on a platter. Or serve the crab in a bowl surrounded by the cucumber slices so that guests can make their own. Garnish platter with sprigs of tarragon and serve.

Mini Crab Cakes with Lime-Pepper Sauce

MAKES ABOUT 24 TINY CAKES; 4 TO 6 SERVINGS

Crab cakes entered the New England food lexicon quite recently. They are seasoned much as they are in Maryland, where crab is king. These tiny cakes make a very elegant and special finger-food hors d'oeuvre. To serve them as a knife-and-fork first course, make the cakes a bit larger and cook them a little longer.

For the sauce:

½ cup regular or lowfat mayonnaise
1 tablespoon fresh lime juice
½ teaspoon grated lime zest
2 teaspoons chopped fresh tarragon
1 teaspoon fresh-ground black pepper

For the crab cakes:

1 egg
1½ cups fresh breadcrumbs
¼ cup minced scallions, including green tops
1 tablespoon regular or lowfat mayonnaise
1 teaspoon fresh lime juice
½ teaspoon Worcestershire sauce
¼ teaspoon Old Bay Seasoning or other Maryland-style seafood
    seasoning mix (see Note)
8 ounces fresh lump-type crabmeat, picked over
2 to 3 tablespoons vegetable oil
Thin lime slices or tarragon sprigs for garnish

1. To make the sauce, whisk together all the ingredients in a small bowl. Refrigerate for at least 2 hours or up to 3 days.
2. To make the crab cakes, lightly beat the egg in a large mixing bowl. Add ¾ cup of the breadcrumbs, the scallions, mayonnaise, lime juice, Worcestershire sauce, and Old Bay Seasoning. Blend well. Add the crabmeat and mix carefully with your clean hands, taking care not to shred the crab entirely.
3. Form the mixture into about 24 tiny patties, using a scant tablespoon for each cake. Place the remaining ¾ cup of crumbs on a plate and lightly dredge each side of the patties in the crumbs. (The cakes can be made a day ahead to this point and refrigerated.)
4. Heat 1 tablespoon of the oil in a large skillet over medium heat. Sauté as many crab cakes as will comfortably fit in the skillet until golden brown and crisp on both sides and hot inside, 4 to 5 minutes total. Repeat with the remaining oil and crab cakes. Serve immediately, or place on a foil-lined baking sheet, wrap well, and refrigerate for up to 24 hours or freeze. If made ahead, remove from the refrigerator

or freezer 30 minutes before reheating. Bake in a preheated 375-degree oven until hot and crisp.

5. Arrange the crab cakes on a platter or on individual serving plates, top with a teaspoonful of the lime-pepper sauce, garnish with lime slices or tarragon, and serve.

Note: Old Bay Seasoning is a mix of salt, pepper, and other spices. There are similar blends sold under the generic term "seafood seasoning mix."

Turkey Hill Taramasalata

MAKES ABOUT 2 CUPS

When I worked for Martha Stewart's catering business on Turkey Hill Road in Westport, Connecticut, we experimented with dozens of dip recipes to serve at big cocktail parties. This creamy, pale salmon pink taramasalata was—and still is—my absolute hands-down favorite of all that we tried. It's made with tarama, tiny, bright pink, salt-packed carp roe, that we bought in the always fascinating Steve's Greek grocery store in nearby Norwalk.

> 4 pieces good-quality white sandwich bread, crusts removed
> ⅓ cup whole or lowfat milk
> ½ cup (1 small jar) carp roe (tarama)
> ⅓ cup fresh lemon juice
> ¾ cup olive oil
> ¼ cup vegetable oil
> 2 tablespoons chopped fresh parsley

1. Combine the bread, broken into pieces, with the milk in a small bowl. Soak for about 30 minutes. Lift the bread out of the milk, gently squeeze it to extract most of the liquid, and place in a food processor.

2. Add the tarama and lemon juice to the work bowl and pulse once or twice to make a coarse paste. With the motor running, slowly pour the olive oil and vegetable oil through the feed tube, processing to make a smooth, slightly fluffy puree. Transfer to a bowl, cover with plastic wrap, and refrigerate. (The dip can be made up to 1 day ahead.)

3. Remove from the refrigerator at least 1 hour before serving. Sprinkle with parsley and serve with crackers, bread, or raw vegetable crudités.

Salt Cod

Before the days of refrigeration and food processing, salt cod was one of the world's most available and affordable fishes. Caught in enormous quantities in the North Atlantic, the cod was heavily salted, then dried on open-air racks in towns all over coastal New England and shipped to Europe, the Caribbean, and South America. Portuguese and Caribbean cooks were particularly skilled at turning this desiccated product that looks like cardboard and smells like day-old gym socks into absolutely delectable dishes. Today, whole sides of bacalao (its Spanish name) are stacked up for sale in ethnic markets in New England cities, and small wooden boxes of salt cod are still sold in the seafood department of many supermarkets. To rehydrate and remove the salt, soak the cod for at least 12 hours in cold water to cover, changing the water 3 or 4 times, and proceed with the instructions in a given recipe.

Caribbean Salt Cod Fritters

MAKES ABOUT 30 FRITTERS

We don't do much deep-frying at home these days, but I do make an exception for these fabulous Caribbean-Yankee fritters. Reconstituting the dried salt cod takes a little time, but its flavor is incomparable. In true West Indian fashion, the dough mixture includes the sharp, citrusy bite of fiery-hot chile peppers, as well as flecks of chopped tomato, scallion, and thyme. I serve these crispy fritters as I had them at Avery's Jamaica Kitchen in South Norwalk, Connecticut, with lemon wedges, and pass a bottle of Jamaican Pickapeppa Sauce (which is kind of like a cross between A-1 Sauce and Worcestershire, but HOT) for dipping.

> 6 ounces dried salt cod
> 1½ cups all-purpose flour
> 1 tablespoon yellow or white cornmeal

1 teaspoon baking powder
3 tablespoons minced seeded tomato
2 tablespoons minced scallions
1 teaspoon chopped fresh thyme or
   ½ teaspoon dried
½ teaspoon minced Scotch bonnet pepper
   or 2 teaspoons minced fresh or pickled
   jalapeño pepper
Vegetable oil for frying
Lemon wedges, optional
Bottled hot pepper sauce

> ### Dried Cod
>
> "Cod meat has virtually no fat (.3 percent) and is more than 18 percent protein, which is unusually high even for fish. And when cod is dried, the more than 80 percent of its flesh that is water having evaporated, it becomes concentrated protein—almost 80 percent protein."
>
> —Mark Kurlansky,
> *Cod, A Biography of the Fish That Changed the World*
> (Walker and Company, 1997)

1. Soak the cod in cold water to cover for at least 12 hours or overnight, changing the water 3 or 4 times. Drain, place in a saucepan, add water to cover, and bring to a boil. Simmer over medium-low heat until the fish is soft and flakes easily with a fork, 20 to 30 minutes. Drain, and when cool enough to handle, strip off and discard the skin and remove the fish from the bones. Finely chop the fish with a large knife or pulse in a food processor. You should have ¾ to 1 cup.

2. Stir or whisk together the flour, cornmeal, and baking powder in a large mixing bowl. Add the cod, tomato, scallions, thyme, and hot pepper and toss together to combine. Make a well in the center, add about 1 cup water, and stir gently but thoroughly to make a loose, sticky dough.

3. Heat about 1½ inches of vegetable oil in a large, deep, preferably cast-iron skillet to 350 degrees. Drop the dough by tablespoons into the hot fat and fry, turning once, until golden brown and crisp outside and cooked in the center, 3 to 5 minutes. Remove the fritters with a slotted spoon and drain on paper towels. Repeat with the remaining dough.

4. Serve the fritters hot, on a doily-lined platter, with lemon wedges if desired, and pass the bottle of hot sauce.

Maine Smoked Salmon and Caper Canapés

MAKES 32 CANAPÉS

This is a lovely way to showcase elegant, wafer-thin slices of the delicately wood-smoked salmon for which New England smokehouses are famous. Other fresh herbs, such as dill, basil, or tarragon, can be substituted for some of the scallions, if you like.

¼ pound (1 stick) unsalted butter, softened
¼ cup finely minced scallions, plus 3 scallion brushes for garnish, if
    desired (see Note)
2 teaspoons coarse-grained mustard
8 pieces thin-sliced dense pumpernickel bread
¼ pound thinly sliced smoked salmon
1 tablespoon small capers, drained
Cracked black peppercorns

1. Blend the butter, scallions, and mustard in a small bowl or food processor until well mixed. Set aside at room temperature for at least 1 hour or refrigerate for up to 3 days. Return to room temperature to soften to a spreadable consistency before using.

2. Lay the bread out on a work surface and spread evenly with the flavored butter. Lay slices of salmon evenly over each slice of bread. Use a sharp knife to cut off the crusts, and then cut each piece of bread diagonally into four quarters. Arrange on a wide, flat serving platter. (Can be prepared up to 3 hours ahead. Cover with damp paper towels and then wrap well in plastic wrap. Store in the refrigerator.)

3. When ready to serve, scatter the capers over the canapés, gently pressing them into the salmon. Sprinkle with cracked pepper and garnish the platters with scallion brushes, if you like.

Note: To make scallion brushes, trim scallions into 4-inch lengths and cut off the roots. Using a small sharp knife, make 4 or 5 1-inch-long cuts in the white end of each scallion. Drop into a bowl of water and ice cubes and let stand for about 30 minutes. The cut ends of the scallions will open up to look like a feathery brush.

Smoked Seafood

Ducktrap River Fish Farm near Camden in midcoast Maine, was founded by Des Fitzgerald in the late 1970s as a rainbow trout farm, and has now transformed itself into one of the leading U.S. producers of high-quality smoked Atlantic salmon, mussels, shrimp, trout, bluefish, scallops, sturgeon, and other fish. Ducktrap employs over one hundred people in a spotless, state-of-the-art smoking plant in Lincolnville, Maine. Each type of seafood is treated with a different brine solution, and smoked with a unique combination of hardwood chips. Small, sweet scallops, for example, are smoked over a delicate wood such as apple, while oilier fish such as salmon and bluefish are smoked over oak or maple. As public appreciation for quality American smoked seafood products increases, this relatively young industry continues to thrive and grow in New England, with other enthusiastic entrepreneurs entering the field to compete for the expanding market share.

Sublime Smoked Salmon Pâté

MAKES 1 CUP; ABOUT 6 SERVINGS

New England now boasts a growing number of fish-smoking operations. When sides of smoked salmon are sliced, the processors will often sell off less-than-perfect end pieces as "ends" or "bits," which are put to excellent use in spreads and pâtés. This one lives up to its name by tasting simply sublime. While you could blend it entirely in the food processor, I like the look of this not-completely-uniform color and hand-mixed texture.

    4 ounces cream cheese, softened
    1/3 cup packed (about 3 ounces) smoked salmon or lox, minced with a
        large knife or in a food processor
    1 tablespoon minced shallot
    2 teaspoons fresh lemon juice
    1 teaspoon grated lemon zest
    1 tablespoon plus 1 teaspoon chopped fresh dill
    1/4 teaspoon cayenne pepper
    1 tablespoon milk, if necessary
    1 tablespoon small capers, drained

1. Combine the softened cream cheese, smoked salmon, shallot, lemon juice and zest, 1 tablespoon dill, and cayenne in a medium-sized bowl. Work the mixture together using a wooden spoon until well combined. If the mixture is too thick to be workable, add a tablespoon or so of milk. Pack into a crock or decorative bowl and refrigerate for at least 2 hours to blend the flavors or for up to 2 days.
2. Remove from the refrigerator at least 1 hour before serving. Sprinkle the top of the pâté with capers and the remaining teaspoon of dill. Serve with crackers.

Broiled Westport Wings with Blue Cheese Dressing

MAKES 4 SERVINGS

A take-off on the famed snack invented in a bar near Buffalo, New York, this version is named in honor of my Connecticut town, wherein dwells a new, health-conscious breed of New Englander, many of whom are somewhat averse to deep-fried foods (or think they are). This broiled rendition of the classic recipe is every bit as lip-searingly, eye-wateringly hot as the original—and actually tastes every bit as delicious.

For the dressing:

½ cup regular or lowfat mayonnaise
½ cup crumbled blue cheese
2 tablespoons white wine vinegar
2 tablespoons minced scallions
½ teaspoon fresh-ground black pepper

For the wings:

3 tablespoons vegetable oil
1 tablespoon bottled hot pepper sauce
1 tablespoon Worcestershire sauce
½ teaspoon cayenne pepper
1½ pounds chicken wings, separated at the joints, tips discarded
4 celery ribs, trimmed and cut into sticks

1. To make the dressing, whisk together the mayonnaise, blue cheese, vinegar, scallions, and black pepper in a small bowl. Refrigerate for at least 1 hour to blend flavors, or for up to 2 days.
2. Stir together the oil, hot pepper sauce, Worcestershire sauce, and cayenne in another small bowl. Place the wings on a shallow, rimmed baking pan, pour the marinade over them, and toss to coat well. Set aside, loosely covered, for 30 minutes.
3. Preheat the broiler.
4. Uncover the pan, place about 6 inches from the heat, and broil, turning the wings once, until the chicken is cooked through and the skin is golden brown, 12 to 15 minutes. Watch closely to avoid burning.
5. Arrange the wings and celery sticks on a platter with the dressing for dipping.

Summer Nights

We'd start when the days grew longer in early June, when Overton's, the clam shack in East Norwalk, Connecticut, opened for the season. Segregated cars full of boys in one, girls in another, radios blasting, casually cruising past the small red-and-white drive-in on the harbor, checking out the action, stopping for a Coke, cruising some more, another stop for french fries, cheap, so a large order for each girl, all the while still casing the shack for boys in or out of their cars. And then finally our hunger for clams would overtake us, canceling out all discretion, all prudence, and we'd figure a way somehow to pool just enough money to buy a single order, lip-scalding hot from the fry vat, childish greasy crunchy batter enshrouding the bold, ocean-briny, adult taste of clam, three extra-tiny pleated paper cups of tartar sauce puh-leese, and we'd each get about two clams, but it was worth it, and just for those few minutes, as we finished licking our fingers, we'd forget to even glance at the boys.

Grilled Cumberland Quail
with Rosemary

MAKES 4 SERVINGS

Quail are farm raised in New England, as they are elsewhere in the country. When I serve these lovely little grilled quail as an appetizer, I suggest that guests pick them up, nibble off the succulent breast meat, and then gnaw on the crisp skin around the almost nonexistent leg and thigh meat. The beauty of the Cumberland sauce, which is a traditional English accompaniment to game, is that it serves here as both a "mopping" sauce and a "sopping" sauce. If guests are sitting around a table to eat these, finger bowls of water with sprigs of rosemary floating on top—along with a stack of napkins—are a thoughtful touch.

For the quail:

8 dressed quail (about 5 ounces each), cut in half along the backbone
¼ cup olive oil
1 garlic clove, crushed
2 tablespoons orange juice
2 tablespoons chopped fresh rosemary
¾ teaspoon salt
½ teaspoon fresh-ground black pepper

For the sauce:

¾ cup ruby port
3 tablespoons orange juice
3 tablespoons red currant jelly
2 tablespoons red wine vinegar
1 heaping tablespoon coarse-grained Dijon mustard
2 teaspoons chopped fresh rosemary, plus sprigs for garnish
2 teaspoons grated orange zest

Wrinkles?

"Wrinkles in Vinegar." I first saw them in a market on the coast of Maine, plastic containers of what looked like plain boiled periwinkles or small whelks. They must mean "winkles," I thought, and someone's made a spelling error on the label but decided to use up the batch before printing more. (This was, after all, New England, land of the archetypal thrifty Yankee). So I bought some—and yes, boiled periwinkles they were indeed, pickled in white vinegar, and absolutely scrumptious, especially when sliced thin and served chilled on crackers or lettuce leaves, sprinkled with a few chopped fresh herbs à la Italian conch salad. And no, by the way, it wasn't a printing error: Mainers do indeed call them "wrinkles."

1. To prepare the quail, flatten the quail with the heel of your hand so they will grill more evenly. Combine the oil, garlic, orange juice, rosemary, salt, and pepper in a shallow pan. Add the quail, turn to coat thoroughly, and set aside at cool room temperature for at least 1 hour or refrigerate for up to 8 hours.

2. To make the sauce, combine the port, orange juice, and jelly in a saucepan. Bring to a boil, stirring until the jelly melts, and cook, uncovered, over medium heat until reduced by about one-third, about 8 minutes. Remove from the heat and whisk in the vinegar, mustard, rosemary, and orange zest. Spoon out and reserve about 3 tablespoons of the sauce to brush on the quail. Set the rest of the sauce aside at room temperature.

3. Build a hot barbecue fire or preheat a gas grill.

4. Remove the quail from the marinade. Grill, turning several times and brushing with the reserved 3 tablespoons of sauce, until the skin is nicely charred and the meat juices run clear, 5 to 10 minutes.

5. Garnish with the rosemary sprigs and pass the remaining sauce for dipping.

Learning to Cook

When asked for advice on how to learn to be a good cook, Cynthia Sewell of the Jamaican-American Little Kitchen in South Norwalk, Connecticut, answered (while frying up a batch of her scrumptious cod fritters), "Just cook. That's the best way to learn. Just do it. And if you keep on doing it, pretty soon you'll begin to be really good at it."

THE CHOWDER, SOUP, AND STEW POT

Nothing, but nothing, better suits the New England winter clime than bracing, soul-satisfying soups and stews.

Chowders of various types, for which there are several exemplary recipes in this chapter, are, of course, quintessential New England. Thinner than stews and thicker than soups, chunky chowders stand smack in the middle of the soup spectrum. On one side are such delicate pureed vegetable potages as Midsummer's Eve Fresh Pea Soup (page 48) or Roasted Pumpkin-Cider Soup (page 45) and somewhat heartier New England brews such as Senator Lodge's Navy Bean Soup (page 51) or Cheddar and Ale Potage de Vermont (page 55). Yankee ethnics contribute many marvelous soups that are now familiar signposts on the region's culinary map. French Canadian *Soupe aux Pois* (page 49), Portuguese *Caldo Verde* (page 74), and Athena Diner Avgolemono (page 40) represent such deliciously satisfying mainstays.

And over on the far end of this continuum are New England's sublime seafood stews. If you've yet to eat the likes of Nantucket Bay Scallop Stew (page 61), Kennebunk Lobster Stew (page 63), or Portuguese Fish Stew (page 67), give yourself a treat by hauling out the stew pot and making one of these memorable classics of New England cuisine.

Athena Diner Avgolemono

MAKES 8 FIRST-COURSE SERVINGS; 4 MAIN-COURSE SERVINGS

Simple, delicious nourishment in a bowl, this Greek version of egg drop soup is my favorite cold-weather lunch—along with a fabulous Greek salad—at the Athena, a local Connecticut diner. The Athena typifies the high standards that we have come to expect from such Greek-run eating establishments: attractive neo-Greek decor, cheerful, professional service, and an extensive selection of good-quality home-style cooking. At home this is what I cook for any family member who might be feeling a tiny bit peaked or who is in need of a quick fix of nutritious comfort food.

>   8 cups chicken broth
>   1 cup orzo or ½ cup long-grain white rice
>   2 eggs
>   5 tablespoons fresh lemon juice
>   Salt and fresh-ground black pepper
>   1 tablespoon minced fresh parsley

1. Combine the broth and orzo or rice in a large soup pot and bring to a boil. Reduce the heat to low and simmer, covered, until the pasta or rice is tender, about 10 minutes for orzo, 20 minutes for rice.
2. Whisk the eggs with the lemon juice in a small bowl until smooth. Whisk about ½ cup of the hot broth into the egg mixture; then slowly and gradually whisk the egg mixture into the gently simmering soup, stirring until the soup achieves a smooth, velvety, lightly thickened consistency, 2 to 3 minutes. Season the soup with salt and pepper to taste.
3. Ladle into soup bowls and sprinkle with parsley before serving.

Marlene's Beauteous Butternut Bisque

MAKES 8 FIRST-COURSE SERVINGS, 4 MAIN-COURSE SERVINGS

Marlene O'Brien, one of Fairfield County, Connecticut's legendary cooks and caterers, whipped up a huge batch of this heavenly soup recently for a friend's supper party. Its vibrant orange-gold hue, the color of autumnal New England foliage, is sparked by just

The Chowder, Soup, and Stew Pot

Crown Pilot Survival

"Nabisco May Crack Down on Crown Pilots." "Losing the Pilot." "Crown Pilotless." "No More Hardtack, Matey?" Thus read some of the headlines in the late 1990s when Nabisco discontinued the cracker that most Yankees define as a necessary accompaniment to or thickener of chowders. A big, rectangular unsalted cracker, the Crown Pilot is a direct descendant of ship's biscuit, or hardtack. In a textbook example of Yankee determination, a grass roots "cracker crusade" convinced Nabisco to reconsider its decision, and, after a nine-month hiatus, headlines proclaimed, "Crown Pilots Are Back by Popular Demand."

---

a whisper of sweet curry powder and sharp ginger. This is more or less how Marlene *thinks* she made the soup that night—but these pureed vegetable soups are so forgiving that you can use this recipe as a basic formula from which to take off in all sorts of creative directions.

3 tablespoons butter
1 large onion, chopped
1 large carrot, peeled and chopped
1 small red bell pepper, chopped
2 garlic cloves, chopped
2 teaspoons curry powder
2 teaspoons ground ginger
8 cups cubed peeled butternut squash (from 1 large squash)
1 celery rib, broken in half
1 large bay leaf, broken in half
5 cups vegetable or chicken broth
1 cup orange juice
Salt and fresh-ground black pepper
1 cup minced unpeeled green apple tossed
    with 1 teaspoon lemon juice, for garnish

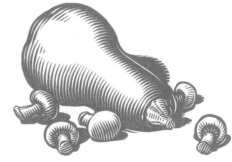

1. Melt the butter in a large, heavy soup pot. Add the onion, carrot, bell pepper, and garlic and cook over medium heat, stirring occasionally, until the onion is well caramelized and quite soft, 10 to 15 minutes. Sprinkle on the curry powder and cook, stirring, for 2 minutes. Stir in the ginger.

2. Add the squash, celery, and bay leaf to the pot, along with 3 cups of the broth. Bring to a boil, reduce the heat to medium-low, and cook, covered, until the squash is tender, 15 to 20 minutes.

3. Remove the celery and bay leaf and discard. Process the cooked squash mixture in a blender or food processor, in a couple of batches, to make a smooth puree. Return the puree to the soup pot. (This soup base can be made a day or two before serving and refrigerated, or it may be frozen. Reheat before proceeding.)

4. Whisk the remaining 2 cups of broth and the orange juice into the soup base. Bring to a simmer and season the soup with salt and black pepper to taste.

5. Ladle the soup into bowls and sprinkle a spoonful of the chopped apple garnish on top before serving. Pass the remaining chopped apple at the table.

Hungarian
Fresh Green Bean Soup

MAKES 8 FIRST-COURSE SERVINGS; 4 MAIN-COURSE SERVINGS

When my Italian friend who happens to be a parishioner at the Hungarian church in Bridgeport, Connecticut, was telling me about some of her favorite Hungarian dishes, she mentioned this fresh green bean soup in the second breath, after reviving from her swoon as she described Hungarian Crêpes with Walnut Filling (page 507). All the Hungarian-Americans from southern Connecticut that I have polled are unanimous in declaring this simple vegetable soup to be one of their favorite Hungarian specialties. After tasting it, I think you might agree that it is extraordinarily delicious.

> 1½ pounds green beans, trimmed and cut in 1-inch lengths
> 1½ pounds (about 3 medium) all-purpose potatoes, peeled and diced
> 1½ teaspoons salt, plus more to taste
> 3 tablespoons butter
> 3 tablespoons all-purpose flour
> 1 teaspoon sweet Hungarian paprika, plus more for garnish
> ¼ teaspoon fresh-ground black pepper, plus more to taste
> 1¼ cups sour cream
> 1½ tablespoons distilled white vinegar or white wine vinegar

1. Bring 8 cups of water to a boil in a large saucepan or soup pot. Add the beans, potatoes, and 1½ teaspoons salt. Return to a boil, reduce the heat to medium-low, and simmer, covered, for about 15 minutes or until the vegetables are tender.

2. Meanwhile, melt the butter in another saucepan. Stir in the flour and cook over medium-high heat, stirring constantly with a wooden spoon, for 2 minutes. Stir in the 1 teaspoon paprika and ¼ teaspoon pepper and cook for 1 minute. Whisk in about 1 cup of the hot soup water and cook, stirring, until smooth and thick, about 2 minutes. Remove from the heat and whisk in 1 cup of the sour cream.

3. Stir the sour cream mixture, a little at a time, into the gently simmering soup. Stir in the vinegar and cook gently, stirring occasionally, for about 5 minutes to blend the flavors. Do not bring the soup back to a rolling boil or it could curdle. Adjust the amount of liquid if necessary and season with salt and pepper to taste before serving.

4. To serve, ladle the soup into bowls and top with a small spoonful of the remaining sour cream and a dusting of paprika.

Martha Kostyra's Polish Wild Mushroom Soup

MAKES ABOUT 10 FIRST-COURSE SERVINGS; ABOUT 6 MAIN-COURSE SERVINGS

Martha Stewart's mother, Martha Kostyra, generously shared her version of this recipe for wild mushroom soup with me several years ago. I was working for "Martha Junior" at the time and was still collecting authentic (though redacted to fit American cooking styles) recipes to serve at the Polish Christmas Eve dinner I put on every year for my Polish-American husband and family. Richard and his knowing relatives proclaimed this soup "absolutely right, just like Nanna's," so it's now become a firmly entrenched part of our menu. The soup is meatless, but the dried wild mushrooms, with their haunting, intensely woodsy flavor, carry one back to a primeval European forest.

1½ ounces dried European mushrooms, such as porcini
8 cups vegetable or beef broth
1 large onion, chopped
4 carrots, peeled and diced
2 celery ribs with leafy tops, minced
2 garlic cloves, chopped

2 tablespoons chopped fresh parsley, preferably flat-leaf
1 pound domestic cultivated mushrooms, sliced
½ pound fresh wild mushrooms, such as shiitakes, sliced
⅓ cup very small pasta, such as squares, orzo, or tiny bows
1½ tablespoons butter
1½ tablespoons all-purpose flour
¾ cup sour cream
5 tablespoons chopped fresh dill
½ teaspoon fresh-ground black pepper, plus more to taste
Salt

1. Pour 2 cups of boiling water over the dried mushrooms in a bowl, and let them soak for about 40 minutes. Lift the softened mushrooms out of the soaking liquid, rinse under running water to remove any lurking grit, and coarsely chop them. Set the mushrooms aside. Strain the liquid through a coffee filter or double layer of cheesecloth and pour it into a large soup pot.

2. Add the vegetable or beef broth to the pot, along with 2 cups of water. Add the onion, carrots, celery, garlic, and parsley. Bring to a boil, reduce the heat to medium-low, and simmer, partially covered, for 20 minutes. Add the sliced fresh mushrooms and the reconstituted dried mushrooms and continue to simmer for about 30 minutes. (The soup can be made up to 3 days ahead to this point and refrigerated or frozen. Reheat before proceeding.)

3. Bring the soup to a full boil and add the pasta. Cook, uncovered, over medium heat for about 5 minutes, until the pasta is tender.

4. Melt the butter in a small saucepan. Whisk in the flour and cook over medium heat, stirring, for 2 minutes. Remove from heat and whisk in the sour cream. Stir in 3 tablespoons of the dill and the pepper. Whisk a ladleful of hot soup liquid into the sour cream mixture; then slowly whisk this mixture into the soup. Return to the heat and cook, stirring occasionally, for about 5 minutes, until the soup is lightly thickened and heated through. Since the sour cream has been stabilized with flour, it is unlikely to curdle, but it is best not to bring it to a rolling boil at this point. Season with salt and additional pepper to taste.

5. Ladle into soup bowls and sprinkle with the remaining 2 tablespoons of dill before serving.

Our Polish-American Christmas Eve

Every year, in an homage to my husband's Polish heritage, our family celebrates the Wiglia (Vigil) supper on Christmas Eve. The tradition is to "fast" on that holy night. Fasting means eating a meatless meal, but the menu is elaborate nonetheless. The table, set with an extra place for "the unexpected visitor," is adorned with the symbolic straw and manger scene, and an offering of coins, along with the *oplatek*, or communion host. Before the meal we pass the wafer from hand to hand around the table, along with good wishes, hugs and kisses, and blessings for the coming year. For the first course, we ladle out steaming bowls of Martha Kostyra's dill-flecked Wild Mushroom Soup (page 43). Next come the pierogi (page 219)—tender, plump little dumplings filled with cheese, potato, mushrooms, cabbage—along with side dishes of pickled herring, cheeses, Composed Winter Salad (page 99), and seeded rye bread and butter. In our version of the Wiglia, we finish the meal with coffee, a poppy seed pastry that I buy at the Polish-Hungarian deli in Bridgeport, Connecticut, and a big plate of assorted all-American Christmas cookies.

■ ■ ■ ■ ■ ■ ■ ■ ■ ■

Roasted Pumpkin-Cider Soup

MAKES 8 FIRST-COURSE SERVINGS; 4 MAIN-COURSE SERVINGS

Pumpkin farms and stands heaped high with this quintessentially American gourd are some of the most beautiful of autumn sights in New England. To make this soup, look for the small cooking pumpkins known as sugar pumpkins, as opposed to the large jack-o'-lantern variety. Long, slow roasting imbues the vegetables with an unbelievable depth of flavor, and when the mellow puree is further augmented by the spicy-sweetness of apple cider, the resulting soup is a dazzling celebration of the season.

> 1 small sugar pumpkin (4 to 4½ pounds), or 4 pounds Hubbard or
>   butternut squash
> 6 tablespoons butter
> ¼ cup packed brown sugar
> 1 large onion, cut in chunks
> 3 large carrots, peeled and cut in chunks
> 4 large garlic cloves, unpeeled
> 1 tart apple, such as Granny Smith, peeled, cored, and quartered
> 1 tablespoon chopped fresh rosemary or 2 teaspoons crumbled dried

Salt and fresh-ground black pepper
7 to 8 cups chicken or vegetable broth
2 cups apple cider or apple juice
1 teaspoon ground ginger
½ teaspoon ground mace
½ cup crème fraîche, yogurt, or sour cream
Fresh rosemary sprigs, optional

1. Preheat the oven to 350 degrees.
2. Cut the pumpkin or squash in half and scoop out the seeds. Place cut sides up in a large shallow roasting pan. Divide the butter and brown sugar among the cavities. Arrange the onion, carrots, garlic, and apple around the pumpkin or squash. Sprinkle with the rosemary and then with salt and pepper. Pour 2 cups of the broth around the vegetables and cover the pan with foil. Roast, stirring once or twice, until the vegetables are all very soft and caramelized, 1½ to 2 hours.

Aunt Menna's Soups

In the Saugatuck, Connecticut, *Festival Italiano* cookbook, Marie Nazzaro's Aunt Menna's thumbnail sketches of various Italian-style soups are a wonderful basic guide to soup making, conveying the kind of casual, breezy attitude that is perfectly appropriate for what should be a very free-form art.

Scudol and Beans:

Wash escarole and put in a pan. Add 2 whole cloves of garlic with 2 tablespoons of olive oil. Add 1 can tomato sauce. Add 1 can cannellini beans. Simmer over low heat stirring occasionally. Before serving, add ½ cup Parmesan cheese, if desired.

Lima Bean Soup:

Place 1 pound of small lima beans, washed, into a pan with 4 stalks of sliced celery, 2 sliced carrots, and 1 medium onion. Add 4 tablespoons butter and 1 can tomato sauce. Add enough water to just cover vegetables. Season with salt and pepper to taste and simmer until cooked. Serve with ½ cup of Parmesan cheese.

Chicken Soup:

Wash chicken parts well, then put into pot with water to cover. Add 3 tablespoons parsley, 1 large onion, sliced, and salt and pepper to taste. Simmer, covered but not tightly, with pan lid. Five minutes before the chicken is cooked, add a box of pastina and 1 cup of Parmesan cheese.

3. Scoop the pumpkin or squash pulp out of the skins. Squeeze the garlic out of its skins. Process the roasted vegetables and apple in a food processor, in batches if necessary, adding enough of the remaining broth to achieve a smooth puree. (This soup base can be made a day or two ahead and refrigerated.)

4. Transfer the puree to a large saucepan and whisk in the cider. Add as much of the remaining broth as necessary to achieve the desired consistency, and season with the ginger and mace. Bring to a boil, whisking, and simmer for a few minutes to blend the flavors. Season to taste with additional salt and pepper.

5. Serve the soup in bowls, topped with a dollop of crème fraîche and a rosemary sprig, if you like.

Hungarian Chilled Sour Cherry Soup

MAKES 8 FIRST-COURSE SERVINGS; 4 MAIN-COURSE SERVINGS

The thousands of Hungarians who have immigrated to New England have brought with them a passion for cherries. In their native Hungary, when cherries begin to come to market, they signal a welcome end to the long, cold winter, and that association with spring persists here in New England's similar climate. This soup is lovely for a light lunch or makes a refreshing starter to almost any meal at any time of year, whether preceding a spicy Hungarian Goulash (page 265) or an all-American roast supper.

> 2 16-ounce cans sour cherries with juice
> 4 tablespoons all-purpose flour
> 2 cups sour cream
> 2 teaspoons confectioners' sugar
> ¼ teaspoon salt
> Pinch of ground cloves
> 2 tablespoons fresh lemon juice
> Thin lemon slices for garnish

1. Heat the cherries with juice in a large saucepan over medium heat.

2. Whisk together the flour, sour cream, confectioners' sugar, salt, and cloves in a small bowl. Whisk in about 1 cup of the hot cherry liquid to temper it, then gradually whisk the sour cream mixture into the cherries in the saucepan. Stir in 4 cups of

water. Cook, stirring, until heated through and thickened. Gradually stir in a bit more water if necessary to thin the soup to the consistency of heavy cream. Add the lemon juice.

3. Transfer to a bowl, place a sheet of plastic wrap directly on the surface, and chill for at least 1 hour or for up to 24 hours.

4. Ladle the soup into bowls and float lemon slices on top.

Midsummer's Eve Fresh Pea Soup

MAKES 6 TO 8 FIRST-COURSE SERVINGS; 4 MAIN-COURSE SERVINGS

Fresh green peas are at their sweet peak in New England just as spring makes her magical leap into summer. Even though it's time-consuming to shell them, I make this lovely light potage with fresh peas once a year in honor of my favorite season. It is unadulterated with extraneous flavors, so the full impact of the primary vegetable comes shining through. Complete the spring theme with a radish salad, crunchy bread-sticks, and Rustic Rhubarb-Raspberry Tart (page 616) for dessert. This is also perfectly delicious made with frozen green peas.

> 4 tablespoons butter, preferably unsalted
> 1 medium onion, preferably a spring onion, chopped
> 4 cups shelled fresh peas or 2 10-ounce packages frozen peas
> 4 cups vegetable broth or chicken broth
> ½ cup dry vermouth or white wine
> ¼ cup coarsely chopped fresh flat-leaf parsley, plus 2 small sprigs or
>   leaves for garnish
> 1 teaspoon salt, or more to taste
> 4 cups torn Boston lettuce
> 1 cup whole milk or half-and-half
> ½ teaspoon white pepper, or to taste
> ⅓ cup crème fraîche, plain yogurt, or lowfat sour cream, optional

1. Melt the butter in a large saucepan. Add the onion and cook over medium heat, stir-ring occasionally, until softened, about 5 minutes. Add the peas, broth, 2 cups of water, vermouth or wine, parsley, and salt. Bring to a boil, reduce the heat to

medium-low, and cook, covered, for about 6 minutes, until the peas are about half cooked. Add the lettuce and continue to cook until the peas are completely tender, 4 to 8 minutes more. (If using frozen peas, they will probably take a few minutes less to cook.)

2. Puree the soup in a blender or food processor, in batches if necessary, until smooth. Return to the saucepan, add the milk or half-and-half, and heat through. Season with white pepper and additional salt if necessary.

3. Ladle into bowls, top with a dollop of crème fraîche, if you like, and garnish with a parsley leaf.

French Canadian Soupe aux Pois

MAKES 4 TO 5 MAIN-COURSE SERVINGS

Please don't be horrified at the amount of salt pork in this recipe. If you've ever had French Canadian yellow pea soup in a can, you'll find lard listed on the label. The salt pork in this recipe lends both its richness and intense flavor to the sweet but otherwise rather bland tasting dried yellow peas.

> 1 pound dried whole yellow peas, rinsed (see Note)
> ½ pound salt pork, cut in 2 or 3 chunks
> 1 large onion, chopped
> 1 large celery rib, chopped
> 1 large carrot, peeled and chopped
> 3 garlic cloves, chopped
> 1 large sprig fresh rosemary
> Salt and black pepper

1. If you like, soak the peas in water to cover for 4 hours or overnight. Drain in a colander. Bring 8 cups of water to a boil in a large kettle or soup pot. Add the soaked or unsoaked peas and the salt pork, return to a boil, and skim off any foam that rises. Add the onion, celery, carrot, garlic, and rosemary, cover, and simmer the soup over low heat until the peas are tender, 1½ to 3 hours. (Unsoaked peas will take the longer cooking time.) Check the water level periodically and add up to 2 cups more water if necessary to keep the peas well covered.

2. Remove and discard the pieces of salt pork and the rosemary. In a food processor, process the soup, in 2 or 3 batches if necessary, to a slightly textured puree. Season with salt and pepper to taste. (The soup can be made up to 3 days ahead and refrigerated, or it may be frozen.)

Note: Yellow split peas can be substituted here, but the skins on the whole dried peas actually do add the requisite authentic texture to the soup.

Salt Pork

"Salt pork is everywhere. Salt pork in the soup. *Soupe aux pois.* Fresh string beans in the pressure cooker with salt pork thrown in *pour donner d'bon gout.* Salt pork as a staple. No French-Canadian, later called Franco-American, cook would be caught without the salt pork in her kitchen."

—Rhea Cote Robbins, *Wednesday's Child* (Excerpted from *A Maine Writers' Cookbook,* Maine Writers Alliance, 1998)

Split Pea Soup with Smoked Ham

MAKES 4 TO 5 MAIN-COURSE SERVINGS

New Hampshire and Vermont produce some of the best smoked ham in the region, much of it cured with maple sugar or syrup. If you're lucky enough to have one of these large bone-in beauties for some special occasion, here's what to do with the ham bone after you've pried off most of the meat.

> 1 pound dried split peas, rinsed
> 1 large meaty ham bone or 2 smoked ham hocks
> 4 cups chicken broth
> 1 bay leaf
> 1 large onion, chopped
> 2 large or 3 small carrots, peeled and chopped
> 1 large celery rib, chopped

1 garlic clove, chopped
2 tablespoons chopped fresh thyme or 2 teaspoons dried
4 tablespoons chopped parsley
½ cup dry sherry
½ teaspoon fresh-ground black pepper
Salt to taste

1. Combine the split peas, ham bone, broth, bay leaf, and 5 cups of water in a large soup pot. Bring to a boil over high heat, cover, and cook over low heat until the peas are almost tender, about 1 hour.
2. Add the onion, carrots, celery, garlic, thyme, and 2 tablespoons of the parsley. Cook, uncovered, over medium heat until the split peas and vegetables are tender, about 30 minutes.
3. Remove the ham bone, strip off the meat, and discard the bone. Chop the ham and return it to the soup. Discard the bay leaf. (You can serve the soup at this point, but I prefer to puree it as follows.)
4. Process the soup in a food processor in batches, pulsing to make a textured, not completely smooth puree. Stir in the sherry, remaining 2 tablespoons of parsley, and the pepper. Season with salt to taste, and adjust the liquid if necessary. (The soup can be made up to 3 days ahead and refrigerated, or it may be frozen.)
5. Ladle the soup into bowls to serve.

Senator Lodge's Navy Bean Soup

MAKES 8 FIRST-COURSE SERVINGS; 4 TO 6 MAIN-COURSE SERVINGS

Massachusetts Senator Henry Cabot Lodge urged a hearty navy bean soup on his fellow legislators after World War I, and it quickly became the deservedly famous Senate Bean Soup. The Capitol Hill dining rooms still can't quite agree on an "official" recipe (and why are we not surprised?); in fact, my research has turned up about a dozen different variations, from an absolutely bare-bones version calling for almost nothing more than beans and water, to very complex concoctions. This, my favorite recipe for the soup, uses small white beans, a smoky ham hock, and a bit of potato for extra body and thickening—perfect for lunch on a chilly winter day, to which many generations of legislators will testify.

1 pound dried navy beans or other white beans, such as Great
   Northern, rinsed and picked over (see Note)
1 meaty ham bone or 2 ham hocks
1 large bay leaf
1 large onion, chopped
1 medium all-purpose potato, peeled and chopped
2 carrots, peeled and chopped
2 celery ribs, chopped
2 garlic cloves, chopped
1 cup tomato sauce
1 teaspoon salt, or more to taste
½ teaspoon fresh-ground black pepper

1. If you like, soak the beans in water to cover for 4 hours or overnight. Drain in a colander. Bring 8 cups of water to a boil in a large soup pot. Add the soaked or unsoaked beans, ham bone, and bay leaf. Bring to a boil, reduce the heat to low, and cook, covered, until the beans are almost tender, 1½ to 2 hours. Strip as much meat off the ham bone or hocks as you can and cut it into small pieces. Discard the bones and return the meat to the soup.

2. Add the onion, potato, carrots, celery, and garlic. Cook at a gentle simmer, uncovered, until the vegetables are very tender, 30 to 40 minutes. Add the tomato sauce and season with salt and pepper. Discard the bay leaf.

3. Process about half the soup in a food processor until fairly smooth. Stir the puree into the remaining soup. (The soup can be made 3 days ahead and refrigerated, or it may be frozen.)

4. Simmer over medium heat until heated through, adjusting the liquid and seasonings if necessary. Ladle into soup bowls to serve.

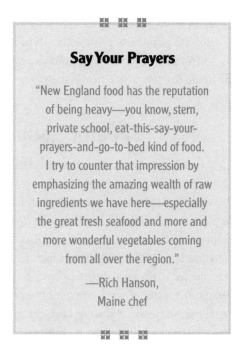

Say Your Prayers

"New England food has the reputation of being heavy—you know, stern, private school, eat-this-say-your-prayers-and-go-to-bed kind of food. I try to counter that impression by emphasizing the amazing wealth of raw ingredients we have here—especially the great fresh seafood and more and more wonderful vegetables coming from all over the region."

—Rich Hanson,
Maine chef

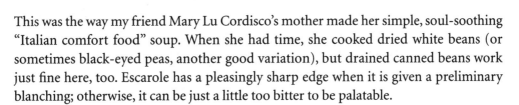

Note: This soup really profits from its long simmering with a ham bone, but you could take a shortcut and use 6 cups of canned white beans, adding them in Step 2 along with about 7 cups of water.

Mrs. Cordisco's Escarole and White Bean Soup

MAKES 4 TO 5 MAIN-COURSE SERVINGS

This was the way my friend Mary Lu Cordisco's mother made her simple, soul-soothing "Italian comfort food" soup. When she had time, she cooked dried white beans (or sometimes black-eyed peas, another good variation), but drained canned beans work just fine here, too. Escarole has a pleasingly sharp edge when it is given a preliminary blanching; otherwise, it can be just a little too bitter to be palatable.

> 1 teaspoon salt, plus more if necessary
> 1 head escarole (about 1½ pounds), rinsed and torn or cut into
>   bite-sized pieces (10 to 12 cups)
> 4 tablespoons olive oil, preferably extra-virgin
> 4 large garlic cloves, finely chopped
> 1¼ teaspoons dried oregano
> ¼ teaspoon red pepper flakes
> 7 cups chicken broth
> 4 cups drained cooked white beans, such as cannellini or
>   Great Northern
> ½ cup fresh-grated Parmesan cheese

1. Bring 12 cups of water to a boil in a large soup pot. Add the 1 teaspoon salt and escarole and boil, uncovered, until the greens are tender, about 5 minutes. Drain in a colander.
2. Return the pot to the stove and add the oil. Add the garlic, oregano, and red pepper flakes and cook over medium heat, stirring, until fragrant, about 1 minute. Add the broth, beans, and cooked escarole. Bring to a boil, reduce the heat to medium-low, and simmer until the broth is slightly reduced and the flavors have blended. Taste

and season the soup with salt to taste. (None may be needed, depending on the saltiness of the broth.)

3. Ladle into shallow soup bowls and pass the cheese at the table for sprinkling over each serving.

Zuppa di Ceci (Chickpea Soup)

MAKES 4 MAIN-COURSE SERVINGS

I love talking food and recipes with my friends Phyllis Diiorio and Ann Marie DeFinis Dustin. Both grew up in large southern Italian–American families in Norwalk, Connecticut; you would think their food memories would be quite similar. Not always. "My grandmother always put ditalini in her *zuppa di ceci* (pronounced 'zupe da cheech'), and just a little tomato," proclaims Ann Marie. "Never pasta," counters Phyllis. "Just the beans. And quite a lot of tomato." I'll settle the argument by adding both pasta *and* quite a bit of tomato to this one—but believe me, if you use fresh garlic, good quality oil, and imported pecorino Romano cheese, any version of this salt-of-the-earth peasant soup is guaranteed to taste fantastic.

> 4 tablespoons extra-virgin olive oil
> ¼ cup chopped celery leaves and tops
> 4 large garlic cloves, minced
> 7 cups vegetable or chicken broth
> 4 cups drained cooked chickpeas (garbanzo beans)
> 1 cup chopped seeded plum tomatoes, fresh or canned
> 4 ounces small pasta, such as ditalini
> 2 tablespoons chopped fresh sage or 1 tablespoon crumbled dried
> ¼ teaspoon red pepper flakes
> Salt
> About ½ cup grated pecorino Romano cheese

1. Heat the oil in a large soup pot. Add the celery and garlic and cook over medium heat, stirring, for 2 minutes. Add the broth, chickpeas, and tomatoes and bring to a boil. Reduce the heat to medium-low and simmer, partially covered, for 10 minutes to develop the flavors. Add the pasta, sage, and red pepper flakes and simmer, uncovered, until the pasta is just tender, about 10 minutes. Season with salt to taste.

2. To serve, ladle into bowls and pass the cheese for sprinkling over the soup at the table.

Cheddar and Ale
Potage de Vermont

MAKES 6 TO 8 FIRST-COURSE SERVINGS; 4 MAIN-COURSE SERVINGS

Even if you make this soup with ordinary supermarket cheddar, it will be delicious; if you use one of the tangy extra-sharp farmhouse cheddars for which Vermont is justly famous, it will be something very special. This does beautifully as a first course for a winter dinner party, or serve it for a supper main course with crunchy sesame-seed breadsticks and perhaps a spinach salad.

3 tablespoons butter
1 large onion, chopped
2 carrots, peeled and chopped
1 celery rib, chopped
⅓ cup all-purpose flour
2 teaspoons dry mustard
4 cups chicken broth
1 cup flat ale or beer, at room temperature
2 cups whole or lowfat milk
4 cups (1 pound) grated sharp or extra-sharp cheddar cheese, such as
   farmhouse cheddar
4 tablespoons chopped fresh dill
¼ teaspoon cayenne pepper
Salt and fresh-ground black pepper

1. Heat the butter in a large saucepan. Add the onion, carrots, and celery and cook over medium heat, stirring occasionally, until the vegetables begin to soften, about 4 minutes. Sprinkle on the flour and mustard and cook, stirring, for 1 to 2 minutes. Whisk in the broth until smooth. Cover the pan and cook over medium-low heat

until the carrots are very soft, 10 to 15 minutes. Transfer this soup base to a food processor and process to make a smooth puree. Return the puree to the saucepan.

2. Whisk in the ale and simmer, uncovered, stirring often, for about 5 minutes. Whisk in the milk. Reduce the heat to low. Add the cheese, a handful at a time, whisking in each addition until it melts before adding another. Add 3 tablespoons of the dill and the cayenne and season with salt and pepper to taste. (The soup can be made 1 day ahead and refrigerated.)

3. When ready to serve, reheat the soup very gently over low heat, stirring until steam rises. Do not boil or the cheese may separate. Ladle into soup bowls and sprinkle with the remaining 1 tablespoon dill.

Thick and Creamy Boston Clam Chowder

MAKES ABOUT 3 QUARTS; 4 MAIN-COURSE SERVINGS

Here is a chowder in the classic Bostonian style—lightly thickened with flour, enriched with a bit of light cream, chock full of chopped hard-shell clams and cubed potatoes, and enhanced with a goodly sprinkling of thyme, the chowder herb. The recipe is adapted from the *Legal Sea Foods Cookbook,* and is essentially the chowder that has been introducing legions of visitors to Boston's "specialty of the house" for a couple of decades. This homemade version makes for an ideal cold-weather supper, especially when served with Pickled Coleslaw (page 85), common crackers, and a dessert of Maple-Ginger Baked Apples (page 499).

¼ pound salt pork, minced (about 1 cup)

1 large onion, chopped

¼ cup all-purpose flour

3 cups whole or lowfat milk

4 cups clam liquor, clam broth, bottled clam juice, or a combination

1½ pounds all-purpose potatoes, peeled and diced (4 to 5 cups)

1 large bay leaf, broken in half

2 teaspoons dried thyme or 2 tablespoons chopped fresh

3 cups coarsely chopped hard-shell clams (see Note)

2 cups half-and-half or light cream

Salt and fresh-ground black pepper

1 tablespoon unsalted butter

1. Cook the salt pork in a large kettle or soup pot over medium heat until the fat is rendered and the pork bits are crispy, about 10 minutes. Remove the pork with a slotted spoon to drain on paper towels, leaving the drippings in the pot.

2. Add the onion to the drippings and cook, stirring frequently, until it begins to soften, about 6 minutes. Sprinkle on the flour and cook, stirring, for 2 minutes. Add the milk and clam liquor, whisking until smooth. Add the potatoes, bay leaf, and dried thyme (if using dried) and cook, uncovered, for 10 minutes, until the potatoes are almost tender. Add the clams and fresh thyme (if using fresh) and stir in the half-and-half. Continue to simmer until the potatoes are tender, about 5 more minutes. Season with salt and pepper to taste. Remove from the heat and let the chowder sit, partially covered, at cool room temperature for at least 1 hour, or refrigerate for up to 2 days. Reheat gently, discarding the bay leaf.

3. To serve, ladle the chowder into soup bowls, add a small square of butter, and stir to swirl in. Sprinkle with the reserved salt pork cracklings, if you like.

Note: You can buy chopped fresh clams from a fish market, or use 5 quarts of scrubbed hard-shell quahogs and steam them in a small amount of water in a large kettle until they open, 5 to 15 minutes, depending on size. Then scrape out the clam meat and chop or cut it with scissors into cranberry-size pieces. Pour the cooking liquid into a glass measuring cup, let any mud settle, and pour off the clean broth to use in the chowder.

> ### Chowder Ageism
>
> Many New England cooks, particularly those from Cape Cod, are adamant about aging their clam chowder, insisting that the chowder should be "cured" for at least 36 hours before even thinking about eating it. This ripening process deepens and intensifies the good clam flavor.

Chowder Wars

Battles over clam chowder have been going on for two or three centuries. Regional distinctions are blurred now, but here are some of the traditional variations.

Boston or New England–Style Chowder:

A milk or cream base, flavored with salt pork, full of diced potatoes and often also thickened with flour; made with chopped hard-shell clams. Clam chowder is the best-known type, but chowders of this stripe can also be made with fish, and in northern New England you can find lots of farmhouse chowders made with corn, chicken, parsnips, and other root vegetables.

Rhode Island–Style Red Chowder:

A clear, milky, or creamy chowder with just enough tomatoes added to color the brew a pretty pink. The occasional Rhode Islander will lay claim to the chowder usually known as Manhattan style, which is like a chunky vegetable soup with clams added, but real New Englanders disdain this as heretical.

Maine-Style Clam Chowder:

A milky, brothy chowder, not thickened with flour. This Down East chowder is made with chopped or small whole steamer (soft-shell) clams, cubed potatoes, and finished with pools of melted butter. A somewhat similar chowder, made with even less milk and more broth (sometimes called "clear" chowder), can still be found at clam shacks in southern New England.

Ethnic Variations I Have Tasted:

One evening at the Kossuth Club, a Hungarian-American social club in Bridgeport, Connecticut, I ate Hungarian-style clam chowder, made blushing pink with liberal doses of sweet paprika and enriched—naturally—with sour cream. And the redoubtable Aunt Menna (see page 46) makes hers Italian-style with chopped tomatoes and seasons the chowder with a little oregano.

❖ ❖ ❖ ❖ ❖ ❖ ❖ ❖ ❖

Milky Maine Steamer Chowder

MAKES ABOUT 3 QUARTS; 4 MAIN-COURSE SERVINGS

In this quintessential Down East chowder, the delicate, subtle sea flavor of soft-shell, or steamer, clams prevails. In fact, if Mainers are building a chowder with hard-shell clams, they specifically label it quahog chowder to differentiate it from the "genuine" article. Never, ever is even a sprinkle of flour introduced; instead, the thickening power of well-cooked floury potatoes gives the chowder its weight. Evaporated milk was used

originally as a convenience but has now become standard in most classic recipes, its smooth creaminess somehow balancing the brininess of the clams. This chowder is one that really benefits from a good long period of aging or ripening to intensify and deepen the clam flavor.

> 2½ pounds (about 50) soft-shell clams (see Note)
> 3 to 4 ounces salt pork, minced (about ¾ cup)
> 1 medium onion, chopped
> 1½ pounds russet or all-purpose potatoes, peeled and diced
>   (4 to 5 cups)
> 6 cups clam liquor, clam broth, bottled clam juice, or a combination
> 3 cups whole milk
> 1 can (12 ounces) evaporated milk
> Salt and fresh-ground black pepper
> 2 tablespoons unsalted butter

1. Scrub the clams well and steam them in a large pot with about 1 cup of water just until they open, 5 to 10 minutes, depending on their size. When cool enough to handle, remove the clams from their shells over the cooking pot to catch the juices. Pull the black skin off the necks and, if the clams are large, separate the soft parts from the firm; chop the firm parts. (If small, leave whole.) Strain the broth through cheesecloth or a dish towel and reserve.

2. Cook the salt pork in a large kettle or soup pot over medium heat until the fat is rendered and the pork bits are crispy, about 10 minutes. Remove with a slotted spoon to drain on paper towels, leaving the drippings in the pot.

3. Add the onion to the drippings and cook until it begins to soften, about 6 minutes. Add the diced potatoes and clam liquor, bring to a boil, reduce the heat to medium-low, and simmer, partially covered, until the potatoes are almost tender, about 10 minutes. Add the clams and simmer until the potatoes are tender, about 5 minutes longer. Stir in the milk and evaporated milk and heat through. Season with salt and pepper to taste. (Remove from the heat and let the chowder sit, at cool room temperature, for at least 2 hours, or refrigerate for up to 2 days.)

4. Reheat over very low heat, stirring frequently, until the chowder steams and is heated through. This chowder should not boil or it could curdle. Stir in the butter until it melts and adjust the seasonings if necessary. Ladle into shallow bowls to serve. Pass the reserved salt pork bits for sprinkling on top, if you like.

Note: Instead of steaming the clams open, as instructed in Step 1, you can shuck the raw clams relatively easily if you prefer. First scrub the clams well to remove as much mud as possible. Use a small sturdy knife to separate the two shells, and then scrape out the bodies, working over a bowl to catch any juices. Strain the flavorful liquor through a double layer of cheesecloth and use it in the chowder. If you use raw clams, cook them about 5 minutes longer in the chowder.

Rhode Island Red Chowder

MAKES ABOUT 2 QUARTS; 3 TO 4 MAIN-COURSE SERVINGS

By the last half of the nineteenth century, the whole of southern New England had begun its enthusiastic love affair with the tomato. Tomatoes began making their way into more and more old-time Yankee dishes, eventually adding their blushing beauty even to traditional chowders, particularly in Rhode Island. This savory chowder, which is tinted an attractive pale orange-pink by its tomato additions, is thickened in one of the classical ways with crumbled crackers. It is wonderful with a crunchy salad such as Crisp Apple Slaw (page 86) and perhaps a platter of fruit and Melanie's Molasses Crinkle Cookies (page 569) for dessert.

3 to 4 ounces thick-sliced bacon or salt pork, chopped
2 medium onions, chopped
3 tablespoons all-purpose flour
4 cups clam broth or a mixture of liquor drained from clams and
    bottled clam juice
3 cups whole milk
1 pound all-purpose potatoes, peeled and diced (about 4 cups)
1½ teaspoons dried oregano
1 large bay leaf, broken in half
2 cups diced seeded plum tomatoes (about 1 pound)
2 cups coarsely chopped hard-shell clams (about 4 quarts; see Note
    page 57)
3 tablespoons ketchup
¼ teaspoon baking soda

Salt and fresh-ground black pepper
1 tablespoon unsalted butter
8 common crackers or saltines, crumbled

1. Cook the bacon or salt pork in a large kettle or soup pot over medium heat until the fat is rendered and the bits are crispy, about 10 minutes. Remove with a slotted spoon to drain on paper towels, leaving the drippings in the pot.

2. Add the onions to the drippings and cook until softened but not brown, about 6 minutes. Sprinkle the flour over the onions and cook, stirring, for 2 minutes. Whisk in the clam broth and milk. Add the potatoes, oregano, and bay leaf and simmer, uncovered, for 10 minutes, until the potatoes are almost tender. Add the tomatoes and clams and simmer, uncovered, over medium heat until the potatoes are very tender, 5 to 10 minutes.

3. Combine the ketchup and baking soda in a small dish, and whisk the mixture into the chowder. Season with salt and pepper to taste. Set aside for an hour or so or refrigerate for up to 2 days.

4. When ready to serve, reheat the chowder gently over medium-low heat. Add the butter and swirl until melted. Adjust the seasonings if necessary. Place the crumbled crackers in the bottom of soup bowls and ladle the chowder over them. Pass the bacon or salt pork bits for sprinkling over the top, if you like.

> ### Moby Dick's Nantucket Chowder
>
> "Fishiest of all fishy places [on Nantucket] was the try pots, which well deserves its name; for the pots there were always boiling chowders. Chowder for breakfast, and chowder for dinner, and chowder for supper, till you begin to look for fish-bones coming through your clothes."
>
> —Herman Melville,
> *Moby Dick* (1851)

Nantucket Bay Scallop Stew

MAKES 4 MAIN-COURSE SERVINGS

A very traditional Nantucket bay scallop stew is white-on-white and completely unadorned (see page 62), tasting of nothing more than its essential ingredients—fresh sweet scallops and pure creamery milk and butter. Here is a slight variation, treated to a

White Marbles

"Each small scallop, no kin either in size or flavor to those we knew elsewhere, was plump and succulent, the size and color of a small white marble. The judicious amount of creamy elixir surrounding them repeated their flavor without obvious distractions . . . bathing them in hot milk and cream. The result was a dish in which tiny, perfect, tender scallops swam gladly in a small creamy sea, with a coral crest of paprika-dusted melting butter."

—Virginia Rich,
The Nantucket Diet Murders
(Delacorte Press, 1985)

contemporary "facelift," but with its beautiful and delicious soul intact. Considering the price of scallops these days, I consider this company fare, and would accompany the stew with Pilot or common crackers and a dark leafy green salad, and finish with Slice of New England Cranberry-Apple-Walnut Pie (page 603).

2 cups whole milk
2 cups half-and-half
1 small onion, quartered
Leafy top of 1 celery rib
4 sprigs fresh parsley, including stems
1 teaspoon salt
1 large bay leaf, broken in half
⅓ cup minced celery
1½ pounds bay scallops
2 tablespoons snipped fresh chives
1 tablespoon chopped fresh tarragon or
    1 teaspoon dried
1 tablespoon chopped fresh marjoram or
    1 teaspoon dried
¼ teaspoon cayenne pepper
4 tablespoons unsalted butter
Fresh-ground black pepper

1. Combine the milk, half-and-half, onion, celery top, parsley, salt, and bay leaf in a large saucepan. Heat over medium heat just until bubbles form around the edges, about 3 minutes. Reduce the heat to very low, cover, and simmer gently for 5 minutes. Remove from the heat and let stand for 10 more minutes to infuse the milk with the flavor of the seasoning vegetables. Strain out the vegetables and discard, returning the flavored milk to the saucepan.

2. Add the chopped celery to the milk and simmer, covered, over low heat until it softens slightly, about 5 minutes. (This base can be made a day ahead and refrigerated. Reheat gently before proceeding.)

3. Add the scallops, chives, tarragon, marjoram, and cayenne. Simmer gently, uncovered, until the scallops are just cooked through, about 3 minutes. Add the butter, stirring until it melts. Season with pepper and adjust the other seasonings to taste.
4. Ladle the stew into shallow soup bowls to serve.

To Freeze Scallops

Scallops, especially sea scallops, freeze better than most other seafood. Place the scallops in a plastic container with a lid, add milk to cover, and put the lid on the container.

Kennebunk Lobster Stew

MAKES 4 MAIN-COURSE SERVINGS

Marjorie Standish writes in *Cooking Down East* that "an old Maine recipe is just as much of an heirloom as a lovely antique," and that's exactly what this stew is. It might sound impossibly rich by today's standards, but when the stew is aged for at least six hours as I suggest here, a kind of alchemy happens, so that by the time you eat it, each spoonful is fully infused with the essence of lobster. I would serve this at a midsummer all-seafood supper, starting perhaps with Crab Cakes with Lime-Pepper Sauce (page 25). Crusty Corn Sticks (page 451) and a simple mesclun salad are good accompaniments to the stew, and Best Maine Blueberry Pie (page 601) a fitting finale.

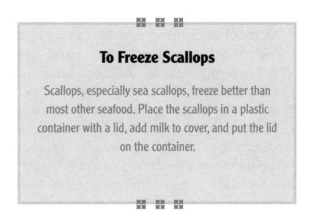

> 3 live 1- to 1¼-pound lobsters
> 6 tablespoons unsalted butter
> ¾ cup dry white wine
> 2 teaspoons paprika
> 2 cups heavy cream
> 3 cups whole milk
> Salt if necessary

1. Boil or steam the lobsters in a large pot in or over salted water until they are just barely cooked, about 8 minutes. Remove with tongs to a rimmed baking sheet.

When cool enough to handle, crack the shells over a bowl, saving as much juice as possible. Extract the tail and claw meat, chop it into 1-inch chunks, and reserve. Scoop the green tomalley (or liver) out of the bodies and reserve it. (The tomalley looks unappealing at this point, but it is full of flavor, and its color will not affect the finished stew.) Reserve 2 of the lobster bodies.

2. Melt the butter in a large heavy soup or stew pot. Add the tomalley and simmer for 5 minutes. Add the wine and cook over medium heat until the liquid is reduced by about half, about 5 minutes. Add the lobster meat along with any saved juices, sprinkle on the paprika, and cook, stirring, for 2 minutes.

3. Slowly add the cream, stirring constantly. Then stir in the milk. Add the reserved lobster bodies to the stew, pushing them down so they're submerged in the liquid. (They lend more flavor to the finished stew.) Cool the finished stew to room temperature, then refrigerate for at least 6 hours or up to 24 hours.

4. When ready to serve, remove and discard the lobster shells. Reheat the stew very slowly, stirring frequently so that it does not curdle. Taste for seasoning, adding salt if necessary. Ladle into deep bowls and serve.

To Clean Mussels and Clams

Both mussels and hard-shell (quahog) clams usually arrive at market these days in a fairly clean state. Hard-shell clams should be soaked in cold water for an hour or so and given a quick scrub with a stiff brush before cooking. Farm-raised mussels are likewise mostly grit free and just need rinsing or a brief scrub. If the tough black filament, or "beard" is still attached, pull it off. Mussels are okay to cook even if their shells are slightly open, but discard any that are still closed after steaming. Attention should be paid, though, to the cleaning of soft-shell, or steamer, clams, whether you buy them from a fish market or dig them yourself. First, rinse the clams well and scrub them with a stiff brush. Then let the clams soak in a large bowl or pot of cold water, along with a couple of tablespoons of cornmeal or flour, which helps the creatures disgorge any internal mud. If the clams are very dirty, let them stand for a couple of hours, changing the water a few times. If they look relatively clean, an hour should do. Then finish with a final scrub and rinse. Discard any open clams.

To Make Basic Fish Stock

Of all the types of homemade stock, fish stock is really the quickest, easiest, and maybe the most rewarding to make. All you need is about 2 or 3 pounds of trimmings, bones, and heads, if you can get them, from fresh, non-oily fish. Place these in a large soup pot with water to cover, add a quartered onion, a sliced carrot, a celery rib, a bay leaf, 6 peppercorns, and about 2 teaspoons of salt. Bring to a boil, skimming off any foam that rises to the surface, and simmer, uncovered, for 25 minutes. Strain out the solids, and that's it! You won't believe the incomparable depth of flavor that fish stock adds to any seafood soup, chowder, or stew.

Down East Bouillabaisse with Dried Cranberry Rouille

MAKES 6 MAIN-COURSE SERVINGS

This marvelous reinterpretation of a French classic is the inspired creation of Maine chef Rich Hanson. Rich is enthusiastically committed to using as many of the rich trove of regional New England ingredients as possible in his cooking. For this Yankee version of bouillabaisse, Rich reinterprets a traditional Mediterranean rouille by using sweetened dried cranberries and walnuts for richness, and adds the local dry apple wine to perfume the soup-like stew with intimations of autumn. Because of the cost of the seafood, this is extravagant—yet very easy—company fare. Complete the meal with a mesclun salad and finish perhaps with Lucetta Peabody's Baked Fudge Pudding Cake (page 522) topped with vanilla ice cream.

For the rouille:

½ cup sweetened dried cranberries
¼ cup broken walnuts
1 shallot, coarsely chopped
¼ cup fresh breadcrumbs
¼ cup orange juice
About ¼ cup safflower oil or other light vegetable oil
¼ teaspoon cayenne pepper
½ teaspoon salt, or to taste

For the bouillabaisse:

24 mussels, scrubbed and debearded
2 cups dry apple wine or fruity white wine
3 tablespoons extra-virgin olive oil
2 leeks, white and pale green parts only, rinsed well and julienned
2 carrots, peeled and julienned
2 parsnips, peeled and julienned
¼ head green cabbage, cut in julienne strips
2 cups fish stock or bottled clam juice
2 tablespoons chopped fresh thyme
2 tablespoons chopped fresh dill
18 medium or large shrimp, shelled and deveined with tails left on
18 sea scallops
½ pound salmon steak, cut in 2-inch chunks
½ pound swordfish steak, cut in 2-inch chunks
Salt and fresh-ground black pepper
12 slices French bread, diagonally cut and toasted
¼ cup chopped fresh flat-leaf parsley

1. To make the rouille, combine the cranberries, walnuts, and shallot in a food processor. Pulse until coarsely chopped. Add the breadcrumbs and, with the motor running, slowly pour the orange juice through the feed tube, processing to a coarse puree. Gradually add enough oil to make a thick, spreadable paste. Season the rouille with cayenne and salt to taste. Set aside until ready to use or refrigerate up to 3 days.

2. To make the bouillabaisse, combine the mussels and wine in a large pot. Bring to a boil over high heat and cook, covered, until the mussel shells open, 5 to 8 minutes. Remove the mussels with a slotted spoon to a plate. If the broth is muddy, strain it through cheesecloth or a clean kitchen towel and reserve.

3. Heat the oil in a large, wide skillet. Add the leeks, carrots, and parsnips and cook over medium heat, covered, for 5 minutes. Add the cabbage and cook, stirring, for 2 minutes. (The mussels and this base can be cooked up to 1 day ahead. Cover and refrigerate.)

4. Add the fish stock to the vegetables, along with the reserved mussel liquid. Add the thyme and dill, and bring to a boil. Add the shrimp and simmer over medium heat

for 1 minute. Add the scallops, salmon, swordfish, and cooked mussels, stir gently, and simmer until the seafood turns opaque, about 5 minutes. Season the stew with salt and pepper to taste.

5. Spread the French bread toasts with the cranberry rouille. To serve, ladle the stew into shallow soup bowls, sprinkle with parsley, and arrange the toasts at the sides.

Portuguese Fish Stew

MAKES ABOUT 6 MAIN-COURSE SERVINGS

Outside, it's a bright sunny Sunday afternoon in New Bedford, Massachusetts. Inside the dimly lit wood-paneled dining room of Antonio's Restaurant, in a friendly Portuguese neighborhood, families gather for a long, leisurely midday dinner. Blue-jeaned and flannel-shirted fishermen, grandparents in silk dresses and neckties, sleeping babies, chattering children, and a handful of us visitors all happily consume course after course of the extraordinarily well-cooked robust Portuguese fare. One of our group orders the fabulous *caldeirada*, or Portuguese seafood stew, a huge, fragrant portion presented in an earthenware crock with a bowl of floury steamed potatoes on the side. When I inquire of the waitress if the potatoes are always cooked separately from the stew, she replies, "Yes, because if you put them in there, they get funny-looking!"

⅓ cup olive oil
2 onions, chopped
1 green bell pepper, chopped
3 garlic cloves, minced
2 bay leaves, broken in half (see Note)
1 16-ounce can plum tomatoes, including some juice, crushed
1 cup fish stock or bottled clam juice
½ cup dry white wine
1 teaspoon salt
½ teaspoon fresh-ground black pepper
18 farm-raised mussels, rinsed
2 pounds boneless firm fish, such as haddock or cod, cut in
    1½-inch chunks

3 tablespoons chopped fresh flat-leaf parsley
 3 tablespoons chopped fresh cilantro
 2 pounds all-purpose potatoes, peeled and cut in 2-inch chunks

1. Heat the oil in a large, heavy kettle. Add the onions, green pepper, garlic, and bay leaves. Cook over medium heat until the vegetables are limp, about 6 minutes. Add the tomatoes, fish stock, wine, salt, and pepper and simmer, uncovered, for 5 minutes, until the liquid is slightly reduced. (The stew base can be made 1 day ahead to this point. Cover and refrigerate or freeze. Reheat before proceeding.)

2. Add the mussels and cook, covered, over medium-low heat until they begin to open, about 5 minutes. Add the fish and continue to cook, covered, until the mussels are all open and the fish is opaque, about 5 minutes. Taste for seasonings and sprinkle with half the parsley and half the cilantro.

3. Meanwhile, cook the potatoes in a saucepan of boiling salted water until tender, about 15 minutes. Drain, transfer to a serving dish, and sprinkle with the remaining parsley and cilantro.

4. Present the stew and potatoes separately and have guests serve themselves.

A Chowder-Off

One recent summer, Dale and John, two ardent foodie friends of mine, decided to embark on a critical evaluation of Cape Cod clam chowders. The critics designed a gridlike chart, placing restaurant names down one side and chowder qualities— thickness, abundance and tenderness of clams, milk-cream-broth balance, potato content, and flavor—across the top. Then they conducted their "research": slurping up copious quantities of chowder in just about every single restaurant, plain or fancy, along the entire length of the Cape. They rated their findings on a scale of 1 to 5. And the results? Dale and John determined that the quintessential Cape chowder uses lots of chopped fresh hard-shell clams and their liquor, salt pork, onions, milk, and some diced potatoes, and has plenty of little pools of melted butter floating on top. Period. Cream makes the chowder too rich, the duo decreed, obscuring the clam taste, and flour thickening, unless it's very restrained, has a similarly counterproductive effect on true sea-briny chowder flavor.

Note: Traditional Portuguese cooks probably would crumble the bay leaves, but, heeding recent admonitions not to ingest them, I prefer to leave the leaves in large pieces for easy removal.

Nor'easter Baked Fish Chowder

MAKES 6 MAIN-COURSE SERVINGS

Chowders need not be limited to the top-of-the-stove variety. This one bakes in the oven, producing an extraordinarily aromatic and flavorful result. Serve with Pilot biscuits, a salad of sharp winter greens, and maybe Chocolate Bread and Butter Pudding (page 515), and you've got the perfect formula for counteracting whatever winter sends your way—even one of New England's infamous "nor'easter" storms.

> ¼ pound salt pork or bacon, cut in ¼-inch dice
> 1 large onion, thinly sliced
> 2 celery ribs, thinly sliced
> 1½ pounds all-purpose or russet potatoes, peeled and thinly sliced
>   (4 cups)
> 1 teaspoon salt, or more to taste
> ½ teaspoon fresh-ground black pepper
> 2 tablespoons chopped fresh thyme or 2 teaspoons dried
> 3 cups fish stock or bottled clam juice
> 3 cups whole milk (see Note)
> ½ cup dry white wine
> 1 large bay leaf, broken in half
> 2 pounds haddock, cod, or other lean white fish, cut in large serving
>   pieces
> 2 tablespoons unsalted butter

1. Preheat the oven to 400 degrees.

2. Cook the salt pork in a large (approximately 6-quart) Dutch oven or heavy flameproof casserole over medium heat until crisp and the fat is rendered, about 10 minutes. Remove the salt pork bits with a slotted spoon, and drain on paper towels. Add the onion and celery to the pan drippings and cook until the vegetables begin to soften, about 4 minutes. (You can do this step in a skillet and scrape the vegetables into a large, deep baking dish.)

3. Layer the potatoes over the onion mixture and sprinkle with the salt, pepper, and thyme. Pour in the fish stock, milk, and wine and add the bay leaf.

4. Cover the cooking vessel (foil is fine if using a baking dish) and bake for 35 to 45 minutes or until the potatoes are nearly tender. (The chowder base can be made ahead to this point and refrigerated. Reheat in the oven before proceeding.) Arrange the fish over the potatoes, gently pushing it down into the cooking liquid. Bake, uncovered, until the fish is just cooked through and the potatoes are very tender, 10 to 20 minutes. Taste for seasonings and adjust if necessary. Discard the bay leaf.

Growing Up Jewish in New England

"There was a sizable Jewish community where I grew up in Springfield, Massachusetts, in the 1950s and 1960s. In my house, Jewish foods were mostly for Shabbos (the Sabbath) and holidays—my aunt made great chicken soup, and my mother made *tsimmes* (sweet potatoes, prunes, and flanken cooked together), chopped liver, matzoh-apple *kugel*, and *latkes*. Otherwise, we ate very American.

"We lived two blocks from the Crown Kosher Market, and even though my mother didn't keep kosher, we shopped there a lot. You couldn't get better gossip than from the lady in the fruit department, or better bread than from the women behind the bakery counter. They had the best rye bread in the world, especially when slathered with Breakstone's whipped butter. But for great deli, you had to go to Gus & Paul's and wait in line. And I mean wait—half of Springfield shopped there. And why not? You couldn't find leaner corned beef or pastrami anywhere. They also had a bakery with

wonderful coffeecake (*babke*) with cinnamon and raisins and walnuts. Also *rugelach* (rich filled cookies) and *schnecken* (literally, snails), sort of like small cinnamon buns.

"Some of the other traditional Jewish foods were cold borscht with sour cream for dinner when it was hot in the summer. Also *schav*, a spinach soup. Knishes were a major treat at Aunt Ida's on holidays. And then there were the foods I had to learn to love, like gefilte fish. I remember once when I was very young, my mother, my grandmother, and my Aunt Sally made gefilte fish at our house—three tight-lipped rivals in the kitchen cooking fish balls in the most enormous pot I had ever seen. The tension was palpable, and the house smelled of fish for days afterward. It was many years before I could eat the stuff, and then only when smothered in horseradish (a.k.a. Jewish Dristan)."

—Elizabeth Freedman Russell

---

5. Use a large spoon to transfer the fish, vegetables, and broth to shallow soup bowls, trying not to break up the fish too much. Add about a teaspoon of butter to each bowl, swirling it into the chowder. Pass the reserved salt pork bits at the table, if you like.

Note: If you have fresh fish bones, you can inject more flavor into the chowder by simmering them in the milk for about 20 minutes and straining them out before proceeding with the recipe.

Quintessential Jewish Grandma Chicken Soup

MAKES 4 TO 6 MAIN-COURSE SERVINGS

Here's the basic formula with which Jewish grandmas all over New England cure whatever ails you, from the common cold to an algebra test to a computer glitch to a broken romance. This, of course, can be tinkered with in all kinds of ways—by adding more vegetables (such as chopped carrots, peas, zucchini, mushrooms), by using rice or dumplings instead of noodles, by varying the herbs and spices. In a medical emergency, I've been known to make this with canned chicken broth, chopped boneless chicken breasts, and Minute rice!

> 3 to 3½ pounds chicken, cut up
> 1 large onion, sliced
> 3 carrots, peeled and cut in 2-inch lengths
> 2 celery ribs with leaves, cut in half
> 2 bay leaves
> 1 teaspoon salt
> ¼ teaspoon black peppercorns
> 1 sprig fresh thyme or 1 teaspoon dried
> 6 ounces egg noodles
> ¼ cup chopped fresh parsley

1. Remove any excess fat from the chicken. Place in a large soup kettle with the onion, carrots, and celery. Add about 8 cups of water, enough to completely cover the chicken. Bring to a boil and skim off any foam and particles that rise to the top. Add the bay leaves, salt, peppercorns, and thyme. Reduce the heat to low and cook, covered, until the chicken is cooked through, about 30 minutes. Remove the chicken from the pot, and when cool enough to handle, strip the meat off the bones. Chop the chicken meat and reserve; return the bones to the pot.

2. Continue to simmer, partially covered, for 2 hours, adding water if necessary to keep level above the bones. Strain the stock through a sieve and return it to the pot.

3. Add the cooked chicken meat to the stock, along with the noodles. Simmer, uncovered, until the noodles are tender, 5 to 15 minutes. Taste for seasoning and correct if necessary and adjust the amount of liquid if necessary. Stir in the parsley.

4. Ladle into bowls to serve.

Vineyard Chicken and Corn Chowder

MAKES 4 TO 6 MAIN-COURSE SERVINGS

I first made this on a rainy, blustery day during a summer vacation on Martha's Vineyard. Though the weather was definitely dictating chowder, there was a clam hater in the group, so we browsed through old cookbooks in the rental cottage and came up with a recipe for chowder using corn and chicken instead of the bivalve. It's been a family favorite ever since. Serve it with toasted country bread, a dark leafy green salad, and a pie such as Frank's Strawberry-Rhubarb (page 610) for dessert.

3 slices thick-cut bacon, coarsely chopped

1 large onion, thinly sliced

3 celery ribs, thinly sliced

1½ to 2 pounds cut-up chicken parts, such as thighs or breasts

3 cups chicken broth

1 large bay leaf, broken in half

1½ pounds all-purpose potatoes (3 to 4 medium), peeled and diced

1 tablespoon dried thyme or 3 tablespoons chopped fresh

4 cups frozen or fresh corn kernels

3 cups half-and-half or light cream

¾ teaspoon salt, or to taste

½ teaspoon fresh-ground black pepper, or to taste

Ishmael's Chowder

"But when that smoking chowder came in, the mystery was delightfully explained. Oh, sweet friends! Hearken to me. It was made of small juicy clams, scarcely bigger than hazelnuts, mixed with pounded ship biscuit, and salted pork cut up into little flakes; the whole enriched with butter, and plentifully seasoned with pepper and salt. Our appetites being sharpened by the frosty voyage, and in particular, Queequeg seeing his favorite fishy food before him, and the chowder being surpassingly excellent, we dispatched it with great expedition."

—Herman Melville, *Moby Dick* (1851)

1. Cook the bacon in a large saucepan or soup pot over medium heat until crisp and the fat is rendered, about 10 minutes. Remove the bacon with a slotted spoon and drain on paper towels, leaving the drippings in the pan.
2. Add the onion and celery and cook until they begin to soften, about 5 minutes. Add the chicken, chicken broth, 1½ cups of water, and the bay leaf. Bring to a boil, reduce the heat to medium-low, and simmer, partially covered, until the chicken is no longer pink, about 20 minutes. Using tongs, remove the chicken to a plate.
3. Add the potatoes and thyme and cook, uncovered, until the potatoes are almost tender, about 10 minutes.
4. Meanwhile, when the chicken is cool enough to handle, strip off and discard the skin. Shred or chop the meat into ¾-inch chunks or strips and return it to the soup. Discard the bones.
5. Add the corn and half-and-half and simmer until all the vegetables are tender and the chowder is lightly thickened, about 10 minutes. Season with salt and pepper. Serve immediately, or set aside for an hour or so and reheat, or refrigerate for up to 2 days. Reheat gently before serving.
6. To serve, ladle into wide, shallow soup bowls and sprinkle with the reserved bacon bits, if you like.

Portuguese Caldo Verde

MAKES 4 MAIN-COURSE SERVINGS

This hearty Portuguese soup appears on the menu of most New England diners and casual restaurants on the coast east of New Haven, and I can righteously claim to have eaten at least a dozen versions, all in the name of scientific research, of course. The soup, variously known as kale soup or Portuguese soup, is true peasant food, with no codified recipe, so its goodness depends entirely on the skill and whim of each cook. The only constants seem to be the glorious deep green leafy kale and the potatoes. This recipe is my attempt to replicate one of the best bowls I found in the colorful fishing-village-turned-artists-colony of Provincetown, Massachusetts.

    2 tablespoons olive oil
    ½ pound garlicky sausage, such as chourico, linguiça, or kielbasa,
        thinly sliced
    1 large onion, chopped
    4 cups chicken broth
    1½ pounds potatoes (Yukon gold, red, or all-purpose), peeled and
        thinly sliced
    1 small bunch (about 1 pound) kale, thick stems removed and thinly
        sliced (see Note)
    Salt and fresh-ground black pepper

Linguiça and Chourico

These two glorious pork sausages are staples of Portuguese-American cookery. In southeastern Massachusetts, with its large Portuguese population, these sausages rival hot dogs and hamburgers in popularity and ubiquity. They are eaten with eggs at breakfast, taking the place of bacon or regular breakfast sausage; they're served broiled with fried potatoes at diners for lunch; they are the essential ingredient in *caldo verde*, the Portuguese kale soup, and are added to the cheesecloth bags of corn and potatoes at local clambakes. Street fairs and festivals feature huge rafts of linguiça and chourico barbecuing on open air grills, sending their heavenly garlicky aromas wafting out to beckon all potential attendees.

Both chourico and linguiça are redolent of garlic and paprika. Hot and spicy, chourico is usually about 1½ to 2 inches in diameter. Linguiça is milder and thinner. They can usually be used interchangeably.

1. Heat the oil in a large saucepan or soup pot. Add the sausage and onion and cook over medium heat, stirring occasionally, until the sausage browns lightly and the onion softens, about 10 minutes.
2. Add the broth, potatoes, kale, and 2 cups of water. Bring to a boil over high heat, reduce the heat to medium-low, and simmer, partially covered, for about 30 minutes, until the potatoes are very soft—almost falling apart—and the kale is tender. Use a large fork or whisk to break up some of the potatoes against the side of the pot to thicken the soup. Adjust the liquid, adding more broth or water if necessary. Season with salt and pepper to taste.
3. Ladle into bowls to serve.

Note: The best way to slice the kale is to roll several of the washed leaves up into a cylinder and use a sharp knife to cut crosswise into ¼-inch-wide ribbons.

SALADS, SIDE AND MAIN

Salads a New England specialty? With those harsh winters and relatively brief summers? Yes! Although we're well aware that New England summers don't stretch very far at either end, while they last, they can be spectacular—warm, often hot, weather, and thanks to our northerly latitudes, longer days with more hours of sunlight than in many other places in the country. And then there is our lush and fertile Connecticut River Valley. The Massachusetts part of the valley, often called the Pioneer Valley, runs from the New Hampshire border through rural Hampshire and Franklin Counties; with its rich bottomland soil and hot, humid summer weather, this valley produces an incredibly luxuriant crop of vegetables and fruits.

All summer long we revel in this bounty, tossing tender lettuces into the salad bowl with abandon to make a Spectacular Greek Salad (page 80), serving up a crisp Cucumber Salad with Shaker Buttermilk-Herb Dressing (page 95), and creating a fabulous free-form Summer Farm Stand Composed Vegetable Salad (page 97).

Picnic and potluck tables are graced with such classic salads as Crispy Creamy Coleslaw (page 84), or a contemporary creation like Crisp Apple Slaw with Honey-Lime Dressing (page 86). And our love affair with the potato also extends to the salad bowl. Perhaps our all-time favorite is a creamy, mustard-enhanced Picnic Potato Salad with Egg and Gherkins (page 93).

Mixed Greens with My Favorite Vinaigrette

MAKES 4 TO 6 SERVINGS

This is my favorite basic French-style vinaigrette formula—the one I use to dress green salads made from a simple combination of lettuces, such as the ones suggested below, or purchased mesclun mix. Vinaigrette comes close to being an all-purpose sauce, good not only on salad but also on roasted or other cooked vegetables, as well as grilled meat or fish. I usually double this dressing recipe so that it's always there in the refrigerator, standing at the ready. If you use the 4 tablespoons of vinegar, this formula veers toward the slightly sharp side, but you can adjust it by using the smaller amount of vinegar if you like. Other variations are given in the accompanying sidebar.

For My Favorite Vinaigrette:

3 to 4 tablespoons good red or white wine vinegar
½ teaspoon salt
¼ teaspoon fresh-ground black pepper
1½ tablespoons minced shallots
2 teaspoons Dijon mustard
½ teaspoon sugar
½ cup extra-virgin olive oil, or a combination of olive and vegetable oils

For the greens:

1 small head Boston or Bibb lettuce, or ½ head romaine, torn into bite-sized pieces
1 bunch arugula or watercress, torn into bite-sized pieces

1. To make the dressing, whisk together the vinegar, salt, pepper, shallots, mustard, and sugar in a small bowl or jar. Whisk in the oil. Use immediately or store in a covered container in the refrigerator for up to a week. Shake or whisk again before using.
2. Combine the greens in a large salad bowl. Toss with enough dressing to coat the leaves and serve.

Vinaigrette Variations

Here are some easy ways to vary My Favorite Vinaigrette (page 79). You can try these ideas alone or in combination.

• Use balsamic vinegar in place of wine vinegar and increase the amount to 4 tablespoons, since the flavor is sweet and mellow. Use to dress sturdier greens, such as romaine.

• Use 2 tablespoons of lemon juice to replace 2 tablespoons of the vinegar. Use all light vegetable oil to replace the olive oil. Use to dress light lettuces.

• For blue cheese dressing, use 2 tablespoons sour cream to replace 2 tablespoons of the oil and stir in ½ cup crumbled blue cheese.

• Add a tablespoon or so of sweetener—maple syrup, honey, more sugar—for use on bitter greens.

• Use a fruit vinegar, such as raspberry or blueberry, in place of the wine vinegar. Use 2 tablespoons nut oil, such as walnut or hazelnut, to replace some of the olive oil. Use to dress salads containing fruit.

• Add 1 minced garlic clove to dress hearty greens.

• Add 1 tablespoon of any minced fresh herb or ½ teaspoon of any dried herb for different ethnic twists.

• Increase the mustard to 1 tablespoon for a thick, creamy mustard dressing.

• Add 1 tablespoon grated fresh ginger and 1 tablespoon soy sauce for an Asian dressing.

• For a spicy dressing, add ½ teaspoon dried red pepper flakes or ¼ teaspoon cayenne pepper.

• Ground spices like curry, five-spice powder, cloves, or cumin can be added in small quantities.

Spectacular Greek Salad

MAKES 4 MAIN-COURSE SERVINGS; 6 TO 8 SIDE-DISH SERVINGS

The primary route through which Greek food has entered the New England mainstream is by way of the dozens and dozens of Greek-American diners and restaurants in the region. The glorious Greek salads served at these family-run establishments—oregano-scented and showered with salty feta, rich Greek olives, and colorful crisp vegetables—have truly raised our salad consciousness, so that now the pallid wedge of iceberg lettuce and orange "French" dressing of yore look sad and sorry. This salad makes a splendid one-dish lunch or supper, along with some warm crusty bread, but it should also definitely be included in any Greek-style feast, such as one featuring Greek Easter Leg of Lamb (page 299).

4 to 6 cups mixed salad greens, such as watercress, romaine, arugula,
 or Boston lettuce
1 cucumber, peeled and sliced
12 cherry tomatoes or tomato wedges
¾ cup sliced celery
1 small red onion, cut into rings
1 green bell pepper, cut into rings
16 Kalamata olives
1½ cups crumbled feta cheese
1 tablespoon small capers, drained
8 anchovy fillets, optional
½ cup My Favorite Vinaigrette (page 79)
2 teaspoons dried oregano
Fresh-ground black pepper

1. Line a good-sized platter or shallow bowl with the greens. Arrange or scatter over the greens the cucumber, tomatoes, celery, onion, green pepper, olives, feta, and capers. Crisscross the anchovies, if you like, over the top. (The salad can be arranged a few hours before serving and stored, covered, in the refrigerator.)
2. Whisk together the vinaigrette and oregano in a small bowl and let the dressing stand for about 10 minutes so the flavors can blend.
3. Drizzle the dressing over the salad, sprinkle with black pepper to taste, and serve.

Salad Greens

Greens are more or less interchangeable within the following categories, so you can freely substitute or mix the best of the daily pick from the garden, farmers' market, or produce department. Look for greens that are vibrant and crisp and show no signs of browning. Mesclun is a mix of tender young greens from all categories.

Mild: Bibb, Boston, iceberg, loose leaf (or green leaf), mâche, oak leaf, romaine, and young spinach

Bitter: Chicory (curly endive), dandelion, endive, escarole, frisée, radicchio

Peppery: Arugula, watercress, mustard

Sicilian Salad of Spinach, Oranges, and Red Onion

MAKES 6 SERVINGS

I found the model for this lovely salad in the Saugatuck, Connecticut, Sons of Italy *Festival Italiano Cookbook.* Inspired by such classical Sicilian ingredients as spinach, oranges, and olives, it's a wonderful accompaniment to soups, pastas, and just about any casserole or other "made" dish.

For the vinaigrette:

3 tablespoons balsamic vinegar
2 tablespoons orange juice
1 tablespoon honey
2 teaspoons Dijon mustard
1 teaspoon grated orange zest
¼ cup extra-virgin olive oil
½ teaspoon salt
½ teaspoon fresh-ground black pepper

For the salad:

1 pound baby spinach, washed well and dried
2 blood or navel oranges, peeled, thinly sliced crosswise, slices cut in
    half
1 small red onion, thinly sliced
½ cup small black European olives, such as Niçoise

1. To make the vinaigrette, whisk or shake together all of the ingredients in a small bowl or jar. (The dressing can be made a day ahead and refrigerated.)
2. To serve, place the spinach in a large bowl and toss with about half the dressing. Arrange the oranges and onion over the greens and scatter with the olives. Drizzle with the remaining dressing and serve.

Sustainable Agriculture

Sustainable agriculture can be defined as a system of farming that is environmentally sound and productive, and at the same time profitable. The long-term goal of sustainable agriculture is to maintain the social fabric of rural communities for generations to come.

The Center for Sustainable Agriculture at the University of Vermont seeks to coordinate a New England–wide education effort in the subject. Kate Duesterberg, director of the center, says, "What we hope is not only to provide additional technical information, but to get people to work closely with their communities to come to a more sustainable way of producing and distributing food. It's our job to push people toward a new way of thinking."

New England Cobb Salad

MAKES 4 MAIN-COURSE SERVINGS; 6 TO 8 SIDE-DISH SERVINGS

Just because Cobb salad was invented in California doesn't mean it can't happily travel east for a visit and, while here, be made with Vermont or New Hampshire double-smoked bacon, locally raised turkey, and one of the several blue-veined cheeses from Massachusetts. This is a take on just such a Cobb salad, created by David Raymer, chef at Tavern on Main in Westport, Connecticut.

8 to 12 slices bacon, preferably double-smoked Vermont bacon

6 cups mixed greens such as Boston, romaine, arugula, watercress, or spinach

2 tablespoons light olive oil

1 tablespoon sherry vinegar

Salt and fresh-ground black pepper

2 cups cooked turkey cut in chunks or slivers

1 large ripe avocado, peeled and sliced

2 cups diced seeded tomatoes

3 hard-boiled eggs, peeled and chopped

1 cup crumbled blue cheese

½ cup My Favorite Vinaigrette (page 79)

2 teaspoons Dijon mustard

2 tablespoons snipped fresh chives

1. Cook the bacon in a large skillet over medium-low heat until it is crisp, about 12 minutes. Drain on paper towels and crumble it coarsely.
2. Spread the greens out on a large platter or 4 individual plates. Drizzle with the oil and vinegar and season with salt and pepper to taste.
3. Make rows or a spokelike design with the bacon, turkey, avocado, tomatoes, and eggs, and scatter the cheese over the top.
4. Whisk together the vinaigrette and mustard in a small bowl. Pour the dressing over the salad in a spiral pattern, sprinkle with chives, and serve.

Crispy Creamy Coleslaw

MAKES 8 SERVINGS

I used to try to make creamy coleslaw using mostly mayonnaise, perhaps combined with sour cream, and little or no sugar, thinking that it was somehow more virtuous to serve a salad that was not sweet. But I became a convert after trying a recipe from a Nashua, New Hampshire, community cookbook, *Liberal Portions*, that called for equal amounts of mayonnaise, vinegar, and sugar. Now people praise my coleslaw instead of eating a polite little pile. This dressing formula offsets and smoothes out the rough edges of cabbage's natural bitterness. The creamy slaw is a natural accompaniment to New Hampshire Maple Baked Beans (page 150) or any other baked beans, as well as all sorts of sandwiches.

> 1 small head green cabbage, shredded, about 7 cups
> 1 carrot, peeled and grated
> ¼ cup minced onion
> ½ cup mayonnaise
> ½ cup sugar
> 1 teaspoon dry mustard
> ½ cup distilled white vinegar or white wine vinegar
> ½ teaspoon salt
> ¼ teaspoon fresh-ground black pepper, or to taste

1. Combine the cabbage, carrot, and onion in a large bowl.

2. Whisk together the mayonnaise, sugar, and mustard in a small bowl. Whisk in the vinegar, salt, and pepper. Pour the dressing over the cabbage mixture and stir gently but thoroughly to combine. Refrigerate for at least 1 hour or up to 6 hours.

3. Before serving, stir the coleslaw to redistribute the dressing and spoon off any excess watery liquid. Correct the seasonings if necessary and serve.

Pickled Coleslaw

MAKES ABOUT 10 SERVINGS

This sweet-tart coleslaw is a refreshing accompaniment to many soups, particularly chowders or bean soups, and is just about the perfect thing to serve with Red Flannel Hash George's Diner (page 188). It's equally good made with green or red cabbage. Just make the choice dependent on which goes better with your menu's color scheme.

For the dressing:

3 tablespoons cider vinegar or white wine vinegar
1½ tablespoons sugar
1½ teaspoons Dijon mustard
6 tablespoons vegetable oil
½ teaspoon salt, or to taste
⅛ teaspoon black pepper

For the coleslaw:

1 small head green or red cabbage, shredded, about 7 cups
1 cup slivered green bell pepper
½ cup chopped or slivered red onion

1. To make the dressing, whisk together the vinegar, sugar, and mustard in a small bowl. Slowly whisk in the oil and season with salt and pepper.

Coleslaw Etymology

Coleslaw derives its name from the Anglo-Saxon word for cabbage, *cal,* and the Dutch word *sla,* meaning salad. Dutch housewives in Manhattan probably made the first coleslaw in America, and it migrated up the New England coast from New York.

2. Combine the cabbage, green pepper, and onion in a large bowl. Pour the dressing over the cabbage mixture and toss until well combined. Cover and refrigerate for at least 1 hour or up to 6 hours before serving.

3. Before serving, stir the coleslaw to redistribute the dressing and correct the seasoning if necessary.

Crisp Apple Slaw with Honey-Lime Dressing

MAKES 10 SERVINGS

I found a version of this recipe while browsing through *The Virginia Bentley Cookbook*, a charming handwritten and illustrated collection of recipes from the author's years spent running a farm in West Lebanon, New Hampshire. The crisp, red-skinned autumn apples add pretty color and a delightfully sweet grace note to the cabbage mixture, and a honey-lime dressing binds it all together beautifully.

For the dressing:

½ cup mayonnaise
1 tablespoon honey mustard
1 tablespoon fresh lime juice
½ teaspoon salt, or to taste
¼ teaspoon fresh-ground black
 pepper, or to taste

For the slaw:

1 cup coarsely chopped pecans
3 red-skinned sweet apples, such as Cortland or McIntosh
1 tablespoon fresh lemon juice
4 cups shredded green cabbage (about ½ head)
¾ cup grated or shredded carrots
½ cup chopped red onion

1. To make the dressing, whisk together the mayonnaise, honey mustard, lime juice, salt, and pepper in a small bowl. (The dressing can be made 1 day ahead and refrigerated.)

2. Toast the pecans in a medium-sized skillet over medium heat, stirring frequently, until fragrant and one shade darker, about 6 minutes. Cool.

3. Core the apples but do not peel them. Cut them into fine shreds or ½-inch cubes. Toss with the lemon juice in a large bowl. Add the cabbage, carrots, and onion and mix well.

4. Pour the dressing over the cabbage mixture and toss gently but thoroughly to combine. Refrigerate for at least 30 minutes or up to 2 hours.

5. Before serving, stir in the pecans and correct the seasonings if necessary.

Salad History

Salads seem to have come full circle in New England. By the mid-1800s, the simple lettuce "sallets" taken for granted in early America began to be replaced by increasingly elaborate concoctions with intricate geometric designs. After gelatin was introduced in the late 1800s, New Englanders developed a fondness for all kinds of vegetables in aspic and other jellied salads. Ironically enough, it was Miss Fannie Farmer, that staunchly conservative New England cook, who helped create the fad for ever-more-fussy salads. The 1912 edition of her cookbook contains such contrivances as Cucumber Baskets, Tomatoes Stuffed with Pineapple, Hindoo Salad, Moulded Russian Salad, and Hawaiian Salad.

This continuum reached its apex in the 1960s, when, after the advent of flavored Jell-O and the availability of such processed foods as sour cream and marshmallows, packaged coconut and canned tropical fruits, increasingly sweet and elaborate Jell-O salad concoctions were the norm.

But now we've come around to the point where simply dressed fresh greens are again the most popular form of salad. Prepackaged or premixed mesclun contains sophisticated combinations of lettuces and other greens that most of us had not even heard of twenty years ago.

Minted Tabbouleh with Toasted Walnuts

MAKES 4 MAIN-COURSE SERVINGS; 6 TO 8 SIDE-DISH SERVINGS

I often get inspired to make this Lebanese salad after browsing in one of the many Middle Eastern neighborhoods scattered around urban New England. Boston's Haymarket has some of the best little Middle Eastern shops and stalls selling meats, produce, spices, dried fruits, and grains. Bulgur is precooked cracked wheatberries, and it softens quickly with just a quick soak in boiling water. Copious handfuls of fresh parsley and mint contribute a fresh summery taste, and this version is finished with a sprinkle of toasted walnuts. An optional pinch of allspice adds an exotic undertone. Other good additions to tabbouleh are chopped cucumbers, other fresh herbs such as dill, and even crumbled feta cheese. Traditionally, the salad is eaten by scooping it up in romaine leaves.

1¼ cups medium bulgur
1 cup coarsely chopped walnuts
1½ cups chopped seeded tomatoes
1½ cups chopped fresh parsley
¾ cup chopped fresh mint
¾ cup chopped scallions
½ cup chopped red onion
½ cup fresh lemon juice
½ cup extra-virgin olive oil
1 teaspoon salt
½ teaspoon fresh-ground black pepper
½ teaspoon ground allspice, optional
1 head romaine lettuce, separated into leaves

1. Combine the bulgur with 2 cups boiling water in a large bowl and stir to combine. Cover the bowl and set aside at room temperature for 30 minutes. Drain in a sieve, pressing out any remaining liquid, and return the soaked bulgur to the bowl.

2. Preheat the oven to 350 degrees.

3. Spread the walnuts out onto a baking sheet and toast in the oven, stirring once or twice, until fragrant and one shade darker, about 8 minutes. Set aside to cool.

4. Add the tomatoes, parsley, mint, scallions, and onion to the bulgur.

5. Whisk together the lemon juice, oil, salt, pepper, and allspice, if you like, in a bowl. Pour the dressing over the salad and stir gently but thoroughly to combine. Set aside at room temperature for 30 minutes or refrigerate up to 6 hours. Return to room temperature before serving.

6. To serve, spoon the tabbouleh onto a platter, sprinkle with the toasted walnuts, and surround with the lettuce leaves.

Harbor View
Many-Bean Portable Salad

MAKES 6 TO 8 SERVINGS

This American classic endures decade after decade for very good reasons. It is attractive and easy to prepare, and it can be made well ahead, and easily transported to a picnic. *And* it tastes great! This is an updated version of my mother's bean salad recipe, the one we ate at countless summer suppers on our porch in Harbor View on the Connecticut shore—usually along with grilled hamburgers or chicken and thickly sliced tomatoes right off the vine.

For the vinaigrette:

¼ cup cider vinegar

2 tablespoons sugar

2 teaspoons grainy Dijon mustard

2 garlic cloves, minced

½ teaspoon salt

¼ teaspoon fresh-ground black pepper

¼ teaspoon bottled hot pepper sauce

½ cup vegetable oil or light olive oil

For the salad:

½ pound green beans, trimmed and cut in 1½-inch lengths

½ pound yellow wax beans, trimmed and cut in 1½-inch lengths

1½ cups drained and rinsed cooked kidney beans

1½ cups drained and rinsed cooked chickpeas

1 red or green bell pepper, seeded and chopped

1 cup chopped red onion

2 tablespoons chopped fresh parsley

1. To make the vinaigrette, whisk together the vinegar, sugar, mustard, garlic, salt, pepper, and hot pepper sauce in a small bowl. Whisk in the oil.

2. Cook the green and wax beans in a large pot of boiling salted water until tender, about 6 minutes. Drain in a colander.

3. Combine the hot cooked beans with the kidney beans and chickpeas in a large bowl. Pour the dressing over and set aside for 15 minutes to cool. Stir in the bell pepper and onion; cover and refrigerate for at least 2 hours or up to 12 hours.

4. Before serving, stir to redistribute the dressing, and taste to correct the seasonings if necessary. Transfer to a serving dish, sprinkle with the parsley, and serve.

Warm Mixed Bean Salad with Pancetta

MAKES 4 SERVINGS

Because cooked dried beans take so well to a variety of seasonings, chefs love to play around with them. This delectable warm bean salad is based on the inspired creation of a chef at one of my favorite Connecticut Italian restaurants, Centro, in Fairfield. Roman beans are a large, relatively soft-textured bean used extensively in Italian cooking. They are pretty widely available in New England as well as around the rest of the country, but if you can't find them, the ubiquitous kidney bean will do just fine as a substitute. Pancetta is Italian bacon that has been cured with salt and spices, but is not smoked. It is available in Italian markets and in some supermarkets.

⅓ cup (1½ ounces) diced pancetta or thick-sliced bacon
6 tablespoons plus 2 teaspoons extra-virgin olive oil
4 garlic cloves, peeled and crushed until flat (see Note)
1 10-ounce package frozen lima beans, cooked and drained
1½ cups drained canned Roman or kidney beans
1½ cups drained canned black beans
2 tablespoons fresh lemon juice
¼ teaspoon fresh-ground black pepper
Salt to taste
1 large bunch arugula
3 tablespoons chopped flat-leaf Italian parsley, plus sprigs for garnish
1 lemon, cut in 4 wedges

1. Cook the pancetta in 2 teaspoons of the olive oil in a large skillet over low heat until crisp and any fat is rendered, about 10 minutes. Remove the pancetta with a slotted spoon and reserve. Pour the grease out of the pan but do not wash the pan.

2. Add the remaining 6 tablespoons of oil and the garlic to the same skillet. Cook over low heat until the garlic turns a pale golden brown, watching carefully so it doesn't scorch, about 10 minutes. Remove the garlic with tongs, leaving the oil in the pan.

3. Add the lima beans, Roman beans, and black beans to the garlic oil in the skillet, raise the heat to medium-high, and toss gently until heated through, about 4 minutes. Add the pancetta and lemon juice and stir gently to combine. Season with the black pepper and salt to taste. (The salad may need no salt as the pancetta or bacon is salty.)

4. Spread the arugula out on a serving platter or individual plates. Spoon the warm beans over the greens and sprinkle with the parsley. Garnish with lemon wedges and parsley sprigs and serve.

> ### A Grand Sallet
>
> "The youngest and smallest leaves of spinage, the smallest also of sorrel, well washed currans, and red beets round the center being finely carved, oyl and vinegar, and the dish garnished with lemon and beets."
>
> —Robert May,
> *The Accomplisht Cook* (1671)

Note: This salad is flavored rather subtly with garlic. For a more assertive garlic flavor, mince one or two of the cooked cloves and stir them into the finished salad.

Classic Mac Salad with Crunchy Veggies

MAKES 6 TO 8 SERVINGS

The traditional "macaroni" (as opposed to "pasta") salad is as popular a fixture on New England picnic tables as it is around the rest of the country. This is a classic version of the recipe, made with old-fashioned elbow macaroni, but you can surely substitute any other similar short, bite-sized pasta shape if you wish. The secret here is mixing the warm pasta with about half the dressing and then chilling it for a while so that the macaroni absorbs its lovely lemony flavor. The chopped vegetables are added with the remaining dressing no more than about an hour before serving time, thus preserving their bright color and crunchiness.

8 ounces elbow macaroni
1 cup mayonnaise
½ teaspoon grated lemon zest
2 tablespoons fresh lemon juice
1 tablespoon grainy Dijon mustard
½ teaspoon salt, or to taste
½ teaspoon fresh-ground black pepper
2 tablespoons milk or cream
1 cup chopped celery
½ cup shredded carrot
½ cup chopped red bell pepper
½ cup thinly sliced scallions
2 tablespoons chopped fresh parsley

1. Cook the macaroni in a large pot of boiling salted water until al dente, 8 to 10 minutes.
2. Meanwhile, whisk together the mayonnaise, lemon zest, lemon juice, mustard, salt, and pepper in a small bowl. Whisk in the milk or cream.
3. Drain the macaroni in a colander and transfer to a large bowl. Pour half the dressing over the hot pasta, stirring gently to combine. Cool to room temperature; then cover and refrigerate the salad and the remaining dressing for at least 30 minutes or up to 6 hours.

Common Ground Fair

The Common Ground Fair, held in Unity every September, has been called Maine's annual party. Sponsored by the Maine Organic Farmers and Gardeners Association (MOFGA) and eschewing the carnival rides and honky-tonk trappings that many New England fairs have acquired over the years, the Common Ground is a successful attempt to bring back the authentic, old-time country agricultural fair.

There are sheep-shearing competitions, fiddling contests, and cider-pressing demonstrations to watch. There are baked beans, pulled-pork sandwiches, fajitas, clam chowder, home-smoked beef jerky, lamb sausages on whole-wheat buns, egg rolls, farmstead goat cheese, barbecued free-range chicken, cheesecake, gourmet cookies, and natural cider to eat and drink. And in the exhibition hall, the displays of organic vegetables, fruits, flowers, and herbs, along with the home-canned and home-baked goods, are a visual feast.

4. Add the celery, carrot, bell pepper, scallions, and parsley to the pasta, along with the remaining dressing, and stir gently but thoroughly to blend well. Taste and correct the seasonings if necessary. Serve immediately or refrigerate up to 1 hour.

Picnic Potato Salad with Egg and Gherkins

MAKES 6 TO 8 SERVINGS

Attend almost any summertime potluck supper or buffet in New England, and you're likely to get this kind of deliciously eggy, slightly sweet (from the pickle juice) potato salad. Comparing potato salad recipes is a favorite picnic pastime, and everybody has a personal tried-and-true formula. This one is mine.

> 2 pounds waxy potatoes, cut in 2-inch chunks
> 3 tablespoons sweet pickle juice
> Salt and fresh-ground black pepper
> ¾ cup minced celery
> ½ cup chopped red or sweet white onion
> ⅔ cup mayonnaise, plus more if necessary
> 2 tablespoons Dijon mustard
> 2 tablespoons milk or cream
> 2 hard-boiled eggs, chopped
> 2 tablespoons chopped gherkins or sweet pickles
> 2 tablespoons minced fresh parsley or dill or a combination

1. Cook the potatoes in a covered pot of boiling salted water over medium heat until just fork-tender, about 15 minutes. Drain well. When they are cool enough to handle, peel and cut the potatoes into ½-inch cubes. You should have about 8 cups. Toss the warm potatoes with the pickle juice and about ½ teaspoon each of salt and pepper in a large bowl. Set aside for 10 minutes. Add the celery and onion and toss.

2. Whisk together the mayonnaise, mustard, and milk or cream in a small bowl. Stir in the eggs and gherkins. Pour the dressing over the potatoes and mix gently but thoroughly to combine. Refrigerate for at least 1 hour. (The salad can be made a day ahead.)

3. Before serving, stir the salad again to redistribute the dressing and correct the seasonings if necessary. Sprinkle with the fresh herbs and serve.

Pickled Beet Salad
New Hampshire

MAKES 4 SERVINGS

Virginia Bentley, a food writer from New Hampshire, says of her similar pickled beet recipe, "In its simplicity lies its goodness." With its sturdy, make-ahead qualities, this classic salad, which is freshened with a garnish of feathery dill, is an excellent candidate for a buffet and is easy to multiply for a crowd.

¾ cup cider vinegar
⅓ cup sugar
¼ cup beet cooking water or
    plain water
½ teaspoon salt
½ teaspoon dill seeds, optional
3 cups sliced cooked beets
2 to 3 tablespoons vinaigrette, such
    as My Favorite Vinaigrette (page 79)
1 tablespoon chopped fresh dill

1. Bring the vinegar, sugar, water, salt, and dill seeds if you are using, to a boil in a medium-sized saucepan, stirring until the sugar dissolves.

Ramps

Throughout New England (as well as in Appalachia and parts of the South) the appearance of green ramp tips in the woods presages spring. Ramps are wild onions, a cousin to garlic and leeks, with a long green leaf and a bulbous white root. They grow in rich forest soil, tending to cluster near groves of sugar maples—and in patches of poison ivy. Since their leaves resemble those of lily of the valley, be sure the plant smells like an onion before you eat it! Ramps need to be washed thoroughly and trimmed of their root ends and outer sheaths of leaves. Then they can be chopped, leaves and all, gently sautéed in olive oil, and used in omelets, risottos, and potatoes. Some Yankees love to eat them raw, their eye-tearing pungency a forceful reminder that one has, indeed, survived another winter.

---

2. Place the beets in a bowl. Pour the hot liquid over and stir gently to combine. Cool to room temperature; then cover and refrigerate for at least 1 hour or up to 1 week.

3. Before serving, spoon beets out of the pickling liquid with a slotted spoon and place in a shallow bowl. Drizzle with the vinaigrette and sprinkle with the fresh dill.

Cucumber Salad with Shaker Buttermilk-Herb Dressing

MAKES 4 SERVINGS

The Shakers, who learned much about culinary and medicinal herbs from the Native Americans, began selling seeds and packaged dried herbs, such as summer savory, marjoram, sage, and thyme, in their 1847 herbal catalog. This tangy, creamy dressing, adapted from Miller and Fuller's *The Best of Shaker Cooking*, is wonderful served over crisp cucumbers and all kinds of greens.

For the dressing:

⅓ cup regular or lowfat sour cream
¼ cup mayonnaise
⅓ cup buttermilk
1 tablespoon white wine vinegar
1 tablespoon sugar
½ teaspoon Dijon mustard
1 tablespoon minced scallions
1 tablespoon chopped fresh tarragon, dill, or thyme
½ teaspoon salt, or to taste
¼ teaspoon fresh-ground black pepper, or to taste

For the salad:

2 medium-large cucumbers, chilled
Sprigs of fresh herbs, for garnish

1. To make the dressing, whisk together the sour cream and mayonnaise in a medium-sized bowl until smooth. Whisk in the buttermilk, vinegar, sugar, mustard, scallions, herbs, salt, and pepper. Refrigerate until ready to use. (The dressing will keep, covered, for 1 to 2 days in the refrigerator.)

2. If the cucumbers are fat, cut them in half lengthwise and scoop out the seeds. If the skin is unwaxed, score the cucumbers with the tines of a fork for a decorative effect; if waxed, peel the skin. Cut the cucumbers into moderately thin slices and arrange on an attractive plate.

3. Spoon the dressing over the cucumbers, garnish with herb sprigs, and serve.

"Peeled, Seeded, and Chopped"

Many other cookbooks call for tomatoes to be peeled, seeded, and chopped. There is no controversy about the chopping part, but I am of the opinion that peeling and seeding are almost always optional. These steps are messy and somewhat time-consuming and sometimes even reduce the flavor and juiciness of the tomatoes. So I rarely peel or seed tomatoes—only when seeds or bits of skin would mar a refined dish.

Tomatoes should always be cored before using by cutting a cone-shaped wedge out of the stem end and removing it.

A Trio of Hungarian Salads

MAKES 4 SMALL SIDE-DISH SERVINGS OF EACH SALAD

These salads—one cucumber, one tomato, one green pepper—are the perfect accompaniments to Chicken Paprika (page 308) or Beef Goulash (page 265). Their pleasing tartness is just right with the sour cream–rich sauces. Or try them with a similarly rich dish such as Cheese-Topped Noodle Casserole with Smoked Country Ham (page 218).

For the dressing:

1 cup very thinly sliced sweet onion, such as Spanish
2 teaspoons sugar
2 teaspoons sweet Hungarian paprika
½ cup distilled white vinegar
½ teaspoon salt, or to taste

For the cucumber salad:

1 large cucumber
1 teaspoon salt

For the tomato salad:

3 medium ripe tomatoes
1 tablespoon minced fresh parsley

For the pepper salad:

1 large green (or other color) bell pepper
2 teaspoons olive or vegetable oil
Salt

1. To make the dressing, combine the onion with the sugar, paprika, vinegar, salt, and ½ cup water in a small bowl. Stir to dissolve the sugar.
2. To make the cucumber salad, peel the cucumber and halve lengthwise. Scoop out the seeds, and cut crosswise into thin slices. Toss with the salt in a bowl and let stand for at least 30 minutes or up to 2 hours. Lift the cucumber slices out of the salty liquid they have exuded and toss them with one-third of the dressing.
3. To make the tomato salad, core the tomatoes, seed if desired, and cut into wedges. Toss with about one-third of the dressing and the parsley in a bowl. Season with salt to taste.
4. To make the pepper salad, seed the pepper and cut crosswise into thin slices. Toss with about one-third of the dressing and the oil in a bowl. Season with salt to taste.

Summer Farm Stand Composed Vegetable Salad

MAKES 4 MAIN-COURSE SERVINGS; 8 SIDE-DISH SERVINGS

This is a gloriously free-form salad that you make with whatever beautiful late-summer vegetables you find at the farm stand, farmers' market, or supermarket. And if you can't resist buying every single vegetable in sight, just cook them all and then have a party. Roasting or grilling (see Note) the vegetables deepens and intensifies their flavor.

¾ to 1 pound each of 2 or 3 of the following: broccoli florets, asparagus, eggplant (sliced ½-inch thick), green or yellow summer squash (cut diagonally ½-inch thick), bell peppers (seeded and cut in ¾-inch wide strips), sweet onions (cut in chunks)

2 tablespoons olive oil

Salt and fresh-ground black pepper

1 pound red- or white-skinned new potatoes, cut in ¾-inch chunks

2 tablespoons white wine or vermouth

About ⅔ cup My Favorite Vinaigrette (page 79)

1 pound ripe tomatoes, sliced

½ cup chopped fresh herbs (parsley, chives, basil, tarragon, and/or dill)

Nasturtium blossoms, optional

1. Preheat the oven to 450 degrees (or see Note).

2. Place the vegetables (except the potatoes and tomatoes) on 2 large rimmed baking sheets, brush or drizzle them with the oil, and sprinkle with salt and pepper. Roast, uncovered, stirring with a spatula once or twice, until the vegetables are softened and tinged with dark brown on the edges, 20 to 35 minutes. Cool the vegetables to room temperature.

3. Cook the potatoes in a large pot of well-salted boiling water, until tender, about 15 minutes. Drain, transfer to a bowl, and sprinkle with the wine. Let stand for 10 minutes. Pour about ¼ cup of vinaigrette over the potatoes and toss to combine.

4. Select an attractive serving platter large enough to display all the elements of the salad. Spoon the potato salad into the center of the platter. Arrange the roasted vegetables around one side and the sliced tomatoes around the other. (The salad can be prepared up to 2 hours ahead. Cover and refrigerate.)

Edible Flowers

A pretty blossom adds a magical note of beauty and surprise to a salad. Some of the edible blooms that have reentered the culinary realm lately include pinks, dwarf marigolds, johnny jump-ups, borage blossoms, chive flowers, and everyone's favorite, nasturtiums. Nasturtiums, which are easily seeded and grow well all summer long in most parts of New England, have a wonderfully addictive taste that is at once pungently peppery and flowery sweet. Their gay, nodding flower caps come in a rainbow of hues and shades—from creamy true yellow, to burnt orange, to pale gently striped pink, to Chinese red, to deep umber. The small, beautifully scalloped leaves of the plant are also deliciously edible.

---

5. When ready to serve, drizzle the salad with more vinaigrette, sprinkle with the herbs, and garnish with the nasturtium blossoms, if you like.

Note: You can also grill the vegetables on a moderately hot barbecue grill, brushing them with oil and turning them until tender and lightly charred.

Composed Winter Vegetable Salad with Peabody Boiled Dressing

MAKES 4 MAIN-COURSE SERVINGS; 6 TO 8 SIDE-DISH SERVINGS

A perusal of Lucetta Upham Peabody's handwritten recipe collection from 1940s Boston yields a flour- and egg-thickened dressing that was a part of every New Englander's repertoire from the late nineteenth century onward. In fact, my 1912 edition of Fannie Farmer's *Boston Cooking School Cookbook* contains three versions of boiled dressing. My adaptation, enriched with tangy sour cream rather than the more traditional heavy cream, is a thick, sweet-tart dressing, just perfect for tossing with cooked winter vegetables for this composed salad. With the optional ham, the salad can become a main course and stand on its own. I make it every year without the meat for our traditional Polish Christmas Eve dinner—a melding of the Yankee and Eastern European strains of the family on one platter.

For the Peabody Boiled Dressing:

1½ tablespoons sugar
1½ teaspoons all-purpose flour
½ teaspoon dry mustard
½ teaspoon salt, or to taste
⅛ teaspoon cayenne pepper
½ cup whole or lowfat milk, plus 2 to 4 tablespoons
2 tablespoons cider vinegar
1 tablespoon fresh lemon juice
1 egg yolk
¼ cup lowfat or regular sour cream
Fresh-ground black pepper

For the salad:

1 pound red- or white-skinned potatoes, cut in ¾-inch chunks

3 tablespoons white wine or vermouth

½ cup thinly sliced celery

¾ to 1 pound each of 2 or 3 of the following: baby beets, sliced fennel,
    slant-cut carrots, broccoli florets, cauliflower florets

About ⅓ cup My Favorite Vinaigrette (page 79) or good bottled
    vinaigrette

⅓ cup chopped fresh flat-leaf parsley

¼ cup chopped fresh dill

Salt and fresh-ground black pepper to taste

2 cups halved cherry tomatoes

1 green bell pepper, cut crosswise into rings

1 small red onion, cut into rings

1 cup diced smoked ham, optional

1. To make the dressing, whisk together the sugar, flour, mustard, salt, and cayenne in a small heavy saucepan. Whisk in about 2 tablespoons of the milk to make a paste. Place the pan over medium heat, whisk in the remaining milk, and cook, stirring, until thickened and smooth, about 5 minutes. Remove from the heat. Whisk together the vinegar, lemon juice, and egg yolk in a small bowl. Gradually whisk the hot milk mixture into the vinegar mixture to temper the eggs and then return the mixture to the saucepan. Cook, stirring, over medium-low heat until smooth and thickened to about the consistency of thin mayonnaise, about 3 minutes. Remove from the heat and cool to room temperature, whisking often; then cover and refrigerate. When cold, gently whisk in the sour cream and season with salt and pepper to taste. (The dressing can be made 2 days ahead and refrigerated. Whisk again before using, and thin with enough additional milk to make a thick yet pourable consistency.)

2. To make the salad, cook the potatoes in a large pot of boiling salted water until they are tender, about 15 minutes. Remove with a slotted spoon and transfer to a bowl. Toss with the wine and stir in the celery. Cook the remaining vegetables separately in the same pot until they are tender, 8 to 20 minutes, depending on their size and shape. Drain in a colander. Toss the hot vegetables in separate bowls with a couple of tablespoons of the vinaigrette and some of the chopped parsley and dill. Refrigerate for up to 8 hours.

3. When ready to serve, toss the potatoes with about ⅓ cup of the boiled dressing and some of the chopped herbs, and season with salt and pepper to taste. Arrange all the cooked vegetables and the cherry tomatoes in a spokelike pattern on a large serving platter. Drizzle with more of the boiled dressing. Arrange the green pepper and red onion over the top and scatter with the ham, if you like. Make a spiral design with the boiled dressing over all, sprinkle with more chopped herbs, and serve.

Jell-O Fever

Jell-O salad frenzy reached a peak during the 1950s, '60s, and '70s, when at many a gathering the array of brightly hued concoctions was almost blinding, and recipe swapping for ever-more-intricate layered creations rose to a fevered pitch. A glimpse into some community cookbooks published during this period—one from Norwalk, Connecticut, one from Auburn, Maine, and another from Burlington, Vermont—reveals some Jell-O salad recipes that these days we might view as rather startling.

• Bing Cherry Jell-O Salad: cherry Jell-O, cream cheese, pecans, and pineapple

• Sunset Salad: orange Jell-O, canned apricots, maraschino cherries, celery, salad dressing, and cottage cheese

• Golden Glow Salad: lemon Jell-O, canned pineapple, vinegar, ground raw carrots, and mayonnaise

• Layered Strawberry Salad: strawberry Jell-O, frozen strawberries, crushed pineapple, sliced bananas, coconut flakes, sour cream, and mayonnaise

• Imperial Salad: lemon Jell-O, chopped cabbage, pimiento, crushed pineapple, and vinegar

• Molded Fruit Salad: lemon Jell-O, bananas, grapes, dates, pineapple, walnuts, and marshmallows

Dilled Seafood Seashell Pasta Salad

MAKES 4 MAIN-COURSE SERVINGS

This super supper salad is simply delicious made with just about any type of seafood—leftover cooked fish or shellfish or canned salmon, tuna, or crab. The seashell pasta shape seems particularly appropriate here, but of course the recipe will work with any other bite-sized pasta. A basket of Best-Ever Buttermilk Biscuits (page 443), or Crusty Cornbread or Muffins (page 451) are all you would need to complete a summer meal.

For the dressing:

¾ cup mayonnaise
1 tablespoon white wine vinegar
2 teaspoons Dijon mustard
1½ tablespoons chopped fresh dill, plus sprigs for garnish
½ teaspoon salt
½ teaspoon fresh-ground black pepper

For the salad:

8 to 10 ounces small or medium pasta shells
Salt and fresh-ground black pepper
3 tablespoons dry white wine
1 green bell pepper, chopped
⅔ cup thinly sliced celery
½ cup chopped red onion
1½ to 2 cups cooked fish or shellfish,
    broken into large flakes or chunks (see Note)
Lettuce leaves
Salt and fresh-ground black pepper
1 to 2 ripe tomatoes, cut in wedges
6 radishes, sliced

1. To make the dressing, whisk together the mayonnaise, vinegar, mustard, dill, salt, and pepper in a small bowl.
2. Cook the pasta in a large pot of boiling salted water until it is al dente, about 10 minutes. Drain in a colander. Transfer to a bowl and, while still warm, toss with the wine. Set aside for 10 minutes.
3. Add the green pepper, celery, and onion to the pasta. Pour the dressing over and stir to combine. Add the seafood and stir gently but thoroughly, taking care to leave some large chunks. Refrigerate for at least 30 minutes, or up to 8 hours.
4. To serve, line a platter with lettuce leaves. Season the salad with salt and pepper. Spoon the salad over the lettuce, arrange the tomatoes and radishes on top, and garnish with dill sprigs.

Note: Use leftover cooked fish or shellfish or a large can of salmon or 2 (6-ounce) cans of tuna or crabmeat.

Plimoth Plantation Fare

On the coast between Boston and Cape Cod, known in Massachusetts as the South Shore, lies Plimoth Plantation (Governor Bradford's own spelling), a living reconstruction of the original Pilgrim settlement as it was in 1627. The site, which also includes a re-created Wampanoag Indian homesite and a facsimile of the *Mayflower II* ship, is peopled by plausible actors impersonating everyone who was there at the time. You meet Edward Winslow, Miles Standish, John Alden, Priscilla Alden, and other women from the *Mayflower*—all settled in but still struggling. They answer visitors' questions in authentic seventeenth-century Shakespeareanese.

The Plantation employs food historians who present an ever-changing array of special events, lectures, and workshops related to foodways, horticulture, and agriculture. Visitors watch as individual house-wives cook the daily meal, which follows the turn of the seasons. They may catch a woman in her kitchen garden, and discover her views on the virtues of medicinal plants or the best way to cook asparagus. They can watch housewives plucking ducks, "raising" pies, laying the board, or doing countless other household chores. Men and women plant and harvest corn, make hay, and tend to animals.

Throughout the spring, visitors can try some of the dishes served at a Pilgrim wedding banquet, including turkey with sorrel sauce, corn pudding with spring herbs, "sallet" of asparagus, fricassee of cod, bride cake, and custard. In the fall, in addition to a re-creation of the first Thanksgiving, a lavish feast like the one served to guests from New Amsterdam is staged. Roast pork, stewed duck with onions and currants, pickled herring, corn pudding with blueberries, stewed pumpkin, and seventeenth-century cheesecake are on the menu.

Grilled Squid Salad a la Al Forno

MAKES 4 SERVINGS

New Englanders by the score regularly make the pilgrimage to Al Forno, Johanne Killeen and George Germon's exceptional trattoria in Providence, Rhode Island. When they get locally caught squid, Johanne and George grill it with abandon on Al Forno's wood-burning grills, turning it into (among other stellar dishes) a vibrant salad made anise-fragrant with chopped fresh fennel. This is my adaptation of the salad, based on a recipe from their book, *Cucina Simpatica*.

For the vinaigrette:

2 tablespoons fresh lemon juice
1 tablespoon sherry vinegar
1 large garlic clove, minced
½ teaspoon salt
½ teaspoon dried red pepper flakes
⅓ cup fruity olive oil

For the salad:

3 tablespoons olive oil
1½ pounds squid, cleaned
Salt and black pepper
2 celery ribs, thinly sliced
½ cup chopped fresh fennel, plus fronds for garnish
Assorted salad greens, about 4 cups

1. To make the dressing, whisk the lemon juice, vinegar, garlic, salt, and red pepper flakes together in a small bowl. Whisk in the olive oil. (Can be made a day ahead and refrigerated.)
2. Build a hot charcoal fire or preheat a gas grill. Place an oiled grill rack as close to the coals as possible.
3. Brush the oil on the squid bodies and tentacles and sprinkle with salt and pepper. Grill until seared and lightly charred on one side, about 1 minute. Turn and sear the second side (see Note). Do not overcook or the squid will be tough.
4. Cut the squid bodies into rings and the tentacles into smaller pieces. Toss the squid, celery, and fennel in a bowl with most of the dressing. Spread the greens out onto a platter, drizzle with a little dressing, top with the squid salad, garnish with fennel fronds, and serve.

Note: To keep the squid flat you can thread them onto metal skewers before grilling.

Carding Brook Farm

Jennifer Schroth and Jonathan Ellsworth operate Carding Brook Farm in Brooklin, in midcoast Maine, single-handedly—with a little help from a couple of draft horses that plow the fields and haul logs from the wood lot, as well as some sheep and chickens that provide not only wool and eggs but also manure to fertilize the organic farming operation.

Jen and Jon are farmers with a vision, one that is both philosophical and aesthetic. They are certified organic farmers and strong proponents of sustainable agriculture. They sell only the vegetables and maple syrup from Carding Brook that look as perfect and beautiful and taste as wonderful as they possibly can.

Carding Brook has made its highly esteemed local reputation on just a few superior products. Their maple syrup, which they collect from "road trees" and boil down in a wood-fired evaporator, is deep amber, smoky sweet, and intensely flavorful. They grow several varieties of specialty potatoes, including skinny red and purple and white fingerlings, round Austrians, an all-red and an all-blue potato, and, best of all, tiny baby versions of all of these, many freshly dug and brought to market when they are no bigger than marbles. Beans, both fresh and dried, are another specialty—little, perfectly matched French haricots verts, sweet yellow wax beans, fat, flavorful Romano beans, cream-colored and maroon-striped Dragon's Tongue beans, cranberry shell beans, favas, black turtle beans, and big white beans. In a recent season Jen and Jon also grew about a dozen varieties of cherry and tiny currant tomatoes, including Gold Nugget, Ruby Pearl, and Sweet Chelsea, and eighteen full-sized tomatoes. In winter they peruse reliable catalogs and order tomato seeds with such irresistible-sounding names as Pineapple, Ida Gold, Green Zebra, Black Prince, Golden Boy, Big Beef, Early Girl, and Aunt Ruby's German Green.

Carding Brook's mesclun mix, which they rotate-plant from late spring right through fall, is an elegant, perfectly balanced, ever-changing combination of mildly sweet, bitter, and sharply peppery greens. The mix usually includes some combination of a lettuce, arugula, a mustard such as mizuna, tatsoi, red Russian kale, baby Swiss chard leaves, a cress, a curly endive, and a few of their signature edible blossoms, such as borage, nasturtiums, violas, or herb or lettuce blossoms. Other choices depend on the season. In spring or fall, it's sorrel; in colder weather, it's mâche. Carding Brook's mesclun is different every day. And it's never not delicious.

Sumptuous Lobster Salad

MAKES 4 SERVINGS

Unlike the utterly simple lobster salad that is de rigueur for Maine-style lobster "rolls" (see page 236), this is a sophisticated contemporary version of the salad using New England's most prized crustacean. The dressing is spiked with lemon zest and cilantro, and the whole gorgeous platter gets garnished colorfully with snow peas and radishes. Add a basket of soft buttery dinner rolls such as Parker House Rolls (page 447), or wedges of Rosemary Focaccia (page 454) for a splendid lunch or supper.

For the dressing:

⅔ cup mayonnaise
2 teaspoons Dijon mustard
1 tablespoon fresh lemon juice
1 teaspoon grated lemon zest
3 tablespoons chopped fresh cilantro, plus sprigs for garnish

For the salad:

1 pound diced cooked lobster meat
⅔ cup minced celery
½ cup minced scallions
Salt and fresh-ground black pepper
Bibb lettuce leaves
1 cup trimmed and blanched snow peas
4 radishes, thinly sliced

1. To make the dressing, whisk together the mayonnaise, mustard, lemon juice, lemon zest, and cilantro in a small bowl. (The dressing can be made several hours ahead and refrigerated.)
2. Toss the lobster, celery, and scallions together in a large bowl. Add most of the dressing and stir gently but thoroughly to mix. (The salad can be made about 2 hours ahead and refrigerated.)
3. To serve, stir the salad, add more dressing if necessary, and season with salt and pepper to taste. Line a large platter or individual plates with the lettuce leaves. Spoon the salad onto the leaves and arrange the snow peas and radishes around the edges. Garnish with cilantro sprigs and serve.

A HARVEST OF VEGETABLES

The first signs that sprout early in a chill New England spring—"Fiddleheads Are Here!" "Dandy-lion Greens," "Locally Grown Asparagus"—are hopeful harbingers of things to come. A bit later it's "Fresh Peas Today," "Cukes, Cukes, Cukes," and rising to a crescendo, "Native Corn—Picked Today," "Red Ripe Tomatoes," and "Free Zucchini!" winding down to "First Potatoes" and "Fresh Dug Parsnips." A long-standing tradition of farm stands thrives in New England today, the farmers' market movement grows stronger every year, and restaurant chefs continue to cultivate intimate relationships with farmers.

Such delicacies as a spring mélange of Sautéed Fiddleheads, Sugar Snaps, and Baby Carrots (page 119), sprightly Dandelion Greens, Modern Maine Style (page 120), and elegant Broiled Asparagus with Asiago (page 110) speak to this bounteous harvest. Minted New Potatoes and Peas (page 124) combines two early summer delicacies; Golden Corn Pudding (page 116) celebrates the plenitude of a mid-summer crop; and Sunny Acres Farm Scalloped Tomatoes (page 143) layers juicy ripe tomatoes with seasoned buttered crumbs.

Root vegetables, especially the venerable potato, are featured in beloved classic New England recipes. And the not-so-classic, such as Spicy Potatoes on the Half Shell (page 128) and Northeast Kingdom Maple-Glazed Braised Turnips (page 129) are also given their due.

Broiled Asparagus with Asiago

MAKES 4 SERVINGS

A man named Diederick Leertower, of Worcester County, Massachusetts, has been credited with bringing asparagus to America from Holland in the eighteenth century. Once here, it proved to grow well in most parts of New England. It seems to be a vegetable that is congenial to the cultural, as well as the physical, climate of the region. Asparagus beds take years of watchful waiting before they produce a good crop, a situation quite compatible with the patient, low-key Yankee temperament. This is one of my favorite ways of preparing the spears during the spring asparagus orgy. Broiling intensifies and deepens the essential flavor of asparagus, and the glaze of sweet, salty cheese is a nice counterpoint to its grassy spring taste. This is a lovely part of any spring menu, either as a side dish or an eat-with-your-fingers hors d'oeuvre.

> 2 pounds asparagus, tough bottom stems removed
> 1½ tablespoons olive oil
> 1 garlic clove, cut in half
> 3 tablespoons fresh-grated Asiago or Parmesan cheese
> Fresh-ground black pepper

1. Blanch the asparagus spears in a large pot of boiling salted water until they are bright green and crisp-tender, 2 to 4 minutes, depending on thickness. Drain in a colander and run under cold water to stop the cooking. Place on a double layer of paper towels and pat dry. (The asparagus can be precooked a couple of hours ahead and refrigerated, covered with plastic wrap.)

2. Preheat the broiler.

3. Coat a large rimmed baking sheet with some of the oil and rub it with the cut sides of the garlic clove halves. Spread the asparagus out in a more or less single layer and drizzle with the remaining oil. Sprinkle with the cheese.

4. Broil about 4 inches from the heat, watching carefully, until the asparagus is tinged with brown and the cheese has formed a melted glaze on top, 1 to 3 minutes.

5. Transfer to a serving platter, sprinkle with a generous grinding of black pepper, and serve.

Greeked Green Beans

MAKES 6 SERVINGS

The Greeks have a wonderful way with vegetables of all kinds. At Greek festivals I have attended around New England, I have often been served this delectable green bean "stew." The beans are parboiled and then treated to a slow, longer-than-usual braise with olive oil and seasonings, which mellows the vegetables so they take on an almost nutty flavor. These beans are particularly tasty eaten as a saucy side dish with roasted meats, such as Greek Easter Dinner Rosemary Roasted Lamb (page 299) or Garlicky Greek Baked Chicken Riganato (page 311).

1¾ pounds green beans, trimmed and cut in half
2½ tablespoons olive oil
1 medium-large onion, cut in half and sliced
3 large garlic cloves, finely chopped
3 cups chopped seeded fresh tomatoes (about 1½ pounds) or
    1 14-ounce can, drained, seeded, and chopped
½ teaspoon sugar
½ teaspoon salt, or to taste
¼ teaspoon fresh-ground black pepper, or to taste
1 tablespoon fresh lemon juice

1. Cook the beans in a large pot of boiling salted water, uncovered, until crisp-tender, about 5 minutes. Drain in a colander, rinse with cold water to stop the cooking, and drain again.
2. Heat the oil in a large skillet with a lid or a Dutch oven. Add the onion and cook over medium heat until softened, about 5 minutes. Add the garlic and cook, stirring, for 1 minute. Add the tomatoes, sugar, salt, and pepper, then stir in the beans. Bring to a simmer, cover, and cook over medium-low heat until the beans are very tender, 10 to 15 minutes. Uncover, and if there is a lot of liquid in the pot, cook briskly for a couple of minutes to reduce it.
3. Stir in the lemon juice, season with additional salt and pepper to taste, and serve.

Ivy League Beets with Orange Sauce

MAKES 4 TO 6 SERVINGS

No one seems to know whether beets in a pleasantly sweet-sour vinegar and sugar sauce were dubbed Harvard Beets after the color of Harvard's jerseys or for some other more obscure reason, but beets have been eaten this way in New England for a long, long time. When I read in John Mariani's *Encyclopedia of American Food and Drink* about Yale beets, which replace some of the vinegar with orange juice, I thought a marriage of these two Ivy Leaguers might taste even better. It does. But I wouldn't dare ask the opinion of anyone from either Cambridge or New Haven.

½ cup sugar
1½ teaspoons cornstarch
6 tablespoons cider vinegar
½ cup orange juice
3 cups diced or sliced cooked beets
 (use 1½ pound fresh beets or
 2 15-ounce cans, drained)
½ teaspoon grated orange zest
Salt and fresh-ground black pepper
2 tablespoons butter

1. Whisk together the sugar and cornstarch in a heavy medium-sized saucepan. Gradually whisk in the vinegar and orange juice. Place over medium-high heat and bring to a boil, stirring. Cook for 2 to 3 minutes, until the sauce is thick and bubbly.
2. Add the beets and stir in the orange zest. Cook over medium heat, stirring occasionally, until heated through. Season with the salt and pepper. Just before serving, cut the butter into pieces and stir it in until it melts.

Saved by Salt Pork

"A string bean, bare, by itself, is a mistake, a sad one. But put a half a pound of sow's belly in with about three times that weight in pole beans, and you have something the angels will fight over. The salt pork brings out the flavors the string beans never knew they had!"

—Robert P. Tristram Coffin,
Maine poet

Church Supper Broccoli and Cheese Bake

MAKES 6 SERVINGS

Broccoli-growing conditions are excellent all over New England but are particularly favorable in the Connecticut River valley farming towns around Northampton, Massachusetts. When one of my sisters lived in that area, almost everything her family ate during the summer came out of the garden. This thyme-flavored cheese-and-crumb-topped broccoli casserole, which can also be made with cauliflower or green beans, is one of those substantial vegetable dishes that should play a starring role at supper. Its make-ahead feature also makes it a perfect candidate for a potluck supper.

1½ pounds broccoli florets (about 7 cups)
3 tablespoons butter
1 onion, chopped
1 tablespoon chopped fresh thyme or 1 teaspoon dried
½ teaspoon dry mustard
¼ teaspoon salt
¼ teaspoon fresh-ground black pepper
1½ cups fresh white or whole wheat breadcrumbs
1 cup shredded cheddar cheese

1. Blanch the broccoli in a large pot of boiling salted water until it is crisp-tender, 3 to 4 minutes. Drain in a colander and refresh under cold water to stop the cooking.
2. Heat 1 tablespoon of the butter in a medium-sized skillet. Add the onion and cook over medium heat until softened, about 5 minutes. Stir in the thyme, mustard, salt, and pepper.
3. Preheat the oven to 375 degrees. Butter a shallow 2-quart baking dish.
4. Layer half the broccoli in the prepared dish and spoon the onion mixture over the top. Sprinkle with half the breadcrumbs and cheese. Repeat the layering, ending with the cheese. Melt the remaining 2 tablespoons of butter and drizzle over the top. (The casserole can be made several hours ahead, covered with foil, and refrigerated.)
5. Bake, uncovered, until the topping is golden and bubbly, about 35 minutes. If the casserole has been refrigerated, bake the foil-covered casserole for 15 minutes. Uncover and bake until the topping is golden, about 35 minutes.
6. Serve directly from the baking dish.

Garlicky Broccoli Rabe

MAKES 4 SERVINGS

Broccoli rabe, also called rappini or rabes (pronounced "rah-bees"), is a flowering variety of broccoli that used to be appreciated only by Italian New Englanders. Now that it appears in supermarket produce aisles all over the country, the rest of us have learned to love its intense, pleasantly bitter flavor. The whole plant—stems, deep-green leaves, and flowering yellow buds—is edible and delicious, particularly when you blanch it to get rid of some of its excess bitterness.

> 1 large bunch (about 1½ pounds) broccoli rabe
> 2 tablespoons extra-virgin olive oil
> 2 large or 3 medium garlic cloves, minced
> ¼ teaspoon red pepper flakes
> Salt and fresh-ground black pepper

1. Trim about 1 inch off the bottom of the broccoli rabe stems, and then cut the entire bunch—stems, leaves, and buds—into 1- to 2-inch lengths. Cook the broccoli rabe in a large pot of boiling salted water, uncovered, until it is just tender, about 5 minutes. Drain in a colander.

2. Heat the oil in a large skillet. Add the garlic and cook over medium heat, stirring, until fragrant but not brown, about 1 minute. Add the broccoli rabe and red pepper flakes and cook, stirring frequently, until the broccoli rabe is thoroughly heated through, 3 to 4 minutes. Season with salt and black pepper before serving.

"Garden Sass"

"Garden sass" was the term New Englanders used for all green vegetables, and the occasional old-time Yankee still uses it. Because vegetables were customarily stewed or covered in a cream gravy, it was natural to think of them as a sort of sauce (or "sass") for meat or fish. These vegetables were usually cooked to the point where they were quite soupy, so they were served in small side dishes (known as "bird baths") and eaten with a spoon. In a few New England hotel dining rooms and country inns, vegetables still appear in little white ironstone dishes served on the side of the main dinner plate.

New England Ladies' Cabbage

MAKES 4 TO 6 SERVINGS

The first English settlers brought cabbage seeds to Plymouth, and they soon discovered that this was one vegetable that flourished in the New England climate. At first the colonists just ate it boiled, English style, but later they learned from the Dutch how to turn cabbage into sauerkraut and coleslaw. Another old New England refinement was this delicate, flanlike cabbage custard known as ladies' cabbage, presumably because it was a rather elegant and genteel way of preparing a common, everyday sort of vegetable.

> 4 cups sliced or chopped green cabbage (about 1 pound) (see Note)
> 2 tablespoons butter
> 1 small onion, sliced
> 2 eggs
> ½ cup heavy cream
> 1 teaspoon sugar
> ¾ teaspoon salt
> ¼ teaspoon black pepper
> Pinch of cayenne pepper

1. Cook the cabbage in a large pot of boiling salted water, uncovered, for 5 to 7 minutes or until tender. Drain in a colander and press out as much of the water as possible.
2. Preheat the oven to 350 degrees. Butter an 8-inch-square baking dish and place the cooked cabbage in it.
3. Melt the butter in a medium-sized skillet. Add the onion and cook over medium heat until softened, about 5 minutes. Scrape the onion into the baking dish with the cabbage. (The vegetables can be prepared several hours ahead and refrigerated.)
4. Whisk the eggs until blended in a mixing bowl. Whisk in the heavy cream, sugar, salt, pepper, and cayenne. Pour the egg mixture over the cabbage mixture and stir gently but thoroughly to combine the ingredients evenly.
5. Place the baking dish in a larger shallow roasting pan and pour into the roasting

pan enough hot water to come halfway up the sides of the baking dish. Bake, uncovered, until the custard is completely set, 25 to 30 minutes.

6. Serve hot or warm, directly from the baking dish.

Note: You can use the precut cabbage sold in bags in the produce department.

Golden Corn Pudding

MAKES 6 SERVINGS

Even though we now can buy asparagus in November and peaches in February, New Englanders still treasure the harvest from our short but intense summer season, savoring every precious bite of sun-ripened flavor, hoarding the memories against the winter darkness. Nothing is as highly prized in this regard as fresh local corn. In middle to late summer, when big bins of bright green ears start to appear at farm stands and in markets, after we've mowed away corn on the cob several nights running, we scrape the sweet golden kernels from some of the ears and make this pudding—one of the all-time great American recipes with New England roots.

> 3 tablespoons butter
> 1 medium onion, chopped
> 1 small green bell pepper, chopped, optional
> 2 tablespoons all-purpose flour
> ½ teaspoon dry mustard
> 2 cups whole or lowfat milk
> 2 teaspoons sugar
> ½ teaspoon salt
> ¼ teaspoon cayenne pepper
> 2 eggs
> 2½ cups fresh, leftover cooked, or frozen corn kernels
> 1 cup grated medium-sharp cheddar cheese
> ⅔ cup fresh breadcrumbs

1. Heat 2 tablespoons of the butter in a large skillet. Add the onion and the green pepper, if you are using it, and cook over medium heat, stirring occasionally, until softened, about 5 minutes. Sprinkle on the flour and mustard and cook, stirring, for

1 minute. Gradually whisk in the milk and cook, stirring, until the sauce comes to a boil. Whisk in the sugar, salt, and cayenne.

2. Lightly beat the eggs in a large bowl. Gradually whisk the hot milk mixture into the eggs.

3. Preheat the oven to 350 degrees. Butter a 1½- to 2-quart shallow baking dish.

4. Combine the corn and cheese in the baking dish, tossing together to mix. Pour the sauce over and stir gently to combine. (The casserole can be made several hours ahead to this point and refrigerated. Add 5 minutes to the baking time if it is cold.)

5. Melt the remaining 1 tablespoon of butter in a small skillet, add the breadcrumbs, and cook over medium heat, stirring, until the crumbs just begin to color. Sprinkle over the casserole.

6. Bake, uncovered, until the custard is set and the top is golden brown, 25 to 35 minutes. Serve directly from the baking dish.

Baked Herbed Eggplant with Fresh Tomatoes and Feta

MAKES 6 TO 8 SERVINGS

It might seem surprising that eggplant grows at all in New England, for this is a vegetable that one usually associates with the hotter climes of southern Italy and Greece. But, in fact, eggplant—particularly the newer slender Japanese and smaller Italian varieties—does thrive in Yankee gardens. Peak season is midsummer to midautumn, coinciding with prime tomato season, so combining these two vegetables is our natural inclination. If the eggplants you are using are fresh and young, they do not really need preliminary salting to draw out bitterness, but I like giving them just a sprinkle of salt because it helps prevent their absorbing quite so much oil. A crumble of stark-white fresh feta finishes the dish with a delightful tang and an attractive contrast in color.

> 2 pounds young eggplants (either Japanese or smaller Italian varieties)
> 1 teaspoon salt
> ½ cup fresh flat-leaf parsley leaves
> ½ cup fresh basil leaves
> 2 garlic cloves, peeled and cut in chunks

6 tablespoons extra-virgin olive oil
Fresh-ground black pepper
2 cups chopped seeded tomatoes (about 3 medium)
1 cup crumbled feta cheese

1. Lightly oil a large baking dish such as a 13-by-9-inch, or two smaller baking dishes. Cut the unpeeled eggplants into ½- to ¾-inch-thick lengthwise slices. Arrange cut sides up, overlapping slightly, in the baking dish(es). Sprinkle with the salt and set aside while preparing the remaining ingredients, about 15 minutes.

2. Combine the parsley, basil, and garlic in a food processor and pulse to coarsely chop. With the motor running, pour the oil through the feed tube to make a coarse puree. (Or, you can chop the herbs and garlic by hand and combine with the oil.)

3. Use several paper towels to blot the surfaces of the eggplant thoroughly dry and to wipe off the excess salt. Sprinkle generously with black pepper. Drizzle or brush the eggplant with the herb mixture and scatter with the tomatoes. Cover the baking dish with foil. (The recipe can be prepared a couple of hours ahead to this point and held at cool room temperature.)

4. Preheat the oven to 350 degrees.

Fiddleheads

New Englanders have been picking fiddleheads for generations. Actually the coiled frond of the ostrich fern, fiddleheads resemble the scroll of a violin—hence the name. They grow wild in Vermont, New Hampshire, and Maine, and for many Yankees, fiddleheads are the first real taste of spring.

Fiddleheads begin to pop up in late April or early May. The tender little rolls of fern should be cut almost as soon as they appear, when the plants are just a few inches off the ground. They can be purchased at roadside stands and lately in supermarkets. Or you can continue the old tradition of foraging for them in the wild; consult a good field guide first.

Once home, unless someone else has already done it for you, fiddleheads must be cleaned of the thin, papery brown membrane that clings to the inner coil. The best way to do this is to immerse the fiddleheads in a sink of cold water, gently rub away the brown skin, and then rinse them in a colander.

Cook fiddleheads by blanching, steaming, or sautéeing for just a few minutes. Season them simply with butter or light olive oil, salt, pepper, and, if you like, a spritz of lemon juice or vinegar. Or include them in a medley of spring vegetables, such as Sautéed Fiddleheads, Sugar Snaps, and Baby Carrots (page 119).

5. Bake for 35 to 45 minutes, or until the eggplant is tender. Uncover, sprinkle with the feta, and continue to bake, uncovered, until the eggplant is very soft and the cheese is slightly melted, 5 to 15 minutes.

6. Serve with a small spatula, directly from the baking dish.

Sautéed Fiddleheads, Sugar Snaps, and Baby Carrots

MAKES 6 SERVINGS

The flavor of fiddlehead ferns, welcome harbingers of northern New England spring, has been likened to that of asparagus, broccoli, artichokes, and even wild rice. None of these comparisons quite works for me. I think fiddleheads have their very own taste, which is like the damp, just-awakening bracken from which they spring. I try to eat them as many times as possible during their fleeting season, and this simple mélange of fiddleheads and other spring vegetables is one of the best. If you cannot get fiddleheads, pencil-thin asparagus cut into 2-inch lengths can be substituted for them in this recipe.

> ½ pound baby carrots
> ½ pound fiddlehead ferns
> ½ pound sugar snap peas
> 1 tablespoon butter
> Salt and fresh-ground black pepper
> Pinch of sugar
> 1 tablespoon snipped fresh chives

1. Peel the carrots, and if the green stems are still attached, leave them on but trim off all but the last ½ inch. Leave the carrots whole or, if the sizes vary, cut the larger ones in half lengthwise.

2. Immerse the fiddleheads in a sink full of cold water and use your fingers to rub off the papery brown skin. Stem and string the sugar snaps.

3. Cook the carrots in a large pot of boiling salted water until they are almost but not quite tender, 3 to 5 minutes, depending on their size. Add the fiddleheads and continue to cook until they are almost tender, about 3 minutes. Add the sugar snaps and cook for 30 to 60 seconds until they are bright green. Drain all the vegetables in a colander and run under cold water to stop the cooking and set the color. (The recipe can be prepared ahead to this point. Wrap in paper towels and refrigerate up to 6 hours.)

4. Melt the butter in a large skillet. Add the vegetables and cook over medium-high heat, stirring frequently, until heated through, 2 to 3 minutes. Season with salt, pepper, and sugar. Add the chives and toss to combine.

5. Transfer to a bowl or platter and serve.

Dandelion Greens, Modern Maine Style

MAKES 6 SERVINGS

In April or May, when you begin to see native Yankees—usually the older generation— out in their yards or in fields, still swathed in winter coats, bending over and rooting in the ground with sturdy old case knives, clutching plastic bags snapping in the chill breeze, you know that spring really might arrive. It's dandelion-digging time. In Maine many old-timers still dig up a big "mess" of dandelion greens and turn them into supper by simmering them for about an hour with salt pork and pared Maine potatoes. Although I prefer a shorter cooking time for tender young greens, the notion of salt pork and boiled potatoes is so appealing that I devised this more modern version of the old Maine recipe. If your greens are actually hand-dug, blanch them first in a large pot of boiling water for about 3 minutes to remove excess bitterness before proceeding with this recipe.

> ¼ cup (2 to 3 ounces) diced lean salt pork
> ½ cup chopped onion
> 2 pounds tender young dandelion greens, rinsed well and cut into
>   1-inch lengths
> 1 tablespoon sugar
> Salt and fresh-ground black pepper
> 1 to 2 teaspoons fresh lemon juice
> 1½ pounds Maine potatoes, peeled and boiled

1. Cook the salt pork over medium heat in a Dutch oven or a large skillet with a lid until the fat is rendered and the lean bits are browned, about 10 minutes. Remove with a slotted spoon and drain on paper towels, leaving the drippings in the pan.

2. Add the onion to the pan drippings and cook until it begins to soften, about 3 minutes. Add the greens, sugar, and about 3 cups of water. Bring to a boil, reduce the heat to medium, and simmer, uncovered, until the greens are tender, 10 to 15 minutes. Drain and season with salt and pepper and the lemon juice.

3. Serve surrounded with the potatoes and sprinkled with the reserved salt pork bits if desired.

Wild Greens

Wild greens thrive in the long, cool, damp New England spring. Of course, "spring" can mean March in Connecticut, but it is usually mid-April to mid-May in northern Vermont, New Hampshire, and Maine before the welcome green shoots begin to poke their heads up through the brown.

Some of the most common New England wild greens are dandelions, fiddleheads, dock, chicory, watercress, milkweed shoots, peppergrass, wild mustard, lamb's quarters, sorrel, yellow rocket, orache, and purslane. All are cooked in a similar manner. Young leaves or shoots are rinsed, trimmed, drained, and simmered in a little salted water for just a few minutes until tender. They may be served with lemon wedges, a cruet of vinegar, or chopped hard-boiled egg. Greens are often delicious cooked in combination with each other, in the true rural "potherb" style. The old-fashioned Yankee way with greens was to add a bit of bacon or salt pork and simmer them for a long time.

As with any plant, younger greens are more tender and less bitter than more mature leaves. Before foraging for wild greens, consult a good field guide to help you identify what you pick. And do not gather greens near major roadways or in chemically treated areas.

Portuguese Limas and Linguiça

MAKES 4 MAIN-DISH SERVINGS

The Portuguese-Americans on Martha's Vineyard, who are descended mostly from sailors from the Azores, cook this dish on the island in winter using dried limas and canned tomatoes. I prefer it decked out in more summery garb, made with the occasional cache of fresh lima beans or the always available frozen beans, and chopped fresh tomato. It's sort of the Portuguese version of *pasta e fagioli*, and it makes a splendid little supper when served with some crusty Portuguese rolls or cornbread for dipping in the delicious garlicky juices.

2 tablespoons olive oil

1 large onion, coarsely chopped

1 garlic clove, minced

½ pound linguiça, or other smoked sausage, such as kielbasa, cut in
   ½-inch slices

1 bay leaf, broken in half

1 pound shelled fresh or frozen lima beans

1 medium tomato, seeded and chopped

2 cups chicken or vegetable broth

Fresh-ground black pepper

1. Heat the oil over medium heat in a Dutch oven or large skillet with a lid. Add the onion, garlic, linguiça, and bay leaf and cook, stirring occasionally, until the onion softens and the sausage browns lightly, about 10 minutes.

2. Add the limas, tomato, broth, and 1 cup of water. Bring to a boil, reduce the heat to medium-low, and simmer, partially covered, until the beans are tender and the flavors blend, 15 to 25 minutes. Season with pepper to taste. (The sausage and broth will probably contribute enough salt.)

3. Spoon into shallow bowls to serve.

New Hampshire Spring-Dug Parsnip Puree

MAKES 4 TO 6 SERVINGS

Because of our long winters, root vegetables have always been an important staple of the New England diet, and Yankees have devised myriad ways of cooking these immensely versatile members of the vegetable family. At one time hardly heard of outside New England, parsnips have, in the past generation or so, come to be appreciated by the rest of the country for their sweet, almost herbaceous flavor and creamy texture. They are harvested both in late fall and early spring, but the "spring-dug" crop stays underground all winter, allowing the natural starches to convert to sugar, resulting in sweeter and somewhat spicier parsnips. At New Hampshire's Canterbury Shaker Village dining room, they serve a similar version of this lovely, pale parsnip puree with roast duckling.

2 pounds parsnips, peeled and cut in 1-inch pieces
4 tablespoons unsalted butter, cut in chunks
½ cup half-and-half
Tiny pinch of ground mace or nutmeg
Salt and fresh-ground black pepper

1. Cook the parsnips in a large pot of boiling salted water until they are very tender, about 20 minutes. Drain in a colander, return to the pot, and place over very low heat until the parsnips are quite dry, 1 minute or so.
2. Transfer to a food processor or leave in the pot to mash. Add the butter and half-and-half and process or mash with a potato masher or electric mixer to make a fairly smooth puree. Season with the mace or nutmeg and salt and pepper to taste. (The puree can be made ahead and reheated in the microwave if desired.)
3. Transfer to a serving dish and serve.

Petite Peas with Prosciutto

MAKES 4 SERVINGS

Called *piselli con prosciutto* in Italian, this way of preparing peas is a favorite among Yankee Italians, particularly the primarily Neapolitan clan living in Saugatuck, Connecticut. This recipe is from their *Sons of Italy Festival Italiano Cookbook*. The little bit of prosciutto delivers a welcome salty counterpoint to the starchy green peas. If you get hold of some fresh green garden peas in spring, try them this way.

3 cups small frozen green peas or fresh-shelled peas
2 tablespoons chicken broth or water
2 large leaves Bibb lettuce
2 tablespoons finely slivered prosciutto (about 1 thin slice)
1 tablespoon butter
1 tablespoon snipped fresh chives
Salt and fresh-ground black pepper

1. Place the peas and broth or water in a medium-large saucepan. Lay the lettuce leaves over the top. Bring to a boil, reduce the heat to medium-low, and cook,

covered, until the peas are tender, about 5 minutes. (Fresh peas will take a few minutes longer.)

2. Discard the lettuce or chop it and add it to the peas. Stir in the prosciutto, butter, and chives and season with salt and pepper to taste.

3. Transfer to a dish to serve.

Minted New Potatoes and Peas

MAKES 4 SERVINGS

This dish unites three of the finest ingredients to be gleaned from a New England spring garden or farmers' market—the first sacrificial gathering of tiny, marble-sized new potatoes, a hard-won handful of freshly shelled green peas, and sprigs of early garden mint. It's a sweetly winning combination that is wonderful with any springtime dinner.

Maine Potatoes

Potatoes first came to New England in the early eighteenth century. Irish Presbyterian immigrants brought them into Boston in 1718, and records indicate that potatoes were also planted at about that time at Londonderry in the New Hampshire colony. They were not to gain wide acceptance in the region, however, for nearly another century.

Scotch-Irish settlers brought potatoes to Maine around 1750. Joseph Houlton is credited with planting the first potato crop—a variety called Early Blue or Blue Nose—in Aroostook County in 1807, where soil and climate combined to create ideal potato-growing conditions. At first potatoes were just a garden and livestock crop, but as rail lines extended into Aroostook, more were grown and exported, and Maine became the nation's biggest potato grower. Much of the crop in the nineteenth

century went not for eating but for stiffening men's shirts and ladies' petticoats. Potatoes were used in the manufacture of laundry starch, which brought more profit than the table crop.

Although Maine now ranks behind several other states in total production, potatoes are still the state's number one agricultural crop, and most of that crop is grown in Aroostook County. Located in the northernmost part of the state, Aroostook, known simply as "The County," is larger than Connecticut and Rhode Island combined. Most of the Maine potato production is in "round whites," a medium-sized, moderately starchy potato that is generally classified as an all-purpose potato. It's an excellent all-round potato, particularly good for scalloped potatoes and for hashed browns.

1 pound tiny whole new potatoes, red- or white-skinned, or a
   combination
2 cups shelled fresh peas, or 1 10-ounce package frozen peas
½ teaspoon sugar
2 tablespoons butter
¼ cup chopped fresh parsley
2 tablespoons chopped fresh mint
1 teaspoon Dijon mustard
Salt and fresh-ground black pepper

1. Scrub the potatoes and leave them whole. Cut any larger potatoes into 1½-inch chunks.
2. Cook the potatoes in a medium-large pot of well-salted water until tender when pierced with a small knife, 15 to 20 minutes. Add the sugar, along with the fresh peas if you are using them, for the last 8 to 10 minutes of cooking time. If you are using frozen peas, add them for the last 3 to 5 minutes. When both vegetables are tender, drain in a colander.
3. Return the vegetables to the pot, add the butter, parsley, mint, and mustard, and season with salt and pepper to taste. Turn into a warm bowl and serve.

Classic Scalloped Potatoes

MAKES 6 SERVINGS

This is for my friend Mary Maynard, who recently misplaced her mother's old scalloped potato recipe and was lamenting the fact that she could not find anything similar in any of her newer cookbooks (not even in that huge compendium, the new *Joy of Cooking*). So here it is, Mary—old-fashioned, lightly flour-thickened scalloped potatoes, not terribly rich, not fancied up with anything more than a light sprinkling of herbs. They go with absolutely everything, including Greek Roast Leg of Lamb (page 299), Baked Ham (page 294), or a plain hamburger.

2½ pounds all-purpose potatoes, such as Maine potatoes or Yukon
   golds, peeled and sliced (about 5 cups)
1 small onion, thinly sliced
2 tablespoons all-purpose flour

1 teaspoon salt

½ teaspoon black pepper

2½ cups whole milk

3 tablespoons butter

1 tablespoon chopped fresh herbs (such as parsley, thyme, sage, or a
combination), optional

1. Preheat the oven to 350 degrees. Butter a shallow 2½- to 3-quart baking dish.
2. Combine the potatoes, onion, flour, salt, and pepper in a large bowl. Toss with your
hands to mix thoroughly, and spread the mixture out in the prepared dish.
3. Combine the milk and butter in a saucepan and heat over medium heat until the
butter melts and steam rises, about 2 minutes. Pour over the potatoes. Cover the
baking dish loosely with foil.
4. Bake for 30 minutes. Uncover the casserole, sprinkle with the chopped herbs, if
you like, and continue to bake, uncovered, until the potatoes are very tender, about
30 minutes.
5. Serve the potatoes directly from the baking dish.

Fluffy Mashed Potatoes and Variations

MAKES 6 SERVINGS

Simple, innocent mashed potatoes are one of my very favorite foods on the planet.
When my mother made mashed potatoes for supper, I'd generally save them to eat at the
very end of the meal, because even when they were stone cold, I loved them better than
dessert. The best mashed potatoes are made with a high-starch, floury potato such as a
russet, but all-purpose potatoes such as the large Maine varieties can also produce a fine
result. Most New England children require mashed potatoes on the plate when any
gravy is present, as with Shaker Roast Pork Loin with Cider-Sage Gravy (page 292) for
example, or Mamie's Little Meatballs with Applesauce Gravy (page 283). I've had fairly
good luck making mashed potatoes ahead, holding them for a few hours at room temperature, and then reheating in the microwave.

> 3 pounds russet or all-purpose potatoes, peeled and cut in 2-inch
>   chunks
> 3 tablespoons butter
> About ⅔ cup whole, lowfat, or skim milk, or light cream
> Salt and fresh-ground black pepper

1. Cook the potatoes in a large pot of boiling salted water until they are very tender, about 15 minutes. Drain the potatoes, return them to the pot, and place over low heat for about 1 minute until they are thoroughly dry. Transfer to a large bowl or leave them in the saucepan to mash.

2. Mash the potatoes with a ricer, potato masher, or electric mixer. Add the butter and most of the milk to the potatoes, and mash until smooth, adding as much more milk as is necessary to make a smooth, fluffy puree. Season with salt and pepper to taste.

3. Serve immediately, or hold for about 45 minutes and reheat in a microwave.

Variations

Mashed Mainers with Mint: A suggestion from Imogene Wolcott, renowned authority on New England cooking. In spring, when suddenly one fine day the garden is full of bright green mint shoots, shred up about 2 tablespoons' worth of the leaves and add them to the potatoes. Add a pinch of sugar, too, to enhance the sweetness.

Garlic Mashed Potatoes: Cook 3 peeled and halved garlic cloves with the potatoes (or roast the garlic separately) and puree along with them.

Scallion or Chive Mashed Potatoes: One of my favorites, especially when chives are thick in the garden. Stir in 3 or 4 tablespoons of snipped fresh chives or minced scallions after the potatoes are mashed. Garnish with a purple chive blossom if available.

Super-Rich Mashed Potatoes: The master recipe is on the lean side, allowing for the potato flavor to shine through. For richer potatoes—say for Thanksgiving dinner—increase the amount of butter in the puree.

Spicy Potatoes on the Half Shell

MAKES 4 SERVINGS

Supermarkets all over the country, including here in New England, now display a panoply of chile peppers. Garden catalogs abound with pepper seeds, and lots of Yankee gardeners are growing them. A gardening chemist in Connecticut is even working on a theory that capsaicin, the heat compound in chile peppers, is actually enhanced by the stressful New England environment and that peppers grown in this climate are even hotter than those grown in the Southwest. Whether you grow or buy peppers, I've found that heat intensity varies all over the place, so adjust the amount according to your taste bud tolerance. The cheese and sour cream filling for these scrumptious baked stuffed potatoes is deliciously enhanced by the pepper's invigorating kick.

A tip of the hat to Imogene Wolcott, the noted New England food historian, who first coined the name "potatoes on the half shell."

4 large baking potatoes
½ cup regular or lowfat sour cream
½ cup shredded cheese, such as medium-sharp cheddar or Colby
2 scallions, minced
1 jalapeño, serrano, or Anaheim chile pepper, or more to taste, minced
1 teaspoon salt, or to taste

Potato Blossom Festival

Maine is the only state in the country where children are still dismissed from school each fall to help harvest a crop. That crop, of course, is potatoes, the great majority of which are grown in the vast Aroostook County. Fort Fairfield in central Aroostook has celebrated potatoes with an annual week-long summer festival since 1937. Held in mid-July, when the potato plants are in full bloom with their beautiful white, pink, or lavender impatiens-like blossoms, the festival attracts thousands of attendees, even in this remote locale.

Food at the Potato Blossom Festival consists of a pancake breakfast, bean-hole baked beans, a pig roast, a chicken barbecue, strawberry shortcake, and . . . potatoes. Potatoes every which way—baked, scalloped, mashed, made into candy, and stuffed with broccoli and cheese, sour cream, bacon and chives, and chili. Events include the Little Miss Potato Blossom Pageant, the Maine Potato Queen Contest, a Potato Picking Contest, a Potato Recipe Contest, and, I kid you not, Mashed Potato Wrestling.

1. Preheat the oven to 400 degrees.
2. Pierce the potatoes in several places, place on an oven rack, and bake until soft, 45 to 55 minutes. Leave the oven on.
3. Whisk together the sour cream, ¼ cup of the cheese, the scallions, the chile pepper, and salt in a large bowl.
4. Cut a long slit in the tops of the potatoes, squeeze open, and scoop out the pulp, leaving a ½-inch-thick shell. Add the pulp to the sour cream mixture and use a potato masher or large fork to mash the mixture together. Taste and adjust seasonings to your preference, adding more hot pepper or salt if you like. Refill the shells with the pulp, sprinkle with the remaining ¼ cup of cheese, and place in a baking pan. (The potatoes can be held for up to 1 hour at cool room temperature before reheating.)
5. Reheat the potatoes, uncovered, in the oven until the filling is hot and the cheese is melted, 15 to 20 minutes.

Northeast Kingdom Maple-Glazed Braised Turnips

MAKES 4 TO 6 SERVINGS

The upper-right quadrant of Vermont, known as the Northeast Kingdom, is good turnip country. And maple syrup is the perfect complementary flavoring for turnips, its smoky sweetness balancing the bite of this distinctive, pleasantly earthy vegetable. A bit of coarse-grain Dijon mustard is stirred in at the end to thicken the lightly caramelized glaze and add a piquant finish. These turnips are a delightful accompaniment to such roasted birds as Autumn McIntosh-Roasted Duckling (page 333) or Christmas Goose with Madeira-Mustard Sauce (page 336).

3 tablespoons butter
1 cup chicken broth
3 tablespoons maple syrup
1½ pounds small young white turnips, peeled and cut in half
1 tablespoon grainy Dijon mustard
Salt and fresh-ground black pepper
1 tablespoon chopped fresh parsley

1. Melt the butter in a large skillet with a lid or a Dutch oven. Stir in the broth and maple syrup, and bring to a simmer. Add the turnips, bring to a boil, reduce the heat to medium-low and cook, covered, until the turnips are tender, 10 to 20 minutes. Remove the turnips with a slotted spoon, leaving the liquid in the pan.

2. Raise the heat and boil the cooking liquid briskly until it is reduced by at least half and is beginning to get syrupy, 2 to 5 minutes, depending on the shape of the pan. Whisk in the mustard. Return the turnips to the sauce, turn to coat, and season with salt and pepper to taste. Reheat gently.

3. Serve the turnips hot, sprinkled with the parsley.

Hashed Browns

MAKES 4 SERVINGS

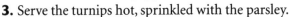

Judith and Evan Jones, in their *Book of New New England Cookery*, speculate that hashed browns may have traveled across America with railroad cooks, but insist that they originated in New England. Generations of coastal Yankees dubbed these potatoes "scootin'-'long-the-shore" because fishermen supposedly cooked them while they worked. Hashed browns can be made with leftover cooked potatoes, but there won't be quite as much starch to make the potatoes stick together in a cake, nor will the flavor be quite as pure. For some reason, hashed browns became a popular breakfast item. They are wonderful with eggs—for breakfast or supper—but also as a side to almost anything else.

> 4 tablespoons bacon fat or vegetable oil or half oil, half butter
> ¼ cup chopped onion, optional
> 4 cups diced or coarsely shredded raw all-purpose potatoes (see Note)
> ½ teaspoon salt, or to taste
> ½ teaspoon fresh-ground black pepper, or to taste

1. Heat the shortening in a large, heavy skillet over medium-high heat. Add the onion, if using it, and cook, stirring, for about 2 minutes until it begins to soften. Add the potatoes and stir in the salt and pepper. Spread the potatoes out evenly and press them down firmly with a spatula. Cover the pan, reduce the heat to medium to medium-low, and cook, pressing down 2 or 3 more times, until golden brown on the bottom, about 15 minutes.
2. Using the spatula, cut down through the middle of the cake and turn each side over. Leave the pan uncovered and cook over medium heat until the potatoes are browned on the second side and cooked through, 10 to 15 minutes.
3. Serve hot.

Note: If you use leftover cooked potatoes, leave the pan uncovered for the first browning, and shorten the total cooking time somewhat.

Maplebrook Farm

"We do things as simply as we can here at Maplebrook Farm. We do not grow exotic or extra fancy items. We feature plain ol' good stuff. Cukes, beans, snow peas, beets and beet greens, summer squash and zucchini, lettuce, spinach, potatoes, and vine-ripened tomatoes.

"We keep our vegetables as fresh as possible. With lettuce, beets and other greens, we leave them right in the ground until the customer wants them.

"Please do drop in if you are in the neighborhood. We'd love to meet you and show you the farm."

—From brochure for the Smith family's Maplebrook Farm, Brooklin, Maine

---

Paprika Potatoes

MAKES 4 SERVINGS

These Hungarian-style paprika-tinted potatoes, which are kind of a cross between sautéed and steamed, taste great as is, but a small dollop of sour cream and a final sprinkling of paprika don't hurt. They are terrific with broiled fish, such as Simple Broiled Boston Scrod (page 362), and are of course a natural accompaniment to anything Hungarian, such as Beef Goulash (page 265) or Chicken Paprika (page 308).

1 tablespoon butter

1 medium onion, chopped

1 teaspoon sweet Hungarian paprika, plus more for sprinkling over
  sour cream

4 medium-large all-purpose potatoes (about 2 pounds), peeled and
  sliced about ¼-inch thick

½ teaspoon salt, plus additional to taste

Sour cream, lowfat or regular, optional

1. Melt the butter in a large heavy skillet or saucepan with a lid. Add the onion and
cook over medium heat, stirring, until it begins to soften, about 5 minutes. Stir in
the paprika and cook, stirring, for 1 minute.

2. Add the potatoes, salt, and about ½ cup of water. Bring to a boil, reduce the heat to
medium-low, and cook, covered, stirring occasionally, until the potatoes are tender,
about 20 minutes.

3. Season with additional salt to taste, and top with a spoonful of sour cream and a
sprinkle of paprika if you like.

Portuguese Potatoes with Cilantro

MAKES 4 SERVINGS

Walk into any Portuguese grocery store in New England and the first thing you're likely
to see is a waist- or shoulder-high stack of 50-pound sacks of potatoes. Order just about
any meal in a Portuguese restaurant, and you're more than likely to see potatoes on
the plate—usually plainly boiled, drizzled with some olive oil and lemon juice, and
sprinkled, surprisingly, with cilantro. Often a salty little black olive or two garnishes
the potatoes, so depending on what else is on the plate, olives are a lovely extra
Portuguese touch.

4 medium-large all-purpose potatoes (about 2 pounds), peeled and
  cut in 2½- to 3-inch chunks

2 tablespoons olive oil

2 teaspoons fresh lemon juice

2 to 3 tablespoons chopped fresh cilantro
Salt and fresh-ground black pepper
Small European-style black olives, such as Niçoise, optional

1. Cook the potatoes in a large pot of boiling salted water, partially covered, until they are tender, about 25 minutes. Drain, return them to the pot, and place over low heat until the potatoes are quite dry, 1 to 2 minutes.

2. Drizzle the potatoes with the olive oil and lemon juice, sprinkle with the cilantro, and stir gently to combine. Season with salt and pepper to taste.

3. Serve garnished with the black olives, if you like.

Haymarket

Every Friday and Saturday morning throughout most of the year, vendors selling vegetables, fruits, meat, poultry, and seafood set up their stands in an open-air market along Boston's Blackstone Street. There has been a market on or near this site since the 1630s, which makes Haymarket just about the oldest public market in the country. Originally it was a farmers' market, but now the food sold by the more than 200 licensed vendors comes not just from New England but from all over the country. In many families vendor's licenses are handed down for generations.

All day long, crowds of shoppers elbow and squeeze their way through the labyrinthine aisles of wooden stalls in search of bargains. Some vendors hawk their wares in that age-old singsong sales pitch: "Hey, look at these apples. Hey, six for a dollar. Hey!"

Most stalls used to be owned by Italian-Americans, but these days you are just as likely to encounter Asian, Middle Eastern, or Caribbean vendors. As you thread your way through the aisles, you'll see boxes of produce from California, cartons of strawberries and blueberries from the Northwest, and crates of oranges marked with a Chinese crest.

Eventually the stalls thin out and shops—mostly one level below the sidewalk—begin to appear. Here can be found some great Middle Eastern ingredients—fresh goat meat (a staple all over North Africa), olives, falafel, hummus, tabbouleh, kafta, fresh cheeses. Another shop is mainly Caribbean, with fruits and tubers from Central America, including yucca, plantain, okra, and eddo (a brown and curly vegetable from Central America), and piles of fresh spearmint.

Ginger-Maple Baked Delicata Squash

MAKES 4 SERVINGS

The delicata is a lovely squash that is grown in New England as well as other parts of the country. It has an oblong shape and pale yellow skin with green striations. The succulent, meaty flesh, which tastes like a cross between sweet potato and butternut squash, is enhanced by this sweet-sharp glaze of butter, maple syrup, and freshly grated ginger. These large and impressively shaped baked squash halves can be the star at an otherwise simple supper of leftover baked ham or roast chicken.

> 2 delicata squash, 1¾ to 2 pounds each
> 2 tablespoons butter
> 2 tablespoons pure maple syrup
> 2 teaspoons grated fresh ginger
> Salt and fresh-ground black pepper

1. Preheat the oven to 375 degrees.

2. Cut the squash in half lengthwise, scoop out the seeds, and place cut side up in a large baking dish. Divide the butter, maple syrup, and ginger among the cavities and sprinkle with salt and pepper. Pour about ½ inch of hot water into the bottom of the pan and lay a sheet of foil over the squash.

3. Bake for 30 minutes. Uncover and brush the squash flesh with the melted filling. Continue to bake, uncovered, until the squash is easily pierced with a fork and the tops are lightly glazed, 10 to 20 minutes.

4. Serve hot.

Shaker Vegetables

The Shakers, most of whose communities were located in New England, were primarily agriculturalists, raising most of their own grains, vegetables, sugar (maple and honey), fruits, meats and poultry, and dairy products. They became skilled horticulturalists too, developing many new and better varieties of vegetables and fruits, including two varieties of potatoes and a very popular species of corn called Shaker Early Sweet Corn. They raised and sold seeds to the "World" (the term for the larger world outside their communities). Even up through the mid-twentieth century, Shakers were farming large tracts of land. Near downtown Concord, New Hampshire, the local Shaker community owned a large piece of real estate, and records show that in 1939 they planted twenty-five of those acres with potatoes.

The gardener at the Canterbury, New Hampshire, Shaker Village grows the same varieties of produce once harvested there by the Shakers, including eight varieties of leaf lettuce, four varieties of tomatoes, three varieties of beets, onions, and cucumbers, three varieties of potatoes, and summer and winter squashes.

Mixed Summer Squash Custard Casserole

MAKES 6 TO 8 SERVINGS

Here's something fabulous to do with that prodigal flood of summer squash. I make this delicate, custardy casserole every summer in August. Somehow it always tastes best when there is a pretty scallop-edged pattypan in the mix. It must be a case of eating with the eyes, since all thin-skinned summer squash taste pretty much alike. Feta cheese adds just enough of a complementary tang to lift the casserole from the plain to the sublime.

> 1½ pounds summer squash, any one type or a mixture of zucchini,
>   yellow crookneck, or pattypan, sliced about ¼-inch thick
>   (6 to 8 cups)
> 1¼ cups shredded medium-sharp cheddar cheese
> ½ cup crumbled feta cheese
> 3 eggs
> 2 cups whole or lowfat milk
> ½ teaspoon dry mustard
> ½ teaspoon salt
> ¼ teaspoon black pepper
> Paprika

1. Preheat the oven to 325 degrees. Butter a shallow 2- to 2½-quart baking dish, such as a 9-inch square or 13-by-9-inch dish.
2. Blanch the squash in a large pot of boiling salted water until it is crisp-tender, 2 to 3 minutes. Drain in a colander. In the prepared dish, combine the squash with the cheddar and feta cheeses and toss gently to mix.
3. Whisk together the eggs, milk, mustard, salt, and pepper in a bowl. (The two parts of the recipe can be made ahead and refrigerated, separately, for up to 6 hours.)
4. Pour the egg mixture evenly over the squash and sprinkle lightly with paprika. Place the baking dish in a larger pan and fill the larger pan with hot water to come halfway up the sides of the baking dish. Bake, uncovered, until the custard is set and a small knife inserted three-quarters of the way to the center comes out clean, 35 to 45 minutes.
5. Serve hot or warm, directly from the baking dish.

Frozen Bean Porridge

Much of New Hampshire was settled on frozen bean porridge, a stew of red kidney beans, beef broth, and yellow cornmeal. It was cooked up in big batches in huge iron kettles and then set out to freeze in the cold winter night. The bean porridge was then hauled on ox sleds into the wilderness to be used as a staple food when men and boys went to clear the land and build cabins for their families, who would follow in the spring. Small amounts of the porridge could be cut from the huge mass and "het" when needed.

Shaker Whipped Winter Squash with Cape Cod Cranberries

MAKES 6 TO 8 SERVINGS

This is my adaptation of an unusual recipe of whipped winter squash and cranberries from the dining room at the Shaker Village in Canterbury, New Hampshire. The cranberries add a pleasant chunky texture to the puree and turn it a gorgeous orange-rose hue. You can use almost any variety of orange-fleshed winter squash—butternut, Hubbard, or delicata are equally good. When cubed peeled winter squash is called for, I recommend looking in the supermarket produce section for fresh squash that has already been cut in chunks. Some even come peeled, which is a real boon. Although cutting up and peeling these heavy, thick-skinned beauties can be done, it's something of a chore, even when you resort to using hammer and saw. Add this splendid and intriguing make-ahead vegetable side dish to your Thanksgiving menu.

> 3 pounds winter squash, peeled and cubed (see Note), about 12 cups
> 2 cups fresh cranberries
> ½ cup light brown sugar
> 6 tablespoons butter, cut in pieces
> 1 tablespoon chopped fresh sage, plus leaves for garnish
> Salt and fresh-ground black pepper

1. Bring about 4 cups of salted water to a boil in a large pot. Add the squash and cook, uncovered, over medium heat until it is almost but not quite tender, about 15 minutes. Add the cranberries and continue to cook until the squash is very tender and the cranberries burst, about 10 minutes. Drain briefly in a large sieve and return to the saucepan.
2. Using a potato masher or electric mixer, mash or beat the mixture to make a coarse puree. Beat in the brown sugar, butter, and sage until smooth, and season with salt and pepper to taste. (If not serving immediately, transfer to an ovenproof or microwave-safe serving dish and set aside at cool room temperature or refrigerate for up to 1 day. Cover with foil and reheat in a 350-degree oven for 15 to 25 minutes, or cover with plastic wrap and reheat in a microwave.)
3. Serve hot, garnished with sage leaves.

Note: In place of the fresh squash, you can use 4 10-ounce bags of frozen cubed winter squash.

Agri-Tourism

Agri-tourism is a growing trend in agriculture. It merges the experiences of farming with the world of travel and tourism. Visitors are welcomed to participating farms, where they get involved in such diverse recreational and educational "ag-tivities" as pick-your-own (PYO) fruits and vegetables, cow and goat milking, cheese making, maple syrup making, and sheep shearing. A recent brochure from Massachusetts titled "Down on the Farms" listed 150 participants, including a "dig your own" clam farm in Provincetown!

❖ ❖ ❖ ❖ ❖ ❖ ❖ ❖ ❖

Herb-Braised Fresh Shell Beans

MAKES 4 TO 6 SERVINGS

Shell beans are the fresh version of dried beans—that is, the mature seeds of the bean plant. In New England most fresh shell beans that I have encountered in farmers' markets in the summertime are one relative or another of the cranberry bean, which is a cream-colored bean with red streaks, housed in a long, knobby, brown- or red-speckled pale yellow pod. Fresh shell beans have a more herbaceous, nutlike flavor and somewhat more delicate texture than their dried counterparts. As they cook, they lose their mottled striations and take on a uniform pink-tan color. The shelling process, while somewhat time-consuming, is well worth it. In this recipe the beans simmer with herb branches and then are finished with a shower of more of those same fresh herbs, minced, along with a luxurious dousing of olive oil and a spritz of lemon juice.

2 pounds shell beans in their pods
2 whole scallions
2 sprigs flat-leaf parsley with stems
2 sprigs summer savory or 1 small sprig rosemary
4 tablespoons extra-virgin olive oil
2 tablespoons chopped scallions or fresh chives
2 tablespoons chopped fresh flat-leaf parsley
1½ tablespoons chopped fresh summer savory or 2 teaspoons
    chopped fresh rosemary
1 tablespoon fresh lemon juice
Salt and fresh-ground black pepper

1. Shell the beans. You should have about 2½ cups of beans.
2. Combine the beans, whole scallions, and parsley and savory sprigs in a medium-large pot of boiling salted water. Reduce the heat to medium-low and cook, covered, until the beans are tender, 30 to 60 minutes, depending on their size and age. Scoop out and reserve ¼ cup of the cooking liquid. Drain the beans in a colander and discard the herb sprigs. (The beans can be cooked ahead and refrigerated for up to 24 hours. Reheat with the reserved cooking liquid in a microwave or over low heat before finishing.)
3. In a large bowl, toss the beans and the reserved cooking liquid with the oil, chopped scallions, parsley, and savory. Stir in the lemon juice and season with salt and pepper to taste.
4. Serve warm.

Lemon-Glazed Sweet Potato Gratin

MAKES 6 SERVINGS

This sweet potato casserole, my adaptation of a recipe that was printed several years ago in the *New York Times*, has become a required part of our Thanksgiving and Christmas dinners. No, there are no marshmallows on top, but it is sweet enough. The surprising addition of layers of cooked whole lemon slices provides a balance to the spiced and spirited brown sugar syrup. If you don't have dry sherry, try it with either rum or bourbon for equally delicious results.

> 6 medium-sized sweet potatoes (about 2½ pounds), scrubbed and
>   quartered
> 4 tablespoons butter
> ½ cup plus 1 tablespoon packed light brown sugar
> 1 large lemon, cut in half lengthwise, very thinly sliced, seeds removed
>   (about 1¼ cups)
> ½ cup dry sherry
> 1 teaspoon salt
> ½ teaspoon fresh-ground black pepper
> ¼ teaspoon grated nutmeg

1. Cook the sweet potatoes in a large pot of boiling salted water until tender when pierced with the point of a sharp knife, about 20 minutes. Drain in a colander.
2. Meanwhile, to make the glaze, melt the butter in a large skillet. Add the ½ cup of brown sugar and cook over medium heat, stirring, until smooth and no lumps remain. Add the lemon slices and sherry, bring to a boil, reduce the heat to medium, and simmer until the lemons are tender, about 8 minutes. Stir in the salt, pepper, and nutmeg.
3. Preheat the oven to 375 degrees. Generously butter a 1½- to 2-quart shallow baking dish.
4. Peel the sweet potatoes and slice half of them into the prepared dish. Spoon half the lemons and syrup over the potato layer. Slice the remaining potatoes over the lemons. Spoon the rest of the syrup and lemons on top in an even layer. Scatter the remaining 1 tablespoon brown sugar over the top of the casserole. (The casserole can be made up to 1 day ahead to this point. Cover with foil and refrigerate.)
5. Bake, uncovered, until the syrup is thickened and bubbly and the potatoes are heated through and lightly glazed on top, about 35 minutes. If made ahead and refrigerated, bake the foil-covered casserole for 20 minutes; uncover and bake another 25 minutes or so until done.
6. Change the oven setting to broil. Place the baking dish 5 inches from the heat and broil 2 to 3 minutes, watching carefully, until the top of the casserole is one shade darker and the edges of some lemons and potatoes are blackened.
7. Serve directly from the baking dish.

Haight Farm Green Tomato Casserole

MAKES 6 SERVINGS

The casserole competition is fierce at public suppers held at the Central Hall in North Brooklin, in midcoast Maine. At a baked bean supper there, I rated (silently, to myself) the vegetable dishes with a critic's eye and awarded my private blue ribbon to a crumb-topped layering of juicy, tangy-sweet green tomatoes with a rich, seemingly intricate filling. Wasn't I surprised to find that the recipe, given to me by Courtenay Haight, owner of nearby Haight Farm, consisted of only a few ingredients, the most crucial of which was a layer of Hellmann's Mayonnaise? It makes sense. Everything's in the mayonnaise, including egg, oil, lemon juice, and seasoning. Although the tart flavor of the green tomatoes should predominate in the casserole, Court says he always tries to add a couple of faintly tinged pink tomatoes because they contribute just a hint of sweetness.

> 3 pounds green tomatoes, sliced (or mostly green and a couple of
>   partly ripe tomatoes)
> ½ cup regular mayonnaise
> Salt and fresh-ground black pepper
> 1 cup dry breadcrumbs
> ⅓ cup grated Parmesan cheese
> 2 tablespoons butter

1. Preheat the oven to 350 degrees. Oil an 11-by-9-inch baking dish.
2. Spread half the tomatoes out in an even layer in the prepared dish. Spread the mayonnaise fairly evenly over the tomatoes and sprinkle with salt and pepper. Spread the remaining tomatoes over the mayonnaise and sprinkle with salt and pepper. (The casserole can be prepared several hours ahead and refrigerated, covered, for up to 4 hours.)
3. Stir together the breadcrumbs and cheese in a small dish and sprinkle evenly over the tomatoes. Dot with the butter. Cover the baking dish with foil and bake for 30 minutes. Uncover and continue to bake until the crumbs are pale golden brown and the tomatoes soften and begin to give off their juice, 15 to 25 minutes longer.
4. Spoon out of the baking dish to serve.

Colonial Produce

"Our Governor hath store of green pease growing in his garden as good as ever I eat in England. This country aboundeth naturally with store of roots of great variety and good to eat. Our turnips, parsnips and carrots are here both bigger and sweeter than is ordinarily to be found in England. Here are also store of pumpions, cowcumbers, and other things of that nature which I know not. Also, divers pot-herbs grow abundantly among the grass, as strawberries, penny-royal, winter savoury, sorrel, brooklime, liverwort, carvel and watercresses; also leeks and onions are ordinary and divers physical herbs. Here are also abundance of other sweet herbs whose names we know not. . . . Excellent vines are here up and down in the woods. Also mulberries, plums, raspberries, currants, chestnuts, filberts, walnuts, smallnuts, hurtleberries, and haws of whitehorn."

—Francis Higginson,
New England's Plantations (1630)

Farming Backwards

Eliot Coleman and Barbara Damrosch sometimes refer to themselves as the "backwards farmers" because at their Four Season Farm in Harborside, in midcoast Maine, they begin much of their planting in the fall. Coleman, a man whose books and lectures have inspired thousands of small farmers to try growing year-round organic crops, and Damrosch, a well-known author of gardening books, have turned the normal northern New England growing season upside down by designing a system of moveable unheated greenhouses and special plant covers that mimic perpetual spring in the dead of winter. An early disciple of fellow New Englanders Helen and Scott Nearing, whose classic work *Living the Good Life* inspired and instructed the back-to-the-land movement of the 1960s and 1970s, Coleman is still excited and entranced by his discoveries. "It's like magic to come out here when there's snow on the ground and lift up a plant cover and see lettuce growing and radishes sprouting. I never get tired of it."

Four Season's enthusiastic customers spur them on. "Despite all our fears that processed foods and tasteless vegetables were going to dull everyone's taste buds, that has not been our experience at all. We focus on the senses, and when we do that, we always get it right. Customers can see, smell, and taste the difference very clearly. People are willing to pay a little extra for the pleasure of that experience. And that's before we even begin to talk about the health benefits of eating good produce."

The proof is in the eating—and in the stunning success of their operation. For instance, Four Season's "candy carrots," so called because of their intense natural sweetness, are actually coveted by kids and bartered for in school lunches. Local markets regularly sell out of them. The farm's elegant, perfectly balanced mesclun mix is picked just hours before it gets to the customers. A few local restaurants and markets sell all that Four Season can produce. Coleman asserts, "We have a passion for feeding our local community."

In summer, Four Season has a farm stand selling beloved seasonal standards such as beets, tomatoes, peas, and eggplant. Sturdy greens are a specialty, and their artichoke fields are now producing perfect green globes. Lovely green and yellow zucchini are harvested when they're big babies—about four inches long. Coleman says, "My favorite way to cook these courgettes is to line them up side by side in a skillet like sausages, roll them around with a little butter, and cook them just until they're tender and very lightly browned." Slender, elongated Asian eggplants also receive a simple treatment. "I usually just halve them, brush with a little olive oil, and slap 'em right on the grill." When vegetables look and taste this good, anything more complicated might almost be heretical.

Sunny Acres Farm
Scalloped Tomatoes

MAKES 6 TO 8 SERVINGS

Mr. Haydn Pearson of Sunny Acres farm in New Hampshire wrote a column in *New Hampshire Profiles* magazine during the 1960s called "Country Fare," in which he dispensed gossip and New Hampshire folk wisdom, as well as home-tested recipes from his farm. In a collection of Mr. Pearson's recipes, the chapter on vegetable casseroles is particularly inspired and includes this wonderful scalloped tomato dish with a baked breadcrumb crust. I have adapted the recipe slightly. His version uses bacon fat, which would indeed taste powerfully good, but because bacon fat is no longer the kitchen staple it once was, I've called for butter or olive oil.

> 4 cups fresh breadcrumbs
> 2 tablespoons chopped fresh parsley
> 2 tablespoons snipped fresh chives or chopped scallions
> 2 tablespoons chopped fresh thyme or marjoram
> ½ teaspoon salt, plus more to taste
> ½ teaspoon fresh-ground black pepper, plus more to taste
> 4 tablespoons melted butter or olive oil
> 6 large ripe tomatoes, cored and sliced about ½-inch thick

1. Preheat the oven to 375 degrees.

2. Stir together in a mixing bowl the breadcrumbs, the three herbs, and ½ teaspoon each of salt and pepper. Drizzle the melted butter or oil over the crumb mixture and toss to combine thoroughly. Spread about half the crumb mixture out in a shallow 2-quart baking dish (such as an 11-by-9-inch dish) and press down firmly to

make an even "crust." Bake until golden, about 10 minutes. Leave the oven on. (The crust can be baked a couple of hours ahead and held, loosely covered, at cool room temperature.)

3. Arrange a layer of sliced tomatoes over the crust and sprinkle with more bread-crumbs. Repeat this process until the tomatoes are used up, finishing with a top layer of breadcrumbs.

4. Return the casserole to the oven and bake, uncovered, until the tomatoes just begin to soften, the juices have started to run, and the crumbs are golden, about 20 minutes.

Farmers' Markets

Not to be confused with roadside stands, the farmers' market is a serious business. Most farmers' markets in New England require that vendors grow or produce what they sell. The foundation of a farmers' market is the standard local vegetables, meats, eggs, and other farm staples, but the list of specialty items keeps growing. Dozens of varieties of lettuce are now sold at farmers' markets around New England. Exotics like garlic curls, shell beans, baby vegetables of all kinds, and herbs galore sit cheek-by-jowl with tomatoes and squash. More and more handmade farmstead cheeses are appearing. These days you are also likely to find long tables filled with bread, muffins, bagels, soused mussels, dilly beans, organic eggs and meats, woolen hats, caned chairs, and decorative gourds. You're also apt to see the family dog, a visiting goat, and pots of calendula, bachelor buttons, zinnias, and lilies. You may overhear tidbits of conversation, such as "I have no regular peas. The raccoons were too hungry for them this year." Or "Next week I can almost

guarantee you some of the first tiny potatoes. In fact, I'll pick some just for you if you'll be here." Recipes are exchanged: "My mother-in-law cooks these shell beans with milk and onions and they're absolutely delicious!" or "I've never seen such beautiful spinach. I cook it in the microwave and it always comes out perfectly."

A weekly visit to the farmers' market becomes a pleasurable and necessary seasonal ritual for many New Englanders. It demonstrates a commitment to supporting small, local, independent growers and the quality goods they produce, and there is tremendous satisfaction and pleasure in seeing and touching lovely peak-season produce and in communicating directly with the people who have grown the food you are going to have for dinner.

Classic All-Season New England Succotash

MAKES 4 TO 6 SERVINGS

Corn and beans were probably the first New World vegetables that the colonists ate when they arrived on these shores, and historians seem to agree that succotash, a combination of the two, was almost certainly brought to the first Thanksgiving feast by the Narragansett Indians. Back in colonial times, succotash was a year-round dish. There was summer succotash, made from tender fresh corn and shell beans or young string beans, and winter succotash, made with cooked dried corn and dried beans. The modern New England version, which is now usually made with lima beans and just a touch of cream, knows no season. Some people like to garnish it with chopped red pepper that has been sautéed in a bit of butter. This addition does indeed look and taste great, but the Puritans would have looked very much askance at this embellishment of their classic dish.

> 2 cups (10-ounce package) frozen regular or baby lima beans
> 2 cups fresh or frozen corn kernels
> 1 teaspoon sugar
> ⅓ cup heavy cream
> Salt and fresh-ground black pepper to taste

1. Cook the beans in a saucepan of boiling salted water for 6 to 8 minutes, until they are almost tender. Add the corn, return to a simmer, and cook, uncovered, over medium heat until both vegetables are just tender, about 5 minutes. Drain well.
2. Return the vegetables to the saucepan and add the sugar, cream, and salt and pepper to taste. Cook over low heat until thoroughly heated through, about 3 minutes.

BAKED BEANS AND OTHER "MADE" DISHES

According to Judith and Evan Jones's *The L.L. Bean Book of New England Cookery*, the term "made" dishes has been used by New Englanders since the seventeenth century. Casseroles or "made" dishes, described by the Oxford English Dictionary as being "composed of several ingredients," have long provided welcome variety to the Yankee table. Some of these one-dish meals, such as cozy Aroostook County Potato and Sausage Skillet Dinner (page 185), make ideal weeknight family fare, while others—Classic Junior League Mixed Seafood Casserole (page 171) or My New England Cassoulet (page 178) to name a couple of my favorites—are absolutely lovely for entertaining.

Boston and baked beans are practically synonymous. (Remember that this is the city affectionately known as "Bean Town.") Boston Baked Beans Durgin Park Style (page 152), made with small pea beans, flavored with salt pork, and long-simmered in bubbling molasses, are the authentic article. However, Boston doesn't have a lock on beans in New England; witness the five other recipes for baked beans in this chapter, each calling for a different bean and using varying flavorings—maple, mustard, rum, brown sugar, spice—and diverse cooking techniques.

French-Americans contribute their fabulous savory meat pie called Acadian Tourtière (page 186); Polish Yankees, the renowned Mrs. Rosinski's Stuffed Cabbage Rolls (page 189); Irish-Americans their peerless Shepherd's Pie (page 180); and the large Cuban population in urban New England, their wonderful, highly seasoned Black Beans and Yellow Rice (Page 160).

New Hampshire Maple Baked Beans

MAKES 6 TO 8 MAIN-COURSE SERVINGS; ABOUT 14 SIDE-DISH SERVINGS

New Hampshire's bean sweetener of choice is pure maple syrup, its dusky smokiness contributing an ineffable dimension that puts one in mind of the north woods. I consulted several cookbooks from the Granite State, including a charming community collection, *The Stoddard Old Home Days Cookbook*, from a town near Keene in the southern part of the state. They all agree pretty much on the seasoning formula I use in this recipe, which calls for a bit of tomato ketchup to cut the sweetness of the maple syrup.

> 1 pound dried navy, pea, or other small white beans, rinsed and
>   picked over
> 1½ teaspoons salt
> ¾ cup pure maple syrup
> ¼ cup ketchup
> 2 teaspoons dry mustard
> ½ teaspoon black pepper
> 1 large onion, peeled and scored with a criss-cross through the root
>   end
> ½ pound lean salt pork, scored up to but not through the rind

1. If you like, soak the beans in water to cover for 4 hours or overnight (see page 159). Drain in a colander. Bring 8 cups of water to a boil in a large soup pot. Add the soaked or unsoaked beans and the salt and bring to a boil. Reduce the heat to low and cook, covered, until the beans are just tender, 1½ to 2 hours. Drain in a colander.
2. Preheat the oven to 325 degrees.
3. Combine the maple syrup, ketchup, mustard, and pepper in a 2½- to 3-quart casserole or bean pot. Add the beans and enough water to cover the beans by about ½ inch. Push the onion and salt pork into the beans.
4. Cover the casserole with foil or a lid and bake for 3 hours. Check the beans every 45 minutes or so, and if the liquid has cooked away, add enough boiling water to keep the beans slightly soupy at all times.
5. Uncover for the last 45 minutes of cooking to concentrate the sauce. Remove the onion before serving.

Prep Time

---

9 am Beans go into oven, *10 am* Prepare sauce for chop suey, *11 am* Put brown bread in steamer, *12 noon* Prepare coleslaw and chill, *3 pm* Put water on to boil for macaroni, *4 pm* Put bread, butter and milk for coffee on tables, *4:10 pm* Put macaroni in boiling water, *4:30 pm* Cut pies and put on tables, *4:35 pm* Drain macaroni and add sauce, *4:40 pm*

Put coleslaw on tables, *4:45 pm* Begin dishing up beans and chop suey, *4:50 pm* Begin cutting brown bread, *5:00 pm* Supper begins.

—Schedule for kitchen volunteers who cook the public supper, for 200 people, at Greenwood Grange in Eastbrook, Hancock County, Maine

---

❈ ❈ ❈ ❈ ❈ ❈ ❈ ❈ ❈

Maine-Style Molasses Baked Yellow-Eyes

MAKES 6 TO 8 MAIN-COURSE SERVINGS; ABOUT 14 SIDE-DISH SERVINGS

Dried yellow-eye beans cook to a smooth creaminess while still holding their shape and have a mellow, earthy flavor that persists even through the long simmering. Yellow-eyes are the bean many Mainers, including me, prefer for making baked beans, but other popular Maine legumes are soldier beans and a spotted beauty called Jacob's cattle. This is my tried-and-true recipe for baked beans, the one that I make regularly and that comes out perfect every time. Its seasoning combines both New England sweeteners—molasses and maple syrup—to wonderful effect. We eat these beans with Pickled Beet Salad New Hampshire (page 94) or Yankee Summer Salsa (page 4), Crusty Cornbread (page 451), and a fruit dessert such as Caramelized Pears with Honey Ice Cream (page 524).

> 1 pound dried yellow-eye or other small beans, such as Great
>   Northern or navy, rinsed and picked over
> 1½ teaspoons salt
> 1 cup chopped onion
> 2 teaspoons dry mustard
> 1 teaspoon ground ginger
> ¼ cup molasses
> ¼ cup pure maple syrup
> ¼ cup cider vinegar
> ¼ pound lean salt pork, scored up to but not through the rind

1. If you like, soak the beans in water to cover for 4 hours or overnight (see page 159). Drain in a colander. Bring 8 cups of water to a boil in a large soup pot. Add the soaked or unsoaked beans and 1 teaspoon of the salt and bring to a boil. Reduce the heat to low and cook, covered, until the beans are just tender, 1½ to 2 hours. Drain in a colander, discarding the cooking water.

2. Preheat the oven to 325 degrees.

3. Combine the onion, mustard, and ginger in a 2½- to 3-quart casserole or bean pot. Add the molasses, maple syrup, vinegar, and remaining ½ teaspoon salt and stir to combine. Add the beans and enough water to cover them by about ½ inch. Push the salt pork into the beans.

4. Cover the casserole with foil or a lid and bake for 3 hours. Check the beans every 45 minutes or so, and if the liquid has cooked away, add enough boiling water to keep the beans slightly soupy at all times.

5. Uncover the baking dish and cook for a final 40 minutes to 1 hour, or until the sauce thickens and the salt pork browns.

Boston Baked Beans
Durgin Park Style

MAKES 6 TO 8 MAIN-COURSE SERVINGS; ABOUT 14 SIDE-DISH SERVINGS

Durgin Park, in Boston's Quincy Market, is a noisy, sprawling, family-style restaurant that has been serving up traditional Yankee fare to locals and "Bean Town" visitors for over 175 years. Many people still say that Durgin Park has the best beans in Boston. This is the recipe that their "chief bean man," a more than century-old position, uses. His preferred bean is the small white California pea bean, which he parboils slightly (with baking soda, thought to help eliminate some of those pesky gas-producing sugars) and then slow-bakes all day with salt pork and molasses. It is the molasses, a by-product of early Boston's sugar-refining industry, that is the distinctly "Boston" part of the dish. Serve this classical Saturday night New England supper with Steamed Boston Brown Bread (page 457), Mustard Chow-Chow (page 473), or Crisp Bread-and-Butter Pickles (page 471) on the side.

A Bean Supper in Maine

"The ladies of the Grange, in their matching aprons, advanced at last with the food.... Bowls and casseroles filled the center of the table. At one end was a big round plate piled with sliced, hot, steamed brown bread, and ... at the other was a great bowl of cole slaw.

"There were two baking dishes of beans. One, the small pea beans, was considered here [in Maine] to be a foreign Massachusetts dish ... these were deep brown with molasses and slow cooking, rich with salt pork, and centered in the pot with a well-browned and tender whole onion....The second bean dish was the favorite of the locality. These were the large yellow-eye beans, also baked long and tender, also rich with salt pork, but sweeter, more golden, and juicier than their Boston cousins.

"The other dishes were passed around and around in their wonderful variety.There was American chop suey ... a casserole of corn and mushrooms with tiny native Maine shrimp....There was a casserole of escalloped potatoes and ham, and another of plain macaroni and cheese, which looked especially tempting with its bubbling golden crust."

—Virginia Rich, *The Baked Bean Supper Murders*
(E.P. Dutton, 1983)

1 pound dried small white beans, such as pea beans, rinsed
   and picked over
½ teaspoon baking soda, optional
½ cup firmly packed light or dark brown sugar
½ cup molasses
1 teaspoon dry mustard
1½ teaspoons salt
¼ teaspoon black pepper
1 medium onion, peeled and scored with a criss-cross through the
   root end
½ pound salt pork

1. Soak the beans in cold water to cover for 4 hours or overnight. Drain in a colander. Bring 10 cups of water to a boil in a large pot. Add the baking soda, if you like, and the beans, return to a boil, and cook over medium heat for 15 minutes. Drain in a colander and rinse the beans.
2. Preheat the oven to 300 degrees.

3. Pour the beans into a 2½- to 3-quart bean pot or other baking dish (see page 162). In a bowl, combine the brown sugar, molasses, mustard, salt, and pepper and stir into the beans. Push the onion into the center of the beans. Pour enough boiling water over the beans to cover them by about ½ inch. Push the salt pork partway into the beans, letting it protrude a bit above the water.

4. Bake the beans, uncovered if in a bean pot, partially covered with foil if in a shallow casserole dish, for 6 to 8 hours, until the beans are softened and the sauce is lightly thickened. Check every hour or so. The sauce should be barely bubbling at the top of the pot. Add boiling water if the liquid cooks down below the level of the beans. When done, the beans will turn a mahogany color and the sauce will be lightly thickened.

5. Remove the onion and serve the beans piping hot.

Shaker Vegetarian Baked Beans with Summer Savory

MAKES 6 TO 8 MAIN-COURSE SERVINGS; ABOUT 14 SIDE-DISH SERVINGS

Eldress Bertha Lindsay (1897–1990) lived most of her long life at Canterbury Shaker Village in central New Hampshire and was intimately involved in the harvesting, processing, cooking, and serving of the food at the self-sufficient community. In the mid-1800s, the Shakers were strict vegetarians for a couple of decades, and this baked bean recipe of Eldress Bertha's reflects and carries on that tradition. The Shakers had a very innovative and modern way with herbs, using them for both medicinal and culinary purposes. Savory is often called the bean herb because it so beautifully complements the flavor of beans. In this recipe, said the Eldress, "I tried adding summer savory because it makes the beans easier to digest."

1 pound dried small white beans, such as
    pea beans, rinsed and picked over
¼ cup pure maple syrup
3 tablespoons molasses
2 teaspoons salt
¼ teaspoon black pepper
1 teaspoon baking soda
1 teaspoon dried summer or winter savory
1 small onion, peeled and scored with a
    criss-cross through the root end
¼ pound (1 stick) butter or margarine

1. Soak the beans in cold water to cover for 4 hours or overnight. Drain in a colander. Transfer to a large soup pot, cover with cold water, and bring to a boil. Simmer until about half cooked, about 40 minutes. Drain again in a colander.

2. Preheat the oven to 225 degrees.

3. Pour the beans into a 2½- to 3-quart bean pot or other baking dish. Combine the maple syrup, molasses, salt, pepper, baking soda, and savory and stir into the beans. Push the onion into the center of the beans. Pour enough boiling water over the beans to cover them by about ½ inch and stir to combine.

4. Bake, uncovered if in a bean pot, partially covered with foil if in a shallow casserole, for about 6 hours, or until the beans are tender and the sauce is thickened. Check the water level periodically and add more boiling water if it falls below the beans.

5. Remove the onion. Cut the butter or margarine into several pieces and stir into the beans until it melts. Taste and adjust the seasonings if necessary.

> ## Maple Syrup Esteem
>
> "Esteem for maple syrup influences much of Vermont's cooking. We use it instead of molasses in our baked beans and these, in consequence, have flavor not to be found elsewhere. Maple sugar gives squash and pumpkin pies additional savor that raises them to ambrosia's level. Maple cream, produced by checking sugaring just before the mass solidifies, is another typical Vermont delicacy."
>
> —Frederic F. Van de Water
> as quoted in Imogene Wolcott's
> *The Yankee Cook Book*
> (Ives Washburn, 1963)

Bean-Hole Cookery

Beans-in-the-hole are the landlocked equivalent of a clambake. The beans are literally cooked underground, in a process that takes at least two days and a lot of muscle power to accomplish. These days bean bakes are staged by community organizations and historical societies around northern New England, with volunteers supplying the labor.

A day before the beans are to be served, the volunteers dig a pit. (Sometimes the pits are maintained year-round and covered over when not in use.) After the pit is lined with rocks, a hardwood fire is built at the bottom. When the fire has burned down, the embers are raked out of the pit, and giant cast-iron pots containing presoaked or cooked beans, seasonings, and large chunks of salt pork are lowered into the ground. The pots are covered with sheets of tin, and a couple of feet of dirt is shoveled over the top.

Then the wait begins. "We prayed all night," says Polly Hutchins of Penobscot, in Hancock County, Maine, who staged bean-hole suppers for years at her local historical society. Prayed for the coals to stay hot, but not *too* hot, and prayed for it *not* to rain and cool things down too much.

Almost twenty-four hours after the beans go in the hole, the dirt is shoveled off, the covers are removed, and the cauldrons are lifted out of the ground. A little more praying, and the bean pots are opened, emitting a smoky-sweet blast of steam redolent of molasses, brown sugar, and pure bean.

Traditional accompaniments to beans-in-the-hole are hot dogs, country ham, coleslaw, eggy potato salad, fresh corn on the cob, rolls, and "tonic" (soda pop) or iced tea.

✠ ✠ ✠ ✠ ✠ ✠ ✠ ✠ ✠

Biba's Spicy "New" Boston Baked Beans

MAKES 6 MAIN-COURSE SERVINGS; ABOUT 14 SIDE-DISH SERVINGS

At the famed Biba restaurant in Boston, chef Susan Regis baked these beans all night long in a brick oven. The same alchemy can also happen with a day-long bake in a home oven set on a very low heat. The sparkling seasonings in these scrumptious beans— jalapeño, cumin, tomato, cilantro—take their cue from the Southwest, but the cooking method is pure New England. I'd serve these as a main dish with Crisp Apple Slaw (page 86), Crusty Cornbread (page 451), and Maple Ginger Baked Apples (page 499) to finish.

1 cup dried kidney beans or other large red beans

½ cup dried cannellini or other large pale beans

½ cup dried Great Northern or other small white beans

2 large sprigs fresh thyme

1 tablespoon whole cumin seeds

1 tablespoon olive oil

½ pound smoked slab bacon or thick-sliced bacon, coarsely chopped

1 large onion, chopped

1 large carrot, chopped

2 large garlic cloves, minced

1 jalapeño pepper, seeded and minced

1½ cups canned plum tomatoes, crushed

¼ cup pure maple syrup

¼ cup packed light brown sugar

1 large bay leaf

1 teaspoon grated orange zest

½ teaspoon salt, plus more to taste

1½ teaspoons cracked black peppercorns

¼ cup cider vinegar

½ teaspoon salt, or to taste

¼ cup chopped fresh cilantro

1. Rinse and pick over the beans. Place them in a large bowl, add cold water to cover by at least 2 inches, and add the thyme sprigs. Set aside to soak for at least 4 hours or overnight.

Salt Pork

Salt pork, so named because it is salt cured, is the layer of fat, usually with some streaks of lean, that is cut from a pig's belly and sides. Salt pork is quite similar to bacon, but it is not smoked.

In early New England salt pork was the Yankee cook's basic cooking fat, far exceeding the use of butter. It was also often the exclusive seasoning, apart from pepper, and accented chowders, gravies, stews, and, of course, baked beans with its rich, incomparable flavor.

Many early cookbooks instruct, at the beginning of a recipe, to "try out" the salt pork. This means to sauté the pork, usually cut into small pieces, slowly to render its fat and crisp the lean.

2. Heat a heavy 3- to 4-quart flameproof casserole over medium-high heat. Add the cumin seeds and toast, stirring, until they dance around and are one shade darker. Remove to a plate.

3. Add the oil and bacon to the pot. Cook over medium heat, stirring occasionally, until some fat is rendered and the bacon begins to brown. Spoon off some of the excess fat. Add the onion and carrot to the pot and cook until the vegetables soften and the bacon is lightly browned, about 10 minutes. Stir in the garlic, jalapeño, and toasted cumin seeds.

4. Preheat the oven to 250 degrees.

5. Drain the beans. Add the beans and thyme sprigs to the pot, along with the tomatoes, maple syrup, brown sugar, bay leaf, orange zest, salt, and cracked peppercorns. Stir in 3 cups of water and bring to a boil. Remove from the heat.

6. Cover the pot and bake for 4 hours. Stir in the vinegar and salt. Return to the oven, and continue to cook, covered, for 3 hours. Uncover the pot, return to the oven, and cook for about 1 hour longer, until the beans are tender and the sauce is thickened and concentrated. Adjust the liquid if necessary.

7. Taste and adjust the seasonings if necessary. Stir in the cilantro and serve.

Baked Bean "Sass"

Take a poll about what New Englanders think is the proper condiment to eat with baked beans, and you'll get very definite opinions, to say the least. Ask a kid—anyone from age five to about twenty-five—and you'll probably get them to admit that they'll only touch the things if they can blanket them with ketchup. Some in the more mature, sophisticated crowd swear by Mustard Chow-Chow (page 473), a delightfully spicy vegetable pickle that is one traditional relish for Boston baked beans. Sweet cucumber pickles (see Crisp Bread-and-Butter Pickles, page 471) are another favorite bean accompaniment, while many add such contemporary toppings as Yankee Summer Salsa (page 4), or, my personal favorite, "New" New England Cranberry-Apple Salsa (page 478).

While some purists will claim that it is heresy to contaminate a good baked bean with any condiment at all, it is my opinion that the beans, while delicious themselves, really do profit from an embellishment of something crisp and crunchy and tart-sweet. Any of the above-mentioned (with the possible exception of ketchup, which I confess to loving when young but have now outgrown) will do very nicely.

No Soak, Quick Soak, or Long Soak?

You don't really need to presoak dried beans before you cook them. The practice of presoaking beans in cold water for several hours or overnight (called the long-soak method) helps to rehydrate the beans, but in fact, after doing a lot of research and testing, I have found that this long soaking shortens the overall cooking time by only about 30 minutes. Quick-soaking dried beans (boiling them for 2 minutes, then letting them stand in the hot water for 1 hour) shortens the final cooking time by only about 15 minutes. So, as a general rule, unless you have lots of time and have planned ahead, there is no need to presoak. Just allow for a few minutes' more cooking time.

Several baked bean recipes in this chapter, however, do give the traditional presoaking instructions. Follow these recipes as written, because they have been tested this way, and the oven-baking times calculated accordingly. Classical, tried-and-true formulas, such as the Durgin Park Beans, Shaker Beans, and Biba's Beans, should not, I feel, be tampered with!

Pantry Bean Bake with Bacon, Rum, and Brown Sugar

MAKES 4 MAIN-COURSE SERVINGS; 6 TO 8 SIDE-DISH SERVINGS

If you don't have time to bake "scratch" beans, may I recommend this casserole of deliciously doctored-up canned baked beans with a spirited rum-enhanced sauce? When I've taken these beans to potluck suppers, the baking dish has been scraped clean every time. You can double or triple the recipe easily by using extra-large cans of beans.

1 tablespoon vegetable oil
1½ cups chopped onions
1 small green bell pepper, finely chopped
2 teaspoons dry mustard
¼ cup packed brown sugar
¼ cup dark rum
3 tablespoons cider vinegar
2 tablespoons ketchup

¼ teaspoon ground cinnamon
3 15- to 16-ounce cans pork and beans in sauce
4 strips bacon, cut in half

1. Preheat the oven to 350 degrees.
2. Heat the oil in a large skillet. Add the onions and cook over medium heat, stirring frequently, until they begin to soften, about 4 minutes. Add the green pepper and cook, stirring, until it begins to soften, about 3 minutes. Add the mustard and cook, stirring, for 1 minute. Stir in the brown sugar until smooth and then add the rum, vinegar, ketchup, and cinnamon. Simmer for 2 minutes.
3. Combine the beans and the onion mixture in a 2-quart baking dish, stirring gently to mix well. Cover the dish with a lid or foil and bake for 30 minutes.
4. Remove the foil and arrange the bacon over the top. Return to the oven and bake, uncovered, until the sauce is reduced and thickened somewhat, and the bacon is brown and crisp, 45 to 50 minutes. (The beans can be baked several hours ahead and held at cool room temperature or refrigerated. Reheat the covered casserole in a 350-degree oven until bubbly, adding a bit of water if necessary.)

Cuban Black Beans and Yellow Rice

MAKES 6 SERVINGS

When Cubans fled their island in the late 1950s, many families found their way to Connecticut, particularly to the town of Stratford, and to Hartford, the capital city. Some of their wonderful full-flavored food has percolated into the New England culinary mainstream, including black beans and rice, the signature Cuban national dish. Here the rice is colored a vibrant yellow, with turmeric (Cubans would use annatto oil). I like to serve this with Yankee Summer Salsa (page 4) or a chunky purchased salsa, Cuban bread, and flan and tropical fruit for dessert.

For the beans:

1 pound dried black beans, rinsed and picked over (see Note)
1 large smoked ham hock
½ teaspoon salt
2 tablespoons olive oil

1 large onion, coarsely chopped
1 large green bell pepper, coarsely chopped
3 garlic cloves, minced
2 teaspoons ground cumin
½ teaspoon cayenne pepper
2 bay leaves
1 teaspoon sugar
2 tablespoons white or red wine vinegar
Fresh-ground black pepper

For the rice:

2 tablespoons olive oil
1¼ teaspoons ground turmeric
2 cups long-grain white rice
1 teaspoon salt
1 cup thinly sliced scallions

1. To prepare the beans, if you like, soak the beans in water to cover for 4 hours or overnight (see page 159). Drain in a colander. Bring 10 cups of water to a boil in a large soup pot. Add the soaked or unsoaked beans, the ham hock, and the salt. Cover and simmer over low heat until the beans are just tender, 1 to 1½ hours. Drain, discarding the ham hock and reserving the cooking liquid. Return the beans to the pot.

2. Meanwhile, heat the oil in a large skillet. Add the onion and green pepper and cook until somewhat softened, about 5 minutes. Add the garlic, cumin, and cayenne and cook, stirring, for 1 minute.

3. Scrape the vegetable mixture into the cooked beans. Add 4 cups of the reserved cooking liquid, along with the bay leaves and sugar. Simmer, uncovered, over low heat for 30 to 40 minutes, until the beans are very tender. They should be quite thick but still soupy enough to ladle over the rice. If they are not thick enough, mash some beans against the side of the pot. Discard the bay leaves and season with the vinegar and black pepper to taste. (The beans can be made ahead and refrigerated for up to 2 days. Reheat before serving, adding a bit more liquid if necessary.)

4. To make the rice, heat the oil in a heavy saucepan. Add the turmeric and cook over medium heat, stirring, for 1 minute. Add the rice and stir until the grains are coated with the oil. Add 4 cups of water and the salt and bring to a boil. Cover and cook over low heat until the rice is tender, about 20 minutes.

5. To serve, mound the rice on a large platter, make a well in the center, and spoon the beans into it, allowing some to spill out over the rice. Sprinkle the scallions over the top.

Note: To make this dish with canned beans, omit the cooking in Step 1. In Step 3, use 6 cups drained canned black beans, about 4 cups of broth or water, and about ½ cup diced smoked ham. Simmer the black bean mixture a few minutes longer to develop the flavors and thicken the sauce.

Vessels for Beans

Much has been made of the classic Boston bean pot, a round, usually brown-glazed, heavy earthenware casserole with a narrow mouth. The shape is ideal for long, slow baking, allowing beans to soften in their sauce while keeping the evaporation of liquid to a minimum. Bean pots are still sold in many hardware stores and some kitchenware shops in New England, and I often see them in antique shops and secondhand stores.

However, in the use-what's-at-hand spirit of Yankee ingenuity, I have found that any vessel appropriate for slow cooking works just fine. This includes enameled cast-iron Dutch ovens, shallow glazed earthenware casseroles, Corningware-type casseroles, large soufflé dishes, and ordinary glass baking dishes. Some of the best beans I have ever made were baked in makeshift fashion in an ancient aluminum pot found in a summer cottage. Here's a tip: When baking "from scratch" beans in an open baking dish, I place a sheet of aluminum foil so that it covers about two-thirds of the top of the casserole, thereby allowing for slower evaporation of liquid.

West Indian Peas 'n' Rice

MAKES 6 MAIN-COURSE SERVINGS; ABOUT 12 SIDE-DISH SERVINGS

I love to eat a big dish of this Jamaican comfort food as a main course, but for the many thousands of West Indian people who have moved to New England, peas 'n rice is also the essential side dish in an all-Caribbean feast, alongside Curried Caribbean Chicken (page 312) or Jerk Pork (page 286). Caribbean Salt Cod Fritters (page 28) could start the meal, and Corina's Sweet Potato Pie (page 612) would be a perfect finale.

½ pound dried red kidney beans (see Note)
1 teaspoon salt, plus more to taste
1 cup canned unsweetened coconut milk
3 garlic cloves, minced
3 tablespoons chopped fresh thyme
½ Scotch bonnet pepper or 2 jalapeño peppers, minced
¼ teaspoon ground allspice
2 cups long-grain white rice
1 cup sliced scallions
1 tablespoon butter
Fresh-ground black pepper

1. If you like, soak the beans in water to cover for 4 hours or overnight (see page 159). Drain in a colander. Bring 7 cups of water to a boil in a large soup pot. Add the soaked or unsoaked beans and 1 teaspoon of salt. Cover, reduce the heat to very low, and cook until the beans are about three-quarters cooked, 1 to 1½ hours.

2. Add the coconut milk, garlic, thyme, minced hot pepper, and allspice to the bean pot and boil, uncovered, for 10 minutes. Stir in the rice, ½ cup of the scallions, and the butter, and reduce the heat to low. Cook, covered, until the rice is tender and most of the liquid is absorbed, about 25 minutes. Adjust the amount of liquid if necessary, adding more if the rice seems dry or cooking for a few minutes uncovered to evaporate the liquid if it is too soupy. Season with black pepper and additional salt to taste.

3. Sprinkle with the remaining ½ cup of scallions before serving.

Note: To make with canned beans, omit Step 1. Bring 4 cups of water to a boil, proceed with Step 2, and then add 3 cups drained canned kidney beans along with the rice. Mash some of the beans against the side of the pot to color the finished dish.

Vermont Cheddar Cheese Strata

MAKES 4 MAIN-COURSE SERVINGS; 6 SIDE-DISH SERVINGS

Well-aged, sharp Vermont farmhouse cheddar, the kind affectionately called "rat cheese" by generations of New Englanders, makes this classic casserole sing with flavor. Any good sharp cheddar will do nicely, though. This dish, which is variously known as cheese scallop, cheese bread pudding, or, modestly, "cheese casserole," makes a sensational lunch, brunch, or supper dish. For entertaining, the base and the custard can both be made ahead and then combined and baked at the last minute.

> 12 slices good-quality firm white bread, preferably day-old
> 3 to 4 tablespoons butter, softened
> 2½ cups (about 10 ounces) grated sharp cheddar cheese, preferably
>   Vermont farmhouse cheddar
> 3 tablespoons thinly sliced scallions
> 4 eggs
> 2½ cups whole or lowfat milk
> 1½ teaspoons dry mustard
> ½ teaspoon salt
> ⅛ teaspoon fresh-ground black pepper
> Paprika

1. Preheat the oven to 350 degrees. Butter a 9-inch-square baking dish.
2. Cut the crusts off the bread and spread each slice with butter. Cut each slice into 3 strips. Layer half the bread in the bottom of the prepared dish and sprinkle with half the cheese and half the scallions. Repeat with the remaining bread, cheese, and scallions. (The casserole can be made ahead to this point and held in the refrigerator, well covered, for several hours.)
3. Whisk together the eggs, milk, mustard, salt, and pepper in a mixing bowl. Pour the milk mixture evenly over the bread, pushing the

Serious Eating in Vermont

"When the food [usually a casserole] is set out, the farmers 'get down to business,' and there isn't much conversation. Vermonters know that good food is to be eaten, not praised or judged or regarded as a delicate art form. Compliments are few but country cooks know that requests for second helpings tell the real story."

—Christopher Kimball,
The Yellow Farmhouse Cookbook
(Little, Brown, 1998)

bread down into the milk to make sure it is all well saturated. Lightly sprinkle with the paprika.

4. Bake, uncovered, until the strata is evenly puffed and golden and a knife inserted near the center comes out clean, 55 to 65 minutes.

5. Serve immediately.

Nonna's Frittata

MAKES 4 SERVINGS

Many of the Yankee Italians I consulted about their food memories recalled eating wonderful egg dishes, like this frittata, for supper. In the multigenerational Italian-American households that were the norm in New England during the middle of the twentieth century, Nonna (the grandmother) was often the cook. Nonna knew that eggs were nutritious and cheap and quick to cook, and with her unfailing ability to work culinary wonders with a handful of simple ingredients, she turned them into memorable suppers. Frittatas are also a great way to use up leftovers. This one contains pasta, but let it be your springboard for experimentation with whatever is in the pantry or the refrigerator, be it potatoes, other vegetables, or just about any type of cheese.

> 4 ounces thin strand pasta, broken in half (see Note)
> 3 tablespoons extra-virgin olive oil
> 1 medium onion, sliced
> 1 green or red bell pepper, chopped
> 2 garlic cloves, minced
> 8 eggs
> 2 tablespoons slivered fresh basil
> ½ teaspoon salt
> ¼ teaspoon black pepper
> 1 cup shredded mozzarella cheese

1. Cook the pasta in boiling salted water until al dente, about 7 minutes. Drain in a colander and set aside.

2. Heat the oil in a 10- or 11-inch skillet with an ovenproof handle. Add the onion, bell pepper, and garlic and cook over medium heat, stirring occasionally, until the vegetables are softened, about 7 minutes.

3. Preheat the broiler.

4. Lightly whisk the eggs with 2 tablespoons of water, the basil, salt, and pepper in a mixing bowl. Stir in the cooked pasta and pour the egg mixture over the vegetables in the skillet. Stir gently to combine.

5. Cook, covered, over low heat until the eggs are almost set, about 10 minutes. Sprinkle evenly with the cheese. Broil, about 5 inches from the heat, until the cheese is melted and the top is lightly speckled with brown, 1 to 2 minutes.

6. Cut the frittata in wedges and serve directly from the pan.

Note: You can use 2 cups leftover cooked pasta and skip Step 1.

Deviled Crab Bread Pudding

MAKES 4 SERVINGS

This soufflé-like savory bread pudding, which uses either fresh or canned crabmeat to excellent advantage, rises above the rim of its baking dish and develops a glorious golden crust in the oven. Delicate crabmeat is beautifully complemented by a mild cheese such as Monterey Jack or muenster. The pudding is also delicious made with just about any mild, cooked and flaked leftover fish, such as sole, haddock, or halibut.

> 4 eggs
> 1½ teaspoons dry mustard
> 1½ cups whole or lowfat milk
> 1 teaspoon salt
> ¼ teaspoon cayenne pepper
> 8 slices good-quality white sandwich bread
> 3 tablespoons unsalted butter, softened
> 2 cups fresh or pasteurized crabmeat or 2 6½-ounce cans, drained and
>   picked over
> 1½ cups shredded Monterey Jack or muenster cheese
> ¼ cup thinly sliced scallions
> Paprika

1. Preheat the oven to 350 degrees. Lightly butter an 8-inch-square glass baking dish.

2. Whisk the eggs with the mustard in a bowl until blended. Whisk in the milk and season with the salt and cayenne.

3. Spread the bread with the butter and trim off the crusts. Cut each slice of bread into 3 strips.

4. Arrange half the bread in the bottom of the baking dish. Sprinkle with half the crab, half the cheese, and half the scallions. Repeat with another layer of the remaining bread, crab, cheese, and scallions. (The recipe can be assembled up to 4 hours ahead to this point. Cover and refrigerate both the milk mixture and the casserole dish.)

5. Pour the milk mixture evenly over the bread, pushing down any bread that is not saturated. Sprinkle with a light dusting of paprika.

6. Bake until the bread pudding is puffed and golden and a knife inserted three-quarters of the way to the center comes out clean, 45 to 55 minutes.

7. Serve immediately from the baking dish.

Stephen King's Favorite Recipe

Author Stephen King, when asked about his favorite recipes, produced one called Lunchtime Ghoul-ash. "My kids love this. I make it when my wife, Tabby, isn't home [home being Bangor, Maine]. She won't eat it; in fact doesn't even like to look at it." Here's how to make this two-ingredient dish: "Take 2 cans Franco American spaghetti (without meatballs) and 1 pound cheap, greasy hamburger. Brown hamburg in large skillet. Add spaghetti and cook 'til heated through. Do not drain hamburg, or it will not be properly greasy. Burn on pan if you want—that will only improve the flavor. Serve with buttered Wonder Bread."

—From *Eating Between the Lines:*
A Maine Writers' Cookbook
(Maine Writers and Publishers Alliance, 1998)

Deep-Dish Cape Cod Clam Pie
with Lemon Béchamel

MAKES 6 SERVINGS

Now that clams are no longer the practically free food that they once were, many dishes made with this bivalve have been elevated from humble fare to the category of special treat. This is certainly the case with Cape Cod clam pie, which in days of yore would have been served for a simple workaday family supper, but is now found on trendy menus and has become one of those recipes over which home cooks compete for fame and glory. My recipe attempts to be true to the straightforward origins of this dish, but the pie filling is invigorated by an infusion of fresh herbs and finished with the refinement of a lemony béchamel sauce.

For the pie:

2 slices bacon
2 tablespoons unsalted butter
1 medium onion, minced
1 celery rib, minced
2 tablespoons all-purpose
   flour
1 cup whole or lowfat milk
4 cups minced or ground
   hard-shell clams, with
   up to ½ cup liquor
   reserved
⅔ cup cracker crumbs made
   from Crown Pilot crackers or
   saltines with unsalted tops
2 eggs
2 tablespoons chopped fresh thyme or 1 teaspoon dried (see Note)
½ teaspoon fresh-ground black pepper
½ teaspoon bottled hot pepper sauce
¼ teaspoon grated nutmeg
Pastry for a single-crust pie, homemade or purchased

For the béchamel:

2 tablespoons unsalted butter
2 tablespoons all-purpose flour
1½ cups whole or lowfat milk
½ teaspoon salt
¼ teaspoon fresh-ground black pepper
1½ teaspoons grated lemon zest
1 tablespoon fresh lemon juice
1 tablespoon chopped fresh parsley

Lemon wedges, optional

1. To make the pie, cook the bacon in a large, deep skillet over medium heat until crisp and the fat is rendered, 8 to 10 minutes. Remove, drain on paper towels, and crumble, leaving the drippings in the pan.

2. Add the butter to the skillet. Add the onion and celery and cook, stirring occasionally, until softened, about 8 minutes. Sprinkle on the flour and cook, stirring, for 2 minutes. Gradually whisk in the milk and bring to a boil, whisking. Stir in the clams and cracker crumbs. Remove from the heat.

3. Whisk the eggs with the thyme, black pepper, hot pepper sauce, and nutmeg in a small bowl. Stir the egg mixture into the clam mixture in the skillet. Stir in the crumbled bacon and up to ½ cup reserved clam liquor. (The filling can be made up to 6 hours ahead and refrigerated.)

4. Preheat the oven to 350 degrees.

5. Transfer the clam filling to a buttered 9-inch deep-dish glass or ceramic pie plate. Cover with the pastry, crimping it securely to the edges of the plate. (The pie can be held in the refrigerator at this point for about 2 hours.) Make several slashes for steam to escape.

6. Bake until the crust is golden brown and the filling is heated through, 45 to 55 minutes.

7. Meanwhile, to make the béchamel, melt the butter in a heavy, medium-sized saucepan. Sprinkle on the flour and cook over medium heat, stirring, for 2 minutes, until pale golden but not browned. Whisk in the milk, bring to a boil over medium-high heat, and cook, whisking continuously, until the sauce is smooth and thickened, about 3 minutes. Remove from the heat, season with the salt and

pepper, and whisk in the lemon zest and juice. (The sauce can be made up to 4 hours ahead. Place a sheet of plastic wrap directly on the surface to prevent a skin from forming and refrigerate. Reheat gently, whisking in a bit of additional liquid if the sauce is too thick.) Stir in the parsley.

8. Cool the pie on a wire rack for 10 minutes before cutting into wedges. Pass a sauceboat of the béchamel and the lemon wedges at the table.

Note: If you are using dried thyme, stir it into the sautéed onion in Step 2.

Rum (or Rink) Tum Tiddy

Recipes for something called Rum Tum Tiddy or Rink Tum Tiddy appear with frequency in old New England cookbooks. The dish is a well-seasoned cheese sauce, similar to Welsh rarebit or rabbit but with chopped tomatoes added, which is served over buttered toast. Food historian Sandra Oliver found a similar recipe in an old Maine Rebekah cookbook that was called "Blushing Bunny." (Like Welsh Rabbit but with the blush of tomatoes, right?) She speculates that these whimsical names, which seem to have been coined beginning in the first part of the twentieth century, were a way of having some fun with something as prosaic-sounding as plain old cheese sauce.

Hank's Heavenly Clam Hash

MAKES 4 SERVINGS

There used to be a diner on Cape Cod, in Orleans, as I remember, called Hank's, I think, where one day I ate a memorable plate of the cook's delectable clam hash, full of chopped hard-shell clams and freshened with lots of chopped parsley. Here is my re-creation of that indelible taste memory. I love hash for supper, with juicy, thick-sliced tomatoes, a romaine salad, and something chocolatey, like Maury's Best Brownies (page 561), for dessert.

1¼ pounds all-purpose or russet potatoes, peeled and cut in 2-inch chunks
6 slices bacon, chopped
1 large onion, chopped

1 green bell pepper, chopped
¾ pound drained fresh, frozen, or canned clams, chopped
1 teaspoon dried thyme
½ teaspoon Worcestershire sauce
¼ teaspoon black pepper
¼ cup chopped fresh parsley
Salt

1. Cook the potatoes in a pot of boiling salted water to cover until just barely tender, 10 to 15 minutes. Drain. When cool enough to handle, cut the potatoes into ½-inch cubes.

2. Cook the bacon in a very large, heavy (preferably cast iron) skillet over medium heat until the fat is rendered and the bacon is crisp, about 10 minutes. Remove the bacon bits with a slotted spoon and drain on paper towels. Pour off the excess fat, leaving 2 to 3 tablespoons of drippings in the skillet.

3. Add the onion and green pepper to the drippings and cook over medium-high heat for about 3 minutes, until the vegetables begin to soften. Add the potatoes, clams, thyme, Worcestershire sauce, and pepper and stir to combine well. Cover the skillet, reduce the heat to medium-low, and cook for 10 minutes, until the hash begins to brown. Uncover, stir in the parsley, and raise the heat to medium-high. Cook, flattening the hash and turning it over in sections as it browns, until it is browned and crisp, about 10 minutes.

4. Season the hash with salt to taste. It may not need any, depending on the saltiness of the clams.

Classic Junior League Mixed Seafood Casserole

MAKES 6 SERVINGS

Picture the scene: A New Year's Day buffet in a Portland, Maine, suburb. The white damask-draped buffet table is arrayed with a slowly baked, maple-basted, clove-studded whole, bone-in country ham, pillowy-soft egg-glazed dinner rolls, homemade bread-and-butter pickles and dishes of mustard, a big bowl of spinach salad, and . . . half-a-dozen seafood casseroles. These casseroles were the potluck part, with various cooks bringing their contributions, and they were what captured my rapt attention. I tasted them all—one like a seafood pie with a pastry crust, one with lots of peppers and pimientos and other vegetables, one topped with melted cheese—but this one, creamy and rich, yet delicate, as honest as an old Yankee soul, was my favorite. The recipe is adapted from a wonderful southern Connecticut Junior League cookbook, *Off the Hook*, which, like the many dozens of such collections published by the League around the country, delivers winning, surefire regional recipes, many of which are pitched perfectly to gracious yet practical entertaining.

For the filling:

5 tablespoons unsalted butter
4 tablespoons minced shallots
3 tablespoons all-purpose flour
1½ cups half-and-half
½ cup bottled clam juice
¼ cup dry sherry
½ teaspoon salt, plus more to taste
½ teaspoon pepper, preferably white
½ pound wild or domestic
   mushrooms (any type), sliced or
   quartered
1 pound medium shrimp, shelled and deveined
½ pound bay scallops
1 cup cooked crabmeat, picked over
1 tablespoon fresh lemon juice

For the topping:

2 tablespoons unsalted butter
1¼ cups fresh breadcrumbs made from about 4 slices white
   sandwich bread
2 tablespoons chopped fresh parsley
1 teaspoon grated lemon zest

1. To make the filling, melt 3 tablespoons of the butter in a large saucepan. Add the shallots and cook over medium heat, stirring, for 1 minute. Stir in the flour and cook, stirring, for 2 minutes. Gradually whisk in the half-and-half, clam juice, and sherry. Bring to a boil, whisking, and cook the sauce until smooth and thickened, about 3 minutes. Season with the salt and pepper.

2. Melt the remaining 2 tablespoons of butter in a large skillet. Add the mushrooms and cook over medium-high heat, stirring frequently, until they are softened and begin to brown lightly, about 5 minutes. Add the shrimp and scallops and cook over medium-high heat, stirring, until the shrimp lose their pink color, about 5 minutes. Gently stir in the crabmeat and lemon juice.

3. Combine the cream sauce with the seafood mixture and transfer to a buttered 2½-quart oven-to-table baking dish. Taste and season with more salt if necessary. (The casserole can be made to this point several hours ahead and refrigerated.)

4. To make the topping, melt the butter in a medium skillet. Add the breadcrumbs and toss over medium heat until just barely colored, about 2 minutes. Stir in the parsley and lemon zest. (The crumbs can be made several hours ahead and stored in a plastic bag.)

5. Preheat the oven to 375 degrees.

6. Sprinkle the casserole with the crumbs. If freshly made, bake the casserole for 20 to 25 minutes, until heated through and bubbly and the crumbs are golden. If refrigerated, bake the casserole, covered with foil, for 20 minutes; then uncover and finish baking for about 15 minutes, until heated through and bubbly.

7. Serve the casserole directly from the baking dish.

Can-Opener Casseroles

Campbell's Cream of Mushroom Soup arrived on the scene in the mid-1930s. It wasn't long before some clever person discerned its potential as the perfect casserole binder, and thus a whole new "cuisine" was born. Some proudly called the concoctions "can-opener casseroles." A spate of can-opener casserole cookbooks appeared, including *Campbell's 100 Best Recipes,* boasting that "over the years Campbell's has provided American families with *thousands* of imaginative recipes using condensed soups." Of course purists would argue that the discovery might, in retrospect, have signaled the beginning of the diminution of cooking skills in America. Creations such as "Chop Soupy," "5-Can Casserole," "Skillet Frankaroni," or "Liver 'n Beans Piquant" did little to raise culinary expectations, but a few cream soup casseroles, particularly the by-now-almost-classic tuna noodle casserole, were on the whole tastier than the TV dinners and frozen microwavable facsimiles that followed.

Vermont Chicken and Leek Pie with Biscuit Crust

MAKES 6 SERVINGS

By now, a couple of generations of Americans have grown up on frozen potpies and have never experienced the pleasure of cooking or eating a homemade chunky chicken and vegetable stew topped with a meltingly tender crust. Grandma's chicken pies, made with a long-simmered stewing hen, were, she would be the first to admit, quite a lot of work. I've tried to streamline and update this recipe in a modern Vermont style, using tender, flavorful boneless chicken thighs in lieu of the hen, adding leeks and woodsy wild mushrooms, and cooking the chicken and sauce all in the same pan. As for the crust, this baking powder biscuit topping is super easy to make and delicious to eat. You could exercise other crust options by using standard pie pastry—homemade or purchased—or even buttermilk baking mix. A salad of dark leafy greens is all you need with this one-pot main course. Complete the Vermont theme by having Maple-Rum Custards (page 510) or Maple-Ginger Baked Apples (page 499) for dessert.

For the filling:

4 tablespoons butter, plus more if necessary

2 tablespoons olive oil

½ pound shiitake or other fresh wild mushrooms, sliced

2 large leeks, white and pale green parts only, rinsed well and thinly sliced

2 carrots, peeled and thinly sliced

1½ pounds boneless, skinless chicken thighs, cut in 1-inch chunks

Salt and fresh-ground black pepper

1 cup frozen green peas

3 tablespoons all-purpose flour

2 cups chicken broth

⅓ cup heavy cream

3 tablespoons chopped flat-leaf parsley

2 tablespoons minced fresh tarragon or 2 teaspoons dried

For the crust:

1½ cups all-purpose flour
1 tablespoon baking powder
½ teaspoon salt
6 tablespoons solid vegetable shortening
About ½ cup whole, lowfat, or skim milk
1 egg yolk

1. To make the filling, heat 1 tablespoon each of the butter and oil in a large skillet. Add the mushrooms, leeks, and carrots and cook over medium heat, stirring frequently, until all the vegetables are softened, about 10 minutes. Remove with a slotted spoon to a large bowl. Do not wash the skillet.

2. Season the chicken on all sides with salt and pepper. Add another tablespoon of butter and the remaining tablespoon of oil to the skillet. Add the chicken and cook until nicely browned outside and no longer pink within, about 10 minutes. Scrape the chicken into the bowl with the vegetables. Do not wash the skillet. Add the peas to the chicken mixture.

3. Melt the remaining 2 tablespoons of butter in the skillet. Add the flour and cook, stirring, for 2 minutes. Gradually whisk in the chicken broth and cream and cook over medium-high heat, stirring, until smooth and thickened, about 3 minutes. Combine the sauce with the chicken mixture, parsley, and tarragon and season with salt and pepper to taste. Transfer to a 2½-quart casserole, such as an 11-by-9-inch or 10-inch round dish. (The recipe can be made 2 days ahead to this point. Cover and refrigerate. Return to room temperature before baking.)

4. Preheat the oven to 400 degrees.

5. To make the topping, whisk the flour with the baking powder and salt in a mixing bowl. Add the shortening and use your fingertips to work it into the flour until most of the pieces are no larger than small peas. Stir in just enough of the milk so that the dough holds together. Knead in the bowl about 6 times. Turn the dough onto a lightly floured board and roll out approximately ½-inch thick and about the same circumference as the baking dish, trimming as necessary. Place the dough on top of the chicken mixture and press it gently to the edge of the dish, making a decorative crimp, if you like. Cut several slashes in the dough to release steam. Beat the egg yolk with 2 tablespoons water in a small bowl and brush over the dough.

6. Bake until the topping is golden brown and the filling is hot and bubbly, about 25 minutes.

Hashed Chicken with Dried Cranberries

MAKES 4 SERVINGS

This is an updated chicken hash made with sweetened dried cranberries. The cranberries are dried with just enough added fructose to make them palatable without sacrificing their pleasingly sour edge. This is the perfect vehicle for using up leftover roast chicken, or you can make it with rotisserie-roasted chicken from the deli. I'd serve a side salad of dark leafy greens or steamed broccoli and maybe a plate of Crisp Maple-Oatmeal Cookies (page 579) for dessert.

4 cups cooked, unpeeled red-skinned potatoes, cut in ½-inch cubes
4 cups (1 pound) diced cooked chicken or turkey
1 cup thinly sliced scallions
¾ cup sweetened dried cranberries
2 tablespoons chopped fresh sage or 2 teaspoons crumbled dried
¾ teaspoon salt, plus more to taste
½ teaspoon coarsely ground black pepper
½ cup plus 2 to 3 tablespoons half-and-half or light cream
3 to 4 tablespoons vegetable oil

1. Toss together the potatoes, chicken, scallions, cranberries, sage, salt, and pepper in a large bowl. Drizzle on ½ cup of the half-and-half and toss to combine well.
2. Heat 3 tablespoons of the oil in a very large, heavy (preferably cast-iron) skillet. Add the hash mixture, spreading evenly and pressing down with a spatula. Cover the pan and cook over medium heat for 15 minutes, uncovering to stir well every 5 minutes. Raise the heat to medium-high and cook, uncovered, stirring often, until the hash is crusty and rich golden brown, about 10 minutes more. If the hash seems too dry, add the remaining tablespoon of oil.
3. Just before serving, stir in the remaining 2 to 3 tablespoons of half-and-half. Taste and add more salt if necessary, then serve.

Public Suppers

The public supper is a two-hundred-year-old New England tradition that not only refuses to fade away gracefully but is currently more popular than ever. On any given weekend in any given corner of the region, you are apt to find at least one supper listed in the newspaper or advertised on a large sign posted in front of the hall where the supper is to be held.

There are Strawberry Suppers in June. In late winter there are Sugaring Suppers, with pitchers of hot maple syrup to pour over pans of packed snow following a ham and beans dinner. There are autumn Hunter's Suppers with rabbit, raccoon, and bear, and there are mostly vegetable Harvest Suppers when the crops come in. There are Chicken and Turkey Suppers because it's a Saturday in the winter, and Spaghetti Suppers on most Friday nights, and there is a Shad Supper in Windsor, Connecticut on a single special day in May.

Firehouses seem to put on lots of Roast Beef Suppers, Meatloaf Suppers, New England Boiled Dinner Suppers, and Potpie Suppers. But the Peach Shortcake Supper in Dummerston, Vermont, is the only one of its kind I know of. In Maine, especially in the summer, it is the Bean Supper that prevails.

The drill for every public supper I have ever attended is the same, whether it is held in a church hall, grange hall, Lions Club, firehouse, or school basement. Most are fund-raisers for a worthy cause, and all paying attendees are welcome. Guests arrive, seat themselves at long, family-style tables, and when the hall is full, an excited, anticipatory buzz fills the air. Brigades of volunteers then emerge from the kitchen to begin dispensing the hot food.

If you're lucky, the supper has been prepared by talented volunteer cooks. But it's not just about the food. It's about the company. It's about families, friends, neighbors, and strangers getting their fill of home-style Yankee casseroles and pies and local news and folk wisdom. As the tables are cleared and hot coffee is sipped, guests often linger for a mysteriously enchanted moment, silently savoring the pleasure of participating in this uniquely American shared experience.

My New England Cassoulet

MAKES 8 TO 10 SERVINGS

Reworking France's celebrated white bean and rich meat casserole by substituting New England ingredients seems completely natural here in baked bean country. To relocate the cassoulet concept to this side of the Atlantic, I've used small white pea beans and left out the traditional French fresh pork rind, goose, and duck confit, using instead a smoky New England country ham bone and a garlicky cured Polish kielbasa or Portuguese linguiça or chourico. An herb-freshened crumb topping lifts and lightens the innate richness of the dish. This cassoulet makes for ideal winter dinner party fare, especially when the meal begins with Maine Smoked Salmon and Caper Canapés (page 30) and finishes with Vermont Pure Maple-Walnut Cream Pie (page 588).

For the beans:

1 pound dried small white beans, such as pea, navy, or Great Northern, rinsed and picked over

1 ham bone, preferably from a Vermont or New Hampshire smoked country ham

1 large onion, coarsely chopped

3 garlic cloves, peeled and crushed

6 sprigs fresh thyme or 1 teaspoon dried

2 bay leaves

For the meats:

1 duck (about 4 pounds), cut in 8 pieces (see Note)

½ teaspoon salt, or more to taste

½ teaspoon fresh-ground black pepper

1 pound linguiça, chourico, or kielbasa, cut in 1-inch pieces

1 pound lean boneless lamb, cut in 2-inch chunks

2 cups sliced onions

4 garlic cloves, chopped

2 cups dry white wine

1 tablespoon chopped fresh rosemary or 1½ teaspoons crumbled dried

1 tablespoon chopped fresh thyme or 2 teaspoons dried

¼ teaspoon grated nutmeg

2 cups beef or chicken broth

1 16-ounce can chopped tomatoes with juice

For the topping:

2½ cups fresh breadcrumbs made from day-old Italian or French bread

¼ cup chopped fresh parsley
1½ tablespoons chopped fresh rosemary
1½ tablespoons chopped fresh thyme
1 teaspoon fresh-ground black pepper
2 tablespoons olive oil

1. To prepare the beans, soak them, if you like, in water to cover for 4 hours or overnight (see page 159). Drain in a colander. Bring 12 cups of water to a boil in a large soup pot. Add the soaked or unsoaked beans, ham bone, onion, garlic, thyme, and bay leaves. Cover, reduce the heat to very low, and simmer until the beans are tender but not mushy, 1½ to 2 hours. Discard the ham bone, thyme sprigs, and bay leaves.

2. To prepare the meats, sprinkle the duck pieces with salt and pepper. Heat a large covered skillet or Dutch oven over medium to medium-high heat, arrange the duck pieces skin side down, and cook until the skin is deep golden brown and some of the fat is rendered, 15 to 20 minutes. Remove to a plate and pour off all but ¼ cup of the drippings.

3. Add the sausage and lamb to the pan drippings and cook until nicely browned on all sides, about 10 minutes. Remove to the plate with the duck, leaving the drippings in the pan.

4. Cook the onions and garlic in the drippings, stirring occasionally, until softened, about 5 minutes. Add the wine, raise the heat to high, and boil, stirring up the browned bits on the bottom of the pan, until the liquid is slightly reduced, about 3 minutes.

5. Return the meats to the pan. Add the rosemary, thyme, nutmeg, broth, and tomatoes. Cook, covered, over medium-low heat until the duck meat is no longer pink, about 30 minutes. Spoon off excess fat that has risen to the surface. (Or refrigerate, and when cold, lift the fat off the top.)

6. Transfer the meat mixture to a shallow 4-quart casserole or 2 smaller baking dishes. Drain the beans, reserving the liquid. Add the beans to the meat mixture, stirring gently so as not to crush them, and add enough reserved bean liquid to come to the top of the solids. Taste and add more salt if necessary. (The recipe can be prepared 2 days ahead to this point, and refrigerated. Return to room temperature before baking, adding a bit more broth or water if all the liquid has been absorbed.) The cassoulet should be somewhat soupy when it goes into the oven.

7. Preheat the oven to 350 degrees.

8. To make the topping, toss the breadcrumbs with the parsley, rosemary, thyme, and pepper in a small bowl. Drizzle with the olive oil and toss until well combined.

9. Sprinkle the casserole(s) with the crumbs and bake, uncovered, until most of the juices are absorbed and the top is crusty and golden brown, 1 to 1½ hours.

10. Serve hot, directly from the baking dish.

Note: You can ask the supermarket meat department to cut up a frozen or fresh duck on a band saw.

Irish Shepherd's Pie

MAKES 4 SERVINGS

Venture into a Boston Irish pub like Donovan's or into a Fairfield, Connecticut, pub like my favorite, the Black Rock Castle, and you're likely to find such superb Irish pub grub as corned beef and cabbage, "bangers and mash," chicken potpie, and my particular favorite, mashed potato-topped shepherd's pie. This one has a savory herb-infused lamb filling, and I'll warrant there is no better supper on a chilly Irish-like New England evening.

For the topping:

2 pounds russet or all-purpose potatoes, peeled and cut in 2-inch
    chunks
¾ cup whole, lowfat, or skim milk
1 tablespoon butter
1 teaspoon salt
¼ teaspoon black pepper

For the filling:

1 tablespoon vegetable oil
1 pound lean ground lamb
1 large onion, chopped
3 garlic cloves, minced
1½ teaspoons dried rosemary
1 teaspoon dried thyme

⅛ teaspoon grated nutmeg
1 tablespoon all-purpose flour
1¼ cups beef broth
Salt and fresh-ground black pepper

2 teaspoons melted butter
Paprika

1. To make the topping, cook the potatoes in boiling salted water until they are tender when pierced with a fork, 15 to 20 minutes. Drain the potatoes, return them to the saucepan, and place the pan over low heat for about 1 minute, until the potatoes are thoroughly dry. Add the milk and butter and whip the potatoes with a potato masher or handheld electric beater until they are fluffy and smooth. Season with the salt and pepper and set aside. (You can substitute about 3 cups of leftover mashed potatoes if you have them on hand.)
2. To make the filling, heat the oil in a large skillet. Add the lamb, onion, and garlic and cook, stirring to break up any large clumps of meat, until the lamb loses its pink color, about 10 minutes. Spoon off and discard any excess fat. Add the rosemary, thyme, and nutmeg. Sprinkle on the flour and cook, stirring, for 2 minutes. Gradually stir in the broth. Simmer the meat mixture, uncovered, until the sauce is lightly reduced and thickened, about 5 minutes. Season with salt and pepper to taste. Transfer to a 9-inch-square baking dish and let it cool for 10 minutes.
3. Preheat the oven to 375 degrees.
4. Spread the mashed potatoes over the filling, using a fork to make peaks in the potatoes. (The recipe can be made a few hours ahead to this point and refrigerated. Return to room temperature before baking.)
5. Brush the potatoes with the melted butter and sprinkle the top with paprika. Bake, uncovered, until the filling is heated through and bubbly and the potatoes are golden brown on top, 30 to 40 minutes.
6. Cool slightly before serving from the baking dish.

Lightened Greek Moussaka

MAKES 8 SERVINGS

New Englanders had been eating sandwiches and burgers, soups and salads in Greek-run diners for years before they suddenly "discovered," in the 1960s, the wonders of the

---

Enough to Eat

"The tending of the bean pot borders on an art form with most Mainers, as they claim that the water must be added to the beans ever so prudently and gently during the long cooking period to ensure that the bean skins remain unsplit and intact."

"Beans at the Dirigo Grange did not disappoint, nor did any of the accompanying homey casseroles. After I had eaten more than my fill and was struggling to finish my piece of rich and sweet butterscotch pie, an elderly male member approached me voicing concern as to whether I had gotten enough to eat. As I assured him I had and thanked him for the generous hospitality of the Grange, he replied, 'If you didn't get enough, then it's your own fault!'"

—Sarah Leah Chase and Jonathan Chase, *Saltwater Seasonings* (Little, Brown, 1992)

---

authentic Greek food that was often listed as an apparent afterthought on the menu. When home cooks learned how to make moussaka, the rich, exotically spiced, layered eggplant casserole, it became the rage for a while, and then seemed to fall out of fashion. I have recently rediscovered its delights and have devised this updated, lightened-up version made with roasted (instead of fried) vegetables, and a somewhat less rich, but nonetheless delicious, custard topping. It's a perfect make-ahead dish for an informal dinner party, perhaps with Turkey Hill Taramasalata (page 27) to start, Spectacular Greek Salad (page 80) as an accompaniment, and a fruit compote and Greek Sugar-Dusted Cookies (page 571) to finish.

For the white sauce:

3 tablespoons unsalted butter
6 tablespoons all-purpose flour
3 cups chicken broth
¼ cup plus 2 tablespoons grated Parmesan cheese
1 whole egg
2 egg whites
¼ teaspoon grated nutmeg
Salt and fresh-ground black pepper

For the vegetables:

Olive oil cooking spray

2 12-ounce eggplants, peeled and cut crosswise in ½-inch-thick slices
1½ medium zucchini, cut in ¼-inch-thick slices
1 pound red-skinned potatoes, cut in ¼-inch-thick slices
Salt and fresh-ground black pepper

For the tomato-meat sauce:

1 tablespoon olive oil
1 large onion, chopped
3 garlic cloves, minced
2 teaspoons dried oregano
1½ pounds lean ground lamb or beef
2 cups bottled tomato sauce
2 tablespoons tomato paste
¼ cup dry red wine
¼ cup chopped fresh flat-leaf parsley
¼ teaspoon ground cinnamon
Salt and fresh-ground black pepper
¾ cup plain breadcrumbs

1. To make the white sauce, melt the butter in a heavy, medium-sized saucepan. Stir in the flour and cook over medium-high heat, whisking, for 2 minutes. Gradually whisk in the broth and cook, whisking, until the mixture is thick and smooth, about 3 minutes. Remove from the heat and stir in ¼ cup of the cheese, whisking to blend. Lightly beat the egg and egg whites together, stir a small amount of the hot cheese sauce in to temper the eggs, and then whisk the egg mixture into the remaining sauce. Season with the nutmeg, and salt and pepper to taste. Set aside. (This sauce can be made a day ahead. Cover and refrigerate. Reheat gently over low heat before using.)
2. Preheat the oven to 425 degrees. Spray 2 large rimmed baking sheets with olive oil cooking spray.
3. To prepare the vegetables, spread the eggplant, zucchini, and potato slices out on the prepared pans, overlapping slightly. Spray generously with olive oil spray and sprinkle with salt and pepper. Roast until the vegetables are tender and beginning to brown, about 40 minutes. Set aside.
4. To make the tomato-meat sauce, heat the olive oil in a large, preferably nonstick

skillet. Add the onion and garlic and cook over medium heat until the onion begins to soften, about 5 minutes. Stir in the oregano and cook, stirring, for 1 minute. Add the ground meat, raise the heat to medium-high, and cook until the pink color is gone. Spoon off and discard any excess fat. Stir in the tomato sauce, tomato paste, and wine. Simmer the sauce, uncovered, until it is reduced and somewhat thickened, about 15 minutes. Stir in the parsley and cinnamon and season with salt and pepper to taste. Stir in ¼ cup of the breadcrumbs. (The sauce can be made 2 days ahead to this point. Cover and refrigerate.)

5. To assemble the moussaka, spray a 13-by-9-inch baking dish with olive oil cooking spray. Sprinkle the remaining ½ cup of breadcrumbs over the bottom of the dish. Arrange the potatoes in a layer over the crumbs. Spoon half of the tomato-meat sauce on top. Arrange the eggplant slices over the sauce. Spoon the remaining tomato-meat sauce on top. Finish with a layer of zucchini, overlapping the slices if necessary.

6. Pour the warm white sauce over the top, smoothing to make an even layer. Sprinkle with the remaining 2 tablespoons of Parmesan cheese. (The casserole can be made up to 3 hours ahead and refrigerated.)

7. Preheat the oven to 375 degrees.

8. Bake, uncovered, until the top is golden brown and set and the filling is heated through, 45 to 60 minutes.

9. Let casserole stand for 15 minutes before cutting into squares to serve.

Aroostook County Potato and Sausage Skillet Dinner

MAKES 4 SERVINGS

Maine's vast Aroostook County, encompassing more land than the rest of the counties in the state combined, grows 90 percent of the large potato crop produced in Maine. "The County," as it is affectionately known by its citizens, holds a week-long Potato Blossom Festival each year to celebrate the Maine spud called the round white, a versatile all-purpose potato. The festival is capped by the crowning of Miss Potato Queen and the awarding of ribbons in a potato recipe contest. This savory skillet-supper dish, made with the garlicky smoked Polish sausage that is so common all over New England, is my adaptation of one of the recent prizewinners. It's perfect for supper on a cold winter evening.

> 1 tablespoon olive oil
> ½ pound kielbasa or similar garlicky smoked sausage, cut in
>   ¼-inch-thick slices
> 1 large onion, sliced
> 2 pounds all-purpose potatoes, peeled and sliced (5 to 6 cups)
> 2 tablespoons all-purpose flour
> 3 tablespoons chopped fresh thyme or 2 teaspoons dried
> ½ teaspoon fresh-ground black pepper
> 2 cups chicken broth
> 1 cup apple juice or apple cider
> ½ cup dry white wine
> 1 bay leaf, broken in half

1. Heat the oil in a very large (11- or 12-inch), preferably nonstick, skillet with sides at least 2 inches high. Add the sausage and onion and sauté over medium heat, stirring, until the onion is softened and the sausage begins to brown, about 6 minutes.

2. Add the sliced potatoes, sprinkle with the flour, thyme, and pepper and toss gently but thoroughly to combine well. Pour the broth, apple juice, and wine over the potato mixture and add the bay leaf. Bring to a boil over high heat, reduce the heat to low, and cook, covered, until the potatoes are tender, 35 to 40 minutes.

3. Remove the bay leaf before serving directly from the skillet.

Acadian Tourtière

MAKES 6 TO 8 SERVINGS

French-Canadians, or Acadians, flocked south by the thousands in the early part of the twentieth century, many to work at the enormous New England mills and factories that turned out essentials from flour to fish hooks, hats to horse-drawn carriages. Many families have stayed, enriching the Yankee culinary melting pot with a soupçon of French flair, with the largest numbers settling in Maine, Vermont, New Hampshire, and Rhode Island. La Kermesse, held in Biddeford, in southern Maine, is one of the many annual Franco-American festivals staged to celebrate and preserve Acadian culture and foodways. I sampled a fabulous tourtière, their savory, stick-to-the-ribs meat pie, there, along with such other wonderful specialties as a thick, smoky dried yellow pea soup, chicken pie, *boudin* (blood sausage), pork spread, fruit-filled crêpes, and that sticky-sweet far-north confection, maple taffy. A wedge of tourtière is delicious with side dishes such as coleslaw and pickled beets with onions.

 2 tablespoons vegetable oil
 2 medium onions, chopped
 2 garlic cloves, chopped
 1½ pounds ground pork, as lean as possible
 ½ pound ground sirloin or round
 2 medium tomatoes, seeded and chopped
 1 tablespoon Bell's seasoning or other poultry seasoning mix
 ½ teaspoon ground allspice
 ½ cup dried breadcrumbs or crushed stuffing mix or ¾ cup fresh
   breadcrumbs
 1 teaspoon salt
 ½ teaspoon black pepper
 1 recipe Old Fashioned Lard Crust (page 585) or Half-and-Half Flaky
   Pastry (page 586) for a double-crust pie or 2 purchased pie crusts
 About 1 tablespoon milk

1. Heat the oil in a very large (11- or 12-inch) skillet. Add the onions and cook over medium heat, stirring frequently, until softened, about 5 minutes. Add the garlic and cook, stirring, for 1 minute. Add the pork and beef, stirring to break up the

La Tourtière

When a tourtière baking contest is held in Woonsocket, Rhode Island, dozens of the French-Canadian immigrants in the area enter their meat pies for judging. Tourtière is a meat pie, typically consisting of a flaky crust that enfolds a mildly seasoned meat loaf–like filling that has been given body with breadcrumbs or mashed or cubed potato.

Louis Dusseault, a retired state trooper from Cumberland, Rhode Island, was a recent prizewinner in the Woonsocket contest. "It's normally a cold weather dish, traditional at Christmas and New Year's. The French go to midnight mass and go home for meat pie afterward," said Dusseault.

Most people like ketchup with their meat pies, according to Dusseault, but the pie judges were told they must taste it plain. Judge Michael Pratt, described as "an avid lover of tourtière," confessed that he'd brought little packets of ketchup anyway.

"They'll throw you out!" fellow judge Michel Coutu, from East Greenwich, Rhode Island, warned Pratt.

Germaine Godfrin was another prizewinner. After fifty years of cooking, Godfrin, whose mother came from Canada, lets other family members host holiday meals now. She just brings her famous tourtière. She serves it with pickled beets. "I also eat mine with butter on top," she admits. "And ketchup."

clumps, and cook until the meat is no longer pink, about 10 minutes. Add the tomatoes, ⅓ cup water, the poultry seasoning, and allspice and simmer, uncovered, over medium-low heat, stirring occasionally, until most of the liquid is reduced and evaporated, about 20 minutes. Spoon off any excess fat that has risen to the surface. Stir in the breadcrumbs and season with the salt and pepper. Cool for at least 20 minutes before using. (The filling can be made up to 2 days ahead and refrigerated.)

2. Preheat the oven to 425 degrees.
3. On a lightly floured surface, roll the pastry out to make 2 12-inch rounds. Line a 9-inch deep-dish pie plate with one of the pie crusts. Spoon in the cooled filling, spreading it out evenly. Top with the second crust, folding the top and bottom together and crimping with the tines of a fork. Slash several vents in the top crust and brush with milk.
4. Bake on the middle rack of the oven for 10 minutes. Reduce the heat to 350 degrees and continue to bake for 35 to 45 minutes, until the crust is an even golden brown.
5. Cool the pie on a wire rack for at least 15 minutes before slicing. Serve hot, warm, or at room temperature.

Red Flannel Hash
George's Diner

MAKES 4 SERVINGS

When I stopped in at George's Diner near Lake Winnipesaukee, New Hampshire, during the midmorning lull, I was intent on ordering a sampler of food from the extensive breakfast menu. Blueberry pancakes, French toast made with thick-sliced homemade bread, and home fries caught my eye. Then I noticed the side-order menu, so I asked for a few items from that list, too: baked beans, coleslaw, corned beef hash, and red flannel hash ("when available," which it turned out to be that day). Made of leftovers from George's New England Boiled Dinner, the hash was the tastiest rendition of the beet-tinged northern New England specialty that I'd ever had. I wangled a recipe out of the management, and here is my adaptation of same. George doesn't put potatoes in his hash ("because they sour" he says, which if you make the mixture ahead of time, they might well do), but I like mine with a few spuds.

2 tablespoons unsalted butter
1 large onion, chopped
1 pound cooked corned beef, roughly chopped into ½-inch cubes
2½ cups cooked potatoes, roughly chopped into ¼-inch cubes
1½ cups minced cooked beets (fresh or canned)
1 cup cooked turnips or rutabagas, minced
¼ teaspoon salt, or more to taste
½ teaspoon coarse-ground black pepper, or more to taste
1 tablespoon Worcestershire sauce
1 teaspoon bottled hot pepper sauce
¾ cup heavy cream
4 poached eggs, optional
Bottled salsa or chili sauce, optional

1. Preheat the oven to 400 degrees.
2. Melt the butter in a large, heavy (preferably cast-iron) skillet with ovenproof handle. Add the onion and cook until it begins to soften, about 5 minutes.
3. Meanwhile, combine the corned beef, potatoes, beets, turnips, salt, pepper, Worcestershire sauce, hot pepper sauce, and cream in a large bowl. Toss gently but

thoroughly to mix well and add to the skillet. Stir to combine with the onion, then press the hash mixture to make a large cake. Cover and cook over medium-low heat until a crust begins to form on the bottom, about 15 minutes.

4. Place the skillet in the oven and bake until the top is crisp and lightly browned, about 15 minutes. If the top is not brown enough, run it under a broiler to finish.

5. Cut into wedges, and top with the poached eggs if you are including them, and serve with the salsa or chili sauce if you like.

Red Flannel Rhapsody

Here is New Hampshire columnist Haydn S. Pearson waxing poetic on one of his favorite subjects: "Red flannel hash . . . is an Oriental-looking, taste-tantalizing dish. Its color is exciting. It has allure and snap. A frying pan full of it on the kitchen stove sends a nostril-tickling aroma through the room. . . . Serve it piping hot with yellow corn-meal muffins and green tomato pickles. For dessert, a wedge of deep-dish apple pie, a piece of old sharp cheese, and a glass of cold, creamy milk are acceptable."

Mrs. Rosinski's Stuffed Cabbage Rolls

MAKES 4 TO 6 SERVINGS

As far as I can tell, stuffed cabbage just might be the Polish national dish, so common is it in all Polish-American households, including the one in Connecticut where my husband was raised. Intense rivalry among wives and mothers- and sisters-in-law comes to the fore when it comes to making the best version of stuffed cabbage. My husband once told his mother (to his lasting regret) that he loved his grandma's best because it was so "juicy," which translates to the fact that she made it with the traditional higher-fat meat mixture that included pork. This recipe is my interpretation and re-creation of Grandma (Nanna) Rosinski's. Using condensed tomato soup as a sauce base has been a firmly entrenched tradition for a couple of generations. It works really well because its sugar adds a nice dimension of sweetness to offset the pungency of cabbage.

1 large head green cabbage
1 cup long-grain white rice
1¾ teaspoons salt
1 tablespoon vegetable oil
1 medium-large onion, chopped
1½ pounds mixed ground meat ("meatloaf mix" of beef, veal, and
    pork)
1 egg, lightly beaten
½ teaspoon fresh-ground black pepper
1 10½ ounce can condensed tomato soup

1. Bring a large pot of salted water to a boil. Discard any tough, dark green outer leaves of the cabbage. Cut out the cabbage core and gently pull off 16 to 20 large leaves. Blanch the leaves in the boiling water until slightly softened and pliable, about 2 minutes. Remove with a slotted spoon and drain on a kitchen towel.

2. Bring 1¾ cups of water to a boil in a medium saucepan. Add the rice and ¾ teaspoon of the salt and stir. Reduce the heat to low and cook, covered, until the rice is just tender, about 18 minutes.

3. Heat the oil in a small skillet. Add the onion and sauté over medium to medium-high heat until softened and beginning to brown, about 8 minutes.

4. Combine the cooked rice, ground meat, cooked onion, egg, remaining 1 teaspoon salt, and the pepper in a large bowl. Use clean hands or a large spoon to mix until all the ingredients are well combined.

Dozynki

The Polish population of New Britain, Connecticut, in the geographic center of the state, still numbers about twenty thousand in a total population of seventy-five thousand people. Dozynki, which means harvest festival in Polish, has been celebrated in Poland since the time of the feudal system, when the lord of the manor invited workers to share in the harvest bounty and New Britain has been celebrating its own Dozynki since the 1930s. The late-summer festival begins with a mass to mark the culmination of the harvest, after which the music making, dancing, drinking, and, of course eating begin. Among the traditional Polish foods are stuffed cabbage, pierogi, kielbasa, stuffed crêpes, hunter's stew, potato pancakes, and filled doughnuts.

5. Preheat the oven to 350 degrees. Lightly oil a 13-by-9-inch baking dish or spray with vegetable oil.

6. Place about 1 tablespoon of filling (more or less, depending on the size of the leaf) at the base of each cabbage leaf. Fold over once; then fold in the 2 sides of the leaf and continue rolling until the filling is enclosed. Place seam side down in the prepared baking dish.

7. Whisk the tomato soup with ½ cup water and pour over the cabbage rolls. Cover the baking dish with foil and bake until the cabbage leaves are very tender and beginning to brown on top and the filling is cooked through, about 1 hour.

8. Serve the stuffed cabbage with a little of the sauce spooned over.

PASTA AND RICE, SIDE AND MAIN

Thanks to the huge influx of Italian immigrants into New England urban centers at the beginning of the twentieth century, we became privy to the virtues of pasta pretty early in the game—in fact, when it was still called, generically, "spaghetti," "macaroni," or "noodles." Such beloved family favorites as Prince Meatballs and Spaghetti (page 211), Mary Gordon's Golden Mac 'n' Cheese (page 198), or, particularly on meatless Fridays in Catholic households, The Very Best Tuna-Noodle (page 216), have been staples of the New England home cook's repertoire for generations.

Rice, which used to be an afterthought served as an occasional starch variation, now plays a starring role on New England plates as colorful Portuguese Rice Garden with Lemon and Garlic (page 223), or creamy Clam and Roasted Tomato Risotto (page 227), or the artful Shaker Baked Rice Pilaf with a Shower of Herbs (page 224).

Pasta casseroles, along with many of the "made" dishes from the previous chapter, are mainstays of New England public suppers, church suppers, and potluck gatherings of all sorts. Dishes like Church Supper American Chop Suey (page 209) or Cheese-Topped Noodle Casserole with Smoked Country Ham (page 218) can be toted to all kinds of gatherings with ease. And because New Englanders, like all Americans, love imaginative pasta creations, I've included a free-form Grilled Farmers' Market Pasta with New England Chèvre (page 200), and a most delectable Herbed Seafood Lasagne with Tomato-Cream Sauce (page 203).

Greek Orzo Pilaf

MAKES 6 SIDE-DISH SERVINGS

Grated carrots add color and a touch of sweetness to this delectable quick and easy garlic-scented orzo pilaf. It's marvelous as an accompaniment to Chicken Riganato (page 311) or any other simple roasted or grilled meat.

>   1 pound orzo
>   3 tablespoons extra-virgin olive oil
>   3 garlic cloves, minced
>   2 carrots, peeled and grated
>   1 teaspoon dried marjoram
>   Salt and fresh-ground black pepper

1. Cook the orzo in a large pot of boiling salted water until al dente, about 10 minutes. Drain in a colander, saving about ½ cup of the cooking water.

2. Return the pot to the stove. Add the oil, garlic, carrots, and marjoram to the pot and cook over medium-high heat, tossing constantly with a wooden spoon, until the carrots are wilted and the garlic is fragant, 2 to 3 minutes.

3. Return the orzo to the pot, add the reserved water, and toss until the pasta is heated through. Season with salt and pepper to taste before serving.

Garlic and Oil Spaghetti

MAKES 4 SERVINGS

Garlic and oil spaghetti (*aglio e olio*) might be called the epitome of minimalist Italian comfort food. You won't find it on many restaurant menus, but all Yankee Italians with legitimate claims to their ethnic heritage know how to make this surefire dish. The spaghetti is simplicity itself, but it is important to cook the garlic slowly so it doesn't get dark brown and give the whole dish a bitter taste. With the ingredients always at hand, this never tastes better to me than when it is consumed while standing or leaning against the kitchen counter at midnight.

1 pound spaghetti
6 tablespoons extra-virgin olive oil
6 large garlic cloves, minced (about
    2 tablespoons)
¼ teaspoon red pepper flakes, or to taste
Salt and fresh-ground black pepper
2 tablespoons chopped fresh flat-leaf
    parsley, optional

1. Cook the spaghetti in a large pot of boiling salted water until al dente, about 10 minutes. Drain in a colander, reserving about 1 cup of the cooking water.
2. Meanwhile, heat the oil in a small skillet. Add the garlic and cook over low heat until it turns a pale golden color (not dark brown), about 6 minutes. Stir in the red pepper flakes.
3. Toss the spaghetti with the garlic oil in a warm bowl or in the pasta cooking pot, adding a bit of the cooking water if it seems dry. Season with salt and black pepper to taste. Sprinkle with chopped parsley, if you like, before serving.

We Cook

"We Italians cook. We've always cooked and we're still cooking. It would never even occur to me in a million years to buy frozen dinners. They taste terrible. Plus, you don't know what they're made from except they have to be loaded with fat and sodium. Why would anyone serve a frozen dinner to their family? I've taught my five daughters to cook, and I myself am going to keep right on cooking."

—Cathy Romano,
Saugatuck, Connecticut

Four-Mushroom Fettuccine

MAKES 4 SERVINGS

New England fields and woodlands abound with wild mushrooms, and Yankee cooks have been drying them and preparing them for the table since settlement began. Nowadays supermarkets and specialty food stores are our source for a dizzying array of wild and cultivated mushroom varieties, inspiring fabulous uses such as this rich and deeply flavored sauce. It is wonderful with fresh or dried fettuccine noodles, but for a different twist, you might try the sauce spooned over Creamy (or Baked) Polenta (page 214). An arugula salad and a dessert such as Cranberry-Orange Upside-Down Cake (page 553) would compliment this main course nicely.

1 cup vegetable or chicken broth

2 ounces dried wild mushrooms, preferably morels

2 tablespoons unsalted butter

1-pound mixture of 3 different types of fresh wild mushrooms, such
as shiitake, cremini, oyster, porcini, or chanterelles, sliced if large,
cut in half or quartered if smaller

⅓ cup chopped shallots

2 garlic cloves, minced

½ teaspoon salt, or to taste

¼ teaspoon fresh-ground black
pepper, or to taste

½ cup dry white wine

¼ cup dry sherry or Madeira

1 cup heavy cream

1½ tablespoons chopped fresh tarragon or 1½ teaspoons dried (see Note)

1 pound fresh or dried fettuccine

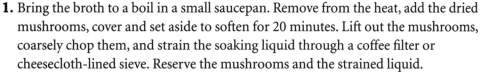

1. Bring the broth to a boil in a small saucepan. Remove from the heat, add the dried
mushrooms, cover and set aside to soften for 20 minutes. Lift out the mushrooms,
coarsely chop them, and strain the soaking liquid through a coffee filter or
cheesecloth-lined sieve. Reserve the mushrooms and the strained liquid.
2. Melt the butter in a very large skillet. Add the fresh mushrooms, shallots, garlic, salt,
and pepper and cook over medium-high heat, stirring frequently, until the
mushrooms have softened and begin to give up their liquid, about 6 minutes. Add
the wine and sherry, bring to a boil, and cook for about 2 minutes to reduce by
about one-third. Add the cream, fresh tarragon, reconstituted dried mushrooms,
and strained mushroom soaking liquid. Simmer, uncovered, for about 10 minutes,
until the sauce is slightly thickened and the flavors blend. Season with additional
salt and pepper if necessary.
3. Meanwhile, cook the fettuccine in a large pot of boiling salted water until al dente,
3 to 5 minutes for fresh, about 10 minutes for dried. Drain in a colander.
4. Serve the pasta with the sauce spooned over.

Note: If using dried tarragon, add it when you sauté the mushrooms, at the beginning
of step 2.

Shiitakes

A once-abandoned nineteenth-century textile mill in North Adams, Massachusetts, may seem an unlikely location for a mushroom farm, but here in the extreme northwestern corner of the state, Delftree Farm uses the vast mill space in a very successful operation to propagate Japanese shiitakes.

In the 1980s a group of dedicated entrepreneurs became frustrated with the lack of mushroom varieties then available in the United States. Experimenting with different nutrient mixes, light and water requirements, and cultivation techniques, Delftree growers were able to mimic the growing conditions of pine forests in Japan, eventually arriving at a complicated high-tech method of producing shiitakes indoors. Their technique involves inoculating grain and sawdust logs with the mushroom fungus in growing rooms created in the restored mill. By the late 1990s Delftree Farm was producing upwards of 8,000 pounds of high-quality shiitakes per week, attempting to meet the growing demand for their certified-organic product.

Shiitakes usually grow to two to three inches in diameter. Good shiitakes, such as those produced at Delftree, have a rich, earthy flavor and a firm yet buttery-smooth texture that can best be likened to that of a tender filet of beef.

Mary Gordon's
Golden Mac 'n' Cheese

MAKES 4 MAIN-COURSE SERVINGS; ABOUT 8 SIDE-DISH SERVINGS

Let's pity the poor souls who believe they're too sophisticated to admit to liking macaroni and cheese. I haven't yet met a person of any age who didn't secretly adore its rich cheddar cheese goodness. This one is a version of my aunt Mary Gordon's oft-requested recipe. The secret lies in beating an egg into the cheese sauce, which results in a somewhat firmer and even richer dish. Using a well-aged sharp cheddar also contributes enormously. Don't be tempted to increase the proportion of macaroni to sauce. The casserole should seem quite soupy when it goes into the oven, or it will be dry when it emerges.

8 ounces elbow macaroni or other small tubular pasta
3 tablespoons unsalted butter
½ cup minced onion
3 tablespoons all-purpose flour
1½ teaspoons dry mustard
2½ cups whole, lowfat, or skim milk
1 egg
3½ cups grated sharp cheddar cheese
¼ teaspoon fresh-ground black pepper
¼ teaspoon cayenne pepper
Salt
¼ cup plain breadcrumbs
½ teaspoon paprika

1. Cook the macaroni in a large pot of boiling salted water until still slightly firm, about 6 minutes. Drain in a colander and transfer to a buttered 2-quart baking dish.
2. Meanwhile, melt the butter in a saucepan. Add the onion and cook over medium heat, stirring frequently, until softened, about 5 minutes. Add the flour and mustard and cook, stirring, for 2 minutes. Whisk in the milk, bring to a boil, and cook, whisking, for about 2 minutes, until smooth, thickened, and bubbly. In a small bowl, lightly beat the egg. Slowly whisk about half of the hot white sauce into the egg to temper it; then whisk the egg mixture into the remaining sauce. Off heat or over the lowest heat, add 3 cups of the cheese, by handfuls, stirring after each addition until the cheese is melted. Season with the black pepper, cayenne, and salt to taste. (The sauce should be salty enough to balance the pasta. The amount needed will depend on the saltiness of the cheese.) Pour the sauce over the cooked macaroni, stirring gently to combine.
4. Preheat the oven to 350 degrees.
5. In a small dish, toss the breadcrumbs with the remaining ½ cup of grated cheese and the paprika. Sprinkle over the macaroni. (The casserole can be made several hours ahead to this point. Cover with foil and refrigerate.)
6. Bake the casserole, uncovered, for 30 to 40 minutes, until the top is golden brown and the sauce is bubbly. If the casserole has been refrigerated, bake, covered with foil, for 20 minutes. Uncover and bake for another 20 to 30 minutes, until golden on top and heated through.

Grilled Farmers' Market Pasta
with New England Chèvre

MAKES 4 SERVINGS

I make this pasta at the glorious height of New England summer, when I just can't resist coming home with bags of every single vegetable I've seen and fallen in love with at the farmers' market. Creamy, fresh local goat cheese, another of the region's splendors, adds zing and body to a simple toss-together sauce. This pasta is a rather free-form affair whose basic proportions you can adapt to other vegetables, other cheeses, and other pasta shapes. Since this dish really constitutes a whole meal unto itself, all you really need is some crusty bread. If you like, finish with a flourish with a delectable summertime dessert such as Blackberry Patch Cobbled Cobbler (page 492).

> 1½-pound mixture of any of the following: asparagus, yellow or green
>   summer squash, bell peppers (any color), broccoli spears, small
>   eggplants, or portobello mushrooms
> Olive oil
> Salt and fresh-ground black pepper
> 1 pound penne or ziti
> 1 cup heavy cream
> 4 ounces fresh goat cheese, cut in cubes
> 2 cups cherry tomatoes, halved
> 1 cup chopped sweet red onion
> ¼ cup chopped fresh herbs, such as basil, tarragon, thyme, chervil, or
>   chives, plus sprigs for garnish
> ½ cup grated pecorino Romano cheese

1. Slice the vegetables into manageable sizes for grilling. Toss with about 2 tablespoons of olive oil and season with salt and pepper. Grill over moderate coals on an outdoor or indoor grill or under the oven broiler, turning with tongs, until somewhat softened and blackened in spots. Remove to a plate.

2. Cook the pasta in a large pot of boiling salted water until al dente, about 10 minutes. Drain in a colander, reserving ½ cup of the cooking water.

3. Return the pasta to the cooking pot and add the cream, goat cheese, and reserved cooking water. Toss, until the pasta is heated through and the goat cheese begins to melt. (The residual heat of the pan should do the job, but use very low heat if necessary.) Add the tomatoes, onion, herbs, and grilled vegetables and toss gently until heated through. Season with salt and pepper to taste.

4. Transfer to a warmed serving platter, garnish with herb sprigs, and serve. Pass the pecorino Romano cheese for sprinkling over the pasta at the table.

Sardines

It's been called "Yankee health insurance," the familiar, distinctive, rectangular can of sardines that is a fixture on New England pantry shelves.

True sardines reside in the Mediterranean and were so named because they were first fished off Sardinia. In the nineteenth century the name was borrowed by New Englanders such as George Burnham of Portland, Maine, who began to process immature herring and market them as sardines. They became a pantry staple, and eventually canneries in Eastport and Lubec on Passamaquoddy Bay in Maine were processing and selling great quantities of sardines.

Sardines also became a popular bar food, and although the adoption of Prohibition dealt the New England sardine industry a severe blow, enough householders remained sardine committed to allow some canning operations to survive. Today a handful of canneries along the Maine coast are still producing tinned sardines, but these days many of the sardines sold in the United States are Norwegian brislings, a small and fatty, lightly smoked sardine, and Portuguese varieties of the fish, which are larger, leaner, and unsmoked.

The tin of sardines stands ever ready to become a satisfying, hunger-assuaging snack lifted straight from the tin and angled diagonally across a saltine cracker, the perfect pick-up lunch when layered between slices of dense bread, perhaps with sliced sweet onion and a little mustard, or a simple and delicious supper such as Sardine Pasta with Fresh Parsley.

Sardine Pasta with Fresh Parsley

MAKES 4 SERVINGS

Canned sardines are an underrated delicacy that should not fall into disuse on the pantry shelf. How comforting, though, to know that that beloved tin of sardines awaits the likes of this dish, which is one of those simple, quick pastas made with ingredients on hand. It is absolutely, irresistibly edible. Try it some night soon when you thought you didn't have anything to make for dinner.

1 pound thin strand pasta, such as linguine or spaghetti
2 3¾-ounce cans small Maine or brisling sardines
2 tablespoons olive oil
4 garlic cloves, minced
½ teaspoon red pepper flakes
1 cup bottled clam juice
1 cup dry white wine
½ cup chopped fresh flat-leaf parsley
2 tablespoons unsalted butter
Salt and fresh-ground black pepper
1 lemon, cut in 8 wedges
Fresh-grated Parmesan cheese, optional

1. Cook the pasta in a large pot of boiling salted water until al dente, about 10 minutes. Drain in a colander.

2. Meanwhile, in a large skillet, heat 3 tablespoons oil, a combination of oil drained from the sardines and the olive oil. Add the garlic and cook over medium heat until fragrant, about 1 minute. Stir in the pepper flakes. Add the clam juice and wine, bring to a boil, and cook, uncovered, until slightly reduced, 3 to 5 minutes. Stir in the parsley and the butter, swirling until it melts.

3. On a serving platter, toss about two-thirds of the sauce with the hot pasta. Arrange the sardines over the pasta, spoon the remaining sauce over the top, and serve.

4. At the table, pass salt and pepper for a final seasoning, along with the lemon wedges and grated Parmesan cheese, if you are using.

Herbed Seafood Lasagne with Tomato-Cream Sauce

MAKES 8 SERVINGS

This sumptuous lasagne, with its layering of a richly suave cream sauce, delicate, herb-infused seafood, and a piquant tomato topping, is just about as elegant and festive as any lasagne can possibly be. Don't be daunted by its rather elaborate preparation. The recipe is based on one from a Worcester, Massachusetts, Junior League cookbook, *The Taste of New England*, and when it comes to gracious yet hassle-free entertaining, the leaguers are masters of the art. You might start such a party meal with Peabody Cheddar Wafers (page 11), serve a spinach salad and crusty bread with the lasagne, and finish with something special like Lemon Buttermilk Pie (page 595).

For the tomato sauce:

2 tablespoons unsalted butter

2 garlic cloves, minced

6 fresh plum tomatoes, seeded and chopped, or canned plum tomatoes, crushed

½ cup dry white wine

¼ teaspoon red pepper flakes

¼ cup thinly sliced scallions

2 tablespoons chopped fresh basil or 1 teaspoon dried

1 tablespoon chopped fresh tarragon or ¾ teaspoon dried

½ teaspoon salt, or to taste

¼ teaspoon black pepper, or to taste

1 teaspoon sugar

For the filling:

2 tablespoons unsalted butter

1 pound bay or sea scallops (if using sea scallops, cut in half)

½ pound shelled and deveined medium shrimp, cut in half

½ cup dry white wine

¾ pound sole or flounder fillets, cut in 1½-inch chunks

1 tablespoon chopped fresh tarragon or 1 teaspoon dried

1 tablespoon chopped fresh thyme or 1 teaspoon dried

½ teaspoon salt, or to taste
½ teaspoon black pepper, or to taste

For the béchamel sauce:

4 tablespoons unsalted butter
4 tablespoons all-purpose flour
2½ cups heavy cream
1 teaspoon salt
½ teaspoon pepper, preferably white
⅛ teaspoon grated nutmeg

1 pound fresh pasta sheets or 12 ounces dried lasagne noodles
½ cup grated Parmesan cheese

1. To make the tomato sauce, melt the butter in a large skillet. Add the garlic and cook over medium heat, stirring, for 1 minute. Add the tomatoes, wine, and red pepper flakes, bring to a boil, and simmer, uncovered, until the tomatoes give off their liquid and the sauce begins to reduce, 7 to 10 minutes. Stir in the scallions, basil, tarragon, salt, pepper, and sugar and simmer for 2 minutes. Set aside until ready to use. (The sauce can be made a day ahead and refrigerated.)

2. To make the filling, melt the butter in a large skillet. Add the scallops and shrimp and cook over medium heat, stirring frequently, until the shrimp begin to turn pink, about 1 minute. Add the wine, bring to a boil, and cook for 1 minute. Add the sole or flounder, along with the tarragon, thyme, salt, and pepper, and continue to cook, stirring gently, just until all the seafood is opaque, 3 to 5 minutes. Remove the seafood with a slotted spoon to a bowl, and reserve any liquid remaining in the skillet.

3. To make the béchamel, melt the butter in a medium-sized saucepan. Add the flour and cook, whisking constantly, for 2 minutes. Gradually whisk in the cream, bring to a boil, and cook, whisking, for 2 minutes. Whisk in the seafood skillet juices and season with the salt, pepper, and nutmeg. Set aside until ready to use. (If not using within 30 minutes, place a sheet of plastic wrap on the surface of the sauce to prevent a skin from forming.)

4. Very fresh pasta sheets do not need to be cooked before the lasagne is assembled. Cook dried pasta (or fresh pasta that has begun to dry out) in a large pot of boiling salted water until still slightly firm, 2 to 5 minutes for fresh, about 8 minutes for dried. Drain in a colander and spread the pasta out on paper or linen towels.

5. Preheat the oven to 375 degrees. Coat a 3- to 4-quart baking dish (such as a 14-by-10-inch lasagne pan) with butter or cooking spray.

6. Spoon about ½ cup of tomato sauce into the prepared dish, tilting to coat the bottom. Make a layer using one-third of the pasta sheets, then half the seafood mixture, then one-third of the béchamel, spreading the filling ingredients evenly. Make another similar layer. Then finish with the last third of the pasta and béchamel. Spread the remaining tomato sauce over the final béchamel layer and sprinkle with the parmesan cheese. (The casserole can be assembled several hours ahead. Cover with foil and refrigerate.)

7. Bake the lasagne, uncovered, until the cheese is golden and the filling is bubbly, 35 to 40 minutes. If the lasagne has been refrigerated, bake the foil-covered casserole for 20 minutes. Uncover and continue to bake for 20 to 30 minutes, until heated through.

8. Let the lasagne rest for about 15 minutes before cutting into squares.

Common Market
Green and White Lasagne

MAKES 8 SERVINGS

The Common Market was a retail food shop in Westport, Connecticut, that was organized by Martha Stewart in the late 1970s to showcase the work of various talented cooks in the area. It was early in the New American "gourmet" revolution, and these were exciting times to be a foodie. I will never forget the first time I saw and tasted the Common Market's gorgeous green and white lasagne, with its layers of tender fresh sheets of pasta (a revelation in itself back then), herb-fragrant spinach and meat filling, and luscious, creamy béchamel sauce. I immediately set about attempting to re-create the dish and, after much experimentation, came up with my own version of the recipe. Eventually this lasagne became something of my signature dish when I had my own small catering business. It makes for exceptional do-ahead party fare, especially when accompanied by a salad of radicchio and mixed greens dressed with My Favorite Vinaigrette (page 79), French bread, and Vermont Chocolate-Potato Bundt Cake (page 550) with coffee ice cream for dessert.

For the filling:

1 tablespoon olive oil
1 pound ground turkey, chicken, or veal
1 medium onion, chopped
2 garlic cloves, minced
2 teaspoons dried tarragon
½ cup dry white wine
1 10-ounce package frozen spinach, thawed and squeezed dry
½ teaspoon salt
¼ teaspoon fresh-ground black pepper

For the sauce:

4 tablespoons butter
4 tablespoons all-purpose flour
1½ cups chicken broth
1½ cups whole or lowfat milk
1 teaspoon salt
½ teaspoon fresh-ground black pepper
¼ teaspoon grated nutmeg
1 cup ricotta cheese

1 pound fresh spinach or egg lasagne noodles or 12 ounces
   (about 12 standard-size) dried egg or spinach lasagne noodles
   or half of each color
3 cups shredded fontina cheese (see Note)
3 tablespoons grated Parmesan cheese

1. To make the filling, heat the oil in a very large skillet. Add the ground meat, onion, garlic, and tarragon and cook, stirring to break up large clumps, until the meat loses its pink color, about 10 minutes. Add the wine, bring to a boil, and cook until most of the liquid is evaporated, about 3 minutes. Stir in the spinach, salt, and pepper and cook to evaporate any remaining liquid if necessary. (The filling can be made a day ahead. Cover and refrigerate.)

Purity Cheese

The cheesemaker at Purity Cheese in Boston's North End wore fisherman's rubber boots and stood ankle deep in water as I watched him early one morning making his daily batches of fresh ricotta, mozzarella, and scamorze, a small braided mozzarella-like cheese.

The difference between Purity's fresh cheeses and packaged supermarket varieties is like the difference between a crusty handmade loaf and soft, squishy supermarket white bread.

By 9:30 A.M. the cheesemaking was finished for the day. The glass cases in the retail shop were stocked. A van pulled up outside to transport Purity's cheeses around the neighborhood and beyond, where they would be transformed into pizza toppings, lasagne fillings, and, at the several neighborhood bakeries, baked into ricotta pies, cannoli, and sfogliatelle, a sublime fan-shaped Neopolitan pastry filled with sweetened ricotta.

2. To make the sauce, melt the butter in a medium-large saucepan. Add the flour and cook, whisking, for 2 minutes. Whisk in the broth and milk and bring to a boil, whisking constantly. Cook for about 2 minutes, until the sauce is thick, smooth, and bubbly. Season with the salt, pepper, and nutmeg. Remove from the heat and whisk in the ricotta cheese. (The sauce can be made a day ahead, refrigerated, and reheated very gently before proceeding.)

3. Very fresh pasta sheets do not need to be cooked before the lasagne is assembled. Cook dried pasta (or fresh pasta that has begun to dry out) in a large pot of boiling salted water until still slightly firm, 2 to 5 minutes for fresh, about 8 minutes for dried. Drain in a colander and spread the pasta out on paper or linen towels.

4. Preheat the oven to 375 degrees. Coat a 3- or 4-quart baking dish (such as a 14-by-10-inch lasagne pan) with butter or cooking spray.

5. Spread a thin layer of béchamel sauce in the bottom of the prepared dish. Begin layering, using one-third of the lasagne noodles, half the meat filling, and one-third each of the béchamel and the fontina. Repeat with another layer, and finish with a layer of noodles, sauce, and fontina. Sprinkle the top with the grated Parmesan. (The casserole can be made 1 day ahead and refrigerated, or it may be frozen. If frozen, thaw in the refrigerator overnight before baking.)

6. Bake the lasagne, uncovered, until the top is pale golden and the filling is hot and bubbly, about 35 minutes. If the lasagne has been refrigerated, cover with foil and bake for 20 minutes; uncover and bake another 20 to 30 minutes, until heated through.

7. Let the lasagne stand for at least 5 minutes before cutting into squares and serving.

Note: Fontina is a flavorful semisoft cheese that is easier to shred if well chilled.

North End Penne with Chicken and Broccoli

MAKES 4 SERVINGS

After a day of walking and eating my way around Boston's Italian North End, I found myself at Pagliuca's Restaurant for dinner—still hungry but by now only for something light and not rich. This lovely, simple pasta dish, along with a plate of their sliced ripe tomatoes dressed with oil and balsamic vinegar, made the perfect supper. Freddy Pagliuca generously shared the recipe.

> 1 pound penne or other similarly shaped pasta
> 4 cups (about 1 pound) broccoli florets
> 3 tablespoons all-purpose flour
> ½ teaspoon salt, plus more to taste
> ½ teaspoon black pepper, plus more to taste
> 1 pound skinless, boneless chicken breasts
> 3 tablespoons olive oil, preferably extra-virgin
> 1 tablespoon butter
> 3 garlic cloves, minced
> 1 teaspoon dried oregano
> ⅓ cup fresh-grated Parmesan cheese

1. Cook the pasta in a large pot of boiling salted water for 8 minutes. Add the broccoli florets and cook for another 3 minutes or until the pasta is al dente and the broccoli is just tender. Drain in a colander, reserving ¾ cup of the cooking water.

2. Meanwhile, combine the flour, salt, and pepper in a shallow dish. Dredge the chicken in the seasoned flour, shaking off the excess. Heat 2 tablespoons of the oil in a large skillet. Cook the chicken over medium heat until golden brown on both sides and no longer pink in the center, about 8 minutes total. Remove the chicken from the skillet, leaving the drippings in the pan, and cut it crosswise into ½-inch-wide slices.

3. Add the remaining 1 tablespoon of oil and the butter to the skillet. Add the garlic and oregano and cook, stirring, for 1 minute. Add the reserved pasta cooking water and bring to a simmer.

4. Toss the hot pasta and broccoli in a large bowl with the sauce and the sliced chicken. Add the cheese and toss again. Season with salt and pepper to taste before serving.

St. Anthony's Feast

Each summer eight saints' festivals are held in Boston's North End, the heart of the city's Italian community. St. Anthony's Feast, held on the last full weekend in August, is the largest. The highlight of the festival is a procession during which a huge statue of St. Anthony is carried on a heavy wooden platform by eight strong, burly men. The statue is festooned with thirteen ribbons symbolizing the date of St. Anthony's death (June 13), and people pin money to the ribbons as the saint passes by.

St. Anthony's Feast is like a giant neighborhood block party, where getting plenty to eat is not a problem. Street vendors vie with each other to entice customers, offering the usual, which includes sausage and peppers, *zeppole* (fried dough sprinkled with powdered sugar), calzone, pizza, and spaghetti and meatballs, as well as the more arcane, such as calamari fried, stuffed, or made into a savory salad.

Church Supper American Chop Suey

MAKES 4 TO 6 SERVINGS

I haven't been able to trace the origin of its quaint name, but I do know from first-hand experience that this ground meat–tomato sauce–macaroni casserole is one of the best-loved and oft-consumed dishes in all of New England. American chop suey has probably been carried to more neighborhood potlucks and public suppers than any other casserole, and when it's made, as this one is, with plenty of rich meat sauce and a cheese topping, it deserves every bit of its popularity.

1 tablespoon olive oil

¾ pound uncooked bulk sausage, such as sweet Italian sausage or
American breakfast-style sausage

1 large onion, chopped

3 garlic cloves, minced

2 teaspoons dried Italian herb seasoning

½ teaspoon red pepper flakes

½ cup dry red wine

1 28-ounce can crushed plum tomatoes in puree

1 8-ounce can tomato sauce

¼ cup chopped fresh parsley, preferably flat-leaf

Salt and fresh-ground black pepper

12 ounces elbow macaroni

1 cup shredded mild cheese, such as Monterey Jack or mild cheddar

¼ cup grated Parmesan cheese

1. Heat the oil in a very large skillet or dutch oven. Add the sausage meat, onion, garlic, Italian seasoning, and red pepper flakes. Cook over medium-high heat, stirring to break up clumps, until the meat loses its pink color, about 10 minutes. Spoon off and discard any excess fat that rises to the surface. Add the wine and boil over high heat until most of the liquid evaporates, about 3 minutes. Add the crushed tomatoes, tomato sauce, and parsley. Bring to a boil, reduce the heat to medium, and cook, uncovered, until the sauce is somewhat reduced and thickened, about 15 minutes. Season with salt and black pepper to taste.

2. Meanwhile, cook the macaroni in a large pot of boiling salted water until it is still slightly firm, about 6 minutes. Drain in a colander.

3. Preheat the oven to 375 degrees. Lightly oil a 2-quart baking dish.

4. Toss the macaroni with the meat sauce in the baking dish. Sprinkle the top evenly with the two cheeses. (The casserole can be made up to 1 day ahead. Cover with foil and refrigerate.)

5. Bake the casserole, uncovered, in the preheated oven for 20 to 25 minutes, until the cheese is melted and browns lightly and the sauce is bubbly. If the casserole has been refrigerated, bake, covered with foil, for 20 minutes. Uncover and bake for another 15 to 20 minutes, until browned and bubbly.

Prince Meatballs and Spaghetti

MAKES 4 SERVINGS

This classical home-style spaghetti and meatballs supper is dedicated to the Prince Spaghetti Company of Lowell, Massachusetts. For several decades the company's memorable commercials declared that "Wednesday is Prince Spaghetti day." The ads worked. In scores of households in Boston's North End and throughout the rest of New England where the pasta was sold, Wednesday did indeed become "spaghetti day." And although, alas, the company no longer exists, their tradition of setting aside a day for spaghetti and meatballs lives on for many New Englanders.

For the sauce:

2 tablespoons olive oil
1 large onion, chopped
3 garlic cloves, chopped
2 teaspoons dried oregano
1 28-ounce can plum tomatoes with juice
1 28-ounce can tomato puree
1 teaspoon sugar
Salt and fresh-ground black pepper

For the meatballs and spaghetti:

1 pound ground chuck or a mixture of chuck, pork, and veal
1 egg
3 tablespoons plain breadcrumbs
2 tablespoons grated Parmesan cheese, plus more for serving
2 tablespoons minced fresh flat-leaf parsley
1 teaspoon dried marjoram
½ teaspoon salt
¼ teaspoon fresh-ground black pepper
1 pound spaghetti

1. To make the sauce, heat the oil in a very large skillet or saucepan. Add the onion and garlic and cook over medium-high heat, stirring often, until beginning to soften, about 5 minutes. Add the oregano and cook, stirring, for 1 minute. Add the tomatoes with juice, tomato puree, and sugar. Bring to a boil, breaking up the tomatoes with the side of a spoon. Cook, uncovered, over medium-low heat for about 20 minutes, until the sauce is somewhat thickened. Season with salt and pepper to taste.

2. Meanwhile, make the meatballs. Combine the ground meat, egg, breadcrumbs, cheese, parsley, marjoram, salt, and pepper in a large bowl. Use your clean hands to mix gently but thoroughly until all the ingredients are combined. Shape into 16 meatballs, about 1½ inches in diameter. As you form each meatball, drop it into the simmering sauce. Spoon the sauce over the meatballs and simmer, uncovered, over medium-low heat until the meatballs are cooked through, 20 to 25 minutes. Skim off any excess fat that rises to the top. (The meatballs and sauce can be made up to 2 days ahead and refrigerated, or they may be frozen. Reheat before serving.)

3. Cook the spaghetti in a large pot of boiling salted water until it is al dente, about 10 minutes. Drain in a colander.

4. Serve the spaghetti with the sauce and meatballs spooned over it. Pass grated Parmesan cheese at the table.

Family-Style "Hamburg" Spaghetti Pie

MAKES 4 SERVINGS

"South Coasters" (people living on the coast in southern Massachusetts and across the border into Rhode Island) have their own food nomenclature, including the habit of calling all ground meat "hamburg." Community cookbooks from this region, such as *The Westport* [Massachusetts] *Heritage Cookbook*, all contain a good many recipes for "hamburg pie," some using a ground meat sauce to top a spaghetti "crust." This version, which is my adaptation of one of these pies, may become a perennial favorite in your family, especially if you finish with a plate of Mom's Harbor View Butterscotch Brownies (page 562).

¾ pound ground beef chuck, pork, or turkey (see Note)
1 medium onion, chopped
1 medium green bell pepper, chopped
2 garlic cloves, chopped
1 tablespoon dried oregano or Italian herb seasoning

South Coasters

"Just where is this South Coast? Well, it's south of Boston, west of Cape Cod and east of Rhode Island proper. I say it's the area between Mount Hope Bay and Buzzards Bay. It includes all the cities and towns between those two bays that are touched by salt water, viz., Swansea, Somerset, Fall River, Tiverton, Little Compton, Westport, Dartmouth, New Bedford, Fairhaven, Mattapoisett, Marion, and Wareham.

"We are sort of a pretense-free zone within the Boston/Newport/Cape Cod triangle.

"We drink 'coffee milk,' call ground beef 'hamburg,' eat chow mein sandwiches, call lobsters 'bugs' and put chourico in our clam boils.

"South Coasters are an ethnic stew. We are English, Irish, Scottish, Italian, Portuguese, French-Canadian, Polish, Cape Verdean, African-American, Lebanese, Greek, Chinese, Vietnamese, Cambodian, Puerto Rican, and Hispanic.

"We are the stewards, for a time, of one of the most beautiful corners of America."

—James W. Clarkin, writing in
The South Coast Insider, May 1997

---

1 16-ounce can tomato sauce
½ teaspoon salt
½ teaspoon black pepper
8 ounces spaghetti, broken in half
1 egg
½ cup whole or lowfat milk
2 cups shredded medium-sharp or sharp cheddar cheese

1. Cook the ground meat with the onion, green pepper, garlic, and oregano in a large, deep skillet or Dutch oven over medium-high heat, stirring to break up clumps, until the meat loses its pink color, about 8 minutes. Add the tomato sauce, salt, and pepper and bring to a boil. Simmer over medium-low heat for about 10 minutes to blend the flavors.
2. Preheat the oven to 375 degrees. Oil a 3-quart (such as a 13-by-9-inch) baking dish.
3. Cook the spaghetti in a large pot of boiling salted water until al dente, about 10 minutes. Drain in a colander and transfer to the prepared dish.
4. In a small bowl, whisk the egg with the milk. Pour over the spaghetti, toss to coat, and spread the pasta out to make an even layer. Spoon the meat mixture over the

spaghetti and sprinkle with the cheese. (The casserole can be made several hours ahead, covered with foil, and refrigerated.)

5. Bake the casserole, uncovered, until the cheese is melted and browns lightly and the sauce is bubbly, 20 to 30 minutes. If it has been refrigerated, bake the foil-covered casserole for 20 minutes. Uncover and continue to cook for about 20 minutes, until heated through.

6. Cut into squares to serve.

Note: If you are using ground turkey, add 1 tablespoon olive oil to the pan when you sauté the meat.

Mike's Polenta

At most veterans' clubs, food is not the draw. But at the V.F.W. Post in Cranston, Rhode Island, a line often stretches outside the building as people wait to eat Mike Lepizzera's gnocchi sorrentina, stuffed artichokes, squid bianco, baccalà salad, and especially his polenta with sausages.

Mike has operated the food concession at the Tabor-Franci V.F.W. Post for almost twenty years, and word of his excellent cooking has spread throughout the area. Mayors and lawyers, young couples and retirees tuck paper napkins under their chins and tuck into Mike's home-style specialties, which, he says, are all based on his mother's recipes from the Depression era. Such fully accredited connoisseurs of fine food as Johanne Killeen and George Germon, owners of the renowned restaurant Al Forno in Providence, count themselves among the fans of Mike's polenta.

Creamy (or Baked) Polenta

MAKES 4 TO 6 SIDE-DISH SERVINGS

As Italian-Americans prospered here in the twentieth century, the cooking of polenta, which was associated with poverty in the old country, began to die out. By the time most of us other New Englanders were exposed to Italian food, we assumed that pasta (or "macaroni," as it used to be known generically) was the one and only Italian starch. Now, it's come full circle, and cooked polenta is again listed proudly on Italian restaurant menus, serving as a savory base for all manner of toppings, particularly tomato or mushroom-based sauces. This recipe first instructs in turning out a cheese-rich, creamy, spoonable polenta, and then, for a somewhat more formal presentation, takes it one step further to the scrumptious baked version.

> 3 cups chicken broth
> 1¼ cups yellow or white cornmeal
> 1 teaspoon salt
> ⅓ cup grated Parmesan cheese, plus more if making baked polenta
> Fresh-ground black pepper

1. Bring the broth to a boil in a large, heavy saucepan over high heat. Whisk the cornmeal with 2 cups of cold water and the salt in a mixing bowl.

2. Gradually whisk the cornmeal mixture into the simmering broth. Bring to a boil, reduce the heat to medium-low, and cook the polenta, uncovered, whisking frequently, until it is very thick, begins to pull away from the sides of the pan, and the cornmeal softens and loses its raw taste, 10 to 20 minutes. (Coarser or stone-ground meals may take longer.)

3. Stir in ⅓ cup of the cheese and season with black pepper to taste before spooning out onto plates to serve as creamy polenta.

4. To bake the polenta, preheat the oven to 375 degrees. Coat a 9-inch cast-iron skillet or 9-inch-square baking dish with olive or vegetable oil cooking spray.

5. Spoon the cooked creamy polenta into the prepared dish, smoothing the top, and sprinkle with about 2 tablespoons more cheese. Bake, uncovered, for about 30 minutes, until the polenta is firm and lightly browned on top and the edges shrink from the sides of the pan. (The polenta can be kept warm, loosely covered, in the turned-off oven for about 30 minutes.)

6. Spoon out of the pan or cut into wedges to serve.

We Called It Macaroni

"We called it macaroni when I was growing up [in Providence, Rhode Island] because that was the generic word that my grandparents used for pasta. Like most of their countrymen, they were eager to adapt to the new land, its people, its culture, its opportunities—but not its food. They clung tenaciously to their own ways of cooking."

—Nancy Verde Barr,
We Called It Macaroni
(Knopf, 1991)

The Very Best Tuna-Noodle

MAKES 4 SERVINGS

Tuna-noodle casserole was the supper of choice for many New England Roman Catholic families during the years of meatless Fridays, maybe because it tasted good even to fish haters. The casserole then went into eclipse for a while, perhaps as a reaction to its overexposure during that era, but is now experiencing a well-deserved revival as folks have remembered what made it a tried-and-true favorite in the first place. Mine is a fairly classic recipe, but with some scallions and dry mustard added to perk up the creamy sauce. It's great for potluck suppers, or serve it to your family with steamed broccoli spears, a garden salad, and a plate of Crisp Maple-Oatmeal Cookies (page 579) for dessert.

> 10 ounces flat or curly egg noodles
> 3 tablespoons butter
> ¼ cup chopped scallions, white parts only
> 2 tablespoons all-purpose flour
> 1 teaspoon dry mustard
> 2¼ cups whole, lowfat, or skim milk
> ½ teaspoon salt
> ⅛ teaspoon black pepper
> 1 large (11- to 12-ounce) can tuna, drained of most oil or water and
>   broken into chunks
> ½ cup fresh breadcrumbs
> ¼ cup chopped scallions, white and green parts

1. Preheat the oven to 375 degrees. Coat a 1½- to 2-quart baking dish with cooking spray or lightly oil it.
2. Cook the noodles in a large pot of boiling salted water until still slightly firm, about 6 minutes. Drain in a colander.
3. Meanwhile, melt 2 tablespoons of the butter in a medium-sized saucepan. Add the white chopped scallion bottoms and cook over medium-high heat, stirring, for 2 minutes. Add the flour and mustard and cook, stirring, for 1 minute. Gradually whisk in the milk. Bring to a boil, whisking, and cook until the sauce is smooth and bubbly, 2 to 3 minutes. Season with the salt and pepper.

4. Transfer the sauce to the prepared baking dish. Add the noodles and the tuna and stir gently to combine.
5. Melt the remaining 1 tablespoon of butter and toss with the crumbs and the green and white chopped scallions. Scatter the seasoned crumbs over the tuna mixture. (The casserole can be made up to 1 day ahead, covered with foil, and refrigerated.)
6. Bake the casserole, uncovered, for 20 to 25 minutes, until the crumbs are lightly browned and the sauce is bubbly. If it has been refrigerated, bake the foil-covered casserole for 20 minutes. Uncover and bake another 15 to 20 minutes, until the crumbs are brown and the sauce is bubbly.
7. Spoon out of the baking dish to serve.

Campbell's Tuna-Noodle

Created by the Campbell Soup Company more than fifty years ago, this casserole has become a beloved can-opener classic. In truth, tuna-noodle made with condensed cream of mushroom soup results in a satisfying, comfortable, quite tasty dish that, taking into account the considerable savings in time, isn't a bad trade-off at all. Here's the formula which serves 4.

1 10¾-ounce can condensed cream of celery or mushroom soup

½ cup milk

2 cups hot cooked medium egg noodles, drained

2 6-ounce cans tuna, drained and flaked

1 cup cooked green peas, drained

2 tablespoons chopped pimiento, optional

¼ cup shredded cheddar cheese, optional

2 tablespoons dried breadcrumbs

1 tablespoon butter or margarine, melted

Preheat the oven to 400 degrees. Lightly butter a 1½-quart casserole. Mix the soup and milk in the casserole. Stir in the noodles, tuna, peas, and pimiento, if you like. Bake, uncovered, 20 minutes; stir. Mix the cheese, if you are using it, with the crumbs and butter in small bowl. Scatter evenly over the tuna mixture and bake 5 minutes more, until lightly browned.

—From *Campbell's Best-Ever Recipes*, 125th Anniversary Edition

Cheese-Topped Noodle Casserole
with Smoked Country Ham

MAKES 4 SERVINGS

This casserole admittedly is somewhat "retro," with its sour cream–rich sauce, but after testing it, I remembered just why this type of dish became so popular in the first place. It tastes wonderful. It's an absolutely perfect use for that leftover holiday ham, but Canadian bacon makes an excellent substitute. Add a salad of dark winter greens and pass some Snickerdoodles (page 568) or Spiced Harwich Hermits (page 559) to complete the meal.

4 tablespoons unsalted butter
1 medium onion, finely chopped
2 eggs
1 cup regular or lowfat sour cream
1½ cups chicken broth, preferably reduced-sodium
1 cup shredded Gruyère or Swiss cheese
3 tablespoons slivered fresh basil, oregano, or parsley
½ teaspoon black pepper
½ pound thinly sliced smoked ham or Canadian bacon, cut in strips
8 ounces thin (¼-inch-wide) egg noodles
¼ cup fine dried breadcrumbs

1. Melt the butter in a medium-sized saucepan. Add the onion and cook over medium heat until softened, about 5 minutes.
2. Lightly beat the eggs in a large mixing bowl. Whisk in the sour cream and chicken broth. Stir in ½ cup of the cheese, 2 tablespoons of the herbs, and the pepper. Stir in the ham and the onion mixture.
3. Cook the noodles in a large pot of boiling salted water until still slightly firm, about 6 minutes. Drain in a colander.
4. Preheat the oven to 350 degrees. Butter a 2-quart baking dish.
5. Place the cooked noodles in the prepared baking dish, add the sauce, and stir until combined.
6. Toss the breadcrumbs in a small dish with the remaining ½ cup cheese and the remaining 1 tablespoon of fresh herbs. Sprinkle over the noodle mixture. (The

casserole can be made 4 hours ahead. Store at cool room temperature or refrigerate.)

7. Bake the casserole, uncovered, until heated through and the top is golden, about 30 minutes. If it has been refrigerated, bake the casserole, covered with foil, for 20 minutes. Uncover and bake for another 15 to 20 minutes, until hot and the top is browned.

8. Serve hot, spooned out of the baking dish.

Polish Christmas

"My father came home just before dark [in western Massachusetts], with his Christmas bonus: an extra day's pay and ten pounds of headcheese. He handed the envelope of money to my mother, and the stinking loaf to my grandmother.

"'The first star is almost out,' he called, signaling it was time to begin our feast.

"I have . . . strong memories of that night . . . how we ate and we ate and we ate: beginning with the soups—beet *barszcz* with tiny mushroom-filled dumplings, and a lighter one of creamed fish; then an almond soup of milk, honey, raisins, and rice. Then pickled herring. And the boiled potatoes with parsley. The green beans, and the cauliflower baked with breadcrumbs. After that, *pierogi* with their hidden fillings of sauerkraut, sautéed mushrooms, onions, sweet cabbage, prunes and cherries. Then the desserts of *blinczyki* cakes fried in oil, *pasteciki* tarts baked around fillings, ginger cakes, fruit compotes of apples, pears, peaches, plums, and the poppyseed coffee cake. And, of course the *krupnik* —the holiday fire-vodka that came to life after months of being hidden in the cellar."

—Suzanne Strempek Shea, *Hoopi Shoopi Donna* (Pocket Books, 1996)

Pierogi with Several Fillings

MAKES 4 TO 5 DOZEN DUMPLINGS

These tender little filled dumplings are the ultimate Polish delicacy. Yes, they're labor-intensive, but if you have a friend or family member or two to help make them, the process can become one of those labor-of-love tasks that creates enduring memories. Pierogi are an important part of the Wiglia supper, the ceremonial Polish Christmas Eve meal, so all of these fillings are meatless, in keeping with the Polish tradition of fasting on this holy night. Each of these filling recipes yields enough to make 16 to 20 pierogi. Make all three, or triple one filling recipe for this quantity of dough.

For the dough:

1 egg
¼ cup sour cream
1 teaspoon salt
½ cup milk
2½ to 3 cups all-purpose flour

For the wild mushroom and sauerkraut filling:

½ ounce dried wild mushrooms
2 tablespoons butter
1 small onion, chopped
1 cup sauerkraut, rinsed, drained, and minced
Salt and fresh-ground black pepper

For the cheese filling:

1¼ cups farmer cheese or ricotta cheese
1 egg yolk
1 tablespoon butter, melted
1 tablespoon sugar
1 teaspoon fresh lemon juice
Salt and fresh-ground black pepper

For the potato filling:

1 cup mashed potato
½ cup farmer cheese or ricotta cheese
1 egg yolk
1 tablespoon butter, melted
Salt and fresh-ground black pepper

1. To make the dough, whisk together the egg, sour cream, salt, milk, and ½ cup water in a large bowl. Add the flour, beating it in with a wooden spoon or the dough hook of a heavy-duty mixer, until a soft dough forms. Turn the dough out on a floured board and knead until smooth, about 8 minutes, or knead with a dough hook for about 3 minutes. Set the dough aside at room temperature to rest for at least 30 minutes, or refrigerate for up to 24 hours. Return to room temperature before rolling.

Millie's Pierogi

As the story goes, the reason so many Polish people ended up settling in Chicopee, Massachusetts, near Springfield, is they thought they were asking directions to Chicago. Polish-American cultural and food mores are still strong in Chicopee, and Millie's Pierogi company is part of that tradition.

A pierogi is a Polish dumpling, a thin layer of tender noodle-type dough wrapped around a filling such as cabbage, potato and cheese, plain cheese, mushroom, sauerkraut, or fruit (see recipe, page 219). Pierogi are a necessary part of every Polish Christmas Eve menu, and they're eaten at other times of year too, particularly at Easter. Millie's brochure suggests that you can serve pierogi plain, with onions or bacon, covered with sour cream, steamed and brushed with butter, baked with a coating of crumbs, made into a casserole with tomato sauce, grilled in butter, or deep-fat fried. "Use as a main dish, hors d'oeuvre, or substitute for potatoes or even dessert!"

Millie's is now owned by Ann Lopuk Kerigan. When she started the business, Ann's father asked, "How do you think you're going to sell pierogi with a name like Kerigan?"

That was more than twenty years and hundreds of thousands of pierogi ago. Millie's produces pierogi in their Chicopee Falls factory year-round, but production increases three-fold at Easter and quadruples at Christmastime. "We have the capacity to make twelve hundred dozen (almost fifteen-thousand) per day," says Mrs. Kerigan. Putting it mildly, that's one heck of a lot of dumplings!

❊ ❊ ❊ ❊ ❊ ❊ ❊ ❊ ❊

2. To make the mushroom filling, soak the mushrooms in 1 cup boiling water for 30 minutes. Drain, leaving any grit behind, and reserve the soaking liquid. Finely chop the mushrooms. Melt the butter in a medium-sized skillet. Add the onion and mushrooms and sauté, stirring, until the onion begins to soften, about 3 minutes. Pour in most of the mushroom soaking liquid, add the sauerkraut, and cook, uncovered, stirring frequently, until most of the liquid is evaporated, about 10 minutes. Season with salt (very little may be needed because of the sauerkraut) and pepper to taste. Refrigerate for up to 3 days.

3. To make the cheese filling, whisk together the cheese, egg yolk, melted butter, sugar, and lemon juice in a bowl. Season with salt and pepper to taste. Refrigerate for up to 1 day.

4. To make the potato filling, whisk together the mashed potato, cheese, egg yolk, and melted butter in a bowl. Season with salt and pepper to taste. Refrigerate for up to 1 day.

5. To make the pierogi, cut the dough into 4 pieces. Roll one piece out on a lightly floured surface until the dough is quite thin, about $1/16$ inch thick. (Or use a hand-cranked pasta roller, decreasing the setting to make a thin sheet of dough.) Using a 2½- to 3-inch cutter, cut out rounds of dough. Spoon about 1 tablespoon of one of the fillings in the center and dampen the edges of the dough. Fold over, pinch to seal, and place the pierogi on lightly oiled baking sheets. Repeat with the remaining dough and fillings. (The pierogi can be frozen at this point.)

6. Bring a large pot of well-salted water to a boil. Cook the pierogi, a few at a time, in the gently boiling water until they float and the dough is tender, about 5 minutes. Remove with a slotted spoon and drain on paper towels. (The pierogi can be made ahead and refrigerated on baking sheets for up to 2 days. Reheat in a microwave or simmer in boiling water for a couple of minutes.)

7. Serve hot, drizzled with melted butter, or follow any of the serving suggestions mentioned in "Millie's Pierogi" (see page 221).

Pasta Primer

The best dried pasta is made from semolina, a flour milled from durum wheat. Most dried semolina pastas have strength and body, but quality can vary. Cheaper pastas, such as store brands, can cook up softer and mushier, without as much volume as better-quality pastas. The best dried pastas are often the imported brands, which usually cost more than domestic ones.

Fresh pasta is sold refrigerated or frozen. The most common fresh pastas are made from white flour and eggs, which produce a tender, delicate dough that is softer and more porous than semolina pasta. Common shapes are flat strands such as fettuccine and stuffed pastas such as ravioli and tortellini.

Noodles are made with flour, water, and eggs or egg yolks. They can be cut into flat thick or thin strips or into squares. Dried egg noodles are sold in packages along with the other pastas in the supermarket.

If you are substituting fresh pasta for dried in a recipe, note that 1 pound of fresh pasta is the equivalent of about 12 ounces of dried pasta because the fresh doesn't absorb as much liquid during cooking.

To cook pasta, use at least 4 quarts of water for each pound. Add 1 to 2 tablespoons of salt to the boiling water, drop in the pasta, and cover the pot. Return quickly to a boil, uncover the pot, and cook until the pasta is al dente, or tender but firm to the bite. Test the pasta after the minimum recommended cooking time by tasting a strand.

Fresh pasta cooks in about one-third of the time that dried semolina pasta takes, roughly 3 to 4 minutes versus 9 to 12 minutes. Because they are made with a softer wheat, dried egg noodles take less time to cook than semolina pasta.

Portuguese Rice Garden with Lemon and Garlic

MAKES 6 SIDE-DISH SERVINGS

Portuguese-Americans' fondness for potatoes, which they eat at just about every meal, tends to obscure their wonderful way with rice dishes. This vegetable-studded preparation is so festive and pretty that it should really star as the main attraction on the plate. Try it when you are serving plain roast chicken or any meat such as ham or a roast of pork.

> 4 tablespoons olive oil
> 1 red bell pepper, diced
> 1 cup diced slender zucchini
> 1 cup thawed frozen or fresh corn kernels
> 3 garlic cloves, minced
> 1 teaspoon ground coriander
> 1 teaspoon ground cumin
> 2 cups long-grain white rice
> 3½ cups chicken broth
> ¾ teaspoon salt, plus more to taste
> 1 teaspoon grated lemon zest
> 2 tablespoons fresh lemon juice
> ¼ cup chopped fresh cilantro
> Fresh-ground black pepper

1. Heat the oil in a very large, heavy saucepan. Add the bell pepper, zucchini, and corn, and sauté over medium heat until the vegetables just begin to soften, about 4 minutes. Remove the vegetables with a slotted spoon and set aside. Add the garlic, coriander, and cumin to the pan and cook, stirring, for 1 minute. Add the rice and cook, stirring, until the grains are coated with oil, about 2 minutes.

2. Add the broth, salt, and lemon zest and bring to a boil. Reduce the heat to very low, cover, and cook until the rice is tender and the liquid is absorbed, about 18 minutes.

3. Stir in the reserved vegetables, lemon juice, and cilantro and fluff the rice with a fork. Season with more salt if needed and plenty of black pepper to taste.

Shaker Baked Rice Pilaf
with a Shower of Herbs

MAKES 4 GENEROUS SIDE-DISH SERVINGS

This recipe is an adaptation of a lovely, simple, herby rice pilaf in Jeffrey Paige's book, *The Shaker Kitchen*. The herb gardens at the Canterbury, New Hampshire, Shaker Village are a constant source of culinary inspiration. The terraced garden beds produce four kinds of mint, assorted basils, tarragon, summer savory, sages, several varieties of thyme, chives, lovage, and rosemary. If you prefer, you can cook this dish in its entirety on top of the stove and simply reduce the simmering time to about 20 minutes. Oven-baked rice, however, is very practical, especially for entertaining. Not only does it free up a stove burner, but the cooked rice will keep warm in the turned-off oven if dinner is delayed.

> 2 tablespoons butter or olive oil
> 1 small onion, minced
> 1 bay leaf
> 1½ cups long-grain white rice
> 2¾ cups chicken broth
> ½ teaspoon salt, or to taste
> 2 tablespoons chopped fresh parsley
> 2 tablespoons chopped fresh herbs, such as thyme, basil, or tarragon
> Fresh-ground black pepper

Is It Gravy or Is It Sauce?

All New England Italians I polled said that their mothers and grandmothers referred to Italian tomato-meat sauce as gravy. "I've got a big pot of gravy on the stove. Want to come over for supper?" Phyllis Diiorio continued to call it gravy until recently. She kept inviting her daughter's non-Italian boyfriend to come for pasta and gravy, and was perplexed that he repeatedly found reasons to politely decline, until she figured out that he thought the meal was going to consist of macaroni topped with American-style brown gravy—admittedly not the most appetizing-sounding concoction! So now Phyllis has trained herself to call it "sauce," except when speaking to other Italians.

---

1. Preheat the oven to 375 degrees.
2. Heat the butter or oil in a large ovenproof casserole such as enameled cast iron (see Note). Add the onion and bay leaf and sauté over medium heat until the onion is wilted, about 4 minutes. Add the rice and cook, stirring, until it begins to turn white and is coated with oil, about 2 minutes. Add the broth and salt and bring to a simmer.
3. Cover the pot and place in the preheated oven. Bake for about 30 minutes, until the rice is tender and the liquid is absorbed. (The rice can be made up to 45 minutes ahead and kept hot in the turned-off oven until you are ready to serve.)
4. Discard the bay leaf. Just before serving, add the herbs and fluff the rice with a fork. Taste, season with pepper and additional salt if necessary, and serve.

Note: You can do the initial sauté in a saucepan on top of the stove; then transfer the rice and liquid to a glass baking dish, cover with foil, and finish in the oven.

Classical Kedgeree with Fresh Herbs

MAKES 4 SERVINGS

Kedgeree, which was originally an East Indian dish that was brought to the New England shores by seamen in the eighteenth century, is still found on diner menus in towns along the coast. Not only is kedgeree a very tasty little lunch or supper dish, but it is the perfect vehicle for using up leftovers of fish and rice. This is the classical recipe, which I have enlivened with some fresh herbs. For a delightful variation, try adding a bit of curry powder—about 1½ teaspoons—stirring it into the butter to cook with the scallions.

2 tablespoons unsalted butter

½ cup plus 2 tablespoons thinly sliced scallions

3 cups cooked white rice

2 cups cooked flaked fish, any type, fresh or smoked

⅔ cup half-and-half, light cream, or heavy cream

½ teaspoon salt, or more to taste

¼ teaspoon fresh-ground black pepper, or more to taste

4 hard-cooked eggs, peeled and coarsely chopped

2 tablespoons chopped fresh parsley

Lemon wedges

1. Melt the butter in a large skillet with a lid or in a saucepan. Add ½ cup of the scallions and cook over medium-high heat, stirring, for 2 minutes. Add the rice, fish, cream, salt, and pepper. Bring to a simmer, cover, and cook over low heat just until heated through, 3 to 5 minutes.
2. Fold in the eggs and parsley and cook for another 2 minutes, until heated through. Season with additional salt and pepper to taste.
3. Transfer to a serving platter or plates, sprinkle with the remaining 2 tablespoons of scallions, and serve with the lemon wedges.

Artisan Cheese

Consumer interest in artisan cheeses rose stunningly in the mid-1990s, and cheesemakers are blooming like a well-aged rind all over New England. Two Massachusetts farms produce exceptional blue cheeses—Westfield Farm in Hubbardston and Great Hill Dairy in Marion. Barbara Brooks of Seal Cove Farm in coastal Maine is one of several Mainers crafting chèvres and salty goat feta out of milk from their own herd of goats.

Vermont is the biggest cheese-producing state in the region, and its recently organized Vermont Cheese Council boasts over twenty cheesemakers, from Cabot's huge dairy cooperative, which produces cheddars and several other cheese varieties in its large, modern facility, to the showcase Shelburne Farms operation, renowned for its well-aged, deep-flavored farmstead cheddars, to Allison Hooper of Vermont Butter and Cheese in Websterville, who makes several superior goat's milk cheeses, to tiny producers like Cindy and David Major, who handcraft eight-pound wheels of a fabulous aged sheep's milk cheese at their farm in Putney.

Clam and Roasted Tomato Risotto

MAKES 4 SERVINGS

Risotto now shows up with regularity on menus all over New England, and it has also become a popular addition to many home cooks' repertoires. Its only drawback is that admonition to stir, stir, stir for the entire 20 minutes of cooking time. Note that the cooking method in this recipe is different. Following the lead of *Bon Appétit* magazine's test kitchen, which experimented with both classic and nontraditional risotto-making techniques, I found that this simplified version produces results that are virtually indistinguishable from—and equally delicious as—the usual stir-constantly method. So, unless you really need a workout for your arms, give this a try. The oven-roasted tomatoes, with their sweet, concentrated flavor, perfectly complement the clams in this risotto and definitely shift the dish into the special occasion category. An arugula salad, seeded breadsticks, and Hester's Sour Lemon Pudding Cake (page 519) would complete the dinner beautifully.

12 small plum tomatoes (1½ pounds), cored and cut in half
   lengthwise
2 tablespoons olive oil
2 dozen small hard-shell (littleneck) clams, scrubbed
4 cups chicken broth, plus more if necessary
3 tablespoons butter
1 medium-large onion, chopped
1¾ cups Arborio or other short-grain rice
1½ cups dry white wine
½ cup slivered fresh basil
½ cup grated Parmesan cheese, preferably imported
Salt and fresh-ground black pepper

1. Preheat the oven to 350 degrees.
2. Toss the tomatoes with the olive oil on a rimmed baking sheet. Roast, stirring once or twice, until the tomatoes soften and are somewhat caramelized, about 35 minutes. Scrape the tomatoes and any blackened or caramelized juices clinging to the baking sheet into a bowl and reserve.

3. Meanwhile, combine the clams with 3½ cups water in a large pot. Bring to a boil, reduce the heat to medium, and cook, covered, until the clams open and the meat is opaque, 4 to 8 minutes, depending on their size. Using a slotted spoon, remove the clams, still in their shells, to a bowl. Cover loosely and reserve. Carefully pour 2 cups of the clam broth into a glass measuring cup, leaving behind any grit or mud.

4. Combine the chicken broth and strained clam broth in a saucepan and bring to a simmer.

5. Melt the butter in a very large, heavy saucepan. Add the onion and sauté over medium heat until it softens, about 5 minutes. Add the rice and cook, stirring, until the grains are coated with butter and slightly translucent, about 2 minutes. Add the wine, bring to a boil, and cook, stirring, until the liquid evaporates, about 2 minutes.

The Villa Correnty

Norwalk, Connecticut, a town in Fairfield County, along the Long Island Sound, was about sixty percent Italian when Frank Correnty was growing up there in the 1940s and '50s. Because it had a strong industrial base, many recent immigrants found work in the Norwalk factories or on the railroad, settling comfortably into the small city to raise families.

Like a good many women, Mrs. Correnty worked all day in a nearby factory. Rather than making supper when she got home each night, she cooked dinner for her husband and children the night before she served it. So on Monday evening, for example, after the dishes were done, Mrs. Correnty cooked for Tuesday's supper. Usually a tomato sauce, sometimes with meat, often with vegetables, occasionally with the crabs caught on a family crabbing expedition to the shore. They ate pasta three nights a week, a different pasta with a different sauce for each meal.

The Correntys' frame house sat on 1½ acres of land. Large vegetable gardens, where Frank's father grew tomatoes, peppers, and eggplants that his mother canned each fall, grew along one side. At the end of the long, narrow backyard stood the chicken coops. And an arbor laden with Concord grapes arched over a corner of the yard near the house, offering welcome shade from the hot Connecticut summer sun. A four-foot-wide table placed under the arbor served, all summer long, as the family gathering place. There they ate all of their meals and then sometimes lingered, sipping wine, talking, storing up memories, and snatching a few richly earned moments of peaceful relaxation from the long New England dusk.

6. Pour all but about 1 cup of the hot broth mixture over the rice. Cook, uncovered, over medium heat, at a constant, barely bubbling simmer, stirring every 4 to 5 minutes, until the rice is swollen and tender but still firm to the bite, about 18 minutes. If the rice has absorbed all the liquid before it is tender, add a bit more broth to finish the cooking. Stir in the basil and cheese and season with salt and pepper to taste.

7. Add the cooked clams to the pot containing the remaining 1 cup of broth mixture, and simmer for about 2 minutes to heat through.

8. To serve, spoon the risotto into shallow soup dishes, arrange the tomatoes and clams in their shells over each serving, and ladle the remaining hot broth over the top.

SANDWICHES
AND PIZZAS

I n summer along coastal New England, there is nothing better than biting into a seafood "roll"—an utterly simple yet sublime creation consisting of nothing more than a butter-grilled flat-sided hot dog bun filled with sweet lobster or crab salad or ocean-fresh fried scallops or clams.

Along about the 1920s, when sliced white bread loaves became a staple of the American diet, sandwiches began to have a huge impact on the New England culinary scene. The relatively small city of New Haven, Connecticut, home of Yale University, proudly claims both the invention of the hamburger sandwich and the first pizzeria in America. The Best "Hamburg" with The Works (page 251) and the Famous New Haven White Clam Pizza (page 253) are re-creations of same.

At Greek-American–run diners and small family restaurants all over the region, sandwiches reign supreme. "Dogs" with Greek Sweet Chili Sauce (page 249) feature the addictive spicy-sweet sauce that gets ladled over frankfurters, and succulent Lamb Souvlaki with Yogurt-Cucumber Sauce (page 246) demonstrates how easy it is to make this Greek-restaurant specialty at home.

A Perfect Scallop Roll

MAKES 4 SERVINGS

Cape Cod's Buzzards Bay Park hosts the Bourne Scallop Fest every September. "This festival," declares the official brochure, is "a celebration of New England's favorite seafood, SCALLOPS!!!" At this three-day event, most of the bivalves served up are very small, sweet, and tender bay scallops. When sautéing these succulent little babies at home, first, dry the scallops on paper towels before cooking if they are damp; second, don't crowd the pan or they will steam instead of browning; and third, salt them after cooking. Taking these simple precautions will help ensure that the scallops brown quickly before they release and lose their sweetly flavorful juices.

> 2 tablespoons vegetable oil or light olive oil
> 2 tablespoons butter
> 1 pound bay scallops
> Paprika
> Salt and fresh-ground black pepper
> 4 frankfurter rolls, preferably top-split, lightly toasted
> Classic Tartar Sauce (page 14) or good-quality bottled tartar sauce

1. Heat half the oil and butter in a skillet large enough to hold half the scallops in a single layer without crowding, over medium-high heat. Add half the scallops and cook without turning or stirring for 1 minute. Shake and toss or stir the scallops to turn them and cook for another minute, or until golden on both sides. Sprinkle lightly with paprika, salt, and pepper, and spoon them into 2 of the buns.

2. Add the remaining oil and butter to the skillet and repeat with the remaining half of the scallops.

3. Pass a small bowl of tartar sauce for spooning over the scallops.

Maine Crab Salad Roll

MAKES 4 SERVINGS

You can get crab rolls in open-air clam shacks and small family-style restaurants up and down the coast of Maine all summer. The classic crab roll is like pure unalloyed gold—a Down East creation consisting of nothing more than fresh-picked locally caught crabmeat and mayonnaise heaped onto a soft grilled hamburger or hot dog bun. Period. Since most of the hard work has already been done by the (expert, we hope) crab picker, crab rolls are great for at-home lunches or suppers, perhaps with a cup of Milky Maine Steamer Chowder (page 58) to start and watermelon wedges and a plate of Melanie's Molasses Crinkle Cookies (page 569) for dessert.

> ¾ pound fresh lump-style crabmeat, picked over
> 1 tablespoon fresh lemon juice
> About ½ cup mayonnaise
> Salt and fresh-ground black pepper
> 4 soft hamburger buns, split
> 2 tablespoons butter, softened
> 4 leaves soft lettuce, optional

1. Toss the crabmeat with the lemon juice in a mixing bowl. Add enough mayonnaise to bind the salad, stirring gently but thoroughly to combine. Season with salt and pepper to taste. (Refrigerate the salad if not using immediately.)

2. Brush the cut sides of the buns with butter and grill on a cast-iron griddle or skillet until lightly toasted on their cut sides.

3. Heap the crab salad on the buns, top with a lettuce leaf, if you like, and serve.

———— A Cheesemaker's Dream ————

Scott Fletcher has been crafting cheddar cheese by hand for the Grafton Village Cheese Company in Grafton, Vermont, for more than thirty years. He admits to nibbling his own product as he makes it, but what he fancies most is what he calls the "cheese dream sandwich." "I take two pieces of white bread, dip them—one side only—into a batter of eggs, milk, and sugar, then brown them on a griddle. Then I put a couple of slices of cheddar on one piece, cover it with the other, and grill the sandwich until the cheese melts. Then I eat it with maple syrup. It's great!"

Whistleville Soft-Shell Crab Sandwich

MAKES 4 SERVINGS

In the early twentieth century, many Italian immigrants found work building the coastal Connecticut rail line. After the railroad was finished, many of these Italians stayed in Connecticut, settling near the tracks in communities that were often dubbed "Whistlevilles." There was a Whistleville in South Norwalk, Connecticut, where I grew up. It felt just like Italy in "my" Whistleville, with vegetable gardens and grape arbors in the backyards, and the narrow shopping streets crowded with small family-run grocery stores, butchers, and fish markets—each with its own memorable and exotic (to a white-bread kid like me) sights and smells. Whistleville's Blue Moon Restaurant was a good place to take a large family for a delicious, inexpensive Italian dinner, and it was there that I was tricked into eating my first soft-shell crab. After getting over being squeamish about eating those spidery-looking claws, I took my first bite and never looked back. This sautéed soft-shell crab sandwich, which is served open-faced, is a simply divine meal served with french fries and coleslaw or, as it is offered at the Blue Moon, with a side of garlic-and-oil spaghetti.

½ cup all-purpose flour
1 teaspoon salt
½ teaspoon black pepper
7 tablespoons butter
4 tablespoons vegetable oil
4 large soft-shell crabs, cleaned
½ cup dry white wine
Dash of bottled hot pepper sauce
4 pieces thick-sliced white bread, lightly toasted
Parsley sprigs
Lemon wedges
Classic Tartar Sauce (page 14) or good-quality bottled tartar sauce

1. Combine the flour with the salt and pepper in a shallow dish.

2. Heat 4 tablespoons of the butter and the oil in a very large (12-inch) skillet over medium-high heat. (If the skillet is smaller, you will need to cook the crabs in 2 batches.) Dredge the crabs in the seasoned flour, and when the foam begins to subside in the pan, add the crabs to the skillet. Cook until golden on both sides, adjusting the heat if necessary, about 7 minutes. Remove to a plate, leaving the drippings in the pan.

3. Add the remaining 3 tablespoons of butter to the pan and cook, stirring, until it melts. Add the wine, bring to a boil, and cook, stirring, for 1 minute. Season with a dash or two of hot pepper sauce.

4. Cut the toast in half diagonally and place 2 diagonals, overlapping, on each dinner plate. Arrange the cooked crabs on the toast and drizzle with the pan sauce. Garnish with parsley sprigs and lemon wedges and serve with the tartar sauce.

Atlantic Lobster Roll

MAKES 4 SERVINGS

Lobster rolls are one of the true glories of New England shoreline cuisine. They range from the almost-virginal "hot lobster roll," consisting of nothing more than chunks of warm, just-picked pink and white lobster meat stuffed into a hot dog roll and drizzled with melted butter, to the more common butter-grilled roll filled with a simple mayonnaise-dressed lobster salad, to fanciful cutting-edge creations with jalapeño peppers or lemon grass or other such heretical ingredients added to the mix. In this, my favorite version of the succulent roll, the otherwise pristine lobster salad has just a little bit of diced celery added for crunch, and the roll is lined with a green lettuce leaf.

2 cups cooked lobster meat, chopped into chunks no smaller than
¾ inch
2 teaspoons fresh lemon juice
¼ cup minced celery
½ cup mayonnaise, or more to taste
Salt
Pinch of cayenne pepper
1 tablespoon butter
4 top-split frankfurter rolls (see Note)
4 leaves green leaf or oak leaf lettuce, optional

1. Toss the lobster meat with the lemon juice and celery in a mixing bowl. Add the mayonnaise and stir gently to combine, adding more if necessary to moisten the salad sufficiently. Season with salt and cayenne.
2. On a cast-iron griddle or in a large, heavy skillet, melt the butter over medium heat. Lay the rolls on their crustless sides on the griddle and toast until golden.
3. Line the rolls with lettuce leaves, if you like. Spoon the lobster salad into the cavities, heaping it high, and serve.

Note: If top-split rolls are not available, use conventional frankfurter rolls, but grill the crusty top and bottom, not the interior.

Lobster Roll

"What's a lobster roll?" Jesse said as they looked at the menus.

"A lobster roll?"

"Yes. Is it a kind of sushi or what?"

Abby smiled.

"God, you California kids," she said. "A lobster roll is lobster salad on a hot dog roll."

[After the food arrives.] "The lobster's in a damn hot dog roll," Jesse said.

"I told you."

"I didn't think you meant an actual hot dog roll."

—Robert B. Parker,
Night Passage (Jove Books, 1997)

Country-Style
Hot Turkey Sandwiches

MAKES 4 SERVINGS

At Hart's Turkey Farm Restaurant in Meredith, New Hampshire, near Lake Winnipesaukee, the motto is "Every day is Thanksgiving at Hart's." Hart's hot turkey sandwich is like the one you or I would make at home a couple of days after the holiday dinner: leftover sliced turkey reheated in gravy, heaped on buttered toast over a layer of reheated leftover stuffing, and finished with a wobbly dollop of sweet-tart cranberry sauce. This recipe, which uses boneless turkey cutlets, sautéed and finished with a quickly made pan gravy, is for the days in the year that *aren't* Thanksgiving. It's a country-style knife-and-fork sandwich that delivers those comforting and nostalgic Thanksgiving flavors.

> 1 pound thin-sliced boneless turkey cutlets
> Salt and fresh-ground black pepper
> 3 teaspoons poultry seasoning
> 4 tablespoons butter, plus more for buttering toast
> ¼ cup thinly sliced scallions
> 2½ tablespoons all-purpose flour
> 2 cups chicken broth
> 4 pieces thick-sliced white or whole-grain bread
> ½ cup cranberry sauce, whole berry or jellied

1. Season the cutlets with salt and pepper and sprinkle on both sides with 2 teaspoons of the poultry seasoning. Melt the butter in a large skillet over medium-high heat. When the foam subsides, sauté the turkey until lightly browned on both sides and just cooked through, about 4 minutes. Remove to a plate, leaving the drippings in the pan.

2. Add the scallions to the pan and cook, stirring, for 1 minute, until softened. Add the flour and the remaining 1 teaspoon of poultry seasoning and cook, stirring, for 2 minutes. Gradually whisk in the broth and cook, whisking constantly, until the gravy boils and thickens, about 3 minutes. Season with salt and pepper.

3. Lightly toast the bread and spread lightly with butter. Place the toast on dinner plates. Arrange the turkey slices over the toast and ladle the gravy over.

4. Top with a spoonful of cranberry sauce and pass the remaining cranberry sauce at the table in a bowl.

The Goat-Cheese Nanny

Alison Hooper has been dubbed the "goat-cheese nanny." Her Vermont Butter & Cheese Company in Websterville, Vermont, produces excellent European-style goat's milk cheeses such as chèvre, impastata, and chevrier. Alison, who helped spearhead a group of about twenty other Vermont cheesemakers to form the Vermont Cheese Council, believes that "cheese can do for Vermont what wine has done for the Napa Valley."

The Vermont Country "Club"

MAKES 4 SERVINGS

All you do to join this "club" is get hold of the right top-drawer ingredients, preferably produced in the Green Mountain state, and then construct this fabulous sandwich. Lean bacon smoked over corn cobs, farm-raised fresh turkeys, well-aged farmstead cheddar, and artisan breads are all specialties of Vermont. Then, if you serve this towering sandwich with Cape Cod potato chips (see page 240) and Prize-Winning Crisp Bread-and-Butter Pickles (page 471), you qualify for membership in the exclusive All New England Club. Fresh fruit from a local farm stand and a plate of cookies such as Spiced Harwich Hermits (page 559) would clinch it.

> 1 cup regular or lowfat mayonnaise
> 3 tablespoons chopped fresh tarragon or 2 teaspoons crumbled dried
> 12 slices bacon, preferably Vermont cob-smoked
> 12 thin slices good-quality white or whole wheat sandwich bread
> ¾ pound sliced roast turkey breast
> 2 ripe tomatoes, thinly sliced
> Salt and fresh-ground black pepper
> 6 ounces sliced well-aged cheese, preferably Vermont farmstead
>   cheddar
> Lettuce leaves or watercress sprigs

1. Stir together the mayonnaise and tarragon in a small dish.

2. Cook the bacon over medium-low heat in a large skillet until browned and crisp, about 12 minutes. Drain on paper towels.

3. Spread one side of 4 slices of the bread with the herbed mayonnaise. Layer with turkey and tomatoes and sprinkle with salt and pepper. Spread 4 more bread slices with mayonnaise and place over the turkey-tomato layer. Layer with bacon, cheese, and lettuce. Spread the remaining bread with mayonnaise and place on top.

4. Carefully cut each sandwich into diagonal quarters and stick a (preferably frilled) toothpick into each quarter to prevent it from toppling.

Cape Cod Potato Chips

The Cape Cod Potato Chip company makes a premium "kettle-cooked" potato chip that is harder and crunchier and a bit less greasy than many chips. At the small Hyannis, Massachusetts, Cape Cod Potato Chip factory, the thin-sliced potatoes, mostly Maine round whites, are fried longer, more slowly, and in smaller batches than those made in huge chip plants. When Cape Cod owner Stephen Bernard started the company back in the 1980s, the crispy delights quickly attracted an almost cultlike following. The company grew, but after Bernard accepted an offer he couldn't refuse and sold the name to the Anheuser-Busch corporation, sales began to plummet, and eventually the Cape Cod operation was closed down. At that point Bernard bought Cape Cod back from Anheuser, reopened the factory, rehired 100 employees, and, by the late 1990s, they were all back in the chips again.

Today Cape Cod Potato Chips, in the distinctive red, white, and blue bag picturing Nauset Lighthouse, have the same good potato flavor and hard crunch that they always had. These chips have a rough-hewn simplicity that makes them the perfect crisp partner to just about any sandwich, particularly The Vermont Country "Club."

The Expert BLT

MAKES 4 SERVINGS

In the mid-1990s I served as a spokesperson for Oscar Mayer bacon for a couple of years. One summer the company's public relations campaign featured the BLT sandwich, so I stood out in a vegetable garden for an entire sweltering July day and made BLT after BLT for a TV satellite media tour. Even after that, I still truly love bacon—*and* BLTs. You can gussy them up any way you like, by adding chives to the mayo, for instance (as I do here), or using basil leaves instead of lettuce. Whatever you do to them, they're always absolutely delicious. How can you go wrong? All the perfect elements are between two slices of lightly toasted bread: the juicy height-of-summer red tomatoes, the crunchy green lettuce leaves, the creamy mayo binding it all together, and, best of all, the incomparable meaty, smoky, salty-sweet flavor of the bacon.

2 tablespoons snipped fresh chives or minced scallions
½ cup regular or lowfat mayonnaise
12 slices good-quality bacon
8 slices good-quality white sandwich bread, lightly toasted
2 tomatoes, thickly sliced
Fresh-ground black pepper
Crisp lettuce leaves, such as romaine or iceberg

1. Stir the chives or scallions into the mayonnaise.
2. Cook the bacon in a large skillet over medium-low heat, separating the slices as they cook, until golden brown, about 12 minutes. Remove with tongs to drain on paper towels.
3. Spread one side of the toast with the mayonnaise. Layer with the tomatoes and bacon and grind black pepper over the top. Add a lettuce leaf, close the sandwiches, cut in half diagonally, and serve.

Portuguese Chourico, Peppers, and Onion Grinder

MAKES 4 SERVINGS

This is the Portuguese version of a grinder, made with chourico, the potently garlicky spicy smoked pork sausage. Portuguese chourico is pretty widely available nationwide now, although in the Southwest you are more likely to find its Mexican cousin, chorizo. Chorizo is made with fresh pork and is a somewhat crumblier sausage, but it can certainly be substituted here. Just be sure to simmer it in the wine and vegetable mixture until the juices run clear.

3 tablespoons olive oil
4 Portuguese chourico sausages, about 4 ounces each
1 large onion, thinly sliced
1 green or yellow bell pepper, thinly sliced

1 red bell pepper, thinly sliced
1 cup dry red wine
Salt and black pepper, optional
4 Portuguese or grinder rolls, sliced horizontally, warmed if you like

1. Heat 2 tablespoons of the oil in a large skillet. Cut the sausages in half lengthwise, place them in the skillet, and cook over medium heat until they are nicely browned on all sides, about 8 minutes. Remove to a plate. If more than a tablespoon or so of fat remains in the pan, pour it off.

2. Add the remaining tablespoon of oil to the skillet. Add the onion and sliced peppers, raise the heat to medium-high, and cook, stirring frequently, until the vegetables begin to brown and soften, about 5 minutes. Return the chorizo to the pan, add the wine, and bring to a boil. Reduce the heat to medium and simmer, uncovered, until the liquid is slightly reduced and the flavors blend, about 4 minutes. Season with salt and pepper to taste if necessary. (It is unlikely to need either one, since the sausage is both salty and spicy.)

3. Place the bottoms of the rolls on plates and divide the sausage mixture among them. Cover with the tops, slice in half diagonally, and serve.

Grinders, Subs, Italians, and Heroes

An oversize sandwich made on a crusty French or Italian loaf split and mounded with everything from meatballs to sausage to cold cuts and cheese, known as a "hero" around much of the country, is called a "grinder" in many parts of New England. It seems to have earned its name because of the tooth-grinding needed to get your teeth through the sandwich. During World War II, around the navy sub base at Groton, Connecticut, grinders came to be known as "submarines." An Italian-American grocer who made a specialty of the sandwiches rechristened them with the name, which is widely used throughout New England. And in Maine many delis proudly advertise the overstuffed sandwiches as "Fresh Italians."

Shaker Grilled Pork Tenderloin Sandwich

MAKES 4 SERVINGS

This maple-grilled pork cutlet sandwich is a re-creation of a fabulous sandwich I ate at the restaurant at Shaker Canterbury Village in New Hampshire. In this version of the recipe, the lean pork tenderloin is brined in a salt solution for several hours before grilling. If you have not tried this treatment, I urge you to put it to the test. The brining process helps the lean meat retain moisture, and the result is a tender and flavorful boneless cutlet. The maple barbecue sauce is made by doctoring up a good-quality bottled sauce with a few judicious additions. Serve with coleslaw, either Crispy Creamy Coleslaw (page 84) or Crisp Apple Slaw with Honey-Lime Dressing (page 86), or buy some from the deli.

For the pork:

1 tablespoon salt
1 pound pork tenderloin, cut in half crosswise

For the sauce:

1 tablespoon vegetable oil
1 small onion, chopped
1 garlic clove, finely chopped
1 teaspoon chili powder
2 cups good-quality bottled smoke-flavored barbecue sauce
1 tablespoon pure maple syrup
2 teaspoons red wine vinegar

Fresh-ground black pepper
1 tablespoon vegetable or light olive oil
About 1 cup coleslaw
4 Portuguese or Kaiser rolls, split

1. To prepare the pork, dissolve the salt in 1½ cups of water in a small deep bowl large enough to hold the pork pieces in a single layer. Add the pork, making sure it is completely covered with brine by 1 inch. Refrigerate, covered, for at least 12 hours or up to 24 hours.

2. To make the sauce, heat the oil in a large saucepan. Add the onion and cook over medium heat until it begins to soften, about 5 minutes. Add the garlic and chili powder and cook, stirring, for 1 minute. Add the barbecue sauce, ½ cup water, and the maple syrup. Bring to a boil, reduce the heat to medium-low, and simmer, uncovered, for 10 to 15 minutes, or until thick. Stir in the vinegar. (The sauce will keep in the refrigerator, covered, for up to 1 week.)

3. Build a medium-hot barbecue fire or preheat a gas grill. Remove the pork from the brine, discard the water, and wipe the meat with paper towels to remove the brine. Cut the pork into ¾-inch-thick slices. Place between sheets of plastic wrap and flatten with a small, heavy saucepan or rolling pin to ¼-inch-thick cutlets. Pat the meat dry, season with pepper, and brush with the oil. Grill the pork on the first side, brush with the barbecue sauce, and turn to the second side. Cook, turning and brushing with more sauce, until just cooked through and the surface is lightly caramelized, about 5 minutes total.

4. Toast the rolls lightly on the edge of the grill and spread the cut sides generously with barbecue sauce. Divide the pork among the rolls, top with coleslaw, and replace the tops. Cut in halves and serve.

Root Beer

"Everybody over forty (unless they were born in the Bronx) has pristine and uncomplicated memories of such places: low, orange-painted wooden bunker boxes with sliding-screen customers' windows, strings of yellow bulbs outside, whitewashed tree trunks and trash barrels, white car tires designating proper parking etiquette, plenty of instructional signs on the trees and big frozen mugs of too-cold root beer you could enjoy on picnic tables by a brook or else drink off metal trays with your squeeze in the dark, radio-lit sanctity of your '57 Ford."

—Richard Ford,
Independence Day
(Vintage Books, 1996)

Cheddar

By the time the Pilgrims landed in America, cheesemaking had been a thriving industry in England for some time, and the English village of Cheddar, in Somerset, was producing a cheese that was considered one of the best in the world. The first variety of cheese made by New Englanders, dubbed "Yankee cheese" after the Revolution, was made in the Cheddar style. Cheesemaking was, at first, strictly a cottage industry based at individual farms. By about 1850 it had evolved into a factory-based industry with wide distribution to retail outlets around the region. Every country store kept a big wheel of the sharp, crumbly cheese, and Yankee cheddar began to be known as "store" or "rat" cheese. Today New England cheesemakers, located mainly in Vermont, market their renowned cheddar cheese nation- and worldwide. In some small towns in New England, it is still called by the vernacular "store" or "rat" cheese but is more commonly given the more dignified and accurate designation of cheddar.

The "Eastern" Egg Sandwich

MAKES 4 SERVINGS

This omelet sandwich, usually known as a Western or Denver, appears on New England diner menus too. Since I've added some grated sharp cheddar to the recipe, and since New England is well known for its wonderful aged cheese, I think it now qualifies as an "Eastern" sandwich. It makes a most agreeable little pick-up supper.

> 3 tablespoons butter, plus more for the toast if you like
> 1 large onion, coarsely chopped
> 1 large green bell pepper, chopped
> 1 cup diced smoked ham or Canadian bacon
> 7 eggs
> ¼ teaspoon cayenne pepper
> 1 cup shredded sharp cheddar cheese
> 8 slices sandwich bread, lightly toasted

1. Melt the butter in a large, preferably nonstick, skillet. Add the onion, green pepper, and ham and sauté over medium heat until the vegetables begin to soften and brown lightly around the edges, about 7 minutes.

2. Meanwhile, whisk the eggs with the cayenne and 2 tablespoons of water until blended in a mixing bowl. Pour the eggs into the skillet with the vegetables and stir gently to combine. Cook, stirring almost constantly with a small spatula, until the eggs begin to set, about 3 minutes. Flatten the mixture evenly with the spatula and sprinkle with the cheese. Cover the pan, reduce the heat to low, and cook until the eggs are set and the cheese is melted, 2 to 3 minutes.

3. Divide the egg mixture into quarters. Place each quarter on a piece of toast, top with the remaining toast, cut in half, and serve.

Lamb Souvlaki with Yogurt-Cucumber Sauce

MAKES 4 SERVINGS

Souvlaki are quintessential Greek street food. In New England souvlaki are on the menus of most of the Greek-run family diners and small restaurants that dot the map of the region. Souvlaki (and other fabulous foods) are also one of the reasons to go to a Greek festival such as the annual "Olympiad" held at Bridgeport, Connecticut's Holy Trinity Greek Orthodox Church. The tented church parking lot is transformed into a little corner of Greece. On the dance floor costumed children and adults perform intricate line dances to the strains of Greek music. In a separate tent, the pastry committee sells a dozen varieties of home-baked cookies, while one committee member fries puffs of dough to dip in honey syrup (*loukoumathes*). Men mill about, sipping from small glasses of ouzo or retsina. And all day long at the large food tent, the mouthwatering scent of grilling lamb is tossed into the air. The souvlaki are lemon- and oregano-marinated grilled lamb cubes cooked kabob-style and served in or on large flat pita breads and garnished with a refreshing yogurt-cucumber sauce called *tzatziki*.

For the sauce:

1 cup plain yogurt
½ cucumber, peeled, seeded, and chopped
1 tablespoon chopped fresh mint
1 garlic clove, minced
2 teaspoons fresh lemon juice
¼ teaspoon salt

For the souvlaki:

3 tablespoons fresh lemon juice

2 tablespoons olive oil

½ teaspoon dried oregano, crushed

1 garlic clove, chopped

½ teaspoon salt

¼ teaspoon fresh-ground black pepper

1 pound well-trimmed boneless leg of lamb, cut in 1-inch cubes

4 pita breads

1 large tomato, seeded and chopped

1 small sweet red or white onion, chopped

1. To make the sauce, stir together the yogurt, cucumber, mint, garlic, lemon juice, and salt in a small bowl. If not using immediately, refrigerate for up to 4 hours.

2. To make the souvlaki, stir together the lemon juice, oil, oregano, garlic, salt, and pepper in a medium-sized bowl. Add the lamb, turn to coat completely, and set aside at cool room temperature for 1 hour or refrigerate up to 12 hours.

3. Build a hot charcoal fire or preheat a gas grill. Thread the lamb cubes onto metal skewers and brush with marinade. Grill, turning occasionally, until the meat is richly browned outside and pink within, about 5 minutes. Warm the pita breads on the side of the grill.

4. Remove the meat from the skewers, serve with the bread, and pass the sauce along with the tomato and onion for garnish.

The Fluffernutter

In the early 1920s two World War I veterans, Allen Durkee and Fred Mower, started a company in Lynn, Massachusetts, selling a sugary confection they dubbed "Marshmallow Fluff." Fluff was an immediate hit with Boston housewives, who put it to all sorts of uses, including as a sandwich spread in combination with peanut butter. Long before this sandwich combo was known around the rest of the country, it had become a New England favorite, beloved by kids for its dessertlike qualities and by their parents, who perhaps appreciated the fact that you can make the sandwich without having to be fully awake. In the 1960s, Durkee-Mower gave the creation a name, "The Fluffernutter," and national sales of Fluff took off. Here's the "official recipe," from *The Yummy Book*, a collection of the company's Fluff recipes: "Spread one piece of bread with Fluff. Then spread another with peanut butter. There you have it: a Fluffernutter!"

A Reuben Update

MAKES 4 SERVINGS

New England Jewish delis and Irish pubs traditionally construct their Reuben sand-wiches using corned beef, Swiss cheese, sauerkraut, and Russian dressing, and then they grill the whole thing like a grilled cheese sandwich. Good, but a bit too salty and fat-laden for modern tastes. Here's a contemporary version made on lightly toasted rye bread, with the corned beef heated in just a little butter, the Swiss cheese laid over the warmed meat so it just begins to melt, and crisp shredded lettuce replacing the sauer-kraut. A good deli or pub will make you an updated Reuben—or "Reubenesque"—like this, and serve it with the traditional giant half-sour or dill pickle on the side.

> 1 to 2 tablespoons butter
> ¾ to 1 pound thin-sliced lean corned beef
> 8 slices sour rye bread, very lightly toasted
> About ¾ cup good-quality bottled Russian dressing (see Note)
> 6 to 8 ounces thin-sliced Swiss cheese
> 1½ cups shredded romaine or iceberg lettuce

1. Melt 1 tablespoon of the butter in a large skillet. Sauté the corned beef, a few slices at a time, over medium-high heat, adding more butter if necessary, until the meat is heated through and the edges just begin to frizzle.

2. Spread the cut sides of the lightly toasted bread with Russian dressing. Heap the hot corned beef on the bread and layer with cheese and shredded lettuce. Top with the remaining bread.

3. Cut in half and serve immediately.

Note: To make your own Russian dressing, combine ½ cup mayonnaise, 2 tablespoons ketchup, and 1½ tablespoons sweet pickle relish.

"Dogs" with Greek Sweet Chili Sauce

MAKES 8 SERVINGS

Chili dogs—hot dogs topped with a sweet-and-sour spicy meat sauce—have been a beloved New England specialty for several generations. The sauce, it turns out, probably immigrated from Greece by way of Coney Island (see page 251). The secret ingredient in this version of the chili sauce (and there are many versions) is a little bit of unsweetened chocolate. It's elusive—you can't really taste it—but it adds a flavor dimension to the sweetly spiced concoction that is almost alchemic. This is similar to the meat sauce that also traveled westward, where it gets ladled over spaghetti for the famous Cincinnati Five-Way Chili.

For the sauce:

1 tablespoon olive oil
¾ pound ground lamb
¾ pound ground beef
1 large onion, chopped
2 garlic cloves, minced
½ teaspoon salt, or to taste
½ teaspoon black pepper, or to taste
1 tablespoon chili powder
1 teaspoon unsweetened cocoa powder
1 teaspoon ground cumin
1 teaspoon dried oregano
1 teaspoon paprika
½ teaspoon ground allspice
½ teaspoon cayenne pepper
1 cup tomato sauce
1 cup beef broth
2 tablespoons honey
2 tablespoons red wine vinegar
½ cinnamon stick
1 bay leaf

For the hot dogs:

8 hot dogs
8 soft hot dog buns
Chopped raw sweet onion, optional

1. To make the chili sauce, heat the oil in a large, heavy skillet or Dutch oven over medium-high heat. Add the ground lamb, ground beef, onion, and garlic, sprinkle with the salt and pepper, and cook, stirring to break up clumps, until the meat loses its pink color, about 10 minutes. Add the chili powder, cocoa powder, cumin, oregano, paprika, allspice, and cayenne; cook, stirring, for 3 minutes. Add the tomato sauce, broth, and 1 cup of water and bring to a simmer. Stir in the honey and vinegar and add the cinnamon stick and bay leaf. Reduce the heat to low and simmer, covered, for about 45 minutes to blend the flavors. Uncover and simmer for another 15 minutes or so, or until the mixture is reduced to a light sauce consistency, adding a little more water if necessary to prevent the sauce from sticking. Adjust the seasonings if necessary. Discard the cinnamon stick and bay leaf. If not using immediately, refrigerate for up to 3 days, or the sauce may be frozen.

2. Simmer the hot dogs in water to cover until heated through, or grill on a moderately hot grill. Place the hot dogs in the buns, ladle some sauce over them, sprinkle with chopped onion, if you like, and serve.

Bright Red Hot Dogs

If you haven't grown up with them, the first time you see red hot dogs, you might think they are some kind of scary joke food. Known as "red hots," hot dogs that have been tinted a bright magenta-red hue with harmless vegetable dye, these unusual-looking (but fine-tasting) franks are a familiar fixture all over the state of Maine. Joe Jordan, of Jordan's Meats in Portland, told me the story.

The move to tint the dogs was originally a marketing ploy. It seems that back in 1895, Schonland Brothers, Jordan's parent company, colored their hot dogs red as an attention-getting bid to differentiate them from the competition. The red dogs, which were distributed all over the state, became the common standard, and, even though Jordan's made both colored and uncolored franks, Mainers developed a fondness, even a preference, for the "red hots."

Jordan says that red hot dogs are sold in other states—particularly in Vermont, New York, and Colorado—but more than sixty percent are still bought by Mainers.

Greek Dogs

Gus Charos's father and uncle owned competing hot dog restaurants—George's Coney Island and Nick's Coney Island—on opposite sides of Fall River, Massachusetts. The "Coney Island" designation for a hot dog smothered with a spicy sweet-sour meat sauce seems to be unique to southern Massachusetts and Rhode Island. Gus says that when his father, George, arrived from Greece, he worked at New York's Coney Island boardwalk during the 1920s or 1930s and brought the name with him when he migrated to Fall River and opened his own place.

Everybody had their own formula for the chili sauce, and Gus won't reveal his family's exact recipe. In general, all were made with meat and onions and spicy seasonings (see page 249). Here's how it worked at George's place: Premium-quality Swift's hot dogs were grilled, snuggled in a steamed "finger-roll" bun (as opposed to the New England top-split bun), topped with a ladle of the spicy sauce, and finished with an optional sprinkling of chopped raw onion or a squiggle of mustard.

At some Rhode Island eateries, if you ask for a Coney Island, you might get what they call "wieners," 3-inch lengths of sometimes-red-tinted hot dogs popped in a small bun, and topped with chili (sometimes called "Coney") sauce. According to real-food connoisseurs Jane and Michael Stern, if you want a lot of them, you order "wieners up the arm," referring to the server's technique of lining several dogs up his arm and then applying the desired condiments. Such a wiener establishment may be termed, mysteriously, a "New York system," referring back, probably, to its Coney Island origins.

❚ ❚ ❚ ❚ ❚ ❚ ❚ ❚ ❚

The Best "Hamburg" with The Works

MAKES 4 SERVINGS

Residents of "South County"—the area of eastern Rhode Island that abuts southwestern Massachusetts—still use some unique colloquial food terms. Ground beef is always called "hamburg," and the patties made thereof are "hamburgs." At Louis Lunch in New Haven, Connecticut, where some say the quintessence of the American sandwich was invented (see page 252), the beef patty was (and still is) always served on white bread toast—a practice still common in southern New England luncheonettes. As all good cooks know, the best hamburg depends almost totally on using good meat. Chuck, preferably freshly ground, has just about the perfect fat-to-lean ratio; sirloin and round are too lean and generic "ground beef" is usually too fatty. Use a light hand to shape the patties and a clean grill or hot pan to cook them on, sandwich between toast or rolls (your preference), and personalize with your favorite garnishes.

> 1½ pounds ground chuck (80 to 85 percent lean)
> Salt and fresh-ground black pepper
> 8 slices white bread or 4 soft hamburger buns or Portuguese rolls,
>   lightly toasted and buttered
> Thick tomato slices
> Thin sweet onion slices
> Lettuce leaves
> Optional condiments: ketchup, mustard, mayonnaise

1. Build a medium-hot charcoal fire, preheat a gas grill, or preheat a large, heavy, preferably cast-iron skillet. Divide the meat into 4 portions and shape into patties about 4 inches in diameter. Try not to compact the meat too much. Season the patties with salt and pepper.
2. Grill or pan-fry the patties until they reach the desired degree of doneness, about 5 minutes per side for medium.
3. Serve the hamburgs on the toast or rolls with the tomato, onion, lettuce, and condiments.

Louis' Lunch

Nestled on a side street in New Haven, Connecticut's downtown, tiny Louis' Lunch still has the original turn-of-the-century leaded windows and wooden booths and benches intact. Whether or not the American hamburger originated here, as some historians claim, Louis' Lunch is just about the cutest little hamburger joint you've ever seen. According to the great-grandson of the original owner, Louis Lassen created a thinly sliced steak sandwich and, as a by-product, then went on to make the first hamburger sandwich in the United States. When you go to Louis' today, you can watch them take a ball of genuine ground chuck, hand-flatten it, and broil the burger in one of the original vertical cast-iron cookers. The hamburger is served on white toast made in an antique toaster, with lettuce, tomato, and onion, if requested. But never, *never* ketchup. That's it. And unlike burgers in most restaurants or fast-food joints, the juicy hand-crafted Louis' Lunch patty-on-toast tastes like just about the best hamburger your mom ever made.

Famous New Haven White Clam Pizza

MAKES 4 SERVINGS

This is a reasonable facsimile of the fabulous thin-crusted, charred-edge White Clam Pie served at Pepe's, the storied landmark pizzeria in New Haven, Connecticut (see page 254). Pepe's enormous coal-fired brick ovens are so deep that the pizza bakers have to use peels with six-foot-long handles to retrieve the pies lurking at the back of the oven. Freshly shucked New England clams, like the ones they use at Pepe's, really do make a superior pizza if you can get them, but canned clams are a perfectly acceptable alternative. To compensate for the lack of a brick oven in most home kitchens, I've boosted the flavors on this topping by adding a bit more oregano and a soupçon of hot pepper flakes.

For the dough:

3 cups all-purpose flour
1 teaspoon salt
1 teaspoon sugar
1¼ ounce package quick-rising dry yeast
1 tablespoon olive oil
1 cup very warm (about 120 degrees) water
About 1 tablespoon cornmeal

For the topping:

2 dozen littleneck clams, shucked and chopped (about 1 cup); 1 cup
   chopped clams from the fish market; or 2 6½-ounce cans chopped
   clams; with juices reserved
3 garlic cloves, minced
1 teaspoon dried oregano or 1 tablespoon chopped fresh
¼ teaspoon red pepper flakes
4 tablespoons olive oil
3 tablespoons grated pecorino Romano cheese

1. To make the dough, whisk together the flour, salt, sugar, and yeast in a large bowl. Add the oil and water and mix with a wooden spoon or the paddle of a heavy duty mixer until a soft dough forms, about 5 minutes. Turn the dough out on a lightly floured board and knead for 10 minutes, or knead with a dough hook for 5 minutes, until the dough is smooth and elastic. (Or make the dough in a large-capacity food processor by pulsing together the dry ingredients, adding the liquid through the feed tube, and processing to mix and knead for about 2 minutes.) Place in an oiled large bowl, turn to coat with oil, and set aside in a warm place, covered, until doubled in bulk, about 30 minutes.

2. Sprinkle 2 baking sheets or pizza stones with the cornmeal. Punch the dough down and divide it into 2 balls. Using a rolling pin or your hands, pull and stretch the dough into 2 rounds, ovals, or rectangles, as thin as you can make them, and place on the baking pans.

3. Preheat the oven to 450 degrees.

4. Distribute the clams and a small amount of their juice over the dough. Scatter the garlic, oregano, and red pepper flakes on top, drizzle with the oil, and sprinkle with the cheese.

Connecticut: The Pizza State

Since Connecticut doesn't do much trade in nutmegs these days, I'd like to petition the state legislature to change Connecticut's nickname to "The Pizza State." It was, after all, the city of New Haven that nurtured Frank Pepe, an immigrant from Salerno, near Naples, Italy, who opened the first (many claim) genuine brick-oven pizzeria in the New World in 1925. Trained as a baker, Frank Pepe went to work at a bakery in New Haven and, on his own time, made "tomato pies" (crushed tomatoes and Romano cheese on bread) and sold them door to door. He soon bought his own shop on Wooster Street in New Haven. Since Frank was a mason, too, he proceeded to build his own huge brick oven—9 feet high by 18 feet wide and 6 feet deep—fired it with wood and coal, and started making "apizza" (pronounced like "ah-beets") on its porous fire-brick floor. It was here that white clam pie, "The Great

White," was created—the pizza that some call the best in the world.

After a while, other pizzerias opened on Wooster Street, but pizza remained pretty much the well-kept secret of Italian-American New Havenites, New Yorkers, and a few other East Coast urban dwellers until World War II, when GIs arrived home from Italy having acquired a hunger for the savory pies.

Even though it has now spread into every corner of the country, if not the world, New Haven pizza remains the pizza of record. "As good as New Haven pizza" is the comparison made all over New England. Indeed, until you have tasted a Wooster Street brick oven-baked pizza, with its yeasty-tasting, crisp yet chewy blackened edge crust and its top-notch toppings, you probably shouldn't try to judge.

5. Bake, rotating the baking sheets, until the crusts are crisp and speckled with brown and the topping is glazed, 12 to 15 minutes.

6. Cut into wedges or squares to serve.

Hot Dog Wanderers

The Hot Dog Wanderers is a group dedicated to the search for the perfect hot dog. At least it *was* such a group, for the Fairfield, Connecticut, chapter of the Wanderers reports that they've now found what they were looking for at Rawley's. Rawley's, a lunch counter in Fairfield, Connecticut, since 1946, sells, according to owner-cook Richard "Chico" Bielik, over two-thousand hot dogs and eight-hundred hamburgers per week. Most frequently ordered is Rawley's "works" hot dog, made by first deep-frying a Roessler's one-hundred percent meat dog, then crisping it further on the grill so the skin cracks. Nestled in a toasted roll, layered with sauerkraut, ketchup, mustard, real crumbled bacon, and, optionally, cheese, the "works" dog tastes a lot better than it sounds (or looks). "When we found Rawley's, we stopped wandering," declares Hot Dog Wanderer Bruce Bunch.

Farmers' Market
Mixed-Grain Pizza with Pesto

MAKES 4 SERVINGS

Pizza toppings can be absolutely free-form and creative these days, especially if you start with a good crust. And this is a very good crust—the bread flour provides sturdiness, the semolina adds crispness and chewiness, the whole wheat flour contributes fiber and a nutty flavor, and the cornmeal gives color and a pleasing grittiness. Pesto, whether it's homemade or purchased, makes an excellent pizza topping, to which you can add whatever the market offers. My suggested topping here includes tender, delicately peppery garlic curls or shoots, which are beginning to make an appearance in New England farmers' markets. If you can't find garlic shoots, slender scallions make a fine substitute.

For the dough:

1¼ cups bread flour
½ cup semolina flour or additional bread flour
½ cup whole wheat flour
¼ cup plus 1 tablespoon yellow cornmeal
1 teaspoon salt
1¼ ounce package quick-rising dry yeast
1 cup very warm (about 120 degrees) water
1 tablespoon olive oil

For the topping:

1 cup Rosemary-Mint Pesto (page 296) or store-bought basil pesto
8 or 10 garlic curls or slender scallions, trimmed
6 ounces goat cheese, broken into rough ½-inch chunks
1 cup meaty black olives, pitted and halved
2 to 3 tablespoons fruity olive oil

1. To make the dough, whisk together the bread flour, semolina, whole-wheat flour, ¼ cup of the cornmeal, the salt, and yeast in a large bowl. Add the water and oil and mix with a wooden spoon or the dough hook of a heavy-duty mixer until a dough forms, about 5 minutes. Turn the dough out on a lightly floured board and knead for 10 minutes, or knead with a dough hook for 5 minutes, until the dough is smooth and elastic. (Or make the dough in a large-capacity food processor by pulsing together the dry ingredients, adding the liquid through the feed tube, and processing to mix and knead for about 2 minutes.) Place in an oiled large bowl, turn to coat with oil, and set aside in a warm place, covered, until doubled in bulk, about 30 minutes.

2. Sprinkle 2 baking sheets or pizza stones with the remaining tablespoon of cornmeal. Punch the dough down and divide into 2 balls. Using a rolling pin or your hands, pull and stretch the dough into 2 rough ovals or rectangles and place on the baking pans.

3. Preheat the oven to 400 degrees.

4. Spread each round of dough with a few tablespoons of pesto, arrange the garlic curls and goat cheese on top, scatter the olives over each round, and drizzle with oil. Bake, rotating the baking sheets, until the dough is crisp and golden and the toppings are heated through, 15 to 20 minutes.

5. Cut into wedges or squares and serve.

A Milk Shake by Any Other Name

What the rest of America knows as a milk shake (ice cream, milk, and syrup whipped in a blender until smooth), Rhode Island and South Coast Massachusetts call a "cabinet." And if you want a cabinet made with locally popular sweet coffee syrup, you ask for a "coffee cab." Farther east along the New England coast, the whipped ice cream drink is known as a "frappe" (especially "down the Cape" on Cape Cod) or sometimes a "velvet." In northwestern Massachusetts, it's known as a "frost." At the Massachusetts-based Friendly's restaurants, a huge oversize version of the ice cream concoction was an "awful-awful."

If you ask for a milk shake in New England drive-ins or sandwich shops, you're likely to be served a drink made with milk and flavored syrup but without any ice cream.

Middle Eastern "Pizza"

MAKES 4 SERVINGS

Lamejun is a thin-crusted Middle Eastern open-faced meat pie, similar to pizza but without cheese. At Eastern Lamejun Bakers in Belmont, Massachusetts, a suburb of Boston, the Armenian-American owners sell all kinds of Middle Eastern delicacies—spinach, cheese, and meat turnovers, hummus, tabbouleh, baba gannoujh, lentil pilaf, and olive salad—and *lamejun*, their signature dish. It comes out on big trays, crisp edged, with toppings of well-seasoned chicken, the traditional spiced ground lamb, and now a vegetarian *lamejun*. It's quite easy to re-create this exotic-seeming pie at home using Syrian bread, pita bread, lavash, or refrigerated pizza crust. It makes a wonderful little supper topped with dollops of cooling plain yogurt and served with a salad on the side.

> 1 pound lean ground lamb
> 1 small onion, chopped
> ½ cup chopped fresh parsley
> 1 teaspoon salt
> ¼ teaspoon black pepper
> ¼ teaspoon cayenne pepper
> ½ teaspoon ground allspice
> 4 large or 8 small Syrian or pita breads or lavash or 2 10-ounce tubes
>   refrigerated pizza dough
> 1½ cups chopped seeded tomatoes
> 2 tablespoons olive oil
> About 1 cup plain yogurt

1. Preheat the oven to 425 degrees.
2. Combine the ground lamb, onion, parsley, salt, black pepper, cayenne, and allspice in a bowl. Use your hands to mix well.
3. Spread the flat breads or pizza dough out on 2 baking sheets. Distribute the lamb mixture over the top and spread it almost to the edges with a spatula. Scatter the tomatoes over the top and drizzle with the olive oil.
4. Bake until the meat is browned and the crust is crisp, about 15 minutes.
5. Cut into wedges or rectangles to serve. Pass a bowl of plain yogurt at the table for spooning over the top.

Baker's Beach Melting Pot

John Abdallah, an educator by profession, takes on a new role every summer as owner-operator of Ahab's, the food concession at Baker's Beach in Westport, Massachusetts. A second-generation Lebanese-American whose parents owned a fruit market in Fall River, John's varied beachside menu reads like a veritable New England smorgasbord, with delicious representation by most of the ethnic groups living around South Coast Massachusetts.

Along with such American familiars as hamburgers, hot dogs, tuna rolls, and fries, Middle Eastern specialties are prominently featured, including savory meat-and-spinach Syrian pies (a pita bread type of dough enclosing well-seasoned fillings), baked kibbe (ground meat and bulgur), creamy, lemony chickpea hummus, and a special tabbouleh salad made with a touch of allspice.

The large Portuguese-American population in the area makes the spicy chourico and pepper grinder an absolute menu requisite.

Good old Yankee fare is represented by fish and chips, chowder, and clam cakes (or "fritters"). In South Coast parlance, "fritters" translates to a clam cake made with chopped hard-shell clams nestled in a flour-and-water batter and deep-fried. A sprinkle of malt vinegar on all fried foods is what differentiates locals from summer visitors.

Finally, there's that most unusual local specialty, the chow mein sandwich. What is it? It's Chinese chow mein and crispy chow mein noodles (bought direct from the noodle factory in Fall River) on a soft hamburger bun, with a soupy gravy poured over the top. Since the bun bottom instantly starts to dissolve, knife and fork are most definitely needed for this popular favorite.

SAVORY MEATS

For the early New England colonists, rich meat dishes furnished fortification against the winter elements. Most small farms raised pigs, and so pork—cured, salted, smoked, and fresh— was an important and succulent mainstay of a sometimes-meager diet. A family counted itself fortunate indeed if, on a chill winter day, dinner took the form of a stew made with pork or mutton or beef simmering in a black iron kettle over the fire.

For some of these same climatic reasons, a love of rich meat dishes persists in New England today. We'll do a Wood-Grilled Steak au Poivre with a Vegetable Bouquet (page 269) or Grilled Lamb Chops with Rosemary-Mint Pesto (page 296) in the summer. But in the colder, darker months, we cook up a big pot of Bildner's Fabulous Five-Alarm Chili (page 271), do a succulent Shaker Roast Pork Loin with Cider-Sage Gravy (page 292), or return to a tried-and-true favorite such as Yankee Pot Roast with a Fresh Face (page 264). These days it's apt to be cooked as a celebratory meal for a crowd of appreciative traditionalists.

Delectable Italian classics such as Sons of Italy Osso Buco (page 279) or Fontina-Stuffed Veal Chops DeRosa (page 278) are now part of the New England culinary mainstream, while Polish Yankees contribute Mellow White Eagles Sauerkraut with Pork and Kielbasa (page 284), and Caribbean–New Englanders proudly offer up Avery's Jamaican Jerk Pork (page 286).

Yankee Pot Roast with a Fresh Face

MAKES 6 TO 8 SERVINGS

Every single New England cookbook, including the 1912 edition of Fannie Farmer's *Boston Cooking-School Cook Book*, instructs us about pot roast. This old-fashioned method of slow-braising tougher cuts such as chuck results in meltingly tender, flavorful meat with savory gravy that is perfect winter fare. This recipe updates the concept by cooking the root vegetables separately so they retain their color and texture, and adding a generous shower of herbs to give the pot roast a "fresh face." A big spoonful of "New" New England Cranberry-Apple Salsa (page 478) is a lovely condiment, and Fluffy Mashed Potatoes (page 126) are the perfect gravy-absorbing accompaniment.

1 4-pound piece beef chuck, rolled and tied if necessary
Salt and fresh-ground black pepper
2 tablespoons olive oil
1 large onion, chopped
4 garlic cloves, chopped
2 tablespoons all-purpose flour
2 cups beef broth
1 cup dry red wine
2 bay leaves
1 sprig fresh thyme
6 carrots, peeled and cut in sticks about 2 inches long and ½ inch
    wide
4 parsnips, peeled and cut in ½-inch-thick slices
2 cups frozen pearl onions
¼ cup chopped fresh parsley
3 tablespoons chopped fresh thyme, plus sprigs for garnish

1. Sprinkle the meat generously with salt and pepper on all sides. Heat the oil in a large Dutch oven. Brown the meat over medium-high heat, turning so that all sides are seared, about 10 minutes. Remove to a plate, leaving the drippings in the pan.

2. Add the onion and garlic to the pan and cook, stirring frequently, until they begin to soften, about 4 minutes. Sprinkle with flour and cook, stirring, for 2 minutes. Stir in the broth and wine and bring the sauce to a simmer, stirring. Add the bay leaves and thyme sprig and return the meat and any accumulated juices to the pot. Bring to a boil, reduce the heat to low, and cook, covered, until the meat is tender, about 2 hours. Spoon off the excess fat that has risen to the surface. (The meat can be cooked 2 days ahead and refrigerated, covered. Lift the hardened fat off the surface before reheating.)

3. Cook the carrots in a large saucepan of boiling salted water for 5 minutes. Add the parsnips and pearl onions and continue to cook until all the vegetables are tender, about 10 minutes. Drain the vegetables, saving 1 cup of the cooking water.

4. Remove the pot roast to a carving board. Cut the meat across the grain into slices and arrange on a serving platter.

5. If necessary, stir some of the reserved vegetable cooking water into the gravy to thin it to a smooth, pourable consistency, stir in the parsley and chopped thyme, and heat through.

6. Arrange the cooked vegetables around the meat, spoon the gravy over the top, garnish with thyme sprigs, and serve.

Hungarian Beef Goulash

MAKES 6 TO 8 SERVINGS

This legendary Hungarian goulash, or shepherd's stew, is what I always eat, if possible, when I go to dinner at the Kossuth Club, a Hungarian-American social club in Bridgeport, a Connecticut coastal city not far from where I live. The neighborhood is a lively, rich ethnic brew that includes an Irish pub, a Japanese noodle shop, a ribs place, and a taco stand. Tempting as this smorgasbord is, my loyalty remains with the cook at the Kossuth, where, for a few dollars, one can eat like Hungarian royalty. Try Potato Dumplings (page 453) or Paprika Potatoes (page 131) and serve little dishes of A Trio of Hungarian Salads (page 96) to conjure up a similar Magyar moment.

> 4 tablespoons butter (see Note)
> 2 large onions, chopped
> 1 celery rib, minced
> 2 garlic cloves, finely chopped
> 3 tablespoons sweet Hungarian paprika
> 3 pounds beef rump or round, cut in 1½-inch cubes

Salt and fresh-ground black pepper
1 large tomato, seeded and minced
5 cups beef broth
¼ cup chopped fresh flat-leaf parsley

1. Melt the butter in a large, heavy skillet with a lid or in a Dutch oven. Add the onions, celery, and garlic and cook over medium heat, stirring occasionally, until softened, about 6 minutes. Stir in the paprika and cook, stirring, for 1 minute.
2. Season the beef with salt and pepper. Add it to the pot and cook, stirring, with the onion mixture until the meat is lightly browned on all sides, about 5 minutes. Add the minced tomato and broth and bring to a boil. Reduce the heat to low, and cook, covered, for 1½ to 2 hours, or until the meat is tender. Uncover and cook over medium heat until the liquid is somewhat reduced and thickened, about 20 minutes. (The stew can be made up to 2 days ahead and refrigerated, or it may be frozen.)
3. When ready to serve, heat through and adjust the seasonings. Serve on rimmed plates or in shallow soup bowls, sprinkled with parsley.

Note: For an even more authentically Hungarian result, cook the onions in lard instead of butter.

The Presidential Beef

MAKES 4 TO 6 SERVINGS

You don't have to be entertaining heads of state (see page 268) to appreciate all the stellar qualities of these succulent wine-braised beef roulades filled with a savory New England root vegetable and greens stuffing. One plus is that the dish can—indeed, should—be made at least a day ahead so the roulades can steep in their flavorful braising liquid overnight. Another is that they are the embodiment of two eminently appealing qualities—a sophisticated touch of class and a gutsy earthiness.

2 boneless beef chuck or "chuck eye" steaks (about 1¼ pounds each),
    cut ¾ inch thick
3 cups chopped broccoli rabe
4 tablespoons olive oil
1 cup diced peeled parsnips

1 cup diced peeled orange sweet potatoes
2 garlic cloves, minced
1 tablespoon chopped fresh thyme
1 tablespoon chopped fresh sage
½ cup breadcrumbs
1 egg, lightly beaten
Salt and fresh-ground black pepper
2 cups dry red wine
6 cups veal stock or canned beef broth
1 tablespoon butter
3 large shallots, chopped
2 tablespoons chopped fresh parsley

1. Using a large, sharp knife, slice each steak horizontally to make 2 thinner pieces of meat. If the pieces are more than ¼ inch thick, place between sheets of plastic wrap and pound with a flat meat mallet or the bottom of a small, heavy pan to an even thickness. Cut the meat into 8 pieces, about 5 by 5 inches each. Set aside.
2. Blanch the broccoli rabe in a large saucepan of boiling salted water for about 3 minutes. Drain in a colander and run under cold water to stop the cooking. Squeeze out any remaining moisture and set aside.
3. In a large skillet with a lid or in a Dutch oven, heat 2 tablespoons of the oil. Add the parsnips and sweet potatoes and cook over medium heat, stirring, until the vegetables begin to soften and brown, about 5 minutes. Add the garlic, thyme, and sage and continue to cook, stirring, for 1 minute. Scrape the mixture into a bowl. Set the skillet aside. Add the broccoli rabe to the vegetable mixture, along with the breadcrumbs, egg, ½ teaspoon salt, and ¼ teaspoon pepper, and mix well.
4. Place the meat on a flat work surface and sprinkle the tops lightly with salt and pepper. Place ¼ cup of the stuffing toward the bottom of each square and roll the meat up to enclose the stuffing. Tie each roll with 2 or 3 pieces of butcher's twine. Season the rolls on the outside with salt and pepper.
5. Heat the remaining 2 tablespoons of oil in the skillet. Sauté the beef rolls over medium to medium-high heat until browned on all sides, about 5 minutes. Add 1 cup of the red wine, raise the heat to high, and boil briskly until the liquid is reduced by about half, about 3 minutes. Add the stock or broth and bring to a simmer. Reduce the heat to low and cook, covered, until the beef is tender when pierced with a sharp knife, 45 minutes to 1 hour. Transfer to a deep container so

that the meat is covered with the liquid, and cool in the braising liquid for at least 2 hours at cool room temperature or up to 2 days in the refrigerator.

6. Melt the butter in a large skillet. Add the shallots and cook over medium heat, stirring, for 1 minute. Add the remaining 1 cup of red wine, raise the heat to high, and cook until the liquid is reduced by half, about 3 minutes. Pour off half the beef braising liquid, add it to the wine mixture, and cook, uncovered, over medium heat until the sauce is somewhat reduced and thickened enough to lightly coat a spoon, about 20 minutes. Strain the sauce, if you like, and return it to the pan.

7. Meanwhile, reheat the beef rolls in the remaining original braising liquid, in a medium-sized covered saucepan, over low heat until just heated through, about 15 minutes. Remove the beef rolls from the liquid and cut the strings. If the rolls are intact, slice them into ¾-inch-thick diagonal slices. If not, simply present them whole.

8. Arrange the beef on a warmed serving platter, nap with the wine sauce, sprinkle with parsley, and serve.

Planning the Presidential Menu

When President Bill Clinton was the guest of honor at a fund-raising luncheon in Connecticut, chef William Lopata of the Restaurant at National Hall in Westport discovered that presidential menu design required the tact of a diplomat and the planning skills of a military strategist. Lopata's mission was to create a meal that would be ready the moment the tightly scheduled leader sat down to eat yet could withstand any delays that might occur on his route to the table. The meal had to satisfy the White House's strict guidelines for a luncheon menu of beef, salad, and dessert (chocolate-free due to possible presidential allergic reactions). Oh yes, the chef also had to feed forty additional guests who happened to be paying $10,000 per plate.

Here is the menu, hammered out over a month-long series of communiqués with the White House:

• Salad of Mixed Winter Greens with Pine Nuts and Brioche-Goat Cheese Toasts and Raspberry Vinaigrette

• Pan-Roasted Arctic Char over Truffled Green Beans

• Braised Beef Roulade Stuffed with New England Root Vegetables and Broccoli Rabe with a Shallot Red Wine Jus

• Strawberry and Champagne Sorbets in a Star Cookie Shell

After lunch the president dropped into the kitchen to say thanks to the staff, and "Everyone just dropped their pots on the floor they were so surprised," says chef Lopata. "He must have loved the meal. At these kinds of occasions many people only eat a token amount, but he cleaned his plate."

Wood-Grilled Steak au Poivre with a Vegetable Bouquet

MAKES 4 SERVINGS

It's a bragging point for some hardy New Englanders when they claim to cook on their barbecue grills right through the winter, even when it means chipping ice to pry open the grill cover. Most of us, though, start thinking about grilling in spring, when standing outside begins to feel more like pleasure than pain. But from late spring through about Halloween, we really go at it, grilling anything that ever walked, swam, or was dug up from the earth. In this lovely presentation, prize selections of both meat and vegetables are wood-grilled to a smoky goodness and featured together on one glorious platter. Tender, well-aged, fully marbled beef filets heavily crusted with potent cracked black peppercorns are surrounded by lightly charred sweet bell peppers, mushrooms, and scallions. The cut of choice here is filet mignon, but rib-eye and strip steaks make excellent steak au poivre, too.

4 filet mignon steaks (about 5 ounces each),
    cut 1 inch thick
Salt
3 to 4 teaspoons cracked black peppercorns
1 large yellow crookneck squash, cut
    diagonally in ¼-inch-thick slices
1 large zucchini, cut diagonally in ¼-inch-
    thick slices
1 large red bell pepper, cut in 2-inch strips
16 scallions, root ends trimmed
8 medium-large mushrooms, such as shiitake, trimmed
¼ cup olive oil
2 tablespoons slivered fresh basil
Fresh-ground black pepper

1. Build a hot charcoal fire or preheat a gas grill. Soak hardwood chips such as hickory in water for 30 minutes and throw on the fire shortly before cooking.
2. Season the steaks with salt. Sprinkle with the cracked pepper, patting it evenly onto both sides of the steaks.

3. Place the yellow squash, zucchini, pepper strips, scallions, and mushrooms in a shallow dish. Drizzle with the olive oil, add the basil, and sprinkle with about ¼ teaspoon each of salt and pepper. Toss to coat evenly; then thread the vegetables onto metal skewers (see Note).

Henry's Hibachi Steaks

Today's gas-fired barbecue grills are so convenient, so efficient, so spacious, so mess free, so odorless, so absolutely simple to operate that even those (dare we say females?) disinclined to muck about with the dirty business of starting a fire can be grill queens with the flick of a switch. Why is it, then, that while I may be unable to remember what I grilled last week, I can close my eyes and instantly recall the taste of the charcoal-grilled steaks of my Connecticut childhood?

Barbecued steak was a big deal meal. The word would go out early, and then we'd anticipate it all the summer day. "Steak tonight!" Sometimes, as a special splurge, T-bones or porterhouse steaks would star; more often than not, to feed a hungry family of six, thick chuck steaks would be coated a few hours ahead with Adolph's meat tenderizer. My father's grill of choice was the hibachi, of ancient Japanese design, made of cast iron, with barely eighteen inches across. It sat on tiny feet, so that the fire builder and grill chef had to hunker down to work, stooping over the fire in a primal stance.

Building the fire involved orchestrating a production to rival the staging of a performance by the Boston Pops. While Mother manned the indoor operation, in charge of baking the Idaho potatoes (with sour cream and chives, of course) and making the tossed salad and sliced tomatoes and dessert, Dad directed the outdoor kitchen. First, the hibachi had to be cleared of the last meal's dead (and often soaking wet) charcoal and wire-brushed clean. Then we received our assignments: one to pick up kindling wood—bone-dry sticks of specifically designated size and shape (petroleum lighter fluid was eschewed, if at all possible); one to twist half sheets of newspaper to feed the fire later; one to locate the bag of briquets in the garage. Oops. That bag was almost empty. One to borrow some charcoal from a neighbor. Then we'd be ready for Dad to construct the fire, squatting over the charcoal, gently nursing the flames with our perfect driftwood kindling, patiently fanning the coals until they began to burn down to the required white-ash coating, expertly feeding in the newspaper twists when the fire seemed in danger of dying.

With any luck, three-quarters of an hour later we were ready to cook, usually in two batches for the large group. As a result, the almost unbearably tantalizing grilling smells lasted so long that by the time we sat down to dinner on the porch, it was usually just about dark, and the potatoes might have begun to shrivel and the salad to wilt. But that steak—that steak was, in my memory at least, altogether the char-crustiest on the outside, the pink-juiciest on the inside, and the most fiercely full-of-flavor meat I have ever eaten.

4. Grill the meat, turning once, to the desired degree of doneness, 3 to 4 minutes per side for medium-rare.

5. Meanwhile, grill the skewered vegetables on the cooler edges of the grill, turning once or twice, until softened and the edges are charred, about 5 minutes.

6. Place the meat on a platter, arrange the vegetables around the sides, and serve.

Note: Alternatively, you can cook the vegetables in a wire grilling basket or simply place them directly on the grill surface.

Bildner's Fabulous Five-Alarm Chili

MAKES ABOUT 6 SERVINGS

The folks from Bildner and Sons, an upscale grocery store in the Boston area that once sold fancy prepared foods by the quarter pound, confess that it was actually their chili that was their biggest-selling item. And no wonder. Bildner's produced a fabulous rendition of a quite standard (non-Texas) chili but spiked it with copious quantities of a good quality chili powder and added a bit of masa harina (you can substitute cornmeal) for thickening. This is my interpretation of their formula. Bildner's suggested serving their chili with toppings of grated cheddar or jack cheese, diced red onion, sour cream, and chopped green chiles. Some folks ladle their chili over plain rice, but I prefer Crusty Cornbread (page 451) on the side.

> 1 tablespoon vegetable oil
> 2 pounds lean ground beef
> 2 onions, chopped
> 6 garlic cloves, chopped
> 1 teaspoon salt
> ½ teaspoon black pepper
> 4 tablespoons chili powder
> 2 teaspoons ground cumin
> 1 teaspoon dried oregano
> ½ teaspoon cayenne pepper
> 2 tablespoons masa harina or cornmeal
> 2 cups beef broth

1 28-ounce can plum tomatoes with juice
2 3-ounce cans green chiles, drained and chopped (or more to your taste)
1 large bay leaf
3 cups drained cooked or canned kidney beans
1 tablespoon sugar

1. Heat the oil in a large Dutch oven or soup pot. Add the meat, onions, and garlic, sprinkle with the salt and pepper, and cook, stirring to break up large clumps, until the meat loses its pink color, about 10 minutes. Add the chili powder, cumin, oregano, cayenne, and masa harina and cook, stirring, for 2 minutes.

2. Stir in 1 cup of water along with the broth, tomatoes, chiles, and bay leaf. Bring to a boil, breaking up the tomatoes with the side of a spoon. Reduce the heat to low and simmer, covered, for 30 minutes. Add the beans and sugar and continue to simmer, uncovered, for about 20 minutes, until the flavors are blended and the chili is quite thick.

3. Discard the bay leaf and adjust the seasonings before serving. (The chili can be made 2 days ahead and refrigerated, or it may be frozen.)

Mrs. Aaron's
Sweet and Sour Brisket

MAKES 4 TO 6 SERVINGS

The large and gregarious Aaron clan, part of the substantial Jewish population that came to the Hartford, Connecticut, area, celebrates the holidays by cooking and sharing special meals that feature the entire fascinating array of traditional Jewish foods. The foods, many of them symbolic, provide a vital link to their history. At Hannukah a version of this splendid, meltingly tender braised brisket of beef is always on the table. The braising liquid is finished with lemon juice and brown sugar, which provide a lovely counterpoint to the rich meat. Classic accompaniments are crisp-fried potato latkes (pancakes) or, as Dorothy Aaron Fox suggests, wide egg noodles and a leafy green salad. Pass a plate of Mrs. Dietz's Fruit-and-Nut Filled Cookies (page 572) for dessert.

1 3- to 3½-pound beef brisket, preferably first cut
Salt and fresh-ground black pepper
1 tablespoon vegetable oil
2 large onions, chopped
8 carrots, peeled, 2 finely diced, 6 thinly sliced
3 garlic cloves, minced
1½ cups beef broth
¾ cup dry red wine
2 teaspoons paprika
1 bay leaf
4 tablespoons fresh lemon juice
3 tablespoons brown sugar

1. Trim any large pieces of fat off the meat. Season on both sides with salt and pepper.
2. Preheat the oven to 350 degrees.
3. Heat the oil in a large ovenproof casserole or in a Dutch oven. Add the meat and cook over medium-high heat until browned on both sides, about 10 minutes. Remove to a plate, leaving the drippings in the pan.
4. Add the onions, diced carrots, and garlic to the pan and cook over medium heat, stirring frequently, until the vegetables are softened, about 8 minutes. Return the meat to the pan and add the broth, wine, paprika, bay leaf, and 1 tablespoon each of the lemon juice and brown sugar. Bring to a boil, scraping up any browned bits in the pan. Cover with a lid or aluminum foil.

"Corned" Beef

Corned beef is a brisket or round of beef cured in brine. It has nothing to do with corn. The name derives from the English use of the word *corn* to mean any small particle, such as the grains of salt used to cure the meat. Northern New Englanders depended on preserved meats such as corned beef and salted and smoked pork products to get them through the long winter and spring, and most householders kept a stoneware crock in the basement to fill with salt-brined beef in the fall. Before chemical preservatives began to be used to cure meat, old-fashioned Yankee home-corned beef was a grayish pink color and was often saltier than today's pinkish red corned beef. Some ardent traditionalists still prefer homemade New England "gray-cured" beef.

---

5. Bake until the meat is fork-tender, 2 to 3 hours. Turn the meat 2 or 3 times during the cooking process.

6. Skim off any fat that has risen to the surface. (The recipe can be made a day ahead to this point. Cover and refrigerate; lift off the fat that hardens on the surface.)

7. Bring the degreased juices to a simmer in a large saucepan. Add the sliced carrots and the remaining 2 tablespoons of brown sugar. Return the meat to the pot and cook, covered, over medium-low heat until the carrots are tender, about 20 minutes. Add the remaining 3 tablespoons of lemon juice to the sauce and season to taste with salt and pepper.

8. Cut the meat into thin slices across the grain and serve with the sauce and carrots spooned over the top.

Classic New England Boiled Dinner with Horseradish Cream

MAKES 6 GENEROUS SERVINGS,
WITH SOME LEFTOVERS

Boiled Dinner for 100 People

"50 lbs. meat (corned beef), 3 lbs. salt pork, 18 cabbages (about 4 pounds each), 4 pecks potatoes, 2 pecks carrots, 4 pecks turnips, 2 bags onions, 2 pecks beets (cooked separately), 1 quart cream, 1 gallon milk, 4 lbs. butter, 15 loaves bread, 35 pies, 3 lbs. coffee, tea. (To make the boiled dinner real good add a cup and a half of molasses to the large kettle of vegetables.)"

—*The Maine Rebekahs Cookbook*, 1939 edition

The traditional New England boiled dinner with all the trimmings is one of those hearty and soul-satisfying, yet celebratory and festive meals that I think is perfect for a large informal gathering. Unique to the Yankee version of boiled dinner (as opposed to Irish corned beef and cabbage, for example) are the beets and parsnips, which are both strictly required. The horseradish-spiked sour cream sauce, while not particularly traditional, provides a welcome piquant counterpoint to the plain meat and vegetables. With boiled dinner leftovers you've got the makings for Red Flannel Hash (page 188), another regional delicacy.

For the sauce:

¾ cup regular or lowfat sour cream
¼ cup prepared horseradish
2 teaspoons grainy mustard
1 tablespoon chopped fresh parsley

For the corned beef and vegetables:

1 5- to 6-pound corned beef brisket or round, gray-cured or regular
2 bay leaves
12 whole black peppercorns
2 whole cloves
1 teaspoon mustard seeds, optional
12 medium whole beets (1½ to 2 pounds)
20 small red-skinned new potatoes (about 2½ pounds), cut in half if
    larger
10 large carrots, peeled and cut in 3- to 4-inch lengths
12 small white boiling onions, peeled
6 parsnips, peeled and cut in 3-inch lengths
1 medium head green cabbage, cut in about 16 wedges without
    removing entire core
Salt and fresh-ground black pepper

1. To make the sauce, stir together the sour cream, horseradish, and mustard. Cover and refrigerate up to 8 hours. Return to room temperature and sprinkle with parsley before serving.
2. Place the corned beef in a very large pot, cover with cold water, and bring to a boil. Skim off the foam that rises to the surface for the first few minutes. Add the bay leaves, peppercorns, cloves, and mustard seeds, if you are using. Reduce the heat to low and simmer, covered, for 2 to 3 hours, until a fork inserted into the meat comes out easily.
3. Meanwhile, cook the beets in a pot of boiling salted water until tender, about 30 minutes. Drain and, when cool enough to handle, peel the beets. Leave whole if small, cut in half or quarter if large. Set aside. (Reheat in a microwave before serving.)
4. About 20 minutes before the corned beef is done, skim off and discard any excess fat from the cooking liquid. Add the potatoes, carrots, onions, and parsnips and simmer, covered, until all the vegetables are tender, about 20 minutes. (See Note.)

5. Cook the cabbage wedges in a separate saucepan in boiling salted water to cover until tender, about 10 minutes. Drain.

6. Lift the meat out of the liquid, carve crosswise into thin slices, and arrange in the center of a large platter. Arrange the vegetables around the sides or on a separate platter, and spoon a bit of the hot liquid over them. Sprinkle the vegetables with salt and pepper to taste.

7. Pass the horseradish cream at the table with the boiled dinner.

Note: If your kettle is not large enough to accommodate all the vegetables, simply cook them in a separate saucepan of boiling salted water.

Corned Beef Night

"Grandpa was a fine figure of a man, with a taste for New England boiled dinners (corned beef and cabbage) that smelled up the house and sometimes the neighborhood. Dinner was at noon. When Grandpa came home, the hired girl staggered into the dining room with an enormous ironstone platter which she placed before him.

"On the platter was the corned beef flanked by cabbage. Grandmother had boiled them together for hours. On the same platter were sliced turnips, whole parsnips, onions, baby carrots, and boiled potatoes. Nearby was a dish of buttered beets. In the center of the table…were saucers of mustard pickle and horseradish. There was also a plate of fresh-baked bread, cut in warm, thick slices.

"Grandpa was a good provider who expected his wife to set a good table, and encouraged her by eating everything in sight. Grandmother wore her fingers to the bone, but I think she liked it. At any rate she thanked God for His abundance and, uncomplaining, cooked His bounty."

—Eleanor Early, *New England Cookbook*
(Random House, 1954)

North End Veal Piccata

MAKES 4 SERVINGS

I was in college the first time I tasted veal piccata, in a tiny, bustling Boston North End trattoria, and I experienced one of those taste jolts that amounts to a culinary epiphany. I'm not sure I'd ever eaten veal before, certainly not veal that had been pounded into thin, delicate, boneless scallops, sautéed to golden perfection, and then napped with such a beautifully balanced butter-rich wine-lemon sauce. It's been one of my favorite dishes ever since—especially after I discovered how absolutely simple veal piccata is to make at home.

> 1 pound veal scallops
> Salt and fresh-ground black pepper
> ¼ cup all-purpose flour
> 3 tablespoons unsalted butter
> 2 tablespoons light olive oil
> 3 tablespoons minced shallots
> 1½ cups dry white wine
> 2 tablespoons fresh lemon juice
> 1 teaspoon grated lemon zest
> 6 lemon slices, cut in half crosswise
> 2 tablespoons chopped fresh parsley, plus sprigs for garnish

1. If the veal is more than ¼ inch thick, place between sheets of plastic wrap and pound with a flat mallet or the bottom of a small, heavy pan to flatten. Dry well on paper towels. Sprinkle both sides of the scallops with salt and pepper and dredge lightly in the flour, shaking off the excess.
2. Heat the butter and oil in a large skillet. Sauté the meat in 2 batches over medium to medium-high heat until nicely browned on both sides and cooked through, about 4 minutes. Remove with tongs to a plate, leaving the drippings in the pan.
3. Add the shallots to the skillet and cook, stirring, for 1 minute. Add the wine and bring to a boil, scraping up any browned bits in the bottom of the pan. Cook briskly until the liquid is reduced by one-third, 3 to 5 minutes. Stir in the lemon juice, lemon zest, and lemon slices. Simmer for 2 minutes.
4. Return the veal and any accumulated juices to the sauce, stir in the parsley, and simmer to heat through before serving the veal, garnished with parsley sprigs.

Fontina-Stuffed Veal Chops DeRosa

MAKES 4 SERVINGS

Saugatuck, Connecticut, is home to DeRosa's, one of those consistently excellent family-run Italian restaurants that retains its rabidly loyal following year after year. The DeRosa brothers were among the first Connecticut restaurateurs to search out pale, milk-fed, tender veal back when this meat was a rare commodity. This veal chop preparation, stuffed with mellow fontina cheese, with its rich, winy sauce, is my adaptation of one of the perennial house specialties at DeRosa's. It's easy to create in the home kitchen—and perfect when you want an impressive special treat meal. Serve the veal with a nest of buttered thin strand pasta, Broiled Asparagus with Asiago (page 110), and Chocolate Bread and Butter Pudding (page 515) to finish.

> 4 loin veal chops (9 to 12 ounces each) (see Note)
> 4 ounces sliced fontina cheese
> Salt and fresh-ground black pepper
> 2 tablespoons olive oil
> 2 tablespoons butter
> 3 cups sliced wild or domestic mushrooms (6 ounces)
> ½ cup finely diced prosciutto (about 2 ounces)
> 2 garlic cloves, minced
> 1 cup dry white wine
> 1 cup chicken broth
> ½ cup Marsala wine
> ½ cup heavy cream
> 2 tablespoons chopped fresh sage, plus sprigs for garnish

1. Cut a deep 1½-inch-wide slit in the side of each chop and stuff the cheese deep into each cavity. Season the chops on both sides with salt and pepper.

2. Heat the oil and 1 tablespoon of the butter in a very large skillet. Add the chops and cook over medium heat, turning once, until golden brown on both sides and just barely cooked through, about 15 minutes. (Do not overcook, or the meat will dry out.) Remove to a platter, leaving the drippings in the pan.

3. Add the remaining tablespoon of butter to the skillet. Add the mushrooms, prosciutto, and garlic and cook, stirring frequently, until the mushrooms wilt and begin to brown, 3 to 5 minutes. Add the wine and broth and bring to a boil, stirring up any browned bits in the bottom of the pan. Boil briskly until the sauce is reduced by about half, about 5 minutes. Add the Marsala and cream and simmer until slightly reduced, 2 to 3 minutes. (The recipe can be made 1 to 2 hours ahead to this point, covered, and set aside at cool room temperature.)

4. Return the veal chops and any accumulated juices to the sauce, add the sage, and simmer until the meat is heated through, 3 to 5 minutes. Taste and adjust the seasonings in the sauce if necessary.

5. Serve the chops with the sauce spooned over, garnished with the sage sprigs.

Note: Veal chops sometimes weigh as little as 8 or 9 ounces but often as much as 12 ounces. A good deal of the weight, however, is comprised of bone.

A Winemaking Brotherhood

On a side street in an old South Norwalk, Connecticut, neighborhood, a dozen men regularly gather for lunch. At a makeshift table in an unheated room, they eat a meal of homemade sausage and pasta, smoked meats, fresh bread, cheese, and cannoli. What brings the men together is their common fascination with making their own wine—and their commitment to carrying on a tradition begun two or three generations earlier by their families in the same neighborhood. Peter Cocchia, who buys the grapes and leads the two-month-long operation, says, "It's definitely not about saving money. It's the whole process. The friendship. The loyalty. That's what this is about."

Sons of Italy Osso Buco

MAKES 4 TO 6 SERVINGS

The Nisticos are an old Westport, Connecticut, family. Not "old" by original Yankee settler standards, of course, but by virtue of having arrived early in the wave of immigration to Saugatuck, Westport's "Little Italy," old by Yankee-Italian standards. By the time I was growing up in the area in the 1950s, the Nisticos' Arrow Restaurant was a venerable institution, and it was there that I had my first taste of many Italian specialties, including their meltingly tender osso buco (braised veal shanks), out of the centers of which I scooped my first transcendent taste of rich, unctuous marrow. This recipe, adapted from the Saugatuck *Sons of Italy Cookbook*, is perfect dinner party fare. Serve it with Creamy Polenta (page 214) or Fluffy Mashed Potatoes (page 126), a mesclun salad, and perhaps Caramelized Pears with Honeyed Ice Cream (page 524) for a fine finish.

For the veal:

8 meaty veal shank slices, cut about 3 inches thick
Salt and fresh-ground black pepper
2 tablespoons olive oil
1 cup chopped onion
½ cup minced carrots
½ cup minced celery
2 garlic cloves, minced
1 cup dry white wine
2 cups chicken broth
1 cup chopped fresh or canned plum tomatoes
1 bay leaf

For the gremolata:

3 tablespoons chopped fresh flat-leaf parsley
2 large garlic cloves, minced
2 teaspoons grated lemon zest
¼ teaspoon salt
¼ teaspoon fresh-ground black pepper

1. To prepare the veal, dry on paper towels if necessary, and season on all sides with salt and pepper. Heat the oil in a very large skillet with a lid or in a Dutch oven. Add the meat and cook over medium-high heat, in batches if necessary, until well browned on all sides, about 10 minutes. Remove to a plate, leaving the drippings in the pan.
2. Add the onion, carrots, celery, and garlic to the pan and cook, stirring frequently, until the onion is softened, about 5 minutes.
3. Add the wine, broth, tomatoes, and bay leaf and bring to a boil. Return the meat and any accumulated juices to the pot, reduce the heat to low, and simmer, covered, turning the shanks once or twice, until the meat is tender and begins to pull away from the bone, about 2 hours. (The osso buco can be made a day ahead and refrigerated. Lift off and discard any fat that congeals on the surface before reheating.)

4. To make the gremolata, stir together the parsley, garlic, lemon zest, salt, and pepper in a small dish.

5. Remove the meat to a warm serving platter. Spoon off and discard the excess fat from the top of the braising liquid. Pour the sauce over the shanks, sprinkle with the gremolata, and serve.

Vermont Smokehouses

Among the Green Mountain state's dozen or more smokehouses, Harrington's of Vermont stands out as the largest and perhaps the longest-running operation. Founded in 1873, the company has earned a reputation in New England—and now around the country—for its high-quality smoked meats and poultry. The smokemaster explains the process. "First the meat is cured with a brine solution of salt and a sweetener that can be maple syrup, maple sugar, or corn sweetener. Then the cuts are transferred to rooms that are really like giant steam-heated ovens, which fully cook the meat as well as smoke it. Ground corn cobs or maple sawdust is set afire to produce the smoke, which is pumped into the smoking chamber with a huge bellows that resembles an upside-down church organ. The cooking/smoking process takes 12 to 14 hours for Harrington's signature spiral-cut hams, about 9 hours for bacon, and about 7½ hours for turkey breasts." In addition to the aforementioned products, the company smokes pork, whole turkeys, chickens, ducks, and pheasants.

My Own Favorite
Glazed Mixed-Meat Loaf

MAKES 6 TO 8 SERVINGS

To my mind, a good meatloaf should be juicy but not crumbly, crusty but not dry, flavorful but not too spicy, and comforting but not boring. This rather classic yet full-of-flavor recipe embodies all these qualities. The secret ingredient is the yogurt, which adds a hint of tanginess to the rich meat flavor. The meat mixture can be baked either in a free-form loaf (giving it a bit more crustiness) or in a loaf pan (making it slightly juicier), so go with your own predilection here. The jelly-horseradish glaze adds a lovely caramelized sheen to whichever shape you choose. My favorite accompaniments are big, floury baked potatoes filled with snipped chives and Ivy League Beets with Orange Sauce (page 112).

> 2 pounds "meatloaf mix" (equal parts of ground beef, veal, and pork)
> 1 cup chopped onion
> 1 cup rolled oats or fresh breadcrumbs
> 1 cup tomato sauce or tomato juice
> ½ cup plain yogurt
> ½ cup chopped fresh parsley
> 2 tablespoons Dijon mustard
> 1½ teaspoons dried thyme
> 1 teaspoon salt
> ½ teaspoon fresh-ground black pepper
> 1 egg
> 2 tablespoons apple or red currant jelly
> 2 teaspoons prepared horseradish

1. Preheat the oven to 350 degrees.
2. Combine the ground meat, onion, rolled oats or crumbs, tomato sauce, yogurt, parsley, mustard, thyme, salt, pepper, and egg in a large mixing bowl. Use your clean hands to work the mixture together gently but thoroughly until it is well blended. Shape the mixture into an oval loaf about 10 inches long and 2 inches high and place in a shallow baking pan or rimmed cookie sheet. (Alternatively, you can pack the meat mixture into a 9-by-5-inch loaf pan.)
3. Bake for 45 minutes.
4. Meanwhile, whisk the jelly with the horseradish in a small bowl. (It doesn't matter if the mixture is not completely smooth.) Brush the top of the meatloaf with the mixture and continue to cook for 20 to 30 minutes, or until the juices run clear and a meat thermometer inserted in the center registers 160 degrees. Pour off any excess fat that has accumulated in the pan.
5. Let the meatloaf stand for 10 minutes before slicing.

Mamie's Little Meatballs with Applesauce-Cider Gravy

MAKES 4 SERVINGS

My mother-in-law, Mamie, who lived all her life in southern Connecticut, loved to try new recipes, and she took particular pleasure in dishes with surprising or unexpected ingredients. If a recipe passed her initial run-through, she often handed it along to me. These savory-sweet little meatballs made with applesauce and crushed cornflakes are one of her real winners. I made them for years, then had almost forgotten about the recipe when I was excited to rediscover it in Mamie's files. Spoon the meatballs and sauce over hot cooked egg noodles, and serve Mixed Greens with My Favorite Vinaigrette (page 79) on the side for a tasty supper.

1 pound "meatloaf mix" (equal parts of ground beef, veal, and pork)
½ cup crushed cornflake crumbs
¾ cup unsweetened applesauce
½ cup minced onion
1 garlic clove, minced
1 egg
1½ teaspoons dried thyme
½ teaspoon salt
½ teaspoon fresh-ground black pepper
1 10¾-ounce can condensed tomato soup
1 tablespoon cider vinegar

1. Combine the meat, crumbs, ½ cup of the applesauce, the onion, garlic, egg, 1 teaspoon of the thyme, and the salt and pepper in a large bowl. Use your clean hands to mix gently but thoroughly. Shape the mixture into about 30 1-inch meatballs.
2. Whisk together the soup, the remaining ¼ cup applesauce, and remaining ½ teaspoon thyme in a very large skillet with a lid or in a Dutch oven. Whisk in 1 cup of water. Bring the sauce mixture to a simmer.
3. Drop the meatballs into the sauce. Return to a simmer, cover, and cook over medium-low heat until the meatballs are no longer pink inside, about 30 minutes.
4. Skim off and discard any excess fat that has risen to the surface of the sauce. Stir in the vinegar and serve.

Mellow
White Eagles Sauerkraut
with Pork and Kielbasa

MAKES 6 TO 8 SERVINGS

In Norwalk, Connecticut, in the 1940s, '50s, and '60s, the White Eagles Hall was the center of Polish-American social life. It was in this simple, old pine-paneled hall that local families gathered for weddings, funerals, harvest festivals, and summer picnics, creating, as they marked these ritual occasions, indelible memories. Kielbasa, the garlicky smoked Polish sausage, was invariably on the menu, frequently cooked in combination with sauerkraut. Fresh sauerkraut, the kind packed in plastic bags in the refrigerator section, is preferable here, but canned will do just fine, too. This is an adaptation of my mother-in-law's peerless rendition of the dish, which she made even more succulent by the addition of pork chops and a bit sweeter with chopped apple. Classic accompaniments are boiled parsley red-skinned potatoes, fresh seeded rye bread, and beer. Pass a pot of Polish mustard at the table.

Shaker Meal Times

Eldress Bertha Lindsay (1897–1990), of the Canterbury, New Hampshire, Shaker Village, describes their mealtimes:

"During the twentieth century, the main kitchen was staffed with a First cook who planned the menus and prepared the main dishes, a Second cook who assisted and prepared side dishes, a Messer who cooked for the sick and elderly with meal restrictions, two cooks in the bakery room, one making breads and the other making desserts, and a couple of young girls as servers.

"The main dining room... had five long trestle tables, each seating twelve, extending the length of the room. An additional table for twelve was set off in the corner near the wood stove for the elderly members. Meals were served family-style, with men and women eating in separate shifts, and you were allowed to eat as much as you liked as long as you 'Shaker[ed] your plate,' taking only what you could eat and leaving nothing to waste."

—Eldress Bertha Lindsay, *Seasoned with Grace* (Countryman Press, 1987)

---

1 tablespoon vegetable oil
6 thin-cut pork loin or shoulder chops
Fresh-ground black pepper
1 pound kielbasa, cut in 1-inch-thick slices
1 large onion, chopped
1 apple, peeled, cored, and chopped
2 pounds sauerkraut, preferably fresh
1 bay leaf
1 teaspoon dried thyme
½ teaspoon celery seeds
¼ teaspoon caraway seeds

1. Heat the oil in a large skillet with a lid or in a Dutch oven. Season the pork chops with pepper and cook the chops and the kielbasa over medium heat, in 2 batches if necessary, until browned on all sides, about 10 minutes. Remove to a plate, leaving the drippings in the pan.

2. Add the onion and apple to the pan drippings and cook, stirring frequently, until softened, about 6 minutes.

3. Drain the sauerkraut in a colander, rinse under warm running water, and squeeze dry. Add the sauerkraut to the pot, along with the bay leaf, thyme, celery seeds, caraway seeds, and 2 cups of water. Return the meat to the pot, nestling it into the sauerkraut. Bring the liquid to a boil, reduce the heat to low, and cook, covered, stirring occasionally, until the meat is tender when pierced with a fork, 45 minutes to 1 hour.

4. Season with plenty of fresh-ground black pepper and serve. (The dish should not need salt, as the sauerkraut is salty.)

Avery's Jamaican Jerk Pork

MAKES 4 SERVINGS

Avery Stephenson, owner and chief cook at Avery's Little Jamaican Kitchen in South Norwalk, Connecticut, serves her delectable jerk pork with coconut-enriched West Indian Peas 'n Rice (page 162), fried plantains, and a cooling shredded lettuce salad. The irresistible smell of her good cooking wafts out of the small storefront restaurant into the street, so that by noon a line for tables or take-out orders often snakes out the door and way down the sidewalk. For a real Jamaican-American feast, precede the dinner with Caribbean Salt Cod Fritters (page 28) and finish with Corina's Sweet Potato Pie (page 612).

3 pounds pork shoulder chops
2 to 4 teaspoons jerk seasoning (see Note)
1 celery rib, finely chopped
1 tablespoon vegetable oil
1 tablespoon grated fresh ginger
1 teaspoon salt, or to taste

1. Trim the meat off the bone, removing the excess fat, and cut into 2-inch cubes. Toss the meat with the jerk seasoning, celery, oil, ginger, and salt in a roasting pan, using your hands to rub the seasonings in well. Set aside in a cool place for at least 30 minutes or up to 3 hours.
2. Preheat the oven to 350 degrees.
3. Pour ½ inch of water over the meat in the pan. Place the pan in the oven and roast the meat, uncovered, stirring occasionally and adding more water if all the liquid cooks away, until the meat is browned, tender, and cooked through, about 1 hour.
4. Remove the meat to a platter. Place the pan on top of the stove, add 1 cup of water, and bring to a boil over high heat, scraping up the browned bits that cling to the bottom of the pan. Simmer for a few minutes to reduce and thicken slightly. Pour the juices over the pork and season with additional salt if necessary.

Note: There are many excellent brands of jerk seasoning on the market now. Avery uses a brand that I love—Walker's Wood—imported from Jamaica. Before you use purchased jerk seasoning, taste a little and adjust the amount according to your heat preference. To make your own, combine ¼ cup chopped scallions with 1 teaspoon each of dried thyme and curry powder, ½ teaspoon each of ground allspice, cayenne, sugar, and salt, and ¼ teaspoon each of ground cinnamon and cloves in a food processor. Process to make a paste. Store it in the refrigerator for up to 1 month.

Portuguese Pork with Clams

MAKES 4 SERVINGS

This is a most unusual and succulent dish that I have eaten in several Portuguese restaurants in New England, including Omanel's in Bridgeport, Connecticut, a coastal city with a substantial number of fairly recent Portuguese immigrants. This pork and clam combination may sound somewhat unlikely, but in fact pork in many forms, whether bacon, salt pork, or ham, enriches a fair number of shellfish preparations, so why not turn the tables and have the briny clams be the embellishment to the meat? Accompany this dish as the Portuguese do, with Portuguese Potatoes with Cilantro (page 132) scattered with some black olives, and finish with eggy Portuguese-Style Caramel Flan (page 509).

For the pork:

1½ pounds boneless pork chops or pork loin, cut in 1-inch cubes
1 onion, chopped
2 garlic cloves, minced
2 teaspoons paprika
1 teaspoon salt
2 bay leaves, broken in half
½ cup dry white wine

For the stew:

1 teaspoon fresh-ground black pepper, plus more to taste
¼ cup olive oil
1 onion, chopped
1 small green bell pepper, chopped
1 celery rib, chopped
2 garlic cloves, minced
1 cup dry white wine
2 plum tomatoes, seeded and chopped
24 small hard-shell clams, scrubbed
2 tablespoons chopped fresh cilantro
Salt

1. To marinate the pork, toss the meat with the onion, garlic, paprika, salt, and bay leaves in a large bowl, rubbing the seasoning into the meat. Add the wine, toss to combine, and set aside to marinate in the refrigerator for at least 8 hours or overnight.
2. Drain the pork, discarding the marinade but reserving the bay leaves. Pat the meat dry on paper towels.
3. To make the stew, season the meat on all sides with the black pepper. Heat the oil in a large skillet. Add the reserved bay leaves and cook over medium heat, turning once or twice with tongs, until they brown. (This releases their flavor.) Remove with tongs and discard the pieces. Add the meat to the pan and cook over medium-high heat until browned on all sides, about 8 minutes. Remove to a plate, leaving the drippings in the pan.
4. Add the onion, green pepper, celery, and garlic and cook, stirring frequently, until the vegetables begin to soften and brown lightly, about 6 minutes. Add the wine and tomatoes and bring to a boil, stirring up any browned bits in the bottom of the pan. Reduce the heat and simmer, uncovered, over medium to medium-low heat until slightly reduced, about 10 minutes. Return the meat to the pan. (The stew can be made several hours ahead to this point. Hold at cool room temperature or refrigerate. Reheat before proceeding.)
5. Add the clams to the simmering stew, cover, and cook over medium heat until the shells open, 5 to 10 minutes. Stir in the cilantro, season with additional salt and pepper to taste, and serve.

Danville Dines

The tiny town of Danville, way up in northeastern Vermont, lays claim to staging the oldest deer-season game supper among dozens of others in the state. It has been held annually since 1921. Other suppers may be more exotic (see page 302), or plainer (in Walden you get deer—boiled, fried, or grilled), but Danville's game pie and samplings of moose, bear, venison, and beaver in their own gravy with sides of garlicky green beans and mashed potatoes is not only the longest-running but also is one of the best-tasting game feasts going. The dessert is always homemade pie.

Maple-Mustard Pork Medallions on Mashed "Sweets"

MAKES 4 SERVINGS

Until relatively recently, lean pork tenderloin has nestled, for the most part unobserved and underappreciated, in the center of a pork loin roast or chop. Now that tenderloins are being separated from the rest of the loin and sold on their own, we have the pleasure of discovering all sorts of new ways to cook and flavor this exquisitely tender and quick-cooking boneless cut of meat. Here it is cut into medallions, seasoned with the smoky essence of pure Vermont maple syrup, and served atop a bed of orange-spiked mashed sweet potatoes.

For the sweet potatoes:

2 pounds sweet potatoes, peeled and cut in 2- to 3-inch chunks
½ cup orange juice, plus 1 to 2 tablespoons more if necessary
2 tablespoons butter
2 teaspoons brown sugar
¼ teaspoon ground mace or nutmeg
Salt and fresh-ground black pepper

For the pork:

1 pound pork tenderloin, trimmed well, cut crosswise into ¾-inch-
thick slices

½ teaspoon salt

½ teaspoon fresh-ground black pepper

2 tablespoons olive oil

½ cup chopped onion

1¼ cups chicken broth

3 tablespoons pure maple syrup

1 tablespoon cider vinegar

1 tablespoon Dijon mustard

1. Cook the sweet potatoes in a pot of boiling salted water to cover until tender, about 20 minutes.

2. Drain the potatoes, return them to the saucepan, and add ½ cup orange juice, the butter, brown sugar, and mace or nutmeg. Mash with a potato masher or large fork, adding more juice if necessary to make a slightly textured puree. Season with salt and pepper to taste. (The sweet potatoes can be made up to 4 hours ahead and transferred to a glass baking dish. When ready to serve, cover with foil and reheat in a 350-degree oven for 20 minutes or cover with plastic wrap and reheat in a microwave for about 8 minutes.)

3. Meanwhile, season the meat with the salt and pepper. Heat the oil in a large skillet. Cook the meat over medium heat until browned on both sides and no longer pink within, about 4 minutes per side. Remove to a platter.

4. Add the onion to the pan and cook until it begins to soften, about 4 minutes. Add the broth, bring to a boil, and cook until it is somewhat reduced, 3 to 4 minutes. Whisk in the maple syrup, vinegar, and mustard. Return the meat and any accumulated juices to the pan and simmer until heated through, about 1 minute.

5. Spoon the sweet potatoes onto a platter or plates and serve the meat and sauce spooned over the top.

Spenser, Hungry Private Eye

Robert B. Parker's Spenser detective novels are set in and around modern-day Boston, in a territory that runs from the city's well-heeled suburbs to its gritty urban neighborhoods. Spenser is a man obsessed—not only with solving crimes using what he views as honorable methods in this often harsh modern world, but also with cooking and eating good food. No matter what plot development unfolds each day, in his spare moments Spenser returns to mulling over his last meal or planning his next.

In *Double Deuce* (Putnam, 1992), Spenser says, "I got a pork tenderloin out and brushed it with honey and sprinkled it with rosemary and put it in the oven. While it roasted I mixed up some corn flour biscuits and let them sit while I tossed a salad of white beans and peppers and doused it with some olive oil and cilantro. When the pork was done I took it out and let it rest while I baked the biscuits. I put some boysenberry jam out to have with the biscuits and sat down to eat."

❖ ❖ ❖ ❖ ❖ ❖ ❖ ❖ ❖

Roast Pork Tenderloin with Spicy Orange Relish

MAKES 6 SERVINGS

Pork tenderloins are often sold two to a vacuum-sealed package. Typically, a single tenderloin is about 12 inches long and weighs about 12 ounces—so the double pack is just about the perfect amount of meat to serve six. I like this cooking method for tenderloins—first a quick browning on top of the stove to seal in juices and create a rich, flavorful crust, and then a brief stay in the oven to roast to juicy tenderness. Just be sure not to overcook the pork, or it will be dry. The spicy orange relish has a refreshing zing, but the pork is also delicious topped with Quick Apple-Tomato Chutney (page 475) or "New" New England Cranberry-Apple Salsa (page 478).

For the tenderloin:

2 pork tenderloins (about 12 ounces each)
Salt and fresh-ground black pepper
2 tablespoons olive oil

For the relish:

2 large oranges, peeled, seeded, and diced
1¼ cups chopped red onions
¼ cup fresh lime juice
1 tablespoon olive oil
1 to 3 teaspoons minced fresh chile pepper
2 teaspoons chili powder
2 teaspoons ground cumin
¼ teaspoon salt
¼ cup chopped fresh cilantro

1. Preheat the oven to 475 degrees.
2. Season the meat on all sides with salt and pepper.
3. Heat the oil in a large skillet over medium-high heat. When the oil is hot but not smoking, add the tenderloins and cook until nicely browned on all sides, about 5 minutes total. Transfer the meat to a shallow roasting pan.
4. Roast the pork in the preheated oven until a meat thermometer registers 150 degrees in the thickest part, about 20 minutes. (If you cut into the pork, you should see just a trace of pink at the center.) Remove to a platter and let the pork rest for about 10 minutes before slicing.
5. To make the relish, stir together in a medium-sized bowl the oranges, onions, lime juice, oil, chile pepper, chili powder, cumin, and salt. Stir in the cilantro.
6. Cut the meat into 1-inch-thick slices and serve topped with the relish.

Shaker Roast Pork Loin with Cider-Sage Gravy

MAKES 6 SERVINGS

Listening to the gentle sputter of meat as it roasts and inhaling the mouthwatering aroma that drifts through the house somehow makes one feel rich in all things good. The New England Shakers were exemplars of goodness too, applying their philosophy of truth, simplicity, and high standards of excellence to all aspects of life lived in their self-sustaining communities. This recipe is based on one from the Shaker village in Hancock, Massachusetts, where apple orchards thrived and gardens proliferated with herbs both medicinal and culinary. This roast makes for a very special dinner, especially when accompanied by Fluffy Mashed Potatoes (page 126), steamed baby carrots, tiny green beans, and Nutmeg-Dusted Rich Custard Pie (page 594).

> 2 tablespoons coarse-grained mustard
> 2 tablespoons olive oil
> 3 tablespoons chopped fresh sage or 3½ teaspoons crumbled dried
> 1 bone-in loin of pork (about 5 pounds) (see Note)
> 1 to 2 tablespoons butter
> 2 tablespoons all-purpose flour
> 1½ cups apple cider or apple juice
> 1 cup chicken or beef broth
> 2 tablespoons fresh lemon juice
> Salt and fresh-ground black pepper

1. Preheat the oven to 400 degrees.
2. Stir together the mustard, oil, and 1 tablespoon fresh sage or 1½ teaspoons dried in a small dish. Spread the paste all over the pork loin.
3. Set the roast, fat side up, on a rack in a shallow metal roasting pan. Place in the oven and immediately reduce the temperature to 325 degrees. Roast for 20 to 25 minutes per pound, until a meat thermometer inserted in the thickest part registers 150 degrees. Remove to a platter, cover loosely with foil, and allow to rest while making the gravy.
4. Place the roasting pan with drippings on a stove burner. You should have 2 table-spoons of fat in the pan. If not, add butter to make up the difference. Sprinkle the flour over the drippings and cook over medium heat, stirring, for 2 minutes. Stir in the cider and broth and bring to a boil, stirring to dissolve the browned bits that cling to the pan. Stir in the remaining 2 tablespoons of fresh sage or 2 teaspoons dried and the lemon juice and season with salt and pepper to taste.
5. Carve the meat, cutting down between the bones. Stir any accumulated juices into the gravy. Pass the gravy in a sauceboat at the table.

Note: Ask the butcher to cut through the chine bone of the pork loin to facilitate carving.

Cider Jelly

When you press apples and squeeze out the juice, you get apple cider. When you boil that cider down, it eventually becomes a thick concentrate called boiled cider, which used to be a staple sweetener on grocery store shelves. If you keep boiling some more, you get natural cider jelly—a mahogany-brown, tangy-sweet jelly that tastes of the essence of apples.

Willis and Tina Wood own a small family farm in southern Vermont, where they grow their own apples, press their own cider, and boil that cider into jelly. "Our family has been pressing cider in the same way on the same Vermont farm since 1882," claims the label on their jelly jar. Their boiled cider is a 7-to-1 concentration (seven gallons of cider are boiled down to make one gallon of boiled cider), and their jelly is 9-to-1, making its flavor especially concentrated.

Cider jelly is excellent spread on toast or hot biscuits, great on turkey or ham sandwiches, fabulous when stirred into the pan juices from a roast pork, but best of all, I think, melted to use as a glaze for a Vermont ham.

❖ ❖ ❖ ❖ ❖ ❖ ❖ ❖ ❖

Vermont-Style Country Ham Bake with Cider Jelly Glaze

MAKES ABOUT 20 SERVINGS, WITH SOME LEFTOVERS

A beautifully glazed whole bone-in ham is perfect party food, whether at a cocktail party, carved into thin slivers to sandwich with sharp mustard between miniature Best-Ever Buttermilk Biscuits (page 443), or as the centerpiece of a dinner buffet alongside a bountiful array of such inviting side dishes as Church Supper Broccoli and Cheese Bake (page 113), New England Ladies' Cabbage (page 115), or Classic Scalloped Potatoes (page 125). New England cider jelly (see above) combines with coarse-grained mustard to make a sweet-sharp paste that burnishes the ham with a spectacular glossy, mahogany-hued glaze.

> 1 12- to 14-pound bone-in fully cooked smoked ham, preferably
>   a Vermont or a New Hampshire ham
> ½ cup cider jelly or apple jelly
> ¼ cup coarse-grained mustard
> Whole cloves

1. Preheat the oven to 300 degrees.
2. Place the ham in a large roasting pan, fat side up. Add about 1 cup of water to the bottom of the pan. Make a tent of aluminum foil over the ham, crimping the edges. Bake for 2 hours.
3. In a small bowl, whisk the jelly with the mustard. (It doesn't matter if the mixture is not absolutely smooth.) Remove the ham from the oven and cut off any thick layers of fat. Brush all over with the jelly glaze. Using a sharp knife, score diamonds in the thin layer of fat and stick a clove in the center of each diamond. Brush with the glaze again.
4. Return the ham to the oven and continue to roast, uncovered, for 30 to 45 minutes, brushing once with more glaze, until the outside is richly browned and a meat thermometer inserted in the thickest part registers 150 degrees.
5. Let the ham rest for 30 minutes before carving into thin slices.

Three More Glazes for Ham

Orange Molasses Glaze: In a small saucepan, stir together ¼ cup molasses, ¼ cup packed dark brown sugar, ¼ cup orange juice, 1 teaspoon dry mustard, and ½ teaspoon grated orange zest. Cook over medium heat, stirring, until the sugar is dissolved. About 45 minutes before the ham is done, score the fat in crisscrossing sets of diagonal lines to make diamonds and insert a whole clove in the center of each diamond. Brush with the glaze, return the ham to the oven, and roast until done.

Cranberry Marmalade Glaze: In a small saucepan, melt together ½ cup orange or lemon marmalade, ½ cup jellied cranberry sauce, 2 tablespoons brown sugar, and 2 tablespoons fresh lemon juice. Score the ham, insert with cloves, and glaze as above.

Mustardy Sherry-Apricot Glaze: In a small saucepan, melt together ½ cup apricot preserves, ¼ cup sherry, 3 tablespoons whole-grained mustard, and ½ teaspoon black pepper. Score the ham, insert with cloves, and glaze as above.

Grilled Lamb Chops with Rosemary-Mint Pesto

MAKES 4 SERVINGS

Like gardeners all over the country, New Englanders produce prodigious quantities of fragrant mint during the high season. Mint sauce is the classical condiment for lamb, another pride of the region, so here I've given the herb sauce a different spin by combining it with rosemary in a pesto take-off. If you don't finish the pesto with this meal, try using it as a baked potato topping or blending it with mayonnaise or sour cream to serve as a vegetable dip.

½ cup lightly packed fresh mint leaves
½ cup lightly packed fresh parsley sprigs
3 tablespoons fresh rosemary leaves, pulled
    from stems
¼ cup grated Parmesan
    cheese
2 garlic cloves, peeled
1 tablespoon fresh lemon
    juice
¼ teaspoon salt, plus more
    to taste
¼ teaspoon red pepper flakes
¼ cup extra-virgin olive oil
8 loin lamb chops, cut 1 inch thick
Fresh-ground black pepper or cracked peppercorns

1. Combine the mint, parsley, rosemary, cheese, garlic, lemon juice, ¼ teaspoon salt, and red pepper flakes in a food processor. Pulse to make a rough paste. With the motor running, slowly pour the oil through the feed tube and process until the sauce is a smooth puree. (The sauce can be stored overnight in the refrigerator, but it will darken in color slightly. Return to room temperature before using.)
2. Build a medium-hot charcoal fire or preheat a gas grill.
3. Season the lamb chops with salt and pepper. Spoon out 2 tablespoons of the pesto and brush it over the lamb chops. Reserve the remainder for passing at the table.

4. Grill the lamb, turning once, until it is cooked to the desired degree of doneness, about 10 minutes for medium.

5. Serve the lamb chops with a bowl of the pesto for spooning over the meat at the table.

Smoked Hams

The mountainous areas of Vermont and New Hampshire are home to several noteworthy ham-smoking operations. Most New England smokehouses use maple sugar for curing and corncobs for smoking, producing a ham that is at once smoky-sweet and yet fresh tasting, quite different from, say, the dense, salty Smithfield hams from Virginia.

Having leftover baked country ham in the refrigerator is the equivalent to having jewels in a vault. After the ham has been the centerpiece of a sit-down or buffet dinner, it can be used in dozens of delicious ways—fried and served with eggs for breakfast, sliced paper thin and draped over melon as an appetizer, made into delicate crustless hors d'oeuvre or tea sandwiches, piled high between slices of fresh rye bread as a "Dagwood" lunch sandwich, arranged with cheeses and fresh vegetables in a dinner salad, or inserted into all manner of potato and pasta casseroles. As its final and possibly most rewarding incarnation, a meaty ham bone can invest such robust wintertime soups as Senator Lodge's Navy Bean Soup (page 51) or Split Pea Soup with Smoked Ham (page 50) with a depth of flavor that ensures their success.

Oregano-Scented Slow-Braised Greek Lamb Shanks

MAKES 4 SERVINGS

Another superlative example of the Greek-American genius with lamb, this succulent braise of meaty lamb shanks is perfumed with dried oregano and then finished with a handful of fresh mint. Greek cuisine has much in common with such eastern Mediterranean countries as Turkey and Morocco—hence the touch of honey and hint of sweet spice in this recipe. Serve the lamb shanks over or alongside Greek Orzo Pilaf (page 195), and then just add a fresh green salad dressed with lemon vinaigrette for a simply splendid dinner.

> 4 meaty lamb shanks (3 to 4 pounds)
> ¼ cup all-purpose flour
> 3 teaspoons dried oregano
> ¾ teaspoon salt
> ½ teaspoon fresh-ground black pepper
> 2 tablespoons olive oil
> 2 onions, chopped
> 3 garlic cloves, minced
> 1 cup beef or chicken broth
> 1 cup dry red wine
> 1 cup chopped seeded plum tomatoes, fresh or canned
> 1 cinnamon stick, broken in half
> 1 tablespoon honey
> 3 tablespoons chopped fresh mint
> 1 tablespoon fresh lemon juice

1. Trim any excess external fat off the meat. In a shallow dish, combine the flour, 2 teaspoons of the oregano, the salt, and pepper. Dredge the meat in the seasoned flour, shaking off the excess. Heat the oil in a large skillet with a lid or in a Dutch oven. Cook the lamb shanks over medium-high heat until browned on all sides, about 10 minutes.
2. Push the meat to one side of the pan and add the onions and garlic. Cook, stirring frequently, until the onions begin to soften, about 5 minutes. Add 1 cup of water along with the broth, wine, tomatoes, cinnamon stick, honey, and remaining 1 teaspoon of oregano. Bring to a boil, reduce the heat to low, and cook, covered, until the meat is tender and begins to pull away from the bone, 1½ to 2 hours.
3. Skim off any fat that has risen to the surface of the braising liquid. (The recipe can be made 1 day ahead to this point and refrigerated. Reheat before proceeding.)
4. Before serving, stir the mint and lemon juice into the sauce and season with additional salt and pepper if necessary.

Greek Easter Dinner
Rosemary Roasted Lamb

MAKES ABOUT 8 SERVINGS, WITH SOME LEFTOVERS

It's a well-known fact that Greek-Americans, who pride themselves on carrying on the rich culinary traditions of their beloved homeland, prize spring lamb above all other meats. Most wouldn't dream of serving anything else for the Easter feast. In years when Easter falls late enough in the spring, a significant number of Greek-American families in New England still gather to spit-roast and baste the paschal lamb outdoors over glowing coals. This oven-roasted leg of lamb, garlic permeated and rosemary scented, is an extraordinarily delicious alternative. Some appropriate accompaniments are Greek Orzo Pilaf (page 195), Spectacular Greek Salad (page 80), and Greek Sugar-Dusted Cookies (page 571) with small cups of espresso to cap the feast.

> 1 leg of lamb (6 to 8 pounds)
> 3 large garlic cloves, peeled and cut in slivers
> 1 tablespoon chopped fresh rosemary, plus sprigs for garnish
> 1 teaspoon salt
> 1 tablespoon fresh-ground black pepper
> 1 tablespoon olive oil
> 1 cup dry white wine
> 2 plum tomatoes, seeded and chopped

1. Preheat the oven to 400 degrees.
2. If necessary, trim the papery filament (called the fell) from the leg by making several small cuts and then pulling it off in pieces. (This is usually quite easy to do.) Then trim off any excess fat from the lamb. Make a good many small slits in the meat and insert the slivers of garlic.
3. Combine the rosemary, salt, pepper, and olive oil in a small bowl. Rub this paste all over the surface of the meat. Place the meat on a rack in a shallow roasting pan, pour the wine into the bottom of the pan, and scatter the tomatoes around in the wine.
4. Place the pan in the oven and immediately reduce the oven temperature to 350 degrees. Roast for about 12 minutes per pound, a total of 1¼ to 1½ hours, or until the desired degree of doneness is reached. A meat thermometer inserted in the

thickest part will register about 135 degrees for medium-rare meat. Remove from the oven, transfer the meat to a carving platter, tent with foil, and let rest for 15 minutes before carving. (The internal temperature will increase about 5 degrees from the residual heat.)

5. Skim any fat off the pan juices and reheat them if necessary.

6. Carve the lamb, garnish the platter with rosemary sprigs, and serve with the pan juices.

Greek Easter Memories

Members of the Greek Orthodox church consider Easter the most significant holiday of the year. Services continue through Holy Week, culminating in the midnight service on Saturday night. Stratti Anagnos of Rutland, Vermont, recounts, "The service extends itself until three o'clock in the morning. Some of the most famous parties have taken place that night; some have lasted until eight, nine o'clock in the morning. And we'd play music and move the tables, and anybody that felt like dancing could dance. All the folk dances. We used to have either lamb shish kabob or legs of lamb. Then there's the traditional eggs that are bright red, denoting the blood of Christ. There's bread made with coins in it. There's also a traditional soup that they make out of lamb brains and intestines. My mother and I would sneak out of church a couple of minutes early and she'd start the avgolemono soup for me. I realize I was so lucky I got both the American and the Greek food."

—*Many Cultures, One People,*
Vermont Folklife Center

New England Venison-Molasses Chili

MAKES 8 SERVINGS

Deer hunting is still very much a part of the culture in northern New England, both for the love of the sport and for the love of eating the full-flavored (and free!) venison meat. One of the best uses, I think, for the less-tender cuts of venison is to stew the meat with bold seasonings to create this unusual, irresistibly vibrant chili. Molasses contributes its dark bittersweetness and the whole cumin seeds add a surprising little crunch and burst of pungent flavor. This is great party food. All you need are bowls of such condiments as sour cream and chopped onion, a big green salad, and something like Sour Lemon Pudding Cake (page 519) for a singularly outstanding meal.

¼ pound bacon, preferably cob smoked, chopped
2 pounds boneless venison meat (see Note), coarsely ground or cut
    into small pieces
1 teaspoon fresh-ground black pepper
½ teaspoon salt
2 large onions, chopped
1 large green bell pepper, chopped
6 garlic cloves, minced
2 tablespoons chili powder
1 tablespoon whole cumin
2 teaspoons dried thyme
1 teaspoon dried oregano
1 teaspoon dry mustard
1 teaspoon cayenne pepper
1 28-ounce can crushed plum tomatoes in puree
1 tablespoon Worcestershire sauce
2 tablespoons molasses
4 cups drained cooked red kidney beans

1. Cook the bacon over medium heat in a large pot stirring occasionally, until the fat begins to render, about 5 minutes. Add the venison to the pot and sprinkle it with the black pepper and salt. Add the onions, green pepper, and garlic and cook, stirring frequently, until the venison loses its pink color and the vegetables are softened, about 10 minutes.

2. Meanwhile, combine the chili powder, cumin, thyme, oregano, mustard, and cayenne in a small, dry skillet. Toast, stirring over medium-high heat for 2 to 3 minutes, or until fragrant and a wisp of smoke appears. Stir the mixture into the pot.

3. Add the tomatoes, Worcestershire sauce, molasses, and 3 cups of water. Bring to a boil over high heat, reduce the heat to low, and cook, covered, for 1 hour, until the meat is almost tender.

4. Add the beans and simmer, uncovered, over medium heat until the chili is thick and the meat is tender, 30 to 45 minutes. (The chili can be made 2 days ahead and refrigerated, or it may be frozen.)

5. To serve, reheat the chili and adjust the liquid and the seasonings if necessary.

Note: Any cut of venison will work, but you'll probably want to save the choice loin portions for a dish like Pan-Seared Venison Steaks with Peppery Beach Plum Sauce (page 303).

Vermont Folklife Game Suppers

The roster of wild game at the Vermont Folklife Center Game Supper in Middlebury, Vermont, reads like a hunter's who's who—and it makes the likes of venison and rabbit sound downright tame. Beaver, bear, moose, elk, antelope, racoon, and such wild birds as Canada goose, wild duck, and partridge are all part of the spread at this annual event. The director of the folklife center says the dinners, which are a continuation of the original Pilgrims' custom of holding harvest festivals, are all about building community and preserving tradition, bringing together old and new New England. Indeed, participants include chefs from the New England Culinary Institute in Vermont and local restauranteurs, as well as volunteer cooks from the community.

Some people seem to attend the game suppers out of simple curiosity, or possibly to score bragging rights. "Game suppers," says one attendee, "are all about getting to say that you ate beaver pate." At a recent supper, there was no beaver pate on the menu, but there was beaver stroganoff and stuffed roast beaver. Most of the dishes received good reviews from the crowd, with the notable exception of the bear. Said one diner, "For once there was a dish about which you couldn't say it tastes like chicken!"

—New York Times, Fall 1997

Pan-Seared Venison Steaks
with Peppery Beach Plum Sauce

MAKES 4 SERVINGS

New England woodlands furnish an ideal environment for farm-raising venison, and a number of north country farmers have formed a consortium through which they distribute and sell their increasingly popular product. Venison, whether wild or farm raised, is a lean meat with very little marbling of fat. Quick-searing, therefore, is the cooking method of choice, particularly for the extra-lean loin or tenderloin. In this elegant preparation, boneless loin steaks are napped with a sweet-tart peppery sauce made from beach plum jelly, which seems to have a natural affinity for venison. (Almost any fruit jelly can be substituted, however.) You might start this meal with Citrus-Glazed Steamed Mussels (page 20), and partner the meat with Classic Scalloped Potatoes (page 125) and a green vegetable. Indulge in Chocolate Bread and Butter Pudding (page 515) for dessert.

> 4 tablespoons butter
> 2 tablespoons chopped shallots
> 1 garlic clove, minced
> ½ cup dry red wine
> 3 tablespoons beach plum or red currant jelly
> 1 teaspoon Dijon mustard
> 2 teaspoons chopped fresh rosemary or 1 teaspoon crumbled dried
> ½ teaspoon cayenne pepper
> 4 boneless venison loin steaks (about 5 ounces each)
> Salt and fresh-ground black pepper
> 1 tablespoon olive oil
> Rosemary sprigs for garnish, optional

1. Melt 2 tablespoons of the butter in a small saucepan. Add the shallots and garlic and cook over medium heat, stirring, for 1 minute. Add the wine, raise the heat to high, and boil for 1 minute. Reduce the heat to medium, add the jelly, mustard, rosemary, and cayenne, and cook, stirring, until the jelly melts. Set aside.

2. Place the meat between 2 sheets of plastic wrap and, using a meat mallet or the bottom of a small, heavy pan, gently pound the meat to an even ½-inch thickness. Season the meat on both sides generously with salt and pepper.

3. Heat the remaining 2 tablespoons of butter and the oil in a large skillet over medium-high to high heat until the foam subsides. Cook the steaks, in batches if necessary, just until seared on both sides but still pink within, about 2 minutes per side. Remove to a warm platter.

4. Add the sauce to the skillet and cook, whisking to incorporate any browned bits in the pan, until the jelly remelts and the sauce is smooth, about 2 minutes.

5. Spoon the sauce over the meat, garnish with rosemary sprigs, if available, and serve.

Note: The steaks can also be grilled. Simply brush them with olive oil and sear over a hot grill. Re-melt the sauce on top of the stove or on the side of the grill and spoon over the meat.

CHICKEN AND OTHER BIRDS

In the tiny town of Adamsville, Rhode Island, a stone monument and plaque commemorate the Rhode Island Red rooster. Today New Englanders in all six states and of all ethnic stripes commemorate the chicken by serving it up frequently—in such appealing dishes as homey Shaker Buttermilk Chicken with Herb Gravy (page 317), Garlicky Greek Baked Chicken Riganato (page 311), light and lovely Marlborough Meetinghouse Lemon Chicken with Thyme (page 318), or, for picnics, incomparable Maine County Fair Barbecued Chicken (page 307).

Indeed, we've come a long way since that cold winter day at Plymouth when Miles Standish and friends shot and roasted an eagle over coals. "Excellent meat, hardly to be discerned from mutton," they are said to have reported bravely (or maybe weakly). One hopes that it wasn't too very long before they happened upon that much tastier native bird, the North American wild turkey. Whether or not roast turkey was on the table for the first Thanksgiving (and records are unclear on the point), we've certainly made up for it in the centuries since.

Farm-raising the wild birds that once abounded in New England woodlands and marshes is now big business. Recipes for game birds, such as Northeast Kingdom Pheasant Fricassee with Riesling (page 339) and Autumn McIntosh-Roasted Duckling (page 333), celebrate this New England culinary inheritance.

Blue Hill Fair

"When they pulled into the Fair Grounds, they could hear music and see the Ferris wheel turning in the sky. They could smell the dust of the race track where the sprinkling cart had moistened it and they could smell hamburgers frying and see balloons aloft.... The children grabbed each other by the hand and danced off in the direction of the merry-go-round, toward the wonderful music and the wonderful adventure and the wonderful excitement, into the wonderful midway where there would be no parents to guard them and guide them, and where they could be happy and free and do as they pleased. Mrs. Arable stood quietly and watched them go. Then she sighed. Then she blew her nose.

"'Do you really think it's all right?' she asked.

"'Well, they've got to grow up some time,' said Mr. Arable. 'And a fair is a good place to start, I guess.'"

—E. B. White, *Charlotte's Web*
(Harper and Row, 1952)

Maine County Fair Barbecued Chicken

MAKES 4 TO 6 SERVINGS

Maine used to produce a lot of chickens. By summer's end, thousands of birds will still be slowly grilled to juicy, golden perfection at barbecue concessions at the dozen or so county fairs around the state. Mainers favor this extremely simple, mild basting sauce that "brings out the fine flavor of the chicken," in the words of Down East food authority Marjorie Standish. We buy some barbecued chicken every year on Labor Day weekend at the Blue Hill Fair (notable as one of the settings for E. B. White's *Charlotte's Web*), and take it home to eat on the deck with Picnic Potato Salad with Egg and Gherkins (page 93), thick sliced tomatoes just off the vine, and maybe Reach House Blueberry Cobbler (page 494).

> 1 cup cider vinegar
> ½ cup vegetable oil
> 1 tablespoon salt
> 1 teaspoon fresh-ground black pepper
> 2 2½- to 3-pound chickens, quartered

1. Stir together 1 cup water and the vinegar, oil, salt, and pepper in a large glass dish. Add the chicken, turning to coat. Set aside for about 1 hour.
2. Build a charcoal fire and let the coals burn down until they are covered with gray ash, or preheat a gas grill to medium heat.
3. Place the chicken on the grill, skin side up, and cook, turning every 5 or 10 minutes and brushing with more of the marinade, until the skin is golden brown and the meat is no longer pink, 30 to 45 minutes. Most of the cooking should be done with the skin side up so that the skin doesn't get too charred.
4. Cut the chicken into smaller parts, if you like, and serve hot, warm, or cold.

Hungarian Chicken Paprika

MAKES 4 SERVINGS

Chicken paprika and beef goulash might well be considered the national dishes of Hungary. When I go to the Kossuth Club, a homey Hungarian-American club in Fairfield, Connecticut, this soul-soothing sour cream–enriched Chicken Paprika is almost always on the menu. Accompany the chicken, as I did recently for a party, with Hungarian Egg Dumplings (page 452) and a Trio of Hungarian Salads (page 96). And then you must splurge with Hungarian Crêpes with Walnut Filling and Warm Chocolate Sauce (page 507) as the appropriately decadent finale to your feast.

> 2 tablespoons butter
> 1 large onion, chopped
> 1 heaping tablespoon sweet Hungarian paprika
> 3½ pounds chicken parts
> 1 large tomato, cored, seeded, and diced
> ¾ teaspoon salt, plus more to taste
> 1 cup chicken broth
> ¼ cup regular or lowfat sour cream
> 1 tablespoon all-purpose flour
> 1 small red bell pepper, thinly sliced

1. Melt the butter in a large heavy skillet with a lid or in a Dutch oven. Add the onion and cook over medium heat until softened but not browned, about 8 minutes. Add the paprika and cook, stirring, for 1 minute.

2. Add the chicken, tomato, salt, and broth. Bring to a boil, reduce the heat to medium-low, and cook, covered, turning the chicken occasionally, until the chicken is tender and no longer pink, about 45 minutes. Using tongs, remove the chicken to a plate.

3. Whisk the sour cream and flour together in a small bowl. Whisk in about 1 cup of the hot cooking liquid. Return this mixture to the pot and stir to blend. Add the red pepper and simmer, uncovered, until it is just softened and the sauce is thickened, about 10 minutes. Do not boil vigorously or the sour cream may curdle. Return the chicken to the sauce, adjust the seasonings to taste, and serve.

Paprika and Sour Cream

Paprika and sour cream are the soul of Hungarian cuisine, equivalent to garlic and tomato sauce in Italian cooking. Hungary produces the world's finest paprika, which ranges from sweet and mild to hot and pungent. The spice adds color and depth of flavor to all manner of Hungarian-American dishes. It's worth searching out genuine Hungarian paprika in Hungarian-American specialty shops or in gourmet stores. My favorite brand is Szeged, a mild, sweet paprika that is packaged in a lovely bright red square can. Sour cream provides richness and a tangy flavor while smoothing out the sometimes-rough edges of paprika. Any good-quality commercial dairy sour cream is fine. If you use lowfat sour cream, the resulting sauce will have slightly less body and richness but will taste very good.

Succulent Braised Chicken Portuguese Style

MAKES 4 TO 6 SERVINGS

This falling-off the-bone chicken stew demonstrates the Portuguese-American genius with seasoning. All the Portuguese flavors are here, including that of linguiça, their wonderful peppery smoked sausage. The stew is finished with a squeeze of orange, punctuating the dish with a delightful burst of bright citrus. This can be a delicious and easy weekday supper, or you could make it the basis for an all-Portuguese feast by partnering it with Portuguese Potatoes with Cilantro (page 132) and a mesclun salad and finishing with Portuguese-Style Caramel Flan (page 509).

2 tablespoons olive oil

½ pound linguiça or other garlicky smoked sausage, such as kielbasa,
    cut in ½-inch-thick slices

1 large onion, cut in half and sliced

1 green bell pepper, coarsely chopped

3½ to 4 pounds chicken parts

1½ teaspoons dried oregano

Salt and fresh-ground black pepper

2 large bay leaves, broken in half

1 cup dry white wine or dry sherry

1 cup chicken broth or water

1 small pickled or dried hot red pepper, minced, or ¼ teaspoon red
    pepper flakes

1 orange, cut in wedges

1. Heat the oil in a large skillet with a lid or in a Dutch oven. Add the sausage, onion, and green pepper and cook over medium heat until the sausage is browned and the vegetables softened, about 10 minutes. Remove with a slotted spoon and reserve, leaving the drippings in the pan.

2. Season the chicken on all sides with the oregano and sprinkle lightly with salt and pepper. Add it to the skillet, raise the heat to medium-high, and cook until browned on all sides, about 10 minutes. Add the bay leaves and cook them in the pan drippings for about 1 minute to release their flavor.

3. Return the sausage and vegetable mixture to the pan and add the wine, broth, and hot pepper. Bring to a boil, reduce the heat to medium-low, and simmer, covered, until the chicken is very tender and cooked through, 35 to 45 minutes. (The chicken can be cooked a couple of hours ahead, held at cool room temperature, and reheated just before serving.) Remove and discard the bay leaves.

Bay Leaves

Portuguese Yankees use a lot of bay leaves in their savory dishes. Try to buy the Turkish variety, which has oval-shaped leaves, as opposed to California bay, whose leaves are long and narrow. The California bay leaves have a stronger taste and can impart an overpoweringly pungent flavor to any dish they inhabit.

4. Serve the chicken with the orange wedges so that guests can squeeze the juice over their portion, if they like.

Garlicky Greek Baked Chicken Riganato

MAKES 4 TO 6 SERVINGS

To cross the threshold of a Greek grocery store is to leave New England behind and embark on a Mediterranean odyssey. Your eye lights on huge crocks of brine- and oil-cured olives, chunks of feta swimming in a salt bath, and orzo, lentils, dried favas, and chickpeas spilling out of burlap sacks. But it's the siren song of fresh and dried herbs strung up in bunches around the store—particularly the potent, resiny Greek oregano—that leaves an indelible impression. This uncomplicated Greek-style baked chicken will taste best if, at the very least, you make sure to use oregano from a fresh jar, not one that is old and tired and musty. Crush the leaves in your fingers before using it to release some of the aroma of a sunny Greek hillside.

> 3½ to 4 pounds chicken parts
> 1 tablespoon dried oregano
> 1 teaspoon salt
> ½ teaspoon black pepper
> 6 large garlic cloves, thinly sliced
> 3 tablespoons fresh lemon juice
> 2 tablespoons olive oil

1. Put the chicken in a large baking dish. Season with the oregano, salt, and pepper, rubbing them into the skin. Scatter the garlic over and sprinkle with the lemon juice. Set aside to marinate for at least 30 minutes at room temperature or for as long as overnight in the refrigerator.

2. Preheat the oven to 350 degrees.

3. Drizzle the chicken with the oil. Bake, uncovered, turning once and brushing with the pan juices once or twice, until the chicken is golden and tender and cooked through, 45 minutes to 1 hour.

4. Serve warm or at room temperature.

───────────── **Caribbean Carnival** ─────────────

Each summer, Boston's Caribbean population holds a week-long party. This Caribbean Carnival is the biggest West Indian festival in New England, drawing upwards of 350,000 people and featuring such fare as Trinidadian roti (flatbread wrapped around various curried fillings), Jamaican jerk chicken, turnover-style beef patties, pudding-like banana bread, and the exotic root and bark drinks for which West Indians are famous. The event features a huge parade, floats, steel bands, contests of several kinds, and the crowning of the queen and king of the festival.

Curried Caribbean Chicken

MAKES 4 SERVINGS

Avery Stephenson, former chef-proprietor of a Jamaican restaurant in Norwalk, Connecticut, who taught me this recipe, says that the secret is rubbing the chicken with vinegar and then with the seasonings. The vinegar not only lifts and sharpens the whole finished dish but removes any "off" flavors in the chicken, too. This simple Caribbean-style curried chicken stew depends very much on the quality of your curry powder. Better curry powders are understandably a bit more expensive, so buy the best you can find. Serve the curry with plain steamed long-grain or basmati rice, mango or other chutney, and a cooling green salad.

3½ pounds chicken parts, skin removed
3 tablespoons distilled white vinegar
1 cup chopped onion
½ cup minced scallions
2 garlic cloves, minced
2 to 3 tablespoons curry powder
2 teaspoons grated fresh ginger
1 teaspoon salt
½ teaspoon black pepper
2 tablespoons vegetable oil
2 cups chicken broth

1. Cut the chicken parts into manageable pieces—separate wings at joints, discarding tips; separate legs into thighs and drumsticks; cut breast halves into 2 or 3 pieces with a large cleaver. Place the pieces in a bowl and sprinkle with the vinegar. Add the onion, scallions, garlic, curry powder, ginger, salt, and pepper, rubbing to coat the chicken evenly with all the seasonings. Set aside for at least 15 minutes or up to 4 hours.
2. Heat the oil in a large skillet. Add the chicken and cook, turning with tongs, until lightly browned, about 5 minutes. Add the broth and bring to a boil, stirring up any brown bits on the bottom of the pan. Cover, reduce the heat to low, and simmer until the chicken is tender, 30 to 40 minutes. (The recipe can be made up to a day ahead to this point. Cover and refrigerate.)
3. Simmer until heated through before serving.

Cooking Caribbean with Avery

Many small Caribbean restaurants, mostly housed in storefronts in urban neighborhoods, now grace the New England food landscape, injecting a welcome infusion of the singularly vibrant, often fiery style of home cooking from the West Indies. Avery's Little Jamaican Kitchen in South Norwalk, Connecticut, is one such establishment, run by Avery Stephenson, who is assisted by Cynthia Sewell. Everything on Avery's menu, which reads like a roster of the best of Jamaican cooking, is homemade, cooked right on the stove as you watch. It includes fried plantains, codfish fritters, pepper shrimp, ackee and salt fish, "brown stew" chicken, jerk chicken and pork, oxtail, cow foot, curried chicken, escovitch fish, stew peas, callaloo (greens), fruitcake, and sweet potato pudding. On weekends Avery cooks a big pot of her specialty, which is curried goat. All are delectable (although I can't say I can vouch for the cow foot), and all are cooked by feel and memory, without real recipes. When I asked Avery where she learned to cook so incredibly well, she said, "Just by cooking. I just did it and that's how I learned."

Avery's "Brown Stew" Chicken

MAKES 4 SERVINGS

A good percentage of the continuous stream of hungry diners arriving at Avery's Jamaican restaurant in South Norwalk, Connecticut, order this succulent West Indian comfort-food dish. Basically a simple stewed chicken, the dish is invigorated with just enough Jamaican sparkle in the form of grated ginger and minced garlic to turn it into a winning blend of vibrant yet soul-soothing food.

3½ pounds chicken parts, skin removed
Salt and fresh-ground black pepper
¼ cup distilled white vinegar
3 tablespoons browning and seasoning base (see Note)
1 cup chopped onion
2 teaspoons grated fresh ginger
2 tablespoons vegetable oil
2 garlic cloves, minced
1 tablespoon butter or margarine
¼ cup minced scallions

1. Cut the chicken into manageable pieces—separate wings at joints, discarding tips; separate legs into thighs and drumsticks; cut breast halves into 2 or 3 pieces. Place the pieces in a bowl and sprinkle them with salt and pepper and then with the vinegar. Add the browning and seasoning base, onion, and ginger and rub to coat the chicken well. Set aside for 15 minutes to marinate.

2. Heat the oil in a large skillet. Add the garlic and cook over medium heat until lightly browned, about 2 minutes. Add the chicken and cook, turning the pieces with tongs, until lightly browned, about 5 minutes. Add the broth and bring to a boil, stirring up any brown bits in the pan. Cover, reduce the heat to low, and simmer until the chicken is tender, 30 to 40 minutes. (The recipe can be made up to a day ahead to this point. Cover and refrigerate.)

3. Before serving, reheat the chicken if necessary, add the butter or margarine to the sauce, and stir until melted. Stir in the scallions. Taste and season with more salt and pepper if necessary.

Note: You will need a browning and seasoning sauce base such as Kitchen Bouquet or Gravy Master, available in bottles in the spice or condiment section of most supermarkets.

Ski-Day Chicken Stew with Herb Dumplings

MAKES 4 SERVINGS

What could possibly taste better after a day on frigid New England ski slopes than chicken and dumplings? This simplified version of one of the most sensational down-home dishes of all time is the perfect recipe to make when everybody's ravenous but so exhausted they can hardly focus well enough to follow a recipe. The stewed chicken base can easily be put together in the morning, and the dumpling mixture is simple to mix up as people are clamoring for food. (I've even been known to use biscuit mix to make the dumplings. It tastes perfectly fine, particularly with the fresh herbs added.)

For the stew:

4 cups chicken broth
6 carrots, peeled and cut in 1-inch lengths
1 medium onion, thinly sliced
2 celery ribs, thinly sliced
1 large bay leaf, broken in half
1½ teaspoons dried thyme
Salt and fresh-ground black pepper
1½ pounds skinless, boneless chicken thighs or breasts, cut in 2-inch chunks

For the dumplings:

1½ cups all-purpose flour
1½ teaspoons baking powder
½ teaspoon salt
2 tablespoons minced scallions or snipped chives
3 tablespoons solid vegetable shortening
½ cup plus 1 to 2 tablespoons whole, lowfat, or skim milk

1. To make the stew, bring the broth to a boil in a large soup pot or Dutch oven. Add the carrots, onion, celery, bay leaf, and thyme. Reduce the heat to medium-low and simmer, partially covered, for 10 minutes. Add the chicken and continue to cook for 5 to 8 minutes, until the vegetables are almost tender. Season with salt and pepper.

2. To make the dumplings, whisk together the flour, baking powder, and salt in a large mixing bowl. Stir in the scallions or chives. Cut the shortening into about 5 pieces and work it into the flour mixture with your fingertips or a fork until most of the pieces are about the size of small peas. Add ½ cup of the milk and stir with a few strokes of a fork or wooden spoon, adding a tablespoon or two more milk, until the dough comes together in a sticky mass.

3. Dip a tablespoon into the simmering stew, then use that spoon to measure out a rounded tablespoon of dough, and drop it onto the top of the stew. Repeat with the remaining dough, making 12 to 14 dumplings. Cover the pot and simmer until the dumplings are slightly shiny on top and firm to the touch, about 15 minutes.

4. Serve the stew and dumplings in shallow soup bowls.

Dumplings

"Dumplings? Oh, yes, dumplings. Why, a whole chapter could be given over to dumplings. A dumpling, you understand, is not necessarily a lump of soggy dough, shaped like a glass paperweight and almost as heavy, tasteless as a rubber bath sponge. A dumpling, a genuine old-fashioned New England 'riz' dumpling, is light and fluffy and flavorsome, something to eat and enjoy. A New England chicken stew with dumplings is—Well, well! A sermon might be preached on dumplings, but 'Dumpling' is not my text just now."

—Imogene Wolcott,
The Yankee Cook Book
(Ives Washburn, 1963)

Shaker Buttermilk Chicken with Herb Gravy

MAKES 4 SERVINGS

Buttermilk, originally a by-product of making butter, has long been a staple ingredient of New England cooks and bakers, who have prized it for its tangy acidity and for its ability to tenderize foods. Nowadays, of course, buttermilk is produced commercially and is available in supermarket dairy cases. This scrumptious chicken is an adaptation of a recipe from the Hancock, Massachusetts, Shaker Village. Fluffy Mashed Potatoes (page 126), Ivy League Beets with Orange Sauce (page 112), and Applesauce-Raisin Hand Cake (page 545) would complete this meal beautifully.

1½ cups buttermilk
4 skinless, boneless chicken breast halves
⅔ cup all-purpose flour
1 teaspoon salt
1 teaspoon black pepper
1 teaspoon dried thyme
Vegetable oil for frying
2 tablespoons butter
2 tablespoons minced shallots
1 cup chicken broth
2 tablespoons minced fresh herbs, such as
    parsley, chives, thyme, or tarragon

1. Pour 1 cup of the buttermilk over the chicken breasts in a bowl, turning the pieces until all are coated. Refrigerate for at least 1 hour or as long as overnight.

2. In a shallow dish, stir together the flour, salt, pepper, and thyme.

3. Heat ½ inch of oil to 350 degrees over medium heat in a large, deep, preferably cast-iron skillet. (The oil is hot enough when a cube of bread browns in about 30 seconds.)

> ### The Shaker Arts
>
> "While the Shakers are particularly famous for beautiful and simple furniture, equal attention should be given to our cooking.... I believe that all people can learn to cook and prepare a good meal.... Indeed, cooking is an art just as much as painting a picture or making a piece of furniture."
>
> —Eldress Bertha Lindsay, Canterbury Shaker Village, Canterbury, New Hampshire, 1990

4. Lift the chicken out of the buttermilk, letting the excess drip off, and dredge well in the seasoned flour. Reserve any remaining seasoned flour. Fry the chicken in the hot oil, partially covered, regulating the heat so the chicken does not burn, until it is golden brown outside and white within, 8 to 10 minutes. Lift out with tongs, drain on paper towels, and transfer to a warm platter. Pour the oil out but do not wash the skillet.

5. Return the skillet to the heat and add the butter. Add the shallots and cook, stirring, over medium-high heat for 1 minute. Add 1½ tablespoons of the remaining seasoned flour and cook, stirring, for 1 minute. Whisk in the broth and the remaining ½ cup of buttermilk, and stir in the herbs. Taste and season with additional salt and pepper if necessary.

6. Serve the chicken with the gravy spooned over.

Marlborough Meetinghouse Lemon Chicken with Thyme

MAKES 4 SERVINGS

The Marlborough Meetinghouse is an elegant old Congregational church in Marlborough, Connecticut. The cookbook assembled by the women's fellowship to commemorate the 250th anniversary of the meetinghouse is full of tried-and-true recipes, bits of historical lore, and free advice, including, on the page with an "easy and delicious" lemon chicken, a reminder that "people rarely succeed at anything unless they have fun doing it." So please have fun making this, my adaptation of their recipe. I like it with Minted New Potatoes and Peas (page 124) and a salad.

4 skinless, boneless chicken breast halves (about 5 ounces each)
3 tablespoons all-purpose flour
1 tablespoon plus 2 teaspoons chopped fresh thyme or
    1¼ teaspoons dried
2 teaspoons grated lemon zest
½ teaspoon salt
½ teaspoon fresh-ground black pepper
2 tablespoons olive oil

1 tablespoon plus 2 teaspoons butter
¾ cup chicken broth
2 tablespoons fresh lemon juice
1 teaspoon sugar
8 thin slices lemon
Thyme sprigs for garnish, optional

1. Place the chicken breasts between 2 sheets of plastic wrap and use a large mallet or the bottom of a small, heavy pan to pound them to an even thickness, about ½ inch thick. Stir together the flour, 1 tablespoon of the fresh thyme or 1 teaspoon of the dried, the lemon zest, salt, and pepper on a plate. Dredge the chicken in the flour mixture, shaking off the excess.

2. Heat the oil and 1 tablespoon of the butter in a large skillet. Add the chicken breasts and cook over medium heat, turning once, until golden brown outside and white but still juicy within, 10 to 15 minutes. Remove to a platter and keep warm in a very low oven while making the sauce.

3. Add the broth and the remaining thyme to the skillet, raise the heat to high, and boil briskly, stirring up any browned bits clinging to the pan, until the sauce is somewhat reduced and lightly thickened, about 3 minutes. Add the lemon juice and sugar and simmer for 1 minute. Cut the remaining 2 teaspoons of butter into small pieces and whisk it into the sauce until it melts.

4. Place the lemon slices on top of the chicken, spoon the sauce over the top, and garnish with thyme sprigs, if you like.

Belfast Bay Festival

Belfast, a town on the midcoast of Maine, used to claim fame as the Broiler Capital of the World. The site of large-scale chicken processing plants during several decades, Belfast began hosting the Belfast Broiler Day festival in 1948. During the inaugural event, four tons of barbecued chicken were served.

Moody's Diner
Orange Chicken Stir-Fry

MAKES 4 SERVINGS

Moody's Diner on U.S. Route 1 in Maine, renowned for its hefty breakfasts and extravagant pie display, also gives a nod to the public's request for occasional lighter fare. Here's an adaptation of their excellent chicken stir-fry, which is endowed with zippy orange flavor along with the more common vegetables. Serve it over plain white rice (as here), vermicelli, or Asian noodles.

> 1 cup chicken broth
> ½ cup orange juice
> 1 tablespoon soy sauce
> 1 tablespoon cornstarch
> ½ teaspoon red pepper flakes
> 1 pound skinless, boneless chicken breasts or thighs
> Salt
> 3 tablespoons peanut or other vegetable oil
> 1 pound broccoli florets
> 1 tablespoon minced fresh ginger
> 2 garlic cloves, minced
> 1 8-ounce can water chestnuts, drained and sliced
> 4 cups cooked white rice
> 1 large seedless orange, peeled and sectioned
> 1 cup thinly sliced scallions, including green tops

1. Stir together the broth, orange juice, soy sauce, cornstarch, and red pepper flakes in a small bowl.
2. Cut the chicken crosswise into thin strips and season lightly with salt. Heat the oil in a large skillet or wok. Stir-fry the chicken and broccoli over medium-high to high heat until the chicken is cooked through and the broccoli is bright green, 2 to 3 minutes. Add the ginger and garlic and stir-fry for 1 minute.
3. Reduce the heat to medium. Stir the broth mixture again and add it to the pan along with the water chestnuts. Bring to a boil and cook, stirring, until the sauce is clear and thickened, about 2 minutes.

4. Spoon the stir-fry over the hot rice and top with the orange sections and scallions before serving.

Atwells Avenue Chicken Cacciatore

MAKES 4 SERVINGS

Atwells Avenue is the main street on Federal Hill, which is Providence, Rhode Island's Little Italy. The avenue begins with a lovely arch over the street and stretches for several wonderful blocks of little Italian cheese shops, bakeries, coffee bars, meat markets, delicatessens, and, of course, restaurants. Angelo's is one of those venerable cavernous, wood-paneled institutions where bankers and construction workers and out-of-town visitors all line up at lunch and dinnertime to partake, elbow to elbow, of superlative country Italian fare. This is my adaptation of a fabulous chicken cacciatore I ate there one blustery fall day, with steaming creamy polenta on the side.

1¼ to 1½ pounds skinless, boneless chicken thighs or breasts
½ teaspoon salt
¼ teaspoon fresh-ground black pepper
3 tablespoons olive oil
1 medium onion, coarsely chopped
2 garlic cloves, minced
½ pound shiitake or other wild or domestic mushrooms, sliced
½ cup dry white or red wine
1 16-ounce can plum tomatoes with juice
2 teaspoons chopped fresh rosemary or 1 teaspoon dried
1 teaspoon chopped fresh sage or ½ teaspoon dried
1 tablespoon fresh lemon juice
3 tablespoons chopped fresh flat-leaf parsley

1. Cut the chicken into 3-inch pieces and season with the salt and pepper on all sides.
2. Heat the oil in a large skillet with a lid or in a Dutch oven. Add the chicken and cook over medium heat until browned on all sides, about 6 minutes. Push the chicken to one side if the pan is large or remove with tongs to a plate. Add the onion, garlic, and mushrooms and cook, stirring frequently, until wilted, about 5 minutes. Add

the wine, tomatoes and juice, rosemary, and sage and return the chicken and any accumulated juices to the pan if you had removed it. Bring to a boil, reduce the heat to medium-low, and simmer until the chicken is tender, about 20 minutes. Uncover and boil the pan juices over high heat until lightly thickened, about 5 minutes.

3. Stir in the lemon juice and parsley and taste for seasoning, adding more salt and pepper if necessary.

Rhode Island Red

Adamsville, Rhode Island, is so proud of its chicken history that it proudly boasts a monument to the Rhode Island Red rooster, right in the middle of town. The bas-relief plaque reads, "To commemorate the birthplace of the Rhode Island Red breed of fowl which originated near this location. Red fowls were bred extensively by the farmers of this district and later named 'Rhode Island Reds' and brought into national prominence by the poultry fanciers."

Crispy Chicken Strips with Pan Gravy Camden Style

MAKES 4 SERVINGS

When the charming Nellie Sweet of Camden, Maine, talks, people listen. So when the winsome Miss Nellie, eleven years old, pronounced these crispy, crusty chicken strips with pan gravy to be up there amongst her all-time favorite chicken dinners, I made sure to include the recipe in this book. If Nellie has her way, she eats this chicken with fluffy mashed potatoes (the better to soak up the gravy) and a small helping of green peas.

½ cup all-purpose flour
2 tablespoons yellow cornmeal
1½ teaspoons dried sage
¾ teaspoon salt
¾ teaspoon black pepper
1¼ pounds skinless, boneless chicken breasts or cutlets

2 tablespoons vegetable oil
2 tablespoons butter
¾ cup chicken broth
¾ cup whole milk

1. Stir together the flour, the cornmeal, 1 teaspoon of the sage, and the salt and pepper in a shallow dish. Cut the chicken crosswise into ½-inch-wide strips and dredge it in the flour mixture, shaking off the excess. Reserve the remaining seasoned flour

2. Heat 1 tablespoon each of the oil and butter in a large skillet. Cook half the chicken over medium-high heat until the strips are crisp and browned outside and cooked within, 3 to 5 minutes. Repeat with the remaining oil, butter, and chicken. Remove the chicken to a plate, leaving the drippings in the pan.

3. Add 1 tablespoon of the remaining flour mixture to the skillet and cook, stirring, for 1 minute. Whisk in the broth and milk and bring to a boil, whisking and scraping up any browned bits in the bottom of the pan. Simmer, stirring, for about 3 minutes, until smooth and thickened. Season with the remaining sage and additional salt and pepper to taste.

4. Serve the chicken with the gravy spooned over.

Skillet Chicken with Cranberry-Vinegar Sauce

MAKES 4 SERVINGS

This is a delightfully quick little sauté of thin-sliced chicken cutlets in a sauce made pleasingly sweet-tart with cranberry and vinegar. Add Shaker Baked Rice Pilaf with a Shower of Herbs (page 224) and steamed broccoli florets for an excellent midweek or informal weekend company supper.

1¼ pounds skinless, boneless chicken cutlets
Salt and fresh-ground black pepper
1 tablespoon plus 2 teaspoons chopped fresh sage or
    1½ teaspoons dried
2 tablespoons butter

1 tablespoon olive oil
½ cup thinly sliced scallions
1 cup chicken broth
¾ cup whole-berry cranberry sauce
1½ tablespoons red or white wine vinegar
Sage sprigs for garnish, optional

1. Season the chicken cutlets on both sides with salt and pepper and rub with 1 tablespoon of the fresh sage or 1 teaspoon of the dried. Heat the butter and oil in a large skillet over medium-high heat. Sauté the chicken, in 2 batches if necessary, until golden brown outside and cooked within, 8 to 10 minutes. Remove to a plate.

2. Add the scallions and the remaining sage to the pan drippings and cook, stirring, for 1 minute, until softened. Add the broth, raise the heat to high, and cook, stirring up the browned bits in the bottom of the pan, until the liquid boils and reduces by about one-third. Reduce the heat to medium. Add the cranberry sauce and stir until it melts. Stir in the vinegar.

3. Return the chicken and any accumulated juices to the sauce and season with additional salt and pepper to taste. Garnish with fresh sage sprigs, if you like.

Cranberry Harvest

The Carver family of Massachusetts has five hundred acres in cranberries, and they have been "berrying" this same land for several generations. Pickers collect the scarlet crop using two different harvesting methods. With water harvesting, which requires first flooding the low-lying cranberry fields, or "bogs," a giant churning machine that they actually call an "egg beater" knocks the cranberries off the vines. The berries that float to the surface are pumped out of the bogs and are immediately shipped to processing plants to be made into cranberry sauce, juice, and other products. Dry harvesting, using a vehicle that pushes steel teeth through the vines and lifts the berries into containers, needs to be done more slowly and carefully to produce the clean, intact berries that are sold fresh in plastic bags in the produce section of the supermarket.

The Carvers still use one old screen harvester to separate their dry-harvest berries. The cranberries are tilted onto seven screen "shelves," and those that bounce all the way down qualify as sound, high-quality, salable cranberries.

Thanksgiving Roast Turkey and Two Stuffings with Giblet Gravy

MAKES 10 SERVINGS, WITH PLENTY OF LEFTOVERS

Central to the Thanksgiving feast, of course, are the turkey, stuffing, and gravy. The well-loved classic New England bread stuffing is supplemented here by a Victorian-style fruit and nut dressing that fills the neck cavity. Giblet gravy is also traditional in New England, but if there are some guests who are not giblet lovers, it's easy to leave the innards out of one gravy boat.

> 1 15-pound fresh turkey
> 2 to 3 cups Fruit and Nut Stuffing (recipe follows)
> About 8 cups New England Sage Bread Stuffing (recipe follows)
> Chicken or turkey broth
> Salt and fresh-ground black pepper
> 4 tablespoons butter, melted
> 5 to 6 cups Giblet Gravy (recipe follows)

1. Remove the bag of giblets and the neck and reserve to make the gravy. Wipe the turkey inside and out with a damp paper towel. Pull off and discard any large pieces of fat around the body cavity.
2. Stuff the neck cavity with the fruit and nut stuffing and close the cavity by using a metal skewer to secure the skin to the body. Then stuff the body cavity with the bread stuffing. Tuck the legs back under the precut band of skin or metal lock to secure them. Tuck the wing tips back under the shoulders of the bird.
3. Put any leftover stuffing in separate baking dishes, sprinkle with a little chicken broth, cover with foil, and refrigerate. Bake leftover stuffing, loosely covered with foil, during the last 45 minutes of the turkey's roasting time.
4. Preheat the oven to 325 degrees.
5. Place the turkey, breast side up, on a rack in a shallow roasting pan. Sprinkle with salt and pepper and brush with 2 tablespoons of the butter.
6. Place the turkey in the oven with the legs facing toward the back. Roast for about 4½ hours, or about 17 minutes per pound, basting with more melted butter and the pan drippings every 20 to 30 minutes. An instant-read thermometer should register

180 to 185 degrees in the thigh of the bird, and the stuffing should register 165 degrees.

7. Remove the bird to a board or platter and let it rest for 20 or 30 minutes before carving. Remove the stuffings and pass them in a bowl. Pass the giblet gravy as well.

Fruit and Nut Stuffing

MAKES 2 TO 3 CUPS

1 4-ounce package dried fruit tidbits or 1 cup coarsely chopped dried
    fruits, such as apricots, apples, and prunes
¼ cup golden raisins
3 tablespoons bourbon
½ cup coarsely chopped walnuts
½ cup coarsely chopped pecans
2 tablespoons butter
1 medium onion, chopped
1 small celery rib, chopped
1 large semisweet apple, such as Empire, unpeeled, cored and chopped
1 teaspoon dried savory
¼ teaspoon ground cinnamon
¼ teaspoon ground ginger
⅛ teaspoon ground allspice
½ cup whole fresh cranberries
3 tablespoons chopped fresh parsley
½ teaspoon salt
½ teaspoon fresh-ground black pepper
1 egg, lightly beaten

1. Toss the dried fruits and raisins with the bourbon in a small bowl. Cover and set aside to soak for at least 1 hour.

2. Toast the walnuts and pecans in a large skillet over medium heat, stirring frequently, until fragrant and one shade darker, about 7 minutes. Transfer to a plate.

3. Melt the butter in the same skillet. Add the onion, celery, and apple and cook, stirring frequently, until well softened, about 8 minutes. Add the savory, cinnamon,

Italian-American Thanksgiving

Italian immigrants were eager to adapt to all things American but were nonetheless adamant about maintaining their own culinary ways. Thus, Thanksgiving, that most American of holidays, began to take on an unusual shape in New England's Italian-American households, where Italian feast-day dishes were simply grafted onto the American tradition to create one huge repast. Here is the Thanksgiving menu that the DeFinis and Diiorio clans from Norwalk, Connecticut, serve every year:

Cold Antipasto Selection

Ravioli Soup

Home-Style Lasagne

Roast Turkey with Bread Stuffing
   and Homemade Gravy

Mashed Potatoes

Candied Sweets

Boiled Diced Turnips

Green Beans Almondine

Steamed Broccoli

Sausage-Stuffed Mushrooms

Date-Nut Bread

Italian Bread

Green Salad

Chocolate Cream Pie

Apple Pie

Pumpkin Pie

Ricotta Pie

Italian Cookies

Champagne

Espresso

ginger, and allspice. Remove from the heat and stir in the macerated fruits, toasted nuts, cranberries, and parsley. Season with the salt and pepper. Cool for 5 minutes, then stir in the egg. (The stuffing can be made a day ahead and refrigerated. If making ahead of time, add the beaten egg just before using the stuffing.)

New England Sage Bread Stuffing
MAKES ABOUT 8 CUPS

10 cups lightly packed bread cubes (from about 1 1-pound loaf) or
   9 cups cubed unseasoned stuffing mix
¼ pound (1 stick) butter

2 large onions, chopped
2 celery ribs, chopped
2 teaspoons poultry seasoning, such as Bell's
½ cup chopped fresh parsley
4 tablespoons chopped fresh sage
¾ teaspoon salt
¾ teaspoon fresh-ground black pepper
¾ to 1 cup chicken or turkey broth
1 egg, beaten

1. Preheat the oven to 400 degrees.
2. Spread the bread cubes out on a baking sheet and toast in the preheated oven, stirring once or twice, until firm to the touch, 8 to 10 minutes. (If you are using packaged stuffing mix, omit this step.)
3. Melt the butter in a large skillet. Add the onions and celery and cook over medium heat, stirring occasionally, until softened, about 10 minutes. Sprinkle with the poultry seasoning, add the parsley and fresh sage, and toss to combine. Season with the salt and pepper.
4. Combine the bread cubes and onion mixture in a large bowl, tossing gently to mix. Add ¾ cup of the broth, along with the egg, and mix lightly but thoroughly again. Add the remaining broth if you want a moister stuffing. (The stuffing can be made a day ahead and refrigerated. If making ahead of time, add the beaten egg just before using the stuffing.)

Giblet Gravy

MAKES 10 SERVINGS (5 TO 6 CUPS)

Turkey giblets, including neck
1 small onion
1 celery rib
1 sprig fresh sage
4 black peppercorns
½ teaspoon salt
6 tablespoons butter

6 tablespoons all-purpose flour
5 to 6 cups turkey giblet broth or canned
    chicken broth
⅓ cup dry sherry
Reserved juices from roasting pan and
    carving board
Salt and fresh-ground black pepper

> ### Easy Turkey
>
> "My favorite way to roast a turkey was to lay on a few strips of bacon, drape the breast with an old handkerchief, pour in broth, and baste away. Who needed a recipe?"
>
> —Karyl Bannister,
> *Cook & Tell* newsletter,
> West Southport, Maine

1. Place all the giblets except the liver in a medium saucepan, cover with 6 cups of cold water, and add the onion, celery, sage, peppercorns, and salt. Bring to a boil, skimming any foam that rises to the surface. Reduce the heat and simmer, partially covered, for 2 hours, until the gizzard is tender. Rinse the liver, add it to the broth, and simmer for 5 minutes, until it is just cooked through.

2. Strain, reserving the broth and discarding the vegetables, sage, peppercorns, and turkey neck. Trim the gizzard and finely chop all the giblets. (This step can be done a day ahead. Cover and refrigerate.)

3. After the turkey has been moved to the carving board, remove the rack from the roasting pan. Pour all the drippings into a large glass measuring cup and let stand for 5 minutes. Spoon off the fat from the top and discard. Reserve the dark juices to add to the gravy.

4. Place the roasting pan over 2 stove burners over medium heat. Melt the butter in the pan. Add the flour and cook, stirring, for 2 to 3 minutes, until lightly browned. Gradually whisk in 5 to 6 cups of the broth and the sherry and bring to a simmer. Cook and stir the gravy for about 5 minutes, until smooth and lightly thickened. Add the reserved turkey juices, including any that have accumulated on the carving board, and season to taste with salt and pepper. Stir in the chopped giblets.

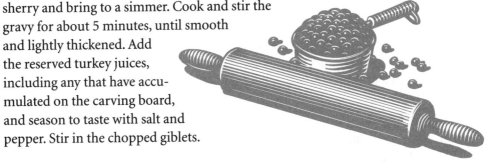

Turkey Breast with Crumbly Cider-Cornbread Dressing

MAKES 4 SERVINGS

Have yourself a scaled-down midweek Thanksgiving dinner by serving this quick and easy crumb-topped turkey cutlet dish with cranberry sauce, a baked sweet potato, green beans, and pumpkin pie for dessert. And naturally, you'll want to drink a toast to New England autumn with some more of that fresh apple cider.

1 pound turkey cutlets, cut about ½ inch thick
Salt and fresh-ground black pepper
1½ teaspoons poultry seasoning, such as Bell's
3 tablespoons butter
1 small onion, chopped
1 celery rib, chopped
1½ cups packaged crumbled unseasoned cornbread stuffing mix
1 cup apple cider or apple juice
1 tablespoon chopped fresh parsley

1. Season the turkey cutlets lightly with salt and generously with pepper, and sprinkle with 1 teaspoon of the poultry seasoning. Melt 1 tablespoon of the butter in a large skillet. Add the turkey and cook over medium heat, in 2 batches if necessary, until barely colored and just cooked through, about 5 minutes total. (Do not overcook the turkey, or it will be dry.) Remove from the skillet, leaving the drippings in the pan, and arrange the turkey in an 11-by-7-inch baking dish.

2. Preheat the broiler.

3. Melt the remaining 2 tablespoons butter in the same skillet, add the onion and celery, and cook over medium heat, stirring frequently, until the vegetables are lightly browned and softened, about 5 minutes. Add the stuffing mix, cider, parsley, and remaining ½ teaspoon poultry seasoning and toss until the liquid is absorbed but the stuffing is still quite moist, 2 to 3 minutes. Season with salt and pepper to taste.

4. Spoon and pat the stuffing over the turkey. Place the dish under the broiler, about 5 inches from the heat, and broil until the stuffing is golden and crispy around the edges, 2 to 4 minutes, watching carefully so it does not burn.

--- **About Cider** ---

"Sweet cider" is the unadulterated juice from apples squeezed through a press. If the juice is filtered and then pasteurized to stop its natural fermentation process, it becomes apple juice. If the alcohol is allowed to develop, after a while it turns into hard cider. Cider, both sweet and hard, was by far the most popular drink in colonial New England. It was either made at home or bought very cheaply by the barrel, and everyone, including children, drank it. President John Adams, who lived to be ninety-one, prided himself on drinking a pitcher of cider every morning. These days cider mills all over the region, using equipment ranging from antique wooden presses to modern hydraulic rigs, still turn out thousands of gallons of cider every fall. Families and field-tripping schoolchildren make pilgrimages to inhale the sweet, spicy, musky apple aroma in the pressing room and to watch as presses with the equivalent of one hundred tons of pressure come down on a fleshy mound of apples, to send a flood of amber juice cascading into a huge vat. Everyone leaves with a plastic jug of the just-made drink, which will keep in the refrigerator for a week to ten days before it gets fizzy and starts to ferment.

Maple-Lacquered Game Hens

MAKES 4 SERVINGS

The robust smokiness of maple syrup enchances the flavor of these lovely little birds, and its sugar content helps to burnish the outside of the hens to a lacquerlike gloss. Serve them as a special meal accompanied, perhaps, by Shaker Whipped Winter Squash with Cape Cod Cranberries (page 136) and herbed rice pilaf.

2 teaspoons butter
1 tablespoon minced shallots
2 tablespoons pure maple syrup
1 tablespoon Worcestershire sauce
2 teaspoons Dijon mustard
¼ teaspoon fresh-ground black pepper, plus more to taste
2 Cornish game hens, cut in half or quartered (see Note)
¾ cup chicken broth
2 to 3 teaspoons fresh lemon juice
Salt

1. Preheat the oven to 425 degrees.
2. Melt the butter in a small saucepan and cook the shallots over medium heat until softened, 1 to 2 minutes. Add the maple syrup, Worcestershire sauce, mustard, and pepper and cook, stirring, until smooth and bubbly, about 2 minutes.
3. Pull off and discard any excess fat on the hens. Use the heel of your hand to flatten the hen pieces somewhat. Place them skin side down in a shallow roasting pan, and brush with some of the maple glaze. Roast for 10 minutes. Reduce the oven temperature to 350 degrees. Turn the pieces, brush again, and continue to roast, brushing once or twice more with the maple mixture, for 35 to 45 minutes, until the thigh juices run clear when pierced with a sharp knife. (You can serve the hens as they are, or proceed to make the sauce.)
4. Remove the hen pieces to a platter and keep warm. Skim the fat off the pan juices. Place the roasting pan over a stove burner, add the broth and any remaining maple glaze, and cook over high heat, scraping up any browned bits on the bottom of the pan, until the liquid is slightly reduced and thickened. Add the lemon juice and season with salt and pepper to taste.

5. Serve the hens with the sauce on the side.

Note: You can ask the meat department of the supermarket to cut the hens on a band saw, or cut them up yourself with a large knife or kitchen shears.

Maple Festival

St. Albans, Vermont, proclaims itself the Maple Capital of the World. St. Albans is the county seat of Franklin County, which makes more syrup than any other county in the United States. On the third weekend of April every year, St. Albans hosts a Vermont Maple Festival. In the demonstration sugarhouse, visitors sniff the sweet-smelling steam and eat maple-glazed chicken and ham, devour hundreds of dozens of doughnuts with maple-cream icing, snack on maple "sugar-on-snow," and try curiosities like maple cotton candy. There are contests for the best maple syrup and for the best apple pie made with maple syrup, along with arts and crafts exhibits, a talent show, a parade, and a supper at which a maple king and queen are crowned.

Cornish Hens

Cornish hens are the result of cross-breeding meaty British Cornish game hens with New England's Plymouth Rock or White Rock chickens. At first the name was Rock Cornish Game Hens, but now it has been shortened to simply Cornish hens. What makes these little birds so appealing is that they're practically all breast and, because of their youth, supremely tender. The hens usually weigh in at about 1½ pounds, making each bird the ideal size to feed two people.

Autumn McIntosh-Roasted Duckling

MAKES 4 TO 6 SERVINGS

Once I discovered this method of cooking duck—first simmering it in water to draw off a lot of its excess fat and then slow-roasting in the oven—I felt much more kindly disposed to cooking these birds. Dealing with all that fat in the roasting pan can be a rather messy business, but this way the meat stays moist and juicy and the skin gets golden and crispy. I usually carve off the breast meat at the table, return to the kitchen to disjoint the birds with shears or a big knife, and then instruct the guests to pick up the bones to gnaw on them—the best way to make the most of that succulent skin.

> 2 4- to 5-pound ducklings
> Salt and fresh-ground black pepper
> 3 sweet apples, such as McIntosh, peeled, cored, and quartered
> 1 large onion, cut in chunks
> Several sprigs fresh rosemary
> 1 lemon, quartered
> ½ cup Madeira or sweet sherry
> 2 cups chicken broth or duck stock (see Note)
> 1 tablespoon chopped fresh rosemary

1. Pull off and discard as much fat as possible from the ducks. Place in a large pot, cover with cold water, and bring to a boil over high heat. Reduce the heat to medium-low and simmer, covered, for 30 minutes. Drain. (This step can be done several hours ahead. Refrigerate.)

2. Preheat the oven to 325 degrees.

3. Place the ducks on a rack in a large shallow roasting pan. Season well inside and out with salt and pepper. Scatter the apples, onion, rosemary sprigs, and lemon over and inside the cavities of the ducks. Tie the legs together, if you like (this is not absolutely necessary but makes for a juicier final result). Roast, uncovered, brushing with the pan juices every 20 minutes or so, until the thigh meat registers 180 degrees, about 1½ hours. Remove to a warm platter.

4. Remove the rack from the roasting pan. Spoon or pour off any excess rendered fat. Squeeze any juice from the lemons into the pan and discard the lemon rinds and the rosemary sprigs, leaving the apples and onions in the pan. Place the pan over 1 or 2 stove burners, add the Madeira, and bring to a boil, scraping up the browned bits that cling to the bottom of the pan and using the back of a spoon to mash the apples and onions into the sauce. Add the broth or stock and boil until slightly reduced and thickened, about 5 minutes. Add the chopped rosemary and season with more salt and pepper to taste.

5. Serve the duck with the sauce on the side.

Note: To make your own duck stock, cover the duck neck and giblets (minus the liver) with water, add a celery rib and a small onion, and simmer for about 2 hours. Strain and season with salt to taste.

My Wild Duck Breast with Fruited Port Sauce

MAKES 6 SERVINGS

My husband has been duck hunting on the islands in Long Island Sound off the Connecticut shore every winter for most of his life. In recent years he has hunted with a group of men around New Year's, and one of the families has turned it into an occasion to throw a big end-of-year hunt feast. The men, who have been up since well before dawn, clean the birds, cook up the livers for a snack, and then retire to nap while the nonhunters take over the cooking. I volunteered the first year to do the duck, and this is the recipe that I have been refining ever since. It works equally well with wild or domestic duck breast. Last year we started with Wellfleet Oysters on the Half Shell with Mango Mignonette (page 22), served the duck with Fluffy Garlic Mashed Potatoes (page 127),

Northeast Kingdom Maple-Glazed Braised Turnips (page 129), and a mesclun salad with toasted walnuts, and ended with Marlborough Apple-Cream Tart (page 614) for dessert.

> 1½ cups port
> 1 cup coarsely chopped dried fruits, such as apricots, prunes, pears,
>   and apples, or 1 4-ounce package dried fruit tidbits, chopped
> 1¾ to 2 pounds skinless, boneless wild or domestic duck breasts
> 1 teaspoon salt
> 1 teaspoon cracked black peppercorns or coarse-ground fresh-ground
>   black pepper
> 4 tablespoons butter
> 2 tablespoons olive oil
> ½ cup chopped shallots
> 1½ cups chicken or beef broth
> 2 tablespoons coarse-grained Dijon mustard
> 2 tablespoons red wine vinegar
> 1 tablespoon minced fresh parsley, preferably flat-leaf, plus sprigs for
>   garnish

1. Combine the port and dried fruits in a bowl. Set aside for about 1 hour.

2. Season the duck breasts with the salt and pepper. Heat 1 tablespoon each of the butter and oil in a large skillet over medium-high heat. Cook half the duck breasts until they are seared on the outside but still rare inside, 3 to 6 minutes, depending on the size and thickness of the breasts. Remove to a plate and repeat with another tablespoon each of butter and oil and the remaining duck. Remove to the plate, leaving the drippings in the pan.

3. Add the remaining 2 tablespoons of butter to the skillet. Add the shallots and cook, stirring, for 1 minute. Add the broth and boil briskly, stirring up the brown bits clinging to the bottom of the pan, until the liquid is reduced by about half, 3 to 5 minutes. Add the port and fruit and boil for 3 to 5 minutes, until the sauce is slightly reduced and thickened. Whisk in the mustard and vinegar. Taste and adjust the seasonings if necessary.

4. Return the duck and any accumulated juices to the sauce and simmer just until warmed through. The duck is best when it is still pink inside.

5. Stir in the parsley and serve, garnished with parsley sprigs.

Steam-Roasted Christmas Goose
with Madeira-Mustard Sauce

MAKES 6 TO 8 SERVINGS

Many New England families, ours included, continue the English tradition of roasting a goose for Christmas dinner, particularly when the holiday gathering is smaller. This unusual goose recipe is adapted from one by Julia Child, the incomparable queen mother of all modern cooks, whose residence for many years happens to have been in the Boston area. With goose, you need to get rid of some of its plenitude of fat. This method of steaming it renders most of the excess fat, and the finish in the oven produces a tender goose with crisp skin. As for stuffing, you could untie the legs and spoon Fruit and Nut Stuffing (page 326) into the cavity when you roast it, if you like, or, preferably I think, bake a pan of the stuffing alongside the bird.

> 1 10-to-12 pound goose
> 1 lemon, cut in half
> Salt and fresh-ground black pepper
> 1 onion, peeled and quartered
> 1 carrot, peeled and coarsely chopped
> 1 celery rib, coarsely chopped
> 4 sprigs fresh thyme or sage, plus sprigs for garnish
> 2 cups chicken broth or goose broth (see Note)
> 1½ tablespoons cornstarch
> ½ cup Madeira or port
> 2 tablespoons coarse-grained mustard

1. Pull away all the visible loose fat on the goose and discard it. Prick the bird all over with a fork or skewer, especially on the underside of the breast and thighs. Rub it inside and out with the cut sides of the lemon and season with salt and pepper. Place the onion, carrot, celery, and herb sprigs in the cavity. Tie the legs together with kitchen twine.

2. Place the bird, breast side up, on a rack in a large metal roasting pan. Place the pan on 1 or 2 burners on top of the stove and pour about 2 inches of boiling water into the bottom of the pan. Bring to a boil. Cover the pan tightly with a lid or aluminum foil. Reduce the heat to medium to medium-low and steam the goose for 1 hour, replenishing the boiling water if it gets low. When cool enough to handle, pour all

---

Bell's Seasoning

In the 1860s Willie Bell from Boston dreamed up the idea of an all-purpose seasoning blend that could be used for everything from turkey stuffing to oysters. This was a young man way ahead of his time, predating by more than a century all the myriad seasoning mixes now crowding our spice shelves. Willie got his mother, who was a good cook, to help him, and they began experimenting with herbs from their kitchen garden and spices from Slade's Mill in Revere, Massachusetts, to create the formula that became Bell's Seasoning. Bell's, packaged in its distinctive yellow box with a colorful turkey on the front, is still used to season poultry stuffing all over New England and indeed is known halfway around the globe. The box lists the ingredients as "rosemary, oregano, sage, ginger, marjoram, thyme, and pepper."

---

the liquid (there will be several cups of liquid and goose fat) out of the pan into a large glass measure. When the fat rises to the surface, you can spoon or lift it off and use this goose broth in your sauce. (You can do the steaming a couple of hours ahead and hold at cool room temperature before proceeding.)

3. Preheat the oven to 325 degrees.

4. Place the goose, breast side down, on the rack. Pour 1 cup of the chicken or goose broth into the pan, cover again, and place in the oven to roast for 1 hour. Replenish with more broth or water if the pan becomes dry.

5. Raise the oven temperature to 425 degrees. Turn the goose breast side up. Uncover, and roast until the skin is golden and the juices run clear, 30 to 40 minutes. Transfer the goose to a cutting board and allow to rest for 30 minutes while making the sauce.

6. Dissolve the cornstarch in the Madeira and whisk in the mustard. Spoon off most of the fat from the pan juices. Place the roasting pan on top of the stove over medium to medium-high heat. Whisk in the remaining 1 cup of chicken or goose broth and cook, stirring up any browned bits, for 2 minutes. Whisk in the Madeira mixture and cook for about 5 minutes, until the sauce is smooth and lightly thickened. Adjust the liquid if necessary. Season with salt and pepper to taste.

7. Carve the goose and arrange the meat on a platter garnished with fresh herb sprigs. Serve the sauce from a gravy boat alongside.

Note: Or, you can make a goose broth by simmering the goose giblets (except the liver) and wing tips, partially covered, in about 5 cups of water for 2 hours. Strain before using.

Thanksgiving

The first Thanksgiving feast is reputed to have taken place in Plymouth Colony on Cape Cod in Massachusetts in 1621, with the Pilgrims and some local Indians, the Wampanoags, in attendance. The celebration, which lasted for three days, was declared by Governor William Bradford to commemorate the survival of the colony through its first difficult year. Although there is doubt about whether they ate roast turkey that first feast day, records list oysters, eel, venison, cornbread, succotash, leeks, berries, and plums. Two years later turkey, pumpkin pie, and cranberries were definitely on the menu—and thus were established the familiar foods that all Americans still associate with the holiday.

Thanksgiving was not then formalized as a regular holiday, but it became popular in New England to give thanks on a day set aside for that purpose. Connecticut had its first official Thanksgiving in 1649, the Massachusetts Bay Colony followed suit in 1669, and President George Washington proclaimed a one-time national Thanksgiving Day in November 1789. Then, after relentless lobbying on the part of Sarah Josepha Hale, the influential editor of *Godey's Lady's Book*, President Abraham Lincoln declared Thanksgiving a permanent national holiday beginning in 1863. Congress passed a law in 1941 fixing the date as the fourth Thursday of November.

From its inception, Thanksgiving has been our most family-centered holiday, drawing generations of

Americans of every ethnic background and faith back home to participate by helping with the cooking, table setting, and, finally, the feasting.

And what a feast it always has been in New England, and still is. Some families begin with soup or oysters, but most just plunge right into the main course so as not to dull the edge of the appetite—and to leave some room for pie.

A New England Thanksgiving Dinner

Thanksgiving Roast Turkey and Two Stuffings with Giblet Gravy (page 325)

Fluffy Mashed Potatoes (page 126)

Lemon-Glazed Sweet Potato Gratin (page 139)

Northeast Kingdom Maple-Glazed Braised Turnips (page 129)

Petite Peas with Prosciutto (page 123)

Ivy League Beets with Orange Sauce (page 112)

Classic Parker House Rolls (page 447)

Shaker Cornmeal Pumpkin Bread with Toasted Walnuts (page 434)

Nantucket Cranberry-Pear Conserve (page 480)

No-Cook Cranberry-Kumquat Relish (page 479)

Richard Sax's Best-Ever Pumpkin Pie (page 607)

Blue-Ribbon Harvest Apple Pie (page 597)

Mince Pie with Decorative Top Crust (page 605)

Northeast Kingdom
Pheasant Fricassee with Riesling

MAKES 4 TO 6 SERVINGS

Since the nineteenth century, pheasant has been hunted and harvested in the huge upper quadrant of Vermont known as the Northeast Kingdom, as well as in other large tracts of woodland in New England. Farm-raised pheasant meat is pinkish white, with a delicate, mild taste. Like the meat of all game birds, it is very lean; hence, I love this method of gently stewing (or fricasseeing) the birds in a fruity white wine, with a finish of cream to round out any rough edges. If you can find a New England apple wine, use it here, but if not, invest in a nice German-style Riesling. Its complex fruitiness elevates the fricassee into something very special indeed.

¼ pound salt pork or bacon, cut in small dice
3 tablespoons butter
2 onions, thinly sliced
2 large leeks, rinsed well and thinly sliced
½ pound wild mushrooms, such as shiitake, sliced
2 2- to 3-pound pheasants cut in 8 pieces, skin removed (see Note)
Salt and fresh-ground black pepper
2 cups slightly sweet white wine, such as
    German or California Riesling, or
    semisweet apple wine
1 large or 2 small bay leaves
1 cup heavy cream
3 tablespoons minced fresh
    flat-leaf parsley

1. Cook the salt pork or bacon in a large skillet with a lid or in a Dutch oven, over medium heat, stirring occasionally, until the fat is rendered and the pork bits begin to brown, about 10 minutes. Remove the pork bits with a slotted spoon, drain on paper towels, and reserve. Pour off all but 2 tablespoons of drippings from the pan.

2. Add the butter to the drippings, along with the onions and leeks, and cook, stirring occasionally, for 5 minutes. Add the mushrooms and continue to cook, stirring occasionally, until the onion and mushrooms are softened, about 10 more minutes.

3. Season the pheasant pieces on both sides with salt and pepper. Add to the pan, turning to coat the pheasant with the onion-mushroom mixture. Pour in the wine, add the bay leaf, and bring to a boil. Reduce the heat and simmer over medium-low heat, covered, turning the pheasant pieces once or twice during the cooking process, until the meat is tender. This will take from 1½ to 2½ hours, depending on the age of the birds. Remove the pheasant to a plate.

4. Uncover the pan, raise the heat to medium-high, and add the cream. Cook at a gentle bubble until the sauce is reduced and lightly thickened, about 30 minutes. (This dish can be made a day ahead and refrigerated. Reheat gently.)

5. Remove the bay leaf, return the pheasant to the pan, and stir in the parsley. Taste the sauce and correct the seasonings if necessary. Reheat the pork bits and sprinkle them over the fricassee before serving, if you like.

Note: If your pheasants are not skinned, cook them with the skin on. Then it will be easy to pull off the skin and discard it before serving the fricassee.

Hart's: A Lot of Turkey

At Hart's Turkey Farm Restaurant in Meredith, New Hampshire, near Lake Winnipesaukee, the menu boasts that "every day is Thanksgiving Day." About half a century ago the Hart family began raising turkeys on their farm and opened a twelve-seat restaurant to merchandise their specialty. Their motto then, and now, is "If you want it done right, do it yourself." Eventually the Harts phased out turkey raising to concentrate on the restaurant business, and their restaurant now seats more than five hundred people. On a typical day they serve over a ton of turkey, forty gallons of gravy, one thousand pounds of fresh potatoes, four thousand dinner rolls, and more than one hundred pies. In addition to turkey dinners with all the trimmings, the menu mentions turkey nuggets, turkey livers, turkey soup, turkey croquettes, turkey pie, turkey stir-fry, turkey salad, turkey leg, BBQ turkey, turkey tempura, turkey divan, turkey club sandwich, turkey burger, hot turkey sandwich, and whole roasted turkey-to-go.

FINFISH

New England's rich history—both mercantile and culinary—rests squarely on the broad, sturdy back of a giant codfish. The first Europeans landed on Cape Cod, insisting on naming the fishhook-shaped peninsula after the cod instead of the king, and survived on the fish teeming around their ship in such numbers they could be scooped up by the bucketful. Descendants of these first settlers then went on to establish the "codfish aristocracy," a mercantile empire based on salting and drying the "sacred cod" and selling it around the globe.

Fishing is still a huge industry in New England, and Yankees, inlanders as well as coast dwellers, dote on fish. We still hold a Simple Broiled Boston Scrod (page 362) in high esteem, but adore, equally, such winning new codfish treatments as Roasted Cod Fillets with a Garlic-Prosciutto Topping (page 365). In spring we cook up a mess of Pan-Fried Mountain Stream Trout (page 375), or indulge in Shad Roe with Bacon and Thyme-Scented Cream Sauce (page 347). We are devoted to fish cakes, both in classic recipes such as Grandmother Maury's Salt Codfish Cakes with Bacon (page 366), and in very contemporary dishes like Ginger-Spiked Smoked Fish Cakes with Herbs (page 345). Meaty steaks cut from the noble swordfish are magnificent as Grilled Block Island Swordfish with Peppery Orange Salsa (page 373), and we happily carry on the splendid New England tradition of serving Fourth of July Grilled Salmon with Egg Sauce (page 358) to commemorate Independence Day.

Yankee Cafe Fresh Fish Cakes

MAKES 4 SERVINGS

According to the knowledgeable New England food writer Allene White, fish cakes, whether made with salted, smoked, or fresh fish, have been a Yankee tradition at least since the early nineteenth century. In Boston fish cakes made with salt cod and potato were a fixture of Sunday morning breakfast menus, along with Saturday's warmed-over baked beans. Not the stuff to inspire rapturous memories. These days, fresh fish cakes can range from very plain to somewhat more deluxe, like this recipe, based on one from the Thomaston Café in midcoast Maine. With such tasty additions as tangy Dijon mustard and fresh herbs, these fish cakes make a scrumptious supper, especially when served with Crispy Creamy Coleslaw (page 84) and Crusty Corn Muffins or Sticks (page 451).

> 3 tablespoons butter
> 1 medium onion, chopped
> 1 celery rib, chopped
> ½ cup heavy cream
> 1 pound boneless haddock or other firm white fish, cut in 2 or 3
>   pieces (see Note)
> ¾ teaspoon salt
> 2½ to 3 cups coarse fresh breadcrumbs
> 1 egg
> 1 egg yolk
> 1 tablespoon coarse-grained Dijon mustard
> 2 tablespoons chopped fresh dill
> 1 teaspoon grated lemon zest
> 1 tablespoon fresh lemon juice
> ½ teaspoon bottled hot pepper sauce
> 2 to 3 tablespoons vegetable oil
> Lemon wedges

1. Melt the butter in a large heavy skillet. Add the onion and cook over medium heat for 2 minutes. Add the celery and continue to cook until the onion is softened and the celery is still slightly crunchy, about 4 minutes. Add the cream, fish, and salt to the skillet. Raise the heat to high, and bring to a boil. Cover, reduce the heat to

The Ocean State

Rhode Island's nickname is the Ocean State. Measuring only 48 miles north to south, and 37 miles east to west, it is the smallest state in the United States. However, a considerable portion of Rhode Island's real estate fronts the Atlantic Ocean and the wide, deeply convoluted Narragansett Bay. Because of all of its inlets, islands, peninsulas, and bays, the coastline of Rhode Island adds up to more than four hundred miles.

medium-low, and simmer until the fish is just cooked through, 6 to 10 minutes, depending on its thickness. Uncover, cool slightly, and flake the fish with a fork. Transfer the mixture to a large bowl.

2. Add 2½ cups of the breadcrumbs to the fish mixture, along with the egg, egg yolk, mustard, dill, lemon zest and lemon juice, and hot pepper sauce. Mix with a large fork, adding the remaining crumbs if necessary to make a mixture that is moist but firm enough to hold its shape. Shape into 8 cakes about ½ inch thick, using about ½ cup of fish mixture per cake. (The cakes can be made several hours ahead. Cover and refrigerate.)

3. Heat the oil in 1 very large or 2 smaller skillets. Cook the cakes over medium heat on the first side until well browned on the bottom, 4 to 5 minutes. Turn, cover the pan(s), and cook until the second side is browned and the cakes are heated through, 4 to 5 minutes.

4. Serve the fish cakes hot, with lemon wedges.

Note: Or you can use ¾ to 1 pound of flaked leftover cooked fish and simmer it in the cream for 2 minutes.

Ginger-Spiked
Smoked Fish Cakes with Herbs

MAKES 4 SERVINGS

The zing of fresh ginger is a refreshing contemporary addition to these potato-based smoked fish cakes, and broiling rather than pan-frying is another delicious variation on the usual theme (and neat, since it means less spattering on the stove). Any one of New England's many varieties of smoked fish can be put to excellent use in these cakes, whether it be smoked haddock, mackerel, salmon, or trout. The broiled cakes are lovely simply served with lime wedges but are also fabulous with a fresh salsa topping such as Triple Tomato and Melon Salsa (page 476). A mixed mesclun salad or Sicilian Salad of Spinach, Oranges, and Red Onion (page 82), seeded breadsticks, and some sliced fresh fruit and Maury's Best Brownies (page 561) are good accompaniments.

1½ pounds russet or all-purpose potatoes, peeled and cut in 2-inch chunks
1½ cups flaked or shredded boneless smoked fish (about 6 ounces) (see Note)
⅓ cup snipped fresh chives or minced scallions
⅓ cup chopped fresh cilantro
1 tablespoon minced fresh ginger
½ teaspoon fresh-ground black pepper, preferably coarse-ground
Salt to taste
1 egg, lightly beaten
2 to 3 tablespoons peanut or other vegetable oil
Lime wedges

1. Cook the potatoes in a large pot of boiling salted water until very soft, about 20 minutes. Drain well and put them through a ricer or mash with a potato masher or a large fork until smooth. (You should have about 4 cups of puree.)

The Richest Town

Provincetown, Massachusetts, was the wealthiest town per capita in New England in the 1840s and 1850s. The source of the town's riches was the commercial fishing business that was concentrated in this small outpost at the very tip of Cape Cod.

2. Combine the potatoes with the fish, chives, cilantro, ginger, and pepper in a large bowl. Stir well to combine. Taste and season with salt if necessary. (Enough saltiness may have been provided by the smoked fish.) Beat in the egg. Shape into 8 ½-inch-thick cakes and place them on a lightly oiled or nonstick baking sheet. (The cakes can be made up to 4 hours ahead. Cover and refrigerate, but add a couple of minutes to the broiling time if they are cold.)

3. Preheat the broiler and position a rack 4 or 5 inches from the heat.

4. Brush or drizzle the fish cakes with some of the oil and broil on the first side for about 3 minutes, until flecked with brown. Turn with a spatula, brush with more oil, and broil on the second side until browned.

5. Serve the fish cakes with lime wedges on the side to balance the saltiness.

Note: If the fish is very heavily smoked, simmer it in boiling water to cover for about 5 minutes before using.

Back Bay Milk-Poached Finnan Haddie

MAKES 4 SERVINGS

Finnan haddie is partially boned, smoked, and lightly salted haddock, named after Findon, the town in Scotland where it was invented, supposedly when a warehouse full of haddock caught fire and inadvertently smoked the entire catch of the day. New Englanders, being lovers of fresh haddock, quickly learned to appreciate the smoked version of this flaky fish as well. Finnan haddie is becoming somewhat hard to find in New England, as well as around the rest of the country, but it is still on the menu of some of Boston's venerable old hotels. Traditionally, poached finnan haddie was served as a breakfast or brunch item, but I love it for supper, with parsleyed boiled red-skinned potatoes in their jackets and a steamed green vegetable such as broccoli.

1½ pounds smoked haddock
3 tablespoons unsalted butter
1 medium onion, thinly sliced
1½ cups whole milk
1 bay leaf, broken in half

½ teaspoon fresh-ground black pepper
Paprika

1. Combine the haddock with about 4 cups of water in a large saucepan or skillet with lid. Bring to a boil, uncovered, over medium-high heat. Remove from the heat and set aside, covered, for 30 minutes (see Note). Drain, discarding the water, and rinse out the pan. Reserve the fish.

2. Return the pan to the stove, melt the butter in it, and add the onion. Cook over medium heat until the onion softens, about 5 minutes. Return the haddock to the pan, add the milk, bay leaf, and pepper, and bring to a simmer over medium heat. Cover, reduce the heat to medium-low, and cook until the haddock is soft and flakes easily, 25 to 30 minutes.

3. Serve in shallow bowls or on rimmed plates with some of the milk spooned over. Sprinkle with paprika. Inform the diners that there will no doubt be a few bones to remove.

Note: Finnan haddie varies in its degree of saltiness. If the fish is very salty, parboil it in 2 changes of water to remove excess salt.

Shad Roe with Bacon and Thyme-Scented Cream Sauce

MAKES 4 SERVINGS

Shad, a member of the herring family, spawns in river estuaries, as salmon do, and then lives out the rest of its life in the ocean. Once so common in Connecticut rivers that townspeople along the big rivers celebrated their abundance with festivals every spring, shad began to diminish because of river pollution. Now they are starting to return. Shad are prized at least as much for their lovely large roe as for their flesh, and shad roe is a delicacy that is almost an addictive taste, once acquired. The eggs are encased in a delicate membrane that, if subjected to high heat, can break and create a real mess in the pan, but this method of poaching the roe solves that problem. Bacon is a classic accompaniment to shad roe; this lovely, light thyme-scented cream sauce is a modern addition. Serve this springtime treat meal with such other seasonal specialties as Sautéed Fiddleheads, Sugar Snaps, and Baby Carrots (page 119) and Shaker Baked Rice Pilaf (page 224). Sugared sliced strawberries spooned over wedges of plain Hot Milk Sponge Cake (page 534) would be an appropriately seasonal dessert.

2 pairs of shad roe (about 1½ pounds)
1 tablespoon fresh lemon juice
¾ teaspoon salt, plus more to taste
4 slices bacon, cut in half to make 8 pieces
4 tablespoons all-purpose flour
¼ teaspoon fresh-ground black pepper, plus more to taste
1 egg
½ cup fine dried breadcrumbs
½ cup dry white wine
½ cup heavy cream
1 tablespoon chopped fresh thyme
4 thin lemon slices

1. Place the roe in a large saucepan or deep skillet and add water to cover, along with the lemon juice and ½ teaspoon of the salt. Bring to a boil, reduce the heat to low, and simmer, uncovered, until the roe begins to firm up, 4 to 7 minutes, depending on size. Using a slotted spoon, lift the roe out of the liquid and drain well on paper towels. Trim the membranes and carefully cut each roe pair into 4 pieces so you have a total of 8 pieces. (The roe can be precooked a few hours ahead. Cover and refrigerate.)

2. Cook the bacon in a large skillet over medium heat until crisp, about 10 minutes. Drain on paper towels, leaving the drippings in the pan.

3. Stir together the flour, ¼ teaspoon salt, and the pepper in a shallow dish. Lightly beat the egg with 1 tablespoon of water in a second dish. Spread out the bread-crumbs in a third dish. Turn the roe in the flour, shake off the excess, then dip in the egg, and turn in the breadcrumbs to coat.

4. Reheat the bacon drippings and cook the roe over medium heat, carefully turning once, until browned and crisp on both sides, 5 to 8 minutes. Transfer to a warm platter and cover loosely with foil.

5. Add the wine and cream to the pan drippings, raise the heat to high, and cook, stirring up any browned bits, until the sauce comes to a boil. Cook, stirring, until

lightly thickened, 3 to 4 minutes. Stir in the thyme and season with salt and pepper to taste, keeping in mind that the bacon garnish will add more salt.

6. To serve, spoon the sauce over the roe, top with bacon, and garnish with the lemon slices.

Shad Bakes

Every spring in the picturesque town of Essex, Connecticut, near the mouth of the Connecticut River, the running of the shad is celebrated with a Shad Bake put on by the local Rotary Club. On Bake Day a bakemaster directs dozens of volunteers in this old New England tradition, which involves "planking" the fish and cooking it outdoors over glowing coals. The boned shad are nailed, along with strips of salt pork, to aged oak boards. The fish is brushed with lemon juice and butter, tilted toward the fire, and baked slowly so that the flesh becomes imbued with the fine flavor of smoke and picks up a subtle suggestion of oak flavoring from the hardwood plank.

Westport Baked Roe-Stuffed Shad with Tarragon Cream

MAKES 6 SERVINGS

For centuries, shad has been synonymous with spring in Connecticut. After a decline during the mid-twentieth century, this luscious, meaty fish and its rich roe are available in fish markets once again. The added bonus these days is that it's mostly sold already boned, presumably by some sort of knife-wielding wizard, for shad is notoriously bony and must be expertly filleted. One year our good friends Dale and Toni, who are both wonderful cooks, prepared one of the most memorable Easter feasts I have ever had the pleasure of eating. The highlight of the elegant meal was this baked roe-stuffed shad with a tarragon cream sauce, based on a Craig Claiborne recipe from a *New York Times* cookbook. If you make this dish, the rest of the menu might be composed of such vernal delicacies as Minted New Potatoes and Peas (page 124), Broiled Asparagus with Asiago (page 110), a salad of baby greens, and Classic Parker House Rolls (page 447). For dessert, try Frank's Strawberry-Rhubarb Pie (page 610).

For the stuffing:

2 tablespoons butter
3 tablespoons minced shallots
2 pairs of shad roe (about 1½ pounds)
1 cup dry white wine or vermouth
1 bay leaf, broken in half
1 tablespoon fresh lemon juice
½ teaspoon salt
¼ teaspoon fresh-ground black pepper

For the fish and sauce:

2 large boned sides of shad (3 to 4 pounds total)
Salt and fresh-ground black pepper
2 tablespoons butter, melted
1 teaspoon cornstarch
1 cup heavy cream
1½ tablespoons chopped fresh tarragon, plus sprigs for garnish

1. To make the stuffing, melt the butter in a large skillet. Add the shallots and sauté over medium heat for 1 minute. Add the shad roe, turn to coat it with butter, and add the wine and bay leaf. Bring to a gentle simmer and cook, uncovered, until the roe is just barely firm, about 10 minutes. Remove the roe with a slotted spoon to a large plate, reserving the poaching liquid. (You can leave the liquid in the pan if you will be finishing the dish right away; otherwise, cover and refrigerate.)

2. Trim off any tough membranes and break the roe into pieces. Add the lemon juice, sprinkle with the salt and pepper, and use a large fork to coarsely mash the mixture. (The roe stuffing can be prepared several hours ahead and refrigerated.)

3. Season the shad on both sides with salt and pepper. Place the stuffing under the natural flaps on each side of the fish. Brush a baking pan large enough to hold the fish with melted butter. Sandwich the stuffed sides together and tie with 2 or 3 pieces of kitchen twine. Brush the top of the fish with the butter. (The recipe can be made ahead to this point and refrigerated for up to 4 hours.)

4. Preheat the oven to 375 degrees.

5. Cover the baking pan loosely with foil and bake until the fish is no longer translucent in the thickest part, 20 to 40 minutes, depending on the thickness.

6. While the shad is baking, boil the reserved roe-poaching liquid over high heat until it is reduced to about ½ cup. Remove and discard the bay leaf. In a small bowl, dissolve the cornstarch in 2 tablespoons of the cream. Whisk the cornstarch mixture and the rest of the cream into the poaching liquid and simmer over medium heat, stirring, until lightly thickened. Stir in the tarragon and season the sauce to taste with salt and pepper.

7. Carefully transfer the fish to a serving platter and remove the strings. Spoon a ribbon of sauce over the fish and garnish with sprigs of tarragon. To serve, cut into crosswise slices to include some of the roe stuffing for each person. Pass the rest of the sauce in a bowl at the table.

The Fishing Industry

New England's coastline comprises only 7.3 percent of the total United States coast, but more than one-third of America's supply of finfish and shellfish comes from New England waters. Of the total number of professional fishermen in this country, 35 percent are employed in the North Atlantic fisheries.

Shallow-Fried
New England "Little Fish"

MAKES 4 SERVINGS

When schools of silvery baby fish, also called minnows or "little fish," teem in Atlantic bays, fishermen sometimes scoop up a whole "mess" and sell them as whitebait, silversides, or alewives. If the fish are really tiny—not more than two or three inches long—they can be eaten bones and all. If they are any larger than that, the flesh can be nibbled off the frame as you would eat corn on the cob. Smelts, which are typically about seven inches long, need to be cleaned before cooking. Simply make a small cut behind the top of the head, pull the head and innards down and back, and rinse the fish. A supper of freshly netted little fish or smelts is something very special. They can be served as an hors d'oeuvre, a snack, or a main course, and we always eat them with our fingers.

¾ cup all-purpose flour
1 tablespoon cornmeal
1 teaspoon salt
¼ teaspoon fresh-ground black pepper
¼ teaspoon cayenne pepper
Peanut or other vegetable oil for shallow-frying
1½ to 2 pounds little fish, gutted and beheaded if longer than
   about 2 inches
Lemon wedges
Classic Tartar Sauce (page 14) or other tartar sauce

1. In a plastic or paper bag, combine the flour, cornmeal, salt, pepper, and cayenne and shake to combine.

2. Heat about ½ inch of oil to 350 degrees in a very large, deep, preferably cast-iron skillet over medium heat. (The oil is hot enough when a cube of bread browns in about 30 seconds.)

3. Shake as many fish as can comfortably be cooked at one time in the bag with the seasoned flour until evenly coated. Ease slowly and carefully into the hot oil and cook, turning once with a long-handled slotted spoon or tongs (it's okay if some of the fish stick to one another), until browned and cooked through, 2 to 5 minutes total. Drain on paper towels. Repeat with the remaining fish. (The fish can be kept warm on a baking sheet in a low oven for up to 30 minutes if necessary.)

4. Transfer to a platter, surround with lemon wedges, and serve with a bowl of tartar sauce.

Never the Twain Shall Meet

Sometimes it seems that Narragansett Bay divides the tiny state of Rhode Island not just geographically but also culturally into two distinct regions, at least culinarily speaking. The dual camps engage in pitched battles over their preference for thick versus thin jonnycakes (see page 414), for example, and over the merits of milky versus "clear" clam chowders. They also skirmish over fried fish condiments. East of the bay, in South County (and across the border into Massachusetts), natives bypass tartar sauce and ketchup and reach for a shaker bottle of cider vinegar to sprinkle on their fish and chips, fried clams, and french fries. Inhabitants of the coastal towns west of Narragansett Bay wouldn't dream of "ruining" their fried shore food with a dousing of vinegar, preferring their condiments in the more standard New England form of tartar sauce and lemon wedges.

Narragansett Beer-Battered Fish 'n' Chips

MAKES 4 SERVINGS

The fishing boats that ply the waters of Narragansett Bay and Rhode Island Sound bring their catch into the docks around the Galilee–Point Judith area. Much of it gets sold to customers right at the pier, destined to reappear hours later on fortunate Rhode Islanders' dinner tables or on the menus of seafood restaurants clustered around the dock (or in the case of one establishment, right on top of the dock). Fish and chips, made with scrod or sometimes with very fresh flounder fillets, are a specialty at every one of these eateries. In this version for the home cook, the fish is shallow- or pan-fried, rather than deep-fried. The beer-and-vinegar batter, somewhat reminiscent of a tempura batter, has a pleasingly sour tang, and the fish emerges with a light, lacy coating and an almost crackling crunch. As for the chips part, my honest recommendation is to pop a batch of frozen french fries into the oven, since deep-frying potatoes in a lot of oil is a messy and somewhat problematic procedure best done with restaurant equipment. Serve the fish and chips with the suggested condiments, along with a side of pickled or creamy coleslaw, for a superb once-in-a-while-treat re-creation of a dockside meal.

> 1 cup all-purpose flour
> 1 teaspoon salt
> ½ teaspoon black pepper
> ¾ teaspoon baking soda
> 1 cup flat beer or ale
> 1 tablespoon cider vinegar
> Peanut or other vegetable oil for shallow-frying
> 1½ pounds firm fish fillets such as scrod, haddock, or pollack, or very
>   fresh flounder, about ½-inch-thick, cut in about 12 pieces
> 6 cups cooked french fries
> Tartar sauce, lemon wedges, and cider or malt vinegar

1. Whisk together the flour, salt, pepper, and baking soda in a large bowl. Gradually whisk in the beer and vinegar. Let the batter stand for 10 minutes and stir gently again before using.

2. Heat ½ to ¾ inch of oil to 350 degrees in a deep, heavy, preferably cast-iron skillet over medium heat. The oil is hot enough when a small cube of bread browns in about 30 seconds.

3. Dip the fish in the batter, letting the excess drip off, and slowly and carefully ease into the oil. (Do not crowd the pan. You will probably have to fry in 2 or 3 batches.) Fry the fish, turning once with a long-handled slotted spoon or tongs, until well browned on both sides and cooked through, 3 to 5 minutes total. Remove carefully and drain on paper towels.

4. Serve the fish with the french fries and pass the condiments at the table.

Tinker Mackerel, Grilled or Broiled, with Honey-Mustard Butter

MAKES 4 SERVINGS

"Tinkers" is the Yankee nickname for small Atlantic mackerel less than 12 inches long. These pretty, bluish gray striped fish are abundant in the bays of Maine, and their run begins in mid-July and usually lasts well into August. Fishing for mackerel can be very rewarding, for when a school comes through, even the most novice (or youngest) angler can pull in a few. Tinkers' small bones can be somewhat pesky, and while it's pretty easy to eat around them, if you happen to have a good fish filleter in the family or can buy the mackerel filleted, so much the better. Tinkers are wonderful broiled or cooked on the grill, especially when a handful of fragrant wood chips such as alder or birch is tossed on the fire. Here a final gloss of this sweet-sharp honey-mustard butter enhances the already-sweet taste of the fish, but, truth to tell, plain, unadorned

Melville's Nantucket

"The area before the house was paved with clam shells. Mrs. Hussey wore a polished necklace of codfish vertebrae; and Hosea Hussey had his account books bound in superior old shark-skin. There was a fishy flavor to the milk, too, which I could not account for, till one morning happening to take a stroll along the beach among some fishermen's boats, I saw Hosea's brindled cow feeding on fish remnants, and marching along the sand with each foot in a cod's decapitated head, looking very slipshod, I assure ye."

—Herman Melville, *Moby Dick* (1851)

Cod Cheeks and Tongues

The thought of eating fish cheeks and tongues might not sound terribly appetizing, but in New England and eastern Canada, these parts of large fish are considered a great delicacy. Cod cheeks are the scallop-sized, sometimes even larger, discs of flesh on each side of the head of the fish; the tongues are not true tongues at all but the meaty part of the throat of the fish. Cheeks and tongues are usually cooked by rolling them in seasoned flour or cornmeal and frying until brown.

❈ ❈ ❈ ❈ ❈ ❈ ❈ ❈ ❈
---

mackerel meat, which turns pearly white when cooked, is superb wearing nothing more than a splash of lemon juice.

> 4 tablespoons unsalted butter, softened
> 2 tablespoons honey mustard
> 4 large to 8 small mackerel (depending on size), cleaned and split, or filleted and boned (see Note)
> 1 to 2 tablespoons peanut or other vegetable oil
> Salt and fresh-ground black pepper
> Lemon wedges

1. Stir together the butter and mustard in a small bowl. Shape into a cylinder, wrap in plastic wrap, and refrigerate until firm.

2. Build a moderately hot charcoal fire, preheat a gas grill, or preheat the broiler. Make sure the grill rack is well oiled.

3. Brush the fish with the oil and sprinkle with salt and pepper. To grill, place in a hinged grill basket or directly on the grill rack, skin side down, and cook for 2 minutes. Flip the basket or turn the fish with a large spatula and cook for 2 to 4 minutes, or until lightly browned and the flesh is cooked through. To broil, place the fish in a broiler pan skin side down. Broil, 4 to 5 inches from the heat, until browned and the flesh is cooked through, 5 to 8 minutes.

4. To serve, transfer the mackerel to a warm platter. Slice the honey-mustard butter into medallions and place atop the hot fish to melt. Serve with lemon wedges.

Note: Allow about a 1-pound whole fish per person, or 2 smaller fish.

At the Sardine Factory

Mildred "Meme" Wilcox has worked at the sardine packing factory in the town of Lubec, at the easternmost tip of the Maine coast, for fifty-eight years. "A lot has changed since I started," she says. "Back then, you had to stake out your own worktable and hang on to it. If you left your table, why, there would be someone else waiting to take over. I worked sealing cans for the first year and then changed to packing, and that's what I've done ever since. In fact, I've had the same table for the last thirty-nine years. They used to cook the sardines first, then pack them. But now they pack and seal first, and then the fish get cooked right in their cans."

"Every year I think this will probably be my last year, but every year I go back again. I really like my job, being with people. It's hard on the back sometimes, but come next morning, I'm up and raring to go again. Me? I'll probably retire when I get old enough."

Rosemary-Grilled Bluefish with Rosemary-Lime Butter

MAKES 4 SERVINGS

Running in large schools in the summer all up and down the Atlantic coast, the bluefish has a high oil content, causing it be unfairly maligned. In fact, the flesh of a very fresh bluefish is deliciously moist and meaty and not at all fishy tasting. If you make friends with a fisherman in the summer in New England, you're apt to be the lucky recipient of bluefish galore. I love this method of grilling the bluefish fillets over a rosemary-perfumed fire and then topping them with a compound butter flavored with the same herb. The pleasantly sharp, resiny tang of rosemary perfectly comple-ments the flavor of this much under-rated fish. The rosemary-lime butter, incidentally, is also fabulous on grilled chicken. You can make a double batch and store it in the freezer.

For the butter:

4 tablespoons unsalted butter, softened
1 tablespoon coarse-grained Dijon mustard
2 teaspoons chopped fresh rosemary
½ teaspoon grated lime zest
1 tablespoon fresh lime juice

For the fish:

4 bluefish fillets (about 6 ounces each), with skin on one side (see Note)
2 teaspoons olive oil
Salt and fresh-ground black pepper
Rosemary sprigs
Lime wedges

1. To make the flavored butter, mash together the butter, mustard, chopped rosemary, lime zest and juice on a plate until well blended. Transfer to a sheet of plastic wrap, shape into a cylinder, and wrap tightly. Refrigerate until firm. (The butter can be stored for several weeks in the freezer. Soften slightly at room temperature before slicing.)

2. Build a moderately hot charcoal fire or preheat a gas grill. Make sure the grill rack is well oiled. Shortly before cooking the bluefish, toss a couple of rosemary sprigs on the fire.

3. Rub the fillets with the oil and season with salt and pepper. Place on the grill, flesh side down, and cook until the bottom begins to brown and the sides begin to turn white, 3 to 5 minutes. Using a large spatula, turn carefully and continue to cook until the flesh is opaque and the skin is crisp, 3 to 5 minutes more, depending on the thickness. (Or use a hinged wire basket to grill the fish.)

4. Transfer to a platter or serving plates. Cut the rosemary butter into medallions and place atop each piece of fish to melt. Garnish with rosemary sprigs and lime wedges and serve.

Note: Removing the dark strip that runs down the center of the fish flesh prevents the rest of the fish from absorbing a strong flavor.

Fourth of July
Grilled Salmon with Egg Sauce

MAKES 6 SERVINGS

It was John Adams, the first president to come from New England, who urged that Independence Day be celebrated with fireworks and parades; it was probably his wife, Abigail, who started the American tradition of serving salmon with egg sauce at her Fourth of July dinner parties. In early New England days, many of the larger rivers in the region, such as the Connecticut, Merrimack, Kennebec, and Penobscot, ran richly with salmon. Early summer was prime salmon-fishing season, and the glorious pink fish was a natural to star as the centerpiece of the Independence Day feast. The rest of this traditional menu is decreed by Mother Nature, who sweetly conspires to produce a garden crop of sweet green peas, the first tiny new potatoes, and our peak native strawberry season to coincide with the date of the national party. Fortunately, salmon are now being farm-raised in Atlantic waters, so this culinary tradition, once in danger of languishing, can now be revived.

For the sauce:

1½ tablespoons butter
½ cup minced onion
1½ tablespoons all-purpose flour
1 teaspoon dry mustard
1½ cups whole or lowfat milk
¾ teaspoon salt
½ teaspoon fresh-ground black pepper
1 hard-cooked large egg, peeled and chopped
1 tablespoon chopped fresh dill
1 tablespoon fresh lemon juice

For the fish:

6 salmon steaks (5 to 8 ounces each), 1 inch thick
2 tablespoons olive oil
Salt and fresh-ground black pepper
Dill sprigs
Lemon wedges

1. To make the sauce, melt the butter in a medium-sized saucepan. Add the onion and cook over medium heat until softened, about 5 minutes. Sprinkle on the flour and dry mustard and cook, stirring, for 2 minutes. Gradually whisk in the milk. Raise the heat to high, bring to a boil, and cook, whisking constantly, for 1 minute. Remove from the heat and whisk in the salt and pepper. (The sauce base can be made up to 24 hours ahead and refrigerated. Rewarm over low heat or in a microwave before proceeding.) Stir in the chopped egg, chopped dill, and lemon juice. Taste and correct the seasonings if necessary.

2. Build a moderately hot charcoal fire or preheat a gas grill. Be sure the grill rack is oiled.

3. Brush the salmon on both sides with oil and season with salt and pepper. Grill the salmon, turning carefully once with a large spatula, until the fish just turns opaque near the bone, about 10 minutes. Transfer to serving plates or a large platter and garnish with dill sprigs and lemon wedges.

4. Reheat the sauce if necessary and pass it in a sauceboat at the table for spooning over the fish.

Grilled Tuna Steaks with Peach–Red Onion Salsa

MAKES 4 SERVINGS

Most of the beautiful bluefin tuna that were fished from the deep Gulf Stream waters off New England used to go to the Japanese, who prize the fish for sushi and sashimi. When we finally began to appreciate this glorious native fish we learned how to cook it at home in all kinds of ways, served with all manner of sauces and toppings. Tuna takes particularly well to grilling, and this dazzling peach salsa, an adaptation of a recipe in Chris Schlesinger and John Willoughby's book *The Thrill of the Grill*, provides a perfect foil for tuna's distinctive, assertive flavor. Wonderful peaches are grown in Massachusetts's Pioneer Valley and are one of New England's little-known summer crops, but this salsa is equally tasty when made with nectarines or plums. In this recipe the tuna takes a one-hour preliminary bath in olive oil, a trick I learned from *Cook's Illustrated* magazine. The oil keeps the lean flesh from drying out, and the resulting grilled tuna is lusciously moist.

For the salsa:

2 or 3 ripe but firm medium peaches, peeled and diced

1 cup chopped red onion

¾ cup chopped red bell pepper

1 large garlic clove, minced

2 tablespoons fruit vinegar or red wine vinegar

2 tablespoons orange juice

2 tablespoons olive oil

½ teaspoon salt, or to taste

½ teaspoon fresh-ground black pepper or cracked black peppercorns

¼ teaspoon red pepper flakes

¼ cup slivered fresh basil

For the fish:

4 tuna steaks (6 to 8 ounces each), 1 inch thick

½ cup extra-virgin olive oil

2 tablespoons slivered fresh basil, plus whole leaves for garnish

½ teaspoon salt

½ teaspoon fresh-ground black pepper or cracked black peppercorns

1. To make the salsa, combine all the salsa ingredients except the basil in a large bowl and mix thoroughly. Set aside at room temperature for about 1 hour or refrigerate for up to 6 hours. Shortly before serving, stir in the basil.
2. Place the fish in a shallow bowl or rimmed dish, pour the olive oil over it, scatter the slivered basil on top, and sprinkle with the salt and pepper. Turn the fish to completely coat it with the oil mixture. Cover and refrigerate for at least 1 hour or up to 3 hours, turning once or twice so the fish stays coated with the oil.
3. Build a moderately hot charcoal fire or preheat a gas grill.
4. Lift the fish out of the oil, letting the excess drain off, and place it on the grill. Cook the fish, turning once, until it reaches the desired degree of doneness, 2 to 3 minutes per side for medium-rare to medium.
5. Transfer the tuna to a platter or serving plates, spoon some of the salsa over the top, garnish with basil leaves, and pass the rest of the salsa at the table.

Portuguese Tuna Escabeche

MAKES 4 MAIN-COURSE SERVINGS; MORE APPETIZER SERVINGS

This mildly spiced pickled tuna, a specialty of Madeira, was transplanted to New Bedford, Massachusetts, and other fishing towns along the New England coast by the Portuguese people who settled there. Pickled tuna has long been popular in Mediterranean countries. This aromatic version of the dish, which is graced with traditional Portuguese garnishes of chopped egg, black olives, and orange wedges makes a delightful summer main course accompanied by chewy Portuguese bread and a light salad. Tuna escabeche also serves well as an hors d'oeuvre or appetizer and makes an impressive addition to a buffet.

For the tuna:

4 tuna steaks (1 to 1½ pounds total), ½ inch thick
1 medium onion, chopped
2 garlic cloves, minced
¼ cup white wine vinegar
1 bay leaf, broken in half
½ teaspoon salt
¼ teaspoon cayenne pepper

For the marinade and garnish:

⅔ cup extra-virgin olive oil
¼ cup white wine vinegar
1 medium onion, chopped
2 garlic cloves, minced
1 teaspoon grated orange zest
½ teaspoon salt
½ teaspoon fresh ground black pepper
4 hard-cooked eggs, peeled and chopped
2 tablespoons chopped fresh flat-leaf parsley
2 tablespoons chopped fresh cilantro
½ cup pitted European black olives, such as Niçoise
1 orange, cut in wedges

1. To poach the tuna, place the steaks in a large skillet. Scatter with the onion and garlic and add the vinegar, bay leaf, salt, cayenne, and 4 cups of water. Bring to a boil, reduce the heat to low, and simmer, covered, until the fish flakes easily, about 10 minutes. Cool in the poaching liquid, about 30 minutes. Remove the tuna from the poaching liquid.
2. To marinate the tuna, combine the oil, vinegar, onion, garlic, orange zest, salt, and pepper in a large bowl. Place the tuna in the marinade, turning to coat well. Cover and marinate in the refrigerator for at least 3 hours or up to 3 days. Remove from the refrigerator about 45 minutes before serving.
3. To serve, lift the tuna out of the marinade, arrange it on a platter, and spoon some of the marinade over the fish. Sprinkle with the eggs and the parsley and cilantro, and scatter the olives around the edges. Garnish with the orange wedges.

Simple Broiled Boston Scrod

MAKES 4 SERVINGS

The origin and definition of the term *scrod* is difficult to pin down. One story has it that *scrod* is a contraction of *Sacred Cod*, the name of the 4-foot wooden sculpture that has hung in the Massachusetts State House since 1748. When the word is spelled *schrod*, some say that the addition of the *h* means the fish is haddock, not cod. Strictly defined, scrod is young cod, from a fish weighing not more than two pounds; it is usually prepared simply broiled with a buttered crumb topping. In some quarters, notably at Boston's more tourist-oriented restaurants, scrod is loosely defined as "catch of the day," which allows an establishment to offer whatever fish is available (and cheap) and call it scrod on the menu. Actually, any impeccably fresh fish in the cod family, whether it be true baby cod or haddock, pollack, or hake, is delicious when cooked in this manner, just to the point when the fragile, moist flesh pulls apart into lovely thick, white flakes.

> 4 tablespoons butter
> 4 young cod fillets (1½ to 2 pounds total)
> Salt and fresh-ground black pepper
> 1½ cups fresh breadcrumbs
> 2 tablespoons chopped fresh parsley, plus sprigs for garnish
> Lemon wedges

1. Preheat the broiler and position the rack 4 to 5 inches from the heat.
2. Melt the butter in a medium-sized skillet. Brush some of it over both sides of the fish and arrange the fillets in a broiling pan or shallow baking dish. Sprinkle with salt and pepper.
3. Add the crumbs to the remaining butter in the skillet and cook over medium to medium-high heat, tossing, until they toast to one shade darker, about 3 minutes. Remove from the heat and stir in the parsley.
4. Sprinkle the crumbs and parsley evenly over the fish. Broil until the crumbs are darkly toasted and the fish flakes and is no longer translucent, about 5 minutes per ½ inch of thickness.
5. Transfer to serving plates, garnish with parsley sprigs and lemon wedges, and serve.

Portuguese New Englanders

Some historians contend that there is evidence that a Portuguese explorer, Miguel Corte Real, and his crew came ashore and lived among the Native Americans in the vicinity of Narragansett Bay a century before the English landed at Plymouth Rock. In the early nineteenth century, New England whaling captains, hearing of the legendary reputation of the Portuguese as expert seamen, departed New England ports intending to fill in the balance of their crew with Portuguese recruits, particularly from the Azores, a cluster of islands off mainland Portugal. After traveling around the globe in pursuit of whales, a good many of these Portuguese sailors signed off back in New Bedford or other New England whaling ports, settling there to raise their families. Other Portuguese immigrated to seaport towns in Rhode Island and Massachusetts, seeking to market their well-honed sea-related skills in the rapidly growing fishing industry in the New World.

For the rest of the nineteenth century and throughout the entire twentieth century, Portuguese have continued to immigrate to New England in large numbers. They have come from mainland Portugal, Brazil, the Azores, Madeira, and Cape Verde, a group of islands off Africa that were once a Portuguese colony.

New Bedford, Portugal

New Bedford, Massachusetts, a small port city about sixty miles south of Boston, proudly boasts the largest Portuguese population of any city in the United States. Almost two-thirds of greater New Bedford's 150,000 residents claim to be of Portuguese descent. Every August for more than eighty years, New Bedford's Portuguese community has celebrated the Feast of the Blessed Sacrament. A large percentage of New Bedford's Portuguese emigrated from the island of Madeira, and this celebration is a re-creation of one of that island's big feast days. Attended by up to 200,000 people (Portuguese and non-Portuguese alike), the annual four-day Feast of the Blessed Sacrament is one of the strongest displays of Portuguese-American cultural identity and pride in the United States.

While a solemn high mass to honor the blessed sacrament is still celebrated at Immaculate Conception Church on Sunday, many of the throngs of attendees come for the big two-hour parade, the live Portuguese band music and songs, the folk dancing, the kids' activities—and the eating and drinking. Before the event New Bedfordites send to Madeira for three thousand liters of the island's sweet fortified wine, also called Madeira. It's sold at the festival by the glass or bottle. There's beer too.

Portuguese cuisine reflects the major role that this small European country played in the Age of Exploration and Discovery. Blending exotic culinary influences from the Far East, Africa, and the New World, Portuguese cooking is rich with surprising

and delicious combinations. Portuguese hot pepper sauce, for instance, is made from a fiery chile discovered in Brazil when it was a Portuguese colony. The sauce then migrated to Portuguese West Africa, where it was adopted, then to Portugal, and finally returned to the New World on the New England coast. A bottle of this *pimenta moida* sits on the table of every Portuguese establishment in New Bedford, and it is available to sprinkle on any or all of the mounds of street food sold at the Feast of the Blessed Sacrament.

Of the dozens of dishes sold at the festival, one of the favorites is *escabeche de atum*, pickled tuna, a Madeiran interpretation of the classic escabeche from around the Mediterranean. Another favorite is *carne de espeto*, meat on a stick, which is beef rubbed with a mixture of coarse salt, crushed bay leaves, and garlic powder. Festival-goers grill the skewers themselves over an open fire. About seven thousand pounds of the meat are devoured in a typical year, and there are sometimes up to one hundred newly acquainted people holding sticks over the 35-foot-long stone grill at one time.

Other favorites are *bacalho*, salted codfish; *carne de vinho de alhos*, pork marinated in wine and garlic and cooked in a big pot, served in a sandwich or as a meal; rabbit stew; goat stew; tuna steaks; *linguiça*; fava and lupini beans; boiled potatoes with everything; and Portuguese sweet breads and pastries.

Roasted Cod Fillets with a Garlic-Prosciutto Topping

MAKES 4 SERVINGS

The simple yet inspired prosciutto, garlic, and herb topping here, created by a Deer Isle, Maine, chef, plays off the clean, neutral flavor of cod, transforming this dish into the centerpiece of what should be a rather elegant meal. Steamed red-skinned potatoes with fresh herbs and Baked Herbed Eggplant with Fresh Tomatoes and Feta (page 117) would be admirable accompaniments to this special fish dish.

For the topping:

½ cup diced prosciutto (about 2 ounces)
¼ cup minced flat-leaf parsley
3 tablespoons chopped fresh basil or chervil
1 garlic clove, minced
2 teaspoons grated lemon zest
¼ teaspoon coarse-ground black pepper

For the fish:

2 tablespoons olive oil
4 cod fillets (about 6 ounces each)
Salt and fresh-ground black pepper
¾ cup dry white wine

1. Combine the prosciutto, parsley, basil or chervil, garlic, lemon zest, and pepper in a shallow dish. (The topping can be prepared a couple of hours ahead and refrigerated.)
2. Preheat the oven to 500 degrees. Brush a shallow rimmed baking sheet or baking dish with some of the oil.
3. Place the fish in the pan and season with salt and pepper. Sprinkle the prosciutto topping over the fish, and pat it on evenly. Drizzle with the remaining oil and pour the wine around the fish in the baking dish.
4. Roast until the fish is no longer translucent and flakes with a fork and the topping is slightly crispy and browned, about 5 minutes for every ½ inch of thickness.
5. Serve with the pan juices poured over the fish.

Grandmother Maury's Salt Codfish Cakes with Bacon

MAKES 4 SERVINGS

My grandmother Martha Aletta ("Allie") Hayward Maury was a lighthouse keeper's daughter from Bermuda who married an American and then lived for most of the rest of her life on Long Island Sound in Connecticut. Fortunately for Allie, the foodways in the two locales were very similar, so at least the transplanted bride didn't have to learn to cook with a whole new set of ingredients. Both Bermuda and coastal New England are influenced by their British roots and also by their proximity to the sea, and in both places dried salt cod played a major culinary role for centuries. Codfish and potatoes, like my grandparents' binational marriage, are natural partners, with the tangy saltiness of the fish being smoothed and tempered by the neutral starchiness of the potatoes. These are Allie's salt codfish cakes—simple, straightforward, sometimes accompanied by the extra richness of smoky bacon (or, at the very least, always fried in bacon drippings)—and there is no better supper. I confess that we all doused them with ketchup as children, but these days I prefer such side dishes as Garlicky Broccoli Rabe (page 114) or sliced ripe tomatoes drizzled with My Favorite Vinaigrette (page 79).

> ### Codfish Cakes
>
> "Salt fish mashed with potatoes, with good butter or pork scraps to moisten it, is nicer the second day than it was the first. The fish should be minced very fine while it is warm. After it has gotten cold and dry it is difficult to do it nicely. There is no way of preparing salt fish for breakfast so nice as to roll it up in little balls after it is mixed with mashed potatoes, dip it into an egg and fry it golden brown."
>
> —Lydia Maria Child, *The American Frugal Housewife* (Boston, 1829)

1 pound boneless salt cod

2 pounds russet or all-purpose potatoes, peeled and cut in 2-inch chunks

4 tablespoons unsalted butter

½ teaspoon fresh-ground black pepper

¼ to ½ cup half-and-half or light cream

Salt, if necessary
8 slices bacon
Vegetable oil or butter, if necessary, for cooking
1 tablespoon minced fresh parsley

1. Follow the directions for presoaking the cod on page 29. After presoaking, simmer the cod in a pan with water to cover by 1 inch for about 20 minutes, until the fish flakes easily with a fork. Drain, pick through to remove any skin or bones, and shred the fish into flakes.

2. Meanwhile, in a large pot, cook the potatoes in salted water to cover until they are very soft, about 20 minutes. Drain the potatoes well and put them through a ricer or return to the pot and mash with a potato masher or a large fork. Add the flaked cod, butter, and pepper and beat with a wooden spoon, adding enough half-and-half to make a smooth but stiff mixture. Season with salt if necessary, keeping in mind that the bacon will add more saltiness. Shape into 8 or 12 ½-inch-thick cakes. (The cakes can be made several hours ahead and refrigerated.)

3. Cook the bacon in a large skillet over medium heat until crisp, about 10 minutes. Drain on paper towels, leaving the drippings in the pan.

4. Cook the codfish cakes over medium heat in the bacon drippings, supplemented with a tablespoon or two of oil or butter if necessary, until they are golden brown and heated through, about 4 minutes per side. If you need to cook the cakes in 2 batches, keep the first batch warm in a low oven.

5. Serve the codfish cakes topped with the cooked bacon and sprinkled with the parsley.

Cod Cakes

"Unfortunately, memories of the Depression have put codfish cakes in bad odor in this country, but call it *brandade de morue* and fine eaters snap to attention. The French blended their salt cod and potato with oil, cream, and garlic. Americans added butter, egg, and pepper, and sometimes pork scraps. Much of the good flavor of codfish cakes came from the pork fat in which they were fried...."

—Betty Fussell,
I Hear America Cooking
(Penguin, 1986)

Baked Greek-Style
Halibut Steaks with Lemon Chunks

MAKES 6 SERVINGS

Majestic halibut, some weighing upwards of three hundred pounds, are fished out of the deep Atlantic waters, and, although its scarcity has driven the price up, halibut's firm, meaty, pearly white flesh is such delectable eating that it's well worth splurging on once in a while. Baking the halibut Greek style, with tomato and chunks of whole lemon, makes for the kind of stylish, colorful, yet earthy presentation that I love for company dinners. A side dish like Greek Orzo Pilaf (page 195), a steamed seasonal green vegetable, and Greek Moist Honey-Walnut Cake (page 542) with a bowl of fresh fruit are perfect accompaniments.

> 2 cups chopped seeded tomatoes
> 1 cup chopped red or white onion
> ¾ cup chopped seeded lemon, including the rind
> 2 large garlic cloves, minced
> 3 tablespoons chopped fresh oregano, plus sprigs for garnish
> 3 tablespoons fruity olive oil
> ¾ teaspoon salt, plus more for sprinkling on fish
> ½ teaspoon fresh-ground black pepper, plus additional for sprinkling
>   on fish
> 6 halibut steaks or fillets (about ½ pound each), 1½ to 2 inches thick
> 1 cup dry white wine

1. Toss together the tomatoes, onion, lemon, garlic, oregano, oil, salt, and pepper in a large bowl. (The topping can be made up to 3 hours ahead. Cover and refrigerate.)

2. Preheat the oven to 400 degrees.

3. Arrange the fish in a lightly oiled large roasting pan and season with salt and pepper. Spread the tomato mixture over the fish and pour the wine around it. Bake, uncovered, until the fish is no longer translucent in its thickest part and the vegetables are lightly caramelized, 15 to 25 minutes, depending on the size of the fish.

4. Transfer to a serving platter, pour the pan juices and vegetables over the fish, and garnish with oregano sprigs before serving.

Fish Sticks

Fish sticks were introduced by Gorton's Seafood Company of Gloucester, Massachusetts, in the early 1950s and were an immediate commercial success nationwide. American homemakers, many of whom had never seen, let alone cooked, a saltwater fish in its fresh and natural state, loved frozen fish sticks for their newfangled convenience and for their decidedly "unfishy" taste, which meant that the kids would eat them, especially if they were dipped in ketchup first. A Gorton's advertisement of the 1950s hailed their product as "the latest, greatest achievement of the seafood industry of today." Fish sticks are produced by cutting a frozen stack of fish fillets into blocks and then into sticks. The sticks are coated with crumbs, deep-fried, and flash-frozen. Created with whatever fillets are most plentiful and cheap, the original fish sticks were made primarily from then-abundant cod. Over the decades cod was replaced first by haddock and then by redfish. Today most fish sticks are made with Alaskan pollack.

Roasted Halibut Fillets
with Herbed Crumb Crust

MAKES 4 SERVINGS

This is a really neat (and also easy) way of cooking halibut or other lean fish fillets. The mustard-and-mayonnaise coating adds a tangy flavor, but its primary function is to insulate the fish from the high oven heat, keeping the flesh moist and allowing the crumbs to brown. It's a rather old method—I remember similar recipes with mayonnaise and cornflake crumbs from the 1960s—but I relearned it recently from the late Richard Sax's last book, finished by his friend David Ricketts, *Get in There and Cook*. This book is a wonderful primer of basic techniques that are designed to take the fear out of cooking. This is a variation of their recipe. Follow Richard's always-sage advice and use this technique with just about any lean fish fillets that are about 1 inch thick. You can't go wrong!

> 4 tablespoons regular or lowfat mayonnaise
> 1 tablespoon Dijon mustard
> 1 tablespoon fresh lemon juice
> 1½ cups fresh breadcrumbs
> 2 tablespoons chopped fresh dill or tarragon, plus sprigs for garnish
> 1 tablespoon chopped fresh parsley, plus sprigs for garnish

½ teaspoon paprika
4 halibut or other lean fish fillets, such as scrod, haddock, or snapper
(about 6 ounces each), 1 inch thick
Salt and fresh-ground black pepper
⅔ cup dry white wine
Lemon wedges

1. Preheat the oven to 450 degrees. Lightly oil a rimmed baking sheet or other large shallow baking pan.
2. Stir together the mayonnaise, mustard, and lemon juice in a shallow dish. Combine the crumbs, dill or tarragon, parsley, and paprika in another dish.
3. Sprinkle the fish with salt and pepper. Dip each fillet in the mayonnaise mixture and then roll in the crumbs, patting them on so they adhere. Place the fillets at least 1 inch apart on the baking sheet. Pour the wine around the fish.
4. Roast until the crumbs are speckled golden brown and the fish is opaque in its thickest part, about 10 minutes.
5. Transfer the fish to plates, pouring any pan juices over it. Garnish with lemon wedges and herb sprigs and serve.

Harbor Fish Market

Nestled on a side street adjacent to Portland, Maine's fishing pier, Harbor Fish Market is a sprawling, noisy, friendly, old-fashioned establishment that has been run by the Alfiero family since 1971. "There's been a fish market out on this wharf since the turn of the century," says Mike Alfiero. "This is what a fish market should look like and this is what a fish market should smell like." Never do you catch a whiff of ammonia—just the clean, sea-breeze aroma of a working fish wharf and just-caught fish. When I visit my sister in Portland, I try never to miss a chance to make a stop at Harbor Fish to admire the stupendous variety of local and exotic seafood carefully presented on heaps of crushed ice—and to help her choose our dinner for that night. Enormous tanks are filled with lobsters and crabs; another contains live Maine brook trout. The glass display cases overflow with fresh fillets of sole and salmon and whole flatfish. Enormous piles of clams, mussels, oysters, and shrimp sit on ice in wooden bins. At Harbor Fish, New England seafood competes with a huge variety of fish and shellfish not only from the rest of the country but from around the world. Depending on the season, you can find shad and shad roe from Connecticut, swordfish from Massachusetts, soft-shell crabs from Maryland, mahi mahi from California, and anchovies or baby octopus from the Mediterranean.

Simple Grilled Dilled Striped Bass

MAKES 4 SERVINGS

Wild striped bass, or "stripers" as they are popularly called, are still being caught by some sport fishermen (under strict size and location guidelines) in the summer from New England rivers and bays. The flesh of the striped bass is firm and meaty, which makes the fillets an excellent candidate for cooking directly on the grill. This simple garlic and herb treatment is favored by residents of coastal New England beachfront communities, who happily turn their catch of the day into one of the highlight meals of the summer.

> 2½ tablespoons light olive oil
> 1 tablespoon chopped fresh dill, plus sprigs for garnish
> 1 garlic clove, minced
> 1 center cut striped bass fillet (about 1½ pounds), about 1 inch thick,
>   with skin on, if desired (see Note)
> Salt and fresh-ground black pepper
> Lemon wedges

1. Build a moderately hot charcoal fire or preheat a gas grill. Make sure the grill rack is clean and well oiled.
2. Stir together the oil, dill, and garlic in a small dish, and let the mixture steep for at least 30 minutes to blend the flavors.
3. Brush the fish on both sides with some of the dill oil and sprinkle with salt and pepper. Place the fish flesh side down on the grill and cook for 3 to 5 minutes, or until it begins to brown lightly and pick up some marks from the grill. Brush with more of the flavored oil and, using a large metal spatula, turn the fish and grill for another 3 to 5 minutes, or until the fish is no longer translucent in its thickest part.
4. Transfer to a platter or serving plates, garnish with dill sprigs and lemon wedges, and serve.

Note: Leaving the skin attached to one side helps hold the fish together as it grills. You can also cook the fish in a hinged grill basket.

Crispy Oven-Fried Flounder
(or Other) Fillets

MAKES 4 SERVINGS

This method of "oven-frying," in which the crumb-wrapped fish crisps in a hot oven, is a wonderful way to cook virtually all flatfish fillets, be they called flounder, fluke, sole, sand dabs, or plaice. The nomenclature of the many varieties of flatfish caught off the New England coast can be confusing, but any mild, relatively soft-fleshed fillets that are about ½ inch thick work well here. If your fillets are ¼ inch thick or less, you can sandwich two together and then dip this "package" into the milk and crumbs. Great accompaniments might be Spicy Potatoes on the Half Shell (page 128) along with a creamed vegetable such as New England Ladies' Cabbage (page 115). A plate of cookies—Crisp Maple-Oatmeal Cookies (page 579) or Spiced Harwich Hermits (page 559)—would be a fitting finish.

> 2 teaspoons vegetable or light olive oil
> ½ cup whole or lowfat milk
> 1 cup fine dried breadcrumbs
> ½ teaspoon salt
> ¼ teaspoon fresh-ground black pepper
> ¼ teaspoon cayenne pepper
> ½ teaspoon crumbled dried marjoram
> 4 flounder or other flatfish fillets (about 6 ounces each), ½ inch thick
> 3 tablespoons butter, melted
> Lemon wedges

1. Preheat the oven to 500 degrees. Use the oil to coat a jelly roll pan or other shallow baking pan with a rim no more than 1½ inches high. (The oven heat needs to circulate freely around the crumbed fish in order to brown it.)
2. Pour the milk into a shallow dish. In another dish, stir together the crumbs, salt, black pepper, cayenne, and marjoram. Dip the fish into the milk and then dredge it in the seasoned crumbs, shaking off the excess. Arrange the coated fish at least 2 inches apart on the prepared pan and brush or drizzle with the melted butter.

3. Bake in the center or upper third of the oven until the outside crust is golden and the fish is opaque in the thickest part when checked with a small knife, about 12 minutes.

4. Transfer with a large spatula to plates and serve the fish with lemon wedges for squeezing over.

Several Ways to Catch Fish

• By a lone individual, using a fishing pole or rod with a baited hook, who will take the catch home to eat that morning for breakfast or that night for supper.

• From commercial fishing boats. A few fish are caught using single *lines*. Caught this way, the fish are brought onto the boat alive and undamaged and are considered to be of the highest, most marketable quality. (Menus at good restaurants often specify "line-caught" fish to alert their customers to its superior quality.)

• Some species of large fish, like swordfish, are *harpooned*. Other methods of catching these big fish are *jig-fishing*, with lines that usually hold about eight baited hooks, and *long-lining*, which involves putting out up to many miles of baited hooks. Shorter lines, frequently checked and carefully tended, generally yield higher-quality fish.

• Much commercial fishing is done with *nets*. With gill-netting, the fish swim through a net and are caught. With dragging, a huge net is dragged along the bottom, sweeping up everything in its path.

Grilled Block Island Swordfish with Peppery Orange Salsa

MAKES 4 SERVINGS

In the deep Gulf Stream waters that run close to Block Island, Rhode Island, fishermen catch some of the best swordfish found anywhere in the world. Chefs on the island are continually experimenting with sauces and toppings to enhance the firm, meaty swordfish flesh without obscuring its delicate flavor. I think this cross-cultural peppery orange salsa with its southwestern seasonings represents a perfect example of East-meets-West and restaurant-meets-home cooking. The salsa is divine on just about any grilled fish and also happens to be a great topping for Ginger-Spiked Smoked Fish Cakes with Herbs (page 345).

For the salsa:

1 teaspoon ground cumin
1 large or 2 small seedless oranges
1 cup diced red bell pepper
1 garlic clove, minced
2 teaspoons minced jalapeño pepper, or more to taste
1 tablespoon fresh lemon juice
2 teaspoons olive oil
½ teaspoon salt, or to taste
¼ teaspoon fresh-ground black pepper, or to taste
4 tablespoons chopped fresh cilantro

For the fish:

1½ pounds swordfish steaks, about 1 inch thick
2 teaspoons olive oil
Salt and fresh-ground black pepper

1. Toast the cumin in a small dry skillet over medium heat, stirring, until it is one shade darker and wisps of smoke begin to rise, 2 to 3 minutes. Scrape into a medium-sized bowl. Grate about 2 teaspoons of zest from the orange and add it to the bowl. Peel the orange, dice it, and scoop the pulp and as much juice as you can save into the bowl. (You should have about 1¼ cups of diced orange.) Add the bell pepper, garlic, jalapeño, lemon juice, oil, salt, and pepper, and stir to blend. (The salsa can be made up to 6 hours ahead and refrigerated.) Shortly before serving, stir in the cilantro.
2. Build a medium-hot charcoal fire or preheat a gas grill.
3. Rub the swordfish steaks with the oil and season on both sides with salt and pepper. Grill the swordfish, turning once, until it is striped with marks from the grill and the flesh has just turned opaque, 8 to 10 minutes.
4. Serve with the salsa spooned over the top.

Julia's Fish Advice

Julia Child, on her long-running Boston-based television show *The French Chef*, awakened an entire generation of neophyte cooks to the pleasures and proper techniques of good cooking. On how to buy fresh fish, her advice was clear, precise, and no-nonsense. "Look into its eyes," said Julia. "Make sure they're clear, never sunken. Touch the fish to make sure it's not slimy. Inspect the gills for good color. And sniff, sniff, sniff. If the fish is already wrapped in plastic, tear it off and smell the fish at the checkout counter before you bring it home. It should have a clean, non-fishy aroma, without a hint of ammonia. Once home, store it on ice or in the coldest part of the refrigerator. Cook it and eat it as soon as possible."

❊ ❊ ❊ ❊ ❊ ❊ ❊ ❊ ❊

Pan-Fried Mountain Stream Trout

MAKES 4 SERVINGS

Corin Hewitt's family has been in Vermont for generations, and, judging from the privately printed *Hewitt Family Cookbook*, the clan has been producing a succession of good cooks in every one of those generations. One spring, Corin and his friend John told me, in glowingly enthusiastic detail, about a day they spent fishing in a cascading mountain stream near their home in East Corinth, in the middle of the state, catching beautiful small brook trout by the dozen, and then pan-frying their catch using this method. When I mentioned that the recipe wasn't in the family's printed cookbook,

---
McLean's Seafood

"McLean's Seafood is a battered two-story building with cement floors for draining fish blood and a rabbit-warren of offices upstairs where deals are cut. Dark, wild-haired young men stomp around in rubber boots and shout to each other in Portuguese as they heave fish around the room. With long knives they 'loin' the fish—carve the meat off the bones—and then seal it in vacuum bags and load it onto trucks. A good worker can loin a full-sized fish in two minutes. McLean's moves two million pounds of swordfish a year, and a million pounds of tuna. They fly it overseas, ship it around the country, and sell it to the corner store."

— Sebastian Junger, *The Perfect Storm*
(W. W. Norton, 1997)

❊ ❊ ❊ ❊ ❊ ❊ ❊ ❊ ❊

Corin said no, it wouldn't be, it's second nature to cook fresh trout this way, we just take it for granted, and there'd be no need to record it. That is the case for much of the best home cooking—the simple, tried-and-true methods are passed almost by osmosis from one generation to the next, and the recipes often never get written down.

> 4 pan-sized trout (about 1 pound each), or 8 small brook trout,
>   cleaned
> ½ cup milk
> ½ cup all-purpose flour
> 2 tablespoons cornmeal
> ½ teaspoon salt
> ½ teaspoon black pepper
> 2 tablespoons vegetable oil, plus more if necessary
> 2 tablespoons butter, plus more if necessary
> Lemon wedges

1. Wash the fish inside and out, and trim off the fins with kitchen shears. Place the milk in a shallow dish. Combine the flour, cornmeal, salt, and pepper in another shallow dish.
2. Heat the oil and butter in 1 very large or 2 medium-sized skillets. You should have about ¼ inch of the oil-butter mixture in each pan. Add more if necessary. Dip the trout in the milk and dredge it in the flour mixture, shaking off the excess. Place in the pan(s) and cook over medium to medium-high heat until well browned and crisp on the first side, 3 to 4 minutes. If the fish curls up, which very fresh trout tend to do, press with a spatula so that it cooks evenly. Turn carefully and cook on the second side until browned and crisp on the outside, and the inside, when checked at the thickest part, tests done, 3 to 5 minutes. Be sure that the flesh has lost all its translucency, but do not overcook, or the trout will lose its flavor.
3. Remove from the pan, letting the excess cooking oil drip off before transferring to plates. Serve with lemon wedges.

Note: The choice of whether to leave the heads on or not is up to you.

Cod in New England History

Boston patriot Samuel Adams said it most succinctly: "The codfish was to us what wool was to England or tobacco to Virginia: the great staple which became the basis of power and wealth."

And it wasn't just economic survival that was dependent on cod. To put it plainly, the early New England colonists' survival depended on cod, as they relied on the fish to stave off starvation during those first desperate years in the New World. Considering that they had presumably planned to stay here awhile, the *Mayflower* pilgrims brought with them scant supplies of food and few of the tools, such as fishing tackle, hunting tools, or farming implements, with which to obtain any food in subsequent years. Very luckily, the waters teemed with codfish in such numbers that they could be scooped up by the bushelful. Bartholomew Gosnold, who dropped anchor off a cape that would soon be named Cape Cod, reported in 1602 that the ship was "pestered so with Cod fish that we threw numbers of them over-bord again." Also luckily, hospitable local Indians taught the new settlers ingenious methods of catching this bounty, which became their essential means for survival.

Cod takes to salting and drying more successfully than any other fish, and salt cod can last for years without spoiling. Dried salt cod could be transported around the globe by ship and traded far inland, away from the coasts. Even before the Pilgrims' landing at Plymouth, European fishermen had made dried and salt cod the region's first export for cash. Already an important part of the diet throughout the Mediterranean region, dried salt cod became a staple in the Caribbean as well, and eventually a huge market developed in New England. English colonists quickly caught on to the commercial possibilities inherent in this abundant, easily caught fish, and commercial fishing for cod began in Gloucester, Massachusetts, in 1623.

Soon great fortunes began to be built from the salt cod trade, and by the eighteenth century, "cod had lifted New England from a distant colony of starving settlers to an international commercial power," states Mark Kurlansky in his fascinating book *Cod: A Biography of the Fish That Changed the World* (Walker and Company, 1997). "The members of the 'codfish aristocracy,' those who traced their family fortunes to the seventeenth-century cod fisheries, had openly worshipped the fish as the symbol of their wealth." Images of codfish began to appear on coins, official crests, and stamps. In 1784, in the ultimate expression of cod homage, a large carved wooden fish, the *Sacred Cod*, was hung in the Massachusetts House of Representatives. It hangs there still, a symbolic reminder of the economic and political importance of the cod to New England.

Cape Cod Turkey

"Cape Cod turkey" is an old-fashioned cooked salt cod dish served on a platter and topped with an egg sauce such as the one served with Fourth of July Grilled Salmon (page 358). Sometimes, like the more traditional boiled New England dinner made with corned beef, the codfish "turkey" was accompanied by boiled carrots, potatoes, and small buttered beets and then garnished with bits of fried salt pork. The origin of the name is obscure, but one explanation has to do with Thanksgiving. From early colonial days, turkey was equated with Thanksgiving and the offering of thanks for a fruitful harvest. But without fish, especially cod, and most especially in lean times, salt cod, Cape Codders did not always have much of a harvest to be thankful for. Perhaps, in a long-ago stab at Yankee humor, this boiled dinner was dubbed "Cape Cod turkey." Another theory is that the term derives from Boston Catholics' attempts to make more palatable the thought of eating fish every week, back when no meat was allowed on Fridays for religious reasons.

SHELLFISH

Early New England colonists wrote home with tales of legions of lobsters piled on the beach within grasping distance, some as big as a small child. They found huge heaps of clam and oyster shells, evidence that local Indians settled in contentedly for summer-long clambakes and then moved on to another shorefront locale the next season. Scallops were easily gathered from the bottoms of shallow bays and salt ponds, and mussels, though considered poor man's food, could sustain people through lean times if all else failed.

In keeping with the Puritan's forthright, plainspoken approach to every task, the cooking of shellfish was mostly done very simply. Modern classics like Magnificent Steamed Lobster (page 399) and North Fork Crusty Pan-Seared Scallops (page 388) are elegant in their unadulterated simplicity. Garlicky Mussels, Italian Style (page 381) and Little Italy Calamari in Spicy Red Sauce (page 395), on the other hand, represent the best of the more robustly seasoned Yankee-Italian way with shellfish.

New Englanders are still partial to treating seafood to a sprinkle of buttered crumbs, adding richness and also protecting the delicate meat from the drying effects of heat. We often "scallop" our shellfish (the term is unrelated to the bivalve—it simply means to layer in a gratin dish with buttered crumbs). Oysters Scalloped with Garlic and Herb Crumbs (page 386) and Baked Crumb-Stuffed Lobster (page 401) are some of the richly rewarding ways of cooking our glorious harvest from the sea.

Garlicky Mussels, Italian Style

MAKES 4 SERVINGS

Growing up along the Connecticut shore, we nonethnic types thought of the abundant mussel flats as simply sharp annoyances to avoid stepping on with bare feet. Not only did it never occur to us to eat the mussels, but, in fact, some people said they were actually poisonous! In early adulthood, after an enlightening eating trip to Boston's North End, as well as a few visits to Portuguese restaurants in Provincetown, Massachusetts, I was disabused of my ignorant notions and became a fervent convert. Cooking mussels at home became even easier (and still very inexpensive), when, about 15 years ago, they began to be farmed, and to appear in fish markets minus their encrustation of barnacles and denuded of that pesky wiry beard. Simmering the mussels in a garlicky tomato sauce is the classic Italian treatment, and is one of the very best ways to eat them. Just open a bottle of red wine, make a green salad, and offer plenty of Italian bread to drag through the sauce.

4 pounds mussels, preferably farm-raised, rinsed
1 cup dry white wine
4 tablespoons olive oil
1 large onion, chopped
4 large garlic cloves, minced
3 anchovy fillets or 1 teaspoon anchovy paste
1 teaspoon dried oregano
½ teaspoon red pepper flakes

Mussels for Chefs

Paul Brayton, who owns Tightrope Seafarms in Blue Hill, in midcoast Maine, grows perfect mussels in his meticulously managed farming operation. He sells two sizes of mussels. The smaller ones, which he calls Blue Hill Bouchons, are favored by French chefs because they are similar to a small mussel variety found in France. Top chefs from New York and California request Tightrope's mussels from wholesalers. "The first time I heard that Wolfgang Puck wanted my mussels," confesses Paul, "I thought it was a joke. I couldn't believe that there really was a grown-up person with that name! We're a little out of the mainstream, I guess, up here in Maine."

1 28-ounce can Italian plum tomatoes, drained, juice reserved
Salt and fresh-ground black pepper
½ cup chopped fresh flat-leaf parsley

1. Combine the mussels with the wine in a large pot. Cover, bring to a boil, reduce the
   heat to medium, and steam until the mussels open, 4 to 10 minutes, depending on
   their size. Use a slotted spoon to remove the mussels to a bowl, discarding any that
   do not open. Let the cooking liquid settle for a few minutes and then pour off the
   clear broth, leaving any sediment in the pot. Reserve the liquid.

2. Heat the oil in a large, deep skillet. Add the onion and cook over medium heat until
   it begins to soften, about 4 minutes. Add the garlic, anchovies, oregano, and pepper
   flakes. Cook, stirring to mash the anchovies, for 1 minute. Add the drained
   tomatoes, along with the reserved mussel liquid, leaving behind any additional sediment at the bottom. Bring to a boil, breaking up the tomatoes into smaller pieces
   with the side of a spoon. Simmer the sauce uncovered over medium-low heat to
   blend flavors and until it is reduced and thickened, about 30 minutes. If the sauce
   begins to look dry, add some of the reserved tomato liquid. (The recipe can be
   made several hours ahead to this point. Cover and refrigerate sauce and mussels
   separately. Reheat the sauce before proceeding.)

Unloved Mussels

Mussels grow in profuse abundance along the New England shore, clumping together in large colonies, making themselves more convenient and easier to harvest than any other indigenous bivalve mollusk. Perhaps they were almost too common to be esteemed in their own region, for until recently mussels were not a popular seafood in New England. From colonial times right through to the last couple of decades of the twentieth century, mussels were viewed with suspicion. At best, they were considered poor people's food, relegated to lean times when little else was available to eat. At worst, they were thought to be poisonous. As filter feeders, mussels have always been the first line of defense against toxins, and indeed, until adequate testing methods were developed, eating shellfish did carry a certain amount of risk. It is speculated that perhaps a few reports of unfortunate experiences with mussels may have given them a bad name with early Yankees. Immigrants, especially the Italians and Portuguese who arrived in the late nineteenth century, always ate mussels, depending on them for a cheap source of protein in their diet, but many of their second and third generation descendants stopped eating them to signal their advancement up the economic and social ladder.

3. Add the mussels in their shells to the sauce and heat gently until heated through, 2 to 4 minutes. Season with salt and fresh-ground black pepper, if necessary.

4. To serve, spoon the mussels and sauce into shallow soup dishes and sprinkle with parsley.

Kenmare Mussels

MAKES 4 SERVINGS

The town of Kenmare, near Cork in Ireland, has sent some of its talented native sons to New England. Some have opened restaurants or pubs, including one of my favorite haunts, the Black Rock Castle, run by the Patrick Smith family in Bridgeport, Connecticut. Irish-Americans, as well as representatives of the entire multiethnic family that comprises Bridgeport, congregate here, drawn by the music, the warm welcome, and the wonderful home-style Irish cooking. The menu is a sample of the best Irish ingredients and dishes—salmon (smoked and fresh), corned beef, chicken pot pies, fresh fish, and these Kenmare Mussels, which showcase the uniformly delicious farm-raised black beauties in an inspired creation involving leeks, cream, and fresh herbs. All you need is a salad and lots of good country bread to sop up every last drop of sauce.

2 tablespoons butter

2 large or 3 small leeks, white and pale green parts only, thoroughly rinsed and thinly sliced

2 garlic cloves, minced

4 pounds mussels, preferably farm-raised, rinsed

1 cup dry white wine

½ cup bottled clam juice

1 bay leaf, broken in half

2 cups heavy cream

3 tablespoons chopped fresh tarragon

Storing Mussels

When cleaning raw mussels, discard any with broken shells. It's okay if mussel shells are open, but the shells should close when lightly tapped. If they don't close, discard them. Store mussels in a mesh bag if possible or in a plastic bag with holes poked in it for air circulation. Wrap the bag tightly around the mussels so the shells will stay closed, and keep in the refrigerator.

2 tablespoons chopped fresh flat-leaf parsley
Salt and fresh-ground black pepper

1. Heat the butter in a very large, deep skillet or saucepan. Add the leeks and cook over medium-low heat until softened, about 10 minutes. Add the garlic and cook, stirring, for 2 minutes. Remove from the heat and set aside.

2. Meanwhile, combine the mussels, wine, clam juice, and bay leaf in a large pot. Cover, bring to a boil, reduce the heat to medium, and steam until the shells open, 4 to 10 minutes, depending on their size. Using a slotted spoon, transfer the mussels to a bowl, discarding any that do not open. Let the cooking liquid settle for a few minutes and then pour off the clear broth, leaving any sediment in the pot. Pour the broth into the skillet with the leeks, leaving behind any additional sediment at the bottom. Add the cream, bring to a boil, and cook over medium-high heat, uncovered, until the liquid reduces by about one-third, 5 to 8 minutes. (The stew can be made several hours ahead to this point. Cover the mussels and broth and refrigerate separately. Bring the broth to the simmer before proceeding.)

3. Return the mussels in their shells to the cream mixture and stir in the tarragon and parsley. Heat gently until the mussels are heated through, 2 to 4 minutes. Season with salt and fresh-ground black pepper to taste. (Salt may not be needed because the broth and mussels may be quite salty.)

4. To serve, divide the mussels among 4 large shallow soup dishes. Ladle the broth over.

Portuguese Clams

MAKES 4 SERVINGS

Some of the Portuguese-Americans who populate the coast of New England still use a traditional oval metal pot for cooking their clam and mussel dishes. The covered vessel, called a *cataplana*, is hinged on one side, held together tightly with clamps, and actually looks a little like the hinged bivalves that simmer happily inside. This clam preparation, made spicy with the traditional Portuguese sausage, is a fabulous way to cook small hard-shell clams. If you can't get chourico or linguiça, Mexican chorizo sausage or even Polish kielbasa are excellent substitutes.

4 dozen littleneck clams, scrubbed
4 tablespoons olive oil
3 Turkish bay leaves
½ pound chourico or linguiça, thinly sliced
1 medium onion, chopped
1 medium green or red bell pepper, chopped
4 garlic cloves, minced
2½ cups chopped seeded tomatoes
1 cup dry white wine
Salt and fresh-ground black pepper
Bottled hot pepper sauce to taste
2 tablespoons chopped fresh cilantro
2 tablespoons chopped fresh flat-leaf parsley

About Clams

There are two basic types of clams in New England—hard-shell and soft-shell (see page 19). Hard-shells are eaten raw on the half-shell, cooked as in Portuguese Clams (page 384), or chopped or ground in chowder. Soft-shells are always eaten cooked, as in Crispy Ipswich Fried Clams (page 13), or Milky Maine Steamer Chowder (page 58).

1. Scrub the clams and soak them in cold water for at least 2 hours or up to 12 hours to help them disgorge any grit. Rinse, drain, and set aside.

2. Heat the oil in a very large, deep skillet or saucepan. Add the bay leaves and cook over medium heat, turning them with tongs, until they are one shade darker, 2 to 3 minutes. Push the bay leaves to the side of the pot, add the sausage, onion, bell pepper, and garlic and cook, stirring occasionally, until the sausage browns lightly and gives off some of its fat and the vegetables soften, about 10 minutes. Add the tomatoes and wine, raise the heat to high, and cook briskly, uncovered, until the liquid is reduced by about half, about 4 minutes. (The recipe can be prepared several hours ahead to this point. Refrigerate the sauce and clams separately. Reheat the sauce before proceeding.)

3. Add the clams to the sauce, cover, and cook over medium heat until they open and are just barely firm, about 10 minutes.

Taste the sauce and season it with salt and pepper if necessary. The dish should be mildly spicy. If not, season with hot pepper sauce to taste. Discard the bay leaves.

4. Spoon the clams, vegetables, and sauce into shallow soup plates, sprinkle with cilantro and parsley, and serve.

Early Aquaculture

New England oysters were the first farmed sea crop. Oysters were so popular in the nineteenth century that overfishing led to the depletion of many New England beds by the 1880s. Because of the nature of the oyster's life cycle, enterprising businessmen figured out how to import oysters from the Chesapeake and beds farther south and use the seed to replant and repopulate fished-out oyster beds from Cape Cod to Long Island Sound. Old oyster shells ("clutch") were laid down on the barren bottoms and larvae brought in to set on the old shells and to spawn there when the water temperature rose. The young oysters were then replanted two or three times, from bed to bed, where they were allowed to grow to their full size before being harvested and brought to market. This early cultivation process is the very same aquaculture method used to farm oysters today, with the modern additions of water testing and health inspections.

Oysters Scalloped with Garlic and Herb Crumbs

MAKES 4 SERVINGS

According to the excellent Time-Life *Foods of the World* volume on New England cooking, scalloped oysters was a dish much favored by Bostonians more than two hundred years ago. Because they have no natural fat of their own, oysters really benefit from this construction, which nestles the delicate bivalves between layers of buttery breadcrumbs, thereby adding richness while at the same time protecting them from the toughening effects of high heat. I've added a touch of freshness and zing with fresh herbs and garlic. All you need to add is steamed broccoli, a mesclun salad, and, perhaps, a bowl of Chunky Windfall Applesauce (page 501) for a really lovely supper.

¼ pound (1 stick) unsalted butter

1 garlic clove, minced

1 cup soft fresh breadcrumbs

1 cup cracker crumbs, from common crackers or saltines

2 tablespoons minced fresh flat-leaf parsley

1 tablespoon chopped fresh thyme

½ teaspoon salt

½ teaspoon fresh-ground black pepper

1 quart shucked oysters with their liquor

3 tablespoons heavy cream

2 tablespoons dry sherry

½ teaspoon bottled hot pepper sauce

1. Preheat the oven to 425 degrees.
2. Melt the butter in a large skillet over medium-high heat. Add the garlic and cook, stirring, for 2 minutes. Add the bread and cracker crumbs and cook, stirring frequently, until pale golden, about 5 minutes. Remove from the heat and stir in the parsley, thyme, salt, and pepper. Spread about one-third of the crumbs in the bottom of a shallow 2-quart baking dish. Drain the oysters, reserving the liquor, and arrange them in a more or less single layer over the crumbs.
3. Stir together the cream, sherry, hot pepper sauce, and 3 tablespoons of the oyster liquor in a small dish. Drizzle this mixture over the oysters, and spread with the remaining crumbs. (The dish can be prepared up to 3 hours ahead and refrigerated.)
4. Bake, uncovered, until the crumbs are a deep golden brown and the liquid around the oysters bubbles, 25 to 35 minutes.

"R" Month Prohibition Repealed

Before the days of efficient and reliable modern commercial refrigeration systems, it was against the law to harvest oysters during months without the letter R (May, June, July, August). It is during these months that oysters and other shellfish spawn, leaving them in a somewhat weakened condition and with a less robust flavor. This prohibition against harvesting them in the summer no longer exists, and oysters (from a reliable source) are considered safe to eat at any time of year. However, for eating raw on the half shell, oysters still taste best during the fall and winter.

North Fork Crusty Pan-Seared Scallops

MAKES 4 SERVINGS

Okay, okay, so eastern Long Island is not *technically* in New England, but that decision was made by political horse traders, resulting in a line drawn arbitrarily on a map. Geologically, geographically, historically, and spiritually, eastern Long Island, particularly its North Fork that seems to reach yearningly out for Connecticut's shore, belongs to New England. Many of its original settlers migrated across the barely fifteen miles of Long Island Sound from New England's shore. The scallops dredged out of Peconic Bay are a match for such other renowned scallops as those from Nantucket Sound. One winter evening my friend Jamie Laughridge pan-seared some of these sweet beauties to

New England Scallops

New England produces two kinds of scallops—small bay scallops, about ½ inch in diameter, and the larger sea scallop, which averages 1¼ inches in diameter. The edible portion of the scallop is the adductor muscle that hinges the two beautiful fan-shaped shells. Europeans also eat the coral, or roe, a large crescent-shaped, yellow-to-orange sac that sits to one side of the muscle. A bottom dweller, the scallop can attach to just about any surface, though it prefers muddy sand. It needs to live in a place where tides sweep in plenty of plankton, which the scallop traps and channels into its mouth.

Bay scallops are gathered in the large bays from Long Island to Nova Scotia. Cape bay scallops, tiny, sweet nuggets of flesh, are considered by many to be the most highly prized. They are gathered close to the shore, and some of the best come from the waters around Nantucket Island. Their season is from November to April.

Sea scallops are harvested two ways. Dragging is done from a boat, using a tall winch rig that drags a metal basket along the ocean bottom. Diving is done by individuals who wear special rubber suits and lower themselves into the frigid, dark Atlantic to search plankton-rich nooks and crannies for the elusive creatures. Sea scallops brought up by divers are often larger, better-quality scallops with remarkably firm, sweet flesh and are highly prized by restaurateurs. Since scallops are harvested in the winter, both draggers and divers brave extreme weather conditions to bring in their prized catch. The season for diver scallops runs only from November to April, whereas draggers can work year-round beyond the three-mile offshore limit.

Scallops are usually shucked on the boat, and their shells and other internal matter are thrown overboard. Scallops freeze uncommonly well, maintaining much of their flavor and texture.

a crusty perfection the likes of which I had never before tasted. It's a simple enough recipe, but the secret, reports Jamie, lies in cooking the scallops on the first side for a full two to three minutes before turning them so that the juices seal themselves inside the lightly floured crust. Serve these scallops with a simple Shaker Baked Rice Pilaf (page 224) and steamed whole green beans for a sublime supper.

> 1½ pounds sea scallops
> ½ cup all-purpose flour
> ¾ teaspoon salt
> ½ teaspoon black pepper
> 3 tablespoons vegetable oil or light olive oil
> 3 tablespoons unsalted butter
> 1 teaspoon grated lemon zest
> 2 tablespoons fresh lemon juice
> 1 small bunch watercress
> Lemon wedges

1. If the scallops are at all watery, place them on a double thickness of paper towels and gently pat them dry.

2. Stir together the flour, salt, and pepper in a shallow dish and mix well.

3. Heat the oil in a large skillet over medium-high heat. Dredge the scallops in the seasoned flour, shaking off the excess. When the oil is hot, place the scallops in the skillet in a single layer, without crowding them. (If the pan is not large enough, cook the scallops in two batches.) Cook them on the first side for 2 to 3 minutes, or until they are a rich, crusty brown on the bottom (jostling or stirring the scallops causes the juices to leak out). Turn to the second side with tongs and cook until the scallops are just firm to the touch and the juices are milky, 1 to 3 minutes. Remove to a warm platter or serving plates.

4. Pour off any oil remaining in the skillet. Add the butter, lemon zest, and lemon juice and cook, swirling the pan, until the butter melts.

5. Surround the scallops with sprigs of watercress, pour the lemon butter over, and serve.

Nantucket Bay Scallops
Gratinéed in Scallop Shells with Tomato

MAKES 4 SERVINGS

This is an adaptation of a recipe I found in an old community cookbook called *From the Galleys of Nantucket*, put out by the Ladies Union Circle of the First Congregational Church on the island. I liked the sound of it, and, once I tested it, I liked the taste even better. Sweet bay scallops nestle in an ever-so-slightly spicy fresh tomato mixture, and roast just until done. It's simple, pretty, and delicious. If you have large scallops shells, use them for this dish, positioning them on large dinner plates surrounded by something like Greek Orzo Pilaf (page 195) or Garlic and Oil Spaghetti (page 195) and spears of steamed broccoli.

1½ cups chopped seeded tomatoes, any type
¼ cup chopped shallots
1 garlic clove, minced
3 tablespoons extra-virgin olive oil
¼ teaspoon cayenne pepper, or more to taste
½ teaspoon salt, plus more to taste
¼ teaspoon black pepper, plus more to taste
1½ pounds bay scallops
Paprika
2 tablespoons minced fresh flat-leaf parsley

1. Preheat the oven to 475 degrees.

2. Combine the tomatoes, shallots, garlic, 2 tablespoons of oil, cayenne, salt, and pepper in a mixing bowl. Divide the tomato mixture between 4 large scallop shells and place the shells in a baking dish, or spread the mixture in the bottom of a shallow 2-quart baking dish. Roast, uncovered, until hot and bubbly and the juices are rendered, 8 to 10 minutes.

3. Remove the dish from the oven and place the scallops atop the tomato mixture. Drizzle or brush the scallops with the remaining 1 tablespoon of oil and sprinkle lightly with salt and paprika. Return to the oven to roast until the scallops just turn opaque, about 5 minutes.

4. Spoon some of the tomato mixture over the scallops, sprinkle with the parsley, and serve.

Job Perk

Sergeant Jeff Gallagher of the Patrol Department of the Maine Department of Marine Resources has a cold job. His boat plies the frigid winter Atlantic, checking to make sure scallop fishermen are complying with state regulations. But there is at least one nice perk to his job: he gets to eat raw scallops right out of the shell. "There's nothing like it," says Sergeant Gallagher enthusiastically. "You just scoop it out of the shell, pick it up with your fingers, grab 'er, and growl. It's still quivering when it goes down." Does he put anything on it first—a squeeze of lemon—I ask. "Nope. Just one more after it. They're better than oysters. Prettier, too. I don't get the scallops free, you understand. Just fresher. But even paying for them, they're really worth it." Spoken like a true Yankee.

Lemon Crumb-Broiled Sea Scallops

MAKES 4 SERVINGS

Meaty sea scallops, dredged or plucked by hand from the frigid Atlantic waters, are another of Maine's glorious contributions to the wild shellfish harvest from the sea. After lobstering season ends in the fall, many Maine fishermen adapt their sturdy boats for scalloping by attaching a special winch that dredges scallops from the sea bottom. A few truly hardy (and, I'll wager, mostly young) men don dry suits and dive with oxygen tanks down into the cold ocean depths, searching out the bivalves hiding in the nooks and crannies of rocks on the sea floor. One of my favorite ways to prepare scallops in season is to broil them with this simple lemon-flavored crumb topping. The buttery crumbs protect the sweet, lean scallops from the drying effects of the heat, and add richness and flavor.

> 6 tablespoons unsalted butter
> 2 garlic cloves, minced
> 2 cups fresh breadcrumbs, preferably made from day-old French or
>   Italian bread
> ½ teaspoon grated lemon zest
> 2 teaspoons fresh lemon juice
> ¼ teaspoon salt, plus more to taste

¼ teaspoon fresh-ground black pepper, plus more for sprinkling
   on scallops
1½ pounds sea scallops
1 large lemon, cut in 4 wedges

1. Melt the butter over medium heat in a medium-sized skillet. Add the garlic and cook, stirring, for 1 minute. Add the breadcrumbs, raise the heat to medium-high, and cook, stirring almost constantly, until they begin to toast and turn very pale golden, about 3 minutes. Remove from the heat and stir in the lemon zest, lemon juice, salt, and pepper.

2. Preheat the broiler.

3. Pat the scallops dry gently on paper towels if they are at all watery. Place them in a single layer in an oiled large shallow baking dish or on a rimmed baking sheet. Season lightly with salt and pepper. Sprinkle with the crumbs, patting them on lightly so they adhere to the scallops. Place the pan 4 to 5 inches from the heat and broil until the crumbs are richly browned and the scallops have just lost their translucency, 5 to 7 minutes.

4. Serve with lemon wedges for squeezing over.

Maine Shrimp

February is the prime month for tiny, popcorn-size Maine shrimp, a.k.a. northern pink shrimp. Maine shrimp are the only shrimp that New Englanders get in a truly fresh state. Peeling the small creatures is labor-intensive, but their sweet, pure taste is utterly addictive. The shrimp can be cooked in their shells, heads and all, or they can be peeled before cooking. If uncooked shrimp are icy cold, they are easier to peel. To cook unshelled shrimp, bring a large pot of salted water to a boil. Add the shrimp, and immediately start testing for doneness, peeling and biting into them. One to 2 minutes is usually long enough. Drain the shrimp in a colander, run cold water over them, and transfer to a bowl. Add ice cubes to the bowl (this helps stop the cooking entirely) and refrigerate until cold. Cook shelled shrimp the same way, but for even less time. The main admonition is to be sure not to overcook them, because overcooked Maine shrimp, even more so than other varieties of shrimp, turn to a mealy mush. Serve the cooked shrimp with any sort of dipping sauce as an hors d'oeuvre, or present as a main course. The yield of peeled shrimp is about half the weight of the original weight in the shell (see the recipe for Jazzed-Up Maine Shrimp Boil, page 23).

Wood-Grilled Darien Shrimp

MAKES 4 SERVINGS

The Junior League of Stamford-Norwalk published an excellent seafood cookbook, *Off the Hook*, a few years ago. I typed and edited the recipes, and in doing so learned a lot from the well-researched book, both about Connecticut seafood and about the history and culture of coastal Connecticut. Gracious, thoughtful, well-planned cooking and entertaining is a hallmark of the "Leaguers," and this adaptation of a wonderful grilled shrimp recipe from a Darien League member exemplifies these talents.

1½ to 2 pounds large or jumbo shrimp
2 tablespoons extra-virgin olive oil
2 tablespoons dry white wine
1 tablespoon honey
1 tablespoon coarse-grained Dijon mustard
1 tablespoon minced garlic
½ teaspoon cayenne pepper
¼ teaspoon salt
¼ teaspoon fresh-ground black pepper
2 tablespoons chopped fresh parsley
Lemon wedges

1. Peel and devein the shrimp, but leave their tails on.
2. Whisk together the oil, wine, honey, mustard, garlic, cayenne, salt, and pepper in a large dish, stirring until the honey dissolves. Add the shrimp, stir to coat with the marinade, and set aside in the refrigerator for at least 30 minutes or up to 3 hours.
3. Prepare a hot charcoal fire or preheat a gas grill to high, and oil the grill rack. Soak some hardwood chips such as oak or apple wood in water for 30 minutes and throw them on the fire or grill rocks a few minutes before grilling.
4. Lift the shrimp out of the marinade, letting the excess drip off, and thread them crosswise onto 4 to 6 metal skewers. Grill the shrimp close to the heat until they are cooked through and are slightly blackened around the edges, 2 to 3 minutes per side. Do not overcook.
5. Arrange the skewers on a serving platter, sprinkle with parsley, and serve with lemon wedges.

Ritzy Stuffed Jumbo Shrimp

MAKES 4 SERVINGS

The only shrimp that is truly native to New England waters is the Maine shrimp, or red shrimp, a tiny, sweet crustacean that is netted and sold fresh during the winter months. (See the recipe for Jazzed-Up Maine Shrimp Boil, page 23.) Although other types and sizes of shrimp are not available fresh, excellent-quality jumbo shrimp that have been flash frozen at the source are sold in virtually every fish market and supermarket in the region. And since everybody loves baked stuffed shrimp, I thought a recipe for this perennial favorite should most definitely be included here. New Englanders are fond of using crushed rich Ritz crackers in their stuffings, and here they are the perfect choice.

14 jumbo or colossal shrimp (about 2 pounds), with shells on
4 tablespoons unsalted butter
2 garlic cloves, minced
1½ cups very fine Ritz cracker crumbs
¼ cup chopped fresh flat-leaf parsley
¼ teaspoon cayenne pepper
Salt and fresh-ground black pepper
¾ cup dry white wine

1. Butterfly 12 of the shrimp by cutting through the legs on the inside curl of the shrimp without cutting through the back shell. Open the shrimp with your fingers and press with the palm of your hand so they lie as flat as possible. Arrange the shrimp cut sides up in a single layer in a shallow baking dish or rimmed baking sheet.
2. Peel and devein the remaining two shrimp and chop them fine. Melt the butter in a medium-large skillet over medium-high heat. Add the garlic and cook, stirring, for 2 minutes. Add the cracker crumbs and cook, stirring frequently, until they turn one shade darker, about 3 minutes. Remove from the heat, stir in the parsley and cayenne, and season to taste with salt and pepper. Stir in the chopped shrimp. (The recipe can be prepared several hours ahead to this point. Refrigerate the shrimp and stuffing separately.)
3. Preheat the oven to 450 degrees.

4. Sprinkle the butterflied shrimp lightly with salt and pepper. Spoon the stuffing over the shrimp, pressing it in lightly. Pour the wine around the shrimp in the bottom of the baking pan.

5. Bake, uncovered, until the stuffing is golden and the shrimp turn pink, about 10 minutes.

6. Spoon the pan juices over the shrimp before serving.

Little Italy
Calamari in Spicy Red Sauce

MAKES 4 SERVINGS

Thanks to the hundreds of wonderful family-run restaurants in the "Little Italies" all over New England, we have now all been exposed to calamari (squid), gotten over being squeamish about their looks, and grown to love their mild, sweet, briny taste. Calamari are delicious cooked in any number of ways—poached for a salad, deep-fried, stuffed, and, one of the simplest and perhaps my favorite way to eat this delicacy, simply stewed in a spicy tomato sauce. Still one of the best bargains around, calamari are readily available everywhere, both fresh and frozen.

3 tablespoons extra-virgin olive oil

4 garlic cloves, minced

1 35-ounce can Italian plum tomatoes
   in puree

1 cup bottled clam juice

1 teaspoon dried oregano

½ teaspoon red pepper flakes

1½ pounds calamari, including tentacles,
   if desired, bodies cleaned and sliced into rings (see Note)

¼ cup chopped fresh flat-leaf parsley

1 tablespoon fresh lemon juice

½ teaspoon sugar

Salt and fresh-ground black pepper

1 pound linguine, cooked and drained

Grated Parmesan cheese, optional

1. Heat the oil in a large, heavy saucepan. Add the garlic and cook over medium heat, stirring, for 1 minute. Add the plum tomatoes and clam juice, breaking the tomatoes up into small chunks against the side of the pot with a spoon. Add the oregano and hot pepper flakes. Bring to a boil, reduce the heat to medium-low, and simmer uncovered until the sauce thickens somewhat and the flavors blend, 20 to 25 minutes.

2. Add the calamari and any of their juices, along with the parsley, lemon juice, and sugar. Bring to a simmer and cook gently until the calamari turn pinkish-white and opaque, about 5 minutes. (Do not overcook or the squid will toughen.) Season to taste with salt and black pepper.

3. Serve the sauce over the cooked pasta and pass the cheese for sprinkling over the top if desired.

Note: You can ask the fishmonger to clean the squid by removing the interior spine and bony parts around the head, or you can do this yourself. Squid are often sold precleaned and frozen.

Calamari Four Ways

At the Daily Catch restaurant on Boston's Fan Pier, calamari is the specialty. When you order a calamari platter it arrives featuring a whole festival of southern Italian-style squid on a single plate—calamari salad doused with a zippy vinaigrette, fried calamari rings and tentacles, stuffed calamari simmered in a marinara sauce, and "meatball"-style calamari, which is a chopped squid and seasoned breadcrumb mixture shaped into compact balls and fried.

Steamed Crabs with Paprika-Lime Butter

MAKES 4 SERVINGS

In New England, lobsters grab the limelight, but if you're lucky enough to be able to catch or buy fresh live crabs, this is an excellent way to cook them. The New England sand crab has wonderfully sweet, delicate, pink-tinged meat that is similar to West Coast Dungeness crab. Present this finger-pickin' and -lickin' feast on a newspaper-covered table, buy some good beer or white wine, and offer such simple sides as Crusty Cornbread (page 451) and Crisp Apple Slaw (page 86), and, for dessert, a platter of cut-up melon and Mom's Harbor View Butterscotch Brownies (page 562) or Native Raspberry Pie (page 609).

> 8 to 12 live crabs (about 1 pound each), or more crabs if they are
>   smaller
> Salt
> ¼ pound (1 stick) unsalted butter
> ¼ teaspoon paprika
> ¼ teaspoon grated lime zest
> 1 tablespoon fresh lime juice

1. Bring about 1 inch of water to a boil in the bottom of 2 large pots. Add about 2 teaspoons of salt to each pot.
2. Place the crabs, undersides down, in the pots. (If their pincer claws are not pegged, use long tongs or wear gloves when handling the crabs.) Cover the pots and return the water to a rolling boil. Reduce the heat to medium and steam the crabs until they are bright pink all over and the meat in the largest claw is no longer translucent, about 12 minutes.
3. Meanwhile, heat the butter with the paprika in a small saucepan or in a microwave until the butter melts. Remove from the heat and stir in the lime zest and juice. Transfer to two or four small dipping bowls.
4. Drain the crabs in a colander and heap them onto a platter to serve. To eat the crabs, begin by cracking and pulling off the top shell. Break off the claws and gently tap them with a mallet to crack the shells without crushing the meat. Remove the

meat from the shells with picks. Break the body into sections and extract the meat with your fingers or a pick. Serve with the paprika-lime sauce for dipping the picked crab into at the table.

New England Crab

Most crabs available in New England are rock or sand crabs, which are close relatives of the Northwest's Dungeness crab. In Maine, crabs are sometimes referred to generically as simply "Maine crabs," but if you ask locals you get different answers. Some Mainers refer to rock or sand crabs as "picked-toe" (local slang for "pointed") crabs, or "peekytoes"; in Massachusetts they are also known as Jonah crabs. Because lobster is such a huge industry in the region, crabs have tended to be overshadowed by their larger crustacean cousins, and it has traditionally been somewhat difficult to buy live crabs in New England. Ironically lobster companies are often the best source for obtaining live crabs because crabs are found in the same traps that catch lobsters.

My Best Crab Cakes

MAKES 4 SERVINGS

By definition, my best crab cakes, or anyone else's, are those with the highest possible proportion of sweet, fresh lump-style crabmeat, bound with the bare minimum of mayonnaise and crumbs, the flavor sparked with just the right amount of complementary seasonings. This is my formula for exactly that. In coastal Maine, where rock or sand crabbing is an informal byproduct of the lobster industry (the crabs go after the same bait and wind up in the lobster traps), superb, freshly picked crabmeat is available all summer. Any good lump or backfin crabmeat, such as blue crab from Maryland, works beautifully in these luxurious yet simple-to-make cakes. A bed of baby lettuces, which should include some peppery bitter greens, is the perfect natural foil for the sweet crab.

½ cup regular or lowfat mayonnaise
1 egg
2 tablespoons snipped fresh chives or minced scallions
2 tablespoons chopped fresh flat-leaf parsley
1½ tablespoons Dijon mustard
¼ teaspoon black pepper

1 cup crushed saltines or packaged saltine crumbs (see Note)
1 pound fresh lump-type crabmeat, picked over
2 teaspoons fresh lemon juice
2 tablespoons light olive oil
2 tablespoons butter
4 large handfuls of mesclun, including some bitter leaves such as
    mizuna or mustard
¼ cup vinaigrette dressing such as My Favorite Vinaigrette (page 79)
Lemon wedges

1. Whisk together the mayonnaise, egg, chives, parsley, mustard, and pepper in a large bowl. Stir in the cracker crumbs. Add the crabmeat and lemon juice and mix with a fork or your clean hands to combine. Stir gently but thoroughly, being careful not to mash the larger lumps of crab too much. Shape into 8 patties, about ½ inch thick. (The patties can be made up to 4 hours ahead and refrigerated.)

2. Heat one tablespoon each of oil and butter in 2 large skillets over medium heat. Cook the crab cakes, uncovered, until the bottoms are nicely browned, about 5 minutes. Turn the cakes, cover the pan, reduce the heat to medium-low, and cook until the undersides are golden and the cakes are hot in the center, about 5 minutes.

3. Meanwhile, arrange the salad greens on a serving platter or on four plates. Drizzle with the vinaigrette. Serve the crab cakes atop the greens, with lemon wedges on the side.

Note: Or you can use unsalted saltines or common cracker crumbs and add ½ teaspoon of salt to the crab cake mixture.

Magnificent Steamed Lobster

MAKES 4 SERVINGS

There is truly no more magnificent feast than this. It has everything: it feels opulent, but is essentially simple; it's glamorous, yet primitive and hands-on; visually, it's cover-photo gorgeous at the start of the meal, and then satisfyingly messy and debris-strewn at the finish. But, above all, a perfectly steamed lobster has an incomparable taste—briny-sweet, rich yet delicate, leaving the essential flavor of deep ocean and summer on

---
To Eat a Lobster

• Grasp the cooked lobster with one hand on the body and one hand on the tail and twist to break in two. Expect a gush of liquid on your plate at this point. You can drain the liquid into the debris bowl for shells on the table.

• Start with the tail. (Some begin with the claws, but I like to save these, my favorite part, for last.) First remove the flat flippers at the end and pull each one through your teeth like an artichoke leaf. Then poke the tail meat out with your finger, or, if the tail has been split, pull it apart with two hands and extract the meat. Remove and discard the black vein running down the center. Dip the meat into melted butter and eat.

• Twist off the two large claw legs where they meet the body. Twist off the pincer claws. Using a nutcracker, crack the claws and the knuckles. The claw meat is easy to get at; sometimes you have to poke out the knuckle meat—some of the sweetest—with a lobster pick or your little finger.

• For the persistent person, there are still the small legs, again best eaten by pulling through your teeth; there are also small nuggets of meat in the joints where the legs meet the body.

• Tucked away deep in the body is the soft green tomalley, or liver, and, if the lobster is female, the bright pink roe, or coral. Some consider these morsels, in particular the rich-tasting tomalley, the very best parts of all.

❋ ❋ ❋ ❋ ❋ ❋ ❋ ❋ ❋
---

the tongue. Steamed lobster should be served simply, just with melted butter, and although it's not traditional everywhere in New England, I add a bit of vinegar to the butter, which nicely cuts the richness of the lobster meat. As for other accompaniments, my menu is almost unvarying. For a real "shore dinner," we start with Connecticut Coast Steamers (page 12) or Citrus-Glazed Steamed Mussels (page 20). With the lobsters, it's corn on the cob, sliced ripe tomatoes drizzled with a little of My Favorite Vinaigrette (page 79), sometimes Crispy Creamy Coleslaw (page 84), and usually garlic bread. Be sure to provide side plates for these accompaniments, since the dinner plate will be too full of drippy lobster and shells to accommodate much else. For a sufficiently grand finale, it should be either U-Pick Native Strawberry Shortcake (page 502), Blackberry Patch Cobbled Cobbler (page 492), or Best Maine Blueberry Pie (page 601). For those outside New England's orbit, lobsters from the cold waters north of Cape Cod can now be airfreighted (see page 619).

Impeccably clean seawater, optional
4 lobsters (at least 1¼ pounds each)
¼ pound (1 stick) butter, melted
About 1 tablespoon cider vinegar or white wine vinegar
Lemon wedges

1. Fill the bottom of a 4- to 5-gallon pot or two 2- to 3-gallon pots with about one inch of seawater or tap water. If using tap water, add about 1 tablespoon of salt to the water. Place the lobsters in the freezer for 10 minutes to numb them. Cover the pot(s) and bring the water to a boil. Place the lobsters in the pot, cover, and return to the boil. Reduce the heat to medium to medium-high and steam until the lobsters are done, approximately 10 minutes per pound (see chart, page 405). When fully cooked, the lobsters are bright red and a sharp tug on one of the antennae pulls it off readily. If there is any doubt about whether the lobster is completely cooked, break one open where the body meets the tail. The tail meat should be creamy white with no translucency.

2. Using tongs, transfer the lobsters to a colander in the sink. If desired, use the tip of a small knife to punch a hole between the lobster's eyes and hold it over the sink to drain off excess liquid. Using a large chef's knife, split the lobster down through the underside of the tail and drain again. Transfer the lobsters to dinner plates.

3. Divide the melted butter between 2 bowls and add vinegar to one or both of the bowls. Pass a plate of lemon wedges.

Baked Crumb-Stuffed Lobster

MAKES 4 SERVINGS

A baked crumb-stuffed lobster is often thought of in New England as the quintessential special occasion restaurant dish. Indeed it is, but if you're bold enough to try preparing a live lobster for stuffing at home—or, if you can get the fish market to perform this operation not more than an hour before you plan to cook—then this really is quite a simple, straightforward recipe. To ready them for stuffing, the lobsters are butterflied, that is partially split and opened up to receive the stuffing, or they can be split completely in half. Either way, when arranged on plates, the presentation really is beautifully butterfly-like. The crumbs, their flavor enriched and enhanced with the pleasantly briny taste of the lobster tomalley, are sprinkled over the cut sides, and the whole is then simply baked in a hot oven for about 20 minutes. It's an absolutely dazzling dish, both to appreciate for its beauty and, above all, to eat. Serve something simple yet pretty on the side, such as Summer Farm Stand Composed Salad (page 97), or Broiled Asparagus with Asiago (page 110) and steamed diced new potatoes tossed with fresh herbs. A dessert such as Rustic Rhubarb-Raspberry Tart (page 616) provides a fitting finale.

4 live lobsters (1¼ to 1½ pounds each)
6 tablespoons butter
½ cup chopped onion
¾ cup dried breadcrumbs
3 tablespoons chopped fresh flat-leaf parsley
Salt and fresh-ground black pepper
Lemon wedges

1. Follow the instructions for splitting live lobsters on page 403. Either butterfly the lobsters and open the tails enough so that they can receive the stuffing, or split them in half. Remove and save the tomalley and roe, if present. Remove the rubber bands from the claws. Arrange the lobsters, cut sides up, on 2 rimmed baking sheets. (The lobsters can be prepared up to 1 hour ahead. Cover with plastic wrap and refrigerate until ready to cook.)

2. Heat 3 tablespoons of the butter in a large skillet over medium heat. Add the onion, along with the tomalley and, if you like, the roe and cook, stirring frequently, until the onion softens, about 5 minutes. Add the breadcrumbs and cook, stirring, until the crumbs are toasted and golden brown, 3 to 4 minutes. Stir in the parsley and season with salt and pepper to taste. (The crumbs can be made several hours ahead and refrigerated. If you make the stuffing before you remove the lobster tomalley or roe, you can simmer it in water to cover for about 3 minutes and add it to the previously prepared stuffing.)

3. Preheat the oven to 450 degrees.

4. Melt the remaining 3 tablespoons of butter. Brush some of the butter over the cut sides of the lobsters and sprinkle them lightly with salt and pepper. Sprinkle the breadcrumb mixture evenly over the body cavity and tail meat. Drizzle with any remaining melted butter.

5. Bake the lobsters, uncovered, until the tail meat is opaque and the crumbs are crisp and deep golden brown, 15 to 20 minutes.

6. Transfer to serving plates, garnish with lemon wedges, and serve.

—— To Prepare a Lobster for Baking or Grilling ——

This process is not nearly as difficult as it may sound. However, if an obliging fishmonger or fisherman will do it for you, so much the better. If you really can't manage it, a brief parboil for 3 to 4 minutes will accomplish the task.

•Wear rubber or other work gloves. Place the live lobsters in the freezer for 10 minutes first to numb them.

•Place the lobster top side up on a cutting board with the face toward you. Grasp the tail. Holding a large chef's knife with the other hand lengthwise over the lobster, insert the point of the blade into the body at the point where the body (thorax) meets the tail. With one swift motion, plunge the knife into the body and split the lobster in half through the head. The lobster is now dead; any twitching is just post-mortem muscle spasms.

•Turn the lobster over so its underside is facing up. Holding the upper body with one hand, cut through the body toward the tail. For Grilled Lobster (page 403), split the lobster entirely in half; for Baked Stuffed Lobster (page 401), cut entirely in half or leave the hard top tail shell intact. To butterfly the whole lobster, hold half of the tail in each hand and crack but do not break the back shell to open it up.

•Remove and save the tomalley and roe, if present, and wrap and refrigerate until you are ready to use. Remove and discard the intestinal tract (black vein) in the tail. Pull the sand sac out of the head and discard. (There might be one in each of the two halves.) With a mallet or rolling pin, crack the top sides of the large pincer claws.

•The lobsters can be prepared up to 1 hour ahead. Place on rimmed baking sheets, cover with plastic wrap, and refrigerate.

—— ❊ ❊ ❊ ❊ ❊ ❊ ❊ ❊ ❊ ——

Grilled Chive-Tarragon Lobster

MAKES 4 SERVINGS, (½ LARGE LOBSTER PER PERSON)

This recipe takes inspiration from two lobster masters, Marion Morash and Jasper White, both legendary New England restaurateurs and cookbook authors. Although it may not appear to be the case, lobster is a perfect candidate for grilling, either split

and grilled raw, or parboiled first. The shells cradle the meat, creating a natural (and spectacular-looking) cooking and serving container, and protect the meat from the intensity of the heat. The sweetness of the lobster flesh is enhanced by the smoky flavor. As fragrant smoke wafts from the grill, whetting appetites, the lobster shells turn a brilliant red and char just a bit, and the whole event takes on a dimension of drama and excitement. This sophisticated presentation calls for an equally brilliant side dish such as Summer Farm Stand Composed Salad (page 97) or Minted Taboulleh with Toasted Walnuts (page 87), some grilled Rosemary Focaccia (page 454), and a smashing finish such as Pioneer Valley Blueberry Bread and Butter Pudding (page 513).

> 4 tablespoons butter
> 1½ teaspoons grated lemon zest
> 2 tablespoons fresh lemon juice
> 2 tablespoons snipped fresh chives
> 1 tablespoon chopped fresh tarragon
> ½ teaspoon salt
> ¼ teaspoon fresh-ground black pepper
> 2 large (1¾- to 2-pound) or 4 smaller lobsters
> 1 tablespoon vegetable oil
> Paprika
> Lemon wedges

1. Build a charcoal fire and let the coals burn down to moderately hot, or preheat a gas grill to medium-high.
2. Melt the butter in a small saucepan or in a glass measuring cup in the microwave. Stir in the lemon zest, lemon juice, chives, tarragon, salt, and pepper. Set aside until ready to use.
3. If you are planning to split the lobsters live, proceed by following the instructions on page 403. If you are parboiling the lobsters, place them in the freezer for 10 minutes to numb them. Bring a large pot of water to the boil and add 2 tablespoons of salt. Drop the lobsters head-first into the boiling water. Cover the pot and boil the lobsters for 3 to 4 minutes, or until they are no longer alive. Lift them out with tongs and hold them head down over a sink for a couple of minutes to drain. Place on a board, and, using a large knife or cleaver, split the lobsters in half lengthwise. Scoop out and discard the gray intestinal tract and the sand sac from the head. Leave any red roe or green tomalley in the lobsters, if desired. Crack the claws in a

couple of places so that the heat can penetrate. Remove the rubber bands. (The recipe could be prepared up to 1 hour ahead to this point. Refrigerate the split raw or parboiled lobsters until ready to cook. Add a few minutes to the grilling time if they are cold.)

4. Rub the lobster shells with the oil. Place the lobsters, shell sides down, on the grill, brush the exposed meat sides with the butter mixture, and sprinkle with paprika. Cover with the grill lid or place a shallow metal roasting pan over the lobsters. Cook, without turning the lobsters (to prevent loss of the juices), brushing 2 or 3 times with the flavored butter, until the meat is a creamy opaque white but still juicy, 10 to 15 minutes if raw, about 8 minutes if parboiled. (If using smaller lobsters, they will take less time to cook.)

5. Transfer the lobsters to a platter or serving plates, and serve with lemon wedges.

To Cook Lobsters

If you like, you can boil lobsters in a large pot of salted water, but I prefer to steam them in just an inch or so of water. There are several advantages to steaming. It takes less time to bring the water to a boil; it is safer because you are not dealing with gallons of boiling water; it is less messy because there are fewer spillovers; the water comes back to a boil faster, so timing is more accurate; and—most important, of course—the lobsters taste better because their flavor is less diluted with water.

If you own a large black enamel pot of the type originally designed for canning, use it for steaming the lobsters. Some people use natural seawater or add rockweed seaweed to the water to create a type of natural rack. I don't do either, nor do I use a rack.

For cooking four lobsters, I bring about 1 inch of water to a boil in the bottom of a 4- to 5-gallon pot or in two 2- to 3-gallon pots, and add 1 tablespoon of salt to the water. While the water heats, place the lobsters in the freezer for 10 minutes to numb them. Bring the water to a rolling boil and add the lobsters. Clamp the lid back on tightly and return to a boil over high heat. Reduce the heat to medium-high and steam according to the following times (hard-shell lobsters take the longer cooking times):

1 pound—9 to 10 minutes

1¼ pounds—12 to 14 minutes

1½ pounds—14 to 16 minutes

1¾ to 2 pounds—17 to 19 minutes

Lobster Lore

• Lobsters must be alive before they go into the pot. When they are dead, they release gastric enzymes that begin to deteriorate the meat.

• Lobsters are invertebrates with very simple nervous systems, similar to grasshoppers. They do not have a brain, so theoretically they do not feel pain. However, feisty lobsters do thrash around for a while when first put into the pot. A 10-minute stay in the freezer numbs them, making the cooking process easier on both the lobster and the cook.

• Lobsters have no vocal cords, so they do not utter sounds. The "scream" some people report is the sound of the body fluids steaming in the pot.

• A "chicken" or "chix" is a 1-pound lobster.

• Unlike much seafood, "rare" or just barely cooked lobster meat is not the best degree of doneness. Lobster meat is more tender and has a more succulent flavor if fully cooked to the creamy, opaque stage.

• There's no noticeable difference in flavor between male and female lobsters. The only reason to request a female is if you want the roe. A female lobster's eggs are dark green when raw and turn red when thoroughly cooked, at which point they are known as "coral." Coral has a mild flavor and is often used as a coloring agent in lobster stew or stuffings.

• The soft, pale green material in the body is called the tomalley. When cooked, tomalley has a rich, slightly sweet taste and is wonderful when added to stuffing or stew. It functions as the lobster's liver, helping protect it against pollutants, so tomalley should not be eaten regularly, but an occasional indulgence should be fine.

• If cooking live lobsters within 3 to 4 hours of purchase, simply store them in a bag in the coldest part of the refrigerator. Do not store them on ice or in tap water. For longer storage, wrap each lobster gently in damp newspaper and store in the coldest part of the refrigerator—usually the bottom shelf. Hard-shells can be stored for a day or so; soft-shells are more perishable and often die if held overnight.

Hard-Shell or Soft-Shell Lobsters

A lobster of legal size (1 pound or larger) is 4 to 7 years old and has molted (discarded its shell in favor of a larger shell) 20 to 25 times. After molting, the shell begins to harden and the meat grows to fill the new shell. Because of the timing of their life cycle, most lobsters we eat in the summer are newly molted soft-shells or are at some stage between soft- and hard-shelled. Very soft-shelled lobsters ("shedders") are watery, with underdeveloped, somewhat spongy claw meat. Very hard-shelled lobsters are packed with meat that I find often borders on tough, and their shells are so calcified that major carpentry is required to open them. I prefer to eat lobsters that are somewhere in between their molting stages. You can feel the difference in the shells when you pick them up by the body. If in doubt, ask a knowledgeable fishmonger. If buying lobsters to travel, choose hard-shells. Soft-shells are too frail to withstand much time out of circulating salt water.

Lobster Fra Diavolo

MAKES 4 SERVINGS

Our friend Mike Elia makes this fabulous Lobster *Fra Diavolo* when he comes to visit us in Maine. Mike is a gifted Italian-American cook, which naturally improves his standing as a welcome houseguest. One recent summer afternoon I looked on, took notes, and inhaled great garlicky smells while Mike meticulously prepared this shellfish masterpiece. It was like watching a composer write a symphony. As a bonus, Mike instructed me in how to split live lobsters, thereby giving me the courage to try it myself. Actually, it's easier than you might think. Although Mike serves his *fra diavolo* over cooked pasta, I think I prefer it just with some hot crusty peasant bread on the side. The number of lobsters you need here depends on their size as well as on the appetites of your guests.

4 small (1¼-pound) or 2 large (1¾- to 2-pound) lobsters
5 tablespoons extra-virgin olive oil
1 medium onion, chopped
4 large garlic cloves, minced
1 teaspoon dried oregano
1 cup dry white wine
2 28-ounce cans Italian plum tomatoes with juice
2 tablespoons tomato paste
1 teaspoon red pepper flakes
Salt and fresh-ground black pepper
3 tablespoons chopped fresh flat-leaf parsley

Italian bread, preferably a semolina bread, warmed

1. Split and clean the lobsters according to the directions on page 403. Remove and save the tomalley and roe, if any. Break or cut off the claws where the knuckles attach to the carcass. Crack the claw shells lightly. Hold the lobster bodies over the sink and allow them to drain well.
2. Heat 3 tablespoons of the oil in a very large, deep skillet or sauté pan. Add the lobster pieces and cook over medium-high heat, turning frequently and pressing down so they don't curl up, until the shells turn bright red, about 7 minutes. Remove all the lobster pieces to a large plate, leaving any drippings in the pan.

3. Add the remaining 2 tablespoons of oil to the pan. Add the onion, garlic, and oregano and cook over medium-high heat, stirring, until the onion begins to soften, about 4 minutes. Add the wine, raise the heat to high, and boil until reduced somewhat, about 3 minutes. Add the tomatoes with juice, tomato paste, and pepper flakes along with the reserved tomalley and roe, if any. Bring to a boil, breaking up the tomatoes, tomalley, and roe into smaller pieces with the side of a spoon. Reduce the heat to medium-low.

4. Twist and break the lobster bodies away from the tails. Set the tails and claws aside. Rinse the body cavities under running water to remove most of the inner matter. Add the body shells to the sauce (to add flavor), partially cover the pot, and simmer for about 45 minutes, stirring occasionally, until the sauce is quite thick. Remove the lobster shells from the sauce and discard them. Season the sauce with salt and pepper to taste. (The sauce can be made several hours ahead. Refrigerate the lobster tails, claws, and the finished sauce. Reheat before proceeding.)

5. Add the lobster tails and claws to the sauce. Simmer, uncovered, until the meat is opaque, 5 to 15 minutes, depending on the size of the lobsters. Stir in the parsley and correct the seasoning if necessary.

6. Serve the lobster in wide shallow bowls with the sauce spooned over, along with the warm Italian bread. Provide plenty of napkins, and nutcrackers and picks for extracting the lobster meat.

Italian Christmas Eve

All the New England Italian-Americans I know celebrate and sanctify Christmas Eve with a meatless, mostly seafood family feast. Many families used to adhere to serving a strict number of dishes, either seven (to signify the seven sacraments) or twelve (for the twelve apostles). These days, while the menu is still strictly meatless, it is likely to be somewhat less ritualized and a little more free-form. A poll of several Yankee-Italian friends elicited a litany of Christmas Eve seafood dishes, including raw clams on the half-shell, deep-fried smelts, fried calamari, lobster *fra diavolo*, sole with capers and brown butter, *frutti di mare* (mixed seafood), and shrimp in garlic sauce. And then there are the pastas, which include such delicacies as mussels marinara, linguine with white or red clam sauce, crab spaghetti, and squid ravioli.

The Grant Family, Fishermen

Bill Grant, son Patrick, and occasionally daughter Sharlene, of Carter Point in Sedgwick, Maine, fish for lobster. One early summer morning, their large, sturdy lobster boat, the *Sharlene IV*, carries us out of the harbor through the fog, heading east in Jericho Bay for a day of lobstering. Conversation is difficult over the thrum of the diesel engines. Within a few minutes Bill is leaning out to snag the first red and white buoy with his gaff, lifting the line over the snatch block. Steering with one hand and operating the winch engine with the other, he kicks the potentially dangerous line off the deck as it reels in, until the 40-pound steel wire trap is dangling over the deck. With a muscle-straining heave, Bill drags the pot up onto the gunwales of the boat, and then with precise, concentrated movements, orchestrated without conversation, he flips up the top of the trap, Patrick empties the remnants of the bait bag into the sea and ties a new one on, Bill removes the lobsters and unhooks the line from the pot hauler, Patrick shoves the pot back in the water, and Bill shifts the engine back into gear. As Bill steers toward the next pot, Patrick sizes the lobsters, throwing any "shorts" back overboard, clips rubber bands around the two large claws of the keepers, and then begins refilling bait bags with more salted herring. He must be ready in a minute or so to haul the next trap.

And so it goes all morning as the fog burns off, the sun moves up in a cloudless blue sky over a glassy sea, and gulls wheel and cry over the boat. By noon, after a five-minute break for lunch, they've hauled more than three hundred traps, and I'm tired and sore just watching. Finally, when we hit a string of particularly full traps, my offer to be put to work is accepted. Wearing rubber gloves, I help with stuffing bait bags and handing Patrick supplies for banding. The sun begins its downward course, the breeze freshens, and we're now in the far easternmost edge of the bay, still snagging lines, hauling traps, shoving them back, and packing seawater-filled barrels and slatted wooden boxes full of beautiful shiny-black *Homarus americanus*.

In midafternoon they shove the last pot overboard. As Bill steers homeward through the bay, Patrick scrubs the boat down and organizes the catch while I sit numbly in a corner, almost too tired to appreciate the beauty of the fir-tipped islands, pink granite ledges, harbor seals, and cormorants that we pass. This was an idyllic weather day, all conditions perfect. How do these fishermen do it day after day, when the boat is pitching in ten- to-fifteen-foot seas, rain pelts their faces, clammy fog obscures up to just a few feet ahead, and cold numbs their fingers and feet? I emerge with heightened respect for the people who are engaged in this arduous, yet often deeply rewarding work.

"This was a good day," Bill says. Hundreds of traps hauled and more than five hundred lobsters to take to market at the wholesaler in Deer Isle. "But our best day ever was a couple of years ago, when my sister Sharlene was working with us," says Patrick. "That day the three of us took almost eight hundred lobsters." "And Sharlene banded every single one of them," Bill smiles, with just a modest Yankee's hint of paternal pride.

The New England Clambake

In Maine it's known as a lobster bake, but everywhere else in New England the ancient, atavistic ritual of cooking lobsters and other shellfish on the beach is called a clambake. We inherit the clambake tradition directly from the Native Americans, who cooked all their food this way in their summer settlements along the New England coast. The basic technique involves digging a deep pit in the sand and lining it with granite rocks, upon which is built a driftwood or charcoal fire. When the coals burn down, the embers are raked away, wet rockweed seaweed is thickly layered over the white-hot rocks, the food is placed on the seaweed, and a heavy canvas tarp is sealed over all. As the rockweed releases water, it steams the food, and when the tarp is lifted the heavenly ocean-sweet aroma of steamed seafood fills the senses. Constructing a clambake takes superb organizational skill and is at least a day-long affair. It's wonderful to do with a few family and (hard-working) friends. A good many local organizations in New England stage clambakes as fund-raisers, such as the famous Allen's Neck Clambake put on every year near Dartmouth, Massachusetts, for five hundred people. Serving as the clambake bakemaster is an honored position that must be earned by serving years of apprenticeship as a helper. New England clambake menus vary considerably from one locale to the next. Some possible candidates for a bake are lobsters, steamer clams, mussels, linguiça (Portuguese sausage), corn, onions, white potatoes, rock crabs, periwinkles, whole fish, tripe, chicken, sweet potatoes, bread dressing, and hen or duck eggs. Accompaniments are butter, lemon, soda, beer, wine, watermelon or other fresh fruit, and blueberry pie. For specific instructions on how to organize a clambake, I suggest you consult Jasper White's book *Lobster At Home* (Scribner, 1998).

SWEET
MORNING BREADS

This chapter is redolent with all the enticing, mouthwatering aromas of an old-fashioned Yankee breakfast. You can serve many of the breads for a midmorning snack or an afternoon tea, too.

When baking powder was introduced in the mid-nineteenth century and more reliable coal-fired stove ovens became the norm, Yankee cooks began a flurry of baking that is still going strong. We flip griddlecakes with abandon, such as egg-rich Golden Rowayton Pancakes (page 416) and Polly's Pancake Parlor Cornmeal Buttermilk Pancakes (page 415). We whip up batches of scrumptious muffins, like Martha's Marvelous Fruit Muffins (page 427), and bake such delectable fruit-and-nut-filled quick breads as Cape Cranberry-Walnut Tea Bread (page 431) and Beautiful Blueberry Cornbread (page 428). A recipe for delicate unleavened Lacy Rhode Island Jonnycakes (page 413) and a journey through jo(h)nnycake history (see page 414) make a deliciously fascinating tale. Greek and Portuguese Yankees add their exceptional yeast-risen sweet breads—the rich Vineyard Portuguese Sweet Bread (page 439) and the spectacular Glorious Greek Easter Braid (page 436)—both significant contributions to the New England bread basket.

Lacy Rhode Island Jonnycakes

MAKES ABOUT 16 PANCAKES, 4 SERVINGS

In this recipe I have compromised between the very thin east-of-Narragansett jonny-cakes and the thicker west-of-Narragansett cakes (see page 414). Jonnycake meal made from white flint corn, ground between old hard granite stones so that the kernels are "flaked" rather than crushed, will produce sturdy cakes that truly taste of corn, but I've found that regular cornmeal works fine too. Just adjust the liquid so that the cakes spread out thin, "making lace curtains around the edges," as Richard Donnelly, a member of the Society for the Propagation of Jonnycake Tradition recommends.

1 cup stone-ground Rhode Island
    jonnycake meal or other cornmeal
1 teaspoon salt
1 teaspoon sugar
1 cup boiling water
1 tablespoon butter, cut in pieces
⅓ to ½ cup whole milk

1. Whisk together the cornmeal, salt, and sugar in a large bowl. Whisk in the boiling water and butter and stir until the butter melts. Let the mixture stand for 15 minutes, until the cornmeal softens somewhat. Whisk in ⅓ cup of the milk. The batter should be thin, like gruel.
2. Heat a griddle or heavy skillet over medium to medium-high heat. Grease the pan well with butter or vegetable shortening.
3. Whisk the batter before making each jonnycake. Make a test cake to check the heat of the pan and the consistency of the batter. Stir in a bit more milk if the batter doesn't spread out onto the griddle to make a thin, lacy-edged jonnycake.

John Thorne on Jonnycake

"Let's be honest: unless you come from Rhode Island, a true jonnycake isn't worth making for anyone but yourself. They're tricky to make and no one will thank you for the effort—at least until they've acquired the taste. Why make them? Well, they taste like that crisp crust that forms on the bottom of the mush pot, a mouthful of hot crunchy corn. If that and the pleasure of working a delicacy out of unpromising and reluctant material is the sort of thing to appeal to you, the effort pays for itself."

—John Thorne, *Simple Cooking* (Viking, 1986)

4. Using about 2 tablespoons of batter for each cake, spoon the batter onto the griddle. Cook until the undersides are golden brown and the tops of the jonnycakes look dry, 3 to 4 minutes. Turn and cook until the undersides are crusted over and the cakes are cooked through, about 3 minutes.

5. Serve hot, with butter and maple syrup.

Jo(h)nnycake Wars

No New England food stirs more debate than the Rhode Island jonnycake. Disagreement rages over the spelling of the name (with or without the *h*, one word or two), the origin of the name (whether a corruption of "journey cake," joniken, or "Shawnee cake"), and, most controversially, how the cakes should be made (with milk or water, thick or thin, dropped on a griddle or baked in a pan).

Rhode Islanders are so fiercely protective of this primitive corn pancake that in the 1970s a group of amateur and professional historians and jonnycake lovers formed the Society for the Propagation of the Jonnycake Tradition in Rhode Island. You can see by the name how they settled the spelling dispute. The only other points not disputed are that true jonnycakes should be made with a local white flint corn called whitecap, that is ground, preferably within the state, between local granite millstones. At least two gristmills, Gray's and Kenyon's, meet those requirements, and their sturdy, intensely corn-flavored, flaky-textured meals are sold around New England and can be mail-ordered (see page 619).

The main line of demarcation in the jonnycake wars is Narragansett Bay. In and around Newport, east of the bay, cooks make a thin batter using cold water or milk, which results in very thin, lacy, crisp-edged pancakes. The people west of the bay, in the area known as South County, scald the cornmeal with boiling water, thereby activating and swelling the starch to make a thick batter, which creates a thick, somewhat fluffy cake.

Whichever way you make them, be sure to eat jonnycakes immediately because, even while still hot, they are dense and can be dry and chewy. John Hart, who was the miller at Gray's Grist Mill in Adamsville, Rhode Island, for sixty-two years, described the best way to eat jonnycakes: "With butter—and good teeth."

World's Largest Breakfast

In 1986 Springfield, Massachusetts, began competing with Battle Creek, Michigan, to see which municipality would lay claim to The World's Longest Breakfast Table. Because of a technical dispute over the table configuration, the cities declared a tie. They also competed to see who could serve the most breakfasts. For additional technical reasons, Battle Creek forfeited and Springfield won. Every May, in a three-hour period, sixty thousand people in Springfield eat a breakfast cooked by four hundred flapjack-flipping volunteers and eat vast quantities of buttermilk pancakes made with six hundred pounds of eggs, and drink more than three thousand gallons of coffee. They sit at a 1,500-foot table that stretches right down the middle of Springfield's main street.

❖ ❖ ❖ ❖ ❖ ❖ ❖ ❖ ❖

Polly's Pancake Parlor
Cornmeal Buttermilk Pancakes

MAKES 12 4-INCH PANCAKES, 2 TO 4 SERVINGS

Helen, daughter of the eponymous Polly, is a lovely lady. In true Yankee form, however, she is parsimonious with her recipes, so I had to re-create this recipe for something akin to the crunchy-delicate yet hefty cornmeal pancakes served at Polly's Pancake Parlor in Sugar Hill, New Hampshire. Sugar Hill, in the White Mountains near Franconia Notch, is a town named for, and dedicated to, maple sugaring. In fact, when "Sugar Bill" Dexter opened Polly's more than sixty years ago, it was primarily to showcase the versatility of their maple syrup, which you must pour with abandon over these golden griddlecakes.

> 1 egg
> 1 cup buttermilk, plus more if necessary
> 2 tablespoons unsalted butter, melted
> 1 cup all-purpose flour
> 3 tablespoons yellow cornmeal
> 1 tablespoon sugar
> 1 teaspoon baking powder
> ½ teaspoon baking soda
> ½ teaspoon salt

1. Whisk the egg with the buttermilk in a medium-sized bowl until blended. Whisk in the melted butter.
2. Whisk together the all-purpose flour, cornmeal, sugar, baking powder, baking soda, and salt in a large bowl. Pour the liquid ingredients over the dry ingredients and whisk them together gently, just until the flour is moistened. Do not overmix. (It's all right if the batter looks lumpy.)
3. Heat a lightly oiled cast-iron griddle or skillet over medium heat. Make a test pancake to check the heat of the pan and the consistency of the batter. Stir in 2 to 3 more tablespoons of buttermilk if the batter is too thick.
4. Spoon about 3 tablespoons of batter onto the griddle for each pancake. Cook until the undersides are golden brown and the tops are speckled with burst bubbles, about 2 minutes. Turn and cook until the undersides are lightly browned and the centers spring back when lightly pressed, 1 to 2 minutes.
5. Serve immediately or keep warm in a low oven while making the remaining pancakes.

Golden Rowayton Pancakes

MAKES 12 4-INCH PANCAKES; 4 SERVINGS

Farm-fresh eggs, with their deep orange-yellow yolks and intense egg flavor, are the reason, I'm sure, that the pancakes of my Rowayton, Connecticut, childhood tasted so good and were such a rich golden color. If you have access to fresh organic eggs, they do make a big difference, but if not, this recipe, which is basically the classic New England pancake but with just a bit more egg than in some recipes, produces superior pancakes that puff up quite high yet are fairly thick and substantial. In New England, butter and pure maple syrup (and a side of smoky bacon or little sausages) are de rigueur.

> 2 eggs
> 1¼ to 1½ cups whole, lowfat, or skim milk
> 3 tablespoons unsalted butter, melted
> 1½ cups all-purpose flour
> 2 tablespoons sugar
> 2 teaspoons baking powder
> ½ teaspoon salt

Sugaring-Off Party

In areas of New England that make maple syrup, a party celebrating the end of the sugaring season is an old and still-beloved tradition. Toward the end of the tapping season (usually in the month of March), when the rush of the work is over, guests are invited to the sugarhouse. Each guest is given a dish of clean snow, often brought out from the dense evergreen woods where snow bands linger in the shade. Syrup is boiled until thick (about 230 degrees) and drizzled over the packed snow, where it instantly hardens into a wonderful waxlike candy, which is eaten with the fingers. The compilers of *A Vermont Cook Book by Vermont Cooks* write, "If you have never attended a Sugaring-Off party you've truly missed something. This is what you would have for refreshments: Sugar on Snow, Sour Pickles, Raised Doughnuts, Coffee. The pickles are served so that you can eat more maple syrup. If snow isn't available, crushed ice will do."

1. Whisk the eggs with 1¼ cups of the milk in a medium-sized bowl until blended. Whisk in the melted butter.
2. Whisk together the flour, sugar, baking powder and salt in a large bowl until well-blended.
3. Pour the liquid ingredients over the dry ingredients and whisk them together gently, just until the flour is moistened. Do not overmix. The batter should still look slightly lumpy.
4. Heat a lightly oiled cast-iron griddle or skillet over medium to medium-high heat. Make a test pancake to check the heat of the pan and the batter's consistency. Stir in a bit of the remaining milk if the batter is too thick.
5. Spoon about ¼ cup of batter onto the griddle for each pancake. Cook until the undersides are golden brown and the tops are pocked with burst bubbles, 1 to 2 minutes. Turn and cook until the undersides are lightly browned, about 1 minute.
6. Serve immediately or keep warm in a low oven while making the remainder of the pancakes.

Berkshire Puffed Apple Skillet-Baked Pancake

MAKES 4 SERVINGS

The Berkshires are a chain of old, worn-down mountains that meander comfortably through northwestern Connecticut and western Massachusetts. The hills are full of farms, old orchards, and charming travel-brochure-perfect New England villages and towns. One such town is Stockbridge, Massachusetts, which was once home to Norman Rockwell, creator of small-town America images that are permanently etched on our collective psyche. At the Red Lion Inn, a large, gracious, old-fashioned New England hostelry in Stockbridge, I once ate a light skillet-baked pancake made with local Macoun apples that engraved an indelible image on my taste memory. Here is my re-creation. Simple and easy to put together, the pancake puffs impressively in the oven like a soufflé, making for the perfect breakfast or brunch dish.

> 4 tablespoons unsalted butter
> 4 cups sliced peeled medium-tart apples, such as Macoun, Crispin, or
>   Jonagold (about 3 medium)
> 3 tablespoons sugar
> 1 teaspoon ground cinnamon
> 4 eggs

Diners Defined

"Diners," write Jane and Michael Stern, in their book *Real American Food* (Knopf, 1986), "were born in the 1890s when Boston, New York, and Philadelphia junked their horse-drawn trolley cars in favor of electric ones. The discarded cars, available cheap, were converted easily into mobile beaneries. Their shape defined the diner look."

The Sterns, who are real diner connoisseurs, identify three types of diners: the original antique wooden dining cars, many of which are in north country New England and along the coast of Maine, serving plain regional food; the stainless-steel and Formica diners built during the 1940s and '50s, many on the outskirts of New England cities, serving a wider variety of standard American fare; and the "post-Hellenic mutations," often located in suburbs, with lengthy, ambitious menus that range from lox and bagels to souvlaki to duck à l'orange.

¼ teaspoon salt
½ cup whole or lowfat milk
1 teaspoon vanilla extract
½ cup all-purpose flour
Confectioners' sugar

1. Preheat the oven to 400 degrees.
2. Melt the butter in an 11- or 12-inch, preferably cast-iron, skillet with oven-proof handle, over medium heat. Spoon out 2 tablespoons of the butter and transfer to a large bowl. Add the apples to the remaining butter in the skillet. Cook, stirring frequently, for 5 minutes. Sprinkle with the sugar and cinnamon and continue to cook until the sugar is dissolved and the apples are almost tender, about 5 more minutes.
3. Meanwhile, break the eggs into the bowl with the reserved butter. Add the salt, milk, and vanilla, and whisk until blended. (The mixture will still be slightly lumpy.) Place the flour in a sieve and sift it over the egg mixture. Whisk gently until just combined. Do not overmix.
4. Spread the apples out in an even layer in the bottom of the skillet and pour the batter over them. Bake until the pancake is puffed and golden and crisp around the edges, 20 to 25 minutes.
5. Sprinkle the pancake heavily with confectioners' sugar and serve immediately, cut in wedges. (Remember that the skillet handle is hot!)

Crispy Scottish Oat Waffles

MAKES 4 8-INCH WAFFLES

The area around Barre, Vermont, in the northern half of the state, attracted a good many immigrants from Scotland who came to work in the granite quarries. Oatmeal is so important in the Scots' diet that one area in Barre that was home to many Scottish people was dubbed "Oatmeal Flats." Doris Macdonald of Barre reports that her grandmother used to tell the children in the family, "If you don't eat your oatmeal you can't have anything else. If you do eat your oatmeal, you don't need anything else." Try these crispy waffles for an absolutely delectable way to eat your oatmeal.

¾ cup quick-cooking rolled oats (see Note)

3 tablespoons unsalted butter, cut in pieces

1¼ cups all-purpose flour

1 tablespoon sugar

1½ teaspoons baking powder

½ teaspoon baking soda

½ teaspoon salt

2 eggs

1 cup buttermilk (see Note)

1. Combine the oats with 1 cup of water in a medium-sized saucepan. Bring to a boil, reduce the heat to medium-low, and simmer, uncovered, whisking often, for 3 minutes. (This porridge will be thicker than oatmeal made from package directions.) Remove from the heat, add the butter, and whisk until it melts.

2. Preheat a waffle iron.

3. Whisk together the flour, sugar, baking powder, baking soda, and salt in a large bowl.

4. Whisk the eggs with the buttermilk in a separate bowl until blended. Whisk the egg mixture into the oatmeal mixture.

5. Add the oatmeal mixture to the flour mixture and stir just until blended.

Buttermilk and Yogurt

Generations of bakers have understood that buttermilk was one of the "secrets" to exceptional baked goods. Early New England farm cooks who used the liquid by-product of churning cream into butter (hence the name buttermilk), knew that buttermilk added a light and pleasing tang that offset the sugars in their baked goods. They may not have been aware that it is the milk solids and natural acids in the buttermilk that tenderized their muffins and pancakes and quick breads.

Plain yogurt has more or less the same properties as buttermilk. These days, although commercial buttermilk is quite readily available in most supermarkets, cooks might be more likely to have plain yogurt on hand in the refrigerator. As a substitute for 1 cup of buttermilk, use ¾ cup of plain yogurt thinned with ¼ cup of any type of milk. You can also substitute soured milk for buttermilk. To make it, add 1 tablespoon of white vinegar or fresh lemon juice to 1 cup of milk and let it stand for 10 to 15 minutes until it curdles and thickens.

6. Spoon about ¾ cup of batter into the hot iron, close the lid, and bake until the steam stops rising or until a light indicates doneness, 3 to 4 minutes. Remove the baked waffle and repeat with the remaining batter.

7. Serve the waffles hot.

Note: Regular old-fashioned rolled oats can also be used, but increase the water to 1¼ cups and increase the cooking time in Step 1 to 3 minutes. Do not use instant oatmeal. Instead of buttermilk, you can use ¾ cup plain yogurt thinned with ¼ cup milk.

Watch Hill Maple French Toast

MAKES 6 SLICES

This recipe is from cookbook author Barbara Lauterbach, who used to run the Watch Hill Bed and Breakfast in Centre Harbor, New Hampshire, on Lake Winnipesaukee. Barbara cut slices from a dense homemade sandwich loaf for this scrumptious French toast.

> 3 eggs
> ¾ cup whole milk
> ¼ cup pure maple syrup
> 3 tablespoons unsalted butter
> 6 slices good-quality sandwich bread (see Note)

1. Whisk the eggs with the milk and syrup in a shallow rimmed dish or pie plate.

2. Melt 1 tablespoon of the butter in a large, heavy skillet over medium heat. Dip 2 slices of the bread into the egg mixture, place in the pan, and cook until the undersides are a crusty golden brown, about 3 minutes. Turn and cook until the bottoms are firm and flecked with brown, about 2 minutes. Remove from the pan and repeat with the remaining butter, bread, and egg mixture.

3. Serve the French toast hot, with more butter and maple syrup.

Note: Use a homemade sandwich bread made with unbleached flour or a sturdy purchased bread such as Pepperidge Farm Toasting White.

Irish Oat Scones with Dried Cranberries

MAKES 12 SCONES

Several Irish–New Englanders offered me their grandmother's scone recipe. It was tempting, but I thought I'd prefer to use this tried-and-true recipe for oat scones that I've perfected over the years, this time with the addition of sweetened dried cranberries. The scones now incorporate a deliciously winning combination that should please all Yankees concerned.

1 cup all-purpose flour
½ cup quick-cooking rolled oats (see Note)
2 tablespoons plus 2 teaspoons sugar
2 teaspoons baking powder
½ teaspoon salt
4 tablespoons chilled unsalted butter, cut into several pieces
½ cup sweetened dried cranberries
1 egg
¼ cup whole or lowfat milk, plus 1 tablespoon more if necessary

---

Cranberry Harvest Festivals

Even though Wisconsin has surpassed Massachusetts in cranberry production, the Bay State is where it all started, and cranberry pride still runs strong. Cranberries remain the commonwealth's number-one agricultural product, so Massachusetts is determined to keep right on celebrating the tart, jewellike berry. At least three different festivals are staged in the state every year. The biggest and most elaborate festival is over Columbus Day weekend in Plymouth County near the Ocean Spray cranberry cooperative. Another is held in early September on Cape Cod in Harwich, near Dennis, where commercial cranberrying began in 1816, and a third cranberry harvest festival takes place on Nantucket island, off Cape Cod's shores on the weekend after Columbus Day. At all these events you can steep yourself in cranberry lore, visit brightly blushing cranberry bogs, participate in cranberry cooking contests, drink cranberry coolers, and sample cranberry breads, muffins, jellies, candies, pies, cobblers, cakes, cookies, salsas, and yes, even cranberry pizzas.

---

1. Preheat the oven to 375 degrees.
2. Combine the flour, oats, 2 tablespoons of the sugar, the baking powder, and salt in a food processor. Pulse once or twice to sift and blend the ingredients. Distribute the butter pieces over the flour mixture. Pulse until most of the pieces of butter are about the size of small peas. Add the cranberries and pulse once to combine.
3. Lightly beat the egg with the milk in a glass measuring cup. With the motor running, pour the liquid through the feed tube and process in short bursts until the dough begins to clump together. If the dough is too dry to shape, add another tablespoon of milk.
4. Transfer the dough to an ungreased baking sheet, gather it together, and shape into a ½-inch-high disc about 9 inches in diameter. Using a large knife, cut the dough into 12 pie-shaped wedges and separate the wedges so they are at least 1 inch apart on the baking sheet. Sprinkle with the remaining 2 teaspoons of sugar.
5. Bake in the center of the oven until the scones are an even golden brown, about 20 minutes.
6. Serve the scones warm.

Note: Use quick-cooking or one-minute rolled oats in this recipe. Do not use regular old-fashioned oats or instant oatmeal.

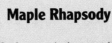

Maple Rhapsody

"Maple sugar is the great New England contentment....It sits so sweetly and lightly on the tongue that it never cloys the palate. It is delicate, and it has a body, in its pure early spring rendering, that is almost ethereal."

—Fred Halliday,
The New England Food Explorer
(Fodor's, 1993)

Baking Powder, Muffins, and Quick Breads

Double-acting baking powder became a reliable, readily available commodity in the late nineteenth century, providing freedom from the dependence on slow-growing yeast to leaven breads. The 1923 edition of *The Boston Cooking-School Cook Book* contained four recipes for baking powder loaves, and by the 1930s quick breads, particularly those filled with fruits and nuts, had increased in variety and popularity.

Plain muffins leavened with baking soda were being made in the nineteenth century, but the invention of baking powder spurred the trend toward more and more elaborate muffins, until finally, in the 1980s, muffin mania took hold. Muffins began to get larger and larger, and the flavor choices were not just bran and blueberry and corn, but also pineapple, papaya, zucchini, and even chocolate chip.

Mimi's Magnificent Blueberry Muffins

MAKES 12 LARGE MUFFINS

Mimi Jennings Boyd is one of the best bakers I have ever known. A native Nutmegger (i.e., a person from Connecticut), Mimi is a self-taught cook who started "helping out" part-time in the early days of the famous Connecticut Hay Day Markets. She went on to become their indispensable head baker, in charge of an operation that, in spite of its eventually enormous size, turned out breads, pies, cookies, cakes, muffins, and short-cakes that always tasted absolutely homemade. The year I worked with her at Hay Day, Mimi slipped me this recipe as I left for a Maine vacation. And sure enough, true to form, it's the best blueberry muffin I (or now, you) will ever eat.

    2 cups all-purpose flour
    ⅓ cup sugar
    ¼ cup packed light brown sugar
    2 teaspoons baking powder
    ¾ teaspoon salt
    2 eggs
    ¾ cup whole or lowfat milk
    5 tablespoons unsalted butter, melted
    1 scant cup fresh blueberries

1. Preheat the oven to 400 degrees. Grease a 12-mold muffin tin (½-cup capacity) or line the cups with paper liners and grease the liners.
2. Combine the flour, two sugars, baking powder, and salt in a large medium-mesh sieve set over a bowl. Use your fingers or a wooden spoon to push the flour-sugar mixture through the sieve into the bowl. (This removes the lumps from the brown sugar.)
3. Gently whisk together the eggs, milk, and melted butter in another bowl.
4. Make a well in the center of the dry ingredients, pour in the liquid ingredients, and stir gently just until the dry ingredients are moistened. (Do not overmix; the batter should still look slightly lumpy.) Fold in the blueberries. Divide the batter evenly among the muffin cups, filling them about three-quarters full.
5. Bake for 18 to 22 minutes, or until the muffins are golden brown and a skewer inserted in the center comes out clean. Cool the muffins in the tin for 5 minutes before removing.
6. Serve warm, if possible.

Cole Farms Date-Bran Muffins

MAKES 12 MUFFINS

Cole Farms is inland, off the coastal tourist trail, in Gray, Maine. It's a big, informal roadside restaurant that serves honest, satisfying food, including such baked goods as a man-size bran muffin, dark and sticky with molasses and chopped dried dates, which can be a meal unto itself. Dates have long been a New England pantry staple because of their remarkable keeping qualities, and they show up in lots of regional recipes, particularly in such baked things as breads and muffins. This is my re-creation of the Cole Farms bran muffin.

> 1½ cups all-purpose flour
> ¼ cup whole wheat flour
> 1 teaspoon salt
> 1½ teaspoons baking powder
> ½ teaspoon baking soda
> 1 teaspoon ground cinnamon
> ½ teaspoon ground ginger

½ teaspoon ground allspice
2 eggs
½ cup sugar
½ cup vegetable oil
¼ cup molasses
1 cup buttermilk
2 teaspoons vanilla extract
1 cup wheat bran
¾ cup chopped dates or raisins

1. Preheat the oven to 375 degrees. Grease a 12-mold muffin tin (½-cup capacity) or line the cups with paper liners and grease the liners.

2. Whisk together the flours, salt, baking powder, baking soda, cinnamon, ginger, and allspice in a large mixing bowl.

3. Whisk the eggs with the sugar, oil, and molasses in a separate large bowl until smooth. Whisk in the buttermilk and vanilla.

4. Make a well in the center of the dry ingredients, add the liquid ingredients, and stir gently just until no specks of flour remain. Stir in the bran and the dates or raisins. Divide the batter evenly among the muffin cups.

Sylvester Graham

In the late nineteenth century the Reverend Sylvester Graham of Connecticut became an early proponent of using whole grains to make bread. He inveighed against milling the bran off wheat, insisting that bread made with the bran was nutritionally superior to white bread. Graham had been inspired by a Shaker manifesto that protested that bread "had been for countless ages the staff of life but has now become but a weak crutch!"

Graham's eloquence inspired "Grahamite societies" in Boston, and bran flour came also to be known as "graham flour." Bronson Alcott was a believer in Graham's philosophy. He took it to the furthest extreme at Fruitlands, a utopian community he established outside Boston, where he exhorted his fellow residents to put their bodies under "utter subjugation." They were to live only on native grains, fruits, herbs, and roots. No fish, fowl, flesh, butter, eggs, milk, cheese, or any drink but spring water was allowed. Many New England cookbooks still refer to whole wheat flour as "graham flour," and graham crackers have fortified several generations of schoolchildren.

5. Bake for 20 to 25 minutes, until the tops are richly brown and a skewer inserted in the center comes out clean. Do not overbake. Cool in the muffin pan for 5 minutes, then turn out onto a wire rack.

6. Serve warm or at room temperature.

Martha's Marvelous Fruit Muffins

MAKES 12 MUFFINS

My sister Martha, who resides in Portland, Maine, is an excellent cook and baker. Her muffins, which the entire family now calls "Martha's marvelous," have achieved legendary status. Martha started tinkering with a basic muffin formula several years ago when she was trying to sneak a few extra wholesome grains into her children's diet. Her recipe has taken on a life of its own, morphing into a moist, fruit-and-nut-filled muffin that is scrumptious. To vary the recipe, Martha suggests substituting blackberries, raspberries, or chopped pears, nectarines, or plums for the apples, and walnuts, hazelnuts, almonds, or sunflower seeds for the pecans.

1½ cups all-purpose flour
⅓ cup wheat bran
¼ cup sugar
¼ cup packed light brown sugar
2 tablespoons wheat germ
2 teaspoons ground cinnamon
2 teaspoons baking powder
1 teaspoon baking soda
½ teaspoon salt
2 eggs
½ cup regular or lowfat plain yogurt
⅓ cup light vegetable oil, such as safflower or canola
1 cup diced cored but unpeeled apple
⅔ cup chopped pecans

Doughnut History

According to legend (and to food writer John Willoughby), a Maine sea captain gave the doughnut its hole when, in a sudden rush to right his ship's course, he thrust a piece of fried bread onto a spoke of his ship's wheel so he could steer the ship with both hands.

1. Preheat the oven to 400 degrees. Grease a 12-mold muffin tin or line the cups with paper liners and grease the liners.
2. Whisk together the flour, bran, two sugars, wheat germ, cinnamon, baking powder, baking soda, and salt in a large bowl.
3. Whisk the eggs with the yogurt and oil in another bowl.
4. Make a well in the dry ingredients and add the egg mixture. Stir until no specks of flour remain. Do not overmix. Stir in the apple and pecans. Spoon the batter into the muffin cups, filling them about three-quarters full.
5. Bake until the muffins are golden brown and a skewer inserted in the center comes out clean, 15 to 18 minutes. Cool in the pan for about 5 minutes, then turn out onto a wire rack.
6. Serve warm or at room temperature. (These muffins can be stored in heavy plastic bags and frozen.)

Maple Grading

Maple syrup is graded by comparing color and flavor to standard USDA samples. Each state has its own grading system. Vermont, which is the largest producer of maple syrup in the region, divides syrups into Grade A and Grade B. Within Grade A, Light Amber is from the earliest sap run, and has a very delicate flavor and light color. Grade A Medium Amber has a moderate maple flavor and is the most popular syrup for table use. Grade A Dark Amber has a dark amber color and a strong maple flavor. This robust flavor makes it good for use in cooking. Grade B has an extremely dark color and intense flavor. It is generally not recommended for table use, but is reserved for commercial purposes.

Beautiful Blueberry Cornbread

MAKES ABOUT 6 SERVINGS

With its sun-drenched golden cornmeal hue and luscious purply blueberries that spurt sweet-tart on the tongue, this bread seems to capture New England summer in a pan. It's lovely for weekend houseguest breakfasts, and, because it's not too sweet, it also happens to pair beautifully with a lunchtime foggy-day clam chowder.

> 1¼ cups plus 2 tablespoons all-purpose flour
> ¾ cup yellow cornmeal

1 tablespoon baking powder
1 teaspoon salt
6 tablespoons unsalted butter, softened
¾ cup sugar
2 eggs
1 cup whole or lowfat milk
¾ cup fresh or frozen blueberries
   (see Note)

1. Preheat the oven to 400 degrees. Grease a 9-inch-square metal baking pan.

2. Combine 1¼ cups of the flour, the cornmeal, baking powder, and salt in a mixing bowl. Whisk thoroughly to sift and blend.

3. Using an electric mixer, beat the butter with the sugar in another bowl until smooth. Beat in the eggs, scraping the sides of the bowl as necessary, until well blended. With the mixer on low speed, add the flour mixture in two batches, alternating with the milk, and beat just until blended.

4. Toss the blueberries with the remaining 2 tablespoons of flour and fold them into the batter. Scrape into the prepared dish, smoothing the top.

5. Bake until pale golden brown on top and a toothpick inserted in the center comes out clean, 25 to 30 minutes.

6. Let the bread rest for 5 minutes before cutting into squares and serving hot.

Note: If you are using frozen blueberries, do not thaw them before adding to the batter.

The Purloined Blueberry

"Once you are in Maine, you can even arrange to pick your own berries. For me, this foraging, which is almost always technically a trespass on somebody's land, is one of the most exhilarating things to do in the outdoors. Robert Frost caught the beauty and mild mischief of it in his horticulturally precise poem, 'Blueberries':

You ought to have seen how it looked in the rain,

The fruit mixed with water in layers of leaves,

Like two kinds of jewels, a vision for thieves."

Raymond Sokolov, *Fading Feast* (Farrar Straus Giroux, 1979) (Poetry excerpt from *The Poetry of Robert Frost*, edited by Edward Connery Lathem (Holt, Rinehart and Winston, 1930))

To Cook Eggs

Overcooked eggs become dry and tough and rubbery, but undercooked unpasteurized eggs can transmit the salmonella bacteria. Here's how to cook an egg properly:

To soft- or hard-cook an egg in the shell: Place the eggs in a saucepan large enough to keep them from knocking into each other too much. Add cold water to cover by 2 inches. Cover the pan and set it over medium heat. Allow the water to come just to a boil. Stir the eggs gently. Remove from the heat and let the pan stand, covered, for about 4 minutes for soft-cooked eggs and 14 to 17 minutes for hard-cooked eggs. Drain off the hot water, then cover with cold water to cool them quickly. Peel soft-cooked eggs when they are cool enough to handle. For hard-boiled eggs, wait until they cool completely, then bang gently on a surface and peel off the shells. (Eggs that are at least 1 week old peel better than very fresh eggs.)

To scramble eggs: Break the eggs into a bowl and whisk them with a small amount of water or milk (about 2 teaspoons per egg) until just blended but not too frothy. Cook in a regular or nonstick skillet over medium heat, in about 1 teaspoon of butter per egg. Stir almost constantly with a wooden spoon or spatula until the eggs are set to your liking, 3 to 5 minutes.

To fry eggs: Melt about 1 teaspoon of butter or oil per egg in a regular or nonstick skillet set over medium-high heat. Break the eggs into the pan, reduce the heat to medium to medium-low and cook, turning the eggs carefully if desired, until set to your liking, 2 to 4 minutes. If you cover the skillet, the eggs will cook a bit faster and somewhat more evenly.

To make an omelet: Whisk the eggs as you would for scrambled eggs, but cook them in a slope-sided pan over medium-high heat without stirring for about 1 minute, or until set enough on the bottom to form a "pancake" that you can then roll over a filling. Ideas for fillings are endless, but some classic ingredients are cheese, lightly cooked vegetables such as mushrooms or asparagus tips, smoked fish, diced ham, or even fruit. This is a great way to use up leftovers. A sprinkling of fresh herbs enhances almost any omelet.

Do not try microwaving eggs, especially eggs in the shell. They inevitably explode, leaving behind an impossible-to-clean mess!

Cape Cranberry-Walnut Tea Bread

MAKES 1 LOAF

This tea bread, adapted from a similar, very classic recipe in a community cookbook called *Flavors of Cape Cod*, compiled by the Thornton W. Burgess Society, is the best I've ever tasted. It's a tried-and-true formula, but toasting the nuts seems to add just the right additional depth of flavor. It's irresistible hot out of the oven, so go ahead and cut yourself a slice right away, but it really is even better if allowed to age for a day.

½ cup coarsely chopped walnuts
2 cups all-purpose flour
1½ teaspoons baking powder
1 teaspoon salt
½ teaspoon baking soda
1 egg
1 cup sugar
3 tablespoons vegetable oil
1 tablespoon grated orange zest
¾ cup orange juice
1½ cups fresh or frozen cranberries (see Note)

1. Preheat the oven to 350 degrees. Grease and lightly flour a 9-by-5-inch loaf pan. (For extra insurance, line the bottom of the pan with parchment or wax paper.)
2. Toast the walnuts in a small, dry skillet over medium heat, stirring frequently, until fragrant and one shade darker, about 5 minutes. Set aside.
3. Whisk together the flour, baking powder, salt, and baking soda in a mixing bowl to sift and combine.
4. Using a large whisk or electric mixer, beat the egg with the sugar and the oil in a large bowl until smooth. Beat in the orange zest and add the orange juice.
5. Stir the flour mixture into the egg mixture, mixing until well blended. Coarsely chop the fresh cranberries and fold them into the batter. Stir in the toasted nuts. Scrape into the prepared pan, smoothing the top.
6. Bake until a skewer inserted in the center comes out clean and the crust is a rich, golden brown, 55 to 65 minutes. Cool in the pan for 10 minutes. Remove from the

pan and cool the bread completely on a wire rack, at least 45 minutes. The bread is best if wrapped and refrigerated for 1 day, or up to 3 days. It can also be frozen.

7. Cut into slices to serve.

Note: If you are using frozen cranberries, do not thaw or chop them; add them to the batter whole.

The Banana Boat Arrives

In 1870 the Boston Fruit Company (later to merge with another fruit importer and eventually to become the colossal United Fruit Company) brought an entire ship loaded with bananas from Jamaica into Boston harbor. It took a little time (another thirty years or so—Bostonians are not famous for leaping immediately onto any bandwagon), but eventually people learned to love the strange-looking exotic fruit. Not only did New Englanders start slicing them onto breakfast cereal and taking them to lunch, but innovative Yankee cooks began inventing a bonanza of banana baked goods, including, most fortuitously, moist, dense banana bread.

The Very Best Banana Bread

MAKES 1 LOAF

When the banana peels are more dark brown than yellow, that's when it's time to make this moist, gently spiced, sweet banana bread. It's heavenly spread with softened cream cheese. This recipe makes a large loaf that will keep very well in the refrigerator for about four days and also freezes well. It truly is one of the very best quick breads there is.

¾ cup coarsely chopped walnuts, optional

2 cups all-purpose flour

1 teaspoon salt

¾ teaspoon baking soda

½ teaspoon ground cinnamon

¼ teaspoon ground cloves

3 to 4 very ripe bananas

2 eggs

Why Brown Eggs?

According to Bill Bell of the Brown Egg Council of New England, brown eggs gained a foothold in New England back in days of the China trade. China has always produced only brown eggs because in that country white is the color of death, while brown signifies virility and life. Clipper ship captains stocked up on chickens in China so they would have fresh eggs on board. Some of these birds made it to New England shores, where, in Little Compton, Rhode Island, the first commercial poultry farm was established. These original brown-egg-laying chickens came to be known as Rhode Island Reds.

Because they were such large and hardy birds, Rhode Island Reds, and related breeds produced from the originals, proved well equipped to withstand New England winters. Thus, brown-egg-laying hens became well established early in New England's history. Barely known outside the region, brown eggs came to be preferred by Yankee housewives, who trusted them because they knew they were local and therefore fresher.

Although chickens are now ensconced in heated poultry barns and lay eggs year-round, brown eggs are still the strong preference of most New Englanders today. At the very least, we know they still have to be fairly local, so they're probably fresher, better-tasting eggs.

½ cup sugar
½ cup packed dark brown sugar
¼ cup regular or lowfat plain yogurt
6 tablespoons unsalted butter, melted
1 teaspoon vanilla extract

1. Preheat the oven to 350 degrees. Grease and flour a large (9¼-by-5¼-inch) loaf pan. (For extra insurance, line the bottom with parchment or wax paper.)

2. If you are using the nuts, toast them in a small, dry skillet over medium heat until they are fragrant and one shade darker, about 5 minutes. Set aside.

3. Whisk together the flour, salt, baking soda, cinnamon, and cloves in a large mixing bowl.

4. Using a large fork or a potato masher, mash the bananas on a rimmed plate or pie dish until they are quite smooth. Measure 1¼ cups of banana puree and transfer it to a large bowl. Add the eggs, sugars, and yogurt and whisk until well blended. Stir in the melted butter and vanilla.

5. Make a well in the center of the flour mixture, add the banana mixture, and stir gently until the batter is moistened and no specks of flour remain. (Do not overmix.) Fold in the nuts, if using. Scrape the batter into the prepared pan, smoothing the top.

6. Bake for 55 to 65 minutes, until the crust is a rich golden brown and a skewer inserted in the center comes out clean. Cool for 10 minutes in the pan. Turn out onto a wire rack and cool completely.

7. Cut into slices and serve immediately. Or wrap and refrigerate for up to 3 days or freeze.

Pumpkin Record Breaker

The southern New Hampshire community of Keene retains the *Guinness Book of Records* championship for "Most Jack-o'-Lanterns in One Place at One Time." Every fall Keene holds a Pumpkin Festival, filling the entire downtown Main Street area with an enormous display of glowing, flickering, candle-lit carved pumkins. The first record was broken in 1992, and a recent count was set at an amazing 17,693 jack-o'-lanterns! The festival includes trick-or-treating, costume parades, entertainment, and . . . food. In addition to pumpkin soup, pumpkin bread, pumpkin mousse, and pumpkin pies galore, one of the most popular food booths features an old-fashioned apple-peeling machine. After peeling, the apples are sliced, dipped in batter, and deep-fried to make apple fritters, or doughnuts."

Shaker Cornmeal Pumpkin Bread
with Toasted Walnuts

MAKES 1 LOAF

The Shakers were brilliant cooks and bakers. I found a recipe similar to this in *Seasoned with Grace*, by Eldress Bertha Lindsay, who was the head cook at the Shaker Village in Canterbury, New Hampshire, until the late 1980s. I love the touch of cornmeal crunch in this quintessentially autumn-in-New England quick bread.

> 1 cup coarsely chopped walnuts
> 1¼ cups all-purpose flour

First American Cookbook

The first American cookbook, *American Cookery*, by Amelia Simmons of Connecticut, was published in 1796. The first edition of the book gave the earliest written instructions for making Indian pudding and jonnycake, and later editions included directions for dealing with knobby native Jerusalem artichokes, introduced the use of *molasses* as a synonym for English treacle, and gave a recipe for pumpkin "slapjacks." The batter used pureed pumpkin, cornmeal, pearl ash or baking powder, salt, sugar, egg, and boiling water. The cakes were fried on a hot griddle and served with maple syrup.

¼ cup yellow or white cornmeal
1 teaspoon baking powder
½ teaspoon baking soda
1 teaspoon salt
½ teaspoon ground cinnamon
¼ teaspoon grated nutmeg
¼ teaspoon ground allspice
2 eggs
1 cup sugar
¼ cup packed brown sugar, preferably dark brown
1 cup canned pumpkin
½ cup vegetable oil

1. Preheat the oven to 350 degrees. Grease a 9-by-5-inch loaf pan.
2. Toast the walnuts in a dry skillet over medium heat, stirring frequently, until they are one shade darker and fragrant, about 5 minutes. Transfer to a plate to cool.
3. Whisk together the flour, cornmeal, baking powder, baking soda, salt, cinnamon, nutmeg, and allspice in a medium-sized bowl until blended.
4. Using an electric mixer or whisk, beat together the eggs, the two sugars, pumpkin, oil, and ⅓ cup water in a large bowl until smooth.
5. Add the flour mixture to the pumpkin mixture and whisk or beat until well mixed, but do not overbeat. Stir in the toasted nuts. Scrape the batter into the prepared pan.
6. Bake for about 1 hour, or until a cake tester or skewer inserted into the center of the bread comes out clean. Cool for 10 minutes in the pan; then invert onto a wire rack and cool completely. (The bread can be stored, well wrapped, in the refrigerator for up to 3 days, or it may be frozen.) Cut into ½-inch-thick slices to serve.

Glorious Greek Easter Braid

MAKES 1 LARGE LOAF

This large braided loaf, with brilliantly colored eggs implanted in the top, is another of the enduring New England Greek Easter traditions. The sweet eggy bread is flavored with orange peel and crushed anise seed, which adds just a faint whiff of licorice. It makes an impressive and delectable edible centerpiece on any Easter table. (But please don't plan to eat the hard-cooked eggs; they're strictly for decoration.)

    1 (¼ ounce) package active dry yeast
    ¼ cup hot tap water (105–115 degrees)
    ½ teaspoon whole anise seed
    ½ cup whole or lowfat milk
    4 tablespoons unsalted butter, cut in pieces
    ½ cup sugar
    1 teaspoon salt
    1 egg
    1 teaspoon vanilla extract
    1 teaspoon grated orange zest
    2½ to 3 cups all-purpose flour
    2 to 3 hard-cooked eggs, colored
    1 egg beaten with 2 teaspoons milk for glaze
    1 teaspoon sesame seeds

1. Sprinkle the yeast over the hot water in a small bowl. Set aside until the yeast is dissolved and bubbly, about 10 minutes.
2. Crush or bruise the anise seed in a mini food processor, mortar and pestle, or by placing them in a plastic bag and pressing hard with the bottom of a small heavy pot. Combine the crushed seeds and the milk in a small saucepan and bring to a simmer over medium heat. Remove from the heat, add the butter, sugar, and salt, and stir until the butter melts.
3. Whisk the egg with the vanilla and orange zest in the bowl of an electric mixer with a dough hook or in a large mixing bowl. Stir in the yeast mixture and milk mixture. Begin stirring in the flour, ½ cup at a time, until the dough reaches a moderately soft but kneadable consistency. Knead with the dough hook for about 5 minutes or

Easter Sweet Breads

Many New Englanders from European backgrounds bake special sweet yeast breads for Easter. You can find English and Irish citron-flecked hot cross buns in Boston, Italian sesame-dusted round braided loaves called *casadella* in New Haven (or the similar *casatiello* in Providence), and the Polish *babka*, a tall, egg-rich, glazed round bread filled with golden raisins and almonds, in Ansonia and other towns in the Connecticut River valley.

Many Polish families still take a basket of holiday foods to the church to be blessed on Good Friday or Holy Saturday. In addition to *babka*, the basket might include such ingredients for the Easter feast as kielbasa, Polish ham, beet horseradish, potatoes, and raw and hard-cooked colored eggs.

by hand for about 10 minutes, until smooth and elastic. Transfer to a buttered bowl, turn so the top is coated with butter, and cover with a towel or plastic wrap. Set aside in a warm, draft-free place until doubled in bulk, about 1½ hours.

4. Punch the dough down. On a lightly floured surface, divide the dough into 3 equal parts. Use the palms of your hands to roll each third into a 20-inch-long rope. Line the ropes up on the work surface and weave them into a fairly loose braid, pinching both ends to seal. Transfer to a buttered baking sheet. Press the colored eggs into the top of the braid. Brush the bread with egg wash, cover loosely, and set aside until almost doubled in bulk, about 1 hour.

5. Preheat the oven to 350 degrees.

6. Brush the bread with another coating of egg wash and sprinkle with the sesame seeds. Bake in the center of the oven for 30 to 40 minutes, or until the crust is a deep golden brown and the bread sounds hollow when tapped on the bottom. Cool on a rack. (The bread can be stored, well wrapped, at cool room temperature for up to a day or frozen.)

7. Cut into slices to serve.

Old-Fashioned Bread

Eleanor Early's *New England Home Cooking* (Random House, 1954) is a treasure trove of recipes, facts, lore, and memories of New England foodways. In a chapter titled "Hot Breads Are a New England Specialty," Ms. Early discourses on some quaint old-fashioned hot breads, including the following.

Hoecakes—early corn cakes baked on a hoe or shingle before the fire.

Wonders—doughnuts without a hole, with a frilled edge that is cut with a "jagger wheel." Jagger wheels, for cutting wonders and fluting pie crust, were made by whalers on long voyages as gifts for the women at home. The tool was crafted from wood or whale tooth. A similar gadget, now simply called a pastry wheel, is made out of metal or plastic today.

Doughgods—doughnut holes, or strips of doughnut dough, that are dipped into deep fat and fried. Doughgods, reports Early, were a treat that children loved to have at doll's tea parties. They were served warm, often with little dishes of maple syrup.

Featherbeds—tiny rolls made from a potato yeast dough, brushed with plenty of melted butter, and baked. Featherbeds are, needless to say, as light as a feather.

Baptist Cakes—small pieces of risen yeast bread dough that are broken off, pulled very thin, and deep-fried in a kettle of hot fat. They are called Baptist cakes because, like the practitioners of that Protestant denomination, they are "immersed." Other New England names for the same fried cakes are holy pokes, huffjuffs, and hustlers.

Seventy-fours—another deep-fried breakfast bread, this one is made of baking powder biscuit dough instead of raised yeast dough. Seventy-fours are rolled very thin, cut with a diamond-shaped cutter, fried in a kettle of hot fat, and sometimes given a final immersion in a second kettle of hot molasses. The cakes are called seventy-fours, they say, because when they were cooked aboard a whaling ship, one sailor ate seventy-four of them.

Jolly Boys—yet another fried bread, made with rye flour, molasses, and sour milk. The dough is shaped into small balls and cooked in hot fat. Jolly boys are often broken in half, a piece of butter sandwiched between the halves, and eaten with maple syrup.

Gems—another name for muffins.

Slapjacks—an early name for pancakes, flapjacks, or griddlecakes.

Vineyard Portuguese Sweet Bread

MAKES 1 ROUND LOAF

Bakeries cluster in Portuguese neighborhoods in New England coastal cities and towns. (I once counted five bakeries in a twenty-block Portuguese section of Bridgeport, Connecticut.) These bakeries dispense egg-rich cookies and custard-filled pastries, but bread is really the main draw. Chewy pointy-ended Portuguese sandwich rolls, crusty open-grained peasant breads shaped into loaves both long and round, and dense, coarse-textured cornbread are popular, but it is probably the sweet breads that have become the most prized Portuguese bakery specialty. This recipe for a round sweet, egg-and-butter-rich, golden-crusted loaf is typical of the kinds of breads on Martha's Vineyard, where many in the large Portuguese community hail originally from the Azores. It's perfect for breakfast or a snack with strong hot coffee. On the Vineyard, beach plum jelly would be required. Portuguese bread also makes great French toast.

 1 (¼ ounce) package active dry yeast
 ¼ cup hot tap water (105–115 degrees)
 ½ cup whole or lowfat milk
 4 tablespoons unsalted butter, cut in pieces
 2 eggs
 ½ cup sugar
 ¾ teaspoon salt
 ¼ teaspoon ground mace
 2½ to 3 cups unbleached or bleached all-purpose flour
 1 egg yolk beaten with 1 tablespoon water for egg wash

1. Sprinkle the yeast over the hot water in a small bowl and set aside until the yeast is dissolved and bubbly, about 10 minutes.

2. Heat the milk and butter in a small saucepan over medium heat until the butter is melted.

3. Whisk the eggs with the sugar, salt, and mace in the large bowl of an electric mixer with a dough hook or in a large mixing bowl. Stir in the yeast mixture and milk mixture. Begin adding the flour, ½ cup at a time, until the dough reaches a moderately soft but kneadable consistency. Knead with the dough hook for about 5 minutes or by hand for about 10 minutes, until smooth and elastic. Transfer to a buttered bowl, turn to coat the top with butter, and cover with a towel or plastic wrap. Set aside in a warm, draft-free place until doubled in bulk, about 1½ hours.

4. Butter a 9-inch pie plate. Punch the dough down and shape it into a tight ball. Place in the center of the pie plate, cover loosely with plastic wrap, and set aside again to rise until doubled in bulk, about 1 hour.

5. Preheat the oven to 350 degrees.

6. Uncover the dough and paint the surface with the egg wash. Bake for 35 to 45 minutes, until the crust is nicely browned and a skewer inserted in the center comes out clean. Cool on a wire rack. (The bread can be baked a day before serving or wrapped well and frozen.)

7. Cut into slices to serve.

SAVORY BREADS

One might trace the history of New England by following a trail of breadcrumbs. Beginning with Crusty Cornbread (page 451), whose ancestor was the first colonists' life-sustaining cornmeal cake, and moist, raisin-studded Steamed Boston Brown Bread (page 457), a direct descendant of the rough-hewn ryan-injun (Rye and Indian) bread of the early settlers. Moving on, there are yeast-risen Multigrain Vermont Loaves (page 466), a delicious throw-back to the nutty whole-grain goodness of nineteenth-century New England breads, and Cape Ann Anadama Bread (page 462), a corn-and-molasses loaf named for the lazy wife of a Gloucester fisherman.

Homemade breads sustain Yankee households still, and the tradition of bread baking remains vibrant and strong. Savory quick breads such as Best-Ever Buttermilk Biscuits (page 443) and Perfect Yankee Inn Popovers (page 450) are perennially popular. Dilly Batter Bread (page 460) is a yeast-risen loaf with a shortcut built into the recipe, and slow-rise breads such as Luella Smith's Maple-Oatmeal Buns (page 445) and Classic Parker House Rolls (page 447) proudly grace the New England feast table.

Best-Ever Buttermilk Biscuits

MAKES ABOUT 16 GOOD-SIZED BISCUITS, 8 SERVINGS

Melanie Barnard and I developed this recipe for our book, *Sunday Suppers*. We worked hard perfecting it, so I include it here, with only a couple of minor changes. A basket of hot biscuits on the table seems to melt hearts and make even the most stoic Yankees beam. Once we actually witnessed these biscuits receive a standing ovation!

> 2 cups all-purpose flour
> 1 teaspoon salt
> 2 teaspoons baking powder
> ½ teaspoon baking soda
> ½ teaspoon sugar
> 4 tablespoons chilled unsalted butter, cut into 8 pieces
> 4 tablespoons chilled vegetable shortening, cut into 8 pieces
> ¾ cup cold buttermilk

1. Preheat the oven to 450 degrees.
2. Combine the flour, salt, baking powder, baking soda, and sugar in a food processor. (To make by hand, see Note.) Process for about 10 seconds to sift and blend. Distribute the butter and shortening over the flour and pulse 8 to 10 times, until most of the shortening is about the size of small peas. With the motor running, slowly pour the buttermilk through the feed tube. Stop the machine when the dough begins to clump together.
3. Turn out onto a lightly floured surface, gather the dough into a ball, and roll or pat to an even ½-inch thickness. Using a floured 2-inch cutter, cut biscuits out of the dough. For crusty sides, place about 2 inches apart on ungreased baking sheets. For soft-sided biscuits, place no more than ½ inch apart. Reroll and cut the scraps once, handling the dough gently so the biscuits don't get tough. (The biscuits can be shaped up to 3 hours before baking. Refrigerate, loosely covered with a sheet of plastic wrap.)
4. Bake for 5 minutes. Reduce the temperature to 400 degrees and continue to bake for 8 to 10 minutes more or until the biscuits are well risen and a rich, golden brown.
5. Serve hot or warm.

Note: To make by hand, whisk together the flour, salt, baking powder, baking soda, and sugar in a large mixing bowl. Add the butter and shortening and use your fingers to rub the mixture until it resembles coarse meal. Add the buttermilk all at once and stir with a fork to make a soft dough. Turn out onto a lightly floured surface and knead for about 30 seconds. Proceed to roll, cut, and bake as directed above.

Shaker Winter Squash Biscuits

MAKES 16 TO 18 BISCUITS

Those clever, resourceful Shakers were continuously thinking up new ways of using the bounty of the land, and of packing more nutrients into their meals. Above all (and this is why I have such fondness for and fascination with them), they really cared about how their food tasted. These biscuits are a perfect example. *The Best of Shaker Cooking* by Amy Miller and Persis Fuller lists at least three different recipes for squash "cakes." The rich orange squash bestows vitamins, to be sure, but also a beautiful golden color, elusive earthy-sweet autumn flavor, and a delicately moist texture.

> 2 cups all-purpose flour
> 2 tablespoons light brown sugar
> 1 tablespoon baking powder
> 1 teaspoon salt
> ¾ teaspoon fresh-ground black pepper
> ¼ teaspoon grated nutmeg
> 4 tablespoons chilled unsalted butter, cut in 8 pieces
> 4 tablespoons chilled vegetable shortening, cut in 8 pieces
> 1 cup winter squash or pumpkin puree (see Note)
> 5 tablespoons whole, lowfat, or skim milk

1. Preheat the oven to 425 degrees.
2. Whisk together the flour, brown sugar, baking powder, salt, pepper, and nutmeg in a large mixing bowl. Add the butter and shortening and use your fingers to rub the mixture until it resembles coarse meal, making sure to break up any lumps of brown sugar.
3. Whisk the squash with the milk in a small bowl. Add to the flour mixture and stir with a fork to make a soft dough.

Kinds of Yeast

Regular and quick-rising yeasts are made from related but slightly differing strains of yeast. The longer, slower rise characteristic of regular yeast gives bread and rolls a deeper, more yeasty flavor than quick-rising yeast does, although some people insist that the difference is barely detectable.

"Instant" yeast is a relatively new product that was developed primarily for making bread in bread machines. In all but a couple of recipes in this book, active dry (regular) yeast is called for, with the option of quick-rising yeast given in a recipe Note.

---

4. Turn out onto a well-floured surface and knead about 6 times. Roll or pat the dough until ¾ inch thick, and cut out biscuits with a floured 2-inch cutter. Reroll and cut the scraps once, handling gently so the dough doesn't become tough. Place the biscuits 2 inches apart on ungreased baking sheets. (The biscuits can be shaped up to 3 hours before baking, loosely covered, and refrigerated.)

5. Bake for 14 to 17 minutes, until golden brown and well risen.

6. Serve hot or warm.

Note: Bake or steam Hubbard or butternut squash and mash with a fork. You can also used canned pumpkin.

Luella Smith's Maple-Oatmeal Buns

MAKES 1½ TO 2 DOZEN ROLLS

Luella Smith and her husband, Arnold, had a maple sugaring farm in Limerick, Maine, in the hills west of Portland. When I visited, I gave the Smiths a loaf of my Very Best Banana Bread (page 432) and one of Cape Cranberry-Walnut Tea Bread (page 431), and, in exchange, Luella rummaged in her freezer and emerged with a cache of her famous oatmeal buns. ("They make her bring them to every single potluck supper around here," boasted Arnie.) Her recipe, originally from a *Better Homes and Gardens* cookbook, calls for molasses, but in tribute to the Smiths' much-prized product, I have also used some smoky-sweet maple syrup in the recipe. The flavor, while just a bit more delicate, is unmistakably present.

¾ cup old-fashioned or quick-cooking rolled oats (not instant oatmeal)
¼ cup pure maple syrup
¼ cup molasses
2 tablespoons vegetable shortening or margarine
2 teaspoons salt
1 (¼ ounce) package regular yeast (see Note)
¼ cup hot tap water (105–115 degrees)
2½ to 3 cups all-purpose flour, preferably unbleached
2 tablespoons butter, melted

1. Bring 1 cup of water to a boil in a medium saucepan. Add the oats, maple syrup, molasses, shortening, and salt and cook, stirring, until the shortening is melted. Remove from the heat and let stand for about 15 minutes, until the oats are somewhat softened and the mixture is lukewarm.
2. Meanwhile, sprinkle the yeast over the hot water in a small bowl. Set aside until the yeast is dissolved and bubbly, about 10 minutes.
3. Combine the oat mixture and yeast mixture in a large mixing bowl, or in the bowl of an electric mixer with a dough hook. Add 2 cups of the flour and beat well with a wooden spoon to combine. Knead by hand on a well-floured board or with the

Fannie Farmer

Fannie Merritt Farmer took to the kitchen after a stroke in her youth left her partially paralyzed. In 1896, she published *The Boston Cooking-School Cook Book*, a collection of recipes and advice that became America's most important cookbook until *The Joy of Cooking* appeared thirty-five years later. The first edition contained more than forty bread recipes, including such New England standards as Graham Bread, Boston Brown Bread, Parker House Rolls, and Raised Squash Muffins. Miss Farmer, who emphasized the value of precision in recording recipes and accuracy in measuring ingredients, earned a lasting reputation as the arbiter of Yankee dining habits.

dough hook until the dough is smooth and elastic, about 10 minutes by hand, or 5 minutes with the mixer, adding enough of the remaining flour to achieve a very soft, slightly sticky dough. Leave the dough in the mixer bowl or transfer to a greased bowl, cover, and let rise until doubled in bulk, about 1½ hours.

4. Lightly oil 2 baking sheets. Punch the dough down and divide into 2 parts. On a floured board, pat or roll out one piece of the dough until about ½ inch thick. Using a 2½- to 3-inch floured cutter, cut out rounds of dough and place them 1 inch apart on the prepared baking sheets. Repeat with the second piece of dough, re-rolling the scraps. Cover loosely with plastic wrap and set aside until the rounds are almost doubled in bulk, 45 to 60 minutes.

5. Preheat the oven to 350 degrees.

6. Bake the buns until they are golden brown, 25 to 30 minutes. Remove from the oven, brush with melted butter, and transfer to a wire rack to cool. (The buns can be stored at room temperature for a few hours or sealed in plastic bags and frozen.)

7. To serve, reheat on a baking sheet in a 350-degree oven for about 5 minutes.

Note: Quick-rising yeast can be substituted. The rising times will be about half as long.

Classic Parker House Rolls

MAKES ABOUT 2½ DOZEN ROLLS

Whether the romantic story of their origin is apocryphal or fact (see page 448), these rolls, which are sometimes called "pocketbooks" for their distinctive, folded-over shape, are rich and buttery yet light, with just a hint of sweetness. A basket of Parker House rolls is essential at every semiformal traditional New England dinner—Thanksgiving being our most famous such occasion.

> 1 (¼ ounce) package regular-rise yeast (see Note)
> ¼ cup hot tap water (105–115 degrees)
> 1¼ cups milk
> ¼ cup sugar
> 11 tablespoons (1 stick plus 3 tablespoons) unsalted butter, melted
> 3 to 4 cups all-purpose flour, preferably unbleached
> 1 egg yolk
> 2 teaspoons salt

1. Sprinkle the yeast over the hot water in a small bowl. Set aside until the yeast is dissolved and bubbly, about 10 minutes.

2. Combine the milk, sugar, melted butter, 2 cups of the flour, the egg yolk, and salt in a large mixing bowl, or the large bowl of an electric mixer with a dough hook. Add the yeast mixture and stir with a wooden spoon to mix well. Add 1 cup more flour and knead by hand on a well-floured board or with the dough hook until the dough is smooth and elastic, about 10 minutes by hand or 5 minutes with the mixer. Continue to add flour as necessary to achieve a soft, workable dough. Leave the dough in the mixer bowl or transfer to a greased bowl, cover, and let rise until doubled in bulk, about 1½ hours.

3. Lightly oil 2 baking sheets. Punch the dough down and divide into 2 parts. On a floured board, pat or roll out one piece of the dough until about ⅜ inch thick. Using a 2½- to 3-inch floured biscuit cutter, cut out rounds of dough. Brush the rounds lightly with melted butter, and using a chopstick or knife handle, press a deep crease across the diameter of each round. Fold the rounds in half, pressing gently to seal slightly. Place the rounds on a baking sheet no more than ½ inch apart. Repeat with the second piece of dough, rerolling the scraps. Brush the rounds with melted butter, cover loosely with plastic wrap, and set aside until almost doubled in bulk, 45 to 60 minutes.

4. Preheat the oven to 350 degrees.

5. Bake the rolls until they are a rich golden brown, 20 to 25 minutes. Remove from the oven, brush with melted butter again, and transfer to a rack to cool. (The rolls can be stored at room temperature for a few hours or sealed in plastic bags and frozen.)

6. To serve, reheat the rolls on a baking sheet in a 350-degree oven for about 5 minutes.

Note: Quick-rising yeast can be substituted. The rising times will be about half as long.

Parker House Rolls

According to legend, these buttery rolls were invented by accident. Soon after the Parker House Hotel in Boston opened in 1855, a pastry chef, angry that his lady love, a chambermaid, had been falsely accused of stealing a guest's diamonds, picked up pieces of bread dough with his fists and slammed them into the oven. Meantime, the diamonds were found. But when these rolls—light and puffy and dented in the middle—were served, they were declared to be so delicious that the recipe was standardized and the rolls have been a fixture on the menu at the Parker House and in other New England hotel dining rooms ever since.

Caprilands Herbed Dinner Muffins

MAKES 12 MUFFINS

Caprilands Herb Farm in Coventry, in the middle of Connecticut, is a rustic eighteenth-century farmhouse surrounded by thirty herb gardens in which over three hundred varieties of herbs flourish. After lunch or tea at this fascinating farm, and a long walk around the beds, an herb-inspired madness takes hold and one wants nothing more than to chuck everything and settle down here, surrounded by fragrant, beneficent herbs, cooking up an endless stream of dishes using the blessed profusion. These delicious herb-scented, green-flecked lunch or dinner muffins are one result of my fantasy.

> 2 cups all-purpose flour
> 3 teaspoons baking powder
> 1 teaspoon salt
> 4 tablespoons sugar
> 1 egg
> 1 cup whole or lowfat milk
> 4 tablespoons melted butter or vegetable oil
> 6 tablespoons chopped fresh herbs, including at least 2 of the
>   following: scallions, chives, basil, dill, sage, flat-leaf parsley,
>   or rosemary

1. Preheat the oven to 400 degrees. Grease a 12-mold muffin tin.

2. Whisk together the flour, baking powder, salt, and sugar in a large bowl.

3. Whisk the egg with the milk in a small bowl. Whisk in the melted butter or oil and chopped herbs until blended. Make a well in the center of the flour mixture, pour in the egg mixture, and stir with a whisk or wooden spoon just until moistened and no specks of flour remain. The batter will be quite thick and somewhat lumpy.

4. Spoon into the muffin molds, filling them about three-quarters full. Bake until the tops of the muffins are rounded and speckled with brown and a tester comes out clean, 18 to 22 minutes.

5. Cool in the pan for a few minutes. Turn out of the pan and serve the muffins hot, warm, or at room temperature. (Muffins are best eaten the same day they are made.)

Perfect Yankee Inn Popovers

MAKES 10 TO 12 POPOVERS

The first time I ever had popovers was at the original Woodstock Inn in Woodstock, Vermont. The old inn was a simple, graceful, white-shingled Victorian-era structure with a charmingly slanted front porch. Sadly, that original building burned down and was replaced by a more formal, somewhat pretentious edifice. Popovers are still served in some of the best traditional New England inn restaurants, arriving at the table hot from the oven, cozily wrapped in a starched white napkin. Leavened only by eggs and air, these crisp, airy, old-fashioned creations seem sort of magical and almost quaint. I like to serve popovers as an accompaniment to a soup or salad meal or for breakfast spread with jam or maple butter.

> 1 cup all-purpose flour
> ½ teaspoon salt
> 2 eggs
> 1¼ cups whole, lowfat, or skim milk
> 1 tablespoon unsalted butter, melted

1. Preheat the oven to 450 degrees. Generously grease a 12-mold muffin tin.

2. Whisk together the flour and salt in a large bowl to sift and blend.

3. Whisk the eggs with the milk and melted butter in another bowl until blended. Pour the liquid ingredients over the flour mixture and whisk just until the batter is smooth. It should be the consistency of thick cream. (The batter can be made a couple of hours ahead and held at cool room temperature or refrigerated. Whisk again before using.)

4. Pour the batter into the muffin cups, filling them about three-quarters full. If any cups remain unfilled, spoon about 2 tablespoons of water into the bottoms of the empty cups.

5. Bake for 15 minutes. Reduce the oven temperature to 350 degrees and continue to bake for 15 to 20 minutes, or until the popovers are risen, browned, and crisp. Do not open the oven until near the end of the baking time.

6. Unmold onto a wire rack and use the point of a small knife to pierce a small hole in the side of each popover to allow steam to escape.

7. Serve immediately.

Crusty Cornbread, Muffins, or Sticks

MAKES 12 TO 16 CORNBREAD SQUARES, 12 MUFFINS, OR 15 CORN STICKS

A basket of hot, crumbly, gorgeously golden cornbread or muffins turns an otherwise routine supper into a treat. All New England cornbreads are descended from the original "spider corn cake," a cornmeal bread that was baked in a black cast-iron "spider," which was a skillet with three legs so it could be placed over hot hearth coals. This recipe is a quickly mixed, standard formula, similar to the delicious corn bread classic printed in *A Taste of New England*, a collection from the Worcester, Massachusetts Junior League. The batter is the same whether making cornbread, corn muffins, or corn sticks.

1¼ cups all-purpose flour
¾ cup yellow cornmeal
2 tablespoons sugar
1 tablespoon baking powder
¾ teaspoon salt
¼ teaspoon fresh-ground black pepper, optional
1 egg
1 cup whole, lowfat, or skim milk
¼ cup melted butter or vegetable oil

1. Preheat the oven to 400 degrees. For cornbread, grease an 8- or 9-inch square baking pan. For muffins, grease a 12-mold muffin tin. For sticks, grease 1 or 2 corn-stick pans (most have 7 or 8 molds); place the corn-stick pans in the oven to preheat.
2. Whisk together the flour, cornmeal, sugar, baking powder, salt, and pepper, if you are using, in a large bowl until well combined.
3. Whisk the egg with the milk and melted butter or oil in a small bowl. Pour the liquid ingredients into the flour mixture and stir gently but thoroughly just until all of the flour is moistened. Do not overmix.

Northern Jo(h)nnycakes

In Maine and parts of Vermont and New Hampshire, jo(h)nnycakes are not pancakes at all. In these northern realms, regular baking powder- or soda-leavened cornbread, the kind that's baked in the oven in a pan, is often called johnnycake or johnny-bread. The only common link between this johnnycake (always spelled with the *h*), and the Rhode Island jonnycake is that they are both made with cornmeal.

4. For cornbread, scrape the batter into the prepared pan and smooth the top. Bake for 20 to 25 minutes until the bread is pale golden brown on top and a tester comes out clean. For muffins, spoon the batter into the prepared muffin tin and bake for 15 to 18 minutes. For corn sticks, fill the molds of the preheated pan almost full of batter and bake about 12 minutes (in 2 batches if using 1 corn stick pan).

5. Cut the cornbread into squares and serve hot.

Hungarian Egg Dumplings

MAKES 4 SERVINGS

There are various names for these small, noodlelike, pastalike Hungarian dumplings. Besides "egg dumplings," they are also sometimes known as "soup dumplings," "little dumplings," or just "dumplings"—or, in the Pearl of Budapest Restaurant in Fairfield, Connecticut, where I have enjoyed many a sumptuous Hungarian meal, they call them by their German name, spaetzle. Whatever the nomenclature, I know that I can eat a very large portion of these Hungarian beauties, adorned with nothing more than butter and salt and pepper, and call it dinner. There are two tricks to making these dumplings: use a light hand when mixing the dough, and don't overcook them. I suggest biting into the first couple that you poach to make sure there is no more raw flour taste.

> 2 eggs
> 1½ cups all-purpose flour
> ¾ teaspoon salt
> ¼ teaspoon baking powder

1. Whisk the eggs with ½ cup water in a large bowl. Add the flour, salt, and baking powder and stir gently but thoroughly to make a smooth, sticky dough.

2. Bring a large pot of salted water or broth to a boil (see Note). Spoon out ½-teaspoonfuls of the dough and drop the dumplings, one at a

Our Cooking Heritage

"We need to value the skills of our mothers and grandmothers. We need every once in awhile to get our hands deep into bread dough, to make a cake from scratch, to preserve the fruits of the summer garden."

—From *Country Kitchen Cookbook*, a community cookbook from Narragansett, Rhode Island

time, into the simmering liquid. (Cook only about one-third of the dough at one time.) Cook at a gentle boil until the dumplings rise to the top of the liquid and are cooked through, about 5 minutes. Remove with a large slotted spoon to a buttered dish and repeat with the remaining dough. (The dumplings can be cooked up to 2 hours ahead and, held, covered, at cool room temperature. Reheat in a microwave before serving.)

3. Serve the dumplings drizzled with melted butter or topped with any sauce.

Note: You can also drop the dumpling dough directly into any soup or stew that has a large quantity of liquid. Just leave them in the soup to serve.

Dynamite Potato Dumplings

MAKES ABOUT 18 DUMPLINGS, 4 SERVINGS

New Englanders with an Eastern European heritage, including Hungarians, Poles, and Czechs, seem to be born with the ability to make great dumplings. There are a few family-run restaurants scattered around New England where you can get a taste of some of the rich, hearty dishes from this region, but by far the best Eastern European food I've ever eaten has been made by such talented home cooks of my acquaintance as Anna Jahelka White, Lottie Dojny Horbal, and Maria Soljek. These dumplings—full of deeply earthy potato flavor, substantial yet delicate—are the quintessential accompaniment to long-simmered goulashes and stews.

> 3 to 4 medium all-purpose or russet potatoes (1½ pounds)
> 1 large egg
> 1 teaspoon salt
> 6 tablespoons all-purpose flour, or more if necessary
> 2 teaspoons chopped fresh parsley

1. Scrub the potatoes, cut them into 2-inch pieces, and cook in a pot of boiling salted water until tender, 15 to 20 minutes. Drain well. While they are still warm, peel the potatoes and put them through a potato ricer or mash in a large bowl using a large fork or potato masher. Stir in the egg and salt and beat in the flour by the tablespoon to make a smooth, soft, only slightly sticky dough.

2. Bring a large pot of water to a rolling boil. Salt the water. Flour your hands and roll the dough into 2-inch balls. Drop the dumplings into the water, reduce the heat to medium, and cook at a gentle boil (in 2 batches if necessary) for about 8 minutes, until they rise to the surface. To test for doneness, taste one. If there is no raw flour taste, the dumplings are sufficiently cooked. Remove with a slotted spoon to a buttered dish. (If not served immediately, the dumplings can be made several hours ahead, and held, covered at cool room temperature. Reheat in a microwave before serving.)

3. Sprinkle the dumplings with chopped parsley before serving.

Rosemary Focaccia

MAKES 1 LARGE RECTANGLE OR 2 SMALLER ROUNDS, 4 TO 6 SERVINGS

This really wonderful focaccia is adapted from a recipe in *Cook's Illustrated*, a magazine dedicated to investigating why and how a recipe works, without relying on preconceived conventional wisdom, and then developing a "master" version of the same. This focaccia dough is streamlined so that it is both mixed and kneaded in a food processor. The resulting flatbread is sublime in summer, especially if you split it and spread it with tangy goat cheese and top the cheese with layers of fresh ripe tomatoes and basil leaves. It is also a wonderful accompaniment to just about any soup, either a robust one, such as Mrs. Cordisco's Escarole and White Bean Soup (page 53) or a lighter potage like Athena Diner Avgolemono (page 40).

For the dough:

2½ to 3 cups all-purpose flour, preferably unbleached
1 (¼ ounce) package active dry yeast (see Note)
1 teaspoon salt
2 tablespoons extra-virgin olive oil
1 cup hot tap water (105–115 degrees)
2 teaspoons yellow cornmeal

For the topping:

2 tablespoons extra-virgin olive oil
2 tablespoons coarsely chopped fresh rosemary leaves
1 teaspoon coarse (kosher) salt

Artisan Bread

Like rapidly rising yeast rolls, artisan bakeries have been springing up all over New England. Steve Lanzalotta, who started Pain de Famille bakery in midcoast Maine, is dedicated, almost fanatically, to baking the best bread he possibly can. This dedication to quality is a trait common among the people attracted to the late-twentieth-century rediscovery of this ancient craft.

Also rather typical are Steve's reasons for becoming a baker—namely, his inability to buy a good loaf of bread near where he and his family were living. "I began baking bread just for my family. I had no intention of selling it, but people would travel up to an hour to inquire about my bread. I needed a new career direction, and this just sort of presented itself."

Born and raised in suburban Connecticut, Steve originally moved to a small town in Maine as a deliberate lifestyle choice—another commonality among many food artisans. When he started down the bread-baking path, Steve became fascinated not only with slowly fermented doughs and sourdough starters and brick hearths but also with the historical role of the baker, who he sees as nothing less than central to the evolution of civilization.

For his first bakery in Brooksville, Maine, Lanzalotta constructed a massive brick wood-fired oven and a trough mechanism that enables him to hand-knead all his dough. "It's important to touch the dough," he says, "although this means that the process takes more time."

Pain de Famille is famous in the region for its crusty, rustic "daily round," its roasted grains loaf, its raisin fennel rye, and its rosemary focaccia, among dozens of other styles they produce.

Artisan breads are, admittedly, a good deal more expensive than commerical loaves, but "it's what I call a cheap luxury," asserts Jim Amaral, owner of the successful Borealis Breads in Waldoboro, Maine. "More and more people recognize and appreciate a handmade product." This is the sort of bread that can become the centerpiece of a meal rather than serving simply something to wrap around a sandwich filling.

He seems to be right. The "proof" is that this is a movement that seems to keep expanding.

1. Combine the 2½ cups of the flour, the yeast, and salt in a food processor. Process for about 10 seconds to blend. With the motor running, add the oil and hot water through the feed tube and process until the dough forms a ball on top of the blade. Continue to process for 45 seconds to 1 minute, adding more flour by the tablespoon through the feed tube, until the dough is smooth and elastic and comes away from the sides of the work bowl.

2. Transfer the dough to a lightly greased bowl and turn to coat the top. Cover loosely and let rise until doubled in bulk, about 1½ hours.

3. Grease a large baking sheet and sprinkle with the cornmeal. Punch the dough down and roll or pat on a lightly floured surface into a rectangle about 10 by 15 inches. Or cut the dough in half and flatten each piece into an 8-inch round. Transfer to the baking sheet. Cover loosely with plastic wrap and set aside until the dough is puffy and somewhat risen, 45 minutes to 1 hour.

4. Preheat the oven to 425 degrees. Adjust an oven rack to the middle position.

5. To make the topping, wet your fingers and make dimples in the risen dough at 1- to 2-inch intervals. Drizzle with the olive oil and sprinkle with the rosemary and salt.

6. Bake until the bottom is golden and the top is just beginning to color, 16 to 22 minutes. (Do not overbake or the bread will tend to be tough.) Transfer to a wire rack to cool for a few minutes. (The focaccia can be stored, covered, at room temperature for several hours and reheated in a 350-degree oven for about 5 minutes before serving.)

7. Serve warm or at room temperature, cut into squares or wedges.

Soft Bread

"I came to America in 1947. I was fifteen years old. My mother and I took an American boat from Palermo, the *S.S. Pierce*, which was carrying back GI soldiers from Europe. On the boat, they served us bread with butter. It was soft bread. I had never had this kind of bread before in my life. I knew the Sicilian loaf bread that was round and dense and you sliced with a knife. I was so disappointed. I said to my mother, 'Ma, what are we doing here? We're going to the wrong country. They don't even know how to make bread!'"

—Antonio Fama as quoted in *We Called It Macaroni* by Nancy Verde Barr (Knopf, 1991)

Note: Quick-rising yeast can be substituted, but the flavor will not be as yeasty. The rising times will be about half as long.

Steamed Boston Brown Bread

MAKES 1 LOAF

In early colonial days, when the Puritan philosophy dominated in Massachusetts, all cooking was forbidden on the Sabbath, which extended from sundown Saturday to sundown Sunday. So Pilgrim housewives baked a big pot of beans and made steamed brown bread on Saturday (or in the oven's burned-down coals all Friday night), which they ate warm for Saturday supper and then cold on Sunday. Evan Jones, in *American Food*, recalls eating this same meal during his childhood in Minnesota. His parents, having migrated from New England a thousand miles away, took this powerful New England tradition with them, thus linking one far-flung region of America with another. Jones describes the bread as "a highly appetizing loaf, as dark as chocolate and rather moist." The fine, moist, tender crumb imparted by the steaming process is distinctive, and greatly appealing. This also happens to be a very easy—and fun—bread to create.

⅓ cup whole wheat flour
⅓ cup yellow cornmeal
⅓ cup rye flour
¾ teaspoon baking soda
½ teaspoon salt
¾ cup buttermilk or sour milk (see Note)
¼ cup molasses
½ cup dark raisins, optional

1. Grease a clean 13- or 14-ounce coffee can.
2. Whisk together the whole-wheat flour, cornmeal, rye flour, baking soda, and salt in a large bowl until blended.
3. Combine the buttermilk and molasses in a small bowl, and stir in the raisins, if you like. Pour the buttermilk mixture into the flour mixture and whisk just until blended. Do not overbeat.
4. Scrape the batter into the prepared can. Cover with a double layer of aluminum foil, pinching it tightly to seal well. Place the coffee can in a large pot with a lid and pour boiling water to come about halfway up the sides of the can. Cover the pot and

steam over low heat until the bread rises and is firm to the touch, and a skewer inserted in the center comes out clean, about 1½ hours.

5. Using oven mitts, remove the can from the kettle and place on a wire rack until cool enough to handle. Tap the bread out of the can or remove the bottom with a can opener and push the bread out. Serve warm or at room temperature, cut into slices. (The bread can be refrigerated for 1 day, or it may be frozen. Reheat in a steamer or in a microwave before serving.)

Note: To sour milk, add 2 teaspoons distilled white vinegar to ¾ cup whole or lowfat milk and let stand at room temperature for about 15 minutes, until curdled.

Niles Golovin, Bread Baker

Keeping his sourdough starter alive and well was so important to Niles Golovin, owner of the Bantam Bread Company near Litchfield, Connecticut, that he was known to take the fermenting yeast mixture with him on family vacations during the early years of the bakery. Indeed, the business of owning your own small bread bakery does tend to tie you down more than a little bit. "I also have to live close by, because I may need to just stop in and feed the sourdough. You have to feed sourdough on a schedule," says Mr. Golovin. In addition to several varieties of sourdough loaves, the Bantam Bread Company turns out multigrain miche (a round loaf), caraway rye, sunny flax bread, and focaccia.

New England Irish Soda Bread

MAKES 1 LOAF

Eleanor O'Sheske (née Hamilton), is a New Hampshire Yankee by birth, a Connecticut Polish Catholic by marriage, and an honorary Irish-American by virtue of years of association with the many colleens in St. Mary's Parish in Norwalk, Connecticut. Not incidentally, Eleanor is a wonderful baker. Every St. Patrick's Day, she and I compare notes on soda bread—whether it's better with or without raisins, with caraway seeds or not. This year she brought me a sample of her version of this soda-raised bread, darkly and chewily crusted outside, moist and ever-so-slightly sweet within, studded with both caraway and raisins. This is my adaptation of her recipe, and it is, indeed, stellar. This soda bread is served at the St. Paddy's Day supper at St. Mary's church hall to accompany the corned beef and cabbage, and then for the rest of the week Eleanor recommends toasting it for breakfast or eating it with soup or salad for lunch or supper.

> 2 cups all-purpose flour
> ¼ cup sugar
> 1 teaspoon baking powder
> ½ teaspoon baking soda
> ¾ teaspoon salt
> 4 tablespoons cold butter
> ¼ cup raisins or dried currants
> 1½ teaspoons caraway seeds
> ¾ cup buttermilk, or more if necessary

1. Preheat the oven to 350 degrees. Grease a baking sheet.
2. Whisk together the flour, sugar, baking powder, baking soda, and salt in a large bowl. Cut the butter into about 10 chunks and use your fingers to rub it into the flour until the largest pieces are about the size of peas. Stir in the raisins or currants and caraway seeds. Make a well in the center, pour in the buttermilk, and stir until a stiff dough forms, adding more buttermilk if the dough is too dry.
3. Turn out onto a lightly floured board and knead until smooth, 2 to 3 minutes. Transfer to the baking sheet and shape into a slightly domed disc about 6 inches in diameter. Use a sharp knife or a razor blade to cut a large criss-cross about ¼ inch deep in the top of the disc to allow for even rising.
4. Bake for 45 to 60 minutes, or until the bread is a deep golden brown and sounds hollow when tapped on the bottom.
5. Cool on a rack before cutting into slices. Serve warm or at room temperature. (This bread is best served on the same day it is made, but it can be frozen for up to 2 weeks.)

Dilly Batter Bread

MAKES 1 LOAF

This quickly mixed batter bread, aromatic with chopped fresh dill and scallions, is adapted from a recipe in a Cohasset, Massachusetts, community cookbook, *Cohasset Entertains*. The cottage cheese and egg in the formula contribute richness, a tender, soft texture, and tangy flavor, and they give the bread a better keeping quality. The open-grained, herb-flecked round loaf also happens to be a pretty fair facsimile of a notable bread made by the Connecticut Hay Day markets in the 1980s. It's a great supper bread, wonderful as an accompaniment to soups and salads, and it also makes super sandwiches, most especially with roast beef.

> 1 (¼ ounce) package active dry yeast (see Note)
> ¼ cup hot tap water (105–115 degrees)
> 1 cup large or small curd cottage cheese
> 1 egg
> 4 tablespoons chopped fresh dill
> 4 tablespoons chopped scallions or fresh chives
> 2 tablespoons sugar
> 2 tablespoons vegetable oil
> 1½ teaspoons salt
> ¼ teaspoon baking soda
> 2 to 2¾ cups all-purpose flour, preferably unbleached

1. Sprinkle the yeast over the hot water in a small bowl. Set aside until the yeast is dissolved and bubbly, about 10 minutes. Grease an 8-inch round cake pan (a disposable foil one is fine).

Batter Bread

Batter bread is a yeast bread that is mixed without kneading. It begins with a dough that is about the consistency of a thick batter. The loose dough is beaten vigorously for a few minutes to develop and stretch the gluten, and then more flour is added to make a soft, workable dough. Generally, batter bread recipes use only 2 to 2½ cups of flour per cup of liquid. The resulting loaves are coarser both in shape and texture than bread made from fully kneaded dough, but their flavor is just as delicious.

---

2. Whisk together the cottage cheese, egg, dill, scallions, sugar, oil, salt, and baking soda in the bowl of an electric mixer with a paddle beater or in a large mixing bowl. Stir in the yeast mixture and 2 cups of the flour. Beat well with the paddle or with a hand-held mixer on medium speed for about 4 minutes, until the dough begins to pull away from the sides of the bowl. (You can also do this by hand, but you need a strong arm.) Stir in the remaining flour, ¼-cup at a time, until the dough is soft and workable.

3. Using dampened hands, gather and shape the dough into a rough ball in the bowl. Transfer the dough to the prepared pan, flattening it so it covers the bottom of the pan. Cover loosely with plastic wrap and set aside in a warm place until it rises to fill the pan, about 1½ hours.

4. Preheat the oven to 350 degrees.

5. Bake for 35 to 45 minutes, or until the crust is evenly browned and the loaf sounds hollow when tapped on the bottom.

6. Remove from the pan and cool on a wire rack. (The bread may be stored, well wrapped, at cool room temperature or in the refrigerator for 2 days, or it may be frozen.)

Note: Quick-rising yeast is not a good substitute in this bread.

Matzoh Workshop

At Passover time, Beth Israel Synagogue in Norwalk, Connecticut, sponsors a hands-on matzoh-making workshop. Workshop leaders thresh wheat stalks, grind the grain to make the flour, mix the matzoh dough, roll it out, and bake it. Participants get one of the crispy, homemade, kosher-for-Passover crackers to take home for their seder.

Cape Ann Anadama Bread

MAKES 1 LARGE LOAF

The legend is that a woman named Anna, who lived in Rockport, on Cape Ann, Massachusetts, was such a poor cook that all she could seem to produce was a meager paste of cornmeal and molasses. One day her long-suffering and very hungry fisherman husband began throwing yeast and flour into her bowl of gruel, all the while muttering under his breath, "Anna, damn her!" This is the classic Anadama loaf—moist, dark-crusted, full of flavor, with the pleasing texture of just a bit of cornmeal. The bread is as delicious as its name is fascinating.

> ½ cup plus 2 teaspoons yellow cornmeal
> 2 teaspoons salt
> 4 tablespoons unsalted butter, cut in pieces
> 1 cup boiling water
> ¼ cup molasses
> 1 (¼ ounce) package active dry yeast (see Note)
> ¼ cup hot tap water (105–115 degrees)
> 2½ to 3 cups all-purpose flour, preferably unbleached

1. Combine the cornmeal, salt, and butter in a large mixing bowl, or in the bowl of an electric mixer. Add the boiling water and the molasses and stir until the butter is melted. Set aside for 15 minutes to soften the cornmeal.

2. Sprinkle the yeast over the hot water in a small bowl. Set aside until the yeast is dissolved and bubbly, about 10 minutes.

3. Stir the yeast mixture into the cornmeal mixture. Add 2 cups of the flour and stir with a wooden spoon to mix well. Add ½ cup more flour and knead by hand on a well-floured board or with the dough hook until the dough is smooth and elastic, about 10 minutes by hand, or 5 minutes with the mixer. Continue to add flour as necessary to achieve a fairly firm, workable dough. Leave the dough in the mixer bowl or transfer to a greased bowl, cover, and let rise until doubled in bulk, about 1½ hours.

4. Grease a 9-by-5-by-3-inch loaf pan and sprinkle the bottom and sides with 1 teaspoon of the remaining cornmeal. Punch the dough down, shape into a loaf, and

Pepperidge Farm

In 1937, a Fairfield, Connecticut, mother with an asthmatic child was convinced that the commercially available squishy white bread that they had been eating did nothing to improve her son's health. So she baked him a loaf made from stone-ground whole wheat flour, whole milk, honey, butter, and molasses. The boy improved, and his doctor, who was impressed, asked the woman to bake more bread for his other patients.

Thus did Margaret "Maggie" Rudkin found one of the most successful bread companies in America. She started baking in her garage, then moved to the stable of her family's farm, named Pepperidge Farm after the black gum trees (also called pepperidge trees) on the property. By the end of her first year of operation, she was selling upwards of four thousand loaves a week.

When she started her company deep in the Depression, Mrs. Rudkin's business philosophy was something of a gamble. Her hope was that if she used the best, most wholesome ingredients, customers would be willing to pay more for her product. That meant that in 1938 Maggie (as she was always known in Connecticut) had to sell her bread for about three times the going rate of a dime a loaf. Enough people were persuaded that it was indeed worth paying more for a better-tasting, nutritionally superior bread, and Pepperidge Farm thrived.

In 1961, a few years before Maggie Rudkin's death, Pepperidge Farm was sold to the Campbell Soup Company. They continue to operate the plant in Norwalk, Connecticut, perfuming the early morning breeze for miles around with gloriousy yeasty bread-baking aromas.

---

place in the prepared pan. Cover lightly and set aside until almost doubled in bulk, 45 minutes to 1 hour.

5. Preheat the oven to 400 degrees.

6. Sprinkle the top of the loaf with the remaining teaspoon of cornmeal. Bake in the center of the preheated oven for 10 minutes. Reduce the oven temperature to 350 degrees and continue to bake for 35 to 40 minutes or until the top is rich golden brown and the loaf sounds hollow when tapped on the bottom.

7. Remove from the pan and cool completely on a wire rack before slicing. (The bread can be wrapped well and frozen. Thaw in the wrapping before using.)

Note: Quick-rise yeast can be substituted. Rising times will be about half as long.

King Arthur Shredded Wheat Bread

MAKES 1 LOAF

The first time I saw a recipe for shredded wheat bread in a New England community cookbook, I assumed it was just one cook's rather eccentric contribution, but when it kept turning up in other sources, I began to gather that maybe this was no anomaly. And when shredded wheat bread appeared in *The Baking Sheet*, a newsletter from the Norwich, Vermont-based King Arthur Flour Company, I knew it had to be legitimate. Here's an adaptation of that recipe, which was published along with this editor's note: "Shredded wheat cereal gives this rich, brown, molasses-scented bread just a hint of whole wheat flavor and texture. We think it originated in the 1950s, because many of us Baby Boomers remember our moms making it, but our moms don't recall having it when they were young." The technique used here is sort of a fusion of both a batter bread and a regular kneading process. The loaf is unexpectedly delicious.

> 3 full-sized shredded wheat biscuits (2½ ounces total)
> 1 cup milk
> ¼ cup molasses
> 2 tablespoons butter
> 1½ teaspoons salt
> 1 (¼ ounce) package active dry yeast (see Note)
> ¼ cup hot tap water (105–115 degrees)
> About 2¼ to 2½ cups unbleached all-purpose flour
> 2 teaspoons softened unsalted butter, optional

1. Coarsely crumble the shredded wheat biscuits into a medium saucepan. Add the milk, molasses, butter, and salt. Bring to a simmer, remove from the heat, and set aside for about 10 minutes, stirring once or twice, until the biscuits are softened, the butter is melted, and the mixture cools to lukewarm.

2. Meanwhile, sprinkle the yeast over the hot water in a large mixing bowl, or the bowl of an electric mixer. Set aside until the yeast is dissolved and bubbly, about 10 minutes.

3. Add the shredded wheat mixture to the yeast mixture and mix well. Using a wooden spoon or the paddle beater of the mixer, add 2¼ cups of the flour and mix well. Set aside in a warm place, loosely covered with plastic wrap, until almost doubled in bulk, about 1½ hours.

4. Turn the dough out onto a floured board, and knead by hand for about 5 minutes, or leave in the mixer and knead with a dough hook for about 3 minutes, adding up to ¼ cup more flour until a cohesive and elastic dough forms.
5. Grease an 8½-by-4½-inch loaf pan. Shape the dough into a loaf and place seam side down in the prepared pan. Set aside in a warm place, loosely covered, until almost doubled in bulk, about 1 hour.
6. Meanwhile, preheat the oven to 350 degrees.
7. Bake for 35 to 40 minutes, until the loaf is well browned on top and sounds hollow when tapped on the bottom. Turn out onto a wire rack to cool completely before slicing. For a softer crust, rub the bread while still hot with softened butter. (The bread can be wrapped well and frozen.)

Note: Quick-rising yeast can also be used. The rising times will be about half as long.

King Arthur's History

The King Arthur Flour Company is America's oldest flour company and the oldest food company in New England. Founded in Boston in 1790 as the Sands, Taylor, and Wood Company, the business has been headed for almost two hundred years by five generations of the Sands family. In 1999 ownership of the company passed to its employees, but the Sands family remains heavily involved.

The King Arthur name was coined in the 1890s when, after seeing a musical production about the Round Table, a savvy marketing manager was inspired to link the legendary Arthurian virtues of strength, purity, honesty, and loyalty with the company's products.

No chemicals, bleaches, or bromates are used in processing King Arthur Flour. "Never Bleached! Never Bromated!" proclaims the slogan on every bag of King Arthur, including the whole wheat flour, all-purpose unbleached flour, and bread flour.

During the 1930s the company marketing strategy included sponsorship of two radio shows, "King Arthur Coffee Club," and "King Arthur Round Table of Song." In an effort to counter a decline in home baking, King Arthur offers classes for home bakers, kids, and professionals in their Baking Education Center, and also supports county fair baking competitions around New England.

In the mid-1990s, King Arthur consolidated its operation, which also includes an extensive mail-order catalog selling baking supplies, into a modern reconstructed round barn complex in Norwich, Vermont, that houses the plant, offices, a café, and a retail store.

--- **Lyndon Grant** ---

"During the Depression, when many a man was earning no more than five or seven dollars a week, we usually had a house full of family on hand to feed because we had the farm. So we had food. We raised everything we ate—potatoes, parsnips, cabbages, other vegetables, chickens, pigs, cows—except wheat for the flour. We bought the flour, fifty-pound sacks at a time, and the sugar, though sugar was dear. My mother baked all kinds of bread and rolls every week, probably a dozen or fourteen loaves every week. And then rolls—plain rolls and cinnamon buns. Oh, that smell of bread baking. I still have it in my mind.

"I was usually the one who got sent to the store a couple of miles away to get the flour. One time I bought the wrong kind. I had to haul that mighty heavy fifty-pound sack the whole way back to the store and bring back the right kind. I can say I never made *that* mistake again!"

—Lyndon Grant, Carter Point, Sedgwick, Maine

■ ■ ■ ■ ■ ■ ■ ■ ■ ■

Multigrain Vermont Loaves

MAKES 2 LOAVES

Vermont has become renowned for reviving and reinvigorating the artisan hearth-style bread-baking tradition. I have sampled truly impressive loaves from bakeries in each of Vermont's "B" towns—Burlington, Brattleboro, and Bennington—as well from bakeries in such smaller villages as Chester and Plainfield. This loaf, which replicates some of the best of those artisan breads, is replete with several whole grains and is amplified with the rich crunch of sunflower seeds. The plain yogurt in the recipe helps produce a home-baked loaf with something akin to the tang and full flavor that are acquired in a long, slow, bakery rise.

⅓ cup cracked wheat cereal or fine bulgur
⅓ cup raw unprocessed wheat bran
⅓ cup plus 1 tablespoon old-fashioned or quick-cooking rolled oats
    (not instant oatmeal)
2 (¼ ounce) packages active dry yeast (see Note)
1¼ cups hot tap water (105–115 degrees)
3½ cups bread flour, plus more for kneading

1½ cups whole wheat flour
½ cup salted sunflower seeds, toasted and coarsely chopped
2 teaspoons salt
1 cup plain regular or lowfat yogurt
¼ cup vegetable oil
¼ cup honey

1. Combine the cracked wheat, wheat bran, and ⅓ cup of the oats in a large, dry skillet. Toast over medium heat, stirring frequently, until fragrant and one shade darker, about 5 minutes. Scrape into a bowl to cool.

2. Sprinkle the yeast over ¼ cup of the hot water in a small bowl. Set aside until the yeast is dissolved and bubbly, about 10 minutes.

3. Stir together the bread flour, whole wheat flour, sunflower seeds, and salt in a large mixing bowl, or the large bowl of an electric mixer with a dough hook. Add the toasted grain mixture, yeast mixture, yogurt, oil, honey, and remaining 1 cup hot water and stir to combine well. Knead by hand on a well-floured board or with the dough hook until the dough is smooth and elastic but still slightly sticky, about 10 minutes by hand or 5 minutes with the mixer. Place the dough in a large oiled bowl, turn to coat with oil, and set aside in a warm place, loosely covered with plastic wrap, until doubled in bulk, about 1½ hours.

4. Punch the dough down. Divide in half and shape into 2 loaves. Place seam side down in 2 oiled 8½-by-5-inch loaf pans. Set aside, loosely covered, until almost doubled in bulk, about 1 hour.

5. Meanwhile, preheat the oven to 350 degrees.

6. Sprinkle the tops of the loaves with the remaining tablespoon of rolled oats. Bake until the loaves are well risen, browned, and sound hollow when tapped, 40 to 45 minutes. Turn out onto a wire rack to cool completely before slicing. (The bread can be stored at cool room temperature for 1 day, or it may be frozen.)

Note: Quick-rising yeast can be substituted. The rising times will be about half as long.

Ken Haedrich on Bread

"I've always tried to emphasize that bread making is intrinsically rewarding in that it allows us to learn something new, no matter how old we are. This learning is deeply satisfying not only because the end product tastes good but also because it restores our faith in ourselves as intelligent human beings. Because bread making is so varied, the potential for new learning is always there.

"If you are an adventurous neophyte, you can probably find your way along with just a few pieces of advice. First, be sure that none of your liquid ingredients is hotter than 115 degrees, or you may kill your yeast. Add the flour to the liquid gradually so you don't end up with a stiff lump of dough to knead. Be patient with the rising; give it ample time to double in bulk. And if you aren't sure if it's done, give your bread a little extra time in the oven."

—Ken Haedrich, *Home for the Holidays*
(Bantam, 1992)
Haedrich is a New Hampshire baker
and award-winning cookbook author

PICKLES, PRESERVES, RELISHES, & CHUTNEYS

Pickles and relishes, which have always been a vital part of the New England culinary scene, have given lift and sparkle to many a homespun meal. There's nothing better with baked beans, for instance, than Crisp Bread-and-Butter Pickles (page 471). Lip-Tingling Dilly Beans (page 472) are the perfect complement to clam chowder, while Mustard Chow-Chow (page 473) is just the thing with corned beef hash.

Pickles and preserves still play a important role on the Yankee table. Modern refrigeration and transportation have made it unnecessary to preserve and pickle food as our forebears did, but pickles and preserves are rewarding, easy, and often quicker to make than you might think. (And we all know that a homemade jar of any condiment makes a much appreciated gift.)

What about preserving your pickles? The recipes for the easily made fresh-pack pickles in this chapter (Pumpkin Pickle [page 474] for example) offer the option of storing the pickles in the refrigerator for up to a month, or putting them up in canning jars. Home canning that employs the boiling-water processing method is not difficult, but there are a few important basic rules to follow, and some special equipment is required. I do not give detailed instructions for water bath processing in this book, so if you plan to put any of these pickles up in jars, first read up on the technique in a reliable, up-to-date reference such as Linda Ziedrich's *The Joy of Pickling* (Harvard Common Press, 1998).

For the jams, jellies, and preserves in this chapter, I suggest following the manufacturer's instructions for sealing them into jars. The fresh salsas and relishes are simply stored in the refrigerator.

Crisp Bread-and-Butter Pickles

MAKES ABOUT 4 PINTS

A venerable community cookbook, *Out of Vermont Kitchens*, yields this classic recipe for crisp bread-and-butter cucumber pickles. Published originally in 1939 by the Women's Service League of St. Paul's Church in Burlington, this is a charming collection that has been reprinted eighteen times and is still a bestseller. Each recipe, including this pickle submitted by Mrs. H. A. Goode, is reproduced in the handwriting of the original donor, and many are accompanied by hand-drawn illustrations. As with other fresh-pack pickle recipes in this chapter, you can put these pickles up in jars or simply treat them as refrigerator pickles and store them in the ice box for up to about a month.

> 3 pounds unwaxed Kirby cucumbers
> ½ pound tiny white onions, peeled, or 1 cup sliced onions
> ¼ cup kosher salt
> 2 cups cider vinegar
> 2 cups sugar
> 1 tablespoon whole mustard seeds
> 1 teaspoon celery seeds
> ¾ teaspoon turmeric
> ¼ teaspoon ground cloves

1. Wash the cucumbers and slice them fairly thin. In a large bowl, toss them with the onions and salt. Add a handful of ice cubes and mix again. Cover and set aside at room temperature for 3 hours, stirring once or twice. Drain well in a colander.
2. Combine the vinegar, sugar, mustard and celery seed, turmeric, and cloves in a large nonreactive saucepan. Bring to a boil, stirring, and add the drained cucumber mixture. Return the liquid just to the boiling point and remove the pan from the heat.
3. Can the pickles in jars while hot, if you like, or let them cool in the brine and refrigerate, covered, for at least 12 hours or up to 1 month.

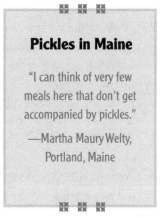

Pickles in Maine

"I can think of very few meals here that don't get accompanied by pickles."

—Martha Maury Welty,
Portland, Maine

Lip-Tingling Pickled Dilly Beans

MAKES 4 TO 5 1½-PINT JARS

Pickled "dilly beans," as they are affectionately known, are a cottage-industry specialty in Maine. You see jars of the beans for sale in practically every tourist-oriented food store in the state—usually at somewhat inflated prices. Here is a recipe for making dilly beans at home. This way you then have the option of canning them in jars or secreting them in a bowl in the back of the refrigerator to await your pleasure. A dozen red chile pepper pods in the recipe add lip tingle to this unusual, pleasingly crisp pickle. If you do decide to "put them up," be on the lookout for 1½-pint canning jars, as they're the perfect height for most green beans.

> 2½ pounds green beans, trimmed to stand upright in the canning jars
> 4 cups cider vinegar
> About 12 small dried red chile peppers
> 3 tablespoons kosher salt
> 1 tablespoon mustard seeds
> 4 garlic cloves, peeled and cut in half
> 8 to 10 large sprigs of fresh dill

1. Blanch the beans for exactly 1½ minutes in a large pot of boiling water. Drain in a colander and refresh under cold running water. Pack the beans upright in sterilized 1½-pint canning jars or, if making refrigerator pickles, transfer them to a large bowl.
2. Combine the vinegar, 2 cups water, chile peppers, salt, and mustard seeds in a large nonreactive saucepan. Bring to a boil, stirring to dissolve the salt, and boil for 1 minute.
3. Divide the garlic and dill among the jars (or add to the large bowl) and pour the hot vinegar mixture over the beans, leaving about ½-inch of headspace if using jars.
4. Can the pickled beans in jars while hot, if you like, or cool and refrigerate the bowl of beans for at least 12 hours or up to 2 weeks.

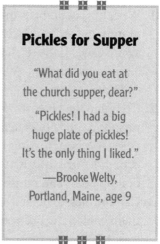

Pickles for Supper

"What did you eat at the church supper, dear?"

"Pickles! I had a big huge plate of pickles! It's the only thing I liked."

—Brooke Welty, Portland, Maine, age 9

Mustard Chow-Chow

MAKES ABOUT 5 PINTS

Some food historians claim this mustardy mixed vegetable pickle came to New England by way of the clipper ship trade from the Far East, while others say it arrived on the western shores of the United States by way of Chinese railroad builders. All agree that the name "chow-chow" derives from the Chinese—possibly from the Mandarin *cha*, which means "mixed." Just to confuse things a bit more, this very same pickle, in its flour-thickened, sweet-sour mustard sauce, is sometimes called Dutch salad in some old Maine and Vermont cookbooks. In any case, the colorful pickle is excellent with hot or cold meats, particularly roast pork.

2 cups sliced Kirby cucumbers
2 cups chopped onion
2 cups coarsely chopped green tomatoes
2 cups small cauliflower florets
1 large red bell pepper, coarsely chopped
½ cup kosher salt
2 cups sugar
½ cup all-purpose flour
3 tablespoons dry mustard
1 teaspoon ground turmeric
2 cups cider vinegar

1. Combine all the vegetables with the salt and 2 cups of cold water in a large bowl. Cover and set aside for 8 hours or overnight. Drain in a colander, rinse well under warm running water, and drain again.
2. Whisk together the sugar, flour, mustard, and turmeric in a large, nonreactive saucepan. Slowly whisk in about 1 cup of the vinegar to make a smooth paste, and then stir in the remaining vinegar and 2 cups of water. Place over medium-high heat and cook, stirring almost constantly, until the mixture comes to the boil and is smooth and thick, about 5 minutes. Add the vegetables to the sauce and cook until the mixture is heated through.
3. Can the pickles in jars while hot, if you like, or let the mixture cool and refrigerate, covered, for at least 12 hours or up to 1 month.

Pumpkin Pickle

MAKES ABOUT 4 CUPS

This pumpkin pickle is a unique and absolutely delicious way to treat New England's prize gourd. You can try using a jack-o'-lantern pumpkin for this pickle, but the small sugar pumpkins that are appearing more and more at roadside stands and markets are considerably easier to handle. The cubed pumpkin first soaks in a salt brine to draw out the liquid, and then simmers in a spiced vinegar-sugar syrup until tender and translucent. The singular result, which is somewhat akin to pickled watermelon rind, is a perfectly lovely condiment, especially on a buffet with Vermont-Style Country Ham Bake (page 296).

> 1 pumpkin, 2½ to 3 pounds
> ¼ cup kosher salt
> 1½ cups cider vinegar

Stolen Sours Are Sweet

Lynn Yobaggy (the Hungarian surname respelled, no doubt, at Ellis Island), whose house was on my long, circuitous walk home from grade school, taught me all about pickles. Her Hungarian grandfather made the pickles, and he stored them in enormous stone crocks "down cellar" of the two-family house that the generations shared.

First Lynn would check to make sure Grandpa was up on the third floor, where he belonged. Then, after determining that her mother was busy enough with the ironing, we'd quietly open the basement door and close it behind us, enveloped suddenly in absolute impenetrable darkness. As our eyes adjusted, we crept down the stairs and groped our way to the dimly spied huge pickle crocks—some chest high on us eleven-year-olds.

The crocks' contents changed periodically, so when we "went fishing," we never knew what pickles we'd catch. After rolling up our sleeves, we plunged our arms into the briny deep, grasped our pickle catch, hauled it up, and ate it, still dripping and almost invisible in the darkness. Sometimes Lynn could detect the pungently aromatic whiff of fermenting sauerkraut. "Stay away from that one," she'd whisper to me. Otherwise, it was an exotic potpourri of delicious stolen pickles, detected by feel. There were big, sour, fermented whole-cucumber dill pickles, pickled sweet bell pepper strips, pretty (but too hot for me then) pickled red cherry peppers, crinkle-cut pickled carrot slices, tiny pickled onions, and my absolute hands-down favorite because they were sweet, knobby pickled cauliflower florets.

1¼ cups sugar
3 slices unpeeled fresh ginger
2 thick slices lemon peel
1 cinnamon stick, broken in half

1. Cut the pumpkin into large wedges, remove the seeds, and peel with a vegetable peeler or small paring knife. Cut into 1-inch cubes.
2. Dissolve the salt in 4 cups of cold water in a large bowl. Add the pumpkin, stir to combine well, and set aside for 6 to 12 hours. Drain in a colander and rinse well.
3. Combine the vinegar, sugar, ½ cup water, ginger, lemon peel, and cinnamon stick in a large, nonreactive saucepan. Bring to a boil, stirring to dissolve the sugar, and add the pumpkin. Cover and simmer over low heat until the pumpkin is tender and translucent, 10 to 20 minutes.
4. Can the pickle in jars while hot, if you like, or cool in the syrup and refrigerate, covered, for at least 12 hours or up to 2 weeks.

Quick Apple-Tomato Chutney

MAKES ABOUT 3 CUPS

Most traditional chutney recipes call for simmering the fruit-spice mixture for upwards of 2 hours. This one, a delectable sweet-hot apple and tomato blend, is all done in less than thirty minutes, start to finish—*and* it lasts for at least two weeks in the refrigerator. It'll be gone well before then, though, eaten with any hot or cold roast meats, especially ham or pork, spread on turkey sandwiches, or spooned atop a curry such as Curried Caribbean Chicken (page 312).

2 tablespoons vegetable oil
1 medium onion, thinly sliced
2 garlic cloves, chopped
2 large tart apples, such as Granny Smith, cored and cut in
　½-inch cubes
1 large tomato, cored and cut in ½-inch cubes (about 1½ cups)
½ cup raisins

1 tablespoon minced fresh ginger

1 teaspoon minced fresh or pickled jalapeño pepper

¼ teaspoon ground allspice

⅛ teaspoon ground cloves

¾ cup distilled white vinegar

⅔ cup packed brown sugar

½ cup orange juice

1 teaspoon salt, plus more to taste

½ teaspoons fresh-ground black pepper, or to taste

1. Heat the oil in a wide, deep skillet (not cast iron), over medium heat. Add the onion and cook, stirring occasionally, until it begins to soften, about 5 minutes. Add the garlic and cook, stirring, for 1 minute. Add the apples, tomato, raisins, ginger, jalapeño, allspice, and cloves and cook, stirring, until the fruit begins to give off its juices, about 3 minutes.

2. Add the vinegar, brown sugar, orange juice, salt, and black pepper, raise the heat to high, and bring to a boil, stirring. Reduce the heat to medium-low and simmer, uncovered, until the apples are softened and the juices are reduced and thickened, about 10 minutes. (Do not cook until dry because the chutney will thicken more as it cools.)

3. Cool and refrigerate for at least 2 hours or up to 2 weeks. Adjust the seasoning if necessary before serving.

Triple Tomato and Melon Salsa

MAKES ABOUT 3 CUPS

Summer salsas or relishes that juxtapose fresh raw vegetables with fruits are great fun to put together. Any number of permutations is possible, as long as the result is a good flavor balance of tart, sweet, and hot, with pretty color and interesting texture. This melon and tomato combination is just that. Yellow tomatoes appear all over New England farm stands in late summer, but if you can't get them, simply use more fresh red tomatoes. And then scoop this refreshing salsa up with chips, spoon it over grilled fish, chicken, or turkey, or serve it with scrambled eggs or a grilled cheese sandwich.

1 cup diced ripe honeydew melon

1 cup diced seeded red tomatoes

1 cup diced seeded yellow tomatoes

¼ cup slivered or chopped oil-packed sun-dried tomatoes, plus 2
tablespoons of the packing oil

½ cup diced sweet yellow or white onion

1 garlic clove, minced

3 tablespoons chopped fresh tarragon

2 tablespoons white wine vinegar

1 tablespoon sugar

¾ teaspoon salt

¼ teaspoon fresh-ground black pepper

½ teaspoon bottled hot pepper sauce, or to taste

1. Combine the melon, red tomatoes, yellow tomatoes, sun-dried tomatoes and oil, onion, garlic, and tarragon in a large bowl. Add the vinegar, sugar, salt, pepper, and hot pepper sauce and toss to combine.

2. Let the salsa stand for at least 15 minutes at room temperature to blend the flavors, or refrigerate for up to 8 hours.

Kenneth Roberts on Ketchup

"In many parts of early New England, tomatoes were called 'love-apples,' and were shunned as being poisonous; but that wasn't true among Maine's seafaring families. Sea captains brought tomato seeds from Spain and Cuba, their wives planted them, and the good cooks in the families experimented with variants of the ubiquitous and somewhat characterless tomato sauce of Spain and Cuba."

"Such was the passion for my grandmother's ketchup in my own family that we could never get enough of it. We were allowed to have it on beans, fish cakes and hash, since those dishes were acknowledged to be incomplete without them; but when we went so far as to demand it on bread, as we often did, we were peremptorily refused, and had to go down in the cellar and steal it—which we also often did. It had a savory, appetizing tang to it that seemed to me to be inimitable. I became almost a ketchup drunkard; for when I couldn't get it, I yearned for it. Because of that yearning, I begged the recipe from my grandmother when I went away from home; and since that day I have made many and many a batch of her ketchup."

—Kenneth Roberts, *Trending into Maine*
(Doubleday, 1949)

"New" New England Cranberry-Apple Salsa

MAKES ABOUT 3 CUPS

This beautiful red, white, yellow, and green fruit salsa has a wonderfully fresh-tasting crunch. It's a piquant accompaniment to grilled chicken, pork, or fish dishes and also makes a marvelous hors d'oeuvre, especially with crackers and a soft cream cheese or goat cheese. You can increase the heat quotient of the salsa by leaving the seeds in the jalapeños.

> 1 large crisp, sweet apple, such as McIntosh, unpeeled, cored, and cut
>   in 1-inch chunks
> ¾ cup fresh cranberries
> 3 tablespoons fresh lime juice
> 2 tablespoons olive oil
> 2 tablespoons honey
> 1 cup chopped onion
> ¾ cup chopped yellow bell pepper
> ⅓ cup chopped fresh cilantro
> 1 garlic clove, finely chopped
> 1 fresh or pickled jalapeño pepper, seeded (optional),
>   and minced
> 1 teaspoon salt
> Fresh-ground black pepper to taste

1. Pulse the apple chunks and cranberries in a food processor until chopped medium fine but not pureed. Do not overprocess.
2. Toss the apples and cranberries with the lime juice, oil, and honey in a medium-sized bowl. Stir in the onion, bell pepper, cilantro, garlic, and jalapeño. Season with the salt and black pepper.
3. Set the salsa aside at room temperature for at least 1 hour to allow the juices to release and flavors to blend, or refrigerate for up to 12 hours. Taste and correct the seasonings if necessary before serving.

Cranberry World

Every year over 340,000 people visit Cranberry World, a museum in Plymouth, Massachusetts, that is entirely devoted to the tart crimson berry. Following a self-propelled tour, Cranberry World leads the visitor through displays that have you activating video screens, pushing buttons to generate color slides, watching early TV commercials—all to provide the complete cranberry education. You get Cranberry History, Geography, Biology, and Social Studies, along with Cranberry Home Ec (or Cranberry Cooking 101). In October, in conjunction with the three-day Cranberry Harvest Festival, you can watch cranberries being harvested from bogs nearby.

Across the street from Cranberry World is the Ocean Spray Cranberry House gift shop, where you can sample all kinds of cranberry goodies or visit the test kitchen to taste the results of experiments in cranberry cooking. The shop sells cranberry-flavored honey, cranberry-chocolate chip cookies, cranberry biscotti, cranberry-orange marmalade, cranberry pancake mix, cranberry syrup, and even cranberry dog bones. Lately Craisins, sweetened dried cranberries, are the hottest seller in the shop.

❖ ❖ ❖ ❖ ❖ ❖ ❖ ❖ ❖

No-Cook Cranberry-Kumquat Relish

MAKES ABOUT 3 CUPS

I always try to have two cranberry sauces on the Thanksgiving dinner table—one cooked, such as the Nantucket Cranberry-Pear Conserve (page 480), and one made with raw cranberries. This unusual combination of raw cranberries, kumquats (which are available most everywhere around holiday time), horseradish, and mint is easily made in about five minutes in a food processor, and has stirred more comment and praise than many a more complicated dish on the groaning board. It has an agreeable fresh, crunchy texture and delightfully piquant flavor.

> 1 12-ounce package fresh cranberries
> 10 large fresh kumquats, quartered
> 1 cup sugar
> 3 tablespoons prepared horseradish
> 3 tablespoons minced fresh mint, plus a sprig for garnish

1. Place the cranberries, kumquats, and sugar in a food processor. Pulse until the mixture is chopped medium fine, but not pureed. Do not overprocess.

2. Transfer the mixture to a bowl and stir in the horseradish. Let the relish stand at room temperature for at least 1 hour, or refrigerate up to 2 days.

3. Up to 30 minutes before serving, stir the chopped mint into the relish, garnish with a mint sprig, and serve.

Nantucket Cranberry-Pear Conserve

MAKES ABOUT 3 CUPS

A recipe in a community cookbook called *From the Galleys of Nantucket* was the starting point for this conserve. Most conserves include nuts in the sweetened cooked fruit mixture, but this Nantucket Island contributor left the nuts out "because they get all gooey." I agree. So I omitted them too, added some pear and candied ginger, and kept the name—mostly because I love the sound of it. This is the cooked cranberry sauce that has become the standard for my Thanksgiving dinner table.

1 12-ounce package fresh cranberries
1 firm, flavorful pear, peeled, cored, and chopped
¾ cup sugar
⅔ cup dry white wine or vermouth
2 tablespoons chopped candied ginger

Cranberry Everything

"'Don't you adore cranberries! Do you think they're Nantucket's most special native food?' Nothing more Nantuckety, they agreed. Cranberry sauce and cranberry conserve, lattice-topped cranberry pie ('Mock cherry, they used to call it,' Gussie said), cranberry nut bread and molded cranberry salad and even cranberry dumplings.

"'Cranberried sweet potatoes,' Beth said yearningly, 'cranberry cake, cranberry cobbler, cranberry pecan pie. And would you believe cranberry soup? It's delicious—sort of a cranberry borscht, with beets and chicken broth. And how about Swamp Fires? Cranberry juice, vodka, and champagne—at least I think that was the general idea of it.'"

—Virginia Rich, *The Nantucket Diet Murders*
(Thorndike Press, 1988)

---

1. Combine the cranberries, pear, sugar, and wine in a large saucepan or deep skillet. Bring to a boil, stirring to dissolve the sugar. Reduce the heat to low and simmer, uncovered, until the cranberries have popped and the sauce is lightly thickened, 10 to 15 minutes. Do not cook the mixture until dry because it will thicken more as it cools. Stir in the candied ginger.
2. Refrigerate, covered, for at least 6 hours, or up to 4 days. Bring to room temperature before serving.

Martha's Wild Blueberry Preserves

MAKES ABOUT 12 HALF-PINT JARS

When the tiny native Maine blueberries have their short season, my sister Martha makes them into these luscious preserves. It's pretty much the recipe on the Certo liquid pectin package, she says, but her addition of the cinnamon stick adds a subtle and very complementary flavor to the blueberries. The tiny amount of butter in the recipe, a recommendation on the pectin package, helps prevent foam from forming while the blueberries are cooking—a plus, since much of the essential fruit flavor resides in the foam.

> 2 quarts wild or cultivated blueberries, rinsed and stemmed
> 7 cups sugar
> 3 tablespoons lemon juice
> ½ teaspoon butter
> 1 cinnamon stick, broken in half or thirds
> 2 3-ounce pouches liquid fruit pectin

1. Crush about one-third of the blueberries with a potato masher in a large bowl. Transfer to a large pot. Repeat with the remaining berries.
2. Add the sugar, lemon juice, butter, and cinnamon stick to the pot. Over high heat, bring the mixture to a full rolling boil, stirring constantly.
3. Add the pectin, return to a boil, and boil for 1 minute, stirring constantly. Remove from the heat.
4. Discard the cinnamon stick and ladle the blueberry mixture into clean canning jars, following the manufacturer's instructions for sealing the jars.

Fruit Butters

They're not butter at all, of course, but smooth pureed fruit cooked down until it thickens to a jamlike consistency, with the spreading qualities of creamy butter. For generations New Englanders have made peach butter and pear butter and tomato butter (doesn't that sound good!) and even cranberry and beach plum butter, but the most popular fruit butter by far is apple butter. You simply take about a dozen McIntosh or Macoun apples, chop them, and cook them, peel, core, and all, with a little water until soft, puree them through a food mill, and then simmer the pulp with 6 to 7 cups of sugar and a little cinnamon and allspice. Then you can add one pouch of liquid pectin to thicken and set the butter, or cook it down so it thickens naturally, and put the butter up in canning jars or refrigerate it for up to several weeks.

In an old cookbook, *New Hampshire Profiles*, I found a recipe for sassafras apple butter. The instructions call for cooking apples, cider, sugar, spices, and sassafras root (for thickening, presumably, like filé powder) for 4 to 5 hours!

Good homemade-style apple butter is sold in lots of gourmet and tourist-oriented gift shops around New England, but making apple butter at home generates some of the finest kitchen cooking aromas you'll ever inhale.

Farm Stand-to-Freezer Strawberry Jam

MAKES ABOUT 5 HALF-PINT JARS

Since it's uncooked—not "put up" or preserved in the traditional sense—this freezer jam retains the true fresh taste of the fruit from which it is made. This preserving method captures the essence of the small sweet New England strawberries during their brief appearance at farm stands in early summer. Do not be tempted to puree the berries in a food processor; they should be mashed by hand so the jam has small chunks of sweet strawberry throughout.

> 1 quart very ripe strawberries, preferably local berries, rinsed and stemmed
> 4 cups sugar
> 1 3-ounce pouch liquid fruit pectin
> 2 tablespoons fresh lemon juice

1. Thoroughly wash 5 half-pint plastic freezer containers or jelly jars (or run them through the dishwasher).
2. Crush the berries with a potato masher or a large fork in a large bowl. Add the sugar and allow the mixture to stand for 10 minutes, stirring once or twice.
3. Stir together the pectin and lemon juice in a small bowl. Add to the fruit and stir constantly until the sugar is dissolved and the mixture is no longer grainy, about 3 minutes.
4. Ladle the jam into the containers to within ¾ inch of the top. Cover with lids and let stand at room temperature until set, up to 24 hours. Store in the refrigerator for up to 3 weeks or in the freezer for 1 year.

Jams and Jellies and Pectin

Jellies gel because of pectin, a substance found naturally in fruit. Commercial pectin, usually distilled from apples or citrus fruits, comes in liquid and powdered forms. In the jelly and jam recipes in this book, I specify liquid pectin, which I much prefer and recommend over the powdered form of the product. When using commercial pectin, be sure to stick to the amounts of sugar and citrus called for in a given recipe, as the gelling process won't happen if the proportions aren't in sync.

Jams, jellies, and preserves can be made without using commercial pectin by following rather precise cooking instructions that involve boiling the fruit and sugar mixture in a widemouth pot or skillet until it "falls in sheets" rather than in separate drops from a spoon, or until a few drops form a soft gel on a chilled plate.

As for processing jams and jellies, because of their high sugar content, they don't need to be subjected to the boiling-water bath method. Most jelly jar manufacturers recommend that the hot filled and capped jars simply be turned upside down for a few minutes until the caps form a seal.

Vineyard Beach Plums

"In its interiors were valleys with winding streams… secret swamps, well-hidden from the sea, great thickets.…One could find the aromatic bayberry, and the beach plum with its gnarled and windbeaten attitudes.…In season the air was perfumed with ecstasy by the wild grape, and Islanders went into the swamps and glades to return with high-heaped baskets.…On the Great Plain, the sweetfern grew, wild-flowers in profusion, and, especially after a spring fire, blueberries and huckleberries of large size and succulence."

—Henry Beetle Hough, *Martha's Vineyard, Summer Resort* in *The Martha's Vineyard Cook Book* by Louise Tate King and Jean Stewart Wexler (Harper & Row, 1971)

Vineyard Beach Plum Jelly

MAKES 6 OR 7 HALF-PINT JARS

Food writer and editor Judith Jones maintains that "a full appreciation of New England food remains incomplete until you've had a taste of beach plum jelly." These tiny wild fruits (see page 485), which grow prolifically along the beaches of Cape Cod and its offshore islands, Martha's Vineyard and Nantucket, make a gorgeous reddish plum-colored jelly, with a deep, well-balanced, tangy tartness. Using a combination of ripe and unripe fruit to make the jelly helps give it its characteristic flavor. Much of the beach plum jelly sold commercially is overly sweetened, so unless you can trust your source, the best way to experience its true taste is to make a batch of your own.

> 3 pounds (about 5 cups) beach plums, a combination of ripe and
>   unripe fruit
> 6 to 7 cups sugar
> 1 3-ounce pouch liquid fruit pectin

1. Wash the beach plums and remove the leaves but don't worry about the stems. Place them in a large pot, press hard on the fruit with a potato masher, and add enough water to barely show through the plums, about 1 cup. Bring to a boil, reduce the heat to low, and simmer, covered, mashing once or twice again during the cooking period, until the fruit is soft, about 20 minutes. Filter the mixture through a damp cloth jelly bag or through a colander lined with a triple layer of rinsed cheesecloth. Do not squeeze the bag if you want clear jelly. (This process takes at least 2 hours. You can leave it to drip undisturbed overnight.)

2. Measure the juice. You should have 3½ to 4 cups. Pour the juice into a large saucepan and add the sugar, starting with 6 cups and adding more if necessary to achieve the desired sweetness. Bring the mixture to a full rolling boil (boiling so hard that you can't stir down the bubbles), stirring constantly. Add the pectin and boil, stirring constantly, for 1 minute.

3. Remove from the heat and skim off any foam that has risen to the surface. Immediately ladle into clean canning jars, following the manufacturer's instructions for sealing the jars.

———— Oh! That Jelly ————

Beach plums grow on shrubby bushes on dunes and coastal plains from Virginia to Nova Scotia. In spring the bushes produce a cloud of fragrant white cherrylike blossoms that infuse the sea air with their sweet scent. By late summer the plants have produced their fruit—olive-size, dark purple plums with a wild flavor that is reminiscent of a grape-plum cross. The fruit is too bitter and tart to be eaten out of hand, but oh! that jelly.

Classic Concord Grape Jelly

MAKES 6 OR 7 HALF-PINT JARS

You have to know where to look, but during September and October around New England there are still old grape arbors and vines sagging heavy with bunches of dusky deep purple-blue Concord grapes. The long-ago-planted vines on abandoned farms (and also the true wild grape vines) produce clusters of small fruit, while the grapes from cultivated arbors are larger and juicier. Any and all Concord grapes make beautiful jelly that, to me, tastes of primeval North American woodlands.

> 3 pounds Concord grapes, including about one-quarter unripe fruit
> 6 to 7 cups granulated sugar
> 1 3-ounce pouch liquid pectin

Vermont Common Crackers

What, exactly, is a Vermont Common Cracker? It's a hard, round, cream-colored biscuit made with wheat flour, potato flour, shortening, water, baking soda, and salt. According to Bob Mills, cracker manager at the Vermont Country Store, where the crackers are made, they're a "bland, almost tasteless cracker"— the perfect vehicle for well-aged Vermont cheddar, as well as for just about any jam, jelly, preserve, or chutney in this chapter.

Common Crackers are one of the direct descendants of ship's biscuit, or hardtack. The towns of Montpelier, Vermont and Arlington, Massachusetts, both lay claim to their invention, in the early part of the nineteenth century. In 1981, when Cross Crackers, as they were then known, were about to be discontinued, Vrest Orton, owner of the Vermont

Country Store in Rockingham, bought the ancient cracker-making equipment and the original recipe, changed the name to Vermont Common Crackers, and started selling them through his shop and catalog.

Common Cracker aficionados become practiced in placing a thumb along the biscuit's side seam and applying the precise amount of pressure to split it in half longitudinally. The halves can then be toasted until lightly golden, spread with a little butter, and topped with a chunk of cheese, perhaps along with a dab of Quick Apple-Tomato Chutney (page 475) or a smear of Martha's Wild Blueberry Preserves (page 481), Vineyard Beach Plum Jelly (page 484), or Classic Concord Grape Jelly (see above).

1. Wash the grapes and remove most of the stems. (You don't have to be too particular because the cooked fruit will be strained.) Place the grapes in a large pot, crush them slightly with a potato masher, and add enough water to barely show through the fruit, about 1 cup. Bring to a boil, reduce the heat to low, and simmer, covered, mashing gently once or twice again during the cooking period, until the fruit is very soft, 10 to 15 minutes. Filter the mixture through a damp cloth jelly bag or through a colander lined with a triple layer of rinsed cheesecloth. Do not squeeze the bag if you want clear jelly. (This process takes at least 2 hours. You can leave it to drip undisturbed overnight.)

2. Measure the juice. You should have 3½ to 4 cups. Pour the juice into a large saucepan and add sugar, starting with the 6 cups and adding more if necessary to achieve the desired sweetness. Bring the mixture to a full rolling boil (boiling so hard that you can't stir down the bubbles), stirring constantly. Add the pectin and boil, stirring constantly, for 1 minute.

3. Remove from the heat and skim off any foam that has risen to the surface. Immediately ladle into clean canning jars, following the manufacturer's instructions for sealing the jars.

Grandma's Storeroom

"Not far from the pork barrel [in this mid-nineteenth century Maine kitchen] were hanging shelves on which were preserves and jelly. Grandma stored them in an orderly fashion. The strawberries, the cherries, the blueberries, the plums, the raspberries, and the blackberries, each had its own enclave. The currant jelly and gooseberry jelly did not touch shoulders. Nor did the elderberry and the apple, the mint, and the quince. Grandmother assigned special shelves to her pickles: the dill and the ripe cucumber; the mustard and piccallili; the sweet and the sour; the beet and the corn relish."

—Esther Wood, *Deep Roots* (Yankee Books, 1990)

COBBLERS, SHORTCAKES, PUDDINGS, AND OTHER DESSERTS

We should pity the poor Pilgrims their dearth of desserts. Why, they counted themselves lucky if they could manage to stir themselves up a pot of maple-sweetened cornmeal mush (the forerunner, incidentally, of Delicate Indian Pudding [page 512]). The minute ovens became more reliable, though, New Englanders rushed to bake all manner of scrumptious desserts, creating, as they went along, such American classics as U-Pick Native Strawberry Shortcake with Egg Biscuit Cake (page 502) and Bethel Inn Maple-Apple Pandowdy (page 495). We're still at it, delighting in fruit cobblers—blackberry, blueberry, rhubarb—and bettys and crisps such as Apple Crisp with Walnut-Oat Topping (page 497).

We're still stirring up those puddings too, only now they might be delicate baked pudding cakes flavored with lemon or chocolate, or smooth Maple-Rum Cup Custards (page 510), or that uniquely delicious northern New England favorite, creamy Finest Kind Grapenut Pudding (page 518).

We agree with Hungarian-Yankees, who, when they want a splurge, make their fabulous Crêpes with Walnut Filling and Warm Chocolate Sauce (page 507), and we concur with Portuguese New Englanders that a Portuguese-Style Caramel Flan (page 509) is a perfect way to end most any meal.

Maine's Own Baking Powder

During World War II a shortage of cream of tartar prompted a Bangor, Maine, chemist to concoct a substitute leavening agent so that Mainers could keep right on baking their beloved biscuits, shortcakes, and cobblers. That product, Bakewell Cream, listed on the label as simply "acid sodium pyrophosphate," is similar to cream of tartar in that it must be mixed with baking soda to create the leavening action. Bakewell Cream was an immediate hit because cooks loved the way it raised their baked goods to new and lighter heights. Sold in a distinctive blue and yellow can, Bakewell Cream is still the preferred leavening agent for most bakers across the state, and it does, indeed, produce exceptionally delicious biscuit doughs. As the product literature states, "It makes a superior, almost no-fail biscuit, even for a heavy-handed amateur cook."

Bakewell Cream can substitute for the baking powder in any of the cobbler or shortcake recipes in this chapter. Simply follow the instructions on the can.

Blackberry Patch Cobbled Cobbler

MAKES 6 SERVINGS

Some of my happiest childhood (and adult) food memories are of berry picking—and somehow, the more uncomfortable the experience, the more indelible is the memory. Blackberries are particularly challenging to wrest from their briery thickets, but those trips home—dusty, thirsty, thorn-scratched, mosquito-bitten, and sunburned—with pails full enough of the fragile, juicy, almost winey-tasting fruit were exhilarating journeys. Those pails did have to be "full enough," though, to make cobbler or shortcake for supper. Often this old-fashioned "cobbled top" cobbler was our well-earned, sweet reward.

For the fruit layer:

4 cups blackberries (see Note)
½ cup sugar
2 teaspoons fresh lemon juice

For the dough:

1 cup all-purpose flour
2 tablespoons plus 1 teaspoon sugar
2 teaspoons baking powder
½ teaspoon salt
6 tablespoons cold unsalted butter, cut in about 10 pieces
⅓ cup half-and-half or light cream, plus more if necessary

Lightly whipped cream or a pitcher of "pouring cream"

1. Preheat the oven to 400 degrees. Generously grease a 9-inch square glass baking dish.
2. To make the fruit layer, scatter the berries in the bottom of the baking dish and sprinkle them with the sugar and lemon juice.
3. To make the dough, pulse the flour, 2 tablespoons of the sugar, the baking powder, and salt in a food processor. Distribute the butter over the flour mixture and pulse until the butter pieces are about the size of small peas. With the motor running, pour the half-and-half through the feed tube and process just until the flour is moistened and a soft dough is formed. (The dough can be made by hand in a bowl by whisking together the dry ingredients, working the butter in with your fingertips, and stirring the cream in with a large fork.)
4. Using a tablespoon, drop spoonfuls of the dough on top of the fruit, spacing fairly close together. Do not smooth out the dough, as you want a "cobbled" texture to the crust. Sprinkle with the remaining teaspoon of sugar.

Irish Moss Blanc Mange

The pure white, feathery seaweed found on New England beaches, called sea moss or Irish moss, was used as a natural thickener for puddings in the nineteenth century. Harriet McKissock gives us the "rule" from her little notebook of "Sakonnet Recipes." "Rinse about ½ cup of moss and soak it in cold water. Pick out any discolored pieces or debris. Add moss to 3 cups milk and cook in a double boiler for about 30 minutes. Strain. Add a pinch of salt and a teaspoon of vanilla. Pour into molds. Chill, unmold, and serve with maple syrup, or, for the youngest generation, chocolate sauce." Harriet gathers the moss from her Sakonnet, Rhode Island, beach and makes this pudding every single summer for her grandchildren as a way of carrying on her own grandmother's tradition.

5. Bake for 25 to 30 minutes, until the fruit is bubbly and the topping is golden brown.

6. Let the cobbler cool for at least 30 minutes, then serve slightly warm or at room temperature, with whipped cream or pouring cream on the side.

Note: Blueberries, huckleberries, raspberries, or a combination can be substituted.

Reach House Blueberry Cobbler

MAKES 4 SERVINGS

The Reach House is the first house our family rented in the coastal town of Sedgwick, Maine. It was a turn-of-the-century shingled cottage with a crumbling porch, a steep, dark staircase, and bats in the bathroom, but there was a splendid, sweeping vista down to the shore of Eggemoggin Reach, blueberry fields out back—and a well enough equipped kitchen so we could cook and bake if we were in the mood. It was here that I first began to appreciate the stellar virtues of the tiny, sweet-tart low-bush Maine blueberry. When on a vacation, a cobbler is just the ticket—easily and quickly put together yet sending forth the kind of heavenly smells from the oven that make a relaxed yet ravenous family feel happy and well loved.

For the fruit layer:

3 cups blueberries
½ cup sugar
2 teaspoons fresh lemon juice
½ teaspoon grated lemon zest
1 teaspoon vanilla extract

For the dough:

1 cup all-purpose flour
2 teaspoons baking powder
½ teaspoon salt
1 tablespoon plus 1 teaspoon sugar
4 tablespoons cold unsalted butter, cut in about 10 pieces
¼ cup whole or lowfat milk

Vanilla ice cream for serving

1. Preheat the oven to 425 degrees. Generously grease a 9-inch glass pie plate or other shallow quart baking dish.

2. To make the fruit mixture, place the berries in the pie plate, add the sugar, lemon juice, lemon zest, and vanilla, and toss to combine.

3. To make the dough, pulse the flour, baking powder, salt, and 1 tablespoon of the sugar in a food processor. Distribute the butter over the flour mixture and pulse until the butter pieces are about the size of small peas. With the motor running, pour the milk through the feed tube, stopping the machine as soon as the flour is moistened and the dough begins to come together. (To make the dough by hand, whisk the dry ingredients together in a mixing bowl, work the butter in with your fingertips, and stir in the milk with a large fork to make a soft dough.) Scrape out onto a lightly floured board, knead a couple of times, and roll or pat the dough into an 8-inch round. (If using another shape dish, simply pat the dough into a shape that is slightly smaller than the interior dimensions of the baking dish.) Trim the edges and crimp them with your fingertips or a fork. Set the dough over the fruit and cut several deep slashes to let steam escape. Sprinkle with the remaining 1 teaspoon of sugar.

4. Bake for 20 to 25 minutes, until the crust is golden and the fruit is bubbly.

5. Serve warm or at room temperature, topped with scoops of vanilla ice cream.

Bethel Inn Maple-Apple Pandowdy

MAKES 6 SERVINGS

This is an old-fashioned New England dessert over which there seems to be absolutely no agreement—whether on the spelling and origin of its name (pandowdy or pan dowdy, "dowdy" for homely, or "dowdy" meaning to slash the pastry?) or on the recipe (cakelike or pancakelike crust, biscuit crust, pastry crust, or bread crust?). None of it matters because this is one of those homey desserts that, if made with juicy, flavorful apples in season, with the right proportion of crust (any type), you really can't go wrong. This maple-flavored pandowdy has a tender, cakelike crust. It is a re-creation of one I ate on a wintry evening in the dining room at the Bethel Inn, a lovely old-fashioned hostelry in the mountains of Maine.

6 cups peeled, cored, and sliced semisweet apples, such as Northern
Spy, Cortland, or Macoun (2 to 2½ pounds) (see Note)
3 tablespoons pure maple syrup
½ teaspoon ground cinnamon
½ teaspoon grated nutmeg
1 cup all-purpose flour
¼ cup sugar
2 teaspoons baking powder
½ teaspoon salt
½ cup whole or lowfat milk
1 egg
6 tablespoons unsalted butter, melted
2 teaspoons vanilla extract

Lightly sweetened whipped cream, optional

1. Preheat the oven to 350 degrees. Grease a shallow 2-quart baking dish.
2. Arrange the apples in the prepared dish, drizzle with the maple syrup, and sprinkle
with the cinnamon and nutmeg. Toss to combine. Cover the dish with foil and bake
for 25 to 35 minutes, or until the apples are moderately tender.
3. Meanwhile, whisk together the flour, sugar, baking powder, and salt in a mixing
bowl. Whisk the milk with the egg in a small bowl. Stir in the melted butter and
vanilla. Stir the liquid mixture into the flour mixture, whisking just until combined.
Do not overbeat.

1880 Apple Pandowdy

Imogene Wolcott quotes this apple pandowdy recipe
from a New England cookbook published in 1880:
"Fill a heavy pot heaping full of pleasant apples,
sliced. Add 1 cup molasses, 1 cup sugar, 1 cup
water, 1 teaspoon cloves, 1 teaspoon cinnamon.
Cover with baking powder biscuit crust, sloping it
over the sides. Bake overnight. In the morning cut
the hard crust into the apple. Eat with yellow cream
or plain."

—Imogene Wolcott, *The Yankee Cook Book*
(Ives Washburn, 1963)

4. Pour the batter evenly over the apples, return to the oven, and bake, uncovered, until the topping is pale golden and a toothpick comes out clean, 25 to 30 minutes.

5. Cool on a rack for about 30 minutes and serve warm, topped with whipped cream if you like.

Note: You can also use a combination of half tart apples, such as Granny Smith, and half sweet apples, such as McIntosh.

Tilly's Pudding

"Meantime Tilly attacked the plum-pudding. She felt pretty sure of coming out right, here, for she had seen her mother do it so many times, it looked very easy. So in went suet and fruit; all sorts of spice, to be sure she got the right ones, and brandy instead of wine. But she forgot both sugar and salt, and tied it in the cloth so tightly that it had no room to swell, so it would come out as heavy as lead and as hard as a cannon-ball, if the bag did not burst and spoil it all. Happily unconscious of these mistakes, Tilly popped it into the pot, and proudly watched it bobbing about before she put the cover on and left it to its fate."

—Louisa May Alcott,
An Old-Fashioned Thanksgiving (1882)

Apple Crisp with Walnut-Oat Topping

MAKES 6 SERVINGS

This apple crisp is the quintessential fall dessert. I love everything about it: the old-fashioned simplicity of the ingredients, the ease with which it is assembled, the way it perfumes the house with its sweet apple fragrance as it bakes, and of course, most of all, the way it tastes. It's a study in delicious contrasts: warm, soft, cinnamon-sweet apples, crunchy, nut-rich crust, and cold ice cream sending vanilla-scented rivulets through the hot dessert so that with each bite, if you're spooning properly, you get something of each element in your mouth. In New England, the scoop of choice would most likely be Ben & Jerry's World's Best Vanilla Ice Cream.

For the topping:

¼ cup broken walnut pieces

½ cup packed light brown sugar

⅓ cup all-purpose flour

½ teaspoon ground cinnamon

⅛ teaspoon salt

4 tablespoons cold unsalted butter, cut in pieces

¼ cup old-fashioned or quick-cooking rolled oats (not instant oatmeal)

For the filling:

8 cups peeled, sliced, medium-sweet apples, such as Cortland, Jonathan, or Macoun, or a mixture of tart and sweet, such as Granny Smith and McIntosh (2½ to 3 pounds)

1 tablespoon fresh lemon juice

2 teaspoons vanilla extract

Vanilla ice cream

1. To make the topping, process the walnuts in a food processor until they are chopped medium-fine. Remove and reserve. Add the brown sugar, flour, cinnamon, and salt to the work bowl and process to remove any lumps in the sugar. Distribute the butter over the flour mixture and process until the mixture resembles coarse meal. Add the oats, along with the reserved walnuts, and pulse just to combine. Set aside. (The topping mixture can be made a couple of days ahead and refrigerated.)

2. Preheat the oven to 350 degrees. Grease a shallow 2-quart baking dish such as a 9-inch square.

3. To make the filling spread the apples in the prepared dish. Combine 2 tablespoons water with the lemon juice and vanilla in a small bowl and drizzle over the apples. Sprinkle with the walnut-oat topping, spreading to make an even layer. (The crisp can be set aside, covered, at cool room temperature for 2 to 3 hours before baking.)

4. Bake for 40 to 50 minutes, until the apples are tender and the topping is browned and caramelized.

5. Serve hot or warm with scoops of vanilla ice cream.

Howard Johnson

At age twenty-seven, Howard D. Johnson borrowed money to buy a small drugstore and newsstand in Quincy, Massachusetts, even though he was already in debt. To increase business, he began making ice cream, borrowing yet more money to engage the expertise of an elderly German master ice cream blender who, cranking away by hand, created a host of new flavor combinations for Mr. Johnson's store. He doubled the butterfat content, used only natural flavorings, and eventually came up with enough new flavors to create the famous "28 flavor" HoJo slogan.

⊞ ⊞ ⊞ ⊞ ⊞ ⊞ ⊞ ⊞ ⊞

Maple-Ginger Baked Apples

MAKES 6 SERVINGS

Oh, that celestial perfume that apples send forth as they bake! The flavorings in this baked apple recipe—maple syrup, candied (or crystallized) ginger, butter, brown sugar, lemon, cinnamon, and cloves—are particularly felicitous ones. The important thing is to use a proper baking apple, meaning one that is good and juicy and doesn't collapse as it cooks. In New England the best baking apples are Cortland, Rome Beauty, or Northern Spy. Golden Delicious apples, available countrywide, are also a good choice. This is a lovely dessert to complete a homey fall supper such as The Very Best Tuna-Noodle (page 216) or more company-type fare like Nantucket Bay Scallop Stew (page 61).

6 large, juicy baking apples
¼ cup packed light brown sugar
3 tablespoons unsalted butter, softened
2 tablespoons minced candied ginger
½ teaspoon ground cinnamon
⅛ teaspoon ground cloves
½ teaspoon grated lemon zest
1 cup hot water
½ cup pure maple syrup
1 tablespoon fresh lemon juice

Lightly sweetened, softly whipped cream or ice cream, optional

1. Preheat the oven to 375 degrees. Grease a 13-by-9-inch baking dish.
2. Core the apples and peel them about halfway down their sides. Arrange in the prepared dish. (If the apples tip over, cut a small slice off the bottoms.)
3. Mash together in a small dish, or process together in a food processor, the brown sugar, butter, candied ginger, cinnamon, cloves, and lemon zest. Stuff this mixture into the apple cavities. Pour the hot water, maple syrup, and lemon juice around the apples and tilt the dish to combine the liquids.
4. Bake, uncovered, 40 to 45 minutes, until the apples are tender but not mushy when pierced with the point of a sharp knife. Brush or spoon with the juice every 10 or 15 minutes.
5. Remove from the oven. Continue to baste with the cooking syrup for 15 minutes to glaze the apples as they cool.
6. Serve warm with whipped cream or ice cream if you like. (The apples will keep warm for an hour or so if covered loosely with foil.)

Apples in Early America

Cato recognized seven different varieties of apples in the third century B.C. According to Eleanor Early's *New England Cookbook* (Random House, 1954), there were hundreds of varieties of apples in Europe when the first colonists came to America. The Pilgrims brought with them both seed and propagating wood of the better English varieties, and it was not long before there were apple orchards in the New World. The number of varieties kept increasing for centuries—more than seven thousand have been recorded in the United States—that is, up until the twentieth, when apple varieties began to drop by the wayside. Renewed interest in old-fashioned apples has spurred a movement to revive some of the heirloom varieties that seemed destined to be lost forever.

Chunky Windfall Applesauce

MAKES ABOUT 4 CUPS; 6 TO 8 SERVINGS

By the side of New England roadways and in overgrown meadows of colonial homesites grow twisted, gnarly, half-dead apple trees. Their fruit litters the ground in the fall, most of it undersized and scarred with rotted spots and insect borings. Often though, these funny-looking, blemished apples have an intensity of spicy, winey, musky flavor that recalls an ancient, collective taste memory. One recent bracing October afternoon, I collected twelve different varieties of windfall apples on our road in Maine. I stuffed my pockets full and made this splendid sauce from the fruit. If you can't get your hands on windfalls, of course, good, flavorful local apples make excellent applesauce, too.

> 4 cups peeled, cored, and quartered windfall apples
> 4 cups peeled, cored, and quartered commercially grown apples,
>   preferably a sweet variety, such as McIntosh or Golden Delicious
> Pinch of salt
> Sugar

1. Combine the apples and salt in a large saucepan. Add water just until it shows around the fruit.
2. Bring to a boil, reduce the heat to medium, and cook, uncovered, stirring the fruit now and then, until the pieces are all quite soft, about 20 minutes. Remove from the heat and beat well with a wooden spoon to make a chunky sauce.
3. While the applesauce is still warm, sweeten to taste with sugar.

Depending on the role of the applesauce in the meal, choose any of the following additions or variations:

• To use as a dessert, sweeten the applesauce more heavily and serve warm with heavy cream poured around the sides.

• If you like a spicy applesauce, add ½ to ¾ teaspoon of ginger, cinnamon, or nutmeg.

• For a richer dessert sauce, stir in about 2 tablespoons of butter along with ½ teaspoon of grated lemon zest.

- For a sophisticated dessert, stir in a couple of tablespoons of cognac or apple or pear brandy.

- To serve as a relish with roast meats, especially pork, cook the apples with a handful of cranberries, use a goodly amount of ground ginger, and stir in about 2 teaspoons of red wine vinegar.

- Stir in prepared horseradish—about 1 tablespoon per cup of applesauce.

- Add finely chopped jalapeños—about 2 teaspoons per cup of sauce—and a squeeze of lime juice.

U-Pick Native Strawberry Shortcake with Egg Biscuit Cake

MAKES 8 SERVINGS

Dead-ripe, fragrant native strawberries, whether picked on your own hands and knees or scored from a roadside stand or farmers' market, are surely one of nature's incalculably priceless seasonal offerings. And the shortcake made from these berries is America's most estimable contribution to the list of the world's great desserts. Simplicity itself, strawberry shortcake—the making of which requires little in the way of culinary expertise—is the epitome of good New England country cooking. The only admonition is to use a light hand with the shortcake dough, lest you overwork it and make it tough. In a perfect world strawberry shortcake would be made only from local berries picked that day, still warm from the sun—and never refrigerated. The "short" egg biscuit, this time made into one large cake for an impressive presentation for a large group, is really best when eaten warm, directly from the oven, but the dough, berry mixture, and even the cream can be made ahead and held for a few hours. At the height of the berry season, I've even fed this to my family for supper—that's the whole supper, folks—skipping any pretense of a main course and heading straight for the glorious finish.

For the filling:

2 quarts ripe strawberries, preferably local berries
¼ to ½ cup sugar
2 teaspoons fresh lemon juice

U-Pick Strawberries

A giant strawberry-shaped balloon greets do-it-yourself pickers at Tate's Strawberry Farm in East Corinth in central Maine. For some, picking is all business. For others, it's all fun. And then there are those for whom it's a little of both. A crew from Dysart's, a restaurant in Hermon, was last season's first customer. They send workers to the 35-acre farm to pick two to three hundred quarts every day for the duration of the picking season—usually about three weeks—to make sure the restaurant will have enough berries on hand for strawberry shortcake all winter.

A retired couple, Mr. and Mrs. Scott, pick for the simple enjoyment of it: "The strawberry fields are so beautiful, and the fruit the best you've ever tasted." They usually pick about fourteen quarts and make a couple of batches of jam, and what they don't eat fresh immediately, they freeze. For another retiree, picking means profits. Philip Gaudette gets up at 2:45 A.M. to make the long drive to East Corinth. He picks about 150 quarts to resell to friends at enough profit to make the task of crouching for several hours in the hot sun amongst the plants worthwhile.

❖ ❖ ❖ ❖ ❖ ❖ ❖ ❖ ❖

For the shortcake:

2 cups all-purpose flour
¼ cup sugar
4 teaspoons baking powder
½ teaspoon salt
6 tablespoons cold unsalted butter, cut in about 10 pieces
1 egg
½ cup milk

1½ cups heavy cream
2 tablespoons confectioners' sugar
3 tablespoons unsalted softened butter

1. To make the filling, choose 8 good-looking berries and set them aside. Hull the remaining strawberries. Place half of the berries in a large shallow bowl or on a large rimmed plate and crush them with a fork or the back of a spoon. Slice the remaining berries and add them to the crushed berries, along with the sugar and lemon juice. (If the fruit is very ripe and sweet, use the smaller amount of sugar.)

Stir well to combine. Set aside at room temperature for at least 30 minutes before serving. (The strawberries can be prepared up to 6 hours ahead and refrigerated. Bring to room temperature before using.)

2. To make the shortcake, preheat the oven to 450 degrees. Generously grease an 8-inch cake pan.

3. Pulse the flour, sugar, baking powder, and salt in a food processor. Distribute the butter over the flour mixture and pulse until the mixture looks crumbly. Whisk the egg with the milk in a glass measuring cup. With the motor running, pour the milk mixture through the feed tube and process just until the dough begins to clump together. (To make the dough by hand, whisk the dry ingredients together in a bowl, work in the cold butter with your fingertips, add the egg and milk, and stir with a large fork to make a soft dough.) Scrape out onto a lightly floured board, knead lightly a few times, and roll or pat to an 8-inch round. (The dough can be prepared several hours ahead and refrigerated at this point. To make individual shortcake biscuits, see Note.)

4. Transfer the dough to the prepared pan, patting it gently to the edges. Place in the oven and immediately reduce the oven temperature to 375 degrees. Bake for 22 to 26 minutes until the shortcake is pale golden brown on top. Cool in the pan on a rack for about 10 minutes.

5. Whip the cream with the confectioners' sugar in a medium-sized bowl until soft peaks form.

6. To assemble, transfer the shortcake to a large serving platter with a large spatula. Using a large serrated knife, split the cake horizontally and lift off the top with a large spatula. Spread the bottom of the cake with the softened butter. Spoon about

The Berry Shortcake Booth at the Blue Hill Fair

The Mountain Rebekah Lodge sells out of blueberry and strawberry shortcake every year at its booth at the Blue Hill Fair in midcoast Maine. Betty Gray, one of the lodge members, explains that the cream is real—Dolly Robertson stands there and whips it right in front of you for three days straight—the berries are local, and the biscuits are homemade. "It's just the regular biscuit that you find on the Bakewell Cream can," according to Betty. Rebekah members bake the shortcakes ahead (in a recent year they made 312 dozen), split them, brush them with melted butter, and freeze them until the fair.

"Working at the fair is fun—until about ten o'clock at night. Even then, we always find something to laugh about. You'd be surprised at some of the things you see at the fair."

half the berry mixture over the bottom layer, and spread the berries with half the whipped cream. Replace the shortcake top, spoon the rest of the berry mixture over, and top with whipped cream. Decorate with the reserved whole berries.

7. Cut into wedges to serve.

Note: To make individual biscuits, roll or pat the dough until ¾ inch thick and cut out 8 biscuits with a 2½-inch cutter. Arrange on a baking sheet and bake for 15 to 18 minutes.

Frank's Rhubarb Shortcake with Almond–Brown Sugar Biscuits

MAKES 4 SERVINGS

My father-in-law, Frank Dojny, was a multitalented man with a gentle disposition who was never pushy about anything—except rhubarb. He had a passion for it. He grew it, but he couldn't cook it, so every spring Frank would bring me large bunches of rhubarb from his garden, and if I didn't get around to it fast enough, he made it plain that he was beginning to get impatient. I'd stew up the rhubarb to stock the freezer and sometimes combine it with strawberries in a pie or cobbler, but after I made this almond-brown sugar shortcake one year, it became Frank's favorite and most frequently requested rhubarb dessert. He was right. The orange liqueur rhubarb sauce is an exquisite pairing with these richly flavored almond biscuits.

For the filling:

1½ pounds rhubarb, trimmed and cut into ½-inch pieces
¾ cup sugar
2 tablespoons Grand Marnier or other orange liqueur

For the shortcake:

¼ cup blanched whole almonds or 3 tablespoons sliced almonds
2 tablespoons sugar
1 tablespoon packed light brown sugar
¾ cup all-purpose flour
2 teaspoons baking powder

½ teaspoon salt
3 tablespoons cold unsalted butter, cut into about 10 pieces
¼ cup whole or lowfat milk

Lightly sweetened whipped cream

1. To make the filling, combine the rhubarb with the sugar and ½ cup water in a medium-large saucepan. Bring to a boil over high heat, stirring. Reduce the heat to low, and cook, covered, stirring occasionally, until the rhubarb is tender but still holds some of its shape, about 10 minutes. Remove from the heat, stir in the liqueur, and cool to room temperature. (The rhubarb mixture can be made a day ahead and refrigerated. Reheat in a microwave to lukewarm to return to a saucelike consistency.)

2. To make the shortcake, preheat the oven to 425 degrees.

3. Combine the almonds and two sugars in a food processor. Process until the nuts are finely ground. Add the flour, baking powder, and salt and pulse to combine. Distribute the butter over the flour mixture and pulse until most of the butter is the size of small peas. With the motor running, slowly pour the milk through the feed tube, stopping just when the dough begins to come together. Scrape out onto a lightly floured board, gather the dough together, knead a couple of times, and roll or pat the dough until about ¾ inch thick. Using a 2¾- or 3-inch cutter, cut out 4 biscuits, recutting scraps if necessary. Place the biscuits on an ungreased baking sheet at least 1½ inches apart. (The biscuits can be made 3 hours ahead and stored, loosely covered, in the refrigerator.)

Tapioca County

More than twenty thousand tons of tapioca arrive in Down East seaports every year to supply the only two tapioca processing plants in the United States. Both plants are located in Maine's Aroostook County.

Apparently tapioca has many more uses than in the traditional "fish eyes and glue" pudding of childhood. Tapioca starch seems to be in just about any processed food you can think of—including puddings, pie fillings, cake mixes, even Gummy Bears. Tapioca is made from the starch root of the cassava plant. It arrives in New England in bags, sent by ship, mostly from Thailand, Malaysia, and other equatorial countries. Before shipping, the root is processed into the tiny white pearls of starch.

---

4. Bake for 15 to 18 minutes, until the biscuits are golden brown. Cool slightly on a rack.

5. To serve, split the biscuits with a serrated knife. Place the bottoms on serving plates, spoon about half the rhubarb mixture over, and replace the tops. Spoon the remaining rhubarb over and top with dollops of whipped cream.

Hungarian Crêpes with Walnut Filling and Warm Chocolate Sauce

MAKES 8 SERVINGS

Crêpes, called *palacsinta* in Hungary, are one of the glories of Hungarian cuisine, and every Yankee-Hungarian I've ever known seems to be genetically programmed with a deft hand for making light, delicate, eggy pancakes. This luscious dessert, in which the crêpes encase a rich ground nut and raisin filling and are drizzled with a warm rummy chocolate sauce, is a fitting finale to any elegant dinner but is especially apt after Hungarian Beef Goulash (page 265) or Hungarian Chicken Paprika (page 308).

For the crêpes:

1 cup all-purpose flour
1 tablespoon sugar
¼ teaspoon salt
3 eggs
1 cup whole or lowfat milk
1 cup club soda or seltzer water

For the filling:

2 cups walnuts
¼ cup dark raisins
½ cup sugar
¼ cup light cream or half-and-half, plus more if necessary
2 tablespoons dark or light rum
1 teaspoon grated orange zest

For the sauce:

1 cup heavy cream
4 ounces semisweet baking chocolate, chopped, or chocolate chips
2 tablespoons sugar
2 tablespoons unsalted butter
2 tablespoons dark or light rum

Confectioners' sugar

1. To make the crêpes, whisk together the flour, sugar, and salt in a large bowl. Whisk the eggs with the milk in a smaller bowl. Make a well in the center of the flour mixture, pour in the egg mixture, and whisk gradually to incorporate the flour into the egg. Gently whisk in the club soda or seltzer. Cover with plastic wrap and set the batter aside for at least 1 hour or up to 3 hours at room temperature. Before cooking the crêpes, whisk the batter again until it is smooth. It should be about the thickness of heavy cream. Add a bit more water or milk if necessary.

2. Heat a 7- or 8-inch crêpe pan or cast-iron frying pan over medium-high heat. Brush lightly with butter. Ladle about 2 tablespoons of the batter into the pan, tilt to make an even layer, and cook until a few bubbles appear on the surface and the edges are dry, 1 to 2 minutes. Turn and cook the second side until the bottom is a speckled brown, about 30 seconds. Remove to a small wire rack or a plate. Repeat with the remaining batter, stacking the crêpes between sheets of plastic wrap or wax paper as you work. You should get about 24. (The crêpes can be made ahead and stored at cool room temperature for 4 hours, refrigerated for 2 days, or frozen. Reheat, covered, in a microwave before serving.)

3. To make the filling, process the walnuts in a food processor until they are finely ground. Add the raisins and pulse until they are chopped.

4. Combine the sugar and the cream in a medium-sized saucepan. Bring to a boil, stirring until the sugar is dissolved. Add the walnut mixture, along with the rum, and simmer, stirring, until the mixture is hot and bubbly, 2 to 3 minutes. Stir in the orange zest. (The filling can be made ahead and refrigerated for 2 days or frozen. Reheat in the microwave to soften slightly before using.)

5. To make the sauce, combine the cream, chocolate, and sugar in a medium-sized heavy saucepan and cook over medium-low heat, stirring almost constantly, until the chocolate is melted, 3 to 5 minutes. Add the butter, stirring until it is melted,

and stir in the rum. (The sauce can be made ahead and stored in the refrigerator for 2 to 3 days. Reheat in a microwave before serving.)

6. To assemble and serve, spoon about 1 tablespoon of the filling on one side of each crêpe and loosely roll the crêpe around the filling. Arrange on dessert plates, allowing 2 or 3 per serving, and spoon the warm chocolate sauce over the top. Finish with a light sprinkling of confectioners' sugar.

Freshman's Tears

The popular early twentieth-century custard pudding made with tiny pellets of pearl tapioca starch was nicknamed "Freshman's Tears" by the undergraduates of Mount Holyoke College, South Hadley, Massachusetts.

Portuguese-Style Caramel Flan

MAKES 8 SERVINGS

A smooth, soothing caramel custard is made in one form or another by all New England Hispanic-Americans, and you will find it on the menu of almost every restaurant in the region, simple or fancy, where South American, Spanish, or Portuguese food is served. As far as I'm concerned, caramel flan is a perfect finish to any hearty, spicy, intensely flavored main course, from whatever ethnic origin. This Portuguese-American version is intensely sweet, but has a pleasingly bitter edge from the almost-burned caramelized sauce. It is wonderful served in small portions by itself or with a bowl of fresh fruits such as strawberries and oranges, to spoon alongside.

½ cup plus ⅔ cup sugar
3 whole eggs
3 egg yolks
3 cups whole milk
2 teaspoons vanilla extract

1. Preheat the oven to 350 degrees. Have ready an ungreased 9-inch round or square 1½- to 2-quart glass baking dish.

2. Cook ½ cup of the sugar over medium heat in a heavy medium-sized saucepan, stirring almost constantly with a long-handled wooden spoon, until it is melted and turns first golden and then very dark brown, about 5 minutes. (Use extreme caution! Cooked sugar is very hot and can burn the skin if it spatters.) Immediately pour the hot caramel syrup into the baking dish and swirl the pan until it coats the bottom. The caramel will harden at this point and melt again later as the flan bakes.

3. Gently but thoroughly whisk together the eggs, egg yolks, and the remaining ⅔ cup sugar in a mixing bowl until smooth. Gradually whisk in the milk and vanilla. Pour the custard mixture into the prepared dish. Set the dish in a larger baking pan and fill the larger pan with hot water to come halfway up the sides of the baking dish.

4. Bake until a knife inserted two-thirds of the way to the center comes out clean, 35 to 45 minutes. The center should still be slightly soft, as the flan will finish cooking after it is removed from the oven. Cool in the water bath, then refrigerate for at least 1 hour or up to 8 hours.

5. Before serving, run a sharp knife around the edge of the flan to release it. Place a large rimmed serving plate over the baking dish and, using both hands, invert both dishes so that the flan and liquid sauce unmold onto the platter. Refrigerate again until serving time.

Note: You can also make this flan in 8 individual 8-ounce ramekins, in which case the baking time would be reduced by about 10 minutes.

Maple-Rum Cup Custards

MAKES 6 SERVINGS

A shot of dark rum enhances the delicate maple flavor of these luscious and smooth cup custards. You can make them in standard custard cups or ramekins or, as my clever recipe tester Debbie Callan does, in ovenproof coffee or cappuccino cups, which add a bit of whimsy to the presentation. This dessert is an exquisite ending to just about any meal at just about any time of year. In summer you might also pass a bowl of mixed ripe blueberries and raspberries at the table, and serve it after a main course of Grilled Lamb Chops with Rosemary-Mint Pesto (page 296). In fall or winter the custards are the perfect finish to something like Autumn McIntosh-Roasted Duckling (page 333), or Down East Bouillabaisse with Dried Cranberry Rouille (page 65).

4 whole eggs
2 egg yolks
½ cup packed dark brown sugar
¼ teaspoon salt
1 cup plus 2 tablespoons pure maple syrup
1½ cups light cream or half-and-half
2 tablespoons dark rum
Fresh-grated nutmeg
¾ cup heavy cream

1. Preheat the oven to 325 degrees. Lightly grease six 6-ounce custard cups or ramekins or ovenproof coffee cups.
2. Whisk together the eggs, egg yolks, brown sugar, and salt in a large bowl until smooth. Whisk in 1 cup of the maple syrup, the cream, and rum. If there are any lumps of brown sugar remaining, strain the mixture through a medium-mesh sieve into a large measuring cup or another bowl. Pour or ladle the custard mixture into the custard cups. Grate fresh nutmeg generously over the tops of the custards.
3. Place the cups in a large baking pan and pour boiling water into the larger pan to come about halfway up the sides of the ramekins. Bake until the surface of the custard appears shiny and the pudding still jiggles slightly when gently shaken, 25 to 35 minutes, depending on the shape of the ramekins.
4. Remove the ramekins from the water bath and refrigerate until completely chilled, at least 2 hours, or up to 24 hours.
5. Whip the cream until soft peaks form and beat in the remaining two tablespoons of maple syrup. Serve the custards topped with a dollop of maple cream.

The Nutmeg State

Connecticut's nickname is the Nutmeg State. It got the appellation not because nutmegs are grown there (they come from the tropics, hardly the climate for which Connecticut is famous) but because the early inhabitants of the state earned a reputation for making and selling fake wooden nutmegs—and for being able to spot the difference. The fact that canny Connecticutters went to all the trouble of carving out nutmeg forgeries demonstrates just how highly prized the hard little spice was in colonial days.

A Delicate Indian Pudding

MAKES 8 SERVINGS

The "Indian" in this recipe title refers not to the fact that Indians made it (they had no cows for milk or butter, nor domesticated chickens for eggs) but from the colonists' habit of calling anything made with corn "Indian." This pudding, English in origin, is a direct descendant of hasty pudding (later of Harvard club fame), which is simply a cornmeal mush made with milk and sweetened with molasses. This recipe for Indian pudding is based on the original standard, such as the famous version served at Durgin-Park restaurant in Boston continuously for about a century, but it is lighter—more custardy and delicate. It also calls for raisins (they're optional, of course), which are not especially traditional either, but I love their extra little burst of sweetness in the mouth.

¼ cup yellow cornmeal
½ teaspoon salt
3 cups whole milk
3 tablespoons unsalted butter
2 eggs
½ cup molasses
2 tablespoons packed light brown sugar
2 tablespoons sugar
¾ teaspoon ground ginger
½ teaspoon ground cinnamon
½ teaspoon grated nutmeg
⅓ cup raisins, optional

Lightly sweetened softly whipped cream or vanilla ice cream or frozen yogurt

1. Preheat the oven to 300 degrees. Lightly grease an 8-inch square glass baking dish.
2. Whisk together the cornmeal and salt in a medium saucepan. Whisk in 2½ cups of the milk until smooth and bring to a boil, whisking almost constantly. Reduce the heat to medium-low, and cook, stirring frequently, until the mixture is thick and creamy, about 10 minutes. Add the butter, whisking until it is melted, and remove from the heat.

3. Whisk the eggs with the molasses, sugars, ginger, cinnamon, and nutmeg in a large bowl. Gradually whisk the hot cornmeal mixture into the egg mixture. Stir in the raisins, if you are using them, and transfer the mixture to the prepared baking dish. Pour the remaining ½ cup of milk over the top of the pudding but do not mix it in.

4. Place the dish in a large roasting pan and pour enough boiling water into the larger pan to come halfway up the sides of the pudding dish. Bake for about 1½ hours, or until the pudding is just set.

5. Cool for at least 20 minutes or for up to 1 hour before serving warm or lukewarm, topped with whipped cream or ice cream. (The pudding can be made up to 8 hours ahead, covered loosely with plastic wrap, and stored at cool room temperature. Reheat the covered pudding in the microwave before serving.)

Coffee Syrup

Autocrat brand coffee syrup, an intensely sweet concentrate of pure coffee essence that is still made in Rhode Island, was a New England novelty early in the twentieth century. Some clever ice cream blender thought to stir a bit of the coffee essence into vanilla ice cream, which turned the frozen confection a pale buff color and gave it a distinctive, pleasantly bitter flavor edge. In fact, it was not until after the middle of the century that coffee ice cream was much known outside New England. Another common use was adding a teaspoon of the sweet coffee syrup to a glass of cold milk. When Susan Capone Maloney, who grew up in Fall River, Massachusetts, went away to college in Burlington, Vermont, she was astonished to find that she couldn't get a good glass of coffee milk anywhere in the Green Mountain State!

Pioneer Valley Blueberry Bread and Butter Pudding

MAKES 6 SERVINGS

The Pioneer Valley in Massachusetts is a section of the Connecticut River valley that stretches from Greenfield in the north to Northampton in the south, and it encompasses not only the bustling, sophisticated college hub that is Northampton, but also some pretty, peaceful villages and towns in more rural Franklin and Hampshire counties. One summer my good friend Susan Young drove miles and miles up into the steep hills near the town of Heath, above Deerfield, and picked quarts and quarts of blueberries at a pick-your-own farm. She was the only person there, and the berries were at their peak, the bushes laden with them, and she just couldn't stop. What would she do with them all? This summer pudding, based on a recipe in the 1984 revision of *The Fannie Farmer Cookbook*, was one of the desserts Susan made, and it instantly became a favorite of everyone who was lucky enough to eat it, including me. It's like a classic English summer berry pudding but more homespun, because you don't bother to try to unmold it.

8 or 9 slices good-quality thin-sliced white bread, such as Pepperidge
   Farm
3 to 4 tablespoons unsalted butter, softened
¼ teaspoon ground cinnamon
5 cups blueberries
½ to ¾ cup sugar
2 teaspoons fresh lemon juice

Vanilla ice cream or lightly sweetened softly whipped cream

1. Cut the crusts off the bread. Lightly butter one side of each slice and sprinkle the butter with cinnamon. Use 6 or 7 slices of bread to line a deep 6- to 8-cup bowl, with the buttered sides facing the center. If there are gaps, cut bread to make rough patches. It doesn't have to be a seamless lining.

2. Combine the blueberries, ½ cup of the sugar, and 3 tablespoons of water in a medium-large saucepan. Bring to a boil, stirring. Reduce the heat to medium and simmer, uncovered, stirring frequently, until the blueberries release their juice and then the sauce begins to thicken slightly, about 10 minutes. Stir in the lemon juice. Taste the blueberry mixture for sweetness and stir in some or all of the remaining sugar if the sauce is not sweet enough.

3. Pour about half the hot blueberry mixture into the bread-lined bowl. Place the remaining buttered bread slices over the blueberries and pour the rest of the blueberries over the bread. Cover with a sheet of plastic wrap; place a small plate on the wrap and place a can on the plate as a weight so that all the bread is submerged in the fruit syrup. Set aside at room temperature for 1 to 3 hours or chill for up to 8 hours.

4. If there is a great deal of excess accumulated juice, pour it off. (This is the cook's bonus. Drink now or save for later.) To serve, spoon the pudding into bowls and top with scoops of ice cream if warm or with whipped cream if chilled.

Blueberry Tips

• Blueberries are 85 percent water, and most of the flavor is in the skin. So bigger is not necessarily better.

• Ice cold water is best for washing berries. Always wash blueberries gently, right before using. If washed before they are refrigerated, the berries end up mushy.

• Store blueberries in their original container in the refrigerator. When stored this way, they are best eaten within a week.

• Check the sides and bottoms of containers for stains. Juice stains are an indication of overripeness, which can lead to mold.

• To freeze raw blueberries, spread them out on a baking sheet and freeze. Then scrape the frozen berries into resealable freezer bags, and seal well.

• Blueberries cooked with some sugar to a thick saucelike consistency until they are soft also freeze well.

Chocolate Bread and Butter Pudding

MAKES 8 SERVINGS

Bread and butter pudding, as it is almost always called in New England (as opposed to simply "bread pudding" as it is known farther south), was originally devised as a way to use up slightly stale leftover bread and concoct a tasty, nutritious egg and milk dessert in the process. Thrifty Yankees took this concept to their collective bosom and began to flavor the pudding with all kinds of intriguing ingredients—maple, cranberries, blueberries—and, of course, once Mr. Baker began selling the exotic comestible in Boston in the nineteenth century, chocolate. This is a very impressive dessert—tender, rich, chocolate custard under the crusty, lightly glazed bread topping. Best served warm or lukewarm, it can be made a couple of hours ahead and presented as a grand finale to an important dinner party. An optional rum custard sauce adds a decadent, lily-gilding finish.

For the sauce:

1½ cups light cream or half-and-half
3 egg yolks
¼ cup sugar
⅛ teaspoon salt
3 tablespoons dark rum

For the pudding:

8 ounces French bread (1 small loaf), preferably day-old
1 tablespoon unsalted butter, softened
6 ounces semisweet baking chocolate, coarsely chopped, or semisweet
    chocolate chips
2 cups heavy cream
1 cup whole milk
4 eggs
¾ cup sugar
⅛ teaspoon salt
2 teaspoons vanilla extract

1. If you are planning to serve the pudding with the rum custard sauce, make the sauce first. Heat the cream in a medium-sized saucepan over medium heat until small bubbles form around the edges.

2. Whisk the egg yolks with the sugar and salt in a medium-sized bowl until blended. Slowly whisk the hot cream into the yolk mixture to temper the eggs; then return the mixture to the saucepan. Cook over medium-low heat, stirring almost constantly, until the custard thickens enough to coat the back of a spoon, about 6 minutes. Transfer to a large bowl, add the rum, and cool for about 15 minutes, stirring occasionally to release steam. Cover and refrigerate for at least 2 hours, until chilled.

Dr. Baker's Cure-All

In 1765 a young Irishman named John Hannon persuaded Dr. James Baker of Dorchester, Massachusetts, to finance the first chocolate mill in America. A few years later, after Mr. Hannon disappeared at sea on a voyage to the West Indies to buy cocoa beans, Dr. Baker purchased the mill from Hannon's widow, founding the company that we know today as Baker's Chocolate. At that time, the product was sold only in liquid form, and promoted mainly as a restorative.

(The sauce can be made 2 days ahead.)

3. To make the pudding, cut the bread into ½-inch-thick slices and remove the crusts. Spread the butter generously over the bottom and sides of a 2- to 2½-quart glass baking dish that is at least 2 inches deep. Arrange the bread in overlapping rows in the bottom of the dish.

4. Combine the chocolate with 1 cup of the cream in a medium-sized, heavy saucepan. Cook over medium heat, stirring frequently, until the chocolate is melted and the mixture is smooth. Stir in the remaining 1 cup of cream and the milk and heat, stirring, until steam rises, about 3 minutes. Do not boil.

5. Whisk the eggs with the sugar and the salt in a large bowl until blended. Slowly whisk in the hot chocolate mixture. Stir in the vanilla. Pour the chocolate custard evenly over the bread in the baking dish. Place a large sheet of plastic wrap on the surface of the chocolate mixture and place another, slightly smaller baking dish on the plastic wrap. Put a couple of small cans or similar objects in the empty baking dish as weights to immerse the bread completely in the milk mixture. Refrigerate for at least 2 hours and for as long as overnight.

6. Preheat the oven to 325 degrees.

7. Remove the empty dish, weights, and plastic wrap from the pudding and cover the dish with foil. Place the pudding dish in a large roasting pan and fill the larger pan with boiling water to come about halfway up the sides of the pudding dish. Bake for 20 minutes. Remove the foil and continue to bake for 35 to 40 minutes more, or until the top is crusty and lightly glazed and a knife inserted two-thirds of the way to the center comes out clean.

8. Cool for at least 30 minutes before serving warm or for up to 2 hours to serve lukewarm. (The pudding can be refrigerated overnight. To reheat, cut into squares, arrange on a platter, and microwave until warm.)

9. To serve with the custard sauce, spoon some of the sauce out on each serving plate. Cut the pudding into squares, and place in the pool of sauce.

Finest Kind
Grapenut Pudding

MAKES 6 SERVINGS

This pudding, which is simply a creamy vanilla-scented baked custard with streaks of crunchy Grape-Nuts cereal running through it, has been a perennially popular, beloved Yankee dessert since the 1930s. Recipes for this comforting homespun pudding appear in many New England community cookbooks, and you can almost use it as a barometer for rating family-run dining establishments: if Grapenut Pudding is on the menu, you can probably trust the place to serve honest home-style food. Finest Kind Dining in Deer Isle, on coastal Maine, was just such an enduring, reliable establishment. This is my adaptation of the recipe for Grapenut pudding that they kindly shared with me. (The discrepancy between the brand name of the Post cereal and the spelling of the dessert is a mystery, but all cookbooks seem to call it Grapenut, rather than Grape-Nuts Pudding.)

> 4 cups whole or lowfat milk
> ¾ cup Grape-Nuts cereal
> 4 eggs
> ½ cup sugar
> ⅛ teaspoon salt
> 2 teaspoons vanilla extract
> About ⅛ teaspoon grated nutmeg

"Finest Kind" Explained

Peter Perez, owner of a restaurant called Finest Kind Dining, on Deer Isle, in midcoast Maine, explains how he chose the name of this family-run establishment. "My brother-in-law suggested it. We have a local saying around here—fishermen use it, everybody uses it. You ask how someone is, they say 'finest kind.' You ask how their day was, they say 'finest kind.' You ask how their boat-building project is going, they say 'finest kind.' Everybody likes the name of this place because it has a good meaning for us around here."

---

1. Preheat the oven to 350 degrees. Lightly grease a shallow 2-quart glass baking dish.
2. Heat the milk in a medium-sized saucepan over medium heat until bubbles form around the edges and steam rises, about 5 minutes. Remove from the heat, stir in the Grape-Nuts, and set aside for about 5 minutes.
3. Whisk the eggs with the sugar, salt, and vanilla in a large bowl until blended. Gradually whisk the milk and Grape-Nuts mixture into the egg mixture. Pour into the prepared baking dish and sprinkle the top generously with nutmeg.
4. Place the prepared dish in a larger baking pan and fill the larger pan with boiling water to come about halfway up the sides of the pudding dish. Bake for 50 to 60 minutes, or until a knife inserted about two-thirds of the way to the center comes out clean. The center should still be somewhat soft.
5. Cool on a wire rack for at least 30 minutes. Serve the pudding warm or lukewarm, or refrigerate and serve chilled.

> ### Louisa's "Slump"
>
> Louisa May Alcott, nineteenth-century author of *Little Women, Little Men,* and *An Old-Fashioned Thanksgiving,* loved a certain traditional apple dessert so much (or perhaps just loved the sound of the word) that she nicknamed her Concord, Massachusetts, home "Apple Slump." The official, serious name for the house was Orchard House. (A slump is an old-fashioned cobbler-like fruit dessert, probably so called because its somewhat misshapen crust "slumps" on the plate.)

Hester's Sour Lemon Pudding Cake

MAKES 4 TO 6 SERVINGS

This lemon pudding cake is one of my mother's wonderful recipes. It typifies the simple virtues of home cooking and is the kind of dessert that trained restaurant pastry chefs rarely match. In fact, I don't believe I've ever seen a pudding cake on a restaurant menu. The cake that rises to the surface is light, the sauce that forms underneath is smooth and slightly rich, and the flavor is an exquisitely pleasing balancing act that teeters on the edge of sour and sweet. It's a perfect finish to a seafood meal such as Ritzy Stuffed Jumbo Shrimp (page 394), a meat main course such as Yankee Pot Roast with a Fresh Face (page 264), or, for that matter, just about any supper you can think of.

2 tablespoons unsalted butter, softened
⅔ cup sugar
3 egg yolks
3 tablespoons all-purpose flour
1 tablespoon grated lemon zest
¼ cup fresh lemon juice
1 cup whole or lowfat milk
4 egg whites
⅛ teaspoon salt

1. Preheat the oven to 325 degrees. Lightly grease a shallow 1½- to 2-quart baking dish.
2. Combine the butter and sugar in a medium-sized mixing bowl. Use an electric mixer or a wooden spoon to mix until crumbly. Add the egg yolks and flour and beat until fairly smooth. Beat in the lemon zest and juice and then whisk in the milk. Set aside.
3. Beat the egg whites with the salt in a separate bowl until firm but not dry peaks form. Pour the lemon mixture over the beaten whites and use a large whisk to stir gently just until no large lumps of egg white remain. (The lemon base is so light that it is difficult to fold the two mixtures together in the traditional manner.)
4. Slowly pour the batter into the prepared dish. Set the dish in a larger baking pan and add boiling water to the larger pan to come halfway up the sides of the pudding dish. Bake 25 to 30 minutes, until the top is lightly colored and springs back when lightly touched.
5. Cool the pudding cake in the water bath for 10 minutes. Serve the dessert warm, at room temperature, or chilled.

Pudding Glossary

The naming of New England's classic desserts has occasionally been poetic but is more often based on plain, straightforward description of a unique look, taste, or cooking technique.

Brown Betty—Layers of buttered breadcrumbs, fruit, and spices, baked until tender. The "brown" in the name is obvious; the "betty" more obscure. (Sometimes known as a "crunch.")

Buckle—A coffeecake-like dessert with berries in the batter and a crumbly topping. The crust was said to look "buckled" as it baked.

Cobbler—A deep-dish fruit dessert topped with a thick layer of biscuit dough or with individual pieces ("cobbles") of dough.

Crisp—Fruit covered with a rich and crusty crumb topping. The topping can be made with flour and/or cookie crumbs or cereal blended with butter, sugar, and sometimes nuts. (Sometimes called a "crumble.")

Deacon Porter's Hat—A spiced suet pudding steamed in a tall cylindrical mold. In 1837, at Mount Holyoke College the pudding was named to honor a favorite deacon, and the shape of his stovepipe hat. The dessert is still served at the college on Founder's Day.

Fool—A mousselike dessert made by swirling together pureed fruit and whipped cream. The name is of English origin.

Grunt or Slump—Similar to a cobbler, but the fruit is usually simmered on top of the stove instead of baked. The biscuit dough is dropped on top and steamed to a dumplinglike consistency. The name derives from the gruntlike sound the fruit makes as it stews or the way it "slumps" on the plate when served. (Sometimes called a "flummery.")

Junket Pudding—A smooth, delicately flavored, custardlike dessert thickened with rennin, a coagulating enzyme obtained from a calf's stomach.

Pandowdy—A deep dish of fruit baked with a pastry topping. Sometimes the crust is cut into pieces halfway through the cooking time and pressed back into the fruit to absorb the juices. The name derives from the homely appearance of the dessert or from the practice of "dowdying," or breaking up the crust before serving it.

Plum Pudding—A steamed pudding made with raisins and other dried fruits but not with plums. A traditional Anglo-Yankee Christmas dessert, served with hard sauce (1 part butter with 1 part confectioners' sugar, and a shot of rum added).

Sailor's Duff—A spiced gingerbread-like pudding steamed in a bag and served to men on Sunday aboard Yankee sailing vessels. "Duff" derives from the old pronunciation for "dough."

Shortcake—Rich (or "short") biscuits, individual or large, sliced in half and filled with sweetened fruit and whipped cream.

Tapioca Pudding—A milk-based pudding thickened with tapioca, a pearl-like starch made from the cassava root.

Tipsy Parson—Similar to English trifle. Sponge cake is moistened with sherry and topped with a custard sauce.

Lucetta Peabody's
Baked Fudge Pudding Cake

MAKES 8 SERVINGS

A collection of handwritten recipes from Lucetta Peabody, a mid-twentieth-century Bostonian, reveals the soul of a truly inspired cook. I wish had known her—and had been able to dine at her table. Lucetta's love of good food radiates from the fading pages of her notebook. Her fudge pudding cake recipe, which I have closely adapted here, has notes such as "tried ground chocolate and cocoa powder—cocoa better, and Reta used, too" and "seems wrong to pour boiling water over batter, but works!" and "batter rises through topping and then rich chocolate sauce forms underneath." All true. Trust Lucetta. This really is delicious.

For the batter:

1 cup all-purpose flour
¾ cup sugar
3 tablespoons unsweetened cocoa powder
2 teaspoons baking powder
¼ teaspoon salt
⅛ teaspoon ground cinnamon
1 teaspoon instant coffee powder
¾ cup chopped walnuts
½ cup milk
4 tablespoons unsalted butter, melted
2 teaspoons vanilla extract

For the topping:

½ cup packed light or dark brown sugar
3 tablespoons unsweetened cocoa powder
1¾ cups hot water

Lightly sweetened whipped cream

1. Preheat the oven to 350 degrees.

2. Whisk together the flour, sugar, cocoa, baking powder, salt, cinnamon, and coffee powder in a large bowl until free of lumps. Stir in the nuts.

3. Stir together the milk, melted butter, and vanilla in a small bowl. Add the milk mixture to the flour mixture and stir just until combined. The batter will be quite stiff. Spread in the bottom of an ungreased 8- or 9-inch square glass baking dish.

4. To make the topping, combine the brown sugar and cocoa powder in a small bowl, mixing with your fingertips or a whisk to break up any large lumps of sugar. Sprinkle evenly over the batter in the baking dish. Pour the hot water evenly over the topping.

5. Bake for 35 to 40 minutes, until the filling is bubbly around the edges and the top is partially set and is a glazed, crusty brown.

6. Cool on a wire rack for at least 30 minutes or up to 4 hours. The sauce thickens considerably as the pudding cools. Serve warm or at room temperature, topped with whipped cream.

Gray's Ice Cream

At Gray's Ice Cream stand in Tiverton, Rhode Island, Marilyn Dennis, proprietor, and a battalion of teenage summer employees man eight take-out windows scooping out as much as a thousand gallons of ice cream a day during the high season. The parking lot is jammed with people slurping, digging, and licking ice cream, and eyeing the gentle Holstein cows in the field next door, who eye them back. Celebrities are often spotted waiting in line along with everyone else at the take-out window. It doesn't faze Marilyn or impress her all that much. She trains her staff to treat everyone equally and to be nice to everyone. Anyway, Marilyn is usually too busy making ice cream out in the back to notice. "I could make ice cream all day and all night," she says. "It's my life."

Caramelized Pears with Honeyed Ice Cream

MAKES 4 SERVINGS

Pears are not a dominant crop in New England, but many an old homestead has a pear tree in the yard, and the pear crop was often cooked and put up as spiced pears, pear butter, or pear chutney to be enjoyed during the dark winter months. Bartletts are one of the more common pear varieties in the region, but just about any type will work fine in this deliciously simple compote, which is spooned over honey-vanilla ice cream.

1 pint vanilla ice cream (see Note)
¼ cup honey, preferably a dark herb honey such as thyme
3 medium-large ripe but firm pears
2 teaspoons fresh lemon juice
3 tablespoons unsalted butter
Pinch of salt
1 to 2 tablespoons light brown sugar
¼ teaspoon ground allspice
1 tablespoon pear or apple brandy or cognac

Ben & Jerry's Ice Cream Factory

Ben Cohen and Jerry Greenfield, two sixties kind of guys, founded an ice cream company in the 1970s that has a reputation for political activism, community service, and punny names for their deliciously super-rich ice cream. The Waterbury, Vermont plant lays claim to being the number one tourist attraction in the Green Mountain state, showing upwards of 300,000 people a year through its large, state-of-the-art facility. You get to watch a slide show complete with corny pictures of Ben and Jerry, corny pictures of cows, with a soundtrack of corny jokes. A trip through the plant reveals a team of men and women in white hats industriously putting the Holstein milk and cream through its paces in huge stainless steel vats and centrifuges, and culminates with a tasting of the "scoop du jour," which might be Heath Bar Crunch (my personal favorite), Totally Nuts, Cherry Garcia, Chunky Monkey, Chocolate Chip Cookie Dough, or, for caffeine lovers, Coffee, Coffee, BuzzBuzzBuzz.

1. Remove the ice cream from the freezer and leave it at room temperature for about 30 minutes to soften slightly. Measure the honey into a glass measuring cup, and set the cup in a basin of hot water, stirring until it is somewhat liquefied but not hot. (Or microwave on low for a few seconds until it is somewhat liquefied.) Scrape the ice cream into a bowl, stir in the honey, and repack into the ice cream carton. Return the carton to the freezer. (This can be done a day ahead.)
2. Core and peel the pears, cut into thin slices, and toss with the lemon juice.
3. Melt the butter in a large skillet over medium-high heat. Add the pears, sprinkle with the salt, and sauté, stirring frequently, until they soften and begin to caramelize around the edges, about 5 minutes. Sprinkle with the brown sugar (use the larger amount if the pears are underripe) and the allspice, and continue to cook, stirring frequently, until the fruit is tender, about 3 minutes. Remove the pan from the heat, add the brandy, and return to the burner to simmer for 1 to 2 minutes to cook off most of the alcohol. (The pears can be cooked a couple of hours ahead and reheated in a microwave.)
4. Scoop the honey ice cream into goblets, spoon the pears over, and serve.

Note: If you find a brand of ready-made honey-vanilla ice cream, use it and skip Step 1.

The Good Humor Man

Like Proust's madeleine, a certain timbre of jingling bell instantly evokes for me a vivid memory of the imminent arrival of the Good Humor truck captained by Steve, the quintessential Good Humor man. Every summer afternoon, promptly at five o'clock, the faint, faraway jingle would sound in our Connecticut community, the peal of the bell gradually growing more crystalline and distinct, 'til the wondrous gleaming-white motorized chariot hove into sight. Out hopped Steve, diminutive and portly, clad in spotless white suit and hat, girded about the waist with a changemaker, primed to dispense the Popsicles (5 cents), Creamsicles (7 cents), and original Good Humor Bars, chocolate-covered vanilla ice cream on a stick (10 cents), to the horde of ravenous, sunburned, barefoot kids clustered around this mid-twentieth-century Pied Piper. If Steve wished to win our affection and loyalty, his late-afternoon timing was impeccable. "Why not *after* supper?" the mothers all wailed as they fished nickels and pennies from their purses. But for us children, it seemed the rightful, most natural order of events to eat dessert first.

❈ ❈ ❈ ❈ ❈ ❈ ❈ ❈ ❈

Concord Grape Sorbet

MAKES 4 TO 6 SERVINGS

According to food chronicler John Mariani, Concord grapes were first propagated from native North American seedling stock in Concord, Massachusetts, by a Mr. Ephraim Bull in 1849. His new grape hybrid eventually became popular for winemaking in New York State, but in New England lots of the vines have reverted to their wild state, producing small, dark bluish-purple fruit with a deliciously intense untamed, almost feral flavor. A taste memory for Concord grapes has been captured by many a New England child by engaging in the annual ritual of chewing on the seedy fruit, sucking out all the sweet flavor that lies next to the skins, and then having spitting contests with the mouthful of seeds. Commercially grown Concord grapes are harder to find these days, appearing only sporadically in specialty markets, so if you have access to an old arbor of the vines, you are among the fortunate. This sorbet, which turns a gorgeous deep rose color when frozen, is a marvelous way of capturing the brilliant Concord flavor.

½ cup sugar
2 to 3 pounds ripe Concord grapes
1 tablespoon fresh lemon juice

1. Combine the sugar and ½ cup water in a small saucepan. Bring to a boil, stirring to dissolve the sugar, and remove the sugar syrup from the heat.

2. Wash the grapes, remove them from the stems, and put them through a food mill or press them through a medium-mesh strainer with a wooden spoon or pestle. Push hard to release the flavorful deep purple pigmentation on the insides of the skins. You should have about 2 cups of juice. Transfer the juice to a bowl. Add half the sugar syrup, taste for sweetness, and continue adding syrup until the juice is slightly sweeter than you want the finished sorbet to be. (The freezing process makes it taste less sweet.) Stir in the lemon juice. Refrigerate the mixture until well chilled.

3. Pour the grape juice mixture into an ice cream machine—any type—and process according to the manufacturer's instructions. Transfer the sorbet to the freezer and freeze until firm, at least 2 hours.

4. Scoop into stemmed glasses such as martini or champagne glasses to serve.

Rum-Walnut Butterscotch Sundaes

MAKES 6 SERVINGS

This homemade version of warm butterscotch sauce, spiked with dark rum and laden with toasted walnuts, is so much better than any similar ice cream topping you can buy in a jar that, once you taste it, you'll never go back. It is amazingly quick and simple to make too. These sundaes could crown just about any autumn or winter meal but seem to me especially suitable after a sandwich supper featuring a Shaker Grilled Pork Tenderloin Sandwich (page 243) or A Perfect Scallop Roll (page 233).

¾ cup broken walnuts
1 cup packed light brown sugar
½ cup heavy cream
3 tablespoons unsalted butter
3 tablespoons light corn syrup
3 tablespoons dark rum
1 tablespoon fresh lemon juice

1 quart good-quality vanilla ice cream

1. Toast the walnuts in a small, dry skillet over medium heat until fragrant and one shade darker, about 5 minutes.
2. Combine the brown sugar, cream, butter, and corn syrup in a medium-large heavy saucepan. Slowly bring to a boil over high heat, stirring constantly until the sugar and butter are melted. Reduce the heat to medium-low and let the mixture bubble and simmer, uncovered, without stirring, for 5 minutes.
3. Remove the pan from the heat, let the sauce cool for 5 minutes, and then add the rum and lemon juice. Stir in the toasted walnuts. (The sauce can be made several days ahead and stored in the refrigerator. Reheat over low heat in a saucepan or in a microwave on low power.)
4. To serve, scoop the ice cream into goblets or dessert bowls and top with the warm sauce.

Five Hundred Gallons of Rum

Rum was being produced in New England as early as 1657. Some of the spirit was sold domestically, but by 1700 vast quantities were being shipped to Europe to be sold or traded for slaves to work the American plantations, which in turn produced the molasses to make more rum—the infamous Triangle Trade. Rum became the predominant alcohol of Yankee working people and sailors, and in 1775 Americans were drinking four gallons of rum per person per year. When Britain passed the Molasses and Sugar Acts, imposing high tariffs on the colonists, and crippling New England rum distilleries, widespread dissent resulted, hastening the American Revolution.

Cranberry-Cointreau Ice Cream Sundaes

MAKES 1¾ CUPS OF SAUCE, ABOUT 6 SERVINGS

This warm orange-liqueur-spiked cranberry dessert sauce offers a brilliant color, texture, temperature, and flavor contrast to the smooth richness of good vanilla ice cream. It is also wonderfully versatile. The sauce takes mere minutes to make and stores well for several days, so it's ideal to have on hand for a quickly assembled dessert, especially around holiday time. Small jars of the sauce also make excellent hostess gifts.

> 1 12-ounce bag fresh cranberries
> 1 cup sugar
> 1 cup orange juice
> 2 tablespoons unsalted butter, cut in pieces
> 2 teaspoons grated orange zest
> ⅓ cup Cointreau or other orange-flavored liqueur
>
> 1 quart vanilla ice cream

1. Combine the cranberries, sugar, and orange juice in a medium-large, nonaluminum saucepan. Bring to a boil over high heat, stirring until the sugar is dissolved. Reduce the heat to medium-low and cook, stirring frequently, until most of the berries pop and the sauce is lightly thickened, 8 to 10 minutes.

Cranberry Etymology

Native North Americans called the tart, bright red berries "sassamanesh" and enjoyed cranberries both raw and sweetened with maple sugar, often adding them to their pemmican. The first English settlers may have called them "fenberries," after a fruit they knew at home. It was probably the Dutch who created the modern name. They called them "kranbeere," or crane berries, because the stamen of the fruit resembles a crane's beak. Others are said to have called them "bounce berries" because of their bouncy quality. Some Cape Codders still call cranberries "bog berries."

2. Remove from the heat and add the butter, stirring until it is melted. Stir in the orange zest and liqueur. (The sauce can be made ahead and stored for several days in the refrigerator. Reheat over low heat in a saucepan or in a microwave.)

3. To serve, scoop the ice cream into pretty dessert dishes and top with the warm sauce.

CAKES AND COOKIES

Nineteenth-century New England women who considered themselves good housekeepers regularly made several cakes a week—all laboriously beaten by hand, in a big ceramic bowl, with a wooden spoon. "A cake," instructs the 1912 edition of Fannie Farmer's *The Boston Cooking-School Cook Book*, "can be made fine-grained only by long beating."

How lucky for us that those Yankee housewives were so industrious, for they have bequeathed us a rich cake legacy, one that includes the likes of the tried-and-true Hot Milk Sponge Cake (page 534), which can be turned into The Best Boston Cream Pie (page 535) or the lovely Old-Fashioned Jelly Roll (page 556). Chocolate came to Boston in the late 1700s, and New England bakers soon grew addicted to using the exotic stuff in such creations as Devil's Food Cupcakes with Angel Icing (page 555) or a towering deeply chocolate Wellesley Fudge Layer Cake with Mocha Frosting (page 547).

Many scrumptious old-fashioned New England spice cookies are enduring favorites, including gingersnap-like Melanie's Molasses Crinkle Cookies (page 569), chewy Spiced Harwich Hermits (page 559), which are a sort of forerunner of bar cookies, and the unusually modern Shaker Giant Rosemary-Ginger Cookies (page 574).

But it's The Justly Famous Toll House Cookie (page 576) that garners most of the press. And with pretty good reason, too. Not only is this superb chocolate-chip-studded brown sugar beauty, which was invented at an inn in the small town of Whitman, Massachusetts, the most popular cookie in America, but now its fame is beginning to span the globe.

Hot Milk Sponge Cake

MAKES 2 9-INCH LAYERS, OR 1 JELLY ROLL SHEET

This light, airy, old-fashioned sponge cake is delicious just as is, sprinkled with confectioners' sugar, and it also makes a wonderful dessert served with fresh ripe summer berries or sliced peaches and a bowl of lightly sweetened whipped cream. This sponge cake is the base recipe for The Best Boston Cream Pie (page 535) and Old-Fashioned Jelly Roll (page 556).

> 1 cup sifted cake flour
> 1 teaspoon baking powder
> ¼ teaspoon salt
> ¼ cup whole or lowfat milk
> 2 tablespoons unsalted butter
> 1 teaspoon vanilla extract
> 5 eggs
> 1 cup sugar

1. Preheat the oven to 350 degrees. Grease the bottom and sides of 2 9-inch layer cake pans and line the bottoms with baking parchment or waxed paper.

2. Sift or whisk together the flour, baking powder, and salt in a small bowl.

3. Heat the milk and butter in a small saucepan over low heat until the butter is melted and the milk is steaming. Remove from the heat and add the vanilla.

4. Using an electric mixer, beat the eggs with the sugar in a small bowl until they are light colored and about tripled in volume, 3 to 5 minutes. Reheat the milk mixture if necessary, until it is steaming. On medium speed, slowly beat the hot milk mixture into the egg mixture.

5. Sift or slowly sprinkle the flour mixture over the egg mixture and fold it in gently with a large spatula. Divide the batter between the prepared pans.

6. Bake until the tops are light golden brown and spring back slightly when touched, about 15 minutes.

7. Cool the cakes in the pans for 10 minutes. Run a knife around the edges and invert the layers onto a wire rack. Cool completely. Use immediately or wrap airtight and store at cool room temperature for 1 day, refrigerate for 2 days, or freeze.

Boston Cream "Pie"

When is a pie not a pie? When it's a Boston cream "pie," which is actually a cake—sponge cake, to be exact, split, filled with vanilla custard, and topped with a shiny fudge glaze. No one's absolutely positive about why this dessert is called a pie, but the best guess of food historians is that pie tins were more common than cake pans when the dessert was invented back in the mid-nineteenth century and the first versions might have been baked in pie tins.

The famous layered confection dates back to 1855, when Harvey Parker, founder of Boston's Parker House, hired a chef from France for the opening of his famous hotel. According to an expert on the early days of the Parker House, the chef, a Mr. Sanzian, who was paid the then-extraordinarily high salary of $5,000 a year, topped a custard cream-filled cake with chocolate frosting.

The Parker House still bakes at least twenty-five Boston cream pies every day. "Technically, this is a cake," admits hotel pastry chef Joseph Ribas. "But I call it a pie. This is our tradition, and I'm not going to be the one to change it."

The Best Boston Cream Pie

MAKES 8 TO 10 SERVINGS

This, of course, is not a pie at all, but a cake. A glorious, custard-filled, chocolate-glazed sponge cake. The misnomer may have come about because the original cake was baked in more readily available pie tins. This is a fairly classic version of the recipe, except that I've added a shot of rum to the custard (since Bostonians were big rum importers and drinkers, a historically accurate touch), and made the glaze with bittersweet chocolate for a wonderfully dark shiny finish.

For the pastry cream:

1¼ cups whole or 2 percent milk
4 egg yolks
½ cup sugar
3 tablespoons cornstarch
Pinch of salt
1½ tablespoons unsalted butter
1 tablespoon light or dark rum
1 teaspoon vanilla extract

For the glaze:

½ cup heavy cream
2 tablespoons light corn syrup
3 ounces bittersweet or semisweet chocolate, chopped

For the cake:

Hot Milk Sponge Cake (page 534) baked in 2 9-inch layers

1. To make the pastry cream, heat 1 cup of the milk over in a heavy, medium-sized saucepan over medium heat until bubbles form around the edges. Whisk the remaining ¼ cup of milk with the egg yolks, sugar, cornstarch, and salt in a medium-sized bowl until pale and light, about 2 minutes. Gradually whisk about half of the hot milk into the egg mixture and then return the mixture to the saucepan. Place over medium heat and cook, whisking almost constantly, until the mixture thickens to a puddinglike consistency and comes to a boil, 2 to 3 minutes. Remove from the heat and add the butter, rum, and vanilla, whisking until the butter is melted. Transfer to a bowl, cool to room temperature, and place a sheet of plastic wrap directly on the surface of the pastry cream to prevent a skin from forming. Refrigerate for at least 2 hours, until cold and firm. (The custard can be made a day ahead.)

2. To make the glaze, heat the cream and corn syrup in a small saucepan over medium heat until the mixture comes to a simmer. Remove from the heat, add the chopped chocolate, and set aside, covered, for about 5 minutes until the chocolate is melted. Stir until smooth. If any unmelted chocolate remains, set the pan over low heat and stir constantly until the glaze is completely smooth. Transfer to a bowl and cool until the glaze is lukewarm and a thick but pourable consistency. (The glaze can be made ahead and refrigerated. Reheat for a few seconds in the microwave and whisk until pourable.)

3. To assemble, if the cake layers are domed, slice off the tops so they are even. (This will also allow better absorption of the pastry cream.) Place a layer on a cake plate or stand. Insert strips of wax paper under the cake to catch drips. Spread the pastry cream thickly and evenly over the cake, coming almost to the edges. Place the second layer on top, cut side down.

4. Pour the glaze over the cake, spread it to the edges with a long metal spatula, and let any excess flow down the sides in a natural dripping pattern. Set aside at cool room temperature or in the refrigerator until the glaze sets completely, about 1 hour. (The cake can be refrigerated for up to 8 hours. Return to room temperature before serving.)

5. Remove wax paper strips, cut into wedges to serve.

Political Dessert Wars

In 1995 a Norton, Massachusetts, teacher took his high school social studies class through a hands-on lesson in the political process. His idea was to come up with a bill and see if the Norton students could get it passed in the state legislature—something like a noncontroversial state symbol, such as a flower, a bird, or . . . a dessert. (Shouldn't he have known that any food-obsessed legislators wouldn't consider a dessert noncontroversial?)

Boston cream pie seemed like a pretty obvious choice to most of the students, for historical as well as culinary reasons, and the bill was introduced. But they hadn't reckoned with a zealous chocolate chip cookie advocate from the Whitman, Massachusetts, Historical Society, where the original Toll House cookie was invented. At a special hearing, the students countered with Boston cream arguments, (along with a pie baked by the Parker House Hotel,

which may have swung some undecideds). The cookie, they declared, was not a full-fledged dessert. The pie, on the other hand, "has something for everyone—chocolate, vanilla, cake, *and* pudding."

More than a year after they introduced the bill, and after beating off a last-ditch challenge from partisans for the more indigenous Indian pudding, the Norton students carried the motion, and Boston cream pie was declared the official dessert of the Commonwealth of Massachusetts. "Politics at its finest," declared their teacher at the bill-signing ceremony, which included a 47-pound Boston cream pie.

P.S. The chocolate chip advocates had their own victory a couple of years later, when the then-governor signed a proclamation declaring the Toll House the official state *cookie* (see page 576).

Cranberry-Walnut Pound Cake

MAKES 12 TO 16 SERVINGS

Black walnuts are a native New England nut with an extremely hard shell. The trees were abundant in the region in early colonial days, and their intensely flavored, slightly bitter nutmeats were much prized for baking—once they were pried open, that is. Black walnuts can still be found here and there around New England, and some specialty food stores carry them in cans. This buttery pound cake, studded with brilliant cranberries and nuts, has evolved considerably from the original "pound of butter, pound of sugar, pound of eggs, pound of flour" formula. The cake is marvelous made with black walnuts if you can get them, but it is nearly as good if you use English (now California) walnuts. It makes a stunning centerpiece for a holiday dessert buffet.

> 1 cup chopped black or California walnuts
> 1½ cups fresh cranberries
> 1¼ cups all-purpose flour
> 1 cup cake flour
> ¾ teaspoon salt
> ½ pound (2 sticks) unsalted butter, softened
> 2 cups granulated sugar
> 5 eggs
> ½ cup buttermilk or plain yogurt
> ¼ cup orange liqueur such as Grand Marnier or Cointreau
> 1 teaspoon grated orange zest
> Confectioners' sugar

1. Preheat the oven to 350 degrees. Grease and flour a 10-inch tube or bundt pan or two 8½-by-4½-inch loaf pans. If using flat-bottomed pans, line the bottoms with parchment or wax paper.
2. Place the walnuts on a baking sheet and toast them in the oven, stirring once or twice, until fragrant and very lightly toasted, 6 to 8 minutes. Cool. Coarsely chop the cranberries with a large knife or by pulsing them briefly in a food processor.
3. Whisk together the two flours and the salt in a large bowl.
4. Using an electric mixer, cream the butter with the sugar in a large bowl until smooth. Beat in the eggs, one at a time, stopping to scrape the sides of the bowl once or twice. Beat in the buttermilk or yogurt, liqueur, and orange zest. With the mixer on low speed, add the flour, mixing just until blended. Stir in the nuts and cranberries by hand. Scrape the batter into the prepared pan(s), smoothing the top.
5. Bake until the top is golden and a tester inserted in the center comes out clean, 45 minutes to 1 hour, depending on the size and shape of the pans. Let the cake cool in the pan on a wire rack for 10 minutes, then turn out onto the rack to cool completely. Wrap and refrigerate for at least 1 day or up to 3 days or freeze.
6. To serve, sift confectioners' sugar heavily over the top and cut into thin slices with a serrated knife.

Blueberry Snack Cake with Toasted Pecan Topping

MAKES 8 SERVINGS

One variation or another of this buttery blueberry cake is made all over northern New England—in Maine, out of the tiny native low-bush blueberries, and in Massachusetts, Vermont, and New Hampshire, where the bushes grow tall enough so that picking can be done in an upright position, with the larger, plumper high-bush blueberries. This is like a rich coffee cake, perfect for snacking, or for toting to potluck teas or suppers. It makes a lovely, not-too-sweet dessert, especially with a scoop of vanilla ice cream or a drizzle of heavy "pouring" cream. Any leftovers are delicious lightly toasted for the next day's breakfast!

1 cup all-purpose flour
3 tablespoons cornmeal
1 teaspoon baking powder
½ teaspoon salt
¼ pound (1 stick) unsalted butter, softened
1 cup plus 1 tablespoon sugar
2 eggs
⅓ cup whole or lowfat milk
1½ teaspoons vanilla extract
½ teaspoon grated lemon zest
2 cups blueberries
1 cup chopped pecans or walnuts

1. Preheat the oven to 350 degrees. Grease a 9-inch square baking pan.
2. Whisk together the flour, cornmeal, baking powder, and salt in a large bowl.
3. Using an electric mixer or a food processor, cream the butter and sugar together until smooth. Add the eggs, milk, vanilla, and lemon zest and process or beat until smooth. Spoon the flour mixture into the processor or bowl and pulse or beat just until the flour is incorporated. If the batter is in a food processor, transfer it to a large bowl.
4. Sprinkle the blueberries over the batter and gently fold them in, just until combined. Scrape the batter into the prepared pan, smoothing the top. Sprinkle with the nuts and then with the remaining 1 tablespoon of sugar.

5. Bake until the nuts are deep brown and a tester inserted in the center of the cake comes out clean, 40 to 45 minutes. Place the pan on a wire rack to cool. (The cake can be wrapped well and stored at cool room temperature for 1 day or frozen.)

6. Cut into squares or wedges in the pan to serve.

Dark and Sticky Gingerbread
with Sherried Foamy Sauce

MAKES 8 SERVINGS

Melanie Barnard (my co-author on several books) and I once listed our requirements for the ultimate gingerbread cake. We agreed that it should be moist (almost to the point of stickiness), dark with molasses, fragrant with spices, and maybe freshened with just a hint of citrus. The texture should be cakey enough for dessert but moist enough to be a good keeper for snacking. This cake, which we developed after more than a few trials and errors, is the result. It can be made without the chopped crystallized ginger, but that really is the kicker that lifts the cake from excellent to extraordinary. Eat this gingerbread plain, for tea, or serve it after an autumn or winter dinner set in a pool of the sherried foamy sauce, a classic New England dessert topper that is somewhat reminiscent of Italian zabaglione.

Special Cakes for Special Days

Two widely observed days of civic obligation in the New England of the early 1800s called for the making of special cakes and cookies. Election Day, or in some places Election Week, was commemorated with sweet yeast-risen fruit-and-nut-filled cakes called election cakes, or, sometimes Hartford election cakes, for they were often associated with that Connecticut capital. These cakes or "buns" were, according to some sources, doled out to those who voted a straight party ballot.

Training Days, or Muster or Militia Days, when citizens traveled from outlying districts to a central town to drill and parade arms, were also occasions for gatherings on village greens and general socializing. According to food historian Betty Fussell, both hard and soft gingerbread were sold by "ginger vendors" who set up concession stands on the parade grounds. The sweet snacks were washed down with mugs of foaming cider or ale.

For the gingerbread:

½ cup molasses
½ cup dark corn syrup
½ cup packed dark brown sugar
6 tablespoons unsalted butter
¾ cup orange juice
¼ cup finely chopped crystallized ginger
2 eggs
1¾ cups all-purpose flour
1½ teaspoons baking soda
1½ teaspoons ground ginger
1 teaspoon ground cinnamon
½ teaspoon fresh-grated nutmeg
½ teaspoon ground cloves
⅛ teaspoon salt

For the sauce:

¼ pound (1 stick) unsalted butter, softened
⅔ cup confectioners' sugar
½ cup boiling water
¼ cup sweet sherry or Madeira
1 egg, lightly beaten

1. To make the gingerbread, preheat the oven to 350 degrees. Grease a 9-inch square baking pan. If you're planning to unmold the cake and present it uncut, line the bottom with baking parchment or waxed paper.

2. Combine the molasses, corn syrup, brown sugar, and butter in a medium-sized saucepan. Bring to a boil over medium-high heat, stirring frequently, until the butter is melted and the mixture is smooth and bubbly. Remove the pan from the heat, stir in the orange juice and crystallized ginger, and let cool for 5 minutes. Whisk in the eggs.

3. Whisk together the flour, baking soda, ginger, cinnamon, nutmeg, cloves, and salt in a large bowl. Make a well in the center, add the molasses mixture, and whisk or beat on low speed with an electric mixer until smooth. (The batter will be foamy and quite thin.) Pour into the prepared pan.

4. Bake until a toothpick inserted in the center comes out clean, 30 to 35 minutes.

5. Cool in the pan on a wire rack. Cut into squares and serve warm or at room temperature, plain or in a pool of the sauce. (The gingerbread can be stored, covered, at room temperature for up to 1 day or frozen.)

6. To make the sauce, cream the butter with the confectioners' sugar until smooth in a medium-sized metal bowl. (The recipe can be made ahead to this step.) Shortly before serving, whisk the boiling water and sherry into the butter mixture. Whisk in the egg. Place the bowl over a saucepan of simmering water and whisk until the sauce is lightly thickened and foamy, about 5 minutes. Serve immediately.

Greek Moist Honey-Walnut Cake

MAKES ABOUT 40 1½-INCH PIECES

Greeks have had a beneficent influence on the New England culinary scene in all kinds of ways, not the least of which is their marvelous tradition of pastry making. To my mind, this rich, moist cake made with ground walnuts and drenched with a lemony brandy syrup is one of the most luscious of the many fabulous Greek pastries or desserts. Cut into traditional attractive diamond shapes or just into small squares, it's a grand finish to any meal, whether Greek or All-American style, especially with a spoonful of lightly sweetened whipped cream. The cake is also a wonderful snack served plain, with cups of strong coffee.

For the cake:

1½ cups plus 1 tablespoon all-purpose flour
2 teaspoons baking powder
½ teaspoon salt
⅛ teaspoon ground cinnamon
1½ cups walnuts
6 tablespoons unsalted butter, softened
¾ cup sugar
4 eggs, separated

For the syrup:

1 cup sugar

1 cinnamon stick, broken in half

2 strips lemon peel

2 tablespoons fresh lemon juice

2 tablespoons brandy or cognac

Lightly sweetened whipped cream, optional

1. To make the cake, preheat the oven to 350 degrees. Grease the bottom and sides of a 13-by-9-inch baking pan.
2. Whisk together 1½ cups of the flour, the baking powder, salt, and cinnamon in a medium-sized bowl. Process the walnuts with the remaining 1 tablespoon of flour in a food processor until the nuts are finely ground. Add the nuts to the flour mixture.
3. Using an electric mixer, beat the butter with the sugar in a large bowl until light and fluffy. Beat in the egg yolks until smooth.
4. Beat the egg whites in another bowl until soft peaks form. Stir about a quarter of the egg whites into the egg yolk mixture to lighten it. Sprinkle the flour-walnut mixture over the batter and use a large spatula to fold gently until most of the flour is incorporated. Fold in the remaining egg whites. Scrape into the prepared pan, smoothing the top.
5. Bake until the cake is golden brown and shrinks from the sides of the pan, and a tester comes out clean, 30 to 35 minutes.
6. While the cake is baking, make the syrup. Combine the sugar, broken cinnamon stick, lemon peel, and 1 cup water in a small saucepan. Bring to a boil, stirring to

---

Looks versus Taste

"Oh! How surprised their mother appeared when she was ushered out to the feast. Her delight in the cake was fully enough to satisfy the most exacting mind . . . then she cut it, and gave a piece to every child, with a little posy on top. Wasn't it good, though! For, like many other things, the cake proved better on trial than it looked, and so turned out to be really quite a good surprise all around."

—Margaret Sidney, *Five Little Peppers and How They Grew* (1880)

---

dissolve the sugar. Simmer, uncovered, over low heat for 5 minutes. Remove from the heat, remove the cinnamon stick and lemon peel, and stir in the lemon juice and brandy.

7. Cool the cake in the pan for 10 minutes. Drizzle about half the warm syrup evenly over the cake. When that syrup is absorbed, pour the remaining syrup over the cake. Set aside at cool room temperature or in the refrigerator for at least 6 hours before serving. (The cake keeps well, refrigerated, for at least 3 days.) Return to room temperature before serving.

8. Cut the cake into diamonds or squares. To make diamond-shaped pieces, first cut into 1½-inch-wide rows parallel to the sides. Turn the pan a quarter turn and cut rows diagonally across. (When the cake is cut this way there will be some scraps at the edges. These are the cook's dividend.)

9. Serve plain or as a dessert with a spoonful of softly whipped cream.

Baking Contest Secrets

Every year the Association of Connecticut Fairs gets together with King Arthur Flour to sponsor baking contests all over the Nutmeg State. All contestants make the same two selected recipes—one for the older generation (such as a chiffon cake) and a simpler recipe for the younger set (perhaps banana muffins)—and take them to a participating fairground for judging. Anna Marie Cwikla, of Lebanon in upstate Connecticut, takes her entries to the Lebanon County Fair. Anna Marie's whole family is involved. Her mother, who used to bake for the competitions, lends encouragement and her well-equipped kitchen, and her daughter and niece participate in the junior baking contest. "It's the challenge; I love to get ribbons," says Ms. Cwikla.

One of her baking secrets is to avoid using appliances. She won a blue ribbon for a carrot cake she made by hand-grating all the carrots and smashing the nuts by hand instead of chopping them.

On the local fair level, Anna Marie enters in several other baking categories. For a recent local competition she made apricot-filled bars, double-chocolate chunk cookies, peanut butter brownies, and cranberry-orange nut bread. "The real secret," reveals her mother jokingly, "is that I haven't cleaned my oven."

"If you win once," says Anna Marie, "you're hooked."

Applesauce-Raisin Hand Cake

MAKES 6 SERVINGS

According to Allene White, eminent New England newspaper columnist and food historian, applesauce cake probably was first created in the late nineteenth century when, Allene speculates, some thrifty Yankee housewife added a cup of applesauce to her spice cake batter to stretch it. This brave baker had excellent instincts, for the fruit puree lends moistness and tenderizes the crumb, as well as contributing its autumnal apple flavor to the mildly spiced cake. This simply made, mix-in-one-pot "hand cake" is perfect for snacking, but that certainly doesn't mean you can't add a scoop of vanilla ice cream and serve it as a fall dessert.

> 6 tablespoons unsalted butter
> ¾ cup packed light brown sugar
> ¾ cup unsweetened applesauce
> 2 eggs
> 1¼ cups all-purpose flour
> 1 teaspoon ground cinnamon
> ½ teaspoon grated nutmeg
> ¾ teaspoon baking powder
> ½ teaspoon baking soda
> ¼ teaspoon salt
> ½ cup raisins
> Confectioners' sugar, optional

1. Preheat the oven to 350 degrees. Grease a 9-inch square cake pan.
2. Heat the butter and brown sugar together in a medium-sized saucepan over medium heat, stirring, until melted and bubbly. Remove from the heat, stir in the applesauce, then whisk in the eggs until well blended.
3. Whisk together the flour, cinnamon, nutmeg, baking powder, baking soda, and salt in a mixing bowl. Add the flour mixture to the saucepan and whisk just until blended. Stir in the raisins. Pour the batter into the prepared pan.
4. Bake until the top springs back when touched lightly and a tester inserted in the center comes out clean, about 25 minutes. Cool the cake in the pan.
5. Sift confectioners' sugar over the top if you like, cut into squares or wedges, and serve.

Cinnamon-Scented Dutch Apple Cake

MAKES 4 TO 6 SERVINGS

My friend Dorothy Caldwell of Norwalk, Connecticut, who gave me this recipe, said she thought it came from her mother, who was Austrian-German. Similar cakes, some labeled "Dutch," others simply called "apple cake," appear in most old New England cookbooks. With its rich, biscuitlike cake layer and spiced apple topping, it's a straight-forward, relatively easy cake to put together, and it perfumes the house with mouth-watering apple and spice fragrance as it bakes. It makes a particularly appealing autumn dessert, especially when served warm, and topped with a big spoonful of softly whipped vanilla-flavored cream. If there should happen to be any leftovers, you'll have to fight over them for breakfast.

For the topping:

2 large semisweet (such as Macoun or 1 Granny Smith and
   1 McIntosh) apples, peeled, cored, and cut into thin slices
   (about 3 cups)
2 tablespoons sugar
2 teaspoons fresh lemon juice
1 teaspoon ground cinnamon
½ teaspoon fresh-grated nutmeg

For the cake:

1 cup all-purpose flour
¼ cup sugar
1½ teaspoons baking powder
½ teaspoon salt
4 tablespoons cold unsalted butter
½ cup half-and-half or light cream
1 egg
3 tablespoons unsalted butter, melted

Lightly sweetened softly whipped cream

1. To make the topping, toss the apples with the sugar, lemon juice, cinnamon, and nutmeg in a large bowl and set aside while making the cake.
2. To make the cake, preheat the oven to 400 degrees. Grease an 8-inch square cake pan.
3. Pulse the flour, sugar, baking powder, and salt together in a food processor. Cut the cold butter into about 8 pieces, distribute it over the flour, and pulse until the mixture resembles coarse meal.
4. Whisk together the half-and-half and egg in a glass measuring cup. With the motor running, pour the liquid through the feed tube, stopping as soon as the batter begins to come together. (Or you can make the batter in a bowl by cutting the cold butter into the flour mixture with a pastry blender and stirring in the half-and-half and egg.) Scrape the batter into the prepared pan, spreading it to the edges with a rubber spatula.
5. Arrange the apples, slightly overlapping, in even rows over the batter and drizzle with the melted butter. Bake until the apples are tender and juicy, 40 to 50 minutes.
6. Cut the cake into squares and serve warm, with a bowl of whipped cream.

Wellesley Fudge Layer Cake with Mocha Frosting

MAKES 10 TO 12 SERVINGS

Chocolate fudge candy was first made in New England women's colleges in the latter part of the nineteenth century. Late-night fudge making grew into such a craze that it was often blamed for the "freshman fifteen"—the poundage put on during the first year away at college. Then, early in the twentieth century, a dark fudge cake, first served in a little tearoom over a shoe store in Wellesley, Massachusetts, became a big hit with Wellesley College students. There doesn't seem to be a codified Wellesley fudge cake recipe—just a definite requirement that the cake be decidedly fudgey and deeply chocolatey, with a rich fudgelike frosting. So I submit herewith my own recipe for my own favorite towering, triple-layer, moist dark chocolate cake with a bittersweet chocolate-mocha frosting. It's our most-often-requested family birthday cake, by far.

For the cake:

4 ounces unsweetened chocolate, chopped
2⅔ cups cake flour
1½ teaspoons baking soda
½ teaspoon salt
12 tablespoons (1½ sticks) unsalted butter, softened
1¼ cups sugar
¼ cup packed light brown sugar
4 eggs
2 teaspoons vanilla extract
1½ cups buttermilk

For the frosting:

6 ounces unsweetened chocolate, coarsely chopped
⅓ cup whole milk or light cream, plus more if necessary
1 tablespoon instant coffee powder, preferably espresso powder
10 tablespoons (1 stick plus 2 tablespoons) softened unsalted butter
4 cups confectioners' sugar
1 tablespoon vanilla extract

1. To make the cake, preheat the oven to 350 degrees. Grease three 8-inch round cake pans and line the bottoms with parchment or wax paper.

2. Melt the chocolate in a microwave, or in a bowl set over simmering water. Sift the flour with the baking soda and salt into a medium-sized bowl.

3. Using an electric mixer, cream the butter with the 2 sugars in a large bowl until light and fluffy. Add the eggs one at a time, beating about 1 minute and scraping the bowl after each addition. Beat in the vanilla and melted chocolate. With the mixer on low speed, add the buttermilk, alternating with the flour mixture, beating just until smooth and no specks of flour remain. Divide the batter among the 3 prepared pans, smoothing the tops.

4. Bake until the cakes are firm to the touch and a tester inserted in the center comes out clean, 25 to 30 minutes. Cool in the pans on a wire rack for 10 minutes, then turn out of the pans, remove the wax paper, and let cool completely. (The cake layers can be made up to 3 weeks ahead and frozen.)

5. To make the frosting, combine the chocolate, milk, and coffee powder. Heat in a microwave or in a bowl set over simmering water until the chocolate is melted.

Using an electric mixer, cream the butter with the confectioners' sugar until smooth in a bowl. Add the chocolate mixture and the vanilla and beat until smooth, light, and creamy. If the frosting seems too thick to spread, beat in additional milk, a spoonful at a time. (The frosting can be made up to 3 days ahead and refrigerated. Return to room temperature and beat until spreadable before using.)

6. To assemble, place one of the cake layers on a cake stand or plate and insert strips of waxed paper under the cake to catch frosting drips. Frost the first 2 cake layers using about ¾ cup of frosting for each. Add the third layer and frost the top and sides with the remaining frosting. (The cake can be assembled a day ahead and refrigerated. Return to room temperature before serving.)

7. Cut into slices to serve.

North End Bakeries

A stroll around any of New England's urban Italian neighborhoods will likely bring you to within sniffing distance of a wonderful old-fashioned Italian bakery. In Boston's North End two of the longest established and best are the Modern and Maria's. If the wind isn't blowing in a favorable direction, Maria's, with its unprepossessing exterior, is easy to miss. But her *sfogliatelle*, a triangular-shaped layering of crisp, flaky dough surrounding a creamy filling flecked with chips of candied citron, is from pastry heaven. Maria's almond biscotti are chock-full of the nuts, and her almond macaroons and *osso di morto*, sweet, crunchy sticks like extra-firm meringues, are also well worth the detour.

The Modern, which has been run by the same family since 1931, specializes in cookies and candies. Their lacy florentines are usually gone by midafternoon; their several flavors of biscotti taste purely of the excellent quality ingredients with which they are made; and the *mostaccioli*, honey-molasses cookies, are an unusual treat. The Modern's freshly made candies, particularly the *torrone*, an Italian confection made with honey nougat and roasted almonds, are a point of pride. They produce several varieties, including plain, chocolate, chocolate covered, and chocolate and caramel covered.

Vermont Chocolate-Potato Bundt Cake

MAKES 12 TO 14 SERVINGS

One might assume, on the face of it, that the addition of mashed potatoes would add heft and heaviness to a cake. On the contrary, the potatoes actually make this lovely, lightly spiced cake lighter, with a more moist, tender crumb. In fact, mashed potatoes were the secret ingredient in many old-fashioned New England baked goods, but most old cookbooks seem to credit the state of Vermont with this winning chocolate-potato combination. In the summer, try presenting this delicate bundt cake with fresh raspberries or small strawberries heaped in the center.

4 ounces semisweet chocolate
1½ cups cake flour
2 teaspoons baking powder
¾ teaspoon salt
½ teaspoon ground cinnamon
½ teaspoon grated nutmeg
¼ teaspoon ground cloves
¼ pound (1 stick) unsalted butter, softened
2 cups plus 2 tablespoons sugar
3 eggs, separated
1 teaspoon vanilla extract
1 cup mashed potatoes, at room temperature (see Note)
½ cup whole or lowfat milk

Confectioners' sugar
Lightly sweetened whipped cream

1. Preheat the oven to 350 degrees. Grease and flour a 10-inch tube or bundt pan or line with baking parchment.
2. Melt the chocolate in a microwave oven or in a bowl set over simmering water.
3. Whisk together the flour, baking powder, salt, cinnamon, nutmeg, and cloves in a medium-sized bowl.
4. Using an electric mixer, cream the butter with 2 cups of the sugar in a large bowl until light and fluffy. Beat in the egg yolks and vanilla. Beat in the mashed potatoes

and the cooled chocolate until smooth. With the mixer on low speed, add the flour mixture, alternating with the milk, mixing just until no specks of flour remain.

5. Beat the egg whites until frothy in a clean bowl. Beat in the remaining 2 tablespoons of sugar until smooth and glossy.

6. Stir one-third of the egg whites into the cake batter to lighten it. Then gently fold in the remaining egg whites just until blended. Spoon the batter into the prepared pan, smoothing the top.

7. Bake for 30 to 45 minutes, depending on the shape of the pan, until a skewer inserted in the center of the cake comes out clean. Begin checking at the minimum baking time and do not overbake.

8. Cool in the pan on a wire rack for 10 minutes. Run a sharp knife around the edges of the pan, turn the cake out of the pan, and strip off the paper, if you used it. Cool completely on a wire rack. (The cake can be wrapped well and stored at cool room temperature for one day, or frozen.)

9. To serve, sift confectioners' sugar over the top of the cake. Serve with the whipped cream on the side.

Note: Instant potatoes work just fine in this recipe. Make the mashed potatoes using potato granules, following the instructions on the box. Or, use leftover mashed potatoes.

Pear-Ginger Upside-Down Cake

MAKES 6 SERVINGS

I clipped a pear and ginger upside-down cake recipe like this one out of a Boston newspaper, thinking that it sounded like an intriguing use of some of my favorite New England ingredients. Then I found a pear and ginger upside-down cake recipe in a King Arthur flour newsletter, and another one in Jasper White's classic *Cooking from New England*. This recipe is closest to the newspaper version. With the sparkling zing of grated fresh ginger and the pleasing tang of plain yogurt, it makes a truly exceptional cake. If you serve this at a fall dinner party after a main course such as Northeast Kingdom Pheasant Fricassee (page 339), Portuguese Pork with Clams (page 287), or Roasted Halibut Fillets with Herbed Crumb Crust (page 369), you will be assured of compliments.

For the pear layer:

2 tablespoons unsalted butter, softened
¼ cup sugar
2 to 3 ripe pears, peeled, cored, and sliced (2 cups)
2 tablespoons dark brown sugar
2 teaspoons grated fresh ginger
2 teaspoons fresh lemon juice

For the cake layer:

1 cup all-purpose flour
1 teaspoon baking soda
½ teaspoon ground cinnamon
¼ teaspoon ground cloves
¼ teaspoon grated nutmeg
¼ teaspoon dry mustard
¼ teaspoon salt
4 tablespoons unsalted butter, softened
½ cup packed dark brown sugar
1 egg
½ cup plain yogurt or buttermilk
¼ cup molasses
1 tablespoon grated fresh ginger

Lightly sweetened softly whipped cream or vanilla ice cream

1. To make the pear layer, thickly coat the bottom and sides of a 9-inch cake pan with the 2 tablespoons of butter. Sprinkle the sugar over the bottom and sides of the pan.
2. Toss the pears with the brown sugar, ginger, and lemon juice in a bowl. Transfer to the prepared pan, smoothing to make an even layer. (For a fancier presentation, arrange the pears in an even pinwheel or spoke pattern.)
3. Preheat the oven to 350 degrees.
4. To make the cake layer, whisk together the flour, baking soda, cinnamon, cloves, nutmeg, mustard, and salt in a medium-sized bowl.
5. Using an electric mixer, cream the butter with the brown sugar in a large bowl until well combined. Beat in the egg, yogurt or buttermilk, molasses, and ginger. With the

mixer on low speed, add the flour mixture, mixing just until blended. Spoon the batter over the pear layer, smoothing the top.

6. Bake until the cake springs back when gently pressed and a tester comes out clean, 35 to 40 minutes.

7. Cool in the pan for 5 minutes. Run a sharp knife around the edge of the cake and invert onto a serving platter. If any pears cling to the bottom of the pan, simply replace them on top of the cake.

8. Serve the cake warm or at room temperature, with whipped cream or scoops of ice cream.

Marjorie Standish Remembers

Marjorie Standish, dean of Maine food writers, wrote in her Foreword to *Cooking Down East* (Down East, 1969), "There is something special about a Maine recipe. . . . Our thoughts hover around the cookie jar and we remember sugar cookies, ginger snaps, brambles, hermits, filled cookies and hard gingerbread. We open our old tin cake boxes and see ribbon cake, applesauce cake, dried apple cake, sponge cake, walnut cake. They may be frosted, more often they are not."

Cranberry-Orange Upside-Down Cake

MAKES 6 SERVINGS

Whole-berry cranberry sauce and orange slices create the gorgeous, glistening topping, the cake layer is a light, not-too-sweet version of an eggy sponge cake with a tiny bit of cornmeal added for a pleasing crumbly texture, and then the whole gets tied together with orange-liqueur-spiked whipped cream. All in all, it's a rather smashing finish for a fall or winter dinner party after a main course such as Yankee Pot Roast with a Fresh Face (page 264) or Maple-Lacquered Game Hens (page 331).

For the fruit layer:

⅓ cup whole-berry cranberry sauce
6 tablespoons unsalted butter, cut into several pieces
6 seedless orange slices

For the cake layer:

1 cup all-purpose flour
4 teaspoons cornmeal
¾ teaspoon baking powder
¼ teaspoon baking soda
¼ teaspoon salt
3 eggs
¾ cup sugar
¼ cup orange juice
1 tablespoon grated orange zest
2 teaspoons vanilla extract

For the orange cream:

1 cup heavy cream
¼ cup confectioners' sugar
2 tablespoons orange liqueur, such as Grand Marnier or Cointreau

1. To make the fruit layer, combine the cranberry sauce, butter, and orange slices in a medium-sized saucepan. Bring to a simmer over medium heat, stirring gently, until the cranberry sauce and butter are melted. Pour into a 9-inch round cake pan and reposition the oranges to create an even layer.
2. To make the cake layer, preheat the oven to 350 degrees.
3. Whisk the flour with the cornmeal, baking powder, baking soda, and salt in a medium-sized bowl.
4. Using an electric mixer, beat the eggs with the sugar in a large bowl until the mixture is light and doubled in volume. Beat in the orange juice, orange zest, and vanilla. With the mixer on low speed, add the flour mixture and beat just until no specks of flour remain. Pour the batter over the cranberry layer, smoothing the top.
5. Bake until the cake is golden and a tester inserted in the center comes out clean, 30 to 35 minutes. Cool in the pan for 3 minutes. Run a paring knife around the edge of the cake to loosen it and then immediately invert the cake onto a serving platter. Leave the pan on the cake for a few minutes; then lift it off. If any topping clings to the pan, simply transfer it to the top of the cake.
6. To make the orange cream, whip the cream with the sugar and liqueur until soft peaks form. Serve the cake warm or at room temperature, topped with the orange cream.

Devil's Food Cupcakes
with Angel Icing

MAKES 24 CUPCAKES

Sinfully dark devil's food cake, at the opposite end of the spectrum from snowy white angel food, has always been popular with Yankee cooks. Here I've made the batter into cupcakes with a moist, springy, open crumb and full-bodied chocolate flavor enlivened by just a tiny bit of black pepper. The white angel icing is a lovely contrast on top.

For the cupcakes:

½ teaspoon instant coffee granules
1½ cups hot tap water
3 eggs
¼ pound (1 stick) unsalted butter, melted
1½ teaspoons vanilla extract
1½ cups all-purpose flour
½ cup unsweetened cocoa powder
1⅓ cups sugar
1½ teaspoons baking powder
1½ teaspoons baking soda
½ teaspoon salt
⅛ teaspoon black pepper

For the icing:

2 tablespoons unsalted butter, softened
2 tablespoons solid vegetable shortening
3 cups confectioners' sugar
3 to 5 tablespoons whole or lowfat milk
1 teaspoon vanilla extract

1. To make the cupcakes, preheat the oven to 350 degrees. Grease and flour 2 12-mold muffin tins or line them with paper liners.

2. Stir together the coffee granules and hot water in a large bowl until the coffee is dissolved. Whisk in the eggs until blended, and then whisk in the melted butter and vanilla. The mixture will look curdled, but that is all right.

3. Whisk or sift together the flour and cocoa in a large bowl until well combined. Whisk in the sugar, baking powder, baking soda, salt, and pepper. Make a well in the center, pour in the egg mixture, and whisk until smoothly and thoroughly blended. Divide the batter among the muffin tins, filling each mold three-quarters full.

4. Bake until the cupcakes have risen evenly and the tops spring back when touched, 20 to 25 minutes. Cool in the pans for 5 minutes, then turn out onto a wire rack to cool completely.

5. To make the icing, pulse the butter and shortening in a food processor until fluffy. Add the confectioners' sugar and process, scraping down the sides of the bowl once or twice, until combined. Add 3 tablespoons of the milk and the vanilla through the feed tube and process until smooth, adding as much more milk as is necessary to reach a spreadable consistency.

6. Frost the tops of the cupcakes with the icing. (The cupcakes can be wrapped well and stored for several hours, but are best served on the day they are made.)

Old-Fashioned Jelly Roll

MAKES 8 SERVINGS

A recipe for a simple jelly roll cake appears in most older New England cookbooks. As I browsed through the *Tarbell, Hartley, Hewitt Vermont Cookbook*, a wonderful handwritten collection of heirloom recipes compiled in 1969 by an East Corinth family clan, it seemed apparent that Grandma Hewitt must have been one of the best and busiest bakers in the family, because many of the most delectable-sounding cake and cookie recipes were hers. Parker House Rolls, Upside-Down Orange Biscuits, Apple Muffins, Raised Doughnuts, Raisin Drop Cookies, Feather Light Cake, Devil's Food Cake, Choice Chocolate Cake, Maple Sugar Pie, Cranberry Pie, and a classic, simple Jelly Roll, which I adapt here, are all attributed to the indefatigable Hewitt matriarch. Pinwheel slices of this delicate, feather-light cake are perfect for tea, and the whole jelly roll makes a lovely display on a dessert buffet table.

> Batter for Hot Milk Sponge Cake (page 534)
> 1 teaspoon grated lemon zest
> 1 cup fruit preserves, such as blackberry, raspberry, strawberry, or
>   apricot, preferably "all-fruit" type
> ¼ cup plus 3 tablespoons confectioners' sugar

1. Preheat the oven to 350 degrees. Grease a 15-by-10-inch jelly roll pan, line with baking parchment or wax paper, and grease the paper.
2. Make the cake batter, adding the lemon zest to the beaten egg yolk mixture. Scrape the batter into the prepared pan, spreading it out to the edges evenly and smoothing with a spatula.
3. Bake until the top is pale golden brown and springs back lightly when touched, 10 to 13 minutes.
4. Spread a tea towel out on a flat surface and sift ¼ cup of the confectioners' sugar onto the towel. Remove the cake from the oven and invert the pan over the sugared towel. Lift off the pan, peel off the paper, and trim off ½ inch of the crisp edges all around the cake so that it will roll more easily. Fold one short end of the towel over the end of the cake, then tightly roll the cake and towel together. Place seam side down on a wire rack until completely cool.
5. Unroll the cake, spread with the preserves, and reroll tightly. (The jelly roll can be wrapped well and stored in the refrigerator for up to 2 days or frozen.)
6. When ready to serve, place the cake on a serving platter, sieve the remaining 3 tablespoons of confectioners' sugar heavily over the top, and cut into slices with a serrated knife.

Apple Harvest Squares

MAKES 24 SQUARES

At Bolton Spring Farm in eastern Massachusetts, apples are the Stephenson family's business. Working with apples harvested from their own orchards and using her grandmother's recipe, Lori Stephenson, the current baker in the family, makes these luscious custardy apple bars, with walnuts and just a bit of coconut added for texture. This is my slightly adapted version of their recipe. Lori recommends tangy Cortland apples because they hold their shape and produce a nice sturdy apple layer, but spicy Macouns or Northern Spys will work equally well.

For the crust:

1½ cups all-purpose flour
⅓ cup packed light brown sugar
½ teaspoon salt
¼ pound (1 stick) cold unsalted butter, cut in about 12 pieces
1 teaspoon grated lemon zest

For the apple layer:

4 cups sliced peeled medium-sweet apples, such as Cortland (about 3
  large apples)
2 tablespoons sugar
2 tablespoons fresh lemon juice
1 teaspoon ground cinnamon

For the custard topping:

1 egg
⅓ cup sugar
⅓ cup heavy cream
1 teaspoon vanilla extract
1 cup chopped walnuts
½ cup flaked coconut

Confectioners' sugar, optional

1. To make the crust, grease a 13-by-9-inch baking pan. Combine the flour, brown
   sugar, and salt in a food processor. Pulse until no lumps of brown sugar remain.
   Distribute the butter and lemon zest over the flour and pulse until the mixture is
   the texture of breadcrumbs. Pour into the prepared pan and use your hands to press
   the dough evenly into the bottom. (Don't worry if it looks a little crumbly; it will
   bind together as it bakes.) Refrigerate until ready to use. (The crust can be prepared
   a day ahead.)
2. Preheat the oven to 375 degrees.
3. To make the apple layer, toss the apples with the sugar, lemon juice, and cinnamon
   in a large bowl. Spread in an even layer over the crust. Bake for 20 minutes, until the
   apples begin to soften.
4. Meanwhile, make the custard topping. Whisk the egg with the sugar, cream, and
   vanilla in a medium bowl until blended. Stir in the walnuts and coconut. Pour the
   egg mixture evenly over the apples, return to the oven, and bake for another 25 to
   35 minutes or until the apples are tender, the topping is golden brown, and a tester
   inserted in the center comes out clean. While still warm, cut into 24 or more
   squares. Cool before removing from the pan. (The squares can be stored in the
   refrigerator for 1 day or frozen.)
5. Dust the tops with confectioners' sugar if you like, before serving.

A Spicy Story

When Columbus stumbled upon the Western Hemisphere, he had been in search of spices. By the eighteenth century the Dutch and English had wrested control of spice importation from the Genoese and Venetians. In the nineteenth century, when American clipper ships began carrying spices from the Far East to New England, they were still a luxury to be hoarded and painstakingly ground or grated by hand. Then, in 1837, two enterprising teenage brothers, David and Levi Slade of Chelsea, Massachusetts, conceived the idea of grinding cinnamon in their father's grist mill. The boys bought half a barrel of cinnamon bark, ground it in the mill for Samuel Pierce, and Mr. Pierce sold the powdered spice in his grocery store (later to become S. S. Pierce) in Boston. The ground cinnamon sold well, and the Slade boys tried grinding dried ginger root and allspice berries and other spices in the mill, eventually founding a spice company bearing their name.

Spices soon became so common in New England that Yankee food became known for its spiciness. When used to excess, spices brought complaints from such well-traveled New Englanders as Harriet Beecher Stowe. Only after living in France for a year was she able to forget, she wrote, "the taste of nutmeg, clove, and allspice, which has met me in so many dishes in America."

❈ ❈ ❈ ❈ ❈ ❈ ❈ ❈ ❈

Spiced Harwich Hermits

MAKES 4 DOZEN 2-INCH SQUARES

These spiced bar cookies originated on Cape Cod in the days of clipper ships—the same ships that brought the spices, fruits, and nuts to New England in the first place. Because these chewy, sturdy cookies kept so well, sailors' wives often packed them into canisters and sea chests for their husbands' long ocean voyages. Eleanor Early, New England food historian, writes that hermits were among the first bar cookies and are probably the direct ancestor of brownies and blondies. They are a tradition well worth keeping alive.

> 2 cups all-purpose flour
> 1 teaspoon baking powder
> ½ teaspoon baking soda
> ½ teaspoon salt
> ¾ teaspoon ground cinnamon
> ½ teaspoon grated nutmeg

¼ teaspoon ground mace
¼ teaspoon ground cloves
¼ pound (1 stick) unsalted butter, softened
½ cup sugar
2 eggs
½ cup molasses
1 cup raisins, coarsely chopped
½ cup chopped walnuts

1. Preheat the oven to 350 degrees. Grease a 15-by-10-inch jelly roll pan.

2. Whisk together the flour, baking powder, baking soda, salt, cinnamon, nutmeg, mace, and cloves in a mixing bowl.

3. Using an electric mixer, cream the butter with the sugar in a large bowl until smooth and fluffy. Beat in the eggs and molasses until very smooth. With the mixer on low speed, add the flour mixture, beating just until blended. Stir in the raisins and nuts. Scrape the batter into the prepared pan, spreading it out evenly to the edges and smoothing the top.

4. Bake until firm on the top and a tester inserted in the center comes out clean, 15 to 18 minutes. Cool in the pan on a rack for 10 minutes, and cut into 1½- to 2½-inch squares. Store the hermits in a tightly covered container for up to a week or so.

Back Door Welcome

"Here in Maine, many of us welcome guests through the back door. Our old houses are simply built so that the most agreeable entrance is through a 'mud room' first (mine has a doormat with the legend 'Wipe Your Paws!') and then into the kitchen where you can immediatey sense what's cooking. It's the lucky guest who arrives just as brownies are being cut."

—From Allene White's "Yankee Sustenance" column, *Maine Sunday Telegram*, January 1999

Maury's Best Brownies

MAKES ABOUT 16 SQUARES

Food historians can't seem to come to a consensus about the origins of the brownie (see page 562), nor do cooks agree on the ideal brownie texture. The cakelike versus fudge-like debate has waged for decades. Here's my favorite brownie—an easy mix-in-one-bowl recipe that my daughter Maury started making for bake sales and sleepover parties back when she was in middle school. As far as we're concerned, *this* is the absolute best brownie, a perfect balance between fudgey and cakey, dense and moist but not too gooey, and without that shiny crust that sometimes makes brownies difficult to cut. The secret ingredient is a pinch of black pepper, which nicely offsets their sweetness.

¼ pound (1 stick) unsalted butter
2 ounces unsweetened chocolate
2 eggs
1 cup sugar
1 teaspoon vanilla extract
½ cup all-purpose flour
¼ teaspoon salt
⅛ teaspoon black pepper
½ cup chopped walnuts, optional

1. Preheat the oven to 350 degrees. Grease an 8- or 9-inch square or 11-by-7-inch baking pan.
2. Combine the butter and chocolate in a heavy medium-sized saucepan over medium-low heat, stirring frequently, until the butter and chocolate are melted. Remove from the heat.
3. Whisk the eggs with the sugar and vanilla in a large mixing bowl until well blended but not foamy. Gradually whisk the melted chocolate mixture into the egg mixture. Sprinkle the flour, salt, and pepper over the chocolate mixture and whisk gently just until combined. Stir in the walnuts, if you like. Pour the batter into the prepared pan, smoothing the top.
4. Bake until a toothpick inserted about two-thirds of the way to the center comes out clean, 25 to 30 minutes. The center should still be slightly sticky. Cool the brownies in the pan on a wire rack for about 20 minutes. Cut into 16 or more squares and cool completely before serving.

Brownies

After a great deal of digging and researching and surmising about the history of brownies, food historian Jean Anderson, in her *American Century Cookbook* (Clarkson Potter, 1997), concludes that the most likely story of their invention is connected to New England and Yankee frugality. It seems that a Bangor, Maine, housewife was baking a chocolate cake one day, and when it fell, instead of chucking it out, she cut the collapsed cake into squares and served it, apparently to high praise. These squares came to be called Bangor brownies.

Although some insist that this story is apocryphal, Ms. Anderson believes that it has the ring of

historical (and culinary) truth—more so than, say, the theory that brownies were invented by a woman named Brownie or the one about brownies being an Americanization of Scottish cocoa scones.

Whatever their original inspiration, the earliest published chocolate brownie recipe seems to have been in the 1906 edition of *The Boston Cooking-School Cook Book*. Once cooks realized just how easy brownies were to make, they started making them like there was no tomorrow, and by the 1920s brownies were on their way to becoming America's most popular homemade baked good.

Mom's Harbor View Butterscotch Brownies

MAKES 16 2-INCH SQUARES

My mother made these moist, chewy brownies so often for her four children—and for their hordes of friends in Harbor View, our island community along the Connecticut shoreline—that she got so she didn't have to consult the recipe. Mother made the recipe pretty much straight from the edition of the *Joy of Cooking* that was published in the 1960s. I have tinkered with the recipe a little, but these fabulous bar cookies have the same deliciously butterscotchy flavor that they've always had.

¼ pound (1 stick) unsalted butter
1 cup packed dark or light brown sugar
2 eggs
1 teaspoon vanilla extract
⅔ cup all-purpose flour
¾ teaspoon baking powder
½ teaspoon salt
½ cup chopped walnuts

1. Preheat the oven to 350 degrees. Grease a 9-inch square baking pan.
2. Combine the butter and brown sugar in a medium-sized saucepan. Cook over medium heat, stirring frequently, until the butter is melted and the mixture is smooth. Remove from the heat, cool for about 5 minutes, and then whisk in the eggs and vanilla until smooth.
3. Whisk together the flour, baking powder, and salt in a large bowl. Add the brown sugar mixture to the flour mixture and whisk just until blended. Stir in the nuts. Pour the batter into the prepared pan.
4. Bake for about 25 minutes or until a tester inserted in the center comes out barely clean. Cool in the pan on a wire rack and, while still warm, cut into about 16 bars. (Wrap well and store in the refrigerator for 2 days or freeze.)

Whoopie Pies

MAKES 12 LARGE FILLED COOKIES

Research as I might, I have yet to uncover much information about the history of whoopie pies, or the origin of the whimsical 1920s-sounding name for these scrumptious sandwich cookies. Whoopie pies are perennially popular in Maine, where many country convenience stores offer them in their tempting homemade goody case near the checkout counter. Marjorie Standish, dean of Maine culinary matters, says her recipe in *Cooking Down East* comes from Bangor, where they were called "whoopsie pies." Gooey-sweet, pure white Marshmallow Fluff, patented by two Boston entrepreneurs in the 1920s (see page 565), is the main ingredient in the buttercream that fills the light cocoa sponge cake cookies. Whoopie pies are an absolutely fabulous, filling-oozing, finger-licking snack—*and* you can stick a candle in the top and turn them into cute little mini birthday cakes.

For the cookies:

2 cups plus 2 tablespoons all-purpose flour
½ cup unsweetened cocoa powder
1 teaspoon baking soda
½ teaspoon salt
1 egg
½ cup flavorless vegetable oil, such as canola
1 cup sugar
1 teaspoon vanilla extract
¾ cup milk

For the filling:

¼ pound (1 stick) unsalted butter, softened
1 cup confectioners' sugar
1½ cups Marshmallow Fluff
1 teaspoon vanilla extract

1. To make the cookies, preheat the oven to 350 degrees. Lightly grease 2 large cookie sheets.
2. Whisk the flour, cocoa, baking soda, and salt together in a medium-sized bowl until well blended.
3. Using an electric mixer, beat the egg with the oil in a large bowl. Gradually add the sugar and beat until the mixture is thick and lemon colored. Add the vanilla. With the mixer on low speed, add the flour mixture and milk alternately, ending with the flour mixture. Beat just until smooth.
4. Using 2 tablespoons of batter for each cookie, make 6 cookies on each baking sheet. The batter will spread, so space at least 2 inches apart.
5. Bake, rotating the position of the baking sheets after 3 minutes, until the cookies are slightly puffy, firm at the edges, and spring back lightly on top when touched, 6 to 8 minutes. Remove with a spatula to wire racks to cool completely. Repeat the process with the remaining batter. You should have a total of 24 cookies.
6. To make the filling, using an electric mixer, cream the butter with the sugar in a medium-sized bowl until smooth. Beat in the Marshmallow Fluff and vanilla. (The filling can be made a day ahead and refrigerated. Rebeat to return to spreading consistency.)

7. To assemble, spread 2 to 3 tablespoons of the filling on half of the cookies and sandwich with the other half. (The whoopie pies can be wrapped individually and stored at cool room temperature or in the refrigerator for up to 2 days or frozen.)

Marshmallow Fluff

In the early 1920s two young men from Lynn, Massachusetts, Allen Durkee and Fred Mower, began whipping up batches of fluffy white marshmallow cream in their kitchens at night, and then selling it door to door during the day. It caught on with Boston-area housewives, and by 1929 the Durkee-Mower company was a going concern, with a large factory in East Lynn turning out the sugary fluff by the barrel. By the mid-1930s, with distribution nationwide, Durkee-Mower sponsored a popular radio broadcast called the "Flufferettes," featuring live music and comedy skits. Their *Yummy Book*, a collection of recipes using Marshmallow Fluff, first published in 1930 and still available in revised form today, includes the famous "Never-Fail Fudge," the Fluffernutter (a kid-friendly sandwich made with fluff and peanut butter), and their recipe for the fabulous Whoopie Pies.

Durkee-Mower still makes Marshmallow Fluff in Lynn, from a formula similar to the one from over eighty years ago, using, the label states, "corn syrup, sugar, dried egg white, and vanillin."

Crackled-Top Sugar Cookies

MAKES ABOUT 2½ DOZEN COOKIES

Exceptional in their utter simplicity, these sugar cookies are the old-fashioned kind that first rise, then fall in the oven to create an attractively cracked top. If you haven't tasted the real thing lately, try them. They're perfect to take on a picnic, to eat after a salad supper such as Spectacular Greek Salad (page 80) in summer, or to follow Roasted Pumpkin-Cider Soup (page 45) or another such simple warming meal in the fall.

> 1¾ cups all-purpose flour
> ½ teaspoon baking soda
> ½ teaspoon salt
> ¼ pound (1 stick) unsalted butter, cut in several pieces
> ¾ cup plus ⅓ cup sugar
> 1 egg
> 1 egg yolk
> 1 teaspoon vanilla extract

1. Pulse the flour, baking soda, and salt in a food processor. Remove to a bowl but do not wash the work bowl.
2. Combine the butter and ¾ cup of the sugar in the food processor and process until creamy and well mixed. Add the egg, egg yolk, and vanilla and process until light and fluffy. Add the flour mixture and pulse just until the flour is blended and a dough forms on top of the blade. (To make the dough by hand, first whisk the flour with the baking soda and salt. Using an electric mixer or working by hand, cream the butter, sugar, egg, yolk, and vanilla. Beat in the flour mixture.) Transfer the dough to a sheet of plastic wrap, flatten into a 1-inch-thick disk, wrap well, and refrigerate for at least 30 minutes or up to 12 hours.
3. Preheat the oven to 350 degrees. Lightly grease 2 cookie sheets.
4. Place the remaining ⅓ cup of sugar in a shallow dish. Shape the dough into 1-inch balls, dredge in the sugar, and place 2 inches apart on the prepared cookie sheets.
5. Bake, rotating the cookie sheets halfway through the baking time, until the cookies are very lightly colored and set on top, 14 to 17 minutes. Cool completely on wire racks. Store in a tightly covered container for up to 3 days.

Grandmother's Brown-Rimmed Butter Cookies

MAKES ABOUT 4 DOZEN SMALL COOKIES

My grandmother made these delectable crisp-edged butter cookies whenever she visited us in Connecticut. Although a basic butter cookie, they get their attractive crunchy snap with the addition of some solid vegetable shortening. When we were very little, Grandmother would flatten out some of this dough and give us her thimble to cut out teeny weeny little cookies—thimble cookies. These were to be served at our doll tea parties, on the miniature blue willow china tea set that my niece still has.

> 1 cup plus 2 tablespoons all-purpose flour
> ½ teaspoon salt
> 4 tablespoons unsalted butter, cut into several pieces
> 4 tablespoons solid vegetable shortening, cut into several pieces
> ½ cup sugar, plus about 2 tablespoons for finishing cookies
> 1 egg
> 1 teaspoon vanilla extract

1. Pulse the flour and salt in a food processor. Remove to a bowl but do not wash the work bowl.

2. Combine the butter, shortening, and ½ cup of the sugar in the food processor and process until creamed and well blended. Add the egg and vanilla and process until light and fluffy. Add the flour mixture and pulse until the dough begins to clump together. (To make by hand, whisk the flour and salt together and set aside. Using an electric mixer or working by hand, cream the butter, shortening, sugar, egg, and vanilla. Beat or stir in the flour mixture.) Transfer to a sheet of plastic wrap, flatten into a disc, and wrap well. Refrigerate for at least 30 minutes or up to 24 hours.

3. Preheat the oven to 350 degrees.

4. Place the remaining 2 tablespoons of sugar on a plate. Using lightly floured hands, shape the dough into ¾-inch balls and place at least 2 inches apart on ungreased cookie sheets. Rinse a clean kitchen towel in cold water and wring out well. Place the damp towel over the bottom of a glass with about a 2-inch diameter, dredge in the sugar, and press on the balls of dough to flatten to about 1¾ inches in diameter.

5. Bake, rotating the cookie sheets halfway through the baking time, until the cookies are deep brown around the rims and pale golden in the centers, 10 to 13 minutes. Cool on wire racks. Store, covered, for up to 5 days or freeze.

Snickerdoodles

MAKES 3 TO 4 DOZEN COOKIES

According to *The American Heritage Cookbook*, when New England cooks weren't giving their cookies very plain, generic cookie names ("sugar cookies," "molasses cookies," etc.), they indulged in a penchant for coining odd and nonsensical monikers, apparently just for the fun of saying them. "Jolly boys," "tangle breeches," "kinkawoodles," and "brambles" are some of the cookies with whimsical-sounding nineteenth-century names. These buttery, cinnamony, nut- and currant-studded cookies were dubbed "snickerdoodles" (or sometimes "snipdoodles"). Don't let their cute old-fashioned name put you off. These are truly excellent cookies, easy to make, and with a perfect balance of sweetness—great for snacking or for dessert with a bowl of fruit.

> 1⅔ cups all-purpose flour
> ½ teaspoon baking soda
> ½ teaspoon salt
> ½ teaspoon grated nutmeg
> ¼ pound (1 stick) cold unsalted butter, cut into several pieces
> ¾ cup plus 2 tablespoons sugar
> 1 egg
> 1 egg yolk
> 1 teaspoon vanilla extract
> ½ cup chopped walnuts
> ½ cup dried currants
> 1 teaspoon ground cinnamon

1. Pulse the flour, baking soda, salt, and nutmeg in a food processor. Remove to a bowl but do not wash the work bowl.
2. Combine the butter and ¾ cup of the sugar in the food processor and process until well blended. Add the egg, egg yolk, and vanilla and process until light and fluffy.

Add the flour mixture and use long pulses until a dough begins to form on top of the blade. Add the nuts and currants and pulse 2 or 3 times to mix, or stir them in by hand. Turn the dough out onto a sheet of plastic wrap, flatten into a 1-inch-thick disc, wrap well, and refrigerate for at least 30 minutes or up to 24 hours.

3. Preheat the oven to 350 degrees. Lightly grease 2 cookie sheets.

4. Stir together the remaining 2 tablespoons of sugar and the cinnamon in a small bowl. Shape the dough into generous 1-inch balls and dredge in the cinnamon sugar. Place 2 inches apart on the prepared cookie sheets. Dip your fingertips in the sugar mixture and flatten the tops of the cookies to about half their original height.

5. Bake, rotating the cookie sheets halfway through the baking time, until the cookies are set and golden around the edges, 10 to 12 minutes. Cool on wire racks. Store in a covered container for up to 3 days or freeze.

Joe Froggers

"Joe froggers" are an old-fashioned New England molasses spice cookie. According to legend, the cookies got their name from their originator, an African-American man known as Uncle Joe, who lived on the edge of a pond full of frogs in Marblehead, Massachusetts. His cookies, reports food historian Eleanor Early, "were plump and dark as the fat little frogs that lived in the pond." Marblehead fishermen would give the old man a jug of rum and he made them batches of froggers to take to sea. But he wouldn't tell how he made them. When Uncle Joe died, everybody was afraid that was the end of Joe froggers. But then a woman called Mammy Cressy, who said she was Joe's daughter, gave the secret recipe to a fisherman's wife, who passed it along to her friends around Marblehead, and Joe froggers were reborn. Being a chewy, substantial sort of cookie, Joe froggers became a favorite Sunday night supper in the town, washed down with a pitcher of cold milk.

Melanie's Molasses Crinkle Cookies

MAKES ABOUT 2½ DOZEN COOKIES

Ginger and spice molasses cookies—both hard and soft—have long been a New England cookie jar favorite. This deeply molassesy, pleasantly chewy version was developed by Melanie Barnard when we worked together at the original *Cook's* magazine. As the balls of dough rise and fall in the oven, the tops develop attractive crinkly fissures.

These cookies make a superb afternoon snack with a glass of cold milk or an excellent dessert accompaniment to lemon sherbet or vanilla frozen yogurt.

>   2 cups all-purpose flour
>   ¾ teaspoon baking soda
>   ½ teaspoon salt
>   ¾ teaspoon ground ginger
>   ½ teaspoon ground cinnamon
>   ½ teaspoon grated nutmeg
>   ⅛ teaspoon ground cloves
>   ¼ pound (1 stick) unsalted butter, cut into several pieces
>   ½ cup plus ⅓ cup sugar
>   1 egg
>   ½ cup molasses

1. Pulse the flour, baking soda, salt, ginger, cinnamon, nutmeg, and cloves in a food processor. Remove to a bowl, but do not wash the work bowl.
2. Combine the butter and the ½ cup of the sugar in the food processor and process until well mixed. Add the egg and molasses and process until light and fluffy. Add the flour mixture and pulse just until a stiff dough forms on top of the blade. (To make by hand, whisk together the flour and other dry ingredients. Using an electric mixer or working by hand, cream the butter with the sugar, egg, and molasses. Beat the flour mixture in just until blended.) Transfer the dough to a sheet of plastic wrap, flatten into a 1-inch-thick disc, and refrigerate for at least 30 minutes or up to 2 days.

A Taste for Molasses

Molasses was the most common sweetener in eighteenth-century America. It was cheaper than sugar because it was brought to New England as part of the triangle trade. The molasses was made into rum, which was shipped to Africa to be traded for slaves, who were in turn traded for molasses in the West Indies. Molasses, along with maple syrup and sugar, remained the most available sweetener through the nineteenth century, but when sugar prices dropped after World War I, their popularity decreased. Many Yankees retained their taste for molasses, continuing to use it more as a flavoring than a sweetener in such signature New England dishes as baked beans, Indian pudding, pumpkin pie, and molasses crinkle cookies.

3. Preheat the oven to 350 degrees. Lightly grease 2 cookie sheets.

4. Place the remaining ⅓ cup of sugar in a small dish. Using lightly floured hands, pinch off pieces of dough about 1 inch in diameter and roll into smooth balls. Roll each ball in the sugar and place on the prepared cookie sheets 2 inches apart.

5. Bake, rotating the cookie sheets halfway through the baking time, until the tops are crinkled and the cookies are set, 12 to 15 minutes. Cool the cookies on wire racks. Store in a tightly sealed container for up to 5 days or freeze.

Greek Sugar-Dusted Cookies (Kourambiedes)

MAKES ABOUT 4 DOZEN COOKIES

No festive holiday or celebratory occasion in a Greek New England household (or the feasting at the numerous Greek festivals that are held around the region) is complete without a piled-high platter of these snowy white, sugar-dusted shortcake cookies. Sometimes studded with a whole clove, which imparts its subtle oil to the dough, these delicate, buttery cookies crumble in the hand and almost melt in the mouth. Their flavor improves with age, and they can be stored in a tightly sealed container for up to a week or so. Try adding them to your holiday baking repertoire—perhaps for a Christmas cookie exchange (see page 581).

> 3 cups all-purpose flour
> ¼ teaspoon salt
> ¾ pound (3 sticks) unsalted butter, softened
> ⅔ cup superfine sugar
> 1 egg yolk
> 2 tablespoons brandy
> 1 teaspoon vanilla extract
> Whole cloves, optional
> ⅔ cup confectioners' sugar

1. Whisk the flour with the salt in a medium-sized bowl.

2. Using an electric mixer, beat the butter in a large bowl until lightened in color and creamy. Add the sugar, egg yolk, brandy, and vanilla and beat until very fluffy and well blended. With the mixer on low speed, gradually add the flour mixture, beating just until smooth and blended. Transfer to a sheet of plastic wrap, flatten into a 1-inch-thick disc, wrap well, and refrigerate for at least 1 hour or up to 24 hours.

3. Preheat the oven to 350 degrees. Lightly grease 2 cookie sheets.

4. Shape the dough into 1-inch balls and place on the prepared cookie sheets, spacing about 1 inch apart. If you like, insert a whole clove about halfway into the top of each cookie.

5. Bake, rotating the cookie sheets halfway through the baking time, until the cookies are very faintly colored, 14 to 16 minutes. Transfer to a wire rack and cool for about 15 minutes.

6. Place the confectioners' sugar in a shallow bowl. While the cookies are still slightly warm, dredge or toss them in the confectioners' sugar until they are liberally coated. Cool completely. Store in a tightly covered container for up to a week or freeze. (These cookies are best made a day or so before you plan to serve them.) Sift more confectioners' sugar over the cookies before serving.

Mrs. Dietz's Fruit-and-Nut-Filled Cookies

MAKES ABOUT 2½ DOZEN COOKIES

The mother of my Connecticut grade-school friend Libby Dietz insisted on baking these cookies early on most weekday mornings before she went to work so that her children would have a welcoming homemade snack after school. Much to my good fortune, Libby's house was on my route home. If the kitchen was redolent with the lingering scent of cinnamon, that was the tip-off. There on the counter, nestled beneath a white linen towel, were these magical cookies. New England drop cookies of all kinds I knew about. Never had I ever seen or tasted a "foreign" delicacy the likes of this: tender spirals of crispy dough with a mysteriously exotic filling that I later learned was fruit preserves, finely chopped nuts, and cinnamon sugar. Made without butter to be "neutral" in accordance with Jewish dietary rules (so they could be eaten with either a dairy or meat meal), these cookies and other such delicate pastries have helped forge links in the immutable culinary chain that binds America to Europe.

For the dough:

2¼ cups plus about ⅓ cup all-purpose flour
1½ teaspoons baking powder
¼ teaspoon baking soda
Pinch of salt
2 eggs
6 tablespoons sugar
¼ cup orange juice
¼ cup vegetable oil

For the filling:

⅓ cup apricot preserves, whirled in food processor if very chunky
½ cup sugar
2 teaspoons ground cinnamon
1 cup finely chopped walnuts

1 egg yolk

1. To make the dough, whisk together 2¼ cups of the flour, the baking powder, baking soda, and salt in a medium-sized bowl.
2. Using a standing or hand-held electric mixer, beat the eggs in a large bowl. Gradually beat in the sugar and then the orange juice and oil until blended. If using a standing mixer, switch to the paddle beater. On low speed, beat the flour mixture into the egg mixture to make a smooth, sticky dough. Transfer to a sheet of plastic wrap, dust well with some of the remaining ⅓ cup flour, and flatten to an 8-inch square. Refrigerate for at least 2 hours, until firm, or overnight.
3. Preheat the oven to 350 degrees. Lightly grease 2 cookie sheets.
4. To prepare the filling, place the preserves in a small bowl. Stir the sugar and cinnamon together and place in another bowl, and place the nuts in a third bowl. Whisk the egg yolk with 1 tablespoon water in another small bowl for the glaze.
5. On a well-floured board, roll out half the dough to a rectangle about 9-by-14-inches and about ⅛ inch thick. Spread with half the preserves, sprinkle with 3 table-spoons of the cinnamon sugar, and finally with half the nuts. Starting from a long side, roll the dough tightly into a cylinder. Place seam side down on the prepared cookie sheet, brush with the egg glaze, and sprinkle the top of the roll with about a

teaspoon of cinnamon sugar. (Refrigerate or freeze if not baking immediately.) Repeat with the remaining dough, fillings, and glaze. Bake for 25 to 30 minutes or until the pastry is an even rich golden brown.

6. Cool for about 20 minutes and while still warm, cut the roll into ½- to ¾-inch-thick slices. Transfer to a wire rack to cool completely. (The cookies keep very well in a sealed container for a day or two or can be frozen.)

Fig Newtons

Fig Newtons are soft cakelike cookies filled with chewy fig jam. They have their name because the company that invented the instantly popular cookies in 1891 was just outside the town of Newton, Massachusetts, near the Kennedy Biscuit Works. Using a newly patented apparatus consisting of an inner funnel that supplied a stream of jam and an outer funnel that made a tubelike stream of dough, the company has produced a seemingly endless rope of Fig Newtons for more than a century. Kennedy Biscuit Works was one of the founding bakeries of Nabisco. A company press release states that "over a billion Fig Newtons are consumed every year, making them the third most popular cookie sold in America."

Shaker Giant
Rosemary-Ginger Cookies

MAKES 2½ TO 3 DOZEN COOKIES

The bake shop at the Canterbury, New Hampshire, Shaker Village is a most beguiling place. As soon as you step inside, a heavenly, mouthwatering buttery, vanilla-y perfume strikes your nose, an aroma more reminiscent of your grandmother's kitchen than a modern bakery. When I was there, I bought several different cookies and bars to bring home for sampling—a "jelly dot" brown sugar cookie, an apple bar cookie, a simple cracked-top sugar cookie—but this crisp, oversize spice cookie, with its intriguing, pleasantly resiny hint of rosemary, was my favorite. A plate of these herbaceous cookies makes a sophisticated dessert or accompaniment to afternoon tea.

2 cups all-purpose flour
1 teaspoon baking soda
1 teaspoon salt
1 teaspoon ground ginger
½ teaspoon ground cinnamon
¼ teaspoon ground cloves
12 tablespoons (1½ sticks) unsalted butter, cut in several pieces
2 tablespoons crumbled dried rosemary
1¼ cups sugar
1 egg
¼ cup molasses
1 teaspoon vanilla extract

1. Pulse the flour, baking soda, salt, ginger, cinnamon, and cloves in a food processor. Remove to a bowl but do not wash the work bowl.
2. Combine the butter and rosemary in the food processor and process until smooth. Add 1 cup of the sugar, the egg, molasses, and vanilla and process until well blended. Sprinkle the flour mixture over the butter mixture and pulse until the flour is blended and a stiff dough forms on top of the blade. (To make the dough by hand, whisk together the flour and spices. Cream the butter with the remaining ingredients using an electric mixer and add the flour mixture on low speed.)
3. Transfer the dough to a sheet of plastic wrap, flatten into a disc, and refrigerate for at least 30 minutes or up to 2 days.
4. Preheat the oven to 350 degrees. Lightly grease 2 cookie sheets.
5. Place the remaining ¼ cup of sugar in a small bowl. Using lightly floured hands, form the dough into balls about 1½ inches in diameter. Roll each ball in sugar and place 3 inches apart on the prepared cookie sheets.
6. Bake, rotating the cookie sheets halfway through the baking time, until the cookies spread, the tops are cracked, and the edges are one shade darker, 17 to 20 minutes. Cool the cookies on wire racks. Store in a tightly covered container for up to 5 days.

The Justly Famous Toll House Cookie

MAKES ABOUT 4 DOZEN COOKIES

This utterly delectable cookie has spread around the world and is justly famous indeed. My recipe deviates slightly from the classic formula from Massachusetts that appears on the back of the Nestle's chocolate chip bag (see page 577). I like to add more vanilla and just a little less brown sugar to balance the sweetness of the chocolate chips. The Nestle recipe does not specify which type of brown sugar, but I'm convinced that dark brown sugar contributes a markedly richer and more appealing color.

2¼ cups all-purpose flour
1 teaspoon baking soda
1 teaspoon salt
½ pound (2 sticks) unsalted butter, softened
¾ cup sugar
⅔ cup packed brown sugar, preferably dark brown
2 eggs
2 teaspoons vanilla extract
2 cups semisweet chocolate chips
1 cup chopped walnuts

1. Preheat the oven to 325 degrees. Line 2 cookie sheets with baking parchment or wax paper.
2. Whisk together the flour, baking soda, and salt in a large bowl. Set aside.
3. Using an electric mixer, cream the butter with the two sugars in a large bowl until smooth and free of lumps. Add the eggs and vanilla and beat until smooth. With the mixer on low speed, add the flour mixture, mixing just until blended. Stir in the chocolate chips and nuts. (If not using immediately, refrigerate the dough for up to 12 hours.) Drop the dough by heaping tablespoonfuls onto the prepared cookie sheets, spacing the cookies about 2 inches apart.

State Cookie Wars

In July 1997, Massachusetts Governor William Weld signed a proclamation declaring the Toll House cookie the commonwealth's official state cookie. The governor, who had lobbied vigorously for the Fig Newton, then tried to create a new category: official state *fruit* cookie, saying "I don't think any other state even *has* a fruit cookie."

Legend of Toll House

By now everybody knows the basics of the story: Back in 1930, Ruth Wakefield, owner of the Toll House Inn near Whitman, Massachusetts, was mixing up a batch of batter for a plain American brown sugar cookie called a Boston or butter drop do cookie. She ran out of nuts. On an inspired whim, she decided to see what would happen if she chopped up a bar of Nestle semisweet chocolate (into "pieces the size of a pea," she later instructed) and added it to the dough. Lo and behold, instead of melting, as she had assumed it would, the chocolate stayed in its nice little chunks, and a classic was born.

Jean Anderson in her *American Century Cookbook*, and John Thorne, in a 1982 issue of his *Simple Cooking* newsletter, add more details to the story. In 1930, when sales of Nestle Yellow Label Chocolate, Semi-Sweet, abruptly soared in the Boston area and then throughout New England, the company sent a salesman around to check into the matter. Eventually this representative traced the sales boom back to Ruth Wakefield at her Toll House in tiny Whitman, a halfway point on the road between Boston and New Bedford. The company was suitably impressed, to the extent that they began manufacturing a scored bar of semisweet chocolate and packaging it with a little chopper. Finally, nine years later, Nestle started making bits of uniformly shaped chocolate chips that they called "morsels" and running Mrs. Wakefield's recipe on the back of every package.

The recipe has changed slightly over the years. Soon after Ruth Wakefield's first startlingly successful addition of chocolate chips, she began baking the cookies with both chocolate *and* nuts, calling them "Toll House chocolate crunch cookies." Ruth always dissolved her baking soda in a teaspoon of water. In the recipe that ran on the package until 1979, Nestle called for the soda to be added to the dry ingredients but still included a mysterious ¼ teaspoon of water in the formula. After their first contract with Mrs. Wakefield expired, Nestle updated the recipe by shortening baking times, calling for unsifted flour, and omitting that cryptic drop of water. (My formula differs by just a tiny bit, see recipe.)

Today, Nestle manufactures more than 240 million morsels every day. Chocolate chip cookies are America's most popular cookie recipe, accounting for half of all cookies baked in this country.

❖ ❖ ❖ ❖ ❖ ❖ ❖ ❖ ❖ ❖

4. Bake, rotating the cookie sheets halfway through the baking time, until the cookies are golden brown around the edges but still soft and puffy in the center, about 14 to 17 minutes. For chewier cookies, cool on baking sheets. For crisper cookies, cool on wire racks. Store in a covered container for up to 3 days or freeze.

Schrafft's of Boston
Chewy Oatmeal Cookies

MAKES ABOUT 3 DOZEN COOKIES

Founded in Boston in the nineteenth century, Schrafft's shops soon became renowned for the quality of their candies, ice creams, and especially their cookies. Eventually they opened several stores in New York City, but according to food writer and food historian Judith Jones, true Schrafft's cookie aficionados believed that the Boston version of their oatmeal cookies was superior, and so they would travel to Boston by train to buy them. This recipe is based on the original Schrafft's formula but I've added some dark brown sugar for the rich color and flavor that it imparts. This is a soft, pleasantly chewy cookie, with plenty of raisins and nuts.

1½ cups old-fashioned or quick-cooking rolled oats (not instant oatmeal)
1¼ cups all-purpose flour
½ teaspoon baking powder
½ teaspoon baking soda
½ teaspoon salt
1 teaspoon ground cinnamon
½ teaspoon ground allspice
¼ pound (1 stick) unsalted butter, softened
¾ cup sugar
¼ cup packed dark brown sugar
2 eggs
1 teaspoon vanilla extract
¼ cup whole or lowfat milk
1 cup raisins
1 cup chopped walnuts

1. Preheat the oven to 350 degrees. Lightly grease 2 cookie sheets.
2. Whisk together the rolled oats, flour, baking powder, baking soda, salt, cinnamon, and allspice in a large bowl.
3. Using an electric mixer, cream the butter with the two sugars in a large bowl until smooth. Add the eggs and vanilla and beat until light and well blended. With the

mixer on low speed, add the oat mixture and the milk, beating until well combined and a stiff dough forms. Stir in the raisins and nuts. (If not using immediately, refrigerate the dough for up to 12 hours.) Drop the dough by tablespoonfuls onto the prepared cookie sheets, spacing about 2 inches apart. Press the tops gently to flatten very slightly.

4. Bake until the edges are brown and the centers are still soft and puffy, about 11 to 14 minutes. Cool on wire racks. Store in a covered container for up to 3 days or freeze.

Crisp Maple-Oatmeal Cookies

MAKES ABOUT 4 DOZEN COOKIES

I developed this cookie for a *Yankee Magazine*–sponsored food festival in Boston about a dozen years ago, and they then reprinted it for a recipe booklet sent to the magazine's subscribers. Several friends told me they had kept the booklet, so when I could not put my hands on this recipe, I just asked Geneva Walsh, a fellow soup kitchen volunteer and a wonderful cook, who not only found the recipe booklet but also baked us all a batch of the cookies! Flavored subtly with maple, these splendid cookies have a lovely coarse texture from lots of oatmeal and a crisp, crunchy bite.

> 3 cups old-fashioned or quick-cooking rolled oats (not instant oatmeal)
> 1½ cups all-purpose flour
> ½ teaspoon baking soda
> ½ teaspoon salt
> ½ teaspoon ground cinnamon
> ⅛ teaspoon grated nutmeg
> ¼ pound (1 stick) unsalted butter, softened
> ½ cup solid vegetable shortening
> ¾ cup sugar
> ¾ cup firmly packed light or dark brown sugar
> 2 eggs
> 3 tablespoons pure maple syrup
> 1 teaspoon vanilla extract
> 1 cup raisins

1. Preheat the oven to 350 degrees. Lightly grease 2 cookie sheets.
2. Whisk together the rolled oats, flour, baking soda, salt, cinnamon, and nutmeg in a large bowl.
3. Using an electric mixer, cream the butter, shortening, and two sugars together in a large bowl until smooth. Add the eggs, maple syrup, and vanilla and beat until light and well blended. With the mixer on low speed, add the oat mixture, beating just until the dough comes together. Stir in the raisins. (If not using immediately, refrigerate the dough for up to 12 hours.) Drop the dough by tablespoonfuls onto the prepared cookie sheets, spacing about 2 inches apart. Dampen 2 fingertips with cold water and flatten each cookie on the top slightly.
4. Bake, rotating the cookie sheets halfway through the baking time, until the cookies spread and are light golden brown, 11 to 13 minutes. (If you have used dark brown sugar, watch carefully to prevent overbrowning.) Cool on wire racks. Store in a covered container for up to 3 days.

The Cookie Exchange

When two women from Wellesley, Massachusetts, Mary Bevilaqua and Laurel Gabel, had the first Christmas cookie exchange back in the 1960s, they started a national trend that now stretches from Maine to Hawaii. The idea was (and is) to host a friendly, usually all-female get-together during the holiday season, serve a dessert and some punch, and request that each guest bring along a batch of her favorite Christmas cookies, and a large empty box. The cookies are arrayed on a table, labeled with the recipe's title and the baker's name. The guests then go down the row, filling their empty boxes with some of each cookie, and sharing, all the while, information and stories (and laughs) about where their cookie recipe came from—so that in the end, warmth and friendship and memories are shared, as well as cookies.

Merrilyn Lewis read about the Wellesley cookie exchange in *Parties!* (HarperCollins, 1992), a book that Melanie Barnard and I coauthored. Merrilyn determined to start her own tradition in the Pioneer Valley in western Massachusetts, where she lives and works. But this party was to be a little different. There would be no hard and fast cookie requirement. Homemade cookies were welcome, of course, but bakery-made were okay, too. So were quick breads, jars of homemade ice cream toppings, even salsas. This was to be an "almost anything edible" exchange.

As hostess, Merrilyn makes the centerpiece dessert, a magnificent mocha bûche de Noel from the *Parties!* book, which goes in the freezer a couple of weekends ahead. Merrilyn serves a few simple hors d'oeuvres with sparkling wine in the living room while the group catches up on weeks' or months' or sometimes a year's worth of news. Then everyone moves to the big kitchen, where the exchange edibles are arrayed.

"It's bedlam," Merrilyn declares. "Funny bedlam. Everybody admires, tells stories about what they brought, laughs about the pitfalls they encountered." One brings lovely traditional sugar cookie cut-outs. Another, who has never ever made a single cookie before, tries a batch of thumbprint cookies and they're beautiful. Someone else tackles an elaborate Styrofoam tree on which to hang decorated cookies. Yet another makes individual cranberry-nut tea breads. A couple of chronically overcommitted people buy jars of the best dessert topping or salsa they can find.

"It's really fun. Somehow I feel free to invite new people I hardly know each year, along with the core of regulars, and it grows. We're all working women, but this is something outside of work. It's become a tradition now that I know will not stop. We tell our children—and maybe someday we'll invite them—in the hope that it will get passed down to the next generation."

PIES AND TARTS

"New England," proclaimed food historian Eleanor Early, "is the famous pie belt of America. New Englanders make not only the best pies in the country, but also the most."

Early made that claim back in 1954, and I guess one could say that since then we've at least held our own in the national pie-making sweepstakes. Yankee bakers no longer bake as many from-scratch pies for weekday meals, but we still pride ourselves on our special occasion pies—witness the Blue Ribbon Harvest Apple Pie (page 597) and Mince Pie with Decorative Top Crust (page 605), which are required on all Thanksgiving dinner tables, and our seasonal pies such as the springtime special Frank's Strawberry-Rhubarb Pie (page 610) and a magnificent midsummer's Best Maine Blueberry Pie (page 601).

You can still be pretty sure of getting a good piece of pie at many of the church and public suppers around New England, sometimes even with that ever-more-scarce commodity, the genuine handmade crust. New England's glorious cream pies, such as Vermont Pure Maple–Walnut Cream Pie (page 588) or Public Supper Banana Cream Pie (page 589), are often the featured dessert at such community gatherings.

And for the fortunate traveler in the region, most Yankee diners and luncheonettes and small family-run restaurants still proudly line their (we hope homemade) pies up in a display case so you can make the agonizing choice among the likes of an old-fashioned Nutmeg-Dusted Rich Custard Pie (page 594) or the perennially popular Maine specialty, Duffy's Graham Cracker Cream Pie (page 591).

To Make Crust by Hand

If you don't have a food processor, make the crust by hand. In a large bowl, whisk together the flour, sugar, and salt. Cut the chilled shortening into small pieces (about 12 slices per stick of butter, or 1-inch chunks of solid vegetable shortening or cream cheese) and add to the flour. Using a pastry blender or two table knives or your fingertips, work the flour and shortening together until most of the shortening is about the size of small peas. (It will never really resemble "meal," except possibly coarse oatmeal.) Sprinkle most of the cold liquid called for in the recipe over the flour mixture and work the dough with a large fork or your hands, adding more water by tablespoons, until it is evenly moistened and begins to clump together. Press the dough together with your hands to make a cohesive ball and flatten into discs.

■ ■ ■ ■ ■ ■ ■ ■ ■ ■

Old-Fashioned Lard Crust

MAKES A DOUBLE CRUST

Lard, which is rendered and clarified pork fat, was the preferred and most available pie crust shortening for generations of New England bakers. Lard makes a meltingly tender pie crust, although I prefer to use it in combination with some unsalted butter to balance its distinctive, mildly nutty flavor. This crust complements fruit fillings, such as apple, blueberry, and rhubarb, particularly well.

   2½ cups all-purpose flour
   2 teaspoons sugar
   1 teaspoon salt
   ½ cup cold or frozen lard, cut in ½-inch chunks
   6 tablespoons cold unsalted butter, cut in ½-inch slices or chunks
   6 to 8 tablespoons ice water

1. Pulse the flour with the sugar and salt in a food processor. Distribute the lard and butter over the flour and pulse until most of the shortening is the size of small peas. Sprinkle 6 tablespoons of the ice water evenly over the flour mixture and pulse just until no dry flour remains and the dough begins to clump together in small balls.

If the mixture is too dry to press into a dough with your fingers, sprinkle on the remaining 1 to 2 tablespoons of water and pulse a few more times. (To make the pastry by hand, see page 585).

2. Divide the dough in half and turn out onto two sheets of plastic wrap. Shape and flatten into 5-inch discs, wrap, and refrigerate the dough for at least 1 hour or freeze. Remove from the refrigerator 10 minutes before rolling it out. If frozen, thaw overnight in the refrigerator before using.

Half-and-Half Flaky Pie Crust

MAKES A DOUBLE CRUST

This recipe, made with half solid vegetable shortening for tenderness and flakiness and half butter for flavor, is a great choice for just about any pie. If you need only a single crust, just halve all of these ingredients.

> 2½ cups all-purpose flour
> 1 teaspoon salt
> 1 teaspoon sugar
> ¼ pound (1 stick) cold unsalted butter, cut in ½-inch slices or chunks
> ½ cup cold solid vegetable shortening, cut in 1-inch chunks
> 6 to 8 tablespoons ice water

1. Pulse the flour with the salt and sugar in a food processor. Distribute the butter and shortening over the flour and pulse until most of the shortening is the size of small peas. Sprinkle 6 tablespoons of the ice water evenly over the flour mixture and pulse just until no dry flour remains and the dough begins to clump together in small balls. If the mixture is too dry to be pressed into a dough with your fingers, sprinkle on the remaining 2 tablespoons of water and pulse a few more times. (To make the pastry by hand, see page 585).

2. Divide the dough in half and turn out onto 2 sheets of plastic wrap. Shape and flatten into two 5-inch discs, wrap, and refrigerate for at least 30 minutes or freeze. Remove from the refrigerator 10 minutes before rolling out. If frozen, thaw overnight in the refrigerator before using.

It's Okay to Buy a Crust—Really!

Millions of otherwise accomplished American cooks cringe when asked to bake a pie. Oh, the fillings can be fun. But that crust can cause angst. So if you're not a born or practiced pie baker, I say it's quite okay to go ahead and buy the crust. Avoid skimpy frozen in-the-pan pie shells that are way too shallow to accommodate most fillings. I recommend the kind of crusts sold fresh, usually in the dairy case. They'll fit in a standard 9-inch dish, and you can crimp or flute your own edge so that the pie *looks* homemade—a crucial psychological element for me. One cautionary note: Because the purchased crusts contain more sugar than homemade, they tend to brown more quickly, so when baking or prebaking, subtract a few minutes from the cooking time.

Cream Cheese Pie Crust

MAKES A DOUBLE CRUST

The cream cheese in this pastry produces a dough that is a pleasure to work with. Even if it becomes slightly overworked, the dough seems more forgiving than some, making a smooth, elastic pastry that always rolls out beautifully and tastes delicious every time.

2¼ cups all-purpose flour
2 tablespoons sugar
1 teaspoon salt
8 ounces cold cream cheese, cut in 1-inch lumps
¼ pound (1 stick) cold unsalted butter, cut in ½-inch slices
5 to 7 tablespoons cold whole, lowfat, or skim milk, or ice water

1. Pulse the flour with the sugar and salt in a food processor. Distribute the cream cheese and butter over the flour and pulse until most of the cheese and shortening is the size of small peas. Sprinkle 5 tablespoons of the milk or water evenly over the flour mixture and pulse just until no dry flour remains and the dough begins to clump together in small balls. If the mixture is too dry to press into a dough with your fingers, sprinkle on the remaining 1 to 2 tablespoons milk or water and pulse a few more times. (To make the pastry by hand, see page 585.)

2. Divide the dough in half and turn out onto 2 sheets of plastic wrap. Shape and flatten into 5-inch discs, wrap, and refrigerate the dough for at least 1 hour or freeze. Remove from the refrigerator 10 minutes before rolling it out. If frozen, thaw in the refrigerator overnight before using.

Vermont Pure Maple–Walnut Cream Pie

MAKES A 9-INCH PIE

This recipe is based on one from Karyl Bannister's *Cook & Tell* newsletter, published out of West Southport, Maine, along with my memory of a sublime maple cream pie I tasted one day at the Wayside Restaurant in Berlin, Vermont. The Wayside is a cheerful, homey lunchroom that has been a stronghold of regional Vermont cooking since it opened in 1918. Their powerfully mapley cream pie alone is worth a detour to north-country Vermont, near Montpelier. Be sure to use pure maple syrup to make this pie. One of the darker grades, such as Medium or Dark Amber, would be a great choice if you can get it.

> Half-and-Half Pie Crust (page 586) or Cream Cheese Pie Crust
>   (page 587) for a single-crust pie
> 3 eggs
> ⅓ cup packed dark brown sugar
> 2 tablespoons all-purpose flour
> 1 cup pure maple syrup
> ½ cup whole milk
> 2 teaspoons vanilla extract
> ¼ teaspoon salt
> 1 cup chopped walnuts, lightly toasted
> ½ cup heavy cream, softly whipped, optional

1. Roll the dough out on a lightly floured surface to a 12-inch round. Ease into a 9-inch pie plate. Trim the overhanging dough to ¾ inch all around. Turn the edges under, flush with the rim of the pie plate, and crimp or flute. Prick the bottom of the shell all over with a fork. Place the prepared shell in the freezer for at least 30 minutes.

2. Preheat the oven to 425 degrees.

3. Bake the frozen pie shell until pale golden brown, 14 to 18 minutes. If the pastry starts to puff up, press the bottom gently with a large spoon or oven-mittened hand to flatten. Fill immediately or cool on a wire rack. Reduce the oven temperature to 350 degrees.

4. Using an electric mixer or whisk, beat the eggs with the brown sugar and flour in a large bowl until smooth. Whisk in the maple syrup, milk, vanilla, and salt. Pour the filling into the prebaked pie shell.
5. Bake until the filling is set around the edges but still somewhat wobbly in the center, about 35 minutes. Cool on a wire rack to room temperature, 2 to 4 hours.
6. Sprinkle the chopped toasted walnuts over the top of the pie. Serve with a spoonful of whipped cream, if you like.

Just a Speck of Pepper

According to food writer and historian Imogene Wolcott, some Vermonters add a speck of black pepper to their Maple Cream Pie filling before pouring it into the pie shell.

Public Supper Banana Cream Pie

MAKES A 9-INCH PIE

I'd heard about Greenwood Grange, inland of Eastbrook, Maine, while on the public supper circuit. The best steamed brown bread, the lady at my table said. They make it right there. And great pies. So I drove up one Saturday evening to glorious, high, rolling farm country, and sky that felt like the roof of the world. It was over an hour's trip and well worth the journey. The bread was good, all right, but oh those pies! Here the custom is to put an entire pie on each table to share. So first thing when he sits down, because he's afraid it might disappear, the man next to me goes and plucks a banana cream pie off the rack and proceeds to serve himself a slice as an "appetizer." And when I got to it after the meal, I had to agree that this was pie worth fighting (and driving) for: layers of homemade vanilla-flecked, egg-rich custard, sliced bananas, whipped cream topping, and a final scatter of buttery crumbs on top. Sublime.

For the crust and topping:

1½ cups graham cracker crumbs (from about 12 double graham
    crackers)
6 tablespoons unsalted butter, melted
1 tablespoon sugar

For the filling:

⅔ cup sugar
¼ cup cornstarch
¼ teaspoon salt
2¼ cups whole or low-fat milk
½ vanilla bean, or 1 tablespoon vanilla extract
3 egg yolks
2 medium bananas, ripe but firm

¾ cup heavy cream, whipped to soft peaks

1. To make the crust, preheat the oven to 350 degrees.
2. Toss together the crumbs, melted butter, and sugar in a bowl until well combined. Remove and reserve ¼ cup of the crumb mixture. Pour the remaining crumb mixture into a 9-inch pie plate and use a large spoon or the heel of your hand to press the crumbs evenly over the bottom and sides of the pie plate. Bake the crust until it is a rich golden brown, 8 to 10 minutes. Cool on a wire rack. (The crust can be made a day ahead and stored, covered, at room temperature.)
3. To make the filling, whisk the sugar with the cornstarch and salt in a medium-sized, heavy saucepan. Slowly whisk in the milk, add the vanilla bean (if you are using), and place the pan over medium-high heat. Cook, stirring constantly, until the mixture comes to a boil and is thick and smooth, about 5 minutes. Boil, whisking, for 1 minute.
4. Lightly beat the egg yolks in a small bowl. Whisk about one third of the hot mixture into the yolks to temper them, then return the mixture to the saucepan. Cook, whisking constantly, until the custard almost returns to a boil, 1 to 2 minutes. Scrape the seeds out of the vanilla bean, and stir them into the custard. If using vanilla extract, stir it in now.
5. Spoon about one third of the filling into the baked pie shell. Slice one of the bananas over the custard layer. Repeat with another layer of filling, the second

banana, and the remaining filling. Place a sheet of plastic wrap directly on the surface of the custard and refrigerate the pie for at least 3 hours, until the filling is firm and cold.

6. Before serving, remove the plastic wrap, spread the whipped cream evenly over the top of the pie, and sprinkle with the reserved ¼ cup of crumbs.

Duffy's Graham Cracker Cream Pie

MAKES A 9-INCH PIE

Duffy's Restaurant in East Orland, Maine, is a comfortable family-run place, proud of all its home-style food but especially its pies. "We have one lady, all she does all day is make desserts," reported Sarah, the enthusiastic owner. When I asked her which was the most popular pie, she said, "Oh, graham cracker, for sure." I wondered how you make a pie filling with graham crackers, but Sarah generously forgave my ignorance and let the piece of pie in front of me speak for itself. It's a graham cracker *cream* pie, with an eggy custard filling and a gossamer light meringue heaped on top, in a darkly baked, crisp, cinnamon graham cracker crust.

For the crust:

1½ cups graham cracker crumbs (from about 12 double graham crackers)
6 tablespoons unsalted butter, melted
½ teaspoon ground cinnamon

For the filling:

½ cup sugar
4 tablespoons all-purpose flour
¼ teaspoon salt
2 cups whole or lowfat milk
½ vanilla bean, or 1 tablespoon vanilla extract
3 egg yolks

For the meringue:

3 egg whites
¼ teaspoon cream of tartar
5 tablespoons sugar

1. To make the crust, preheat the oven to 350 degrees.

2. Toss together the crumbs, melted butter, and cinnamon in a bowl until well combined. Remove and reserve ¼ cup of crumb mixture. Pour the remaining crumb mixture into a 9-inch pie plate and use a large spoon or the heel of your hand to press the crumbs evenly over the bottom and sides of the pie plate. Bake until it is a rich deep brown, 8 to 10 minutes. Cool on a wire rack. (The pie crust can be made a day ahead and stored, covered, at cool room temperature.) Reduce the oven temperature to 325 degrees.

3. To make the filling, whisk the sugar with the flour and salt in a medium-sized, heavy saucepan. Slowly whisk in the milk, add the vanilla bean, if you are using, and place the pan over medium-high heat. Cook, stirring constantly, until the mixture comes to a boil and is thick and smooth, about 5 minutes. Boil, whisking, for 1 minute.

4. Lightly beat the egg yolks in a small bowl. Whisk about one third of the hot mixture into the yolks to temper them, then return the mixture to the saucepan. Cook, whisking constantly, until the custard almost returns to the boil, 1 to 2 minutes. Scrape the seeds out of the vanilla bean and stir them into the custard. If using vanilla extract, stir it in now. Pour the filling into the baked pie crust and immediately place a sheet of plastic wrap on the surface to prevent a skin from forming.

5. To make the meringue, using an electric mixer, beat the egg whites in a large bowl until foamy. Add the cream of tartar and beat until very soft peaks begin to form. Gradually add the sugar and continue beating until the meringue is stiff, smooth, and glossy. Immediately spread over the custard filling (after removing the plastic wrap), beginning at the edges to anchor it to the crust and filling in the center. Sprinkle with the reserved ¼ cup of crumbs.

6. Bake until the meringue is a very pale gold, about 15 minutes. Cool on a wire rack for at least 2 hours before serving.

Mary Ross's Chocolate Cream Silk Pie

MAKES A 9-INCH PIE

This recipe is based on one from the 1950s files of my mother-in-law, Mary Ross Dojny, who would make this pie as an extra-special treat for her son when he was growing up in Connecticut. Mary's background was Polish, so her culinary repertoire ranged from adaptations of traditional Polish dishes to the best American standards. Chocolate cream pie is a New England favorite, but this recipe, with its buttery chocolate crumb crust and deep-chocolatey, almost fudgy filling, represents a delectable twist on the classic.

For the crust:

About 30 plain chocolate wafer cookies, such as Nabisco wafers
6 tablespoons unsalted butter, melted

For the filling:

¾ cup sugar
3 tablespoons cornstarch
2 tablespoons all-purpose flour
¼ teaspoon salt
2 cups whole milk
1 cup half-and-half
4 egg yolks
4 ounces semisweet chocolate, finely chopped, or chocolate chips
2 teaspoons vanilla extract

¾ cup heavy cream, whipped to soft peaks

1. To make the crust, preheat the oven to 350 degrees.

2. Process the chocolate wafers in a food processor until finely ground. Toss the crumbs with the melted butter in a small bowl. Press the crumbs over the bottom and sides of a 9-inch pie plate, using the heel of your hand to make an even crust. Bake for 6 to 8 minutes until the crust is set and barely one shade darker. Cool on a wire rack. (The shell can be made a day ahead and stored, covered, at cool room temperature.)

3. To make the filling, stir together the sugar, cornstarch, flour, and salt in a medium-sized, heavy saucepan. Slowly whisk in the milk and half-and-half. Place the pan over medium-high heat and cook, stirring, until the mixture comes almost to a boil, about 5 minutes.

4. Lightly beat the egg yolks in a small bowl. Whisk about ¼ cup of the hot mixture into the yolks to temper them, then return the mixture to the saucepan. Cook, whisking constantly, until the mixture comes almost back to a boil, about 3 minutes. Remove the saucepan from the heat, add the chocolate, and let stand for 30 seconds; then stir until smooth and melted. Stir in the vanilla. Cool, whisking occasionally, for about 5 minutes.

5. Pour the filling into the baked pie shell. Place a sheet of plastic wrap directly on the surface of the filling and cool to room temperature. Refrigerate for 2 to 3 hours or overnight.

6. Before serving, remove the plastic wrap. Spread the whipped cream evenly over the top of the pie, if you like, or serve each slice of pie topped with a spoonful of whipped cream.

Nutmeg-Dusted Rich Custard Pie

MAKES A 9-INCH PIE

Custard pies and meringue-topped pies used to be known as "nervous pies" in New England because of their tendency to quiver and shake. I once made this nutmeg-dusted custard pie for a friend who had been going through a rough patch, and she confessed later that she'd eaten the entire thing by herself, mostly by sneaking into the refrigerator to pare off slices late at night, at one point literally weeping with gratitude. Can you think of any better recommendation? As with all custards, the center of this filling should emerge from the oven looking slightly underbaked so that it will remain satiny smooth as it cools and firms.

> Pastry dough such as Half-and-Half Flaky Pie Crust (page 586) or
>   other dough for a single crust pie
> 2 cups whole milk
> 3 eggs
> 3 egg yolks

½ cup sugar
¼ teaspoon salt
2 teaspoons vanilla extract
¾ teaspoon fresh-grated nutmeg

1. Roll the dough out on a lightly floured surface to a 12-inch round. Ease into a 9-inch pie plate. Trim the overhanging dough to ¾ inch all around. Turn the edges under, flush with the rim of the pie plate, and crimp or flute. Prick the bottom and side in several places with a fork. Place the prepared shell in the freezer for at least 30 minutes.

2. Preheat the oven to 425 degrees.

3. Bake until pale golden brown, 14 to 18 minutes. If the pastry starts to puff up, press the bottom gently with a large spoon or oven-mittened hand to flatten. Fill immediately or cool on a wire rack. Reduce the oven temperature to 325 degrees.

4. Heat the milk in a small saucepan over medium heat until steam rises, 2 to 3 minutes.

5. Gently whisk together the eggs, egg yolks, sugar, salt, and vanilla in a large bowl until blended. Gradually whisk in the warm milk. Pour the custard mixture into the baked pie shell and sprinkle the top evenly with the nutmeg.

6. Bake on the middle rack of the oven 25 to 35 minutes, or until a knife inserted two-thirds of the way to the center comes out clean. The center should still be jiggly. Cool completely on a wire rack, 2 to 3 hours.

7. Serve immediately or refrigerate for up to 8 hours. This pie is best served on the day it is made, or the crust will tend to get soggy.

Lemon Buttermilk Sponge Pie

MAKES A 9-INCH PIE

This recipe is my version of a lemon pie that often shows up at public suppers in New England and is especially well loved by the ardent regular attendees of same. The filling is similar to the enchanting old-fashioned lemon sponge pudding that separates, magically, into a lemon curd layer on the bottom and a sweet cakey crust on top. This one, though, uses buttermilk, which adds its own delightfully mysterious tang.

Half-and-Half Flaky Pie Crust (page 586) or other dough for a single
   crust pie
3 egg whites
½ teaspoon salt
1 cup sugar
3 tablespoons unsalted butter, softened
3 egg yolks
1 tablespoon all-purpose flour
1½ teaspoons grated lemon zest
1 cup buttermilk

1. Roll the dough out on a lightly floured surface to a 12-inch round. Ease into a
9-inch pie plate. Trim the overhanging dough to ¾ inch all around. Turn the edges
under, flush with the rim of the pie plate, and crimp or flute. Prick the bottom and
sides in several places with a fork. Place the prepared shell in the freezer for at least
30 minutes.

2. Preheat the oven to 425 degrees.

3. Bake the shell until pale golden brown, 14 to 18 minutes. If the pastry starts to puff
up, press the bottom gently with a large spoon or oven-mittened hand to flatten. Fill
immediately or cool on a wire rack. Reduce the oven temperature to 350 degrees.

4. Using an electric mixer, beat the egg whites and salt in a medium-sized bowl until
frothy. Slowly add ¼ cup of the sugar and beat until soft peaks form. Do not wash
the beaters.

5. Using the same beaters, beat the remaining ¾ cup of sugar with the butter in
another bowl until granular and well blended. Beat in the egg yolks, flour, and
lemon zest. On low speed, beat in the buttermilk until smooth. Stir one-third of the
egg whites into the yolk mixture to lighten; then fold in the remaining whites,
leaving a few streaks of white. Pour into the baked pie shell.

6. Bake until the top is golden brown and the custard is set near the center, 25 to 35
minutes. Cool the pie on a wire rack for at least 1 hour before serving.

7. Serve barely warm or at room temperature. Refrigerate leftovers.

Apples for Your Pie

My apple pie recipe calls for a combination of tart Granny Smiths and sweet McIntosh, two varieties of cooking apples that are available countrywide, year-round. Several varieties of New England apples found at local farm stands in the fall, such as Macouns and Jonathans, make excellent pies on their own (or sweetened with a little extra sugar) because they offer a superior balance of sweetness, tartness, and juiciness. Here are some common baking apples, along with substitutes you can use:

- **Granny Smith** (tart and crisp; needs to be sweetened with extra sugar or balanced with a sweeter apple in pies)—substitute Greenings (including Rhode Island), Pippin, York, Winesap

- **Macoun** (medium-sweet, crisp, medium-juicy, good used alone in pies)—substitute Crispin, Gravenstein, Rome Beauty, Northern Spy, Cortland, Jonathan, Mutsu, Baldwin

- **McIntosh** (sweet, aromatic, juicy; needs to be balanced with a tarter apple in pies)—substitute Golden Delicious, Gala, Fuji, Empire, Idared

---

Blue-Ribbon Harvest Apple Pie

MAKES A 9-INCH PIE

Twice I've been invited to help judge apple pie contests in Connecticut, and on both occasions the panel was unanimous in choosing its first-place blue-ribbon winner. Simplicity is the key. A classic apple pie like this one should taste like nothing more or less than the essence of the good *apples* with which it is made (see above). Too much spice can muddy up the flavors. If all the apple peeling seems too onerous for one cook, recruit the family to help. They're usually more than willing if they get to eat the results!

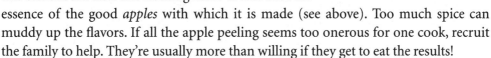

Old-Fashioned Lard Crust (page 585) or Half-and-Half Flaky Pie
    Crust (page 586) for a double-crust pie
1 cup sugar
2 tablespoons all-purpose flour
¼ teaspoon salt
½ teaspoon ground cinnamon
¼ teaspoon fresh-grated nutmeg

Pinch ground allspice

3 cups cored, peeled, and thinly sliced tart crisp apples, such as
    Granny Smith (about 1 pound)

3 cups cored, peeled, and thinly sliced sweet juicy apples, such as
    McIntosh (about 1 pound)

2 tablespoons fresh lemon juice

1 teaspoon grated lemon zest

1 tablespoon unsalted butter, cut into several pieces

1. Roll half of the dough out on a lightly floured surface to a 12-inch round. Ease into a 9-inch pie plate. Roll out the second disc of dough and slip onto a rimless cookie sheet. Refrigerate while making the filling.

2. Whisk together the sugar, flour, salt, cinnamon, nutmeg, and allspice in a large bowl. Add the apples, lemon juice, and lemon zest and toss to thoroughly coat the apples with the sugar mixture. Set aside for 15 minutes, until the apples soften slightly.

3. Preheat the oven to 425 degrees. Position a rack in the lower third of the oven.

4. Spoon the apple mixture into the pie shell and distribute the butter over the apples. Cover with the top crust and trim the overhanging dough to ¾ inch all around. Turn the edges under flush with the rim of the pie plate, and crimp or flute to seal. Use a sharp knife to cut several steam vents.

Dwight Miller Orchards

The Miller family has been farming the same land in Dummerston, Vermont, for eight generations, and they claim to have one of the oldest apple trees in the state growing on their property. Dwight Miller Orchards harvests about twenty kinds of apples, including a number of old-fashioned varieties, all grown organically. Some of the more unusual are Tolman Sweet, Pound Sweet, Snow, Blue Pearmain, and the 20-Ounce, or Blessing, apple. The 20-Ounce, a huge, tart, green apple, is a superior pie apple, one that holds its shape in the pie and allows for a harmonious blending of apple and spice flavors. Dwight Miller supplies all the apples for the up to fifteen hundred pies for the famous Dummerston Congregational Church Apple Pie Festival every year. Gladys Miller is the pie maker in the family. Cathy, her daughter, admits she has yet to make a pie. "Why should I when my mother is so good at it?" she protests. Early in the season, Gladys uses Paula Reds; later, the 20-Ounce; and in winter, Northern Spys, a great keeping apple.

5. Bake for 30 minutes. Reduce the oven temperature to 350 degrees and bake until the crust is a rich golden brown and juices bubble through the vents, 25 to 35 minutes. Cool on a wire rack for at least 1 hour.

6. Serve slightly warm or at room temperature.

Something Missing

"Apple pie without the cheese is like a kiss without the squeeze."

—Neil Shaw

Apple Pie with Cheddar–Brown Sugar Crumb Crust

MAKES A 9-INCH PIE

When I lived in California and a friend and I were into competitive cooking (an excellent training ground for a food writer, incidentally), she made a pie from *Gourmet* magazine with this sort of cheddar cheese crumb crust. The taste lodged permanently in my memory bank. It's a brilliant reworking of the New England apple-pie-with-wedge-of-sharp-cheddar-cheese concept. The cheese tang is discernible but elusive, contributing a subtle, pleasing flavor dimension.

For the crumbs:

⅔ cup all-purpose flour
2 tablespoons brown sugar
2 tablespoons cold unsalted butter, cut in ½-inch pieces
⅓ cup shredded sharp cheddar cheese

For the crust:

Half-and-Half Flaky Pie Crust (page 586) or Old-Fashioned Lard
  Crust (page 585) for a single-crust pie

For the filling:

¾ cup sugar
2 tablespoons all-purpose flour
¾ teaspoon cinnamon
¼ teaspoon nutmeg, preferably freshly grated

3 cups peeled, cored, and thinly sliced tart
crisp apples, such as Granny Smith
(about 1 pound)

3 cups peeled, cored, and thinly sliced
sweet apples, such as McIntosh (about
1 pound)

1 tablespoon fresh lemon juice

1. To make the crumbs, pulse the flour and brown
sugar in a food processor until no large lumps
of sugar remain. Add the butter and pulse until
it is the size of small peas. Add the cheese and
pulse briefly, just until the entire mixture is the
texture of rolled oats. Refrigerate in a covered
container for up to 3 days.

2. To prepare the crust, roll the dough out on a
lightly floured surface to a 12-inch round. Ease
into a 9-inch pie plate. Turn the edges under,
flush with the rim of the pie plate, and crimp or
flute. Prick the bottom and sides in several
places with a fork. Freeze for at least 30 minutes.

3. Preheat the oven to 425 degrees.

4. Bake the frozen pie shell until pale golden brown, 14 to 18 minutes. If the pastry
starts to puff up, press the bottom gently with a large spoon or oven-mittened hand
to flatten. Cool on a rack for at least 15 minutes. (The crust can be baked 1 day
ahead. Cover and store at room temperature.) Reduce the oven temperature to 375
degrees.

5. To make the filling, whisk together the sugar, flour, cinnamon, and nutmeg in a
large bowl. Add the apples and lemon juice, toss to combine, and let the mixture
stand for 15 minutes, until the apples begin to soften.

6. Spoon the apples into the prebaked pie shell. Sprinkle with the crumb mixture,
making sure to cover all the apples thoroughly and filling up any gaps and holes
where the apples have sunk. Bake until the crust is golden brown and the filling is
soft and bubbly, 50 to 60 minutes. Cool on a wire rack for at least 30 minutes.

7. Serve warm or at room temperature.

Vermont Pork (Apple) Pie

Old-time New Englanders
used salt pork in everything
from soup to dessert, including,
occasionally, their pies. A pie
made with salt pork and
apples, called both Pork Pie
and Pork Apple Pie, became a
popular dish in Vermont, and
was often served for the
Sunday evening meal. While
in the White House, Vermonter
Calvin Coolidge is said to have
extolled its goodness.

Best Maine Blueberry Pie

MAKES A 9-INCH PIE

This blueberry filling is as pure and pristine as a crisp, cloudless Maine late-summer day. Mainers don't *like* it when you try to tamper too much with the lovely tiny tart berries of which they are justifiably proud. And I agree. Just a smidgen of cinnamon and a spoonful of fresh lemon juice are required to allow the blueberry flavor to shine forth. If you use the larger high-bush blueberries, you might want to decrease the sugar by a tablespoon or so to balance their sweetness.

Old-Fashioned Lard Crust (page 585) or Half-and-Half Flaky Pie
  Crust (page 586) for a double-crust pie
¾ cup sugar
2 tablespoons all-purpose flour
¼ teaspoon ground cinnamon
⅛ teaspoon salt
4½ cups blueberries
1 tablespoon fresh lemon juice
1 tablespoon unsalted butter, cut into several pieces

——— Maine Wild Blueberries ———

Maine wild blueberries are low-bush blueberries. The plants grow only 6 to 18 inches high, as opposed to the much taller cultivated berries, which are called high-bush (or "tame" by the USDA). Wild blueberries are smaller and usually a little less sweet (depending on the growing conditions in a given year) than cultivated blueberries and with a distinctly more intense wild berry flavor.

Blueberries are one of North America's few native berries, and the low-bush variety grows thickly on treeless sandy "barrens" in coastal Maine. The berries are still largely hand-harvested with a steel rake invented in 1883 that looks like a dustpan with teeth. After harvesting, they're canned or flash-frozen and shipped around the United States and overseas. (The Japanese are crazy about them.)

In Maine wild blueberries are picked and sold in their fresh state for a few brief shining August weeks, in heaping pints and quarts, mostly from roadside honor stands. Then, in the Down East version of a bacchanal, they are eaten for breakfast, lunch, dinner, and snacks, slurped by the handful, scattered on cereal and ice cream, stewed into jam, and baked into breads, muffins, cobblers, cakes, puddings, and, of course, pies.

1. Roll half of the dough out on a lightly floured surface to a 12-inch round. Ease into a 9-inch pie plate. Roll out the second disc of dough and slip onto a rimless cookie sheet. Refrigerate while making the filling.

2. Whisk together the sugar, flour, cinnamon, and salt in a large bowl. Add the blueberries and lemon juice and toss gently to combine. Set aside for 10 minutes, until the berries begin to soften.

3. Preheat the oven to 425 degrees. Position a rack in the lower third of the oven.

4. Spoon the blueberry mixture into the pie shell and distribute the butter over the top. Cover with the top crust and trim the overhanging dough to ¾ inch all around. Turn the edges under, flush with the rim of the pie plate, and crimp or flute the dough to seal. Use a sharp knife to cut several steam vents in the crust.

5. Bake for 30 minutes. Reduce the oven temperature to 350 degrees and bake until the crust is a rich golden brown and juices bubble through the vents, 25 to 35 minutes. Cool on a wire rack.

6. Serve slightly warm or at room temperature. This pie is best eaten on the day it is made.

Pie-Eating Contest

In order to compete in the Machias, Maine, Wild Blueberry Festival pie-eating contest, an entrant has to relish the notion of plunging his or her entire face into a fresh blueberry pie. Andy, age 8, took his Dad's advice—"Don't breathe"—and won his age division. His sister Susie, 13, with a spirited performance that covered her entire front with the sticky blue filling, tied for first place in her age category. But victory comes at a cost. "This is one of my favorite shirts," Susie said, looking down at her now-blue-spangled jersey. "I hope this comes out."

Slice of New England
Cranberry-Apple-Walnut Pie

MAKES A 9- OR 10-INCH PIE

Apples, cranberries, walnuts, spices, orange, and rum—all are here together, composing a harmonious symphony of New England seasonal flavors. This pie makes a sensational Thanksgiving or Christmas dessert, especially when served with a scoop of vanilla ice cream.

Old Fashioned Lard Crust (page 585) or Half-and-Half Pie Crust
    (page 586) for a double-crust pie

For the cranberry filling:

1 cup fresh cranberries
⅓ cup sugar
¼ cup packed brown sugar
⅓ cup orange juice
1 teaspoon grated orange zest
⅛ teaspoon grated nutmeg
2 tablespoons dark rum

For the apple filling:

½ cup plus 2 teaspoons sugar
2 tablespoons all-purpose flour
¾ teaspoon ground cinnamon
⅓ cup chopped walnuts
3 to 4 cups thin-sliced peeled and cored semisweet apples, such as
    Cortland, Macoun, or Empire (about 1¼ pounds)
2 tablespoons unsalted butter
1 tablespoon whole, lowfat, or skim milk

1. Roll out half of the dough on a lightly floured surface to a 12-inch round. Ease into a 9- or 10-inch pie plate. Roll out the second disc of dough and slip it onto a rimless cooking sheet. Refrigerate while making the fillings.

2. To make the cranberry filling, combine the cranberries, sugars, and orange juice in a medium-sized nonreactive saucepan. Bring to a boil over high heat, stirring frequently. Reduce the heat to medium-low and simmer, uncovered, until the berries pop and the mixture is reduced and thickened, about 10 minutes. Stir in the orange zest, nutmeg, and rum. Set aside.

3. To make the apple filling, stir together ½ cup of the sugar, the flour, cinnamon, and walnuts in a large bowl. Add the apples and toss until well combined.

4. Preheat the oven to 425 degrees. Position a rack in the lower third of the oven.

5. Spoon the cranberry filling into the prepared pie shell and spread to make an even layer. Top with the apple filling, mounding it in the center. Cut the butter into several pieces and distribute it over the apples. Drape the top crust over the apples and trim the overhanging dough to ¾ inch all around. Turn the edges under, flush with the rim of the pie plate, and crimp or flute to seal. Use a sharp knife to cut several steam vents. Brush the top crust with the milk and sprinkle with the remaining 2 teaspoons of sugar.

6. Bake for 30 minutes. Reduce the oven temperature to 350 degrees and bake until the crust is a rich golden brown and juices bubble through the vents, 25 to 35 minutes. Cool on a wire rack for at least 1 hour.

7. Serve slightly warm or cool for several hours and serve at room temperature.

Mincemeat

Richard Sax, in *Classic Home Desserts* (Chapters, 1994), says that mincemeat has its roots in Elizabethan England, when cooked meats were potted under a layer of butter to preserve them. Eventually the meat was chopped into finer pieces ("minced") and copious amounts of spices and other dried fruits were added. The mixture traveled to America, where New England colonial housewives stored it in crocks in the cellar, ready to be turned into pies or tarts. It's the rare modern mincemeat recipe that actually contains meat, though some still call for beef suet. Most, however, are simply made with fruit, both fresh and dried; citrus peel, often in the form of candied citron; fragrant sweet spices, such as cinnamon, nutmeg, mace, allspice, and cloves; and usually spirits such as brandy or sherry.

Mince Pie with Decorative Top Crust

MAKES A 9-INCH PIE

If you really, really want to make your own mincemeat, a good standard cookbook, such as *The Fannie Farmer Baking Book*, will provide a lengthy, detailed recipe for the spiced dried-fruit mixture. Here's what I do, though, and what I recommend: buy a jar of good-quality mincemeat, and doctor it up as in this recipe. To pay homage to my family's English heritage, a mincemeat pie is obligatory on our New England Thanksgiving Day table. Since this filling is now so easy to make, I take the opportunity to spend a little more effort on crafting a pretty top crust made from easy decorative cutouts.

> Cream Cheese Pie Crust (page 587) or other dough for a
>   double-crust pie
> 1 ripe but firm pear, such as Bosc or Comice, peeled, cored, and finely
>   chopped (1 cup)
> ½ cup orange juice
> ¼ cup dark rum or bourbon
> 3 cups prepared mincemeat (1 28-ounce jar)
> 2 tablespoons fresh lemon juice
> 1 teaspoon grated lemon zest
> 1 teaspoon grated orange zest
> ¼ teaspoon fresh-grated nutmeg
> 1 egg lightly beaten with 1 tablespoon water

1. Roll half of the dough out on a lightly floured surface to a 12-inch round. Ease into a 9-inch pie plate. Trim the overhanging dough to ¾ inch all around. Turn the edges under, flush with the rim of the pie plate, and crimp or flute. Place the prepared shell in the freezer for at least 30 minutes. Roll out the second disc of dough to a 12-inch round. Using a cookie cutter or working freehand, cut out enough shapes (see Note) to almost completely cover the top of the pie. Slip onto a cookie sheet and refrigerate, or freeze.

2. Combine the chopped pear with the orange juice and rum in a medium-sized saucepan. Bring to a boil, stirring, and simmer over medium heat for 8 to 10 minutes, until the pear is softened and most of the liquid is evaporated. Stir in the mincemeat, lemon juice, lemon zest, orange zest, and nutmeg and simmer for 5 minutes to blend the flavors. Cool to room temperature before using or cover and refrigerate for up to a week.

3. Preheat the oven to 425 degrees.

4. Prick the bottom of the frozen pie shell all over with a fork. Bake until pale golden brown, 14 to 18 minutes. If the pastry starts to puff up, press the bottom gently with a large spoon or oven-mittened hand to flatten. Fill immediately or cool on a wire rack. Reduce the oven temperature to 350 degrees.

5. Spoon the filling into the prebaked pie shell. Arrange the cutouts over the filling, overlapping slightly to cover most of the top, but leaving small spaces for vent holes. Brush the top crust with the egg glaze.

6. Bake until the crust is a rich golden brown and the filling is bubbly, 35 to 45 minutes. Cool on a wire rack.

7. Serve barely warm. If the pie cools completely, reheat in a 350-degree oven for a few minutes before serving.

Note: Use whatever shapes you like—leaves, hearts, turkeys, pumpkins, stars, or a purely decorative shape.

Roberts on Mincemeat

"In my grandmother's house, mincemeat was made in bulk and kept in a stone crock in the chilly storeroom where unused garments, blankets, comforters and bed linen were stored.

"The fragrance from that mincemeat percolated through the locked door, since it was redolent of rum and richness; and whenever the door was carelessly left unlocked, I helped myself to a cupful and for the remainder of the day was more offensively active than usual."

—Kenneth Roberts, quoted in Marjorie Mosser's *Good Maine Food* (Down East Books, 1974)

Richard Sax's Best-Ever Pumpkin Pie

MAKES A 9-INCH PIE

Richard Sax was right, as usual! This recipe from his *Classic Home Desserts* is truly the *best-ever* pumpkin pie I have tasted. After baking it once, I haven't used another recipe since. The only significant change I made when adapting his recipe is to call for prebaking the pie shell, as I always do. Richard worked and worked to get this formula just right, and indeed he found it, achieving a perfect blend of soft yet cuttable custard, complex spices, and balanced sweetness with, most important, the true flavor of pumpkin predominant. This makes a generous amount of custard, so be sure to use one of the larger capacity 9-inch pie plates, not a shallow, skimpy one (see page 608).

> Half-and-Half Flaky Pie Crust (page 586) or other dough for a single
>   crust pie
> 1¾ cups canned pumpkin puree (not presweetened pumpkin pie
>   filling)
> ⅔ cup packed brown sugar
> ¼ cup sugar
> 1 tablespoon all-purpose flour
> ½ teaspoon salt
> 1½ teaspoons ground cinnamon
> ½ teaspoon fresh-grated nutmeg
> ½ teaspoon ground ginger
> ¼ teaspoon ground allspice
> ⅛ teaspoon fresh-ground black pepper
> 2 eggs
> ¾ cup heavy cream
> ⅓ cup whole or lowfat milk
> 2 tablespoons bourbon or rum
> 1 teaspoon vanilla extract
>
> Softly whipped cream flavored with maple syrup

1. Roll the dough out on a lightly floured surface to a 12-inch round. Ease into a 9-inch pie plate. Trim the overhanging dough to ¾ inch all around. Turn the edges

---

Pie Plate Capacity

How I wish the manufacturers would get together on this and establish some kind of standard! "Bake in a 9-inch pie shell" can mean anything from the meager 2½- to 3-cup capacity of a frozen crust in a flimsy disposable foil pan to the 4- to 5-cup capacity of a glass or heavy metal pie plate. *All the pie fillings in this book are designed to fill the latter.* Store-bought crusts are fine (see page 586), but only if you fit them into the larger-capacity pie pan. A pox on those skimpy frozen pie shells!

❖ ❖ ❖ ❖ ❖ ❖ ❖ ❖ ❖

---

under, flush with the rim of the pie plate, and crimp or flute. Prick the bottom and sides in several places with a fork. Place the prepared shell in the freezer for at least 30 minutes.

2. Preheat the oven to 425 degrees.

3. Bake until pale golden brown, 14 to 18 minutes. If the pastry starts to puff up, press the bottom gently with a large spoon or oven-mittened hand to flatten. Fill immediately or cool on a wire rack. Reduce the oven temperature to 375 degrees.

4. Whisk together the pumpkin, sugars, flour, salt, cinnamon, nutmeg, ginger, allspice, and pepper in a large bowl. Add the eggs and whisk until smooth. Whisk in the cream, milk, bourbon or rum, and vanilla. Pour into the prebaked pie shell.

5. Bake for 10 minutes. Reduce the heat to 325 degrees and continue baking until the custard is set and a knife inserted two-thirds of the way to the center comes out clean, 35 to 50 minutes. Cool on a wire rack.

6. Serve at room temperature, topped with the maple-flavored whipped cream.

Native Raspberry Pie

MAKES A 9-INCH PIE

To those who must pay dearly for every half pint of raspberries, this pie may seem like an extravagant use of the ruby-red beauties. But raspberries do have a brief but prolific season (sometimes two) in New England, so I make this opulent, country-elegant pie when I find a bountiful display of the summertime jewels at a roadside stand or farmers' market. Black raspberries can substitute nicely for the red raspberries.

Old-Fashioned Lard Crust (page 585) or Half-and-Half Pie Crust
    (page 586) for a double-crust pie
1 cup plus 2 teaspoons sugar
4 tablespoons all-purpose flour
¼ teaspoon salt
5 cups fresh raspberries
2 teaspoons fresh lemon juice
2 tablespoons unsalted butter, cut into
    small pieces
1 tablespoon milk, for glaze

1. Roll half of the pastry out on a lightly floured surface to a 12-inch round. Ease into a 9-inch pie plate. Roll out the second disc of dough and slip it onto a rimless cookie sheet. Refrigerate while making the filling.
2. Whisk together 1 cup of the sugar, the flour, and salt in a large bowl. Add the raspberries and lemon juice and toss to coat well with the sugar mixture.
3. Preheat the oven to 425 degrees. Position a rack in the lower third of the oven.
4. Spoon the raspberry mixture into the pie shell and distribute the butter over the fruit. Cover with the top crust and trim the overhanging dough to ¾ inch all around. Turn the edges under, flush with the rim of the pie plate, and crimp or flute to seal. Use a sharp knife to cut several steam vents. (Or cut strips and weave a lattice.) Brush the top crust with the milk and sprinkle with the remaining 2 teaspoons of sugar.
5. Bake for 30 minutes. Reduce the oven temperature to 350 degrees and bake until the crust is a rich golden brown and the berry juices bubble through the vents, 25 to 35 minutes more. Cool on a wire rack for at least 1 hour.
6. Serve slightly warm or at room temperature.

The Pie Plate Game

The Frisbee is believed to have originated in Bridgeport, Connecticut, where William Russell Frisbie started the Frisbie Pie Company in 1871. The story is that Yale students in nearby New Haven began playing a game of tossing empty pie tins to each other, crying out, "Frisbie!" When a West Coast company started mass-producing plastic flying discs in 1948, they named their product Frisbee after hearing about the Yale tradition.

Frank's Strawberry-Rhubarb Pie

MAKES A 9-INCH PIE

Nothing is as emblematic of a New England spring as these two fruits, and they couldn't possibly be greater opposites. Sweet, juicy, pretty-looking strawberries, and sour, hard (until cooked), unpromising-looking rhubarb. When baked together, they form the perfect marriage—sort of like Frank and Mamie, my Connecticut-born-and-bred in-laws, for whom I baked one of these pies every spring, because sweet tough-guy Frank had such an overweening fondness for both fruits—and for Mamie!

Half-and-Half Flaky Pie Crust (page 586) or Old-Fashioned Lard
    Crust (page 585) for a double-crust pie
1 cup plus 2 teaspoons sugar
⅓ cup flour
¼ teaspoon salt
¼ teaspoon ground cinnamon
2½ cups sliced rhubarb (about 1¼ pounds)
2½ cups hulled strawberries, halved or quartered if large
2 teaspoons fresh lemon juice
1 teaspoon vanilla extract
2 tablespoons unsalted butter, cut in several pieces
1 tablespoon milk
Vanilla ice cream, optional

Shaker Pie Ovens

I was just about to leave the Shaker Canterbury Village in Canterbury, New Hampshire, after taking the formal tour and eating an incredibly delicious "tasting" lunch cooked by chef Jeffrey Paige. While browsing in the bookstore, I mentioned my *New England Cookbook* project to a friendly volunteer staff member, whose face immediately lit up with enthusiasm. "You've got to see this kitchen!" she said, taking me by the hand and leading me to a building-restoration-in-progress that had not been on the official tour. Here was the original kitchen for the compound, completely intact, as if Eldress Bertha Lindsay, the renowned last Shaker head cook, had just stepped out for a day. Its dark, perfectly tongue-and-grooved paneled walls, scrubbed pine worktables, beautifully built cupboards and shelving, and clever labor-saving gadgets neatly placed on galvanized tin counters bespoke the Shakers' attention to detail and passion for taking the commonplace and creating something extraordinary. But then guide Suzanne Slater gestured to the ovens. "More than sixty pies could be baked in these at one time," she said. This was a very large brick box constructed in 1878, woodfired, with four circular shelves that slowly revolved over the firebox so that the pies (and pots of beans placed over the dying embers to cook overnight) baked evenly.

1. Roll half of the dough out on a lightly floured surface to a 12-inch circle. Ease into a 9-inch pie plate. Roll out the second disc of dough and slip onto a rimless cookie sheet. Refrigerate while making the filling.

2. Whisk together the sugar, flour, salt, and cinnamon in a large bowl. Add the rhubarb, strawberries, lemon juice, and vanilla and toss until the fruit is well coated with the sugar mixture. Set aside for 10 minutes, until the fruit softens slightly.

3. Preheat the oven to 425 degrees. Position an oven rack in the lower third of the oven.

4. Spoon the rhubarb mixture into the pie shell and distribute the butter over the fruit. Cover with the top crust and trim the overhanging dough to ¾ inch all around. Turn the edges under, flush with the rim of the pie plate, and crimp or flute to seal. Use a sharp knife to cut several steam vents. (Or cut 1-inch strips and weave a lattice crust, crimping the edges.) Brush the top crust with the milk and sprinkle with the remaining 2 teaspoons of sugar.

5. Bake for 30 minutes. Reduce the oven temperature to 350 degrees and bake until the crust is a rich golden brown, the fruit is tender, and juices bubble through the vents, 25 to 35 minutes. Cool on a wire rack for at least 1 hour.

6. Serve warm or at room temperature, with ice cream, if you like.

Corina's Sweet Potato Pie

MAKES A 9-INCH PIE

You can almost always get a smile out of nine-year-old Reggie Johnson of Bridgeport, Connecticut, but his face fairly glows when you get him talking about his grandmother Corina's sweet potato pie. Usually associated with southern cooking, sweet potato pie traveled to New England on the waves of northward migration in recent decades and is now a favorite dessert in households and on restaurant menus all over the region, particularly in urban areas. This pie is a delectable kissing cousin to our native Yankee pumpkin pie, but with a somewhat richer flavor and sturdier texture.

Half-and-Half Flaky Pie Crust (page 586) or Old-Fashioned Lard
    Crust (page 585) for a single-crust pie
2 eggs
¾ cup sugar
2 tablespoons unsalted butter, melted
2 tablespoons molasses
2 cups cooked mashed sweet potatoes or yams (see Note)
¾ teaspoon fresh-grated nutmeg
½ teaspoon ground cinnamon
½ teaspoon ground ginger
½ teaspoon salt
1 teaspoon vanilla extract
1½ cups half-and-half

Softly whipped cream, optional

Too Many Pies

"All around Almonzo were cakes and pies of every kind, and he was so hungry he could have eaten them all....

"When he began to eat pie, he wished he had eaten nothing else. He ate a piece of pumpkin pie and a piece of custard pie, and he ate almost a piece of vinegar pie. He tried a piece of mince pie, but could not finish it. He just couldn't do it. There were berry pies and cream pies and vinegar pies and raisin pies, but he could not eat any more."

—Laura Ingalls Wilder, *Farmer Boy*
(HarperTrophy, 1979)

1. Roll the dough out on a lightly floured surface to a 12-inch round. Ease into a 9-inch pie plate. Trim the overhanging dough to ¾ inch all around. Turn the edges under, flush with the rim of the pie plate, and crimp or flute. Prick the bottom and sides of the shell in several places with a fork. Place the prepared shell in the freezer for at least 30 minutes.

2. Preheat the oven to 425 degrees.

3. Bake the frozen shell until pale golden brown, 14 to 18 minutes. If the pastry starts to puff up, press the bottom gently with a large spoon or oven-mittened hand to flatten. Fill immediately or cool on a wire rack. Reduce the oven temperature to 350 degrees.

4. Whisk together the eggs, sugar, melted butter, and molasses in a large bowl until smooth. Whisk in the mashed sweet potatoes and add the spices, salt, and vanilla. Gradually whisk in the half-and-half. Pour the filling into the prebaked pie shell.

5. Bake until a knife inserted two-thirds of the way to the center comes out clean, 45 to 55 minutes. Cool on a wire rack.

6. Serve slightly warm or at room temperature, with whipped cream, if you like.

Note: Scrub 2 large yams, cut into 2-inch chunks, and boil in lightly salted water until tender, 15 to 20 minutes. Drain, peel, and mash with a fork. Or use drained canned sweet potatoes or yams.

> ### Maine Pies
>
> "The finest products of old-time Maine cooks may have been fruit pies. They had a whole repertory of them—apple, blueberry, cherry, rhubarb, raspberry, lemon, cranberry, as well as mincemeat, pumpkin, molasses, maple syrup, raisin, custard, date custard, chocolate, and often meat pies, usually baked in a flavorful lard crust."
>
> —Ed Behr,
> *The Art of Eating* newsletter
> (Summer 1994)

Priscilla the Pie Lady

Right there on Route 1 in Bucksport in midcoast Maine, you see Priscilla's signs. "Pies. Homemade. Strawberry, Blueberry, Raspberry, Blackberry. Come On In." So we do, climbing her back steps to check out the contents of the old-fashioned pie safes lining the porch, chatting with the amiable Priscilla and her husband, a retired merchant mariner, who built her the cozy modern kitchen where she bakes all those pies in an oven that doesn't look any bigger than yours or mine. When we inquire about her flaky, melt-on-the-tongue crust, she replies, "The secret's in the lard, dear." And in the love she lavishes on each one, sticking strictly to in-season ingredients and to the simplest possible formulas, thereby achieving absolute pie perfection.

Marlborough Apple-Cream Tart

MAKES A 9-INCH TART

Popular in nineteenth-century Massachusetts, Marlborough pie is an open-faced apple cream pie that food historians have traced to an old British recipe. Here the classic lemony, custardy applesauce filling is baked in a shallow tart crust, which turns it into a decidedly elegant dessert. This is luscious served still slightly warm from the oven, accompanied by a scoop of vanilla ice cream.

Half-and-Half Flaky Pie Crust (page 586) or Cream Cheese Pie Crust
  (page 587) for a single-crust pie
2 eggs
1 cup unsweetened applesauce
⅓ cup packed light brown sugar
2 teaspoons fresh lemon juice
½ teaspoon grated lemon zest
⅛ teaspoon ground mace
2 tablespoons unsalted butter, melted
½ cup heavy cream
1 teaspoon vanilla extract
1 tablespoon sugar
½ teaspoon ground cinnamon
Vanilla ice cream, optional

1. Roll the pastry dough out on a lightly floured surface to an 11- or 12-inch round. Ease into a 9- or 10-inch tart pan with a removable bottom. Press the dough against the sides of the pan and trim the edges. Prick in several places with a fork. Place in the freezer for at least 30 minutes.
2. Preheat the oven to 425 degrees.
3. Bake the frozen shell for 14 to 18 minutes, until light golden brown. If the pastry starts to puff up, press the bottom gently with a large spoon or oven-mittened hand to flatten. Fill immediately or cool on a rack (see Note). Reduce the oven temperature to 350 degrees.
4. Whisk the eggs with the applesauce and brown sugar in a large bowl until blended. Add the lemon juice, lemon zest, and mace and stir until well combined. Whisk in the butter, cream, and vanilla. Pour the filling into the prebaked tart shell. Stir together the sugar and cinnamon in a small bowl and sprinkle evenly over the top of the tart.
5. Bake until the custard is set near the center and the top is golden brown, 25 to 30 minutes. Cool on a wire rack.
6. Serve slightly warm or at room temperature. Add a scoop of vanilla ice cream, if you like.

Note: If there are cracks in the baked crust, wrap the outside of the tart pan with foil before filling to stop any leaks.

New England Apples

The first English colonists carried apple seeds with them on the *Mayflower*, and it was Reverend William Blaxton who planted some of America's first apple orchards on the slope of what would become Boston's Beacon Hill. When the Reverend Mr. Blaxton moved to Rhode Island in 1635, he created the first American hybrid seedling type, the Rhode Island Greening, and soon the colonies had dozens of their own varieties. Judith and Evan Jones, in their *Book of New New England Cookery* (Random House, 1987), list the following old-time New England apple names: Baldwin, Black Gilliflower, Duchess, Fameuse, Greening, Jonathan, Northern Spy, Pippin, Red Astrachan, Roxbury Russet, Westfield Seek-No-Further, Spitzenburg, Sweet Paradise, Tompkins King, Williams Nothead, Winter Banana, Winesap, Yellow Transparent.

Pie Crisis

Many observers of the New England culinary scene, such as Leslie Land, *Yankee Magazine* food writer and cookbook author, have commented on the decline of pie making in the region. Barbara Haber, curator of the culinary collection at Radcliffe's Schlesinger Library, a primary resource for scholars interested in the history of home cooking, says, "I think it's fear of pastry making. There's a kind of mystique about who has a fine hand at pastry, so a lot of people opt for the frozen. Even good cooks no longer aspire to make a great pie from scratch."

Rustic Rhubarb-Raspberry Tart

MAKES A 9-INCH TART

Whether you harvest your own rhubarb as it pushes its pink stalks hopefully up out of a still-brown New England garden, or buy the hothouse variety that appears every year to herald springtime in the supermarket, this splendid free-form tart evokes the new season. Raspberries are not often paired with rhubarb, but their intense berry taste is a lovely counterpoint to the more assertive rhubarb flavor. Serve with vanilla ice cream on the side, perhaps for an Easter or Passover dinner.

For the pastry:

1¼ cups all-purpose flour
2 teaspoons sugar
½ teaspoon salt
¼ pound (1 stick) cold butter
About 4 tablespoons ice water

For the filling:

1 pound rhubarb
1 cup raspberries
¾ cup plus 2 teaspoons sugar
2 tablespoons cornstarch
½ teaspoon ground cinnamon

1 egg beaten with 2 teaspoons water
⅓ cup sliced almonds
1 tablespoon cold unsalted butter, cut in 3 to 4 pieces
Confectioners' sugar, optional

1. To make the pastry, pulse the flour, sugar, and salt in a food processor. Cut the butter into about 12 pieces, add to the flour, and pulse until most of the butter pieces are the size of small peas. Sprinkle the ice water over the flour mixture and pulse just until the mixture begins to clump together and form small balls. Turn out onto a sheet of plastic wrap, gather into a ball, flatten into a 5-inch disc, and refrigerate for at least 30 minutes.

2. To make the filling, trim the ends of the rhubarb and cut in half lengthwise if the stalks are more than 1 inch thick. Cut into inch-long pieces. You should have a generous 2 cups of rhubarb. In a large bowl, toss the rhubarb with the raspberries, ¾ cup of the sugar, the cornstarch, and cinnamon. Set aside for about 15 minutes, until the fruit softens somewhat.

3. Preheat the oven to 425 degrees.

4. Roll the pastry dough out on a lightly floured surface to a 13-inch round. Do not trim the edges; they are supposed to be ragged. Transfer the dough to a large rimmed baking sheet, patching any tears by pressing the dough together with your fingers. Brush the dough with the egg glaze and sprinkle with the almonds. Spoon the fruit mixture onto the dough, mounding it slightly higher in the center and leaving a 2-inch border all around the edge. Scatter the butter over the fruit. Fold the border in, pleating it as necessary, to make an uneven 1½-inch-wide edge. Brush the edge with egg glaze and sprinkle the top with the remaining 2 teaspoons of sugar.

5. Bake for 15 minutes. Reduce the oven temperature to 375 degrees and continue baking for 25 to 30 minutes, until the pastry is golden brown and the fruit is soft and bubbly. Cool on a wire rack.

6. Serve warm or at room temperature, with confectioners' sugar sprinkled over the top, if you like.

MAIL-ORDER SOURCES

Apple Ledge Company
170 South Road
Holden, Maine 04429
207-989-5576

Source for Bakewell Cream, a unique
leavening agent.

The Baker's Catalogue
King Arthur Flour Company
P.O. Box 876
Norwich, Vermont 05055
www.kingarthurflour.com

Baking ingredients and equipment.

Bascom Maple Farms
RR1, Box 137
Mount Kinsbury Road
Alstead, New Hampshire 03602
603-835-6361

Maple syrup, maple sugar, and other
maple products.

Cabot Creamery
P.O. Box 128
Cabot, Vermont 05647
800-639-3198
www.cabotcheese.com

A large line of Vermont-made cheese and
other dairy products.

Cavendish Game Birds
396 Woodbury Road
Springfield, Vermont 05156
800-805-2251

Pheasant and quail.

Cotuit Oyster Company
P.O. Box 563
Cotuit, Massachusetts 02635
508-428-6747

Farm-raised Cape Cod oysters and
quahog clams.

Delftree Farm
234 Union Street
North Adams, Massachusetts 01247
800-243-3742

Shiitake mushrooms.

Ducktrap River Fish Farm
57 Little River Drive
Belfast, Maine 04915
800-828-3825
www.ducktrap.com

Smoked seafood products.

Gaspar's Sausage Company
384 Faunce Corner Road
North Dartmouth, Massachusetts 02747
800-542-2038
www.gasparssausage.com

Portuguese linguiça and chourico.

Gray's Grist Mill
P.O. Box 364
Adamsville, Rhode Island 02801
508-636-6075
www.graysgristmill.com

Stone-ground jonnycake meal.

Great Hill Dairy
160 Delano Road
Marion, Massachusetts 02738
888-748-2208
www.greathillblue.com

Great Hill blue cheese.

The Harrington Ham Company
210 E. Main Street
P.O. Box 288
Richmond, Vermont 05477
802-434-3415
www.harringtonham.com

Cob-smoked hams and bacon.

Kenyon Corn Meal Company
21 Glenn Rock Road
West Kingston, Rhode Island 02892
800-753-6966
www.kenyonsgristmill.com

Jonnycake and other stone-ground meals.

New England Venison Co-op
RR1, Box 73
Abbot, Maine 04406
207-997-3922

Information on mail-ordering farm-raised venison.

Sakonnet Vineyards
162 West Main Road
Little Compton, Rhode Island 02837
800-919-4637
www.sakonnetwine.com

Vinifera wines.

Shelburne Farms
Shelburne, Vermont 05482
802-985-8686
www.shelburnefarms.org

Aged farmhouse cheddar.

Somerset Bean Company
RFD 1, Box 1575
Skowhegan, Maine 04976
207-474-8865

Dried beans, including soldier, yellow eye, jacob's cattle, cranberry, and pea beans.

The Spanish Table
1427 Western Avenue
Seattle, Washington 98101
206-682-2827

Portuguese products, including pimienta moida, sardines, salt cod, cheeses.

Stonewall Kitchen
York Corners
Route One
York, Maine 03909
800-207-5267
www.stonewallkitchen.com

Preserves and condiments.

Stonington Lobster Co-op
P.O. Box 87
Stonington, Maine 04681
800-315-6625

Fresh lobster and crabmeat, shipped overnight.

Tightrope Seafarms
HCR64, Box 397
Brooklin, Maine 04616
207-359-9802

Farm-raised rope-cultured mussels.

Vermont Butter and Cheese Company
Pitman Road
P.O. Box 95
Websterville, Vermont 05678
800-884-6287
www.vermontcreamery.com

Specialty European-style cow and goat cheeses.

The Vermont Country Store
RR 1, Box 231
North Clarendon, Vermont 05759
802-776-5730
www.vermontcountrystore.com

Source for Vermont Common Crackers.

Westfield Farm, Inc.
28 Worcester Road
Hubbardston, Massachusetts 01452
877-777-3900
www.chevre.com

Natural goat and cow cheeses.

Westport Rivers Vineyard and Winery
417 Hixbridge Road
Westport, Massachusetts 02790
508-636-3423
www.westportrivers.com

Vinifera wines.

Wood's Cider Mill
1482 Wethersfield Center Road
Springfield, Vermont 05156
802-263-5547
www.woodscidermill.com

Cider jelly and maple syrup.

BIBLIOGRAPHY

I have quoted (with much appreciation) from some of these books, cited others, and used many for background reference.

American Cooking: New England (*Foods of the World*). Time-Life Books, 1970.

Anderson, Jean. *The American Century Cookbook*. Clarkson Potter, 1997.

Anderson, Jean. *The Food of Portugal*. William Morrow, 1994.

Anderson, Jean. *The Grass Roots Cookbook*. Doubleday, 1992.

Bannister, Karyl. *Cook and Tell* newsletter. West Southport, Maine.

Barr, Nancy Verde. *We Called It Macaroni*. Knopf, 1990.

Barron, Rosemary. *Flavors of Greece*. William Morrow, 1991.

Behr, Ed. *The Art of Eating* newsletter. Peacham, Vermont.

Best of the Best From New England. Quail Ridge Press, 1994.

Blue, Anthony Dias. *America's Kitchen*. Turner, 1991.

Blue, Anthony Dias, and Kathryn K. Blue. *Thanksgiving Dinner*. HarperCollins, 1990.

Cameron, Angus, and Judith Jones. *The L.L. Bean Game and Fish Cookbook*. Random House, 1983.

Carlson, Barbara. *Food Festivals*. Visible Ink, 1997.

Chase, Sarah Leah and Jonathan Chase. *Saltwater Seasonings*. Little, Brown, 1992.

Cummings, Rebecca. *Turnip Pie*. Puckerbrush Press, 1986.

Cunningham, Marion. *The Fannie Farmer Baking Book*. Knopf, 1984.

Doiron, Paul, ed. *Eating Between the Lines: A Maine Writers' Cookbook*. Maine Writers and Publishers Alliance, 1998.

Early, Eleanor. *New England Cookbook*. Random House, 1954.

Farmer, Fannie Merritt. *The Boston Cooking-School Cook Book*. Little, Brown, 1896.

Favorite Greek Bazaar Recipes. Holy Trinity Greek Orthodox Church, 1975.

Ford, Richard. *Independence Day*. Vintage Books, 1996.

From the Galleys of Nantucket. First Congregational Church, 1982.

Fussell, Betty. *I Hear America Cooking*. Penguin, 1986.

Fussell, Betty. *The Story of Corn*. North Point Press, 1999.

Gunst, Kathy, and John Randolph. *The Great New England Food Guide*. William Morrow, 1988.

Haedrich, Ken. *Home for the Holidays*. Bantam, 1992.

Halliday, Fred. *Halliday's New England Food Explorer*. Fodor's Travel, 1993.

Herbst, Sharon Tyler. *The New Food Lover's Companion*. Barron's, 1995.

Hometown Cooking in New England. Yankee Books, 1994.

Hornblower, Malabar. *The Plimoth Plantation New England Cookery Book*. The Harvard Common Press, 1990.

Jones, Evan. *American Food: The Gastronomic Story*. The Overlook Press, 1990.

Jones, Judith, and Evan Jones. *The L.L. Bean Book of New New England Cookery*. Random House, 1987.

Junger, Sebastian. *The Perfect Storm*. W.W. Norton, 1997.

Kimball, Christopher. *The Yellow Farmhouse Cookbook*. Little, Brown, 1998.

King, Louise Tate, and Jean Stewart Wexler. *The Martha's Vineyard Cook Book*. Harper & Row, 1971.

Kurlansky, Mark. *Cod: A Biography of the Fish That Changed the World*. Walker and Co., 1997.

The Legal Sea Foods Cookbook. Legal Sea Foods, 1975.

Lindsay, Eldress Bertha. *Seasoned With Grace*. The Countryman Press, 1987.

MacDonald, Duncan, and Robb Sagendorph. *Old-Time New England Cookbook*. Dover Publications, 1993.

Mariani, John. *The Dictionary of American Food and Drink*. Ticknor & Fields, 1983.

Marlborough Meetinghouse Cookbook. Congregational Church of Marlborough, Connecticut, 1997.

Miller, Amy Bess, and Persis Fuller. *The Best of Shaker Cooking*. Macmillan, 1985.

Mosser, Marjorie. *Good Maine Food*. Down East, 1974.

Murphy, Martha Watson. *A New England Fish Tale*. Henry Holt, 1997.

Off the Hook: A Cook's Tour of Coastal Connecticut. Junior League of Stamford-Norwalk, 1988.

Oliver, Sandra L. *Saltwater Foodways*. Mystic Seaport Museum, 1995.

Out of Vermont Kitchens. St. Paul's Cathedral, 1994.

The Oyster Epicure. White, Stokes, and Allen, 1883.

Paige, Jeffrey S. *The Shaker Kitchen*. Clarkson Potter, 1994.

Platt, June. *June Platt's New England Cookbook*. Atheneum, 1971.

Rhode Island Cooks. American Cancer Society, 1992.

Rich, Virginia. *The Baked Bean Supper Murders*. E.P. Dutton, 1983.

Rich, Virginia. *The Nantucket Diet Murders*. Thorndike Press, 1985.

Root, Waverly. *Eating in America*. William Morrow, 1976.

Sax, Richard. *Classic American Desserts*. Chapters, 1994.

Schlesinger, Chris, and John Willoughby. *The Thrill of the Grill*. William Morrow, 1990.

Shea, Susan Strempek. *Hoopi Shoopi Donna*. Pocket Books, 1996.

Sokolov, Raymond. *Fading Feast*. Farrar Straus Giroux, 1981.

Standish, Marjorie. *Cooking Down East*. Down East, 1969.

Stern, Jane, and Michael. *Real American Food*. Knopf, 1986.

Stern, Jane, and Michael. *Road Food*. HarperPerennial, 1992.

Stoddard Old Home Days: Our Favorite Recipes. Fundcraft, 1978.

The Taste of Gloucester: A Fisherman's Wife Cooks. The Fishermen's Wives of Gloucester, 1976.

Thorne, John. *Simple Cooking*. Viking, 1987.

A Vermont Cook Book by Vermont Cooks. Green Mountain Studio, 1958.

Walker, Barbara M. *The Little House Cookbook*. Harper & Row, 1979.

Waters, Alice. *Chez Panisse Vegetables*. HarperCollins, 1996.

Westport Sons of Italy Cookbook. Westport Sons of Italy, 1973.

White, E. B. *Charlotte's Web*. Harper & Row, 1952.

White, Jasper. *Jasper White's Cooking From New England*. Harper & Row, 1989.

White, Jasper. *Lobster At Home*. Scribner, 1998.

Wolcott, Imogene. *The Yankee Cookbook*. Ives Washburn, 1971.

Wood, Esther. *Deep Roots*. Yankee Books, 1990.

The Yankee Magazine Cookbook. Yankee Books, 1981.

Yankee Magazine's Favorite New England Recipes. Yankee Books, 1972.

INDEX